Principles of Business: Marketing

Principles of Business: Marketing

The Editors at Salem Press

SALEM PRESS

A Division of EBSCO Information Services, Inc.

Ipswich, Massachusetts

GREY HOUSE PUBLISHING

Publisher's Cataloging-In-Publication Data
(Prepared by The Donohue Group, Inc.)

Names: Salem Press, editor.
Title: Principles of business. Marketing / the Editors at Salem Press.
Other Titles: Marketing
Description: [First edition]. | Ipswich, Massachusetts : Salem Press, a
   division of EBSCO Information Services, Inc. ; Amenia, NY : Grey House
   Publishing, [2017] | Includes bibliographical references and index.
Identifiers: ISBN 978-1-68217-599-6 (hardcover)
Subjects: LCSH: Marketing.
Classification: LCC HF5415 .P75 2017 | DDC 658.8--dc23

FIRST PRINTING
PRINTED IN THE UNITED STATES OF AMERICA

CONTENTS

PUBLISHER'S NOTE

Everything you need to know about marketing is addressed in this comprehensive introduction: strategies, principles, issues, and key ideas. *Principles of Business: Marketing* is the third of a six-volume series covering important topics in business. Titles already published in the *Principles of Business* series are *Finance* (2017) and *Management* (2017). Forthcoming titles are *Entrepreneurship* (2017), *Economics* (2018), and *Accounting* (2018). The set introduces students and researchers to the fundamentals of business with brief but comprehensive articles written in easy-to-understand language. We hope that these books will become your go-to resource for information on these important and far-reaching topics.

The entries in this volume are arranged in an A to Z order, from "Advertising Campaigns" to "Value-Based Strategies for Business Marketing," making it easy to find the topic of interest. The entries are written in a uniform format:

- an *abstract* gives a brief introduction to the topic;
- an *overview* presents key terms and concepts;
- a clear, concise *presentation of the topic* includes a discussion of applications and issues;
- a helpful list of *further reading* appears at the end of every article.

Added features include helpful illustrations and diagrams of relevant topics. The back matter in *Principles of Business: Marketing* contains a thorough and valuable glossary of terms as well as an index.

Salem Press extends its appreciation to all involved in the development and production of this work. The signed entries have all been written by scholars and experts in business. Without these expert contributions, a project of this nature would not be possible. A full list of contributor's names and affiliations follows this Note. *Principles of Business: Marketing* is available in print and as an e-book.

INTRODUCTION

For most people, the first thing that comes to mind when the subject of marketing comes up is advertising, in forms such as television commercials, newspaper inserts, or billboards on the side of the road. Modern society has become so permeated by advertising that it is not difficult to conjure up numerous examples. However, important as it is, there is more to the field of marketing than finding new ways to draw consumer attention to products. Ultimately, marketing is about managing relationships between providers of products and services and those who purchase and/or consume those products.

Marketing is concerned with a particular type of relationship called an exchange relationship. This may sound like an abstract concept, but its definition is a straightforward one. An exchange relationship is one in which two or more parties voluntarily exchange products, services, or units of value such as currency. The place, whether physical or virtual, where these exchanges occur is the market, so the act of managing the exchanges is known as marketing.

More specifically, marketing seeks to encourage particular types of exchanges to encourage exchanges involving particular parties or both (Kurtin, 2016). For example, if the state of California launches an advertising campaign to encourage people in other parts of the world to visit California on their vacations, this would be encouragement of a particular type of exchange: tourism, in which consumers spend money in exchange for memorable experiences. If, instead, a hotel chain with locations throughout California created a commercial to encourage people to come and stay at its hotels, this would be an example of encouraging an exchange involving a particular party, the hotel chain. In the first case, the goal is to get tourists to come to the state and spend money, while in the second case the goal is to get tourists to come to a specific hotel chain and pay to stay there.

Many people assume that marketing always involves getting people to spend money. However, marketing is often performed by nonprofit organizations, governments, and other entities wishing to spread their messages without necessarily implicating a purchase of some kind. A government might, for example, wish to use marketing to remind people to vote in upcoming elections or to file their taxes on time. Similarly, a nonprofit organization might market itself to raise awareness in the community about who the organization is and what it does (Wendt, Griesbaum & Kölle, 2016).

MARKETING ORIENTATIONS

There are different approaches or orientations that may be taken to marketing, and marketers may have reasons to prefer one orientation over the others. To some extent, the different orientations are concerned with different phases of the product life cycle.

Product Orientation. The most straightforward marketing orientation is a product orientation. When an organization has a product orientation for its marketing, its focus is on making sure that the product being produced is consistently of high quality. Product orientation reached its height during the 1950s and 1960s, and is based on an assumption that consumers do not really need to be convinced to purchase the product. As long as the product is high in quality, then people will seek it out and purchase it. This type of marketing orientation tends to be observed more frequently during periods of economic prosperity and expansion, when consumers have money to spend and producers can rely upon large numbers of people wanting to have the latest and most highly regarded items available for purchase, with little or no convincing necessary (Zwick & Bradshaw, 2016).

Customer-Oriented Marketing. A more contemporary orientation to marketing is customer-oriented marketing. Instead of focusing on the product and assuming people will want to buy it, a customer-oriented approach begins by trying to figure out what consumers want. This process involves the identification of gaps in the marketplace. To identify these gaps, organizations conduct market research, collecting information from consumers through surveys, interviews, focus groups, observations, and other methods. The information is then used in the research and development process to design new products or services that will fulfill consumers' unmet needs. Developing products in this fashion can take months or even years, as prototypes are built, tested, refined, and tested again, and then piloted in the market to see how consumers respond to them. If the response is favorable, then the product may go into production. At this time, marketing efforts will ramp up to make consumers aware of the new product and its features. The customer orientation is a much more labor intensive marketing approach. The hope is that by more closely studying consumer desires, sales figures will be much higher than they otherwise would be, because the final product will more closely resemble what consumers feel that they need in their lives. This approach tends to be employed by larger organizations because they are more likely to have the resources needed to support market research campaigns.

Relationship Marketing. The trend in marketing over the last few decades has been to shift the focus from the product to the sales process. Companies that use the relationship-marketing approach view a sale not as the end of the company's interaction with the customer, but as the beginning. Relationship marketing doesn't focus so much on individual products and purchases, but seeks to build feelings of loyalty and identity.

This approach can require companies to expand their customer support resources so that when there are issues with products, customers do not feel that the company was only interested in taking their money. It can also affect the behavior of sales teams. For example, sales staff may be instructed to focus less on making the sale and more on listening to the customer and helping them figure out what they need, even when that turns out to be a product or service that the company does not offer (Metcalf, Neill, Simon, Dobson & Davis, 2016).

THE INTERNET AND MARKETING
Marketing has undergone a significant transformation with the advent of the Internet. The Internet has provided myriad new communication platforms that companies may use to reach out to their customers.

E-Mail Marketing. One of these platforms is e-mail, which companies use regularly to inform customers about new products, sales, and other developments. Often, however, these messages are unsolicited and are being sent to a huge list of people in the hope that a small percentage will respond. Most consider these unsolicited sales e-mails to be junk, or "spam,"

and the proliferation of junk e-mail has given rise to a whole industry of software developers, marketers, and salespeople who offer customers e-mail filtering software to help them avoid receiving so much spam (Grundy, Bero & Malone, 2016).

Pay-per-Click. Many social network applications derive a significant amount of their financial support from advertising messages displayed to users. Many of the advertisements placed on social networks by marketing teams are set up on a pay-per-click basis, meaning that each time a user clicks on an ad to find out more about it, the company that paid for the advertisement pays the marketing company a small amount of money, which is shared with the social network site as well. (In some cases the money is paid directly to the social network).

The pay-per-click revenue model works because of the huge numbers of people that participate in social networks (Jiang, Ramkissoon & Mavondo, 2016). If even one out of every thousand users of the social network decides to click an ad, income can amount to millions of dollars per year. Marketing teams are often drawn to this type of online advertising because it has the potential to reach such a large audience. Anyone on Earth with an Internet connection becomes a part of the audience for the advertisement, meaning that the ad is highly cost effective.

SEO Optimization. Marketing online has also created some new career options for those with technical skills, through the creation of the field of search engine optimization (SEO) under the broader umbrella of marketing. SEO is the process of configuring a website so that search engines such as Google and Yahoo will give that web page greater relevance, and therefore a higher ranking, when they index it (Ahmed, 2016). These days, people all over the world perform millions of searches every day, many of them looking for information that marketers would like to connect them with. In many cases, a user will search for a generic product to solve a particular problem. They do not have a specific brand or manufacturer in mind but simply want something that will "get rid of grey hair," or "clean hardwood floors." When these types of searches are entered into an online search engine, there are many different websites that the search engine could choose to display. Those sites that have been optimized by a specialist for SEO will be placed higher in the list of results, meaning that users will see them first and are therefore more likely to click on them.

CONCLUSION: THE FUTURE OF MARKETING

Online marketing reaches an enormous population by relying on statistics and the law of averages to get people to click. Under this approach, marketers usually see inquiries from only a tiny segment of the population that received the ad. Yet, because so little effort had to be expended to obtain those inquiries, the marketing effort is perceived to be a success.

For many years, the emphasis was for companies to focus their attention on the product and on the consumer. The general idea was to better understand what people wanted and thereby gain an advantage by designing products better suited to people's desires. SEO, pay-per-click ads, and e-mail solicitations, however, work differently. They use an approach that has been likened to a fisherman casting a wide net. No one knows for sure for how long this type of marketing will remain sustainable, but some observers think that the returns produced by Internet ads will diminish as users become less tolerant of the distraction of online marketing.

—*Scott Zimmer, J.D.*

BIBLIOGRAPHY

Ahmed, T. (2016). Countering counterfeit branding. Implications for public-sector marketing. *Journal of Nonprofit & Public Sector Marketing, 28*(3), 273–286. Retrieved October 23, 2016, from EBSCO Online Database Business Source Ultimate. http://search.ebscohost.com/login.aspx? direct=true&db=bsu&AN=117876758&site=ehost-live

Barton, E. K. (2016). Social media marketing: Do this, not that. *IDC Quarterly, 26*(3), 69–70. Grundy, Q., Bero, L. A., and Malone, R. E. (2016). Marketing and the most trusted profession: The invisible interactions between registered nurses and industry. *Annals of Internal Medicine, 164*(11), 733– 740.

Jiang, Y., Ramkissoon, H., & Mavondo, F. (2016). Destination marketing and visitor experiences: The development of a conceptual framework. *Journal of Hospitality Marketing & Management, 25*(6), 653–675. Retrieved October 23, 2016, from EBSCO Online Database Business Source Ultimate. http://search.ebscohost.com/login.aspx? direct=true&db=bsu&AN=116620527&site=ehost-live

Kurtin, K. S. (2016). Social media strategy: Marketing and advertising in the consumer revolution. *Journalism & Mass Communication Quarterly, 93*(3), 694–695. Retrieved October 23, 2016, from EBSCO Online Database Business Source Ultimate. http://search.ebscohost.com/login.aspx? direct=true&db=bsu&AN=117270218&site=ehost-live

Metcalf, L. E., Neill, S., R. Simon, L., Dobson, S., & Davis, B. (2016). The impact of peer mentoring on marketing content mastery. *Marketing Education Review, 26*(3), 126–142. Retrieved October 23, 2016, from EBSCO Online Database Business Source Ultimate. http://search.ebscohost.com/login.aspx? direct=true&db=bsu&AN=117575084&site=ehost-live

Saetang, W., & Pathomsirikul, Y. (2016). Marketing strategy model for building customer loyalty in feed wholesale business. *International Journal of Behavioral Science, 11*(2), 109–126.

Wendt, L. M., Griesbaum, J., and Kölle, R. (2016). Product advertising and viral stealth marketing in online videos. *Aslib Journal of Information Management, 68*(3), 250– 264.

Witkowski, T. H., & Jones, D. B. (2016). Historical research in marketing: Literature, knowledge, and disciplinary status. *Information & Culture, 51*(3), 399–418.

Zwick, D., & Bradshaw, A. (2016). Biopolitical marketing and social media brand communities. *Theory, Culture & Society, 33*(5), 91–115.

CONTRIBUTORS

MICHAEL P. AUERBACH

Mr. Auerbach holds a bachelor's degree from Wittenberg University and a master's degree from Boston College. Mr. Auerbach has extensive private and public sector experience in a wide range of arenas including political science, business and economic development, tax policy, international development, defense, public administration and tourism.

SETH M. AZRIA

Mr. Azria earned his J.D., magna cum laude, from New York Law School where he was an editor of the Law Review and a research assistant. He has written appellate briefs and other memoranda of law on a variety of legal topics for submission to state and federal courts. He is a practicing attorney in Syracuse, New York.

TRACEY BISCONTINI

Tracey Biscontini is the president and CEO of Northeast Editing, Inc. Tracey holds bachelors' degrees in secondary education and mass communications from King's College and a master's degree in English from the University of Scranton. In 2009, she was named one of the Top 25 Women in Business in Northeastern Pennsylvania by the National Association of Women Business Owners (NAWBO).

BRIAN BURNS

Brian Burns has worked in a number of writing positions including editor and columnist for the *Franklin Times*, reporter for the *Walpole Times*, and marketing consultant for the *Town of Walpole Trade and Commerce Magazine*. Brian currently works within the marketing department of an industry-leading pet supply company.

JOSEPH DEWEY

Joseph Dewey holds a Ph.D.

MICHAEL ERBSCHLOE

Michael Erbschloe is an information technology consultant, educator, and author. He has taught graduate level courses and developed technology-related curriculum for several universities, and he speaks at conferences and industry events around the world. Michael holds a master's degree in sociology from Kent State University. He has authored hundreds of articles and several books on technology.

SIMONE I. FLYNN

Dr. Simone I. Flynn earned her doctorate in cultural anthropology from Yale University, where she wrote a dissertation on Internet communities. She is a writer, researcher, and teacher in Amherst, Massachusetts.

JOHN MARK FROILAND

Dr. Froiland is an assistant professor in the Department of School Psychology at the University of Northern Colorado. Dr. Froiland earned his Ph.D. at Michigan State University, where he developed expertise in promoting intrinsic motivation and positive behavior. He has authored over 50 articles and book chapters.

MARIE GOULD

Marie Gould is an associate professor and the faculty chair of the Business Administration Department at Peirce College in Philadelphia, Pennsylvania. She teaches in the areas of management, entrepreneurship, and international business. Although Ms. Gould has spent her career in both academia and corporate, she enjoys helping people learn new things — whether it's by teaching, developing or mentoring.

STEVEN R. HOAGLAND

Dr. Hoagland holds bachelor's and master's degrees in economics, a master's degree in urban studies, and a doctorate in urban services management with a cognate in education, all from Old Dominion University. His background includes service as senior-level university administrator responsible for planning, assessment, and research. He has consulted in the health care, information technology, and education sectors and taught as an adjunct professor of economics.

TRUDY MERCADAL

Trudy holds a Ph.D. in comparative studies from Florida Atlantic University.

ELIZABETH RHOLETTER PURDY

Elizabeth Rholetter Purdy earned a B.A. in political science graduating summa cum laude from Columbus

College, an M.A. from Emory University as a Phi Kappa Phi fellow, and a Ph.D. in political science from Georgia State University. She has published articles on subjects ranging from political science and women's studies to economics and popular culture.

VANESSA A. TETTEH

Dr. Tetteh earned her doctorate from the University of Buckingham in England, U.K., where she wrote a dissertation on tourism policy, education, and training. She is a teacher, writer and management consultant based in Ghana, West Africa. Her work has appeared in journals such as *International Journal of Contemporary Hospitality Management, The Consortium Journal,* and *Ghana Review International.*

RICHA S. TIWARY

Dr. Richa S. Tiwary holds a doctorate in marketing management with a specialization in consumer behavior from Banaras Hindu University in India. She also holds a master's degree in library sciences from the Department of Information Studies, University at Albany-SUNY.

RUTH A. WIENCLAW

Dr. Ruth A. Wienclaw holds a Ph.D. in industrial/ organizational psychology with a specialization in organization development from the University of Memphis. She is the owner of a small business that works with organizations in both the public and private sectors, consulting on matters of strategic planning, training, and human/systems integration.

SCOTT ZIMMER

Scott Zimmer has earned a master's degree in library science, a master's degree in computer science, and a Juris Doctor. He is both an attorney and a librarian at Alliant International University.

A

ADVERTISING CAMPAIGNS

ABSTRACT

An advertising campaign is a series of messages on the same idea and theme that constitute consistent, seamless, one-voice Integrated Marketing Communications (IMC). The global advertising industry is a large and growing one that uses virtually every type of media and promotional opportunity available. Advertising campaigns require a thorough process, from the setting of objectives to campaign evaluation. Although most advertising is for commercial purposes, an increasing amount of advertising campaigns are designed to serve noncommercial purposes. Advertising itself can be a controversial activity that many have come to view as detrimental to society, and as such, industry regulation has become necessary.

OVERVIEW

Advertising is the paid promotion of a cause, an idea, an opinion, a product, or a service by an identified sponsor attempting to inform or persuade a particular target audience through a nonpersonal medium. Advertising also refers to the profession and the business of designing and writing advertisements, along with any related techniques and practices. An advertising campaign is a series of advertisement messages on the same idea and theme that constitutes consistent, seamless, one-voice Integrated Marketing Communications (IMC). As a marketing tool, advertising can be combined with other marketing tools, such as sales promotions, branding, personal selling, publicity, and public relations.

Advertising has become a ubiquitous phenomenon in modern society, where a single individual can be bombarded with thousands of advertising messages each day. Industry, companies, nonprofit organizations, and individuals all use advertising media such as the print media, broadcast media, electronic media, direct mail, logos on products, promotional items, product placement on television shows and in films, and outdoor advertising (via wall paintings, billboards, posters, automobiles, subway trains, skywriting, bus-stop benches, town criers, roof mounts, and so on). These media are used to communicate messages that are meant to influence the behavior and/or thought patterns of a specific target audience.

Advertising expenditure in the United States alone exceeded $192 billion in 2016, while worldwide advertising spending surpassed $542.55 billion in 2016 (*eMarketer*, 2016). It is not surprising, therefore, that advertising is the most important source of income for many of the world's media organizations today.

The firms that generate advertising are mainly profit-making corporations, with the largest groups being retailers, the automotive industry, and financial services (*eMarketer*, 2015).

Advertising can be traced back to ancient times, when means such as rock paintings, wall paintings, and human criers were used to advertise events and products for sale. In those days, political campaign displays, papyrus wall posters, and even papyrus lost-and-found announcements were in use. As the centuries progressed, technological advances made more media available for advertising. In the fifteenth and sixteenth centuries, for instance, the development of printing paved the way for handbill advertising. Subsequently, in the seventeenth century, newspaper advertisements began. As national economies grew toward the end of the nineteenth century, advertising grew significantly, to the extent that this period is said to have marked the beginning of modern advertising.

Other forms of advertising were developed, such as classified advertising and mail-order advertising. A major milestone was achieved in the late 1880s, when manufacturers began to advertise their own branded products themselves, after taking packaging and branding away from the wholesalers.

The advertising agency sector also underwent its own developmental changes. Initially, the first advertising agencies were established in the nine-teenth century to serve as brokers for newspaper advertising space, but by the early twentieth century, the advertising agencies were handling the production of advertising messages, including, among others, copy and artwork. As the number of advertising agencies grew, more advancements were made in such areas as copywriting and research.

Thanks to the new technology of broadcasting, radio advertising was thriving by 1930, and television advertising was also introduced in the 1950s. Cable and satellite television were introduced between the late 1980s and early 1990s, carrying new broadcasting channels wholly devoted to advertising.

Internet advertising bloomed in the 1990s, creating novel advertising opportunities in various forms, such as popup, flash, banner, advergaming, email advertisements, embedded advertising, and so on. In the twenty-first century, Internet advertising has been the fastest-growing form of advertising and is projected to surpass television commercials in terms of ad spending in 2017 (*eMarketer*, 2016). Interactive advertising allows advertising to be tailored to individuals' own interests. Other recent advertising innovations include guerrilla promotions, which employ sensational and unusual tactics such as expensive product giveaways and staged encounters in public places. As the Internet has evolved, advertising has increasingly been dotted with niche and targeted advertisements. Consumers are increasingly able to choose which advertisements they come into contact with, and advertisers are increasingly relying on data mining to target very specific audiences.

FURTHER INSIGHTS

The Advertising Campaign Process. The advertising campaign process consists of five main stages. These are:
- Objective setting
- Budget preparation
- Selection of the right advertising approach
- Copy testing
- Evaluation of the campaign's effectiveness

Objective. Every advertising campaign must have an objective stating what the campaign should accomplish with specific customers over a particular time frame, and there must also be a campaign theme, which is the central message to be communicated through the campaign.

The advertising objective is usually selected on the basis of a product's stage in its life cycle. It should address four key points:
- The basic message to be delivered.
- The target audience to whom the message is to be delivered.
- The intended effect of the advertising campaign.
- The specific criteria to be used later on to measure the campaign's effectiveness.

Types of Campaigns. There are various types of advertising campaigns, each with its unique objective. They include the following:
- **Informational Advertising Campaigns:** These are used to introduce a new cause, idea, product, or service, placing emphasis on promoting its name, benefits, and possible uses.
- **Trial Advertising Campaigns:** These are used to encourage customers to make an initial purchase of a new product.
- **Persuasive Advertising Campaigns:** These are used to generate sales within a particular target market after a product has already been introduced to the public.
- **Continuity Advertising Campaigns:** These are used to keep existing customers using a particular product, building customer loyalty by typically providing new information about a product.
- **Brand Switching Advertising Campaigns:** These are used to convince customers to switch from competitors' brands, usually by comparing price or quality.
- **Comparative Advertising Campaigns:** These are used to directly or indirectly compare one brand with one or more of its competitors.
- **Reminder Advertising Campaigns:** These are used to remind customers and maintain awareness of products that have entered the mature stage of the product life cycle.
- **Switchback Advertising Campaigns:** These are used to get back former customers, by highlighting new product features, price reductions, or other important information.
- **Advocacy Advertising Campaigns:** These are used to persuade the public on a specific economic, political, or social issue.

- **Cooperative Advertising Campaigns:** These are used to enable manufacturers and distributors to share advertising costs.
- **Institutional Advertising Campaigns:** These are used to promote the benefits, concept, idea, or philosophy of a particular industry, in a fashion similar to public relations.
- **Product Advertising Campaigns:** These are simply used to promote specific products to the general public.

Advertising Campaign Budget. Once the advertising objective is selected, the advertiser must set an advertising budget for each product. The budget-setting stage is another key step in the advertising campaign process, since the campaign budget is significantly related to the campaign's success. However, an advertiser seeking a true IMC approach should base budget allocations on the marketing communications objectives that need to be achieved, rather than being constrained by budgets imposed by management.

The advertising campaign budget should fit in with overall company objectives and must take into consideration other market factors, such as the following:

- Advertising frequency. This refers to the number of times an advertisement is repeated during a given time period. The higher the desired advertising frequency, the higher the advertising budget required. It has been estimated that a consumer must come into contact with an advertising message nine times before he or she will remember that message.
- Competition intensity. This refers to the degree of competition in the market. The more competitive the market, the higher the advertising budget required to simply remain at par with a product's or brand's competitors.
- Clutter of the market. The more cluttered a market, the more necessary the advertising interventions and the higher the advertising budget, in order that the advertised product will stand out.
- Desired market share. Companies desiring to increase market share typically require a large advertising budget, since their competitors are likely to react defensively with their own advertising campaigns. A company seeking to be the market leader must have a substantial advertising budget.

- Product differentiation. In competitive markets where the products are so similar that customers find it difficult to tell them apart, aggressive advertising campaigns with higher budgets may be required in order to help make customers aware of the product's availability and unique features.
- The product's stage in its life cycle. In general, advertising budgets are highest for products in the introduction stage. Advertising budgets typically decline gradually as products mature.

Advertising Approach. After choosing which type of advertising campaign to use and after drawing up a budget, an advertiser must decide which advertising approach to use. The advertising approach will specify the frequency goals, media impact, media timing, and reach of the campaign.

- The frequency goals specify the number of times that the average consumer should be exposed to the message during the campaign period.
- Media impact considers the effectiveness of each media outlet by analyzing the strengths and weaknesses of each outlet vis-à-vis its cost. Evaluating the media impact helps advertisers determine which media outlets will maximize the interest and awareness of the consumer.
- Advertisers must also consider media timing, which simply put, refers to the timing of the advertisements: For instance, advertisers must consider whether a campaign should be run during a specific season or whether the advertisements should run in a continuous pattern (scheduled in a regular manner) or pulsing pattern (scheduled disproportionately over a period of time).
- An advertiser must specify the reach of any advertising campaign: That is, the percentage of customers within the target market who will be exposed to the campaign during a given time period. The aim is to reach as close to 100 percent of the target market as possible, since the chance of future sales is directly related to the exposure of the target audience.

Before running any advertising campaign, all advertisements must be copy tested and, if necessary, improved upon. This is to ensure that the advertisements contain the best-quality messaging, captivate the audience's attention, and lead to the desired behavioral change.

Advertising for Noncommercial Purposes. Advertising can be used for noncommercial purposes as a tool for informing, educating, and motivating large audiences. Such advertising is often referred to as advocacy advertising, cause marketing, non-commercial advertising, public-interest advertising, public-service advertising, or social marketing.

Increasingly, the advertising campaigns of profit-making companies contain social dimensions, as companies affiliate with noncommercial public-interest issues and initiatives such as health concerns, human-rights advocacy, crime prevention, and environmental preservation. This type of advertising is also known as cause marketing, cause-related marketing, corporate issue promotion, corporate social marketing, social issues marketing, mission marketing, or passion branding. Such advertising appears to be well received by consumers, especially when the cause is one that the customers care about. Therefore, corporate advertising with a social dimension helps to create a positive corporate image.

Advertising campaigns that aim to serve social goals face many challenges and obstacles, including these:

- First, social advertising campaigns involve more complex and longer creative and production processes, since they have multiple objectives and require more research than normal.
- Second, social advertising campaigns typically face resistance from salespeople and retailers, either because of lower-than-expected sales or because the salespeople and retailers do not care about the social agenda and do not appreciate the strategic benefits that may be derived from being associated with the cause.
- Third, social advertising campaigns are also prone to resistance from company management, especially when management is uncertain about how the social agenda can help meet the company's economic goals and the company does not have a history of innovative advertising, risk-taking, or civic-mindedness.
- Fourth, some would argue that company advertising with social dimensions is tantamount to exploitation, depending on the campaign's objectives and motivations.

Advertising campaigns with a social agenda are most likely to succeed when there is compatibility between the cause and the company, with the cause bearing some relationship to the company's core business; when internal and external shareholders also have some affinity to the cause; and when the campaign has the support of nonprofit organizations and associations affiliated with the cause.

Advertising Campaign Effectiveness. It is virtually impossible to generalize which factors may favor the success of any advertising campaign. The conditions favoring the success of any campaign will vary depending on the advertising objective of that particular campaign. Therefore, even before developing an advertising campaign, an advertiser must first find a match between attributes of the product or service advertised and the needs of the consumer. The chances of success will be higher if the advertised product has features perceived as unique by the target market.

In addition, the more consumers are satisfied with the products of a company's competitors, the lower the likelihood that the company's campaign will be successful; therefore, companies must conduct regular customer satisfaction surveys to monitor their own market performance and identify the weaknesses and strengths of their competitors. Furthermore, the degree of advertising expertise of the corporate staff assigned to the campaign will also impact the success of the campaign: The greater the advertising know-how of the team assigned to the campaign, the greater the chances of campaign success.

Advertising campaigns can be evaluated based on their initial objectives, as well as through a comparison of pre-campaign and post-campaign sales of the product or service that was advertised. Advertising campaign effectiveness can also be measured by a means known as ad tracking. This involves measuring shifts in the target market's perceptions and analyzing these shifts in relation to the levels of exposure that the consumers have had to the company's advertisements and promotions.

ISSUES

Advertising clearly has many benefits, and although some argue that advertising is necessary, for example, as a tool for economic growth, advertising campaigns have several limitations. For instance, they cannot focus on the specific needs of individual consumers. Again, most advertising campaigns cannot provide in-depth information about the products, services, or causes that are being promoted. Even when information is provided, the advertising messages often convey partial truths, and the advertising campaigns themselves do not provide the means for consumers to verify the advertising claims. In comparative advertising, for example, the lack of accurate information tends to leave customers confused and in doubt about an organization's or a brand's integrity.

Advertising campaigns are also not cost-effective for small companies. In fact, economists believe that advertising raises barriers to entry for new firms, and therefore it distorts competition. They argue that advertising distracts consumers from price. In this regard, advertising has been said to create false values and make consumers purchase items they do not need or want. Worse still, consumers are often led to purchase and consume products that may be harmful to them, such as cigarettes, alcohol, and prescription drugs, leading to government regulation of the advertising of such products.

Sociologists complain that advertising promotes materialism and suggests that the possessions one has are more important than who one is. Consumer advocates maintain that advertising victimizes and exploits children and can be offensive to the elderly, minorities, and women. Unsolicited advertising such as spam is a nuisance to consumers and Internet service providers. Even advertisers themselves have their concerns about whether their advertising campaigns are yielding value for money: Due to the difficulties in predicting or evaluating the effectiveness of advertising campaigns, advertisers often cannot tell whether their efforts have been worthwhile, though tracking advertising success has become easier in the Internet era.

Advertising also impacts the content, visions, and actions of the media, particularly in those media outlets that generate most of their revenue from advertising. Such media organizations often seek first and foremost to make their medium as attractive to advertisers and consumers as possible, to the extent of airing programs that, by their nature, are low in mental stimulus and require little concentration, in order to heighten the attractiveness of the advertisements and prevent the target audience from switching to another media outlet.

Due to the negative impacts of advertising, efforts have been made to regulate the content and reach of advertising through regulation on the part of governments, the advertising industry, and other industries. Some countries have therefore imposed bans on the advertising of particular products on specific media and to specific audiences, particularly children.

On the positive side, however, advertising can actually create new markets for products and services, and through free competition, advertising can lead to continuous product improvement, as different brands try to gain advantage over each other.

BIBLIOGRAPHY

Britt, S. (2000). Are so-called successful advertising campaigns really successful? *Journal of Advertising Research, 40,* 25. Retrieved from EBSCO Online Database Business Source Complete. http://search.ebscohost.com/login.aspx?direct=true&db=bth&AN=4009765&site=ehost-live

Dinner, I. M., Van Heerde, H. J., & Neslin, S. A. (2014). Driving online and offline sales: The cross-channel effects of traditional, online display, and paid search advertising. *Journal of Marketing Research, 51*(5), 527–545. Retrieved from EBSCO Online Database Business Source Complete. http://search.ebscohost.com/login.aspx?direct=true&db=e6h&AN=98472595&site=ehost-live&scope=site

Drumwright, M. (1996). Company advertising with a social dimension: The role of noneconomic criteria. *Journal of Marketing, 60,* 71–87. Retrieved from EBSCO Online Database Business Source Complete. http://search.ebscohost.com/login.aspx?direct=true&db=bth&AN=9610251921&site=ehost-live

eMarketer. (2016, March 8). Digital ad spending to surpass TV next year. *eMarketer.* Retrieved December 28, 2016 from https://www.emarketer.com/Article/Digital-Ad-Spending-Surpass-TV-Next-Year/1013671

eMarketer. (2016, March 25). US spending on paid media expected to climb 5.1% in 2016. *eMarketer.* Retrieved December 28, 2016 from https://www.emarketer.com/Article/US-Spending-on-Paid-Media-Expected-Climb-51-2016/1013739

eMarketer. (2016, April 21). Worldwide ad spending growth revised downward. *eMarketer.* Retrieved December 28, 2016 from https://www.emarketer.com/Article/Worldwide-Ad-Spending-Growth-Revised-Downward/1013858

Ghose, A., & Todri-Adamopoulos, V. (2016). Toward a digital attribution model: Measuring the impact of display advertising on online consumer behavior. *MIS Quarterly, 40*(4), 889-910. Retrieved December 28, 2016 from EBSCO online database Business Source Ultimate. http://search.ebscohost.com/login.aspx?direct=true&db=bsu&AN=119473689&site=ehost-live&scope=site

Korgaonkar, P., Mosehis, G., & Bellenger, D. (1984). Correlates of successful advertising campaigns. *Journal of Advertising Research, 24*, 47. Retrieved from EBSCO Online Database Business Source Complete. http://search.ebscohost.com/login.aspx?direct=true&db=bth&AN=6560186&site=ehost-live

QSR magazine. (2011, Feb). Don't interrupt your consumer; engage them. *QSR.* Retrieved from http://www.qsrmagazine.com/outside-insights/don-t-interrupt-your-consumer-engage-them

Richards, L. (n.d.) What industry spends the most on advertising? *Houston Chronicle.* Retrieved from http://smallbusiness.chron.com/industry-spends-advertising-22512.html

Story, L. (2007, Jan. 15). Anywhere the eye can see, it's likely to see an ad. *The New York Times.* Retrieved from http://www.nytimes.com/2007/01/15/business/media/15everywhere.html?pagewanted=all

Wang, G., et al. (2013). Advertiser risk taking, campaign originality, and campaign performance. *Journal of Advertising, 42*, 42–53. Retrieved from EBSCO Online Database Business Source Complete. http://search.ebscohost.com/login.aspx?direct=true&db=bth&AN=89358978

ZenithOptimedia. (2014, June). Executive summary: Advertising expenditure forecasts. *ZenithOptimedia.* Retrieved from http://www.zenithoptimedia.com/wp-content/uploads/2014/06/Adspend-forecasts-June-2014-executive-summary.pdf

PriceWaterhouseCoopers. (2007). Global entertainment and media outlook: 2007–2011. New York: Author.

SUGGESTED READING

Chapter 5: The tools of corporate reputation: Integrated marketing communications (IMC). (2003). Managing corporate reputation. London: Thorogood Publishing, Ltd. Retrieved from EBSCO Online Database Business Source Complete. http://search.ebscohost.com/login.aspx?direct=true&db=bth&AN=22377418&site=ehost-live

Cornelissen, J. (2003). Change, continuity and progress: The concept of integrated marketing communications and marketing communications practice. *Journal of Strategic Marketing, 11*, 217–234. Retrieved from EBSCO Online Database Business Source Complete. http://search.ebscohost.com/login.aspx?direct=true&db=bth&AN=11763013&site=ehost-live

Davis, Brent. (2017). Negative Political Advertising: It's All in the Timing." *Australian National University,* https://mpra.ub.uni-muenchen.de/79449/1/MPRA_paper_79449.pdf

Fill, C. (2001). Essentially a matter of consistency: Integrated marketing communications. *Marketing Review, 1*, 409. Retrieved from EBSCO Online Database Business Source Complete. http://search.ebscohost.com/login.aspx?direct=true&db=bth&AN=5776082&site=ehost-live

Gonring, M. (1994). Putting integrated marketing communications to work today. *Public Relations Quarterly, 39*, 45–48. Retrieved from EBSCO Online Database Business Source Complete. http://search.ebscohost.com/login.aspx?direct=true&db=bth&AN=9412092110&site=ehost-live

Jankovic, M. (2012). Integrated marketing communications and brand identity development. *Management, 63*, 91–100. Retrieved from EBSCO Online Database Business Source Complete. http://search.ebscohost.com/login.aspx?direct=true&db=bth&AN=83926216

Langley, T. E., McNeill, A., Lewis, S., Szatkowski, L., & Quinn, C. (2012). The impact of media campaigns on smoking cessation activity: A structural vector autoregression analysis. *Addiction*, 107, 2043–2050. Retrieved from EBSCO online database, Business Source Complete. http://search.ebscohost.com/login.aspx?direct=true&db=sih&AN=82211730&site=ehost-live

Rotfeld, H. (2002). The social harm of public service advertising. *Journal of Consumer Marketing, 19*, 465–467.

Sasser, S., Koslow, S., & Riordan, E. (2007). Creative and interactive media use by agencies: Engaging an IMC media palette for implementing advertising campaigns. *Journal of Advertising Research, 47*, 237–256. Retrieved from EBSCO Online Database Business Source Premier. http://search.ebscohost.com/login.aspx?direct=true&db=buh&AN=26976941&site=ehost-live

Wharton, C. (2015). *Advertising: Critical approaches.* Abingdon: Routledge.

Yadav, M. S., & Pavlou, P. A. (2014). Marketing in computer-mediated environments: Research synthesis and new directions. *Journal of Marketing, 78*(1), 20–40. Retrieved from EBSCO Online Database Business Source Premier. http://search.ebscohost.com/login.aspx?direct=true&db=e6h&AN=93641514&site=ehost-live&scope=site

Vanessa A. Tetteh, Ph.D.

ADVERTISING MANAGEMENT

ABSTRACT

The basic intent of advertising is to persuade a potential customer to purchase the goods or services of the advertiser or to otherwise respond in the way that the advertiser desires. Advertising management is the application of the principles, concepts, and research of management science, marketing, and communications to the design and evaluation of advertising. Advertising management comprises three general types of activities. Strategic planning comprises activities that help determine ways in which the advertising department can support the organization in meeting its goals. Research and evaluation comprises efforts to determine how best to reach a target market, including general research efforts as well as specific pre- and post-testing. Design and development comprises the actual design and development of the ad or advertising campaign, including writing copy and designing artwork and layouts.

OVERVIEW

Advertising management is the application of the principles, concepts, and research of management science, marketing, and communications to the design and evaluation of advertising. Advertising management comprises research to determine the needs and characteristics of the target market, strategic planning to determine advertising goals and objectives and how to reach them, advertising design, and evaluation of advertising and campaign effectiveness. Advertising is just one element of the Integrated Marketing Communications (IMC) process, which is an approach to marketing communications that combines and integrates multiple sources of marketing information (e.g., advertising, direct response, sales promotions, public relations) to maximize the effectiveness of a marketing campaign.

Sending the Message

In order to understand how to manage the advertising function, one must first understand the nature of advertising as a communications process. At its most basic, the communication process begins when the organization (i.e., the sender) decides to transmit a message to potential customers (i.e., receivers). After the organization decides what it wants to convey to the customers (e.g., Acme Corporation produces superior widgets), the message is transmitted using a medium or mix of media that the organization thinks will best reach the target market (such as television commercials, newspaper advertisements, etc.).

However, the information does not reach the prospective customer directly; it first goes through a series of filters that screen the message. These filters may alter the meaning of the intended message. For example, suppose that Acme Corporation is not the only organization that is trying to reach the customer; two competitors are also sending messages to say that their widgets are superior and less expensive. The customer may unconsciously screen the message for other reasons, as well. For example, the customer may be a loyal customer of Gizmo Corporation and, therefore, only consider Gizmo's ads for widgets. Or, the customer may not like the background music played in the commercial or the layout of the print advertisement run by Acme and so chooses to ignore them.

The potential customer in these cases will decode the filtered message rather than the intended message. The potential customer then encodes an appropriate response, sending either positive or negative feedback to the organization that sent the message (e.g., the customer does or does not buy a widget).

Part of the function of advertising management is advertising communication. Research gives advertising managers the data that they need in order to understand how best to communicate with the members of the target market. For example, a local company wanted to advertise its products in its area. They designed two radio ads: one for the local rock station and one for the local classical station. The message of both advertisements was the same. However, the accompanying music was chosen to appeal to the target audience of each station. Unfortunately, someone mixed the ads, and the rock ad was sent to the classical station and the classical ad to the rock station, and the ads were aired. Not only did the advertiser not receive the influx of business that it had expected, but it also had to pull the ads and pay for new messages of apology to be aired on both stations.

FURTHER INSIGHTS

Although numerous activities fall under the aegis of advertising management, these can be grouped together into three general functions: (1.) strategic planning, (2.) research and evaluation, and (3.) design and development.

Strategic Planning

In most organizations, the strategic planning function is the process of determining the long-term goals of an organization and developing a plan to use the company's resources – including materials and personnel – in reaching these goals. One of these resources is the advertising personnel and the ads they develop. One of the purposes of strategic planning within the advertising management function is to determine ways in which the advertising department can support the organization in meeting its goals.

In general terms, the purpose of advertising is to persuade potential customers to purchase the products or services of the organization. Another part of the strategic planning function of advertising management, therefore, is to create an advertising campaign that will meet this goal in terms of the higher-level strategy of the organization. Traditionally, this has meant determining the best way to persuade potential customers to purchase the product or service offered by the organization. However, increasingly, advertising is becoming more closely aligned with public relations. Therefore, advertising departments may be called upon to develop ads that manage the public image or reputation with outside agencies and groups.

Budgeting. Another aspect of advertising management is developing the advertising budget (Egelhoff,

2004). For the most part, the greatest proportion of the budget needs to be allocated with those areas that have the highest potential return on investment. For example, one would probably not spend a significant proportion of one's advertising budget to purchase ad space in a professional scientific journal to advertise skateboards. To determine how the budget for an advertising campaign should be allocated, therefore, one needs first to determine what the expected outcome of the ads will be both in the short term and in the long term. Although one might not advertise skateboards in a scientific journal, one might advertise skateboards on a website that is targeted to adolescents and does not already carry similar advertising in order to build a new market. Similarly, one must estimate the revenue that the ad will produce. It is typically bad strategy to spend more on an advertising campaign than the campaign will generate in revenues in the short and long terms. Another question to ask when developing an advertising budget is what kinds of ads competitors are using. For example, if one's main competitor is taking out a half-page ad in the local paper to sell their similar product, buying one column-inch in that paper to advertise one's own product is likely to do little good (and may even do harm). The monies would be better allocated to a larger competitive ad or to another part of the ad campaign.

Media Selection. Another aspect of strategic planning for advertising management is the development of a media strategy. This is often done as part of an IMC approach in which multiple sources of marketing information are combined and integrated in order to develop an effective marketing campaign. For example, advertisements for skateboards might be placed in periodicals that are read by likely customers, on websites frequently viewed by likely customers, and on radio stations listened to by likely customers. The specific media used to advertise skateboards, however, are likely to be different than those used to advertise scanning technology to scientists. Media selection models are available to help advertising managers select the appropriate media for an effective advertising campaign.

Research & Evaluation

Research and evaluation for advertising management consists of a number of different types of activities. First, research takes place continually at universities and in research and advertising firms to determine the best ways to develop and implement an advertising campaign. This level of research can be used to great profit by an advertising manager in setting research strategy, selecting media, and designing advertising materials and campaigns. Research is also part of the strategic planning process. Research is necessary in order to determine the characteristics of the average consumer in the target market and what would make members of the target market want to purchase the organization's products or services.

In order to get feedback from members of the target demographic about the effectiveness of the materials, research is typically conducted in-house to determine the effectiveness of messages and advertising materials before they are generally released. Although the above example of the misplaced musical ads stems from a clerical error, it illustrates the importance of research to understand how best to reach one's target market. Pretesting an ad helps advertising managers determine how effective the copy may be in the intended market, point out weak spots in the ad copy, and select the appropriate images or music. Advertising research pretesting also includes pretesting of the entire ad campaign, not just an isolated advertisement. The reason for this expansion of pretesting is because ads designed for one medium (e.g., print) do not necessarily translate precisely into another medium (e.g., television). Research pretesting can be used to determine the effectiveness with which the intended message comes across to the potential customer, to compare alternate draft ads to determine which one is more effective, and to obtain feedback from representative members of the target market to determine how and if an ad or advertising campaign needs to be refined.

Research can be used not only on the front end of a management campaign, but also during the research campaign and on the back end as well. Tracking research is often used after an ad campaign is launched to determine how well the campaign is working, including whether members of the target market are showing an increased preference for the product or brand. This information can help advertising managers make better decisions about the ad or advertising campaign, including whether or not to extend the run of the ad or pull it. In addition, posttesting can be used to evaluate the effectiveness of an ad or advertising campaign. This information can be used to help design future campaigns.

Design & Development
The third major group of activities in advertising management is the actual design and development of the ad or advertising campaign. Once the strategy—including the product concept and media selection—has been determined and the target market analyzed, the next step is to craft the message. This is the core of any ad or advertising campaign. At the design and development phase, the message should be directed at the specific target audience with the intention of meeting specific goals as laid out in the strategic planning stage. The message should include the communication of the product's or service's unique features and why this product or service is better than those offered by the competition (although this latter is often implied rather than stated). The message should also take into consideration how potential customers are likely to evaluate the product or service and what might make them more likely to purchase.

Once the message has been crafted, the actual advertising copy needs to be written and the artwork and layout for the ad created. Often, an outside advertising agency is used to write the copy and do the layout and artwork. Given the fact that people are inundated with messages on screen, in print, and over the air, it is important that advertising catch and hold the potential customer's attention. This is done in different ways depending on the medium being used to carry the message. However, in general, direct, simple language and clean presentation work best. Although modern technology allows the creation of eye-catching animations and artwork and memorable storylines for advertisements, in the end it should always be the message, not the story, the audience should remember.

ISSUES
Advertising Management for the Global Company
It can be a complicated task to determine the best way to market a product to differing subgroups of potential customers with one culture. This task becomes even more complex, however, when marketing the same product in the global marketplace among differing cultures. What is an appropriate advertisement for a product in the United States, for example, may utterly fail in Sweden or Japan for any of a wide variety of factors. Reflecting these complexities, there has been a long-standing debate in the literature

regarding whether advertising management should be centralized or decentralized. One of the aspects of advertising management in the international arena that needs to be taken into account is the perspective of the local manager.

Global management of the advertising function makes sense at one level. Such an approach can help ensure a consistency of message and branding in all markets. However, when some of those markets are in different cultures, regional expectations need to be taken into account. In addition, advertising copy cannot merely be translated from one language to another. To be effective, advertising management of global campaigns needs to be managed for consistency and also take into account individual differences.

Jeong, Tharp, and Choi (2002) explored the importance of local managers in multinational advertising agencies with branches in the United States and Korea. The researchers found that when local managers in global firms were dissatisfied with standardized advertising approaches, difficulties tended to arise. To help attenuate such problems, the researchers suggested that managers be rotated through various locations so that they can better understand the thinking and issues associated with advertising in the other locales. Frequently, local managers are not made to feel part of the advertising team and do not perceive their input as being valued by managers at headquarters. Implementation of training programs and better use of the organization's intranet to include local managers can go a long way to alleviating this problem. The researchers also found that when local managers were brought into the process rather than just seeing copy that could be adapted for local use, the end result was more effective advertising efforts that better reflected the local culture.

CONCLUSION

Advertising management is the application of the principles, concepts, and research of management science, marketing, and communications to the design and evaluation of advertising. The goal of advertising is to communicate with potential customers and persuade them to purchase the product or service offered by the organization. The advertising management function is responsible for overseeing and coordinating all the activities of the advertising process in order to produce an effective ad or advertising campaign. Although there are many individual activities within the advertising department that need to be managed, in general, these can be classified into three general categories:

- Strategic planning is necessary to provide the baseline information for a successful ad or advertising campaign that not only wins customers, but also advances the organization's goals and objectives. This should be coupled with research in order to determine the best target market and the best way to reach that market.
- Advertising messages and copy should be developed in support of these goals and designed not only to show the advantages of the organization's offerings over those of their competitors, but also to do so in a way that is easily understood and memorable and that communicates the message.
- Research and evaluation are useful tools throughout the development and implementation processes in order to provide feedback to help develop better advertising both in the short and long terms.

BIBLIOGRAPHY

Egelhoff, T. (2004). How to advertise: Planning your ad budget strategy. Retrieved October 6, 2009 from Eagle Marketing Website http://www.small-townmarketing.com/adbudget.html

Jankovic, M. (2012). Integrated marketing communications and brand identity development. Management (1820-0222), (63), 91-100. Retrieved November 20, 2013 from EBSCO online database Business Source Premier. http://search.ebscohost.com/login.aspx?direct=true&db=buh&AN=83926216

Jeong, J., Tharp, M., & Choi, H. (2002). Exploring the mission point of view in international advertising management: Local managers in global advertising agencies. International Journal of Advertising, 21(3), 293-321. Retrieved September 22, 2009 from EBSCO Online Database Business Source Premier http://search.ebscohost.com/login.aspx?direct=true&db=buh&AN=7256031&site=ehost-live

Laurie, S., & Mortimer, K. (2011). 'IMC is dead. Long live IMC': Academics' versus practitioners' views.

Journal of Marketing Management, 27(13/14), 1464-1478. Retrieved November 20, 2013 from EBSCO online database Business Source Premier. http://search.ebscohost.com/login.aspx?direct=true&db=buh&AN=67698755

Mazharul Haque, S. M. (2011). Introduction: Global advertising and values. In E. C. Alozie (Ed.), Advertising in developing and emerging countries: The economic, political and social context (pp. 1-17). Farnham, England: Gower. Retrieved November 20, 2013 from EBSCO online database eBook Academic Collection (EBSCOhost). http://search.ebscohost.com/login.aspx?direct=true&db=e000xna&AN=398278&site=ehost-live

Percy, L. (1997). Strategies for implementing integrated marketing communications. Lincoln, IL: NTC Business Books.

Schultz, D. E., Tannenbaum, S. I., & Lauterborn, R. F. (1993). Integrated marketing communications. Lincoln, IL: NTC Business Books.

Sirgy, M. J. (1998). Integrated marketing communications: A systems approach. Upper Saddle River, NJ: Prentice Hall.

Wind, Y., Sharp, B., & Nelson-Field, K. (2013). Empirical generalizations: New laws for digital marketing – How advertising research must change. Journal of Advertising Research, 53(2), 175-180. Retrieved November 20, 2013 from EBSCO online database Business Source Premier. http://search.ebscohost.com/login.aspx?direct=true&db=buh&AN=88284642

SUGGESTED READING

Balnkenburg, W. B. (1970). Successful advertising management by Henry Obermeyer [Book Review]. Public Relations Quarterly, 14(4), 42. Retrieved September 22, 2009 from EBSCO Online Database Business Source Premier http://search.ebscohost.com/login.aspx?direct=true&db=buh&AN=6570982&site=ehost-live

Biehal, G. J., & Sheinin, D. A. (1998). Managing the brand in a corporate advertising environment: A decision-making framework for brand managers. Journal of Advertising, 27(2), 99-110. Retrieved September 22, 2009 from EBSCO Online Database Business Source Premier http://search.ebscohost.com/login.aspx?direct=true&db=buh&AN=1287062&site=ehost-live

Chan, Christopher (2016). Your mileage may vary: Facebook advertising revisited. College & Research Libraries. Retrieved June 29, 2017 from http://crln.acrl.org/index.php/crlnews/article/view/9478/10744.

Cohen, S. I. (1966). The rise of management science in advertising. Management Science, 13(2), B10-B28. Retrieved September 22, 2009 from EBSCO Online Database Business Source Premier http://search.ebscohost.com/login.aspx?direct=true&db=buh&AN=7351772&site=ehost-live

Hall, B. F. (2004). On measuring the power of communications. Journal of Advertising Research, 44(2), 181-187. Retrieved September 22, 2009 from EBSCO Online Database Business Source Premier http://search.ebscohost.com/login.aspx?direct=true&db=buh&AN=13039259&site=ehost-live

Helgesen, T. (1992). The rationality of advertising decisions: Conceptual issues and some empirical findings from a Norwegian study. Journal of Advertising Research, 32(6), 22-30. Retrieved September 22, 2009 from EBSCO Online Database Business Source Premier http://search.ebscohost.com/login.aspx?direct=true&db=buh&AN=9301270947&site=ehost-live

Massey, C. S. (2011). Advertising management: Media challenges and lesson learnt. Advances in Management, 4(12), 38-45. Retrieved November 20, 2013 from EBSCO online database Business Source Premier. http://search.ebscohost.com/login.aspx?direct=true&db=buh&AN=69973547

Pollack, I. (2002). The 8 golden rules of winning advertising campaigns. Fort Worth Business Press, 15(43), 7. Retrieved September 22, 2009 from EBSCO Online Database Regional Business News http://search.ebscohost.com/login.aspx?direct=true&db=bwh&AN=7723516&site=ehost-live

Sheehan, B. (2011). Marketing management. Lausanne, Switzerland: AVA Pub. Retrieved November 20, 2013 from EBSCO online database eBook Academic Collection (EBSCOhost). http://search.ebscohost.com/login.aspx?direct=true&db=e000xna&AN=390499&site=ehost-live

Ruth A. Wienclaw, Ph.D.

Applications for Business Consulting in Marketing

ABSTRACT

This article will focus on how an individual may effectively market a new consulting practice. The development of creative and unique marketing strategies used to be the lifeline of business for start-up consulting companies. Although the budding entrepreneur may be an expert in his or her field, the individual needs to make sure that others understand the benefit of doing business with the new consultant. Most consultants utilize the basic marketing plan that everyone else uses. However, in order to be successful, consultants must distinguish themselves from the pack.

OVERVIEW

Finer (2002) suggests that new businesses have a marketing budget of $10,000 in their first year of business. A typical first-year budget would include budget items such as (Finer, 2002):

- Website
- Web hosting and maintenance and url
- Search engine positioning (expert)
- Newsletter—either e-distribution or print
- Logo design
- Letterhead
- Business cards
- Brochure design and layout and some writing
- Brochure printing for 200 pieces
- Advertisements
- Memberships
- Networking expenses

Levinson and McLaughlin (n.d.) suggest a marketing formula for the budget once the business has been established. It is referred to as the 60/30/10 Marketing Formula. The approach advocates a balanced budget distributed among current clients (60 percent), prospective clients (30 percent) and the broader market (10 percent).

Current Clients. Although this is the smallest group, as a consulting practice is developed, there is an expectation that this group will generate the most profits. Therefore, a significant amount of time and money should be allocated toward cultivation efforts to secure revenue from this group.

Prospective Clients. Consultants should strive to convert this group into current clients. There is potential that some of the targeted clients will have a need for a consultant; therefore, consultants should spend at least 30% of their marketing efforts securing business from this group.

The Broader Market. This is everyone else who does not fit into the first two categories.

New consultants may adjust the percentages until they have built up their businesses. The distribution will be different among consultants, and each businessperson should customize an approach for his or her practice.

One of the best ways to get the "first" clients is to network. Most consultants find their first clients through networking activities, professional or personal. Relationship building is essential to the business consultant. It is an opportunity for the new consultant to showcase his or her capabilities, strengths, and uniqueness. It helps to distinguish the individual from others who may offer the same service. Finer (2002) developed a list of tips to assist consultants with being effective networkers.

Tips for Effective Networking:
1. "Have a crisp elevator pitch" that includes why and how your business can add value. Have three or four bullet points "about your background that relate to why you will be successful in this endeavor" (Finer, 2002).

2. "Make sure you are having a conversation in which you are listening for ways you can help the other person and talking less than 50 percent of the time. Give the person your undivided attention" (Finer, 2002).

3. "Be proactively helpful—send an email with some info that the person may be interested in" (Finer, 2002).

4. "Go to events where people in your industry go and where your clients may go; volunteer to help the organization, write articles, speak on your area of expertise" (Finer, 2002).

Even with following the steps to starting a consulting business, the entrepreneur should focus on how to effectively market his or her craft. When potential clients are looking for a consultant, they want the best. Although it is important to get a consultant exposure, one must make sure that unique qualities of the business are highlighted in order to differentiate one consultant from other consultants in the field. Competition is great in the consulting field. Therefore, it is imperative that a new consultant develops a strategic marketing plan that emphasizes strengths and weaknesses.

APPLICATION

Guerilla Marketing
Most consultants utilize the basic marketing plan that everyone else uses. However, in order to be successful, consultants must distinguish themselves from the pack. One way to accomplish this is to employ guerilla marketing techniques. According to Levinson (1984), the following principles are the foundation of guerilla marketing:

- Guerilla marketing is specifically designed for small businesses, especially consultants.
- Guerilla marketing should focus on human psychology versus experience, judgment, and hunches.
- A consultant should consider his or her time, energy, and ideas as the primary investment. Money is a secondary investment.
- Success should be defined in terms of profits, not revenue.
- A monthly goal should be the number of new relationships secured per month.
- Consultants should focus on developing the current client base and getting more business versus soliciting new customers by cold calls. Referrals are an important aspect of keeping existing clients.
- Consultants may want to build relationships with other consultants versus seeing them as competition.
- A combination of various marketing methods is the preferred approach when creating a marketing campaign.
- Staying abreast of technology is crucial in empowering the marketing campaign.

When meeting with potential clients, it is important to keep the sales pitch simple so that more time can be devoted to listening to the client explain his

or her needs for the project. The sales pitch could be a one-page plan consisting of seven sentences describing:

1. Purpose of the consultant's marketing efforts.
2. How the consultant plans to achieve the purpose by explaining the benefits the consultant can provide the client.
3. Consultant's target market.
4. Consultant's niche.
5. The marketing techniques the consultant will use.
6. The identity of the consultant's business.
7. The consultant's marketing budget (Levinson & McLaughlin, n.d.).

Once the plan has been developed, the consultant may start to discuss the different techniques and strategies he or she may use in order to solve the client's problems.

VIEWPOINT
Home-Based Business Consulting
Entrepreneurship has grown into a very lucrative business. Although the general classification for a small business is a company that has $5 to $100 million in annual sales, Tunwall & Busbin (1991) describe a small business as one "with both moderate size and managerial sophistication" (p. 16). Making the transition from a full-time permanent job to entrepreneurship can be difficult for thriving entrepreneurs. However, many will start their business on a part-time basis and work from their homes to minimize overhead costs. In order to grow the business, an entrepreneur should develop a strategy for how he or she intends to solicit new customers.

Ted Harwood was a college professor when he decided that he wanted to use his expertise to start a consulting business. He understood that potential clients would be interested in how he could use his skill set to add value to their organizations. As he developed his home-based consulting business, he reflected how gaining visibility was as important as having an established client base. Harwood (1996) recognized that he needed to create a visibility strategy for his specialty niche consulting business, and some of his tips include:

- Networking. Networking provides advantages for the work-from-home consultant in two different ways. First, it gives the individual the opportunity to get outside of the house and mingle with people. Working at home can be a lonely experience, so it is important that these individuals get outside and mingle with the public. Secondly, networking provides the budding consultant with an opportunity to make verbal sales pitches, follow up on leads, get a pulse on the environment, and make sure that he or she is positioned to be in alignment with the current trends in the field. Finer (2002) suggested having an elevator pitch that highlights who you are and what you do.

- Cold Call Pitching. One recommendation would be to invest in a current database directory in order to get initial leads. The next step would be to create a letter introducing yourself and discussing your credits. When you send your publicity piece to the identified companies, it is essential that you include a business card so potential clients can put it in their rolodex or contact list. If an individual is new to the business, it is best to send this type of introduction package prior to attempting to schedule a face-to-face meeting.

If the consultant is new to this process, Galper (n.d.) suggests seven tips on how to reap the most benefits from cold calling. The seven steps are:

- Change your mental objective before making the call. Potential clients can pick up when the consultant is only concerned about what he or she needs. Therefore, it is important to the consultant to shift into thinking about what the needs are for the potential client.
- Understand the mindset of the person who is being called. The consultant should put him- or herself in the place of the client and think about how to engage the potential client in a conversation versus getting the sales pitch out.
- Identify a core problem that can be solved. As the consultant listens to the potential client, he or she can determine key issues that the potential client may be facing.
- Start with a dialogue, not a presentation. Create a two-way dialogue that engages the potential client in the conversation.
- Start with a core problem. Introduce a topic that may be problematic for the business and ask the potential client if he or she has identified the issue as a concern for the organization.

- Recognize and diffuse hidden pressures. Make the conversation natural versus a sales pitch where the potential client may be placed on the spot.
- Determine a fit. Once the consultant and potential client agree on the problem, the consultant needs to determine the appropriate time and importance of resolving the issue. For example, the client may agree on the problem, but may not have the budget to contract a consultant to fix it at the time of the conversation.
- Writing. Another way to attract potential clients is to start writing. Some individuals have contacted journals to find out the guidelines for submitting articles, created a newsletter and sent it via email to potential clients, or developed a website and posted a regular newsletter section on the site. Another good idea is to link the business's email address and homepage information to the work that you submit and post. Potential clients must have the ability to get in touch with you. Also, if a website is to be used, having it reviewed by some friends is valuable. They could provide constructive feedback as to whether or not changes need to be made. Levinson and McLaughlin (n.d.) provided seven questions that should be asked about the site:

1. What is distinctive about the site?
2. Is the content valuable?
3. Does the site convey a clear understanding of what the business is about?
4. Is the site's content helpful in addressing the clients' issues?
5. Is the site focused on the clients' needs?
6. Would a potential client bookmark the site?
7. Would a potential client be encouraged to call based on the material located on the site? (p. 8).

- Presentations. Many successful consultants have found that they were able to solicit business when they engaged in speaking events. A budding consultant can identify different trade organizations and offer to speak for a low fee. At the presentation, the consultant would share generic tips on a topic with the hope that members from the audience would request additional meetings with the consultant's organization.

■ Business Cards. Business cards are a way to stay in a potential client's mind. The client would have the information even when you are not in the person's presence. In addition, the client could be a source of additional referrals as he or she passes your business card around. Finer (2002) also recommends putting a slogan on the business card. It can be short and describe the image that the consultant wants to leave in the minds of potential clients.

CONCLUSION

Harwood (1996) provided some valuable tips on how consultants can market their business when they are first starting out. In addition to the basic tips, he stressed the importance of setting a fee structure that is fair and realistic. He believed that every consultant should charge at least $70 to $80 an hour. However, once a consultant has been established, the individual can move up to charging $100 to $120 an hour for stable clients who do business on a regular basis. This practice will encourage steady cash flow into the business.

In order to differentiate a consulting practice, the consultant may elect to utilize a guerrilla marketing strategy. The guerilla marketing strategy is different from the traditional marketing strategy based on focus (Levinson & McLaughlin, n.d.).

However, some have found it difficult to develop marketing strategies when they are first starting out. Therefore, they have solicited the assistance of professional strategic marketers. Sometimes, it is important to make an investment in order to generate income. Hiring experienced marketers can fast track a new business and provide the company with new clients. In addition, the new consultant must be able to avoid the classic slogans/clichés when developing the marketing plan so that the service/product catches the attention of the potential client. Levinson & McLaughlin (n.d.) listed some of the typical clichés (buzzwords) as:
■ Quality service
■ Best price
■ Methods, tools, and approaches
■ Service responsiveness
■ Consultants' credentials
■ Importance of the client
■ Testimonials and references

Table 1

Traditional Marketing	Guerilla Marketing
Central to the business	Is the business
Consultant-focused	Insight-focused
Invest money	Invest time, effort and energy
Show up and throw up	Listen and serve
Grow revenue	Grow profit
One size fits all	One size fits none

BIBLIOGRAPHY

Christensen, C. M., Wang, D., & Bever, D. (2013). CONSULTING ON THE CUSP OF DISRUPTION. Harvard Business Review, 91, 106-150. Retrieved November 20, 2013 from EBSCO online database Business Source Complete with Full Text:http://search.cbscohost.com/login.aspx?direct=true&db=bth&AN=90326068&site=ehost-live

Finer, B. (2002, October 23). Marketing tips for starting your consulting business. Retrieved June 20, 2007, from http://westorg.org/nl/featured%5farticles/marketing%5fbf%5f102202.html

Galper, A. (n.d.). 7 cold calling secrets even the sales gurus don't know. Retrieved June 7, 2007, from http://www.unlockthegame.com/April-Article-2005/

Harwood, T. (1996). Marketing a home based consulting business. In Business, 18, 31-33. Retrieved June 6, 2007, from EBSCO Online Database Business Source Complete. http://search.ebscohost.com/login.aspx?direct=true&db=bth&AN=9609131824&site=ehost-live

Levinson, J. (1984). Guerilla marketing. Boston: Houghton Mifflin Company.

Levinson, J., & McLaughlin, M. (n.d.). A guide to guerrilla marketing for consultants. Retrieved June 7, 2007, from www.guerrillaconsulting.com

Tunwall, C., & Busbin, J. (1991). Consulting effectiveness in smaller companies: Guidelines for the consultant and user. Journal of Organizational Change Management, 4, 16-24. Retrieved June 7, 2007, from EBSCO Online Database Business

Source Complete. http://search.ebscohost.com/login.aspx?direct=true&db=bth&AN=6552325&site=ehost-live

SUGGESTED READING

Benazi?, D., & Došen, ?. (2012). SERVICE QUALITY CONCEPT AND MEASUREMENT IN THE BUSINESS CONSULTING MARKET. Trziste / Market, 24, 47-66. Retrieved November 20, 2013 from EBSCO online database Business Source Complete with Full Text:http://search.ebscohost.com/login.aspx?direct=true&db=bth&AN=78350612&site=ehost-live

Godkin, L., Valentine, S., Mosley, G., Silver, L., & Flores, F. (2002). Marketing orientation and organizational learning Mexican small business: The role of consulting support. *International Journal of Management, 19*, 68-79.

Industry vet starts marketing consulting business. (2006, September 25). *Travel Weekly.*

The Boston Consulting Group SWOT Analysis. (2013). Boston Consulting Group SWOT Analysis, 1-8. Retrieved November 20, 2013 from EBSCO online database Business Source Complete with Full Text:http://search.ebscohost.com/login.aspx?direct=true&db=bth&AN=91549806&site=ehost-live

Marketing your consulting services: A business of consulting resource. (2005). *Consulting to Management- C2M, 16*, 62. Retrieved June 7, 2007, from EBSCO Online Database Business Source Complete. http://search.ebscohost.com/login.aspx?direct=true&db=bth&AN=16310557&site=ehost-live

Nolsøe^Grünbaum, N., Andresen, M., Hollensen, S., & Kahle, L. (2013). Industrial Buying Behavior Related to Human Resource Consulting Services. IUP Journal Of Marketing Management, 12, 27-51. Retrieved November 20, 2013 from EBSCO online database Business Source Complete with Full Text:http://search.ebscohost.com/login.aspx?direct=true&db=bth&AN=91675208&site=ehost-live

Wheals, J., & Petch, M. (2013). A fresh look at consulting and collaboration. International Journal Of Market Research, 55, 320-322. doi:10.2501/IJMR-2013-027 Retrieved November 20, 2013 from EBSCO online database Business Source Complete with Full Text:http://search.ebscohost.com/login.aspx?direct=true&db=bth&AN=86742735&site=ehost-live

Marie Gould

APPLIED PROBABILITY MODELS IN MARKETING

ABSTRACT

To understand, explain, and predict the behavior of businesses and consumers in the workplace, marketing departments frequently apply probability theory to model the reality of the marketplace. These models allow marketing managers and analysts to run "what if" scenarios and manipulate variables in order to better utilize marketing resources to influence consumer behavior. Marketing models fall into three categories: explanatory models that attempt to explain how some part of the marketing process works; predictive models that help the marketer forecast buyer behavior; and decision support models that help managers make decisions about various marketing problems. Many marketing models are based on behavioral economics, which take into account insights from both psychology and economics, and use the principles of statistics and probability to model the real-world situation.

OVERVIEW

It is the responsibility of the marketing function within an organization to create, communicate, and deliver value to customers and manage customer relationships in ways that benefit the organization and its stakeholders. This means that the marketing department is concerned with two constituencies: customers—who want value for their money—and the organization—which wants to increase its profitability. In some ways, the two constituencies are in conflict. As long as the value is high, most customers would be perfectly happy to have the lowest price possible. Most organizations, on the other hand, would be perfectly happy to charge as much as possible in order to reach their goal. In the tension between these two disparate sets of needs and desires, there is a middle ground where both the customer and the organization win. Part of the task of the marketing function is to determine where this middle ground lies and how to best attract more customers for the organization's products or services.

To this end, many marketing departments rely on the use of mathematical models to help them forecast consumer buying behavior under various sets of variables and "what if" scenarios. Marketing is concerned with both the description of actual behavior (e.g., when we marketed the widget as a home tool, more people bought it than when we marketed it as a business tool) and the prediction of behavior (e.g., if we price the widget at $X, will more people buy it than if we price it at $Y?). A mathematical model is a mathematical representation of the system or situation being studied.

Marketing Models

There are three basic types of models used in marketing: explanatory models, predictive models, and decision support models.

Explanatory Models

This model attempts to explain how some aspect of a marketing process works. For example, a model could be developed to explain how various factors such as product features, packaging, or perceived benefits affect consumers' perceptions of the product and their likelihood of purchasing it. This information can help marketers better understand how to best position a product or brand to gain a larger market share. Marketers use the results observed in the model to explain such factors as customer perceptions and to develop marketing strategies for the brand or product.

Predictive Models

Predictive models are designed to help the marketer forecast buyer behavior, future marketplace trends, or other factors of interest. For example, a simulation model could be developed to predict sales for a new product for the first six months. This information could be used to support the marketing department and the supply chain in estimating how many units to produce, warehouse, etc.

Decision Support Models

Decision support models are computer-based information systems that help managers make decisions about semi-structured and unstructured problems. For example, a decision support model could be developed to investigate a series of "what if" scenarios to determine the optimal marketing mix for the introduction of a new product in the marketplace. Decision support systems can be used by individuals or groups and can be stand-alone or integrated systems or web-based.

Application of Marketing Models

Marketing models are firmly based on the contributions of two disciplines. The applied psychology of consumer behavior helps marketers better understand how businesses and customers behave within the marketplace and better know how to influence them as a result. In addition, most marketing models are applications of economic theory. Both of these disciplines use mathematical modeling tools that take advantage of probability theory to explain and predict behavior in the marketplace. Many marketing models use the approach of behavioral economics, which integrates the insights of both of these disciplines. This approach allows marketers to link the psychology of consumer behavior to the economics of consumer choice and activities.

Ideally, a marketing model should be able to explain, predict, and support decision making. In reality, however, this is not always the case. Models—particularly comprehensive ones—are frequently expensive to develop. Many organizations find that it is better to develop a model that will meet its primary objectives well and cost-effectively rather than trying to develop a more comprehensive model that will do multiple things. In addition, some marketing problems are more difficult to model than others (e.g., isolation of the long-term effects of advertising or measurement of factors that currently do not exist in the marketplace). Such factors set a limit to how much one can do with one model as well as detract from the development of a sharply focused model. Further, measurement of variables can limit the validity of a model. Not only are some variables difficult to measure, but various measurement errors can also affect the validity of the data. For example, the collection of subjective data (e.g., answers to questionnaires) is liable to contain several types of errors that can skew the results and negatively impact the effectiveness of the resultant model.

The Mathematical Models

No matter their application, the mathematical models used in marketing attempt to succinctly describe reality and clarify important relationships between variables. To do this, models simplify the relationships observed in the real world. For example, if one wanted to find out whether a proposed new logo projected a more positive image than the current logo, marketing research might be done to collect consumers' opinions on the two logos. Some people would say that they liked the new logo more than the current logo, and others would not. However, there could be a number of reasons why some people disliked the new logo that were extraneous to the logo itself. Such extraneous variables affect the outcome of research but are not related to the independent variable. For example, one consumer might not like the proposed new logo because it was red, and she had had a fight with her husband that morning while he was wearing a red tie. Another consumer might prefer the current logo because it is blue, and blue is his favorite color. Neither of these reasons has anything to do with the research question: whether or not the new logo projects a more positive image than the current logo. However, these extraneous variables—reactions for or against a particular color—affect the outcome of the research.

Impact of Variables on Marketing Models

The number of extraneous variables that can affect the outcome and effectiveness of a model are legion. Although it is important to control as many of these variables as possible, it is not possible to control them all. The design of a comprehensive model that takes into account all possible extraneous variables is not only a virtual impossibility, but also not feasible from a practical standpoint. Even if a model complex enough to take into account all variables could be designed, sufficient detailed data could be operationally defined and collected, and the research subjects willing and able to discriminate on such minutia, the cost of developing such a model would be prohibitive, and the model probably could not be designed until after the research question had become moot. Therefore, one of the goals of mathematical modeling is to be able to explain the relationship

between variables elegantly; that is simply and parsimoniously expressing the relationship between the important variables rather than trying to explain all possible permutations of the problem in all possible conditions.

The question, of course, is how to best choose which variables need to be included in the model and which can be excluded without negatively affecting the validity of the model. The best models hit the right note between being able to predict in all circumstances and predicting accurately. A model that leans too far to one side or the other will not have much applicability. A model that fits the real-world situation with its multitude of extraneous variables would more than likely be too general to be of much practical use. For example, to know that women 35 years of age who are currently dating but are not engaged and who prefer to eat a hot breakfast like the new logo design may be an accurate picture of reality, but unless the marketer is trying specifically to reach that target demographic, the observation is not of much help. A model with these parameters might be a better predictor, but too narrow to be helpful.

In part, choosing which variables to include or exclude in the model-building process should be done based on the relevant literature. In most situations, the theorists and researchers will have given serious thought to the relationship between variables and corresponding literature and will express the state-of-the-art thinking about various aspects of the universe of data at which one is looking. Similarly, observations of trends and relationships by the marketing personnel or management in the organization can lead to other strong assumptions that are good points of departure for building a model of consumer behavior. However, strong assumptions alone are insufficient. A useful model also needs to be testable. No matter how good the assumptions seem in theory or the relationships look on paper, it is important that marketers or analysts be able to actually collect data to test the validity and reliability of the model. Model building is an iterative process. Based on empirical observation, one posits a theory and develops a model based on its assumptions. The model is then tested with real-world data and modified to better reflect the real-world experience. This process is repeated as necessary to refine the model and improve its accuracy.

Factors Influencing Customer Behavior

It is also important to remember that models are not set in stone: The factors influencing customer behavior change over time, and the marketing model needs to be flexible to reflect those changes. For example, fifty years ago the concept of a store-bought frozen dinner that one could eat in front of the television was a novel concept. Not only was the television a relatively new technology in most households, but most women did not work outside the home and cooked from scratch. A few decades later, however, the opposite situation is true in many households. As a result, the frozen-food aisles in grocery stores today offer an amazing array of frozen dinners and even the fresh-food departments offer conveniences such as pre-sliced onions to cook with one's liver, marinated meat that only needs to be thrown on the grill, or bags of pre-washed and chopped lettuce that were unheard of in the mid-twentieth century. The important assumptions and variables for grocery store marketing of fifty years ago (e.g., fresh food; full-time homemaker) are no longer appropriate today (e.g., convenience foods; bi-vocational or single parents).

APPLICATIONS

Mathematical models can be used for many applications in marketing. Generic models to forecast customer lifetime value can help marketers better understand how to spend their budgets to both acquire and retain customers. In addition, expert systems utilize the power of artificial intelligence to develop models that are more flexible and integrate numerous sources of data.

Customer Lifetime Value

To improve the cost-effectiveness of their efforts, the objective of many marketing departments is not just to win the customer for a one-time purchase, but also to gain customer loyalty to the business or brand and thereby win continuing sales over the long term. This approach to marketing is called customer relationship management. In this process, the business identifies prospective customers, acquires data concerning prospective and current customers, builds relationships with customers, and attempts to influence their perceptions of the organization and its products or services. One statistic that is helpful in this endeavor is customer lifetime value. This is an estimate of how much a customer will spend with a business or brand over his or her lifetime. This information is of interest because it theoretically allows a business to know how much each customer is worth in terms of dollars of income which, in turn, allows businesses to better know how to spend their marketing budget. For example, if the 20-35 year-old demographic will potentially spend ten times as much money on widgets during their lifetime than the 60-75 year-old demographic, then the business is well advised to focus its efforts on the younger demographic (although not necessarily excluding the older demographic). This approach to weighting marketing emphases, however, is not without its drawbacks. Calculating customer lifetime value tends to be complex (e.g., the customer's need or desire for the product may change, the competition may bring out a product that better fits the customer's needs), and reliable data to build a usable model and net cash flow from the customer are difficult to gather.

Particularly where markets are mature and there is significant competition, it would be helpful to be able to forecast the lifetime value of a customer to a business or brand. This is a good example where mathematical marketing models can be of use. Berger and Nasr review five general marketing models of customer lifetime value. The simplest case assumed one sale per customer a year with both the cost of marketing efforts to retain customers and their actual retention rate remaining constant over time. The second approach removed the assumption of once-yearly sales and allowed examination of time periods both longer and shorter than one year. The third and fourth cases examined the effects of gross contribution margin and promotion costs that vary over time. Case 4 examined a model that takes into account the added complexity of continuous rather than discrete cash flows. The final model assumed a shrinking customer base in which customers are lost over time and treated as new customers when they return. These models can be used by marketers for a variety of purposes including decisions concerning the allocation of marketing dollars for advertising campaigns and forecasting the effect of a marketing strategy particularly *vis a vis* acquisition and retention of customers and the associated costs and tradeoffs.

Expert Systems

Mathematical models today can do more than mere number crunching. Expert systems—decision support systems that utilize artificial intelligence technology to evaluate a situation and suggest an appropriate course of action—can help marketers better understand the marketplace and forecast consumer behavior. The use of expert systems in modeling in support of marketing processes can consider both qualitative (judgmental) and quantitative data. These hybrid models (sometimes referred to as knowledge-based systems) can utilize multiple sources of data. As opposed to standard mathematical models that rely solely on the inputs of quantitative data, knowledge-based systems allow the user to specify the constraints and objectives under which the model should process the data. The model then synthesizes both quantitative and qualitative data to develop a potential solution. The major difference between standard mathematical models and knowledge-based models is that in the former, the marketing environment needs to be represented mathematically. The model also needs to be complex enough to represent the real-world situation accurately but simple enough to be solvable. A knowledge-based system, on the other hand, relies not just on mathematical rules but on heuristics—rules based on empirical relationships—generated from non-quantifiable sources such as experience or insight.

There are several steps to building a knowledge-based model. First, a decision needs to be made as to when to develop a model. Some of the situations in which it may be of use to develop a knowledge-based model include when the organization has a recurring problem, experts are retiring or leaving the organization and their replacements do not have the same skill based on long experience, or decision-making processes could be aided by the consideration of qualitative data. Once it is determined that a model needs to be built, the next step is to decide who needs to be involved in the model-building process. The individuals involved should understand the discipline of marketing, have experience building models, understand probability and statistics, and be familiar with expert systems. After the model-building team has been developed, the shell for the model needs to be chosen. There are a number of readily available shells for model building on the market. First-time users are well advised to select a shell that is easy to learn at the cost of sacrificing some flexibility rather than a very flexible shell that is difficult to learn. Once the shell has been selected, the next step is to structure the problem domain. This involves defining

the variables that need to be considered and anticipating the relationship that will be impacted by the analysis. This will allow one to establish a framework within which to work. The next steps are to gather and process the data. To maintain the usefulness of the model, it also needs to be updated on a regular basis.

BIBLIOGRAPHY

Berger, P. D. & Nasr, N. I. (1998). Customer lifetime value: Marketing models and applications. *Journal of Interactive Marketing, 12*, 17-30. Retrieved June 12, 2007, from EBSCO Online Database Business Source Complete. http://search.ebscohost.com/login.aspx?direct=true&db=bth&AN=348356&site=ehost-live

Coussement, K., & Buckinx, W. (2011). A probability-mapping algorithm for calibrating the posterior probabilities: A direct marketing application. *European Journal of Operational Research, 214*, 732-738. Retrieved November 15, 2013, from EBSCO Online Database Business Source Complete. http://search.ebscohost.com/login.aspx?direct=true&db=bth&AN=62844526&site=ehost-live

Ho, T. H., Lim, N., & Camerer, C. F. (2006). Modeling the psychology of consumer and firm behavior with behavioral economics. *Journal of Marketing Research, 43*, 307-331. Retrieved June 12, 2007, from EBSCO Online Database Business Source Complete. http://search.ebscohost.com/login.aspx?direct=true&db=bth&AN=21945242&site=ehost-live

Keon, J. W. (1991). Point of view: Understanding the power of expert systems in marketing—when and how to build them. *Journal of Advertising Research, 31*, 64-71. Retrieved June 12, 2007, from EBSCO Online Database Business Source Complete. http://search.ebscohost.com/login.aspx?direct=true&db=bth&AN=9202171002&site=ehost-live

Shugan, S. M. (2002). Marketing science, models, monopoly models, and why we need them. *Marketing Science, 21*, 223-228. Retrieved June 12, 2007, from EBSCO Online Database Business Source Complete. http://search.ebscohost.com/login.aspx?direct=true&db=bth&AN=17463152&site=ehost-live

Wyner, G. A. (2006). Why model? *Marketing Research, 18*, 6-7. Retrieved June 12, 2007, from EBSCO Online Database Business Source Complete. http://

search.ebscohost.com/login.aspx?direct=true&db=bth&AN=20577118&site=ehost-live

Yi, Q., & Hui, X. (2011). No customer left behind: a distribution-free bayesian approach to accounting for missing xs in marketing models. *Marketing Science, 30*, 717-736. Retrieved November 15, 2013, from EBSCO Online Database Business Source Complete. http://search.ebscohost.com/login.aspx?direct=true&db=bth&AN=65097007&site=ehost-live

SUGGESTED READING

Barns, D. M. (2005). Comment on the value of simple models in new product forecasting and customer-base analysis. *Applied Stochastic Models in Business & Industry, 21*(4/5), 475-476. Retrieved June 12, 2007, from EBSCO Online Database Business Source Complete. http://search.ebscohost.com/login.aspx?direct=true&db=bth&AN=18071419&a,p;site=ehost-live

Fader, P. S. & Hardie, B. G. S. (2005). The value of simple models in new product forecasting and customer-base analysis. *Applied Stochastic Models in Business & Industry, 21*(4/5), 461-473. Retrieved June 12, 2007, from EBSCO Online Database Business Source Complete. http://search.ebscohost.com/login.aspx?direct=true&db=bth&AN=18071420&site=ehost-live

Gilbride, Timothy J. (2016). A model for inferring market preferences from online retail product information matrices. *Journal of Retailing*. Retrieved June 29, 2017. http://www.sciencedirect.com/science/article/pii/S0022435916300227

Hanssens, D. M., Leeflang, P. S. H., & Wittink, D. R. (2005). Market response models and marketing practice. *Applied Stochastic Models in Business & Industry, 21*(4/5), 423-434. Retrieved June 12, 2007, from EBSCO Online Database Business Source Complete. http://search.ebscohost.com/login.aspx?direct=true&db=bth&AN=18071428&site=ehost-live

Ho, T. H., Lim, N., & Camerer, C. F. (2006). How "psychological" should economic and marketing models be? *Journal of Marketing Research, 43*, 341-344. Retrieved June 12, 2007, from EBSCO Online Database Business Source Complete. http://search.ebscohost.com/login.aspx?direct=true&db=bth&AN=21945228&site=ehost-live

Jones, S. & Eden, C. (1981). Modelling in marketing: Explicating subjective knowledge. *European Journal of Marketing, 15*, 3-11. Retrieved June 12, 2007, from EBSCO Online Database Business Source Complete. http://search.ebscohost.com/login.aspx?direct=true&db=bth&AN=5117933&site=ehost-live

Ruth A. Wienclaw, Ph.D.

B

Brand Management

ABSTRACT

Brand management is the practice of managing all aspects of a brand, from tangibles such as logo and package design to the intangible tenor of the emotions a consumer experiences when purchasing a brand product or service. First used in its modern form by Procter & Gamble in 1931, brand management has become a standard method used by virtually all organizations marketing any type of product or service. This article begins by reviewing the history of brands and the origins of brand management. It then turns to the two main types of brand management, exploring the philosophies and organizational strategies associated with each. Next, it examines how the rise of Internet commerce and advertising has affected brand management. Finally, it turns to the future of brand management, anticipating what changes the field will likely undergo as the 21st century continues.

OVERVIEW

In today's highly competitive marketplace, brand management has become one of the primary tools used by organizations to gain a sustained competitive advantage over rivals (Louro, M. & Cunha P., 2001; High, 2004). While all products or services can eventually be copied, brands are not easily imitated. If marketers successfully endow a brand with associations that tap into consumers' emotional states, then branded products retain some degree of product differentiation, even if the products themselves are copied by competitors (Bengtsson & Firat, 2006). This is the primary goal of brand management: to use a brand to add value to the intrinsic value of a product or service (Keller & Richey, 2006). This added value is called brand equity.

The term "brand" is understood to have a number of different meanings. Some people use the word

brand interchangeably with "logo" or "label." In these contexts, the term brand refers to the legally protected trademarks, trade names, and trade symbols used to differentiate products. Others use the term in a more expansive sense, to denote the larger bundle of trademarks associated with intellectual property, including product design and packaging, advertising content, sounds, domain names, as well as innumerable other items. Finally, still others use "brand" in an even more holistic sense, to indicate the company that owns a given brand. The terms corporate brand and corporate brand personality are often used interchangeably with "reputation" (High, 2004). The field of brand management accepts and engages with all of these different meanings of the term.

Since the beginning of the twenty-first century, brand management has expanded its scope to deal with the challenges and opportunities presented by the Internet. As a global marketplace, the Internet poses new legal questions about brand names and trademarks; questions that were long ago resolved in the traditional marketplace. So long as brand managers are aware of these legal issues, they can use the Internet to exponentially increase consumer awareness of brands (Loosley & Gregory, 2004).

The future of brand management will likely include many other changes besides those instigated by the Internet. The field has long been criticized for a lack of accountability, as no reliable measurements have yet been devised to measure the performance of brand managers. New research into brand metrics promises to change this situation (Keller, 2001).

APPLICATION

History of Brands & Brand Management
The roots of brand management can be traced to the late nineteenth century, when a number of business owner-entrepreneurs working independently of one another established the first successful, nationally

recognized branded products (Low, 1994). Before this time, brands and advertising in general had been associated with disreputable vendors, such as quack medicine salesmen. But beginning in approximately 1870, and facilitated by Civil War-era improvements in long-distance transportation and communication, as well as advancements in the art of packaging, the first hugely successful brands were born. By the turn of the twentieth century, consumers were beginning to associate brands with quality and consistency, two characteristics largely missing in unbranded manufactured goods of the period (Low, 1994).

During these early years in the history of brands, what we would now refer to as brand management was carried out exclusively by firm owners or presidents. The creators of the first successful brands were visionaries, and the novelty of branding made managing newly created brands the personal project of these forward-looking business owners. Often these men developed brands despite resistance at every level of their organization; from the board of directors to the sales force, company employees were hesitant to embrace changes they did not fully understand (Low, 1994). No single management philosophy or organizational structure predominated during this period. Rather, brands were managed with an "intuitive and common-sense approach" by their entrepreneurial-minded creators (Low, 1994, p. 177).

Only after the market leadership of branded products was established did the management of brands become the domain of professionals. Between 1915 and 1930, the management of brands was transferred from the chief executive suite to the control of specialized managers, who worked with advertising agencies to promote existing brands and bring new brands into being (Low, 1994). During this period, a functional style of managing brands emerged. This first generation of middle managers entrusted with managing brands represented "an entirely new class of businessmen," which was not made up of independent, creative entrepreneurs, but of salaried professionals trained in functional specialties and rational problem-solving (Low, 1994, p. 177). These men used their pragmatic skill-set to conduct market research and product testing, create appropriate advertising, develop attractive packaging, prepare sales manuals, and run sales promotions. Managing brands became team-based and highly reliant on a functionally organized company model. Team members, each with

their own specialty, worked together in order to develop and market a company's brands (Low, 1994).

While this functional method achieved extraordinary results during the early twentieth century, problems soon became apparent. First, poor coordination between team members (and often an outside advertising agency as well) could be disastrous. Second, companies had no formal system for promoting more than one brand in any given market. And, most importantly, no single person was held accountable for the overall success or failure of a brand (Low, 1994). It was this last grievance that Neil McElroy, of Procter & Gamble (P&G), sought to address in his now famous 1931 memo that invented both the idea of modern brand management and the term "brand management." McElroy suggested that instead of organizing marketing and advertising departments functionally, P&G should organize these departments by brand, with each brand run by its own set of brand managers. P&G adopted this new system in 1932, with most other advertising firms following suit during the 1950s and 1960s (Low, 1994).

Between 1930 and 1950, P&G's brand manager system was adopted by very few other agencies. However, in the two decades following World War II, it was adopted en masse until, in 1967, 84 percent of large consumer goods manufacturers in the United States had brand managers (Low, 1994). This large-scale shift from a functional organizational structure to the modern brand manager system was largely due to the proliferation of brands. As it became increasingly common for companies to have multiple brands, it became more difficult to manage these brands with a functional system. Delegating responsibility for a brand to a single brand manager became the only system that seemed to make sense in this environment (Low, 1994). Once the shift was made, a company's various brands became nearly autonomous entities, run by brand managers with a remarkable degree of autonomy, "like a mini-company" (Pearson, 2004, p. 76).

The rapid assimilation to the brand manager system that so many companies underwent during the 1950s and 1960s contributed to a backlash against this system during the 1970s. Companies complained that the system increased the size of bureaucracies and brand managers had too vague a job description and too little authority to be truly effective. During this period, companies did not abandon brand management altogether, but merely adapted the brand manager system to their own company culture and needs (Low, 1994). From this time onward, brand management became a far less rigid field, dominated not by just the brand manager paradigm, but accommodating to countless new organizational approaches. Beginning in the 1980s and continuing to the present, brand management has become both more heterogeneous and more pervasive. Brand management is now viewed as vital to the future success of all corporations and is accordingly carried out by virtually all corporations in a variety of ways (Louro & Cunha, 2001).

Different Types of Brand Management

In today's business world there is "a cacophony of simultaneously competing and overlapping approaches to brand management" (Louro & Cunha, 2001, p. 850). This "cacophony" is partly due to the previously mentioned multiple understanding of the term "brand." Different ideas about what a brand is have understandably led to different styles of managing brands. The two types of brand management described below each encapsulate a philosophy of brands as well as a style of brand management. Some of these philosophies and styles are in direct contrast with one another; others complement one another without complication. In reality, most firms do not adhere strictly to any one type of brand management but utilize a mix of strategies derived from each.

Brand as Trademark

Some brand managers define a brand as a name, logo, or symbol (Felgner, 2007). For these brand managers, a brand serves two main purposes. First, in the form of a trademark, trade name, or trade symbol, a brand establishes legal ownership of a product and protects the product from the most direct forms of imitation. Second, a brand enables consumers to differentiate a branded product from its competitors (Louro & Cunha, 2001; High, 2004).

This understanding of brands leads to a product-oriented style of brand management. In order for brands defined in this particular sense to be valuable, they need to carry and retain positive associations with consumers. More simply, a brand name or trademark must establish and maintain a reputation for excellence (High, 2004). This task is the principal goal of brand management. It is achieved mainly through vigorous and sustained oversight of production and monitoring of quality control (Pearson, 2004). Advertising and marketing also play an important role in creating brand associations with consumers.

In this type of brand management, success is measured by the marketplace performance of branded products. If quality control in combination with advertising achieves an increase in sales revenue, then brand management has been successful. The most significant weakness with this type of brand management is that it leaves a brand vulnerable to imitation. If a brand is identified with little more than the product itself, then consumers are less likely to exhibit brand loyalty if competitors enter the market with similar products (Louro & Cunha, 2001).

Holistic Brand Management

When a brand is defined either as the entire bundle of the intellectual property associated with its trademark or as a company's reputation/corporate brand personality, then brand management becomes a much more complex and diversified undertaking. When a brand is considered to be "a whole greater than the sum of its parts," brand management must likewise supervise every aspect involved with the traditional functions of a brand and more (Keller & Richey, 2006, p. 80).

Besides managing the marketplace products and services that carry a brand's name, brand managers must also manage a brand's intangible identity, or personality (Kelley & Richey, 2006; Louro & Cunha, 2001). Such a personality is built out of human traits, such as integrity, compassion, or creativity. Brand managers establish a brand's identity through traditional methods such as advertising, as well as through internal brand management. This latter task necessitates that brand managers become "brand ambassadors" who teach company employees at every level about brand personality and values (Hulberg, 2006, p. 61). Brand management becomes "culture management," or an attempt to direct the entire organizational culture so that it aligns with the brand personality (Hulberg, 2006, p. 64). If this is done effectively, then everyone from the chief executive officer to the sales force to the customer relationship team will operate in alignment with brand identity.

This type of brand management offers several distinct advantages over a more product-oriented system. Focusing on corporate brand personality is a way of reducing the costs associated with brand management, as it can promote many products at the same time (Hulberg, 2006; Louro & Cunha, 2001). Additionally, a corporate brand personality is less vulnerable to imitation than a traditional brand. Once a brand has engaged with consumers on an emotional level, consumers are much more likely to stay loyal to that brand in the face of competition (Bengtsson & Firat, 2006). However, a brand is also made vulnerable by this type of brand management in the sense that consumers can more easily associate one troubled product with the entire brand.

Brand Management & the Internet

The dawn of the Internet age raised many new issues in the field of brand management. In particular, several new legal complications arise when brands migrate from the real world of commerce into the virtual world of Internet commerce. The Internet represents a global marketplace in which national boundaries are faint or nonexistent. This fact becomes problematic for brand management because different nations have very different laws governing advertising, trademarks, and domain registration (Loosley & Gregory, 2004).

Advertising

This is by far the most nebulous area with regards to Internet brand management. Virtually every country has its own national legislation concerning advertising. When advertising in the global marketplace of the Internet, it is sometimes necessary to abide by these various regulations. Specifically, when directing advertising at the population of a particular nation, it is necessary to abide by that nation's advertising laws. Criteria for determining who advertising is directed toward is still rather opaque. Anything from the content of an advertisement to the language it is written in or the placement of the advertisement on a particular website can be taken as evidence that the advertisement was directed toward a particular population. Brand managers should navigate this difficult legal territory by first prioritizing markets and then only directing advertisements to markets given top priority. This approach allows brand managers to ensure that they are in legal compliance with the laws and regulations of each national market they choose to target (Loosley & Gregory, 2004).

Trademarks

When promoting a brand on the Internet, brand managers must first secure special additional trademark protection. Along with the brand name, any icons or designs used to denote brand identity must also be registered. As with advertising, because of the global nature of the Internet marketplace, brand managers must apply for protection in the various national markets they expect to do the most Internet business in (Loosley & Gregory, 2004).

When nationally recognized brands migrate onto the Internet, they often face challenges from local brands operating under the same brand name in other nations. These local businesses often infringe on brand trademarks and may have to be dealt with in their own nation's legal system (Loosely & Gregory, 2004).

Domain Registration

Domain names, which may include a brand name or slogan, must also be registered. This should always be done as soon as possible in order to prevent "cyber squatting" (Loosley & Gregory, 2004, p. 192). Cyber squatting is a relatively prevalent practice and consists of opportunists registering a famous brand name as a domain and then attempting to sell this domain back to the company that owns the brand. Although cyber squatting is illegal in many nations (the United States passed the Anticybersquatting Consumer Protection Act in 1999), the easiest way to avoid it is through prevention (Loosley & Gregory, 2004).

VIEWPOINTS
The Future of Brand Management

As the business world moves forward, brand management will continue to evolve. One factor that will certainly affect the field's evolution is globalization. In the past, brand production was largely outsourced because it proved too expensive to maintain factories in developed countries. Now, however, entrepreneurs in the developing countries that serve as manufacturing hubs for brands are themselves founding brands that they can both manufacture and produce (Pearson, 2004). It is only a matter of time before these new brands pose as serious competition to existing brands in global markets.

At the beginning of the twenty-first century, some onlookers pointed to the most common criticism of brand management—a lack of accountability—and suggested that the field had to move toward greater accountability in the future (Hinshaw, 2005). Many charged that the principal problem with brand management was the lack of uniformly tracked brand-related metrics (Keller, 2001). Without such data, it was difficult to evaluate the effectiveness or productivity of brand managers (Hinshaw, 2005). However, in the second decade of the century, charting brand management metrics has become easier, as companies offer software that is able to chart the effectiveness of brand advertising; Vizu's Brand Lift is one such example. New metrics have been developed to measure brand management's effects on critical areas such as customer experience and loyalty, brand profitability, and brand value.

Brand management is poised to become only more important as the twenty-first century progresses. It also promises to become even more diverse, changing to meet the evolving future needs of all businesses and organizations.

BIBLIOGRAPHY

Batra, R., Ahuvia, A., & Bagozzi, R. (2012). Brand Love. *Journal of Marketing, 76*, 1–16. Retrieved November 21, 2013 from EBSCO online database, Business Source Complete. http://search.ebscohost.com/login.aspx?direct=true&db=bth&AN=71960581&site=ehost-live

Bengtsson, A & Firat, A. (2006). Brand literacy: Consumers' sense-making of brand management. *Advances in Consumer Research, 33*, 375-380. Retrieved March 19, 2007, from EBSCO Online Database Business Source Premier. http://search.ebscohost.com/login.aspx?direct=true&db=buh&AN=23585722&site=ehost-live

Felgner, B. (2007) New challenges in branding. *Home Textiles Today, 28*, 1-31. Retrieved March 19, 2007, from EBSCO Online Database Business Source Premier. http://search.ebscohost.com/login.aspx?direct=true&db=buh&AN=24101418&site=ehost-live

Hanna, S., & Rowley, J. (2011). Towards a strategic place brand-management model. *Journal of Marketing Management, 27*(5/6), 458–476. Retrieved November 21, 2013 from EBSCO online database, Business Source Complete. http://search.ebscohost.com/login.aspx?direct=true&db=bth&AN=60041215&site=ehost-live

High, D. & Knowles, J. (2004). How to define your brand and determine its value. *Marketing Management, 13*, 22-28. Retrieved March 23, 2007, from EBSCO Online Database Business Source Premier. http://search.ebscohost.com/login.aspx?direct=true&db=buh&AN=13468247&site=ehost-live

Hinshaw, M. (2005). A survey of key success factors in financial services marketing and brand management. *Journal of Financial Services Marketing, 10*, 37-48. Retrieved March 19, 2007, from EBSCO Online Database Business Source Premier. http://search.ebscohost.com/login.aspx?direct=true&db=buh&AN=18315948&site=ehost-live

Hulberg, J. (2006). Integrating corporate branding and sociological paradigms: A literature study. *Journal of Brand Management, 14*(1/2), 60-73. Retrieved March 19, 2007, from EBSCO Online Database Business Source Premier. http://search.ebscohost.com/login.aspx?direct=true&db=buh&AN=23521028&site=ehost-live

Keller, K. (2001). Editorial: Brand research imperatives. *Journal of Brand Management, 9*, 4-6. Retrieved March 22, 2007, from EBSCO Online Database Business Source Premier. http://search.ebscohost.com/login.aspx?direct=true&db=buh&AN=6906941&site=ehost-live

Keller, K & Richey, K. (2006). The importance of corporate brand personality traits to a successful 21st century business. *Journal of Brand Management, 14*(1/2), 74-81. Retrieved March 19, 2007, from EBSCO Online Database Business Source Premier. http://search.ebscohost.com/login.aspx?direct=true&db=buh&AN=23521027&site=ehost-live

Loosley, R., Richards, S., & Gregory, J. (2004). The effect on brand management when a business migrates onto the internet: A legal perspective. *Journal of Brand Management, 11*, 183-196. Retrieved March 22, 2007, from EBSCO Online Database Business Source Premier. http://search.ebscohost.com/login.aspx?direct=true&db=buh&AN=12061306&site=ehost-live

Louro, M. & Cunha, P. (2001). Brand management paradigms. *Journal of Marketing Management, 17*(7/8), 849-875. Retrieved March 19, 2007, from EBSCO Online Database Business Source Premier. http://search.ebscohost.com/login.aspx?direct=true&db=buh&AN=5482283&site=ehost-live

Low, G. (1994). Brands, brand management, and the brand manager system: A critical-historical evaluation. *Journal of Marketing Research, 31*, 173-189.

Retrieved March 19, 2007, from EBSCO Online Database Business Source Premier. http://search. ebscohost.com/login.aspx?direct=true&db=buh &AN=9411112938&site=ehost-live

Naylor, R., Lamberton, C., & West, P.M. (2012). Beyond the "like" button: The impact of mere virtual presence on brand evaluations and purchase intentions in social media settings. *Journal of Marketing, 76*, 105–120. Retrieved November 21, 2013 from EBSCO online database, Business Source Complete. http://search.ebscohost.com/login.aspx?di rect=true&db=bth&AN=82680221&site=ehost-live

Pearson, D. (2004). Changes in brand management. *Journal of Brand Management, 12*, 76-80. Retrieved March 19, 2007, from EBSCO Online Database Business Source Premier. http://search.ebsco- host.com/login.aspx?direct=true&db=buh&AN= 14975939&site=ehost-live

Quinton, S. (2013). The community brand paradigm: A response to brand management's dilemma in the digital era. *Journal of Marketing Management, 29*(7/8), 912–932. Retrieved November 21, 2013 from EBSCO online database, Business Source Complete. http://search.ebscohost.com/login.aspx?direct=tr ue&db=bth&AN=89358318&site=ehost-live

Satomura, T., M. Wedel, & R. Pieters. (2014). Copy alert: A method and metric to detect visual copycat brands. *Journal of Marketing Research, 51*, 1–13. Retrieved November 24, 2014, from EBSCO On- line Database Business Source Complete. http:// search.ebscohost.com/login.aspx?direct=true&d b=bth&AN=95682563

Xueming Luo, et al. (2013). Make the most of a po- larizing brand. *Harvard Business Review, 91*, 29–31. Retrieved November 24, 2014, from EBSCO On- line Database Business Source Complete. http:// search.ebscohost.com/login.aspx?direct=true&d b=bth&AN=91570267

SUGGESTED READING

Blankson, Charles, et al. (2016). The Routledge com- panion to contemporary brand management. *Routlege.* Retrieved June 29, 2016. https://books. google.com/books?id=pq2uDAAAQBAJ&dq=bra nd+management&lr=&source=gbs_navlinks_s.

Burmann, C. & Zeplin, S. (2005). Building brand commitment: A behavioural approach to internal brand management. *Journal of Brand Manage- ment, 12*, 279-300. Retrieved March 19, 2007, from

EBSCO Online Database Business Source Premier. http://search.ebscohost.com/login.aspx?direct=t rue&db=buh&AN=16515522&site=ehost-live

Hankinson, G. (2007). The management of des- tination brands: Five guiding principles based on recent developments in corporate branding theory. *Journal of Brand Management, 14*, 240-254. Retrieved March 19, 2007 from EBSCO Online Database Business Source Premier. http://search. ebscohost.com/login.aspx?direct=true&db=buh &AN=24245775&site=ehost-live

Hatch, M. (2006). The hermeneutics of branding. *Journal of Brand Management, 14*(1/2), 40-59. Re- trieved March 19, 2007, from EBSCO Online Da- tabase Business Source Premier. http://search. ebscohost.com/login.aspx?direct=true&db=buh &AN=23521029&site=ehost-live

King, C. & Grace, D. (2006). Exploring managers' perspectives of the impact of brand management strategies on employee roles within a service firm. *Journal of Services Marketing, 20*(6/7), 369-380. Re- trieved March 19, 2007, from EBSCO Online Da- tabase Business Source Premier. http://search. ebscohost.com/login.aspx?direct=true&db=buh &AN=23357533&site=ehost-live

Reppel, A., Szmigin, I., & Gruber, T. (2006). The iPod phenomenon: Identifying a market leader's secrets through qualitative marketing research. *Journal of Product & Brand Management, 15*(4/5), 239-249. Retrieved March 19, 2007, from EBSCO Online Database Business Source Premier. http:// search.ebscohost.com/login.aspx?direct=true&d b=buh&AN=22868389&site=ehost-live

Uggla, H. (2013). The nature and scope of brand portfolio signals within brand portfolio manage- ment. *IUP Journal of Brand Management 10*, 7–16. Retrieved November 24, 2014, from EBSCO On- line Database Business Source Premier. http:// search.ebscohost.com/login.aspx?direct=true&d b=bth&AN=91675189

Uggla, H. (2004). The brand association base: A con- ceptual model for strategically Leveraging partner brand equity. *Journal of Brand Management, 12*, 105- 123. Retrieved March 19, 2007, from EBSCO On- line Database Business Source Premier. http:// search.ebscohost.com/login.aspx?direct=true&d b=buh&AN=14975918&site=ehost-live

Richa S. Tiwary, Ph.D., M.L.S.

BRAND PERSONALITY

ABSTRACT

"Brand personality" refers to ascribing elements of human personality to a brand so that it may appear more attractive and engaging to an audience. Some companies may create brand personalities that reflect their founder or CEO; others reflect the culture of the organization. Whichever strategy a firm undertakes to develop its brand personality, it is understood that carelessness in developing a brand personality may lead to failure and culture and technology have become crucial factors in developing a strong and durable brand personality.

OVERVIEW

The concept of "brand personality" has generated a great deal of interest since the late 1990s. A brand personality is a dynamic thing, in which organizations create and imbue a brand with anthropomorphic characteristics. Consumers give the brand symbolic value through their interactions with, use of, or consumption of the brand. Brand personality, then, refers to human characteristics allocated to the brand by both its creators and consumers.

Among the reasons found by marketing managers to develop the concept of brand personality was the growing proliferation or excess number of brands in the market. In order to stand out from the crowd and fight against a target market increasingly desensitized to conventional advertising cues, firms had to find better ways to express and communicate their message. For instance, they found that it was crucial that content be relevant and provide a differential added value. This content should be created in a way that is relevant not only to the brand but also to the needs of its target market and other interest groups. To achieve this, they began to give brands a gloss or appearance of personality so that consumers are able to relate to the brand as if the brand has the capacity to relate to them. The challenge for marketers is to define the specific personal characteristics that reflect the key values firms want the brand to express.

Because human beings are complex, the best brand personalities are those able to encompass human complexities and even contradictions. In other words, a successful brand personality usually includes nuances or shades of meaning to better reach a larger number of consumers who will feel a personal connection with the brand. However, although in theory it is possible for firms to add as many nuances as they desire to a brand, it is also convenient to limit characteristics to those that are coherent with its attributes and with the company's general values and discursive aspects.

A common example of a successful brand personality is that of Coca-Cola. Coca-Cola successfully integrated and disseminated the concept of happiness as part of its brand philosophy. Happiness has long been a part of its differentiation strategy and one that has been consolidated throughout its marketing campaigns for decades. Nevertheless, although it may reflect the idea of happiness, the brand itself is incapable of feeling joy. It is merely part of a conscious marketing strategy.

There is, in fact, a very real difference between brand personality and that of human beings. People develop personalities as an admixture of traits and assimilation by learning behavioral models from the world around them. This includes all sorts of external influences, such as human relationships—parents, relatives, friends—but also pervasive elements such as the media, through advertising and celebrity culture. A brand's personality, on the other hand, is created internally, through research, trial and error, and seeking those values and attributes deemed by a marketing team as the most convenient for its goals and representative of the brand's "essence."

However, both human and brand personalities are imbued by tangible and intangible elements, those that reflect material objects and personal feelings. In the case of a brand, tangible and intangible elements are those offered to its target market, consumers, stakeholders, and all other interest groups. The end goal is differentiation, and the means to differentiation include offering better prices than the competition, offering added value, being a unique product, incorporating flexible policies, and implementing customer relations strategies.

When speaking of differentiation, elements that make a product different and unique should also reflect organizational values. This commitment of the firm to the brand is part of the intangible elements that contribute to added value, the elements that a customer receives beyond the product itself—in this case, trust in the brand and the sense of having acquired a quality product. Usually, upon creating or renewing a brand, brand managers and their teams make a list of the values and benefits they wish to be reflected. These are then organized in order of priority according to interest and relevance and distilled into the essence of the brand. It makes a difference, for instance, if customer satisfaction is among the topmost priorities. Being able to satisfy customers' needs and wants for that brand and product makes for much better long-term sustainability. The commitment to customer satisfaction, however, must come across as real or customers will, in time, eventually see through the façade and lose trust in the brand. There are many products, however, that for a variety of reasons do not need to place customer satisfaction as the topmost priority and instead favor other factors that better align with their brand profile.

There are a great many ways in which brand managers sort out personality factors in order to develop brand personalities. Among the most common ways to characterize brand personality elements or concepts are the following: (a) rational—measurable and tangible concepts; (b) emotional—related to moods, able to conjure abstract ideas and feelings; (c) internal—used in connection to internal factors such as employees and company stakeholders; and (d) external—necessary to generate a favorable opinion among audiences and other external interest groups.

FURTHER INSIGHTS

Once the basic "personality traits" have been decided upon, these must translated or expressed through the stage of verbal identity, which includes content-based elements such as brand voice, tone, and style. These are important to establishing an emotional connection with the brand's target market. According to experts, the success of a brand is dependent—in about 90 percent of cases—to successfully establishing an emotional connection with the audience and consumer groups.

Reaching this goal is challenging, because a vast array of human relationships and ways of connecting exist, as well as symbolic meanings that customers can assign to a brand. Many brand managers, then, strive to assign something extra, an added value, to

that relationship between the brand and its target. One of the most effective strategies used to achieve this, is verbal identity. Once the brand personality's "essence" or core values have been identified, the marketing team must implement ways to communicate the values and its attributes. Besides the visual components of a brand—its logo, for example—experts use the principle of "the 3 Cs" to develop its verbal identity.

- Clarity. Strong or successful brands are able to express very clearly how they wish to be perceived. The image and message remain clear and understandable across interest groups and, in some cases, across languages and nations. This differentiates them from their competitors and is a useful platform to cultivate brand loyalty among its target groups, as well as name recognition among the general audience. A strong brand personality can be based on the bold and unique personality of its major representative, such as Virgin Airlines and its CEO Richard Branson, or it may be a company brand that remains strong in the public consciousness, such as Coca-Cola.

- Consistency. Even constant change may become consistent if a brand or celebrity becomes known for constant reinvention. In fact, human beings can be a brand; one can think of such celebrities as Madonna, the Kardashian sisters, or Angelina Jolie. Each change may start a new trend and thus, the brand becomes known a trendsetter. Most brands, however, do better by remaining consistent in image and message, while adapting to social changes and developments. In other words, successful brands ensure that their essence remains true, despite sometimes necessary change and adaptation. A powerful idea—and its values—will endure.

- Constancy. It is known among successful firms that strong brands are constant. That is, their message is heard frequently and repeatedly, ideally through a variety of channels and platforms. They are always "available" to their public, even if the feeling of nearness or closeness they provide is an illusion. These brands may include famous television talk show or reality show celebrities, company CEOs, or brands such as Pepsi or including government agencies, such as USAID, which has been successful in many of its foreign relations campaigns abroad furthering humanitarian aid in the form of educational and health services aid.

Alternatively, some brand managers have interpreted the 3 Cs as consistency, culture, and content or communication. Content refers to verbal communication—in its written or spoken form—to promote a message. Culture, however, is a novel element that speaks of shared values, beliefs, behaviors, languages, and ways of life; it includes the way people interpret and engage with slogans and symbols as presented through a brand personality. Many cases of brand failure have been ascribed to focusing on the visual aspect of a brand but failing to take into account the verbal and cultural aspects of their brand strategy.

Important brand personality elements, such as brand voice, then, are directly related to culture. Each organization has a specific or unique culture, which should be reflected in its brand: what makes it unique, what it stands for, and why its product is important. Guidelines such as the 3 Cs help brand managers be more accurate in visualizing a long-term branding strategy, including the personality that a brand should have—that is, what characteristics such a personality should have and how to make it relate to its customers, both local and global. It is for these reasons that experts insist verbal identity must always be an integral part—a clear, coherent, and culturally relevant part—of a brand's personality.

Issues

According to experts, iconic brands—those that have risen to become the most successful at representing the ideals and desires of a society—follow principles known as "cultural branding." These precepts, developed in the 1990s, are different than traditional branding strategies established around the 1950s and sometimes even contradict established advertising conventions. As such, it remains a relatively new and sometimes controversial field that demands new mindsets and innovative models. Conventional branding practices include a dependence on cognitive models, whereas the novel strategies were based on "emotional branding." Rather than appeal to rational responses, emotional branding appeals to its audience's emotions, feelings, and aspirations. In the contemporary marketing field, however, brand managers who seek to create or strengthen a brand's personality usually draw upon a combination of these approaches.

In the 1970s, the idea that most took hold among brand managers was that for a brand to become successful, it must keep its marketing approach simple and position each product in consumers' minds as offering a single, specific benefit. This idea, known as "mind share," was directly related to the concept of "brand positioning," which, at the time, related to occupying a preferred place in the consumer's mind, as compared to the competition, based on reasons and benefits to buy. In other words, it relied on the mind to make the connections between the specific realities and functions of the service or good as the focus of the brand, and secondarily, factors such as status, benefits, or brand personality attributes. An example of a distinctive benefit of a product, for instance, might be the specific cavity-fighting ingredients of a specific brand of toothpaste or the added vitamins in a brand of children''s cereal. These elements are secondarily supported by emotional appeals, such as the natural desire of people to provide the best for their family.

Mind share—also known as "brand identity" and "brand essence"—remains useful and valued among brand managers. Its strategy seeks to identify the concepts that are important in an individual's mind and create the necessary connections between these and the brand. Once identified, these concepts should be clearly and consistently recalled in the mind of a customer in relation to the brand.

Emotional branding seeks to differentiate a brand from its competition by making strong emotional connections with consumers. Brand personality is developed accordingly. An emotional connection might be better able to overrule rational arguments against purchasing a product. Creating an emotional bond with consumers requires understanding that contemporary customers define their identities through the brands they consume, places they frequent, colleges they attend, music they listen to, and other consuming behaviors. Emotional branding is centered on its customers' material and emotional needs. Critics, however, warn of the risks of manipulating the emotions of audience members to the extent that they may overrule the call of reason or disregard their better nature.

Both mind share and emotional branding can be combined with cultural branding, a highly innovative model that seeks not only to be relevant and appropriate to the culture in which it develops, but also to identify opportunities unique to each market. Although the spread and reach of technology has to some extent equalized much of a brand's audience, media users remain embedded in their cultural environment, which inevitably influences how they respond to brands.

The phenomenon of social media has become an important player in developing brand personalities, highlighting the need to build personal connections with individuals through a variety of platforms. Social-media outlets exist for every single aspect of social life. Successful brand managers use the vast array of social media to establish its brand in a variety of media platforms. Social media not only makes for a ubiquitous brand presence, but also is an extremely cost-effective way to position and promote almost any kind of product or service, due to its relatively low cost and its capacity to reach vast numbers of users.

It is important to note, however, that the relentless pervasiveness of social media illuminates, more than ever, the importance of employing clarity, consistency and good practices of cultural communication. For example, essential elements of brand personality should remain consistent throughout different social-media platforms and media outlets in general. These include visual elements, brand voice and style, and message tone. Individuals, however, use a variety of media, and inconsistent branding across outlets results in consumer confusion and a diffused brand message. One of the most important factors in building a loyal customer base is not only trust, quality, and image, but also coherence and consistency.

BIBLIOGRAPHY

Bechter, C., Farinelli, G., Daniel, R., & Frey, M. (2016). Advertising between archetype and brand personality. Administrative Sciences, 6(2), 1–11. Retrieved October 23, 2016, from EBSCO Online Database Business Source Ultimate. http://search.ebscohost.com/login.aspx?direct=true&db=bsu&AN=116380833&site=ehost-live

Ghosh, S. (2016). Modeling the personality construct of brands: A study on apparel brands in India. *IUP Journal of Brand Management, 13*(2), 57–74. Retrieved October 23, 2016, from EBSCO Online Database Business Source Ultimate. http://search.ebscohost.com/login.aspx?direct=true&db=bsu&AN=117397840&site=ehost-live

Holt, D. B., & Cameron, D. (2012). *Cultural strategy: Using innovative ideologies to build breakthrough brands.* Oxford, UK: Oxford University Press.

Kastiya, S. (2016). The impact of consumer personality traits on luxury brand market: An empirical study on closet consumers. *IUP Journal of Brand Management, 13*(1), 20–33. Retrieved October 23, 2016, from EBSCO Online Database Business Source Ultimate. http://search.ebscohost.com/login.aspx?direct=true&db=bsu&AN=114187528&site=ehost-live

Shehu, E., Becker, J., Langmaack, A., & Clement, M. (2016). The brand personality of nonprofit organizations and the influence of monetary incentives. *Journal of Business Ethics, 138*(3), 589–600. Retrieved October 23, 2016, from EBSCO Online Database Business Source Ultimate. http://search.ebscohost.com/login.aspx?direct=true&db=bsu&AN=118555338&site=ehost-live

Thomas, B. J., & Jenifer, S. C. (2016). Measurement model of employer brand personality. *Journal of Contemporary Management Research, 10*(1), 58–78. Retrieved October 23, 2016, from EBSCO Online Database Business Source Ultimate. http://search.ebscohost.com/login.aspx?direct=true&db=bsu&AN=113644338&site=ehost-live

Vegheş, C., & Popescu, I. C. (2016). The Proust Questionnaire as tool of studying the brand personality: an exploratory approach. *Romanian Journal of Marketing, *(2), 77–78. Retrieved October 23, 2016, from EBSCO Online Database Business Source Ultimate. http://search.ebscohost.com/login.aspx?direct=true&db=bsu&AN=117267260&site=ehost-live

SUGGESTED READING

Ferguson, Graham, et al. (2016). Brand personality as a direct cause of brand extension success: does self-monitoring matter? *Journal of Consumer Marketing.* Retrieved June 29, 2017. http://www.emeraldinsight.com/doi/abs/10.1108/JCM-04-2014-0954

Kang, C., Bennett, G., & Welty Peachey, J. (2016). Five dimensions of brand personality traits in sport. *Sport Management Review, 19*(4), 441–453. Retrieved October 23, 2016, from EBSCO Online Database Business Source Ultimate. http://search.ebscohost.com/login.aspx?direct=true&db=bsu&AN=117734766&site=ehost-live

Mann, B. S., & Rawat, J. (2016). The role of consumer personality trait and brand personality trait in creating customer experience. *IUP Journal of Brand Management, 13*(3), 23–42. Retrieved October 23, 2016, from EBSCO Online Database Business Source Ultimate. http://search.ebscohost.com/login.aspx?direct=true&db=bsu&AN=119548845&site=ehost-live

Roy, P., Khandeparkar, K., & Motiani, M. (2016). A lovable personality: The effect of brand personality on brand love. *Journal of Brand Management, 23*(5), 97–113. Retrieved October 23, 2016, from EBSCO Online Database Business Source

Ultimate. http://search.ebscohost.com/login.aspx?direct=true&db=bsu&AN=119206809&site=ehost-live

Sundar, A., & Noseworthy, T. J. (2016). Too exciting to fail, too sincere to succeed: The effects of brand personality on sensory disconfirmation. *Journal of Consumer Research, 43*(1), 44–67. Retrieved October 23, 2016, from EBSCO Online Database Business Source Ultimate. http://search.ebscohost.com/login.aspx?direct=true&db=bsu&AN=115648580&site=ehost-live

Trudy Mercadal, Ph.D.

BUSINESS MARKETING

ABSTRACT

This article will focus on business marketing, especially business-to-business (B2B) marketing and e-commerce. The foundation of business marketing strategy is based on three concepts: segmentation, targeting, and positioning. Many forecasters have predicted that B2B markets can expect purchases to net several trillion dollars a year, which is why many are predicting that the growth will outpace business-to-consumer (B2C) marketing. Although business-to-consumer electronic commerce captures the attention of the industry, business-to-business electronic commerce is the format that is predicted to reap most e-business activity.

OVERVIEW

When marketing is mentioned, many think of the function as it relates to consumers. However, there is another side that is expected to blossom during the next decade—business-to-business marketing. According to the 2007 Marketing Priorities and Plans survey conducted by the trade journal *B to B*, marketing efforts will grow as business-to-business marketers increase budgets, do more business online, and try new technologies (Maddox, 2006). Respondents shared some of their goals for 2007, and the top three goals were customer acquisition (62.3 percent of the respondents), brand awareness (19.5 percent) and customer retention (11 percent).

"New market growth, product penetration, research and positioning the company as a thought leader" were other goals listed in the survey (Maddox, 2006). Although email, search, and webcasts were listed as still being important and worthy of some funding, website development was allocated the biggest percentage of online marketing funds. It was also illustrated that "67.7 percent of advertisers plan to launch new ad campaigns in 2007" (Maddox, 2006).

Many forecasters have predicted that the business-to-business market can expect purchases to net several trillion dollars a year, which is why many are predicting that the growth will outpace business-to-consumer marketing. However, the marketing industry will respond accordingly by providing both markets with sufficient attention even though both have different focuses.

Business Marketing Versus Consumer Marketing

There are many differences between the two forms of marketing, such as business marketing using shorter and more direct channels of distribution (Dwyer & Tanner, 2006), and consumer marketing aiming at larger demographic groups through mass media and retailers. In addition, the negotiation process is more personal between the buyer and seller in business marketing. Business marketers tend to use direct mail and trade journals as the preferred method of advertising and only commit a small portion of their budgets to do so (Hull & Speh, 2001).

According to Oliva (n.d.), some of the unique features between the two methods are:

Business-to-Business (B2B) Marketing:

- Transactions among and within value chains
- Value primarily determined by business economic use
- Small numbers of customers, many requiring personalized marketing, including customized products and prices
- Large customers with strong market power (a business's customers tend to be its competitors)
- Diverse and varied customer types and customer needs
- Large unit transactions
- Complex and lengthy selling processes involving many players creating a demand decision chain
- Deeper partnerships with members of the value chain, including customers
- Channel management oriented up and down the supply chain
- Sales focused on key account management and multiple purchasing influencers

Business-to-Consumer (B2C) Marketing:

- Transactions through the dealer to the end consumer
- Value determined by end-consumer perception
- Focus on brand management
- Large number of generally similar consumers
- Small transactions
- Linear selling process, usually of short duration
- Channel management oriented toward retail
- Sales activity focused on the end user

Business marketing's foundation is based on "building profitable, value-oriented relationships" between two organizations and their workforces (Oliva, n.d.). Business marketers focus on a small number of customers by using sales processes that are large, complex, and technical. Due to new marketing and communication technologies, B2B and B2C marketing efforts cross many industries. Business marketers must understand how the two methods work together in order to create and deliver value.

Importance of Value

Value is central to all marketing practices, especially business marketing. In business markets, the real value of a product or service can be understood by "analyzing the product's use in the marketplace and comparing the product or service to the next best alternative for the customer" (Oliva, n.d.). For example, Microsoft has introduced Office 2013. However, many companies are still using Office 2010. Many organizations tend not to update to the newer version until the bugs are worked out. The value concepts for both of these products can be calculated in monetary terms. In consumer markets, value is based on perception. For example, the value of coffee is based on brand symbolism, loyalty, experience, and taste preference.

Some business marketers have made the mistake of pricing their products and services too low. Many believe that price and costs are directly related. However, pricing based on cost may create pricing errors, which may lead to missed profit opportunities with business-to-business efforts. In order to avoid this costly mistake, value-based pricing should be used by companies. Value-based pricing occurs when a company creates a marketing and sales program geared toward educating potential customers on the value of the product or service they are receiving. If this goal is successful, potential customers tend to be willing to pay more for the product or service. Oliva (n.d.) believes that "studying the impact of value on profitability is one of the most important analyses a business marketer can conduct. Value in business markets can be examined on many levels" such as:

- The actual economic value of the offering delivered to the typical customer.
- The value of the supplier to the customer and the brand strength and relationship value of the supplier.
- How value differs among actual and prospective customers and among the individuals who collectively make a buying decision.
- How specific marketing activities influence customer recognition of value.
- How value builds through the industry supply chain and how much of that value is actually captured in the prices charged by supply chain members (Oliva, n.d.).

Once the importance of value in business marketing has been established, value-based strategies should be developed. Value-based pricing aims to match the price of a product with the value that product imparts. Some value-based pricing strategies consider the break-even point and tend to be subjective. According to SmallBusinessNotes.com

("Value-based pricing," 2007), three of these types of strategies are:

- Price the same as competitor. This strategy is useful when offering a commodity product, when prices are well established or when there are no other means to set prices. Organizations will be challenged to develop a plan that will lower their costs so that they can receive a higher profit than their competitors.
- Establish a low price on a product in order to capture a large number of customers in that market. This strategy is useful if the organization's goal is to achieve non-financial objectives such as creating product awareness, meeting the competition, or establishing an image of having a low cost. This strategy will work if the organization can maintain profitability at the low price or is able to maintain an acceptable level of sales in the event that it wants to raise prices at a later date.
- Charge a high price relative to cost if the product has a uniqueness that is valuable to the customers. This strategy is useful when the target market is affluent, and the product is positioned as being upscale. In this type of situation, the organization may be able to mark up the price because there will be a demand. The organization charges what it believes potential customers are willing to pay.

Business Marketing Strategy

The foundation of business marketing strategy is based on three concepts: segmentation, targeting, and positioning.

Segmentation. Customers are not the same. They have different needs and place different values on products and services. In order for organizations to respond to the various demands, they may group similar customers together in order to customize a marketing campaign geared toward each group. This process is an example of market segmentation. Marketers predict that each segment will have similar feelings about specific products. Therefore, there is a high probability that the individuals in the group will be receptive to the marketing campaign.

The purpose of marketing segmentation is to identify groups of similar and potential customers; prioritize which groups a business will focus on; understand the potential customers' wants, needs and behavior patterns; and respond to the different preferences with the appropriate marketing strategy. If the goal is met, businesses are expected to increase their revenue and marketing effectiveness.

Successful segmentation is characterized by the ability to recognize similarities within segments and differences between segments as well as the ability to create identifiable and measurable groups, accessible groups, and groups that are large enough to positively affect profits. The variables used for segmentation include geographic variables, demographic variables, psychographic variables, and behavioral variables. When a marketer collects information on the various variables, he will combine the information to create a buyer profile. In business-to-business marketing, market segmentation can be tricky because market researchers must work with smaller customer populations that are not conducive to large-group statistical analysis (i.e. data mining).

Targeting. Once the segments have been identified, the organization must determine which markets it will focus on. This is the next step and it is called targeting. Targeting involves the selection of customers. At this level, the organization must decide "which segments to target, how many products to offer, and which products to offer in which segments" ("Target market," 2008). Targeting decisions are based on market maturity, diversity of buyers' needs and preferences, strength of the competition and the volume of sales required for profitability. Business marketers have to decide which segments are the most profitable, how to assign the sales staff to the various segments, and how to develop distribution channels. Targeting can be selective (i.e. niche marketing) or extensive (i.e. mass marketing).

Positioning. Once segmentation and targeting have been completed, the organization is ready for the final step – positioning. The way potential customers perceive a product is referred to as a product's "position." Organizations have the power to actively position their products through the fostering of image creation and association amidst target markets. There are two ways to achieve this goal. They are re-positioning and de-positioning. When an organization changes a product's identity to differentiate it from competing products, it is called re-positioning. When an organization changes the identity of competing products to affect the identity of its own product, it is called de-positioning.

According to Ries and Trout (n.d.), the positioning process involves:

- Defining the market in which the product will compete
- Identifying the characteristics that define the product
- Collecting information from a sample of customers about their perceptions of each product on the relevant characteristics
- Determining each share
- Determining each product's current location in the product category
- Examining the fit between the position of the organization's product and the ideal vector

In the positioning phase, organizations are challenged with deciding which elements of their value proposition they will highlight in order to make their product the preferred choice for potential customers. The three elements are uniqueness, differences, and similarity. Uniqueness is when the organization can say it is the only company with the product. Differences are highlighted when the organization compares its product to the competitor's product (e.g. a Sony television has more features than a Toshiba television). Similarity occurs when an organization advertises that its product has the same features, but at a lower price. Organizations may highlight different parts of its value proposition to different target markets. The objective is to position the product or service so that it is the first thing that pops into the mind of the potential customers.

APPLICATIONS

E-commerce

Although business-to-consumer electronic commerce captures the attention of the industry, business-to-business electronic commerce is the format that is predicted to reap most of e-business activity. B2B e-commerce has exploded. This market became a trillion-dollar market by 2003 and was expected to have a 90-percent compound annual growth rate (Sprague, 2000). According to Sprague (2000), "B2B e-commerce represents another revolution that is reshaping business relationships and is causing dramatic shifts in channel power as information and communication imbalances disappear" (p. 1). B2B e-commerce provides "buyers and suppliers with value

propositions that can lower transaction costs and increase the value obtained in business relationships" (Sprague, 2000). These value propositions provide opportunities for new players to enter the process of facilitating buyer and supplier adoption of e-commerce capabilities.

One of the most important objectives of B2B e-commerce is to change the cost and benefits of transactions. Kaplan and Garicano (2001) developed a framework that describes how B2B e-commerce can change transaction costs. The model presented five ways that this could be done":

- Changes in the processes. B2B e-commerce can improve efficiencies by reducing the costs associated with existing business processes. Improvements may occur in two different ways. The first way is to reduce the cost of an activity that is currently being conducted (e.g. catalog orders being taken online versus by telephone or fax). The second way is to use the Internet to redesign the existing process (e.g. Autodaq creates online auctions for used cars without having to ship the cars to a physical auction). Each process improvement effort should be measured and evaluated to ensure that there are cost savings. This effort can be assessed by documenting the time and costs involved in both the existing process as well as the proposed process. The difference between the two is the savings from the process improvement.
- Changes in the nature of the marketplace. Use of the Internet can reduce a buyer's cost of finding suppliers, provide buyers with better information about product characteristics, and provide better information about buyers and sellers.
- Changes in indirect effects of transaction cost reductions. Better information about future demand through B2B e-commerce may allow a seller to improve its demand forecasts and use that information to change its production decisions to better match demand. As a result, a buyer may obtain better information about existing and future supplies and use the information to change its inventory decisions. Also, if the Internet is able to produce decreases in the costs of processing transactions in the market, fewer transactions may be processed inside organizations.
- Changes the degree of information incompleteness. Since buyers and sellers tend to not have the same information about a particular transaction,

one or both parties may be at a disadvantage when evaluating the desirability of a transaction. The Internet has the potential to change the informational positions of buyers and sellers.

- Changes the ability to commit. B2B e-commerce has the ability to both increase and decrease the ability of buyers and sellers to commit to transactions. The Internet has the ability to increase a buyer's ability to commit by standardizing the process of the transaction and leaving an electronic trail.

VIEWPOINT
Left-Brain Approach

Marketing should be based on two goals: making sales in the present and driving organizations to create strategies that will define what is next. Unfortunately, most organizations do not have that focus. According to Anderson (2005), the marketing function in most B2B organizations are:

- **Siloed.** Most organizations have a decentralized marketing department where various aspects of the marketing function report to different departments such as sales or a line function. The marketing professionals in organizations with this type of structure are concerned that they cannot develop relationships with existing customers. However, organizations with a centralized marketing department have a different challenge. The marketing professionals in this type of structure are concerned with their ability to build an effective relationship with the sales department. Regardless of the structure, the silo approach does not work in either environment.

- **Tactically focused.** Many departments have a service-oriented approach where they implement strategies that have been defined by other departments (e.g. sales, line management or senior management), and they are not a part of the planning process. As a result, the goals and objectives are short term versus long term. The focus tends to be on opportunities and deals that can be made on a quarterly basis versus relationships that can be built for long-term profit. This type of strategy can backfire on an organization, especially if the market experiences paradigm shifts or changes in customer behavior.

- **Not accountable.** Marketers tend to use response analysis, annual attitudinal and usage studies, and post-buy media reports to measure return on invest-

ment. Unfortunately, these methods do not align and measure the areas that senior management focuses on. For example, many executives are interested in top-line revenue growth and the above-mentioned methods do not measure this area.

If B2B professionals want to be taken seriously by the other major players in the organization and desire a place in the organization's strategic planning process, they will need to shift their strategies from qualitative to quantitative measures. This type of philosophy is referred to as the Left-Brain Marketing approach. Anderson (2005) believes that this type of transformation will require a more data-driven approach that will allow the major players to see bottom-line results. The process requires:

- **Deep audience knowledge.** Instead of relying on information obtained from direct sales and channel partners, organizations must develop strategies that will assist them with collecting information about their target audiences. This step will assist marketing professionals with developing strategies that can reach their target markets.

- **Analytic techniques.** Organizations have realized that the information they have in their CRM systems is very valuable and should be analyzed and evaluated. The results could identify "patterns and trends, profile and segment contacts, model customer profitability and potential, and the best prospects" (Anderson, 2005).

- **Closed-loop measurement practices.** Many marketing executives believe one of their biggest challenges is tying their efforts to end results. Unfortunately, most of their time is spent on putting processes, data, and tools in place so that they can measure the results. They must develop a plan that will allow them to close the loop by measuring the results, then analyzing what it means.

CONCLUSION

For many years, business marketing took a back seat to consumer marketing (Morris, Pitt & Honeycutt, 2001), but times have changed. B2B e-commerce has exploded and surpassed the profitability of B2C e-commerce. The new tools and techniques of the digital era have allowed these organizations to understand, develop, and implement processes in a more effective and efficient manner. As a result, they are able to understand, develop, and implement products with a greater value as well as create new channels for communication, supply-chain integration, demand forecasting, and transaction management.

B2B marketers who work within brick-and-mortar organizations are leading the way by building digital business designs and portfolio-based strategies. They are exploring how the new technologies can expand the options that they will have for improving the organization's marketing strategies. The processes and relationships of business-to-business marketing can be changed with the new technologies. In the future, complex digital networks will be used to supply customer needs. As the field progresses, business marketing will become a more defined discipline in marketing. Business marketers and scholars will be asked to contribute their findings to organizations so that they can continue to provide quality services to the growing customer base.

BIBLIOGRAPHY

Anderson, E. (2005, April). *Making B2B marketing work.* Retrieved on May 3, 2007, from http://www.forrester.com/Research/Document/Excerpt/0,7211,36434,00.html

Dwyer, F., & Tanner, J. (2006). *Business Marketing: Connecting Strategy, Relationships, and Learning* (3rd ed.). New York: McGraw-Hill/Irwin.

Hosford, C. (2013). E-commerce growing as b-to-b sales channel. *B to B, 96,* 1. Retrieved November 20, 2013, from EBSCO Online Database Business Source Premier. http://search.ebscohost.com/login.aspx?direct=true&db=buh&AN=66796947&site=bsi-live

Hosford, C. (2013). B-to-b e-commerce taking hold. *B to B, 98,* 3. Retrieved November 20, 2013, from EBSCO Online Database Business Source Premier. http://search.ebscohost.com/login.aspx?direct=true&db=buh&AN=88213611&site=bsi-live

Hutt, M., & Speh, T. (2001). *Business Marketing Management: A Strategic View of Industrial and Organizational Markets* (7th ed.). Dryden, TX:Harcourt, Inc.

Kaplan, S., & Garicano, L. (2001). The effects of business-to-business e-commerce on transaction costs. *The Journal of Industrial Economics, 44,* 463–485. Retrieved May 3, 2007, from http://ssrn.com/abstract=252210

Maddox, K. (2006). Outlook 2007: The future looks bright, with marketing expanding and online exploding. *B to B, 91,* 28–30. Retrieved May 3, 2007, from EBSCO Online Database Business Source Complete. http://search.ebscohost.com/login.aspx?direct=true&db=bth&AN=23601887&site=ehost-live

Morris, M., Pitt, L., & Honeycutt, E. (2001). *Business-to-Business Marketing: A Strategic Approach.* Thousand Oaks, CA:Sage Publication

Oliva, R. (n.d.). Business-to-Business marketing overview. Retrieved on May 3, 2007, from http://www.marketingpower.com/content1488.php

Ries, J. & Trout, J. (n.d.). The marketing strategy gurus on positioning. Retrieved May 3, 2007, from Easy-Strategy.com. http://www.easy-strategy.com/al-ries-jack-trout.html

Ryan, J., & Silvanto, S. (2013). The critical role of corporate brand equity in B2B marketing: An example and analysis. *Marketing Review, 13,* 39–50. Retrieved November 20, 2013, from EBSCO Online Database Business Source Premier. http://search.ebscohost.com/login.aspx?direct=true&db=buh&AN=89761598&site=bsi-live

Sprague, C. (2000). B2B eCommerce comes of age and drives shareholder value. ASCET, 2. Retrieved on May 3, 2007, from http://www.ascet.com/documents.asp?grID=149&d%5fID=246

Target market. (n.d.). Retrieved May 3, 2007, from Answers.com. http://www.answers.com/target%20market

Value-based pricing. (2007). Retrieved May 3, 2007, from Small Business Notes. http://www.smallbusinessnotes.com/operating/marketing/pricing/valuebased.html

SUGGESTED READING

Brennan Ross, et al. (2017). Business-to-business marketing. *SAGE.* Retrieved June 29, 2017.

Eid, R., Elbeltagi, I., & Zairi, M. (2006). Making Business-to-business international internet marketing effective: A study of critical factors using a case-study approach. *Journal of International Marketing, 14,* 87–109. Retrieved May 13, 2007, from EBSCO Online Database Business Source Premier. http://search.ebscohost.com/login.aspx?direct=true&db=bth&AN=23047726&site=ehost-live

Ordanini, A. (2011). The ties that bind: How cooperative norms and readiness to change shape the role of established relationships in business-to-business e-commerce. *Journal of Business-to-Business*

Marketing, 18, 276–304. Retrieved November 20, 2013, from EBSCO Online Database Business Source Premier. http://search.ebscohost.com/login.aspx?direct=true&db=buh&AN=64854567&site=bsi-live

Ryals, L., & Humphries, A. (2007). Managing key Business-to-business relationships: What marketing can learn from supply chain management. *Journal of Service Research, 9*, 312–326. Retrieved May 13, 2007, from EBSCO Online Database Business Source Premier. http://search.ebscohost.

com/login.aspx?direct=true&db=bth&AN=24835946&site=ehost-live

Salminen, R., & Moller, K. (2006). Roles of references in business marketing—towards a normative theory of referencing. *Journal of Business-to-Business Marketing, 13*, 1–48. Retrieved May 3, 2007, from EBSCO Online Database Business Source Premier. http://search.ebscohost.com/login.aspx?direct=true&db=bth&AN=20492412&site=ehost-live

Marie Gould

BUYER BEHAVIOR

ABSTRACT

Buyer behavior is based on a complex process by which consumers choose, acquire, use, and dispose of goods and services in order to fulfill their needs and desires. To understand why a buyer makes a purchase, it is important to understand his or her needs and motivations. This knowledge enables the seller to better develop a strategy for convincing the potential buyer that the product or service will meet his or her needs. In addition, in order to better target one's marketing strategy, it is important to understand the buying situation, including the routineness with which the particular purchasing decision is made as well as the importance of the decision to the buyer. When the buyer is an organization, it is also important to recognize that although there may be one decision maker, there are typically many parties who can influence the final buying decision.

OVERVIEW

No matter how good the product or service, no matter how satisfied the employees, no matter how well the communications within an organization, if the customer does not buy what the business is selling, these factors are irrelevant. Although people may band together for all sorts of reasons – the need to feel a part of a group, the need to contribute to the welfare of society, the need to connect with friends – businesses are by definition commercial, industrial, or professional enterprises that seek to make a profit. Even nonprofit organizations need to make money

in order to continue to provide the service that they are offering to their market. The question, of course, is how is this best done?

Interest in understanding buyer behavior has been going on since there first were buyers and sellers. Philosophers have long wondered why consumers buy things. Aristotle, for example, wondered about consumption and its effects on both the individual and society. Eighteenth-century philosopher Adam Smith pondered the same and concluded that in the end, resources would be optimally allocated.

However, business organizations are interested in more than philosophical musings about buyer behavior: They need to know what makes a consumer purchase a product or service and how to reach the consumer and convince him or her to buy. Toward this end, the study of buyer behavior has become more systematic in the past few decades, applying insights from the social sciences in an attempt to help businesses better understand the consumers in the marketplace and determine ways to best reach them.

One of the areas of study that has been applied to the prediction of buyer behavior is motivation. There are several approaches to explaining this important determinant of human behavior. Instinct theories emphasize the innate biological impulses that motivate behavior (e.g., a bird flies south for the winter; a human automatically tries to protect his or her children). Drive-reduction theories are based on the assumption that behavior is a response to biological needs for the organism's physiological system to remain stable and organisms learn to reduce the drives or motivating tendencies that arise from those needs (e.g., if thirsty, one looks for something to drink). Arousal theories posit that organisms are motivated to seek and maintain an optimal level of arousal in various physiological systems (e.g., a cat enjoys playing with a catnip mouse; a human enjoys the adrenaline rush of wind surfing). Incentive theories of motivation are based on the assumption that behavior is performed in response to the possibility of rewards or punishments (e.g., the dog learns to sit up to get a treat; the child learns to do homework assignments after school in order to watch TV in the evening).

One of the most enduring and popular theories of motivation that has been applied to the understanding of buyer behavior is Abraham Maslow's hierarchy of needs. In this theory, Maslow hypothesizes that people are motivated by different things at different times in their lives depending on what needs have been met or not met. This theory also hypothesizes that needs lower on the hierarchy (such as physiological needs for food, shelter, and warmth) must be satisfied before higher-level needs (such as love and self-actualization) can be satisfied.

As shown in Figure 1, the most basic level of needs is physiological needs. This category includes the needs to satisfy hunger and thirst, sleep, and sex. From a buyer behavior point of view, this means that a salesperson would most likely be unsuccessful in selling a new luxury car to someone who is living from paycheck to paycheck and is struggling to put food on the table. The need to eat is more important than the need to impress one's friends. Once the physiological level of needs has been met, people become more concerned with safety needs. These needs include the need to feel safe, secure, and stable in life (e.g., having a job so that one not only has food for today but can also buy food for the foreseeable future). At this level of need, people want to feel that their world is organized and predictable. From a buyer behavior point of view, this could mean that someone is unlikely to buy a house if he or she is working a temporary job with no future prospects. In this situation, there is no way to predict whether or not one will be able to continue to make mortgage payments. Once the security and safety needs of the individual are satisfied, the next level of needs is for belongingness. This level includes such factors as the need to feel accepted and part of a group, to love or feel affection and be loved in return, and to avoid

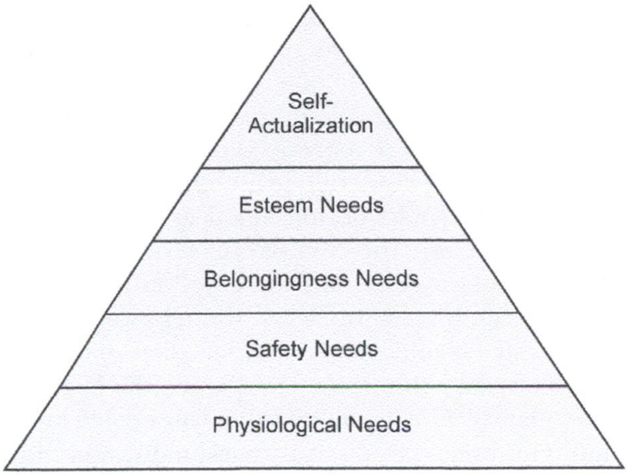

Figure 1: Maslow's Hierarchy of Needs

loneliness and alienation. From a consumer behavior point of view, if someone is at the level of belongingness needs, he or she is less likely to invest in the purchase of a status item than if these needs have been met because of the lack of a group to affirm the person's status. The next level of needs in Maslow's hierarchy is the esteem needs. These include the needs to achieve and to be competent and independent. In addition, the needs at this level of the hierarchy include the needs for self-respect and to develop a sense of self-worth as well as the need for recognition and respect from others. From a buyer behavior point of view, someone at this level in the needs hierarchy would be likely to buy the aforementioned luxury item as a symbol of his or her status because the lower level needs have been met.

The final level on Maslow's hierarchy of needs is self-actualization. This is a complex concept that basically means the need to live up to one's full and unique potential. Associated with self-actualization are such concepts as wholeness, perfection, or completion; a divestiture of "things" in preference of simplicity, aliveness, goodness, and beauty and a search for meaning in life. People at this level in the hierarchy would be less interested in the acquisition of things but would more likely be interested in acquiring things that enable them to reach other goals such as learning, spiritual development, or enjoying the wonders of nature.

One of the implications of Maslow's hierarchy of needs for understanding buyer behavior is that one has to approach selling the same thing in different ways depending on where the buyer is on the hierarchy. For example, one would be unlikely to sell a world cruise to someone who was at the physiological or safety levels of motivation. However, at the belongingness level of the hierarchy, the trip could be marketed as a group venture to be enjoyed with friends or fellow college alumni. At the esteem level, the trip could be marketed as a luxury item that will make one the envy of one's friends. Neither approach, however, would work well at the level of self-actualization. At this level, the trip would more successfully be sold as a way to broaden one's horizons, learn new things, or experience the beauty of foreign lands. The trip in all three cases could be the same. However, the way it is marketed would differ depending on the needs of the individual.

Several other things can be learned from Maslow's hierarchy of needs that have direct application to understanding buyer behavior. First, one can move not only up the hierarchy, but down as well. For example, although most adults are not worried about the safety and security needs (i.e., they have a regular paycheck and live in a safe neighborhood), the situation can change. Over time, a once safe neighborhood may start having a problem with crime. Therefore, someone who once felt secure at home in a quiet, middle-class neighborhood and felt no need for protection, might now feel less secure and would be interested in purchasing an alarm system. In addition to moving up and down the hierarchy, people can experience multiple needs at once. So, for example, the person in the gourmet store buying food for a dinner party may have several simultaneous motivators: hunger (e.g., if he or she has not eaten before going shopping or is on a diet that will be broken for the dinner party), esteem (e.g., the need to impress the people who are coming over to the party), or safety (e.g., the need to buy fresh, untainted food) might come into play.

From a marketing point of view, understanding the needs of the potential buyer can help focus the marketing effort to better demonstrate how the product or service will meet his or her particular needs. As discussed above, marketing to a potential buyer by targeting needs above where he or she currently is on the hierarchy (e.g., the luxury car to the unemployed person) is unlikely to meet with success. In addition, Maslow's hierarchy provides a method of identifying needs of classes of potential buyers so that successful marketing programs can be crafted to target these needs.

APPLICATIONS

Buying Situations

Although a number of models are available for predicting consumer buying behavior, most theorists believe that buyers' behavior changes depending on the buying situation. This term is most frequently used to refer to factors that cannot be predicted from knowledge of either the buyer or the situation alone. For example, buying a widget as a present for someone else might entail an additional level of decision-making factors than if the widget were being purchased for oneself (e.g., I like the widget, but will my friend, who has different tastes, like it?). Similarly, the purchase of a dessert from a bakery might differ depending on whether it was being purchased for the family, a formal dinner party, or a child's birthday party. Although some decisions can be made spontaneously (e.g., I want chocolate cake for dessert), others cannot (e.g., I need to hire a new accountant). Therefore, people frequently use different problem-solving processes for the different types of situations.

Some models of buyer behavior theorize that consumers may change their behavior depending on the reason for the purchase. Any one of three levels of problem solving may apply to the purchasing decision depending on how routine or important the purchase is. At the lowest level is routine problem solving, used when the buyer knows the product well, needs little information, the price is low, or the risk of making a wrong buying decision is low. For example, when grocery shopping, I am most likely to grab a quart of skim milk and put it in my shopping cart without much thought: I know that I want skim milk and not whole milk; I have been quite happy with the store brand in the past and see no need to change; and the cost of a quart of milk is negligible compared to my total food budget. On the other hand, if the manufacturer of my favorite breakfast cereal discontinues that variety, I may have to employ limited problem solving to the situation. These skills are important when buying a new or unfamiliar brand or considering a more expensive item. For example, I may want to compare the fiber, sodium, sugar, and carbohydrate contents of the various cereals under consideration. I may prefer cereal that has both crunchy nuggets and flakes rather than either one alone. I will probably also compare prices to see which is the better bargain. Although I may not walk out of the grocery store ecstatic because of my decision to buy a new cereal, buying the wrong one will not be an earth-shattering event, and the decision can be made in a matter of several minutes comparing labels while standing in the grocery-store aisle. Other decisions, however, require extensive problem-solving processes, particularly where the price is high, the item is rare, or the purchase requires a significant investment of time. For example, the decision to buy a new television set probably cannot be made in a few minutes' time in the aisle of a big-box store. This is not a minor purchase, and I need to consider a number of factors. Do I want a high-definition set or is a digital set sufficient? Are there size limitations for fitting the television into an existing space or for being able to see the screen from a distance? Is an investment in a plasma screen worth the cost at this time? The more information that is needed, the more complicated the decision-making process becomes.

Similarly, buyer behavior can change depending on the type of buying situation. For example, a routine purchase such as buying another ream of copy paper or instructing one's accountant to prepare this year's tax return does not require much decision making on the part of the buyer or marketing on the part of the seller. The office-supply salesperson may just ask if I want to place the same order as last time or the accountant may ask if anything has changed since last year. Other than that, the decision has been made. Other buying situations, however, are more complicated. If the usual brand of copy paper is no longer available or if an equivalent brand goes on sale, the office-supply salesperson will have to be more proactive in trying to get me to buy the product. If my former accountant retires and I hire a new one, we may need to sit down together and discuss the situation and the nature of my business before we mutually agree to proceed with the process. If this situation is exacerbated and if the purchase is for a product or service that I have not purchased before—a will, a new piece of office equipment—the seller will have to use considerably more skill than for the other two types of purchases.

Organizational Buying Behavior
It is not only individuals who are consumers. Businesses, too, purchase both goods and services. In a small business, this may be done by the founder of the organization. However, in many businesses, the sales transaction may involve the formal and informal inputs and many different parties. To successfully market to organizations, one must understand not only the individual behaviors of each of these parties, but also their interactions in order to convince them to buy. This means that there is not a single best approach to selling to an organization. Sometimes, in fact, different selling approaches must be tailored to different departments or executives within a single organization.

One model that attempts to explain the complexity of this situation examines the roles of different parties in the decision-making process so that the seller's market strategy can be appropriately focused. As shown in Figure 2, this model recognizes that the organizational buying process may include the inputs of several types of people: gatekeepers, users, buyers, influencers, decision makers, and sponsors and anti-sponsors.

The obvious person to target in a sales pitch is the decision maker. For major purchases, this is often a senior-level executive (e.g., the chief executive officer, chief financial officer, chief operating officer) or a person high up in the functional chain who has the final authority for deciding whether a product or service will be procured (e.g., the head of the department in which the product or service will be used). Decision makers at these levels tend to take a high-level view of the decision-making process rather than get mired down in the technical details. In addition, persons at these levels are typically influenced by various other parties within the organization who help shape the final decision. These parties may include

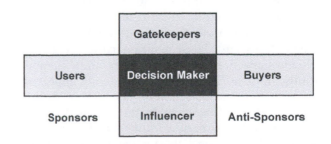

Figure 2: The Decision-Making Unit

gatekeepers, users, buyers, influencers, and sponsors or anti-sponsors.

Gatekeepers are the people within the organization who control access to the decision makers. These may be people like administrative assistants, receptionists, or mid-level managers on the organization management or functional hierarchies. Although these individuals do not make the purchasing decisions, they can keep the prospective seller from reaching the people who do. Therefore, it is important to develop a rapport with the gatekeepers so that one will be granted access to the decision makers. In addition to gatekeepers, there are other people in the decision-making process who, although technically without power, are important players in the decision. These are the users; the actual people who will be using the product or service. For example, although the decision to replace the current printers, copiers, and scanners with multi-functional units that provide all three capabilities may be attractive to decision makers because they require less financial investment in equipment, the proposition may not be as attractive to the actual users. They may not want to give up the equipment with which they are familiar or know that if a multifunction machine breaks down, they will lose the equivalent capabilities of three of their current machines. Although these individuals may not have a direct say in the decision-making process, they may influence the purchase. On the other end of the spectrum are the buyers, those individuals who actually purchase the product or service but do not use it. Their goal is to maximize the benefit to the organization of the purchase by making sure that it meets technical standards and is done at an acceptable price according to their criteria. Although they may not make the final decision per se, they can be quite influential on the decision maker.

In addition, decisions can be influenced by other advisors not directly affected by the decision. Influencers are individuals in whom the decision maker places trust. These may be a trusted peer at another organization, a spouse or other family member, or other advisor. These individuals do not appear on the organizational chart and may be hard to identify. However, their influence in the decision-making process is nonetheless real. Another set of parties that influence the buying behavior of organizations are

sponsors and anti-sponsors of the firm attempting to sell the product or service. Sponsors are those who have dealt with the selling organization before or have successfully used this particular product or service before. They demonstrate brand loyalty and encourage the decision maker to purchase the product not necessarily on its comparative merits, but because they are familiar with it or with the company that provides it. Anti-sponsors are sponsors for another company or product with which they are familiar. In the same way, they will attempt to influence the decision maker based not on comparative merits, but on past experience.

All these parties are important in the decision-making process for organizational buyers. The savvy seller understands these levels of organizational buyer behavior and takes them into account when developing an effective marketing strategy.

BIBLIOGRAPHY

Arndt, J. (1968). Insights into consumer behavior. Boston: Allyn and Bacon.

Banyte, J., Rutelione, A., & Kazakeviciute, A. (2012). Relationship between industry and capital determinants of compulsive buyers' behaviour: the case of retail clothing market in Lithuania. International Journal of Management Cases, 14(1), 359-373. Retrieved November 20, 2013 from EBSCO online database Business Source Premier. http://search.ebscohost.com/login.aspx?direct=true&db=buh&AN=89546205

Horton, R. L. (1984). Buyer behavior: A decision-making approach. Columbus, OH: Charles E. Merrill Publishing Company.

Kothandaraman, P., Agnihotri, R. (2012). Purchase professionals' cynicism about cooperating with suppliers: does it impact top management efforts to induce relational behaviors in buyer-supplier relationships? Marketing Management Journal, 22(2), 1-18. Retrieved November 20, 2013 from EBSCO online database Business Source Premier. http://search.ebscohost.com/login.aspx?direct=true&db=buh&AN=87023184

Larson, J. S., & Billetera, D. M. (2013). Consumer behavior in "equilibrium": how experiencing physical balance increases compromise choice. Journal of Marketing Research, 50(4), 535-547. Retrieved November 20, 2013 from EBSCO online database Business Source Premier. http://search.ebscohost.com/login.aspx?direct=true&db=buh&AN=90046033

Myers, D. G. (2001). Psychology (6th ed.). New York: Worth Publishers.

Newell, S. J., Belonax, J. J., McCardle, M. W., & Plank, R. E. (2011). The effect of personal relationship and consultative task behaviors on buyer perceptions of salesperson trust, expertise, and loyalty. Journal of Marketing Theory and Practice, 19(3), 307-316. Retrieved November 20, 2013 from EBSCO online database Business Source Premier. http://search.ebscohost.com/login.aspx?direct=true&db=buh&AN=61988855

Shahraki, A., Zarea, H., & Jannesari, A. (2012). Decision making with multi criteria through hierarchic analysis technique and its effect on customer decision procedure. Information Management and Business Review, 4(4), 153-158. Retrieved November 20, 2013 from EBSCO online database Business Source Premier. http://search.ebscohost.com/login.aspx?direct=true&db=buh&AN=74607675

Tasso, K. (2003). Adopting the buyer's point of view: An introduction to buyer behaviour and relevant psychology. In Tasso, K. Dynamic Practice Development: Selling Skills and Techniques for the Professions. Retrieved May 1, 2007, from EBSCO Online Database Business Source Complete. http://search.ebscohost.com/login.aspx?direct=true&db=bth&AN=22366820&site=bsi-live

SUGGESTED READING

Arndt, J. (1968). Insights into consumer behavior. Boston: Allyn and Bacon.

Baca-Motes, K., Brown, A., Gneezy, A., Keena, E. A., & Nelson, L. D. (2013). Commitment and behavior change: evidence from the field. Journal of Consumer Research, 39(5), 1070-1084. Retrieved November 20, 2013 from EBSCO online database Business Source Premier. http://search.ebscohost.com/login.aspx?direct=true&db=buh&AN=85132937

O'Shaughnessy, J. (1992). Explaining buyer behavior: Central concepts and philosophy of science issues. New York: Oxford University Press.

Nunes, P. F. (2003). The customer has escaped. Harvard Business Review, 81 (11), 96-105. Retrieved May 1, 2007, from EBSCO Online Database Business Source Complete. http://search.ebscohost.com/login.aspx?direct=true&db=bth&AN=11187645&site=bsi-live

Semenik, R. J. (2002). Promotion and integrated marketing communications. Cincinnati, OH: South-Western/Thomson Learning.

Trinh, Giang, et al. (2016). Benchmarking buyer behavior towards new brands. *Marketing Letters*. Retrieved on June 29, 2017. https://ideas.repec.org/a/kap/mktlet/v27y2016i4d10.1007_s11002-015-9376-8.html

Ruth A. Wienclaw, Ph.D.

C

CHANNEL MANAGEMENT

ABSTRACT

To be effective, the provider of a product or service needs not only to be able to offer something of value to the customer, but also be able to deliver it to market. Although direct marketing can do this effectively in many situations, an increasing number of organizations are offering their products or services through multiple channels – networks involved in delivering the product or service to market. To effectively add value to the product or service for the customer and to optimize the value of the channel to all its partners, the channel needs to be effectively managed through the development and implementation of policies and procedures that gain and maintain the cooperation of the various organizations in the channel and coordinate their activities. The major factors influencing both the short-term action of the channel as well as its long-term evolution are the requirements of the demand chain, the capabilities and costs of the channel, the power of the channel, and competitive actions.

OVERVIEW

No matter how effective or efficient an organization is in producing a product, if that product cannot be put into the hands of consumers, the organization will not be successful. Although cottage industries may produce goods and sell them directly to the customer, for most larger businesses, this is no longer true. For example, a patient is not allowed to purchase medication directly from a pharmaceutical company and must go through a pharmacy to get a prescription filled. Similarly, although one may visit a tailor from time to time to have clothes altered or the occasional garment made, most people purchase clothes from businesses that not only offer a selection of garments, but also a selection of garments from different manufacturers for comparison and convenience. Although some stores sell their own brand of products such as canned goods or over-the-counter medications, these products tend to take up a minority of their shelf space. However, it is not only tangible products that need to be delivered to the customer. Organizations in the service sector also need to market and distribute their services. For example, hotels may sell their rooms through any number of media and methods including travel agents, tour operators, tourist boards, centralized reservation systems, and online travel services.

Distribution Channels

The network involved in delivering a business's product or service to market is called the distribution channel. A channel is a route used by a business to market and distribute its products or services (e.g., wholesalers, retailers, mail order, Internet). The simplest channel, of course, involves only the organization itself selling directly to the consumer. However, many other channels are available. Direct marketing is a customer relationship management strategy to help the organization identify prospective customers, acquire data concerning these prospective and current customers, build relationships with customers, and influence their perceptions of the organization and its products or services. In direct marketing, the provider of the product or service delivers the promotional message directly to potential customers on a one-to-one basis rather than through the use of mass media. This can be done by the organization itself (e.g., sales call by a marketing representative) or through an agent (e.g., telephone marketing through a third-party agency). Another marketing channel uses mass media (e.g., newspaper or television advertisements). Although mass marketing can reach more potential customers more economically than direct marketing, the personal approach of direct marketing often results in a higher response rate. An organization's products can also be sold

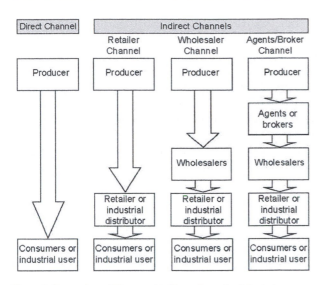

Figure 1: Comparison of direct and indirect channels of distriution

through distributors or wholesalers who sell to re-tailers or through retailers who sell directly to customers. Figure 1 illustrates some of the channels that may be used by organizations.

Channel Management

Just as an organization needs management in order to run smoothly, so do the partnerships within a channel. Channel management – also referred to as channel relationship management or partner relationship management – is the development and implementation of policies and procedures to gain and maintain the cooperation of the various organizations in the channel and coordinate their activities. Channel management helps organizations manage activities and the flow of information among the channel partners.

Although channel management is necessary for effectiveness of the marketing strategy and of the organization as a whole, many channels are dysfunctional. Stronger channel members often impose their will on other members in the channel and the weaker members suffer as a result. One of the objectives of channel management is to optimize the benefits for all members of the channel; policies and processes need to be developed and implemented that will minimize this problem. In addition, good channel management needs to consider the needs of the customer – the ultimate user of the processes in the value chain – which are often ignored in the design of the distribution channel.

Channel Stewardship

A recent development in channel management is the concept of channel stewardship. This approach to channel management is the ability of a given partici-pant in the distribution channel to design a strategy that addresses both the problem of optimizing ben-efits for channel members and considering the needs of the customer. In channel stewardship, the channel processes and communication flows are designed to take into account the best interests of the customer and optimize profits for all partners in the channel. A channel steward – the channel partner given this task – can be any member of the channel including the manufacturer or service provider, the maker of a key component of the final product, the supplier or as-sembler, or the distributor. Effective channel steward-ship has two outcomes. First, stewardship can help in-crease the value of the end product or service for the customer as well as the value of the relationship for the channel steward. Second, stewardship results in a stronger yet more flexible channel. In an effectively managed channel under this paradigm, the channel partners that contribute to the utility are rewarded and the less valuable partners are weeded out.

Designing Effective Marketing Strategies

In designing an effective marketing strategy, a number of factors need to be considered. These fac-tors tend to be the same regardless of the industry or the specifics of the channel. The major factors influ-encing both the short-term action of the channel as well as its long-term evolution are the requirements of the demand chain, the capabilities and costs of the channel, the power of the channel, and competitive actions.

Demand

Traditionally, demand is defined narrowly as the de-sire of the customer for a product or service. However, for effective channel management, demand needs to be viewed in a broader context. In addition to the desire of the customer for the product or service, demand can also include the customer's desire for supplemental or supporting products or services, maintenance of the product, training about the product's use, etc. For example, when purchasing a new computer, there may also be a demand for a new printer or other peripheral, an extended service con-tract, or training or consulting in how to use the new computer. Effective channel management should include consideration of all such demands, not just for the main product or product line.

Capabilities & Costs

Another factor to be considered in channel design is channel capabilities and costs. An effective channel needs to be a value chain where each partner adds value to the product or service before it is offered to the customer. Channel partners who do not add to the value of the product or service raise its cost without raising its value. Value can be added to a product or service by adding information (e.g., writing a user's guide or technical manual), inventory or warehousing the product, convenience for the customer (e.g., delivering the product to the customer's door or making it available in a retail outlet where the customer can examine or compare products), and so forth. However, these activities not only add value to the customer, but also add cost to the channel partners. The comparative benefits of these additions must be estimated to determine whether or not the additional capabilities are of benefit to the channel members.

Distribution of Power

Another factor to be considered in the design and management of a channel is the distribution of power among the channel partners. More powerful partners exert more influence over the policies and procedures governing the relationships within the channel. This power can come from two sources. A channel partner may have power because it has a unique product or technology that is necessary for the effectiveness of the channel (e.g., in a channel distributing computers, the computer manufacturer will have significant power). Power can also come from a channel partner's access to the market or intelligence about the market (e.g., although the computer manufacturer may have power because of its product, if it does not know how to effectively market its product, the other partners in the channel that have this skill also have power). Power is often also correlated with other factors such as the partner's size. While in some ways this can be an advantage for the partner exerting the power, it can also be disadvantageous not only to the weaker partners but also to the channel as a whole. Channels should foster cooperation and communication among the partners

if they are to be effective. Channel management requires the coordination and facilitation of these relationships.

Actions of the Competition

Finally, it is imperative that channel design and management take into account the actions of the competition. No matter how well an organization or channel markets a product, most customers make their purchasing decisions after some level of comparison with similar products. Therefore, the policies and procedures associated with the channel structure and management need to be flexible so that the channel cannot only respond quickly and appropriately to the demands of the customer, but also to meet or exceed the offerings of the competition.

APPLICATIONS

E-Commerce Pros & Cons

The advent of the Internet led some observers to predict that online retailing would become a superior channel to store-based retailing. After all, in e-commerce, the customer can shop from the comfort of home, compare prices and products, and have items delivered directly to the front door. In reality, however, although the Internet is a potent marketing channel for getting goods into the hands of consumers, it is not without its drawbacks. Although one can compare prices and items online, it is impossible to try on a garment, compare two physical items (as opposed to pictures or descriptions) side by side, or see if the blue in the oriental rug is compatible with the blue on the living-room wall. Although some organizations have developed various ways to overcome these obstacles (e.g., free return shipping for exchanges; virtual models for "trying on" clothes), the bottom line is that these approaches add significant time to the transaction. When a product is needed quickly, promises of free returns do not suffice. However, the Internet continues to be a viable channel for reaching the customer.

Strategies for Conducting Online Business

Organizations take several different strategies to do some or all of their business online. These strategies vary in the extent to which they use either or both online and offline channels. In the offline-focused strategy, the primary channel used is offline with online marketing efforts playing only a supporting role. In the offline focused strategy, a website may be published that provides customers with information about store hours and locations, describes the range of products sold, or offers customer-service options. For example, many grocery stores use this strategy. One can go online to read the weekly sales flyer, send a comment to the store or corporate manager, or find driving directions to the store, but one cannot buy groceries online. This strategy is often used when a sophisticated distribution system is needed to provide goods, personal consultation services are offered that can only be done in person (e.g., interior-decoration services), or there are contractual restrictions among the channel partners that prohibit more online involvement. On the other end of the spectrum are organizations that primarily use the online channel for their marketing efforts. Some businesses only do business online and use traditional marketing methods (e.g., television advertisements; infomercials) to point the customer to their website. This strategy can be an effective way to bypass the "middleman" or take advantage of the lower costs associated with the online channel (i.e., no need for the overhead associated with a physical retail store).

Multi-Channel Strategies

In addition to these two ends of the spectrum, some organizations use a more balanced approach to using both online and offline channels. In the isolation strategy, the online and offline channels are distinct entities, often managed separately or even offered as independent brands. In this approach, the organization does not offer any incentive to customers to switch between one channel and the other. This approach can be effective in situations where the two channels are used to appeal to different market segments (e.g., a younger or more technologically savvy target market for the online channel and an older or more traditional target market for the offline channel). Another way to utilize both physical and virtual channels is to integrate them. In this strategy, the two types of channels are viewed as complementary rather than as independent. This type of multi-channel approach is typically used to provide convenience to customers. For example, some retailers allow customers to order online and pick up their purchases in the store. Other retailers may offer the same products through traditional catalog/mail-order sales, the Internet, or in retail stores.

Despite the initial predictions that online channels would become superior to offline channels, this has not proven to be true. Traditionally, many theorists posited that multi-channel strategies work best when they are extensively integrated. As a result, many organizations attempt an extensive use of online channels and integrate them with more traditional channels. Some theorists go so far as to say that such approaches are best no matter what the retailer's individual situation.

However, Müller-Lankenau, Wehmeyer, and Klein found that the range of combinations of physical and virtual channels in multi-channel strategies suggest that no one approach is universally superior. Based on the literature and their observations of multi-channel management, they developed a model to examine how organizations use physical and virtual channels in multi-channel strategies. Their analysis led to the conclusion that differences in retailers' business activities and marketing strategies can impact their choice of multi-channel strategies.

Significant Factors for Aligning Multi-Channel Strategies

Their analysis found four factors to be significant in the alignment of multi-channel strategies: business scope, distinctive competencies, governance, and technology scope. For purposes of the model, business scope is shaped by the organization's decision concerning the arenas in which it should compete. These considerations include product and service type, customer segmentation, and geographical reach. Distinctive competencies are those factors that distinguish one business competitor from another as well as their differing skills and abilities in providing products or services to the customer. These factors help determine whether or not the customer will choose to make a purchase from a given provider. These factors are influenced by the organization's competitive strategy (e.g., cost leader, differentiation, and niche strategy), established channel system (i.e., retailers have less flexibility to use online-focused strategies than do Internet-only retailers), and competitive environment (i.e., how the competition is using the various channels). Governance also plays a part in which multi-channel strategy is most appropriate for a given business. Specifically, the governance of retail outlets differs from organization to organization. In some companies, each retail outlet is required to use the same channels as the other outlets in the group. In other companies, however, the various outlets have more flexibility as to how they will manage their channels. This allows them to better target the demographics of their particular market. Similarly, the structure of the organization can impact the best multi-channel strategy. In addition, multi-channel approaches can be restricted or promoted by government regulation (e.g., regulations concerning the legal store opening hours; consumer-protection laws). Finally, the scope of technology can affect how an organization can best manage multi-channel strategies. For example, the value chain – the network of businesses working together to bring a product or service to the market – can affect the strategic role of information technology across industries. Similarly, the development of multi-channel strategies may be limited or supported by the organization's current information technology infrastructure and competencies.

Using this model, Müller-Lankenau, Wehmeyer, and Klein examined the multi-channel strategies of four grocery-store chains. They found that each chain used different strategies based on the four factors discussed above. They concluded that the extensive integration of physical and virtual channels proposed by some theorists is not necessary and the organization needs to choose its multi-channel strategy based on its own situation. This model better explains the diversity of approaches that can be observed in the real world.

BIBLIOGRAPHY

Avery, J., Steenburgh, T., Deighton, J., & Caravella, M. (2012).
Adding bricks to clicks: Predicting the patterns of crosschannel elasticities over time. Journal of Marketing, 76(3), 96-111. Retrieved November 15, 2013, from EBSCO Online Database Business Source Complete. http://search.ebscohost.com/login.aspx?direct=true&db=bth&AN=74749677&site=ehost-live

Columbus, L. (2005/2006). Avoiding the pitfalls of channel management. Manufacturing Engineer, 84(6), 16-19. Retrieved June 5, 2007, from EBSCO Online Database Business Source Complete. http://search.ebscohost.com/login.aspx?direct=true&db=bth&AN=19677139&site=ehost-live

Kuruzovich, J. (2013). Sales technologies, sales force management, and online infomediaries. Journal of Personal Selling & Sales Management, 33(2), 211-224. Retrieved November 15, 2013, from EBSCO Online Database Business Source Complete. http://search.ebscohost.com/login.aspx?direct=true&db=bth&AN=86457301&site=ehost-live

Kushwaha, T., & Shankar, V. (2013). Are multichannel customers really more valuable? The moderating role of product category characteristics. Journal of Marketing, 77(4), 67-85. Retrieved November 15, 2013, from EBSCO Online Database Business Source Complete. http://search.ebscohost.com/login.aspx?direct=true&db=bth&AN=88790001&site=ehost-live

Lichung, J., & Han-Kuang, T. (2013). Ascertaining the dynamic competition in channel relationship management. International Journal of Marketing Studies, 5(3), 36-47. Retrieved November 15, 2013, from EBSCO Online Database Business Source Complete. http://search.ebscohost.com/login.aspx?direct=true&db=bth&AN=88382365&site=ehost-live

Müller-Lankenau, C., Wehmeyer, K., Klein, S. (2006). Strategic channel alignment: An analysis of the configuration of physical and virtual marketing channels. Information Systems & E-Business Management, 4(2), 187-216. Retrieved June 5, 2007, from EBSCO Online Database Business Source Complete. http://search.ebscohost.com/login.aspx?direct=true&db=bth&AN=20253392&site=ehost-live

Rangan, K. (2006). The promise and rewards of channel stewardship. Supply Chain Management Review, 10(5), 42-49. Retrieved June 5, 2007, from EBSCO Online Database Business Source Complete. http://search.ebscohost.com/login.aspx?direct=true&db=bth&AN=21691541&site=ehost-live

SUGGESTED READING

Brown, M. D. & Smith, R. W. (2004). The role of channel management. Adhesives & Sealants Industry, 11(6), 16-18. Retrieved June 5, 2007, from EBSCO Online Database Business Source Complete. http://search.ebscohost.com/login.aspx?direct=true&db=bth&AN=13803615&site=ehost-live

Foreman, S. (2006). Power conflict and control in distribution channels. Henley Manager Update, 17(3), 11-18. Retrieved June 5, 2007, from EBSCO

Online Database Business Source Complete. http://search.ebscohost.com/login.aspx?direct=true&db=bth&AN=20770548&site=ehost-live

Garcia, Daniel and Janssen, Maarten. (2016). Retail channel management in consumer search markets. *International Journal of Industrial Organization.* Retrieved on June 29, 2017. http://www.sciencedirect.com/science/article/pii/S0167718716302843

Harreld, H. (2001). Channel management. InfoWorld, 23(41), 47-51. Retrieved June 5, 2007, from

EBSCO Online Database Business Source Complete. http://search.ebscohost.com/login.aspx?direct=true&db=bth&AN=5335842&site=ehost-live

Manjunatha, K. V. (2006). Channel management. The Journal for Decision Makers, 31(2), 179-184. Retrieved June 5, 2007, from EBSCO Online Database Business Source Complete. http://search.ebscohost.com/login.aspx?direct=true&db=bth&AN=21559060&site=ehost-live

Ruth A. Wienclaw, Ph.D.

CONSUMER AND ORGANIZATIONAL BUYER BEHAVIOR

ABSTRACT

Consumer and organizational buyer behavior are subcategories of marketing. Research in both fields has enabled manufacturers and distributors to understand the needs, preferences, and behavior of buyers, as well as the internal and external factors that influence buyer behavior. Although much has been written about the differences between consumer and organizational buyer behavior, it appears that the demarcations between the two fields are not as clear as they may seem to be.

OVERVIEW

Buyer behavior is concerned with the selection and purchase of products or services to satisfy a need for individuals or groups. It is focused on the needs of individuals, groups, and organizations. Buyer behavior occurs either for an individual consumer on his or her own; an individual consumer in the context of a group (where others in the group influence how a person behaves); or an organization (where employees make decisions about which products or services the firm should use).

Although economists were the first academic group to offer a theory of buyer behavior, the field of buyer behavior is a subcategory of marketing that blends elements from economics, psychology, sociology, social psychology, anthropology, and other sciences, such as physiological psychology, biochemistry, and genetics. The two main areas of buyer behavior are consumer buyer behavior, and organizational buyer behavior.

Consumer buyer behavior has developed, since the 1960s, as a separate discipline within marketing, to enable manufacturers and distributors to research and understand the needs and preferences of the increasingly sophisticated customer, and to respond accordingly. The field of organizational buyer behavior—initially called industrial buyer behavior—also surfaced in the 1960s, but most of the research in this area has taken place since 1980. Progress in this field has led to a new occupation of professional buyers.

Buyer behavior is influenced by many factors, namely the internal mental processes of individuals; external factors; the availability of resources; the characteristics of the product, service, or idea required; the availability of the requisite skills; and the socio-demographic variables.

FURTHER INSIGHTS

There are four typical types of buyer behavior based on the nature of the product, service, or idea to be purchased. Complex buyer behavior involves a high-value brand and involves an intense information search before the purchase is made. Habitual or routinized response buyer behavior is where a product is regularly purchased out of habit, and as such, the buyer needs relatively little information. Variety-seeking buyer behavior describes the situation where the buyer shops around and experiments with different products. In some purchases, buyer dissonance is reduced because the purchase is large or infrequent, thus reducing the number of differences between brands; the buyer becomes more highly involved with the purchase.

Consumer Buyer Behavior

As individuals or as households, consumers undergo various stages in making the decision to purchase. These stages occur in varying degrees, depending on the complexity of the purchase and the buyer's purchasing behavior (Zahorsky, n.d.). At the most, many experts agree that the consumer buying decision process can have six stages: problem recognition, information search, evaluation of alternatives, purchase decision, purchase, and post-purchase evaluation.

First Stage of Consumer Buying Decision Process

The first stage, problem recognition or need awareness, occurs when a potential buyer becomes aware of a need, which may have been established by encountering a problem or may have been prompted by a company's marketing efforts. Consumer needs are either biological, that is, relating to primary or physiological elements; or psychological, that is, emotional. Needs change as individuals satisfy their basic needs and move along the path toward self-actualization.

Second Stage of Consumer Buying Decision Process

The second stage of buying is the information search. Information often facilitates purchasing. There are two types of information searches: internal and external. With an internal information search, the consumer searches the information stored in his or her memory. If more information is needed after the internal search, the consumer may consult external information sources such as friends and relatives for word-of-mouth; marketing information; comparison shopping; and public sources. This information search stage is usually bypassed when the consumer is buying out of habit, wants to experiment, or is buying on impulse.

Third Stage of Consumer Buying Decision Process

A successful information search leaves a needy consumer with possible alternatives collectively called the evoked set. Armed with an evoked set, the consumer embarks on the third stage of the buying decision process: evaluation of alternatives (also known as information evaluation). Here, the consumer may need to establish the criteria for evaluation, such as features of the product or service that the buyer wants or does not want, pricing, and company credibility. The consumer may rank or weight the alternatives to arrive at a choice or resume searching if a satisfactory choice is not arrived at.

Fourth & Fifth Stages of Consumer Buying Decision Process

The fourth stage in the consumer buying decision process is the purchase decision. Here, the consumer makes the decision to buy; he or she has selected from the available alternatives, making decisions on details such as the specific product or service, its packaging, retail outlet, and method of purchase. The fifth stage, which some authors do not recognize as a separate stage, is the purchase, which at times occurs simultaneously with the purchase decision. When the product or service is not readily available, there is likely to be a time lapse between the purchase decision and the actual purchase.

Sixth Stage of Consumer Buying Decision Process

The sixth and last stage in the consumer buying decision process is post-purchase evaluation (also known as post-acquisition evaluation, post-buying behavior, or after-purchase evaluation), which may consciously or subconsciously occur to the buyer. The buyer may look to the media, friends, and other sources for reinforcement to confirm that he or she has made the right decision.

At the end of his or her evaluation, the buyer may experience satisfaction or dissatisfaction. Dissatisfaction, also known as cognitive dissonance or buyer's remorse, may result from many factors, such as unmet brand expectations. Dissatisfaction may also cause the consumer to lodge a complaint. Satisfaction, on the other hand, may result in a customer becoming loyal to a particular brand or retail outlet.

FACTORS THAT AFFECT CONSUMER BUYER BEHAVIOR
Internal Mental Processes & the Consumer

Consumer buyer behavior is affected by internal mental processes such as behavioral intention, past experience, behavior in similar settings, perceptions, habit, and genetic heritage. According to the Theory of Planned Behavior, behavioral intention is the most influential predictor of behavior. According to Pavlou and Fygenson (2006), "Behavioral intentions are motivational factors that capture how hard people are willing to try to perform a behavior" (p. 4). They are derived from attitude, subjective norm (one's desire to act as others act or think one should act), and perceived behavioral control (the perception of how easy or difficult it would be to carry out a behavior). Most consumer behavior is learned from experience, and the lessons learned from past experience have been found to influence consumer buyer behavior. Consumer buyer behavior is also affected by the way the consumer tends to behave in similar settings; as well as by perceptions, habit, and genetic heritage (Pavlou and Fygenson, 2006).

Trust & the Consumer
Trust is another important factor in consumer buyer behavior, since it reduces uncertainty. First of all, "trust is important for getting information, since consumers tend to assess whether the information obtained is valid, credible, and accurate." Trust is also important for product purchasing, especially in cases such as online purchasing, where consumers tend to be vulnerable, as they cannot see or touch any products or vendors (Pavlou and Fygenson, 2006).

External Factors & the Consumer
The common external factors that influence consumer buyer behavior are other people; the setting or situation; one's upbringing, culture and religion; marketing and advertising; and the media. According to Wilson (2000), "many consumer purchasing decisions are probably more accurately seen as collective decisions, in that they are influenced by many others." As such, purchasing decisions are influenced by family members, friends and other peer groups, reference groups, and other groups.

Reference groups are particular groups of people that an individual looks up to. These groups of people are used as a standard of reference against which individuals compare themselves. Reference groups come in various forms. For example, the aspirational reference group is made up of those others with whom one would like to be compared, such as role models.

Associative reference groups include those who more realistically represent an individual's peers or equals. Specifically, these groups can be coworkers, neighbors, or members of churches, clubs, and organizations. The final group, the dissociative reference group, includes people to whom the individual would not like to be compared. Marketers use the various groups to bring pertinent messages home to their actual and potential consumers.

Reference groups can have different levels of influence on consumer behavior. Primary reference groups are those with the greatest amount of influence on an individual. Secondary reference groups tend to have less influence—they may not enjoy very close relationships with the individual, and therefore their influence on buyer behavior will be minimal.

Another external factor influencing consumer buyer behavior is the setting or situation. A theoretical model known as the Behavioral Perspective Model views the actions of customers as determined by the setting or situation in which consumption takes place rather than by internal mental processes such as attitudes or intentions. According to the Behavioral Perspective Model, behaviors such as product or brand choice are determined by two situational factors: the consumption or purchase setting (including physical surroundings, social surroundings and time) and the sentiments evoked by features of the setting as determined by the consumer's past experience. The consumer's economic environment (for example, whether the consumer has a secure job and regular income to spend on goods) also has an impact on his or her buyer behavior.

Consumers do not exist in a vacuum; they are a part of their society. Consumer attitudes and beliefs are shaped by their upbringing, culture, and religion. Marketing, advertising, and the media in general also constitute important external forces that shape a person's buyer behavior. Consumer buyer behavior is also influenced by the availability of resources, mainly time and money. The consumer requires time to get information about a product, a service, or an idea; and in addition, the consumer must also have the time to be able to use and enjoy the purchase.

Consumer Expertise & Skill
Additionally, the consumer may require personal skills and expertise to undertake a new behavior, and the availability or lack of such skills may influence purchase behavior. Additionally, consumers' socio-demographic status often dictates what and how they buy. Key socio-demographic variables include age, gender, personality, income, marital and family status, type of job, education, and experience with the product, service, or idea under consideration.

Product Characteristics & Buyer Behavior
The characteristics of the product, service, or idea sought after also affect consumer buyer behavior. Product value, which is the attractiveness of the

combination of quality and price, has a strong impact on buyer behavior. "Product value favorably predisposes consumers by allowing them to expect a high quality product at a low cost" (Pavlou and Fygenson, 2006, p. 15). Likewise, price discounts have been shown to influence purchase intentions.

ORGANIZATIONAL BUYER BEHAVIOR
Decision-Making Units
Much of the buying and selling in advanced economies takes place between organizations. In buying transactions within large organizations, buying decisions tend to be made by a group of people in the organization collectively known as the decision-making unit (DMU), or buying center, rather than by an individual. Those in the DMU share the same objectives and risks in making the purchase.

Webster and Wind (1972) write that, "major purchases typically require input from various parts of the organization, including finance, accounting, purchasing, information technology management, and senior management. Highly technical purchases also require the expertise of technical specialists" (p. 17). Thus, in some cases, the DMU is an informal loose group, but in other situations, it is a more formal group with specific mandates, criteria, and procedures.

Roles within Decision-Making Units
DMUs include people with different roles. In a general sense, there are five roles within any DMU:
- End users of the item being purchased
- Buyers who are responsible for the contract
- Influencers who try to affect the outcome decision with their opinions
- Deciders who make the final decision
- Gatekeepers who act to prevent or discourage a purchase by controlling the flow of information and/or access to people in the decision-making unit (Webster and Wind, 1972, p. 17)

The various roles are aptly labeled with titles such as "users," "influencers," "deciders," "policymakers," "purchasers," "technologists," "analysts," "spectators" and "gatekeepers." The composition of a DMU varies by organization and also according to the buying situation or item to be purchased (Lewis & Littler, 1999). In addition, "different roles and functional representatives are likely to have varying influence at different stages of the purchasing process" (Wilson, 2000).

Character Profiles of Organizational Buyer Behavior Research has also revealed three character profiles of buyer behavior in organizations: the hard bargainer, the sales job facilitator, the straight shooter, and the socializer. The hard bargainer describes buyers with whom salespeople may find it difficult to conduct business with and finalize a sale. A sales job facilitator, on the other hand, is open to salespeople's solicitations and even attempts to make the sales transaction go smoothly. The straight shooter describes industrial buyers who behave with integrity and decency (Dubinsky and Ingram, 1982).

Stages of Organizational Buyer Behavior
The buyer decision-making process applied above to consumer buyer behavior can also be applied to organizational buyer behavior. In the need recognition stage, it is the initiators in the DMU who recognize a need for new solutions, such as new products, while buyers are more likely to identify the need to repurchase products. After a need is recognized, a specifications document may be generated by the DMU describing the requirements of the product or service.

In the information search stage, the search for alternatives to consider is one of the most important differences between consumer and organizational buying. This is because an organization is motivated to reduce costs, and it is at this stage where professional buyers are most beneficial. They can identify multiple suppliers that meet product specifications. Then, after a screening process, they may offer a select group the opportunity to present their products.

In simple repurchase situations, the process usually goes from need recognition directly to purchase, with little search activity performed. Once a search has produced options, members of the DMU may choose from the alternatives. In more complicated purchase situations, the DMU may evaluate each option. In government and non-profit markets, suppliers must submit bids, and the lowest bidder is awarded the order, providing that his or her products or services meet the required specifications.

The next stage in the organizational buyer decision making process is the purchase decision, which is sometimes simultaneous with the purchase. Placing an order usually requires the completing paperwork (or electronic documents). Getting the necessary approvals can delay the order for an extended period of time. For capital purchases, such as buildings or equipment, financing options may also need to be explored.

In the final stage, post-purchase evaluation, (once the order is received) the organization should review the results of the purchase. This may involve the buyer discussing product performance with users. If the product is well received, it may be moved to a straight repurchase status, thus eliminating much of the evaluation process on future purchases ("Business Buying," n.d.).

VIEWPOINTS

Although much has been written about the differences between consumer and organizational buyer behavior, Wilson (2000) argues for the development of a rigorous theory of buyer behavior that can generally be applied to both consumer and organizational markets. He notes that the demarcations between organizational and consumer buyer behavior are founded on several assumptions:

- Consumers buy as willful individuals while organizations purchase as a rational group.
- The same individual behaves differently as a consumer and as an organizational buyer.
- The same individual behaves differently in a social context and in a professional context.

Wilson explains that "individual consumers purchase not only for themselves, in response to their own perceptions and wishes, but also collectively on behalf of others and under many powerful societal (organizational) influences." Furthermore, in routine purchasing, which is the case with the majority of organizational purchasing transactions, the more typical pattern is that purchasing managers act as individual decision makers having been delegated to do so within the prescribed limits and cultures of the organization.

The reality, according to Wilson, is that "organizational purchasing is both professional and behavioral, to differing degrees, just as is consumer buying. The professionalism of organizational buying is often put forward as one of the main factors distinguishing it from consumer buying, but it could be argued that this trivializes and underestimates the degree of professionalism that is also involved in consumer buying."

Wilson also points out that organizations, just like consumers, indulge in therapeutic buying from time to time. They do so to help them recover from bad experiences or ease undesirable tensions. There are many "examples of organizations spending in order to meet the expectations of involved peer groups or stakeholders, for example, in purchasing elaborate IT systems, corporate jets, landscaping grounds, revamping corporate logos and letterheads, refurbishing offices and premises." In organizations, such activity is usually presented as rational and commercially sensible, yet paradoxically, similar behavior in individual consumers appears as "self-indulgent, therapeutic, imitative, and even conformist" (Wilson, 2000).

BIBLIOGRAPHY

Anderson, E., Chu, W., & Weitz, B. (1987). Industrial purchasing: An empirical exploration of the buyclass framework. Journal of Marketing, 51(3), 71-86. Retrieved May 21, 2007, from EBSCO Online Database Business Source Complete. http://search.ebscohost.com/login.aspx?direct=true&db=bth&AN=4996446&site=ehost-live

Business buying behavior. (n.d.). *Principles of Marketing Tutorials*. Retrieved May 26, 2007, from Know This.com: http://www.knowthis.com/tutorials/principles-of-marketing/business-buying-behavior/11.htm

C., M. (2009). Buyer behavior in business markets: A review and integrative model. *Journal of Global Business Issues, 3*, 129-138. Retrieved November 15, 2013, from EBSCO Online Database Business Source Complete. http://search.ebscohost.com/login.aspx?direct=true&db=bth&AN=44900543&site=ehost-live

Demirdjian, Z., & Senguder, T. (2004). Perspectives in consumer behavior: Paradigm shifts in prospect. *Journal of American Academy of Business, Cambridge, 4*(1/2), 348-353. Retrieved May 21, 2007, from EBSCO Online Database Business Source Complete. http://search.ebscohost.com/login.aspx?direct=true&db=bth&AN=12704394&site=ehost-live

Dubinsky, A., & Ingram, T. (1981/1982). A classification of industrial buyers: Implications for sales training. *Journal of Personal Selling & Sales Management, 2*, 46-51. Retrieved May 21, 2007, from EBSCO Online Database Business Source Complete. http://search.ebscohost.com/login.aspx?direct=true&db=bth&AN=6349873&site=ehost-live

Gao, T., Joseph Sirgy, M., & Bird, M. (2005). Reducing buyer decision-making uncertainty in organizational purchasing: can supplier trust, commitment, and dependence help? *Journal of Business Research, 58,* 397-405. Retrieved May 21, 2007, from EBSCO Online Database Business Source Complete. http://search.ebscohost.com/login.aspx?direct=true&db=bth&AN=16540343&site=ehost-live

Harris, C. (2013). A metric to drive lean purchasing. *Industrial Management, 55,* 10-14. Retrieved November 15, 2013, from EBSCO Online Database Business Source Complete. http://search.ebscohost.com/login.aspx?direct=true&db=bth&AN=91914537&site=ehost-live

Hirschman, E. (1989). Consumer behavior theories as heroic quest. *Advances in Consumer Research, 16,* 639-646. Retrieved May 21, 2007, from EBSCO Online Database Business Source Complete. http://search.ebscohost.com/login.aspx?direct=true&db=bth&AN=6487778&site=ehost-live

Hirschman, E., & Stern, B. (2001). Do consumers' genes influence their behavior? Findings on novelty seeking and compulsive consumption. *Advances in Consumer Research, 28,* 403-410. Retrieved May 21, 2007, from EBSCO Online Database Business Source Complete. http://search.ebscohost.com/login.aspx?direct=true&db=bth&AN=6686449&site=ehost-live

Ho, T., Lim, N., & Camerer, C. (2006). Modeling the psychology of consumer and firm behavior with behavioral economics. *Journal of Marketing Research (JMR), 43,* 307-331. Retrieved May 21, 2007, from EBSCO Online Database Business Source Complete. http://search.ebscohost.com/login.aspx?direct=true&db=bth&AN=21945242&site=ehost-live

Krapfel Jr., R. (1982). An extended interpersonal influence model of organizational buyer behavior. *Journal of Business Research, 10,* 147-157.

Lewis, B. & Littler, D., Eds. (1999). *Blackwell Encyclopedic Dictionary of Marketing.* Malden, MA: Blackwell Publishers.

Lusch, R., & Vargo, S. (1998). Multiplex retailers versus wholesalers. *International Journal of Physical Distribution & Logistics Management, 28,* 581. Retrieved May 21, 2007, from EBSCO Online Database Business Source Complete. http://search.

ebscohost.com/login.aspx?direct=true&db=bth&AN=1438007&site=ehost-live

Pavlou, P., & Fygenson, M. (2006). Understanding and prediction electronic commerce adoption: An extension of the theory of planned behavior. *MIS Quarterly, 30,* 115-143. Retrieved May 21, 2007, from EBSCO Online Database Business Source Complete. http://search.ebscohost.com/login.aspx?direct=true&db=bth&AN=19754863&site=ehost-live

Powers, T.L., & Hopkins, R.A. (2013). Altruistic motives and socially responsible purchasing behavior. *AMA Summer Educators' Conference Proceedings,* 2496-103. Retrieved November 15, 2013, from EBSCO Online Database Business Source Complete. http://search.ebscohost.com/login.aspx?direct=true&db=bth&AN=90022231&site=ehost-live

Upah, G., & Bird, M. (1980). Changes in industrial buying: Implications for industrial marketers. *Industrial Marketing Management, 9,* 117-121.

Webster, F., & Wind, Y. (1972). A general model for understanding organizational buying behavior. *Journal of Marketing, 36,* 12-19. Retrieved May 21, 2007, from EBSCO Online Database Business Source Complete. http://search.ebscohost.com/login.aspx?direct=true&db=bth&AN=4994960&site=ehost-live

Wilson, D. (2000). Why divide consumer and organizational buyer behaviour? *European Journal of Marketing, 34,* 780-796.

Zahorsky, D. (n.d.). Break the resistance of consumer buying behavior. Retrieved May 26, 2007, from About.com: http://sbinformation.about.com/od/advertisingpr/a/behavior.htm

SUGGESTED READING

Ward, S. & Webster, F. (1991). Organizational buying behavior. In T. Robertson & H. Kassarjian (Eds.), *Handbook of consumer research and theory* (pp. 419-58). Englewood Cliffs, NJ: Prentice-Hall.

Wilson, D. (2000). Why divide consumer and organizational buyer behaviour? *European Journal of Marketing, 34,* 780-796. Retrieved May 21, 2007, from EBSCO Online Database Business Source Complete. http://search.ebscohost.com/login.aspx?direct=true&db=bth&AN=3497726&site=ehost-live

Vanessa A. Tetteh, Ph.D.

CONSUMER BEHAVIOR

ABSTRACT

The study of consumer behavior involves elements of economics, the social sciences, and the physical sciences. An endless and diverse field of research and applications, consumer behavior considers such areas as buying decision making, internal influences, and external influences on the consumer. An understanding of consumer behavior can lead to improved marketing strategies on the part of firms and organizations and can also lead to improved public policy.

OVERVIEW

In marketing, consumer behavior is the study of the acquisition, consumption, use, and disposal of products, services, experiences, or ideas by consumers. When considered in greater depth, consumer behavior can be defined as the study of how and when individuals, groups, and organizations select, purchase, use and dispose of products, services, experiences, or ideas to satisfy their needs. It also involves the study of why consumption decisions are made. In addition, consumer behavior looks at the impacts that the processes of selection, purchasing, use, and disposal have on consumers and society.

Consumer behavior studies the characteristics of individual consumers by looking at variables such as demographics, psychographics, and behavior in an attempt to understand the consumer and his or her world. Demographics include factors such as race, age, income, mobility (travel time to work or number of vehicles available), educational attainment, home ownership, employment status, and location. Psychographics are attributes related to personality, values, attitudes, interests, or lifestyles. Behavioral variables include usage rate and loyalty. Consumer behavior also tries to assess influences on the consumer from groups such as family, friends, reference groups, and society in general (Perner, 2003).

Consumer behavior is a subcategory of marketing that blends elements from economics, psychology, sociology, social psychology, anthropology, and other sciences, such as physiological psychology, biochemistry, and genetics. The field of economics actually provided the foundation for marketing, but it wrongly assumed "that consumers are rational decision makers who actively seek information, objectively evaluate alternatives available to them, and make rational selections of products or services to maximize their benefits." By neglecting the emotional side of the customer, among other psychological factors, economists "failed to provide marketing with all of the concepts needed to understand the complexities" of what motivates consumers(Demirdjian & Senguder, 2004, p. 349).

Realizing these limitations, marketing scholars began to seek an "understanding of consumer behavior from other sciences. Psychology—the study of individual behavior—was one of the earliest and most extensively used fields from which concepts have been borrowed. Motivation, perception, learning, beliefs, attitudes and so on, have all been used to explain why the consumer behaves the way he or she does" (Demirdjian & Senguder, 2004, p. 349). "Social psychology is yet another source from which many concepts have been borrowed, as this field is concerned with the behavior of individuals in the presence of other individuals or groups." Research into other sciences such as physiological psychology, which is the "study of the interaction of the body with the mind," and which studies the "extent to which behavior is caused by physical and chemical phenomena in the body," is relatively recent (Demirdjian & Senguder, 2004, p. 349).

It has been said that the basic nature of consumer behavior is diversity: the field is characterized by diversity in theories and diversity in research methods (Demirdjian & Senguder, 2004). Although early related research can be traced back much farther, the attempt to theorize consumer behavior began in 1962, first looking at the type of behavioral processes consumers typically used in adopting new products; then addressing consumer problem-solving, buyer behavior, and buyer decision processes. Subsequent research has looked into information processing of consumer choice and the experiential consumer.

Since the early 1980s, research has been conducted in areas as wide and varied as deviant behavior, consumer perception, planned behavior, intention-behavior discrepancy, environmentally responsible behavior, consumer judgment, attitudes, dependence, international and cross-cultural consumer behavior, impulsive buying, personality-behavior relationships, the role of imagery, web-browsing habits, and social and political marketing issues.

APPLICATIONS

Behavior occurs either for an individual on his or her own; for an individual in the context of a group (where others in the group influence how a person behaves); or for an organization (where people on the job make decisions as to which products the firm should use). The study of consumer behavior attempts to understand the buyer decision-making process for individuals, groups, and organizations.

Consumer decision making comes about as an attempt to solve consumer problems, both major and minor. A consumer buying decision process can have up to six stages. Actual purchasing is only one stage of the process, and not all decision processes may lead to a purchase. The number of stages involved in a particular decision depends on the degree of complexity of that decision. The six stages are problem recognition, information search, evaluation of alternatives, purchase decision, purchase, and post-purchase evaluation.

The first stage, problem recognition, is when a consumer becomes aware of a need. The need is manifest because there is a difference between the consumer's desired state and his or her actual condition. The second stage is the information search. There are two types of information searches: internal and external. With an internal information search, the consumer searches the information stored in his or her memory. If more information is needed after the internal search, the consumer may consult external information sources such as friends and relatives for word-of-mouth, marketing information, comparison shopping, and public sources.

A successful information search leaves a needy consumer with possible alternatives collectively called the evoked set. Armed with the evoked set, the consumer embarks on the third stage of the buying decision process: evaluation of alternatives. Here, the consumer may need to establish the criteria for evaluation, such as features of the product or service that the buyer wants or does not want. The consumer may rank or weigh the alternatives to arrive at a choice or resume searching if a satisfactory choice is not arrived at. Information from different sources may be treated differently.

The fourth stage in the consumer buying decision process is the purchase decision. Here, the consumer selects from the available alternatives, making decisions on details such as the specific product or service, its packaging, retail outlet, and method of purchase. The fifth stage is the purchase, which at times occurs simultaneously with the purchase decision. Sometimes product availability issues may cause a time lapse between the purchase decision and the actual purchase.

The sixth and last stage in the consumer buying decision process is post-purchase evaluation (also known as post-acquisition evaluation), which may occur to the buyer consciously or subconsciously. At the end of his or her evaluation, the buyer may experience satisfaction or dissatisfaction. Dissatisfaction may result from many factors, such as unmet brand expectations, and at times may lead to the consumer lodging a complaint. A satisfied consumer may end up becoming loyal to a particular brand or retail outlet.

A plethora of variables affect consumer behavior and not all have been even discovered or explored yet. While it is not possible to discuss many of these variables here, it is possible, however, to look at the following:
- Group influences
- Family influences
- Attitudes
- Perceptions
- Planned behavior
- Deviant consumer behavior

In consumer behavior, the Behavioral Influence Perspective assumes that strong environmental forces propel consumers to action without them necessarily first developing strong feelings or beliefs about a product, a service, an experience, or an idea. The consumer is impacted by many external influences: as a member of society, for instance, one acquires, through one's culture, knowledge, beliefs, morals, values, customs, and other capabilities and habits.

Apart from cultural and sub-cultural (such as African American, Hispanic and Asian) influences, the consumer is also subject to situational influences, which are temporary environmental factors and include physical surroundings, social surroundings, and time. Consumers are also subject to cross-cultural influences and group influences.

The literature on group influence is as extensive as its role in consumer decision making. One useful framework of analysis of group influence on the individual is the reference group. This is a group of people used by an individual as a standard of reference against which to compare him- or herself, such as role models. Reference groups come in several different forms. The aspirational reference group refers to those others against whom one would like to compare oneself (Perner, 2003).

According to Perner (2003), associative reference groups "include people who more realistically represent an individual's current equals or near-equals." Specifically, these include "coworkers, neighbors, or members of churches, clubs, and organizations. The final group, the dissociative reference group, includes people that the individual would not like to be like" (Perner, 2003). Marketers use the various groups to bring pertinent messages home to their actual and potential consumers.

Reference groups have various degrees of influence. Primary reference groups are those with the greatest amount of influence on an individual; secondary reference groups tend to have less influence—they may not enjoy very close relationships with the individual.

As Perner notes, in families, individual members "often serve different roles in decisions that ultimately draw on shared family resources. Some individuals are information gatherers or information holders: they seek out information about products of relevance. These individuals often have a great deal of power because they may selectively pass on information that favors their chosen alternatives" (2003). There are also the influencers: "they do not ultimately have the power to decide between alternatives, but they may make their wishes known by asking for specific products or causing embarrassing situations if their demands are not met" (Perner, 2003).

The next role is that of the decision maker(s), who have the power to determine issues such as whether to buy; which product to buy; which brand to buy; where to buy it; and when to buy it. The last role in family decision making is that of the purchaser. The fact that the purchaser and the decision maker may be different people often poses problems for marketers, since the purchaser can be targeted by point-of-purchase marketing efforts that cannot be aimed at the decision maker (Perner, 2003).

Apart from external factors and influences as described above, the consumer is also prone to internal influences, such as attitudes, perception, and intention. Consumer attitudes are the sum of a consumer's positive, negative, or neutral beliefs about, feelings about, and behavioral intentions toward an object, which, in the context of marketing, is usually a brand or retail outlet. The components of attitude are considered "together since they are highly interdependent and together represent forces that influence how the consumer will react to the object" (Perner, 2003).

Perception is one of the personal factors that determine consumer behavior. The term "personal factors" refers to the closest environment of a person, including everything that is inside the person, his or her head and soul, characterizing him or her as a personality. Using his or her sensory receptors and being influenced by external factors as discussed above, the person receives information, accepts and adapts it, forms a personal attitude, an opinion, and a motive, which can be defined as factors that will influence his or her further activity and behavior (Banyte, J., Paunksniene, Ž., & Rutelione, A., 2007).

The Theory of Planned Behavior suggests that behavioral intention—the motivation that determines how hard people are willing to try to perform a behavior—is the most influential predictor of behavior: it assumes that a person does what he or she intends to do (Pavlou & Fygenson, 2006). However, this is not always the case. Sometimes there is a discrepancy between intention and behavior. This is referred to as the intention-behavior discrepancy.

Other factors that influence behavior include past experience or past behavior, habit, and even the information-gathering process, which has been found to have a significant impact on purchasing (Pavlou and Fygenson, 2006).

When consumer behavior differs from the norm or the standard, it is termed "deviant." Deviant behavior veers away from established customs, manners, rules and regulations, laws, and mores—which themselves are sometimes poorly defined or unclear. Depending on the extent to which an individual's behavior deviates from such norms, it may be considered by society to be either undesirable, unacceptable, or dysfunctional (which is another word for "deviant").

Another way in which deviancy can be defined is in terms of the frequency or the degree to which a consumer deviates from society's norms and pre-scribed behaviors (Moschis and Cox, 1989). Deviant behavior does not only pertain to individuals: it can also emanate from firms and organizations, for instance, through deceptive advertising, advertising harmful products to children, and telemarketing fraud.

Similarly, some consumers display negligent consumer behavior through the misuse of products and the consumption of hazardous products.

To conclude, those organizations that understand what would appeal to the current and potential consumers of their products and services can tailor their advertising and other marketing efforts accordingly. Understanding consumer behavior helps firms and organizations improve their marketing strategies by understanding issues such as:

- How consumers think, feel, reason, and select between different alternatives, such as brands and products
- How consumers are influenced by their environment, for instance, by culture, family, signs, and the media
- The behavior of consumers while shopping or making other marketing decisions
- How limitations in consumer knowledge or information-processing abilities influence decisions and marketing outcomes
- How consumer motivation and decision strategies differ between products that differ in their level of importance or interest for the consumer
- How marketers can adapt and improve their marketing campaigns and marketing strategies to more effectively reach consumers (Perner, 2003).

Apart from assisting in the area of marketing, the study of consumer behavior also aids policymakers in formulating rules and regulations concerning the uses and abuses of certain products and services. Likewise, the study of consumer behavior also helps environmentalists put measures into place to reduce the occurrence of improper waste disposal. By understanding consumer behavior, social marketers are also able to improve their marketing strategies, so as to get their ideas across to their target audience.

BIBLIOGRAPHY

Banyte, J., Paunksniene, Ž., & Rutelione, A. (2007). Peculiarities of consumer perception in the aspect of marketing to women. *Engineering Economics, 51,* 50–58. Retrieved April 22, 2007, from EBSCO Online Database Business Source Complete. http://search.ebscohost.com/login.aspx?direct=true&db=bth&AN=24496667&site=ehost-live

Bertrand, G. (2013). Social media research: developing a trust metric in the social age. International Journal Of Market Research, 55, 333-335. doi:10.2501/IJMR-2013-032 Retrieved November 19, 2013 from EBSCO online database Business Source Complete with Full Text:http://search.ebscohost.com/login.aspx?direct=true&db=bth&AN=87975673&site=ehost-live

Dahlström, P., & Edelman, D. (2013). The coming era of 'on-demand' marketing. *Mckinsey Quarterly,* 24–39. Retrieved November 19, 2013 from EBSCO online database Business Source Complete with Full Text:http://search.ebscohost.com/login.aspx?direct=true&db=bth&AN=87315649&site=ehost-live

Demirdjian, Z., & Senguder, T. (2004). Perspectives in consumer behavior: Paradigm shifts in prospect. *Journal of American Academy of Business, Cambridge, 4*(1/2), 348–353. Retrieved April 02, 2007, from EBSCO Online Database Business Source Complete. http://search.ebscohost.com/login.aspx?direct=true&db=bth&AN=12704394&site=ehost-live

Moschis, G., & Cox, D. (1989). Deviant consumer behavior. *Advances in Consumer Research, 16,* 732–737. Retrieved April 02, 2007, from EBSCO Online Database Business Source Complete. http://search.ebscohost.com/login.aspx?direct=true&db=bth&AN=6487793&site=ehost-live

Mowen, J., & Minor, M. (2003). *Consumer Behavior: A Framework.* Retrieved April 26, 2007, from http://www.consumerbehavior.net/.

Pavlou, P., & Fygenson, M. (2006). Understanding and prediction electronic commerce adoption: An extension of the theory of planned behavior. *MIS Quarterly, 30,* 115–143. Retrieved April 02, 2007, from EBSCO Online Database Business Source Complete. http://search.ebscohost.com/login.aspx?direct=true&db=bth&AN=19754863&site=ehost-live

Perner, L. (2003). *The Psychology of Consumers.* Retrieved April 2, 2007, from http://www.consumer-psychologist.com/.

Quinn, L., & Patterson, A. (2013). Storying marketing research: The twisted tale of a consumer profiled. *Journal Of Marketing Management, 29*(5/6), 720-733. doi:10.1080/0267257X.2013.771203 Retrieved November 19, 2013 from EBSCO online database Business Source Complete with Full Text:http://search.ebscohost.com/login.aspx?direct=true&db=bth&AN=88212135&site=ehost-live

Scaraboto, D., Carter-Schneider, L., & Kedzior, R. (2013). At world's end: Exploring consumer-marketer tensions in the closure of adverworlds. *Journal Of Marketing Management, 29*(13/14), 1518-1541. doi:10.1080/0267257X.2013.833968 Retrieved November 19, 2013 from EBSCO online database Business Source Complete with Full Text:http://search.ebscohost.com/login.aspx?direct=true&db=bth&AN=91900379&site=ehost-live

Steenkamp, J. M., & Maydeu-Olivares, A. (2015). Stability and change in consumer traits: Evidence from a 12-year longitudinal study, 2002–2013. *Journal of Marketing Research (JMR), 52*(3), 287–308. doi:10.1509/jmr.13.0592. Retrieved December 3, 2015, from EBSCO Online Database Business Source Complete. http://search.ebscohost.com/login.aspx?direct=true&db=bth&AN=103236329&site=ehost-live&scope=site

Wong, J., & Sheth, J. (1985). Explaining intention-behavior discrepancy—A paradigm. *Advances in Consumer Research, 12*, 378-384. Retrieved April 02, 2007, from EBSCO Online Database Business Source Complete. http://search.ebscohost.com/login.aspx?direct=true&db=bth&AN=6430998&site=ehost-live

SUGGESTED READING

Demirdjian, Z., & Senguder, T. (2004). Perspectives in consumer behavior: Paradigm shifts in prospect. *Journal of American Academy of Business, Cambridge, 4*(1/2), 348–353. Retrieved April 02, 2007, from EBSCO Online Database Business Source

Complete. http://search.ebscohost.com/login.aspx?direct=true&db=bth&AN=12704394&site=ehost-live

Kardes, F. R., Cronley, M. L., & Cline, T. W. (2015). *Consumer behavior.* (2nd ed.). Stamford, CT: Cengage Learning.

Mowen, J., & Minor, M. (2003). *Consumer Behavior: A Framework.* Retrieved April 26, 2007, from http://www.consumerbehavior.net/

Mandel, Naomi, etal. (2016). The compensatory consumer behavior model: how self-discrepancies drive consumer behavior. *Journal of Consumer Psychology.* Retrieved June 29, 2017. https://papers.ssrn.com/sol3/papers.cfm?abstract_id=2787451

Perner, L. (2007). *The Psychology of Consumers.* Retrieved April 2, 2007, from http://www.consumer-psychologist.com/

Vernette, E., & Hamdi-Kidar, L. (2013). Co-creation with consumers: who has the competence and wants to cooperate?. International Journal Of Market Research, 55, 2–20. Retrieved November 19, 2013 from EBSCO online database Business Source Complete with Full Text:http://search.ebscohost.com/login.aspx?direct=true&db=bth&AN=89071271&site=ehost-live

Wong, J., & Sheth, J. (1985). Explaining intention-behavior discrepancy—A paradigm. *Advances in Consumer Research, 12*, 378–384. Retrieved April 02, 2007, from EBSCO Online Database Business Source Complete. http://search.ebscohost.com/login.aspx?direct=true&db=bth&AN=6430998&site=ehost-live

Vanessa A. Tetteh, Ph.D.

CONSUMER DEMOGRAPHICS

ABSTRACT

This article will provide an overview and analysis of the history and current relevance of the consumer demographics movement and related practices, such as psychographics, in market research. Business applications of consumer demographics will be discussed. In addition, the issue of globalization's effect on consumer demographics, and market research in general, will be covered. The phenomena of global consumers, global brands, and consumer ethnocentrism will be introduced.

OVERVIEW

Consumer demographics, which include categories such as age, ethnicity, gender, income, mobility, education, and social class are considered to be predictors of consumer behavior, habits, and patterns. For example, variances in customer gender and income predictably result in higher sales in certain markets and lower sales in others. Consumer demographics are generally considered to be either antecedent or non-antecedent in nature. Antecedent demographics, such as gender, race, and nationality refer to socio-developmental processes that may influence an individual's intellectual and emotional responses to consumer choices. Non-antecedent demographics, such as student-status, home-ownership status, and political affiliation, refer to identities added during the lifecycle.

The field of market research uses consumer demographic data, and related tools, to accomplish the following value-added processes (Claxton, 1995, ¶1):

- "Identify meaningful new market segments."
- "Fit products to individual needs more closely."
- "Build better relationships with the many facets of today's complex consumer."

Consumer demographics, as a tool or a statistical grouping, are part of a larger effort to study and gather information about the consumer. Areas of related consumer study include consumer behavior, consumer characteristics, lifestyle attributes, life-cycle consumption, market segmentation, target demographics, psychographics, and consumer price knowledge. Market researchers use polls, surveys, and tracking technology to gather demographic data.

Consumer demographic data is an important tool used by marketers and advertisers in the brand-making process. Marketers create brand through a two-step process: marketing mix and marketing implementation. Marketing mix refers to the process of researching customers and "formulating the policies for new product and service developments, distribution channel choice, pricing strategy, marketing communications, and customer servicing. Marketing implementation refers to the process of delivering products and services to consumers, and involves such activities as production, supply chain management, logistics, employee training and motivation, advertising and promotions, and sales and after-sales service" (Gelder, 2004).

Consumer demographic data is gathered in the private and public sectors alike. Multinational corporations, such as Citibank and Coca Cola, depend on consumer demographic profiles to target

segments of the population with appropriate advertising campaigns and estimate consumption and distribution needs. Nonprofits such as the Association for Consumer Research exist to advance consumer research in areas such as consumer demographics and facilitate the exchange of information among members of academia, industry, and government. Government agencies, such as the U.S. Department of Labor's Bureau of Labor Statistics, collect consumer demographic data on the U.S. population. The Bureau of Labor Statistics collects consumer demographic data on thirteen standard characteristics such as income quintile, income class, age, size, composition, number of earners, housing tenure, type of area, race, Hispanic or Latino origin, region, occupation, and education. The Bureau of Labor Statistics creates the Consumer Price Index, which is a measure of the average variation over time in the prices paid by urban consumers to buy a market basket of consumer goods and services in order to quantify urban consumption of food and beverages, housing, apparel, transportation, medical care, recreation, education and communication, and other goods and services.

Consumer demographics, and market research in general, is increasingly important in the new global economy. Consumer demographics in the global market are a tool used by applied market researchers and corporations to maintain or increase market share. Controlling market share, which refers to the fraction of industry sales of a good or service controlled by a certain company, is becoming increasingly competitive in the global marketplace.

The following section will provide an overview and analysis of the history and current relevance of the consumer demographics movement in market research. This section will serve as a foundation for later discussions of the business applications of consumer demographic and the rise of global consumers and global brands.

History of Consumer Demographics
The study and use consumer demographic data as a marketing and advertising tool began in the early twentieth century. Studies of consumer behavior began at the same time as mass-circulating, advertising-sponsored magazines. Consumer information became crucial currency in advertising and media industries of the early twentieth centuries. From

1910-1940, weekly magazines, such as *Ladies' Homes Journal, Woman's Home Companion,* and *Harper's Bazaar,* promoted their magazines to advertisers as being representative of a certain kind of consumer. Magazines and publishers established research departments to collect data on the income and demographics of their audience. Magazine surveys in which readers were asked to report information on family size, occupation, size of home, gardens, domestic help, car type, meal planning, leisure time, and food preparation became common. These surveys were transmuted into reports on consumer demographics, behavior, and purchasing patterns.

During the 1930s, the growth in radio broadcasting facilitated the growth of national consumer rating research and the development of a standardized consumer typology, called the ABCD system, used to differentiate households according to income. Income data was thought to provide associated information about lifestyle and politics. The ABCD consumer income typology included the following categories:

A: Homes of substantial wealth
B: Comfortable middle-class homes
C: Industrial homes of skilled tradespeople
D: Homes of unskilled laborers

The ABCD income system influenced the development of the Cooperative Analysis of Broadcasting (CAB) survey approach and the Nielsen ratings index. The ABCD, and its later incarnations, allowed for standardized and targeted marketing efforts. The ABCD system's popular use in market research declined in the years following World War II. At this time, American society changed in three major ways:

- **Creation of consumer culture:** Post WWII years were characterized by a rise in the standard of living, new materials and designs, shopping malls, and new appliances.
- **Popularity of television:** Post WWII years were characterized by the ubiquity of television in American households. The rise in the popularity of television transformed American media consumption habits and patterns. Television became the main conveyor of advertising messages.
- **Focus on lifestyle:** Post WWII years were characterized by the emerging awareness of lifestyle. The rise of consumer culture and new media culture created new focus on youth culture and leisure time.

In response to these three changes or shifts in American society, market research grew in size and sophistication. In the 1950s and 1960s, market research expanded in an effort to gather more and better information about consumer behavior. During the 1960s, market researchers began to abandon the idea (as typified in the ABCD income system) that demographic data was the only or most important measure of consumer patterns or predictor of consumer behavior.

Market researchers began to conduct consumer motivation research that was characterized by the notion that consumer action and decision was motivated by the consumer's unconscious. The consumer motivation research approach, which depends on in-depth information to gather consumer information, asserts that consumers are engaged in a dynamic consumption process in which they are active, rather than passive, actors. Motivation research is based on the following beliefs:

- Consumer needs and desires are independent of environment.
- Consumer preferences are not created through structural determination.

While motivation research was responsible for the recognition that consumers have subjective experiences and are actors in their own rights, motivation research, based on interview data, was considered to be methodologically anecdotal and unscientific. Motivation research became the foundation for a field called psychographics (Arvidsson, 2004).

Psychographic research refers to quantitative research intended to place consumers on psychological, rather than demographic, dimensions. Psychographics involves quantitative research on consumer attitudes, opinions, and interests. Consumer data was generated from computer analyses of more than 300 variables. Consumer habits and profiles became highly individualized. Segments and consumers were no longer determined by small numbers of categories. Variety characterized this new approach. Psychographic research, with its hundreds of variables, allows for new insights and unexpected conclusions. Market researchers who collect psychographic data are interested in the complexities of consumer personality and behavior. Psychographic research, also referred to as lifestyle, activity, and attitude research, attempts to move beyond demographic data collection and analysis. Psychographic variables include activities, interests, opinions, needs, values, attitudes, and personality traits. Ultimately, consumer motivation research and psychographics, which remain market research tools today, account for the complexity of the modern consumer when the ABCD income typology, and consumer demographics in general, cannot (Wells, 1975).

APPLICATION

Data on consumer demographics is crucial information for nearly every industry including retail, insurance, finance, advertising, and consumer goods. The connection between subsets of demographic particulars and consumer behaviors and action are long established. For example, there is an established relationship between consumer socio-economic demographics and consumer price knowledge (Rosa-Diaz, 2004). In addition, there is an established relationship between shopper's demographic characteristics, retailer reputation, shopping expenditure, and frequencies of store patronage (Ou, 2007).

Demographic data, along with other market research tools such as psychographic data, competitive data, shopping-center data, brand sales, and site-related data, allows an organization or industry to understand and predict consumer behavior. Demographic data can be used for the following business analyses:

- Comparison of demographic data and sales regions helps to connect sales to neighborhoods and aids in creating a distribution of sales map.
- Comparison of demographic data and sales levels helps identify which characteristics are associated with high, medium, and low sales.
- Comparison of demographic data and site characteristics helps to analyze and determine which variables contribute positively or negatively to sales potential.

Regional, national, and international organizations alike depend on consumer demographics data but, at this point in the development of market research and brands, consumer demographics are rarely used as the exclusive tool to plan an advertising or marketing campaign. Instead, marketers use consumer demographics *and* other tools such as psychographics.

For example, the financial industry depends on market research of all kinds to understand and segment its customers or consumer base into target groups. In 1999, Citibank hired Fallon Worldwide as its bank marketer. Fallon Worldwide combined demographic and psychographic research and data to understand Citibank customers. Citibank's use of consumer demographic and psychographic data can be seen in Citi's "Live Richly" campaign. This campaign cut across traditional demographic categories and targeted consumers with a "healthy" attitude toward money who sought to fulfill their values of family, friends, and shared happiness. Ultimately, demographic data, discovered through focus groups, surveys, polls, and interviews, are at their most useful when combined with consumer behavior data (Sausner, 2006).

ISSUE
Consumer Demographics & Globalization

The forces and processes of globalization affect established approaches to market research such as consumer demographics data. The advent of global markets and global brands challenges the fixed categories of consumer demographic profiles. The intersection of marketing and diverse cultures has created the need for new demographic tools that reflect cultural, economic, and social contact and transitions. For example, the traditional demographic category of nationality is challenged by transnationalism. The traditional demographic categories of race and ethnicity are challenged by multiracial and multiethnic identities. The traditional demographic category of gender is challenged by transgender identities.

Global markets are characterized by an increasing mobility in capital, research and design process, production facilities, customers, and regulators. Global markets, created through socio-economic changes, political revolutions, and new Internet and communication technology, have no national borders. The modern trend of globalization, and resulting shifts from centralized to market economies in much of the world, has created opportunities for increased trade, investment, business partnerships, and access to once closed global markets. Economic environments around the world are changing due to the forces of globalization. Globalization is characterized by the permeability of traditional boundaries of nations, culture, and economic markets. The fundamental economic forces and events influencing globalization around the world include the end of communism; the move away from an economy based on natural resources to one established on knowledge industries; demographic shifts; the rise of a global economy; increased trade liberalization; advances in communication technology; and increased threats of global terrorism (Thurow, 1995).

Globalization creates a turbulent global sociopolitical environment characterized by competing political actors, shifting power relations, and politically driven changes in national economies around the world. Businesses work to find opportunity and profit in the political and economic changes. The political turbulence and upheaval has resulted in a move from centralized economies to a decentralized global economy and has created numerous emerging markets. These emerging markets are capital markets within developing countries that have decided to liberalize their financial system to increase capital flows from external investors.

In a fast-moving global environment, cultures around the world are changing. Economic and social migration causes individual members of various cultural groups to move from one country to another. People bring their interests, values, and distinctive behavior patterns, which result in cultural interpenetration (Craig & Douglas, 2006). Economic globalization, the first step of globalization, is followed by political, cultural, and psychological globalization. In response to the processes of globalization, individual consumer demographic categories need to be expanded as does the overall definition of the consumer (Suh & Kwon, 2002). Scholars debate whether globalization fosters renewed nationalism or national and cultural homogenization. While people do not seem to be transcending their cultures, people engaged in cultural contact and interpenetration do seem to be creating some degree of world citizenship (Cannon & Yaprak, 2002). World or global citizenship is strongly connected to the growing trend of global brands.

Businesses participating in the new global economy continue to seek out new manufacturing and sales opportunities in foreign markets and countries (Sites, 1995). Economic globalization has resulted in the creation of global or world brands. The growth of world brands is challenged by the specific norms and values of individual cultures. Marketers of international or global brands face problems of consumer ethnocentrism, or reluctance to buy a foreign product. National values are shifting due to cultural interpenetration. Market research studies are increasingly incorporating international consumer demographic data to gain insight on global processes and preferences.

In many instances, cultural norms and values often conflict with a company's desire to obtain brand consistency across markets. For example, a local culture's values and norms can influence areas such as the "volume of mineral water and soft drinks consumed, ownership of pets, of cars, the choice of car type, ownership of insurance, possession of private gardens, readership of newspapers and books, TV viewing, ownership of consumer electronics and computers, usage of the Internet, sales of video-cassettes, usage of cosmetics, toiletries, deodorants and hair care products, consumption of fresh fruit, ice cream and frozen food, and usage of toothpaste" (de Mooij, 2000). The management of brands across multiple societies and geographical areas is a fast growing area within market research. Market researchers, and the corporations who hire them, are committed to reaching the full potential of brands in diverse markets (Gelder, 2004).

CONCLUSION

Market research during the twentieth century incorporated nearly all the disciplines and related tools of social science research (including anthropology, sociology, economics, psychology, and political science) to understand and predict consumer behavior and choices in the marketplace. Market research, which was originally based on simple demographic systems such as the ABCD typology described in this article, has expanded over the last century into every industry and market. Today, data on consumer demographics contribute to nearly every market research process including "target marketing, customer profiling, site evaluation, demographic analysis, market segmentation, color mapping, business and competitive analysis and sales forecasting, marketing and advertising campaign development, and strategic business planning" (Hoffman, 1987, ¶3).

Demographic profiles are standard practice in modern market research. Consumer demographics are believed to influence every part of consumer behavior. Demographic profiles, which were the foundation of market research conducted in the early twentieth century and remain an influential and much-used market research tool today, are criticized for the rigidity and fixity of consumer categories and variables. Consumer demographic data is increasingly augmented with consumer behavior and consumer motivation data. Market research is increasingly interested in collecting and analyzing multi-variable consumer data on demographics, motivation, psychology, and behavior.

In the late twentieth and early twenty-first centuries, market research is characterized by single-source information services such as barcode scans and Internet tracking software. Twenty-first century market research is concerned with knowledge, mobility, post-modern consumer, virtual communities, branding revolution, and brand value that transcended place. The twenty-first century consumer is virtual, mobile, and highly aware of corporate behavior and actions (Arvidsson, 2004). Demographics were found to be an important factor in some kinds of purchasing behaviors, such as for electronics, and demographics were shown to have superior predictive potential (Sandy, Gosling, & Durant, 2013) in Internet commerce. With the near ubiquity of smartphones and tablets, researchers and marketers began to look at differences in e-commerce, which allows collection of data tracked to an IP address, and mobile transactions, or m-commerce, which allows collection of real-time data tracked to a device's serial number, including location, "social relationships, life style, preferences, or behavior patterns" (Zhang, Chen, & Cajaejung, 2013).

BIBLIOGRAPHY

Arvidsson, A. (2004). On the 'pre-history of the panoptic sort': mobility in market research. *Surveillance and Society, 1,* 456-474.

Cannon, H. & Yaprak, A. (2002). Will the real-world citizen please stand up! The many faces of cosmopolitan consumer behavior. *Journal of International Marketing, 10,* 30-53.

Carpenter, J.M., Moore, M., Alexander, N., & Doherty, A. (2013). Consumer demographics, ethnocentrism, cultural values, and acculturation to the global consumer culture: A retail perspective. *Journal of Marketing Management, 29*(3/4), 271-291.

Retrieved October 31, 2013, from EBSCO Online Database Business Source Complete. http://search.ebscohost.com/login.aspx?direct=true&db=bth&AN=87341771&site=ehost-live

Claxton, R. (1995). Birth order as a market segmentation variable. *Journal of Consumer Marketing, 12,* 2-38. Retrieved Monday, April 23, 2007, from http://www.emeraldinsight.com/journals.htm?articleid=856206&show=html

Craig, C., & Douglas, S. (2006). Beyond national culture: implications of cultural dynamics for consumer research. *International Marketing Review, 23,* 322-342.

Demographics. (2007). U.S. Department of Labor's Bureau of Labor Statistics. Retrieved April 20, 207 from http://www.bls.gov/.

de Mooij, M. (2000). The future is predictable for international marketers Converging incomes lead to diverging consumer behavior. *International Marketing Review, 17,* 103.

Gelder, S. (2004). Global brand strategy. *Journal of Brand Management, 12,* 39-49.

Heffetz, O. (2012). Who sees what? Demographics and the visibility of consumer expenditures. *Journal of Economic Psychology, 33,* 801-818. Retrieved October 31, 2013, from EBSCO Online Database Business Source Complete. http://search.ebscohost.com/login.aspx?direct=true&db=bth&AN=76306000&site=ehost-live

Hoffman, B. (1987). Databases help companies with target marketing efforts. Quirk's Marketing Research Review. Retrieved 29 July 2010 from http://www.quirks.com/articles/a1987/19870304.aspx?searchID=18015093&so

Orton, J. (2006). Making demographics, research and modeling work for a franchise system. *Franchising World, 38,* 34-38.

Ou, W. (2007). Moderating effects of age, gender, income and education on consumer's response to corporate reputation. *Journal of American Academy of Business, 10,* 190-195.

Rosa-Diaz, I. (2004). Price knowledge: effects of consumers' attitudes towards prices, demographics, and socio-cultural characteristics. *The Journal of Product and Brand Management, 13,* 406.

Sandy, C.J., Gosling, S.D., & Durant, J. (2013). Predicting consumer behavior and media preferences: The comparative validity of personality traits and demographic variables. *Psychology &*

Marketing, 30, 937-949. Retrieved October 31, 2013, from EBSCO Online Database Business Source Complete. http://search.ebscohost.com/login.aspx?direct=true&db=bth&AN=90577043&site=ehost-live

Sausner, R. (2006). Beyond demographics: tracking buying trends. *U.S. Banker, 116,* 24-24. Retrieved Monday, April 23, 2007, from EBSCO Online Databse Business Source Complete. http://search.ebscohost.com/login.aspx?direct=true&db=bth&AN=21463171&site=ehost-live

Sites, J. (1995). Going forward with global investments. *Risk Management, 42,* 12-17.

Suh, T., & Kwon, I. (2002). Globalization and reluctant buyers. *International Marketing Review, 19,* 663-681.

Thurow, L. (1995). Surviving in a turbulent environment. *Planning Review. 23,* 24.

Wells, W. (1975). Psychographics: a critical review. *Journal of Marketing Research (JMR), 12,* 196-213. Retrieved Monday, April 23, 2007, from EBSCO Online Database Business Source Complete. http://search.ebscohost.com/login.aspx?direct=true&db=bth&AN=5001322&site=ehost-live

Zhang, R., Chen, J.Q., & Cajaejung, L. (2013). Mobile commerce and consumer privacy concerns. *Journal of Computer Information Systems, 53,* 31-38. Retrieved October 31, 2013, from EBSCO Online Database Business Source Complete. http://search.ebscohost.com/login.aspx?direct=true&db=bth&AN=90111068&site=ehost-live

SUGGESTED READING

Bellman, S., Lohse, G., & Johnson, E. (1999). Predictors of online buying behavior. *Communications of the ACM, 42,* 32-38. Retrieved Monday, April 23, 2007, from EBSCO Online Database Business Source Complete. http://search.ebscohost.com/login.aspx?direct=true&db=bth&AN=11872116&site=ehost-live

Black, G. (2005). Is eBay for everyone? An assessment of consumer demographics. *SAM Advanced Management Journal, 70,* 50-59. Retrieved Monday, April 23, 2007, from EBSCO Online Database Business Source Complete. http://search.ebscohost.com/login.aspx?direct=true&db=bth&AN=17063790&site=ehost-live

Estelami, H. (1998). The price is right...or is it? Demographic and category effects on consumer price knowledge. *Journal of Product & Brand Management, 7,* 254. Retrieved Monday, April 23, 2007, from EBSCO Online Database Business Source Complete. http://search.ebscohost.com/login.aspx?direct=true&db=bth&AN=4043329&site=ehost-live

Subitia, Pattanaik, et al. (2017). How consumer demographics is associated with shopping behavior, a study on indian consumers. *Indian Journals.* Retrieved June 29, 2017.

Simone I. Flynn, Ph.D.

CONTENT MARKETING

ABSTRACT

Content marketing is a form of advertising and product promotion that has existed in rudimentary form at least as far back as the late nineteenth century but has recently been revitalized by the popularity of the Internet, which provides a simple, global platform for worldwide content distribution. In essence, content marketing differs from traditional marketing in its value proposition—that is, what it offers the consumer. Traditional marketing functions by creating a need and then convincing consumers that they have this need. Content marketing develops a commodity that consumers want and draws consumer attention to the products.

OVERVIEW

Content marketing is an intriguing approach to building a customer base and maintaining it over a long period of time. Traditional marketing uses a broadcasting strategy in which the target audience for a product is seen as being scattered throughout the general population and therefore difficult to communicate with directly. When marketing teams operate under this paradigm, they usually conclude that the best way to convey their message to the target audience is by broadcasting it to as much of the general population as can be reached, given the limits of their budget, their schedule, and the available technology. This has traditionally included advertising across all forms of media, from print and radio to television, street signs, and the Internet, to the point that advertising has become so ubiquitous that people often fail to notice it even when it is staring them in the face.

Traditional marketing does not come cheap—billions are spent each year to promote everything from diapers to solar panels. However, marketers have realized that there are a number of problems with this approach, aside from the significant expense it entails: The public becomes desensitized to it, many people are bombarded by messages that they have no interest in, and above all else it is inefficient because it communicates a message intended for a few to everyone (Odden, 2013).

Content marketing provides an alternative to this model. Instead of sending a marketing message to everyone, the idea behind content marketing is to create some type of resource—the content—that will attract those who are interested in the resource and cause them to build a stronger connection with the company or product. The content can take almost any form and is usually chosen based upon the resources that are available, the nature of the product or service being promoted, and the interests of the target audience. Content marketing for senior citizens generally does not involve the intense use of complex technology, for example, because many older people are not comfortable with computers and the Internet.

Some content used for marketing takes the form of a monthly magazine; an online forum; a smartphone application that people download, install, and use; or an online service that people sign up for. In fact, many of the Internet-based services that people use on a daily basis are actually complex forms of content marketing, disguised as free services. These include free online email services, file-storage services, online calendar and productivity suites, and many more. Companies offering these services do so not out of a purely charitable impulse, but as a way to encourage potential customers to "buy into their ecosystem."

Buying into an ecosystem means that if customers are using Company X's "Xmail" service for their email and then find a need for online file storage also, the first option they consider will probably be "Xdrive" because it is offered by a company that they already recognize and trust with their communications. During the dotcom boom in the early part of the twenty-first century, free online services proliferated, offering contact management, calendars, email, and even photo storage (Syzdek, 2014). Some of these services survived and grew, boasting millions of users. They also generated billions in advertising revenue because such services are typically tied into pay-per-click advertising mechanisms that provide the funding needed to support the platform.

Many people have come to rely on these services in their daily lives, yet they do not realize that by using the service, they are benefitting the company that supports it, even if not through a direct payment. A phrase often used to describe this situation is If you are not paying for it, then you are the product." This sums up many of the essential features of content marketing: It is essentially an exchange of value-bearing commodities. The customer receives the content, whatever form it happens to take, while the company receives the customer's time and attention (and perhaps loyalty). Provided that customers are aware they are giving at the same time they receive, there is nothing inherently wrong with this type of transaction.

The character of a content-marketing campaign is determined largely by the purpose for which the campaign is undertaken. Some content marketing is created in order to establish a community of users for the first time, bringing together people from disparate locations to share their common interests (Forouzandeh, Soltanpanah & Sheikhahmadi, 2014). In other cases, content marketing has been used even though there is an existing base of users; in these situations, content marketing tends to appear as an added feature that has the unspoken purpose of either recruiting new users or making the existing base of users more diverse. Where a company's product has mostly been used by middle-aged consumers, that company might develop and release a free smartphone application tied to the product as a way of appealing to younger consumers and bringing them into the user community.

Content marketing can even play a role in increasing customers' respect for and faith in the product by making the product appear more official and established. Some grocery stores have tried this approach by creating their own monthly or quarterly newsletters, which are then mailed to regular customers and contain information about new products, recipes, and similar types of content. Even to the seasoned and cynical consumer, this can create the impression that the store cares enough about its customers to produce this information and distribute it and the store is sophisticated enough to be able to provide this service in addition to simply selling groceries (Wylie, 2014).

Further Insights

Content marketing has grown rapidly since the dawn of the Internet, and this rapid growth has brought its share of challenges. The most pervasive challenge has been the widespread lack of expertise in media creation and distribution. To put this more plainly, most companies are experts at a particular type of service, whether that is making hamburgers or building jet engines. The company is extremely good at that one thing and not very good at anything else (Ahmad, Musa & Harun, 2016). Content marketing involves creating content that is interesting, useful, or otherwise engaging, and it often happens that companies face a steep learning curve as they explore what it means to create media that meets these user expectations.

As a result, many content marketing efforts have produced decidedly uninteresting content—glossy magazines full of tedious stories, poorly designed online portals and web-based services, and smartphone apps that barely function, much less do anything useful. Not surprisingly, these content-marketing campaigns tend to have a negative effect, causing users to distance themselves from the company. Some companies have been quick to learn this harsh lesson, and as a consequence, they have outsourced their content-marketing efforts to firms that specialize in this area. Content-marketing specialists are familiar with understanding a product and its target audience and then designing creative and effective ways to bring the two closer together (Pažėraitė & Repovienė, 2016).

Specialists in content marketing continue to develop new and unexpected forms, as media and entertainment keep evolving. An example of this can be found in the relatively new phenomenon of video game play-throughs on online video streaming sites such as YouTube. In the early years after the invention of video games, people would purchase the games and play them on their computers without interacting with others. The Internet made it possible for people to play games online with others, with all players interacting in a shared, online environment as they played the game. A huge part of the video-gaming community involves people who, instead of playing the video game themselves, tune into a video streaming site to watch someone else—a "YouTuber"—play the game, while providing entertaining commentary (Holliman & Rowley, 2014).

This phenomenon seems to have developed on its own, but video-game companies have been quick to capitalize on it by turning it into a content marketing platform in which the video-game maker pays a famous YouTuber (some have millions of followers all over the world) to play the company's game, with the goal of causing the YouTuber's viewers to become interested in purchasing the game for themselves. The viewers receive what appears to be free entertainment, while the YouTuber is paid by the company, and the company receives increased awareness and interest in its products, which often translates into increased sales (Harad, 2016).

Issues

While there are many advantages to content marketing, there are also pitfalls that must be avoided. Perhaps the foremost of these is the possibility that the content that has been created may be interpreted by some as biased or misleading, resulting in accusations that misinformation or thinly disguised advertising is being distributed, rather than objective and useful information. This can lead to users of the content targeting the company as behaving dishonestly, which can negatively effect all aspects of the company's business and may erode the benefits of the content-marketing campaign.

For example, if a manufacturer of personal electronics creates an online user community as part of its content-marketing strategy, but then suppresses forum posts within this community that tout the advantages of other companies' gadgets, users of the forum will quickly sour on the platform and either criticize it in other venues, cease to participate in it, or both. If content marketing is to be worth the effort, it must be authentic and provide something of real value to its target audience (Patrutiu Baltes, 2015).

In the example of the electronics forum, the company should realize that it has far more to lose by censoring the posts of its users than it does by allowing other electronics makers' products to be discussed or even praised. If a number of customers use the forum to point out the ways in which competitors' products exceed those of the firm hosting the forum, there are two ways for the firm to respond. First, it could see the posts as criticism that may cut into sales and which must therefore be suppressed. On the other hand, the more strategic interpretation is to view such postings as valuable customer feedback that is being collected at no cost, without the need to convene focus groups, send out surveys, or incentivize people to provide their views. The first interpretation is likely to lead the company into taking draconian actions that reflect poorly upon it, while the second can produce long-term benefits for the brand (Harad, 2013).

In addition to controversies over control and free speech, online forums used as content marketing must also be wary of the potential for liability that may arise from hosting the forum but failing to manage it appropriately. This can happen when users of the forum interact with one another in inappropriate ways, as when one user cyberbullies another. If the company that created the forum for content-marketing purposes does not have adequate safeguards in place to protect users from this type of behavior, such as having forum moderators who can monitor users' behavior to make sure that it remains civil, then there is the possibility that persons suffering a harm of some sort could see the company as being partially responsible in a moral or even in a legal sense. This is a danger faced by almost any kind of activity that relies upon crowdsourced content: Members of "the crowd" do not operate under the same types of controls and incentives as regular employees do, so there is the potential for their behavior to deviate from what is expected in polite society (Alsip, 2013).

BIBLIOGRAPHY

Ahmad, N. S., Musa, R., & Harun, M. M. (2016). The impact of social media content marketing (SMCM) towards brand health. *Procedia Economics & Finance, 37,* 331.

Alsip, J. (2013). 3 keys for a successful content marketing campaign. *English Teaching: Practice & Critique, 12*(2), 20. Retrieved October 23, 2016, from EBSCO Online Database Business Source Ultimate. http://search.ebscohost.com/login.aspx?direct=true&db=bsu&AN=89421420&site=ehost-live

Forouzandeh, S., Soltanpanah, H., & Sheikhahmadi, A. (2014). Content marketing through data mining on Facebook social network. *Webology, 11*(1), 1.

Harad, K. C. (2013). Content marketing strategies to educate and entertain. *Journal of Financial Planning, 26*(3), 18–20. Retrieved October 23, 2016, from EBSCO Online Database Business Source Ultimate. http://search.ebscohost.com/login.aspx?direct=true&db=bsu&AN=86444581&site=ehost-live

Harad, K. C. (2016). Don't avoid content marketing. *Journal of Financial Planning, 29*(7), 20–22. Retrieved October 23, 2016, from EBSCO Online Database Business Source Ultimate. http://search.ebscohost.com/login.aspx?direct=true&db=bsu&AN=116592969&site=ehost-live

Holliman, G., & Rowley, J. (2014). Business to business digital content marketing: marketers' perceptions of best practice. *Journal of Research in Interactive Marketing, 8*(4), 269.

Odden, L. (2013). Engaging more influencers and buyers with content marketing. *Public Relations Tactics, 20*(8), 18. Retrieved October 23, 2016, from EBSCO Online Database Business Source Ultimate. http://search.ebscohost.com/login.aspx?direct=true&db=bsu&AN=101658770&site=ehost-live

Patrutiu Baltes, L. (2015). Content marketing - the fundamental tool of digital marketing. *Bulletin of the Transilvania University of Brasov. Series V: Economic Sciences, 8*(2), 111–118. Retrieved October 23, 2016, from EBSCO Online Database Business Source Ultimate. http://search.ebscohost.com/login.aspx?direct=true&db=bsu&AN=112384428&site=ehost-live

Pažėraitė, A., & Repovienė, R. (2016). Content marketing elements and their influence on search advertisement effectiveness: Theoretical background and practical insights. *Management of Organizations: Systematic Research,* (75), 97–109. Retrieved October 23, 2016, from EBSCO Online Database Business Source Ultimate. http://search.ebscohost.com/login.aspx?direct=true&db=bsu&AN=117016412&site=ehost-live

Syzdek, N. C. (2014). Going native: Will content marketing work for you. *Public Relations Tactics, 21*(9), 14. Retrieved October 23, 2016, from EBSCO Online Database Business Source Ultimate. http://search.ebscohost.com/login.aspx?direct=true&db=bsu&AN=101636346&site=ehost-live

Wylie, A. (2014). The awwwww factor: How content marketing messages go viral. *Public Relations Tactics, 21*(4), 7. Retrieved October 23, 2016, from EBSCO Online Database Business Source Ultimate. http://search.ebscohost.com/login.aspx?direct=true&db=bsu&AN=95465050&site=ehost-live

SUGGESTED READING
Anatheunis, et al. (2016). Content marketing on social network sites. A study on brand-related social media behavior and its motives. *Tijdschrift voor Communicatiewetenschap,* 44-4. Retrieved on June 29, 2017.

Iglesias, O., Ind, N., & Alfaro, M. (2013). The organic view of the brand: A brand value co-creation model. *Journal of Brand Management, 20*(8), 670.

Kuenn, A. (2016). Successful content marketing in 8 steps. *Brand Quarterly,* (24), 16–20. Retrieved October 23, 2016, from EBSCO Online Database Business Source Ultimate. http://search.ebscohost.com/login.aspx?direct=true&db=bsu&AN=119802503&site=ehost-live

Metcalf, L. E., Neill, S., R. Simon, L., Dobson, S., & Davis, B. (2016). The impact of peer mentoring on marketing content mastery. *Marketing Education Review, 26*(3), 126–142. Retrieved October 23, 2016, from EBSCO Online Database Business Source Ultimate. http://search.ebscohost.com/login.aspx?direct=true&db=bsu&AN=117575084&site=ehost-live

Murthy, A. (2011). Content Marketing. *PRIMA: Practices & Research In Marketing, 2*(1), 31.

Rowley, J. (2008). Understanding digital content marketing. *Journal Of Marketing Management, 24*(5–6), 517–540.

Santos, M. (2016). Learning about content marketing. *Sign Builder Illustrated, 30*(254), 16–20. Retrieved October 23, 2016, from EBSCO Online Database Business Source Ultimate. http://search.ebscohost.com/login.aspx?direct=true&db=bsu&AN=117049015&site=ehost-live

Scott Zimmer, J.D.

COPYRIGHTS

ABSTRACT

This article examines copyright laws and the process of protecting works by registering copyrights. The history of copyrights is reviewed along with the types of works that can be copyrighted. International trends and activities in copyright law and copyright protection are explained. The concept and process of fair use of copyrighted materials is examined along with some of the problems that creators have encountered when using the copyrighted material of others to create a parody. Issues in combating piracy and copyright infringement are reviewed along with some of the social issues surrounding various antipiracy efforts.

OVERVIEW

A copyright gives the owner of a created work the right to use, sell, or license the creation and prohibits others from doing so without appropriate approval from the copyright owner. A copyright extends protection for the work as long as the author is alive and 70 years after the author's death. This duration enables the author's estate to collect royalties from the work (U.S. Copyright Office, 2008). Central to the concept of copyright are economic rights that are recognized by copyright laws around the world and generally apply to any commercial activity including physical reproduction of books, public performances, and electronic distribution (UNESCO, 2009).

The U.S. Copyright Office

The U.S. Copyright Office has several strategic goals and responsibilities:.

- First, the office works to support Congress, the executive branch, and the courts on issues related to copyright policy and regulations.
- Second, the office serves the public with registration services and information on copyright processes and issues.
- Third, the office is responsible for acquiring copyrighted works to be deposited in the Library of Congress. Since 1870, copyright deposits have formed the bulk of the library's best-in-class collections of books, sound recordings, photographs, motion pictures, and other creative works.
- Finally, the office strives to be a leader in educating the public about copyright issues such as piracy and the affect of emerging technologies on copyrights (U.S. Copyright Office, 2008).

In 2007, the U.S. Copyright Office registered more than 500,000 claims to copyright. More than one million items were transferred to the Library of Congress and were valued at more than $45 million, half of which were obtained through the mandatory deposit requirements set in copyright law. The office collected licensing royalties of $234 million and distributed $280 million in royalties. In addition, the office responded to more than 300,000 inquires for information (U.S. Copyright Office, 2007).

U.S. Copyright Law

The Copyright Act of 1976 is the basis of copyright law. In the United States, the federal Copyright Office manages the process of registering copyrights. Once a work is filed with the Copyright Office, a public record of the copyright claim is established (U.S. Copyright Office, 2008) According to the Copyright Office, "Copyright protection is available for original works or authorship in a tangible medium. Works of authorship include: Literary works; musical works, including any accompanying words; dramatic works, including any accompanying music; pantomimes and choreographic works; pictorial, graphic, and sculptural works; motion pictures and other audiovisual works; sound recordings; and architectural works" (U.S. Copyright Office, 2007). Copyright protection is also available for computer chip designs and vessel hull designs. In addition, computer programs or software packages sold for commercial or private use can also be copyrighted (U.S. Copyright Office, 2008).

International Copyright Law

International action on the protection of copyrights dates back to the Berne Convention for the Protection of Literary and Artistic Works held in 1896. The convention has been revised and updated several times since it was first developed. International activity and cooperation on copyright administration and protection accelerated after World War II. With the support of the United Nations Educational, Scientific, and Cultural Organization (UNESCO), the Universal Copyright Convention was adopted in 1952 (UNESCO, 2009).

The World Intellectual Property Organization (WIPO) continues to work on copyright issues with countries around the world. The WIPO Standing Committee on Copyright and Related Rights (SCCR) meets frequently to discuss ongoing as well as emerging issues, including the protection of broadcasting organizations and the protection of audiovisual performances. Work is also continuing on the WIPO Copyright Treaty, and discussions have focused on software, databases, and Internet distribution and content (WIPO, 2009).

Similar to the patent process, the copyright process is becoming more harmonized around the world. Most countries have an established copyright office and a registration process. The procedures for managing copyrights at the national level, as with managing patent applications and grants, are evolving consistently toward the recommendations and standards of WIPO. However, not all countries are in step with international efforts to protect copyrights, especially those copyrights that are registered in other countries (Crockford, 2008).

Under U.S. law, copyright protection is automatic when an original work is created and is put into a tangible form. The work does not need to be published or registered with the Copyright Office (Dames,

2009). However, many people feel that it is prudent to register their creation with the Copyright Office, and national offices are in virtually every country in the world where they can accomplish this.

The Copyright Process
The process of registering a copyright is not overly complicated and can be done online or by competing paper forms and filing them with the Copyright Office. The electronic process and the paper process are not substantially different but the electronic process is not equipped to handle all items that can be copyrighted at this time. Each method requires three basic steps: completing a form, paying a fee, and submitting a copy of the work (U.S. Copyright Office, 2009).

Fees for registering a copyright vary, and other fees are applicable for a variety of services provided by the Copyright Office. These services include searches, copying, and bulk registration (U.S. Copyright Office, 2009).

Economic Implications of Copyright Law
The economic importance of copyrights cannot be overstated. The International Intellectual Property Alliance (IIPA), a coalition of seven trade associations with members that produce and distribute copyrighted materials, contends that in 2010, the value added to the U.S. Gross Domestic Product (GDP) by copyrighted materials was $1.627 trillion. This is equivalent to about 11.1 percent of the 2010 GDP (IIPA, 2011).

IIPA members are very serious about protecting their industry and the economic benefit of their members as derived from copyrights. The members of the IIPA are the Association of American Publishers (AAP), the Business Software Alliance (BSA), the Entertainment Software Association (ESA), the Independent Film & Television Alliance (IFTA), the Motion Picture Association of America (MPAA), the National Music Publishers' Association (NMPA), and the Recording Industry Association of America (RIAA) (Siwek, 2011).

An Ever-Evolving Prospect
Copyright laws will continue to evolve. More countries will adopt mainstream copyright practices and copyright protection. New technologies will continue

to change how the distribution of copyrighted material is managed and licensed (Kaushik & Prakash, 2009) (Quint, 2009). As distribution systems such as cable and satellite television add more features and services, lawmakers will be faced with more copyright protection issues as well as more regulatory challenges ("Cable, satellite," 2009).

APPLICATIONS

Balancing Owner Rights & Creativity through Fair Use
There has been ongoing debate, as well as numerous court cases, regarding the concept and practice of the fair use of copyrighted material. The purpose of the fair use process is to allow creativity, scholarship, and research to continue and promote the creation of knowledge and the perpetuation of culture (Kirsch & Klett, 2009). As new technologies emerge and consumer demand for content continues to grow, the boundaries of fair use have often become blurred and violated.

The goal of copyright protection is to provide the owner "the right to reproduce or to authorize others to reproduce their work" and to receive economic gain for doing so (UNESCO, 2009). The primary limitations to these rights are established in sections 107 through 118 of the Copyright Act (title 17, U.S. Code) and are centered in the doctrine of "fair use." Section 107 provides "a list of the various purposes for which the reproduction of a particular work may be considered fair, such as criticism, comment, news reporting, teaching, scholarship, and research" (U.S. Copyright Office, 2006) (Mattingly & Samardzija, 2009).

Section 107 also provides four factors that need to be considered in determining whether or not a specific use is fair:
1) The purpose and character of the use, including whether such use is of commercial nature or is for nonprofit educational purposes
2) The nature of the copyrighted work
3) The amount and substantiality of the portion used in relation to the copyrighted work as a whole
4) The effect of the use upon the potential market for or value of the copyrighted work (U.S. Copyright Office, 2006)

Determining Copyright Infringement

The determination as to whether use is a copyright infringement or use is fair is not easily defined. There is a lack of structure and formula in making the determination. For example, there is not a specific number of words, lines, or notes that automatically constitute fair use. In addition, citing the source does not also automatically constitute fair use (U.S.Copyright Office, 2006).

The courts have agreed that a use is fair in many generic circumstances including excerpts in a review or criticism and brief quotations in a news report. Other court rulings have included reproduction by a library of a portion of a work to replace part of a damaged copy and reproduction by a teacher of a small part of a work for use in a lesson or to illustrate a lesson. Not surprisingly, fair use has also been expanded to include reproduction of a work in legislative or judicial proceedings or reports (U.S. Copyright Office, 2006).

On November 14, 2013, a federal judge ruled that Google did not violate copyright with its massive book-scanning project, arguing that the project was fair use under copyright law and provided significant public benefits (*The Authors Guild, Inc. v. Google, Inc.,* 2013).

Parodies & Copyright Infringement

Over time, the use of copyrighted material in a parody has also been covered under the concept of fair use (U.S. Copyright Office, 2006). The creation of parodies has also been considered free speech and is protected by the First Amendment (Celedonia and Doyle, 2007). However, because the goal of a parody is basically to make fun of a person, a product, an idea, or a belief, it is not likely that a copyright owner would grant a parody creator permission to use the work. Thus, any parody creator that uses the original work of another person or company will assume some risk of being accused of infringement (Johnson & Spilger, 2000).

The parody creator faces many challenges in avoiding or maintaining innocence in an infringement lawsuit. First, the court must determine that a work is indeed a parody. Second, the parody creator must be able to demonstrate that the use of the material falls within the guidelines and is consistent with previous court rulings as to what is fair use (Johnson & Spilger, 2000). It is important that the parody

creator note that courts have anguished over the fair use defense when dealing with works of parody, and just because the creator thinks something is a parody does not dissolve possible litigation and rather costly legal fees (Eisenstein, 2000).

Case Study: Al Franken's *Lies and the Lying Liars Who Tell Them*

One of the many parodies to draw backlash in the 2000s was Al Franken's book *Lies and the Lying Liars Who Tell Them: A Fair and Balanced Look at the Right* (a parody of Fox News). Fox did not appreciate the title and chose to file a lawsuit for trademark infringement (similar to copyright infringement). The suit claimed that the publisher, Penguin, did not have the right to use the term "Fair and Balanced." The suit also stated that the design of the cover of the book, which included a picture of Fox commentator Bill O'Reilly and mimicked the look and style O'Reilly's books, was an infringement. Part of what may have fueled the fire in this case was that Franken and O'Reilly had a confrontation at the 2003 BookExpo America, where they broke into a shouting match during a panel discussion. The animosity was played out in the court filings, which reportedly include repeated personal attacks on Franken (Holt, 2003). Ultimately, the court threw out the suit, stating it was without merit. Book sales soared, and Fox did not appeal the ruling.

Case Study: Alice Randall's *The Wind Done Gone*

Another high-profile parody suit involved Alice Randall, who in 2001 was about to have her first novel, *The Wind Done Gone*, published by Houghton Mifflin. The book was a parody of *Gone With The Wind*, an American icon of literature authored by Margaret Mitchell. Randall's version blatantly expounded upon the racism of the old South. U.S. District Judge Charles A. Pannell decided that Randall's version was unabated piracy. Randall and Houghton Mifflin then planned to appeal (Kniffel, 2001).

The American Library Association's Freedom to Read Foundation, the American Booksellers Foundation for Free Expression, and the PEN American Center, among others, defended the right of the author and the publisher. The debate and the attention it caused reached a fever pitch. Advance galleys of *The Wind Done Gone* were in distribution during the trial. Four of those copies showed up in eBay auctions. Bidding reached $485 for one copy when eBay removed all of them, supposedly at the request of lawyers from the Margaret Mitchell Trust (G.M.E., 2001).

In 2002, Houghton Mifflin and the estate of Mitchell publicly announced that they had reached a settlement in the infringement case. Some interpretations of the settlement's language suggest that Randall would face even more litigation should she try to sell movie rights or create new adaptations (Reid, 2002). The Wind Done Gone was published and lives on. It was another test, and a rather emotional and complex one, of the fair use concept (Grossett, 2002).

ISSUE
Combating Piracy of Copyrighted Materials

Piracy, or illegal copying, distribution, and sales of copyrighted works including books, music, software, and videos has become an international business (Einhorn, 2000). In the United States, federal law protects against the unauthorized use of copyrighted works. In addition, many copyrighted works feature embedded technology designed to hinder copying. Federal law also prohibits willfully creating or selling technology to circumvent such protections (U.S. Department of Justice, 2006).

Under these laws, copyright infringement for profit is a felony that is punishable by a maximum penalty of five years in prison and a $250,000 fine or twice the gain/loss for an individual first-time offender and double that for a second offense. Large-scale copyright infringement even without a profit motive is a felony punishable by a maximum penalty of three years in prison and a $250,000 fine or twice the gain/loss for an individual first-time offender and double that for a second offense. Developing technology to circumvent antipiracy protections is also a felony punishable by a maximum penalty of five years in prison and a $500,000 fine or twice the gain/loss for an individual first-time offender and double that for a second offense (U.S. Department of Justice, 2006).

The U.S. Federal Bureau of Investigation (FBI) actively pursues investigations and indictments of copyright infringement crimes. It handles more than 300 cases per year and participates in more than 100 indictments per year. Many of these cases have been international in scope and have resulted in thousands of arrests and the seizure of hundreds of millions of dollars in pirated works. The FBI has also developed a label that producers of copyrighted works can place on their products:

"Warning: The unauthorized reproduction or distribution of this copyrighted work is illegal. Criminal copyright infringement, including infringement without monetary gain, is investigated by the FBI and is punishable by up to five years in federal prison and a fine of $250,000" (FBI, 2009).

File Sharing

The big cases with hundreds of arrests are impressive. But other situations have brought criticism to law enforcement and industry groups that are attempting to stop piracy. In the United States and many countries around the world, peer-to-peer sharing or exchanging of files has become almost ubiquitous. Due to the ubiquity of this activity in the United States, many feel that the lines which separate general law-abiding citizens from criminals are blurred (Adamsick, 2008).

Efforts to stop file sharing have been compared to the past efforts to stop the distribution of alcohol during U.S. prohibition in the 1920s. The Recording Industry Association of America (RIAA) has sued thousands of individuals alleging millions of dollars in damages. Schools across the nation are implementing strict policies to stop file sharing and halt an activity that the U.S. Supreme Court declared presumptively illegal in 2005 (Schlesinger & Lessig, 2008).

University students are said to illegally download well over one billion music files every year. The RIAA and others are putting the pressure on universities to stop the illegal downloading. Universities are responding by installing filtering appliances to prevent downloads or are offering a free service with a wide range of music choices (Pike, 2008).

In 2006, the RIAA informed university officials that it was initiating a process to bring lawsuits against students for the illegal downloading of music. In this effort, the RIAA had identified students they considered violators and were sent letters offering out-of-court settlements. The RIAA accepted credit cards for the fines (Read, 2007).

User-Generated Content

Internet users, mostly younger users, are creating user-generated content at an astonishing rate. Much of this content now consists of videos and sometimes results in lawsuits (Beckerman, 2009). YouTube and Viacom had a legal battle because YouTube videos were found to include a mix of copyrighted video material with some of their original creations. This battle has cost a considerable amount for both sides. YouTube has agreed to put in place video content filters to protect copyrighted video; however, the ability of it to stop YouTube users or to satisfy Viacom is not guaranteed (Meisel, 2009).

The list of copyright crimes and criminals continues to grow. As long as new technology continues to emerge, Internet users will increase their consumption of content, copyright protected or not.

CONCLUSION

The copyright process and copyright law have evolved over the last two centuries. New technologies including electronic mediums and the Internet have presented challenges for policy makers, creators, and sellers of copyrighted works. It is likely that technologies will continue to expand the options for distribution of works and that copyright law will continue to evolve along with the new technologies.

Some aspects of copyright law are ambiguous, especially the concept and process of fair use. The courts continue to grapple with fair use as creators push the envelop on how they use works created by others while copyright owners, for a variety of reasons, attempt to minimize the value of their work being diluted.

In the case of *Lies and the Lying Liars Who Tell Them* by Al Franken and *The Wind Done Gone* by Alice Randall, it may have been far more than just the protection of a copyright that motivated the owners to pursue litigation. The political and social motivations of those lawsuits may have well outweighed the economic gain that the copyright owners could have reaped.

Protecting copyrights or stopping the piracy of works has become a major challenge in the global, technically advanced marketplace. Massive international efforts are making some progress in the fight against piracy. On the other hand, the pursuit of litigation against consumers who copy small quantities of copyrighted work has created considerable social

backlash and may also be creating an entirely new generation of criminals.

BIBLIOGRAPHY

Adamsick, C. (2008). "Warez" the copyright violation? Digital copyright infringement: Legal loopholes and decentralization. *TechTrends: Linking Research & Practice to Improve Learning, 52*, 10-12. Retrieved April 12, 2009, from EBSCO Online Database Academic Search Complete http://search.ebscohost.com/login.aspx?direct=true&db=a9h&AN=35622988&site=ehost-live

Beckerman, R. (2009). Content holders vs. the web: 2008 U.S. copyright law victories point to robust internet. *Journal of Internet Law, 12*, 16-21. Retrieved April 12, 2009, from EBSCO Online Database Business Source Complete. http://search.ebscohost.com/login.aspx?direct=true&db=bth&AN=36066990&site=ehost-live

Cable, satellite tv executives battle in Congress over copyright laws. (2009). *Satellite News, 32*, 1. Retrieved April 12, 2009, from EBSCO Online Database Business Source Complete. http://search.ebscohost.com/login.aspx?direct=true&db=bth&AN=36845199&site=ehost-live

Celedonia, B., & Doyle, K. (2007). Trademark parody, statutory and nominative fair use under the Lanham Act. *Computer & Internet Lawyer, 24*, 11-27. Retrieved April 14, 2009, from EBSCO Online Database Business Source Complete. http://search.ebscohost.com/login.aspx?direct=true&db=bth&AN=26633515&site=ehost-live The Authors Guild, Inc., et al. vs. Google, Inc. (2013). United States District Court, Southern District of New York. http://www.documentcloud.org/documents/834877-google-books-ruling-on-fair-use.html

Crockford, P. (2008). EU copyright developments and enforcement in European Countries. *IP Litigator, 14*, 9-15. Retrieved April 13, 2009, from EBSCO Online Database Academic Search Complete. http://search.ebscohost.com/login.aspx?direct=true&db=a9h&AN=34617841&site=ehost-live

Dames, K. (2009). Information business meets copyright policy. *Information Today, 26*, 16-17. Retrieved April 12, 2009, from EBSCO Online Database Academic Search Complete. http://search.ebscohost.com/login.aspx?direct=true&db=a9h&AN=37191477&site=ehost-live

Einhorn, B. (2009, March 2). Microsoft has hope in Asian piracy fight. *Business Week Online*, 23. Retrieved April 12, 2009, from EBSCO Online Database Academic Search Complete. http://search.ebscohost.com/login.aspx?direct=true&db=a9h&AN=36822257&site=ehost-live

Eisenstein, M. (2000). An economic analysis of the fair use defense in Leibovitz V. Paramount Pictures Corporation. *University of Pennsylvania Law Review, 148*, 889. Retrieved April 14, 2009, from EBSCO Online Database Academic Search Complete. http://search.ebscohost.com/login.aspx?direct=true&db=a9h&AN=2937890&site=ehost-live

Fakler, P. (2013). Music copyright royalty rate-setting litigation: Practice before the copyright royalty board and how it differs from ASCAP and BMI rate court litigation. *Licensing Journal, 33*, 9-16. Retrieved November 15, 2013, from EBSCO Online Database Business Source Complete. http://search.ebscohost.com/login.aspx?direct=true&db=bth&AN=89389487&site=ehost-live

G.M.E., G. (2001). Wind Done Gone Called 'unabated piracy'. *American Libraries, 32*, 30. Retrieved April 14, 2009, from EBSCO Online Database Academic Search Complete. http://search.ebscohost.com/login.aspx?direct=true&db=a9h&AN=4525666&site=ehost-live

Grossett, J. (2002). The Wind Done Gone: Transforming Tara into a plantation parody. *Case Western Reserve Law Review, 52*, 1113. Retrieved April 14, 2009, from EBSCO Online Database Academic Search Complete. http://search.ebscohost.com/login.aspx?direct=true&db=a9h&AN=6870900&site=ehost-live

Holt, K. (2003). Franken gets a big, fat publicity boost. *Publishers Weekly, 250*, 16-16. Retrieved April 14, 2009, from EBSCO Online Database Academic Search Complete. http://search.ebscohost.com/login.aspx?direct=true&db=a9h&AN=10615867&site=ehost-live

Holt, K. (2003). With court victory, Penguin ups Franken run. *Publishers Weekly, 250*, 12-12. Retrieved April 14, 2009, from EBSCO Online Database Academic Search Complete. http://search.ebscohost.com/login.aspx?direct=true&db=a9h&AN=10708648&site=ehost-live

Hugenholtz, P. (2013). Fair use in Europe. *Communications Of The ACM, 56*, 26-28. Retrieved November 15, 2013, from EBSCO Online Database Business Source Complete. http://search.ebscohost.com/login.aspx?direct=true&db=bth&AN=87500045&site=ehost-live

Johnson, M., & Spilger, U. (2000). Legal considerations when using parodies in advertising. *Journal of Advertising, 29*, 77-86. Retrieved April 14, 2009, from EBSCO Online Database Business Source Complete. http://search.ebscohost.com/login.aspx?direct=true&db=bth&AN=4224209&site=ehost-live

Kaushik, A., & Prakash, N. (2009). Google library project: Following the copyright debate. *ICFAI Journal of Intellectual Property Rights, 8*, 74-80. Retrieved April 12, 2009, from EBSCO Online Database Academic Search Complete. http://search.ebscohost.com/login.aspx?direct=true&db=a9h&AN=36350168&site=ehost-live

Kirsch, E., & Klett, A. (2009). US and European courts split over fair use. *Managing Intellectual Property, 3*. Retrieved April 12, 2009, from EBSCO Online Database Academic Search Complete. http://search.ebscohost.com/login.aspx?direct=true&db=a9h&AN=36824874&site=ehost-live

Kniffel, L. (2001). The perils of birthin' a parody. *American Libraries, 32*, 50. Retrieved April 14, 2009, from EBSCO Online Database Academic Search Complete. http://search.ebscohost.com/login.aspx?direct=true&db=a9h&AN=4525696&site=ehost-live

Meisel, J. (2009). Economic and legal issues facing You Tube and similar internet hosting web sites. *Journal of Internet Law, 12*, 1-16. Retrieved April 12, 2009, from EBSCO Online Database Business Source Complete. http://search.ebscohost.com/login.aspx?direct=true&db=bth&AN=36511957&site=ehost-live

Nichols, J. (2009). The big lie on Franken. *Nation, 288*, 6-7. Retrieved April 14, 2009, from EBSCO Online Database Academic Search Complete. http://search.ebscohost.com/login.aspx?direct=true&db=a9h&AN=35973368&site=ehost-live

Quint, B. (2009). Books, books, books: Going, going, Google. *Information Today, 26*, 7-8. Retrieved April 12, 2009, from EBSCO Online Database Academic Search Complete. http://search.ebscohost.com/login.aspx?direct=true&db=a9h&AN=36344103&site=ehost-live

Read, B. (2007). Recording industry will sue students but let them settle. *Chronicle of Higher Education, 53*, A1-A40. Retrieved April 12, 2009, from EBSCO

Online Database Academic Search Complete. http://search.ebscohost.com/login.aspx?direct=true&db=a9h&AN=24514203&site=ehost-live

Reid, C. (2002). Suit done gone, for now. *Publishers Weekly, 249*, 17. Retrieved April 14, 2009, from EBSCO Online Database Academic Search Complete. http://search.ebscohost.com/login.aspx?direct=true&db=a9h&AN=6693490&site=ehost-live

Samuelson, P. (2013). The quest for a sound conception of copyright's derivative work right. *Georgetown Law Journal, 101*, 1505-1564. Retrieved November 15, 2013, from EBSCO Online Database Business Source Complete. http://search.ebscohost.com/login.aspx?direct=true&db=bth&AN=90613565&site=ehost-live

Schlesinger, R., & Lessig, L. (2008). Don't make kids online crooks. *U.S. News & World Report, 145*, 15. Retrieved April 12, 2009, from EBSCO Online Database Academic Search Complete. http://search.ebscohost.com/login.aspx?direct=true&db=a9h&AN=35864181&site=ehost-live

Siwek, S. (2011) Copyright industries in the U.S. economy: The 2011 report. Retrieved November 14, from the International Intellectual Property Alliance. http://www.iipa.com/pdf/2011copyrightindustriesreport.PDF

The United Nations Educational, Scientific, and Cultural Organization (UNESCO). Basic notions about copyright and neighboring rights. (2009). Retrieved April 13, 2009, from http://portal.unesco.org/culture/en/files/30671/11443368003faq%5fen.pdf/faq_en.pdf

United States Copyright Office. (2006). *Copyright fair use.* Retrieved April 12, 2009, from The Register of Copyrights. http://www.copyright.gov/fls/fl102.html

United States Copyright Office. (2007). *Annual report of the Register of Copyrights fiscal year ending September 30, 2007.* Retrieved April 13, 2009, from The Register of Copyrights http://www.copyright.gov/reports/annual/2007/ar2007.pdf

United States Copyright Office. (2007). *Circular 92 Copyright Law of the United States and Related Laws Contained in Title 17 of the United States Code.* Retrieved April 12, 2009, from The Register of Copyrights. http://www.copyright.gov/title17/circ92.pdf

United States Copyright Office. (2008). *Circular 1 copyright basics.* Retrieved April 12, 2009, from The Register of Copyrights. http://www.copyright.gov/circs/circ1.pdf

United States Copyright Office. (2008). *Strategic plan 2008-2013.* Retrieved April 13, 2009, from the United States Copyright Office. http://www.copyright.gov/reports/s-plan2008/s-plan2008-2013-i.pdf

United States Copyright Office. (2009). *Current fees.* Retrieved April 12, 2009, from http://www.copyright.gov/docs/fees.html

United States Copyright Office. (2009). How to register a copyright. Retrieved April 12, 2009, from The Register of Copyrights. http://www.copyright.gov/register/index.html

United States Department of Justice. (2006). *Progress report of the department of justice's task force on intellectual property.* Retrieved April 14, 2009, from Computer Crime & Intellectual Property Section United States Department of Justice. http://www.cybercrime.gov/2006IPTFProgressReport(6-19-06).pdf

United States Federal Bureau of Investigation (FBI). (2009). Investigative programs, cyber investigations. Retrieved April 14, 2009, from United State Federal Bureau of Investigation (FBI). http://www.fbi.gov/ipr/

World Intellectual Property Organization (WIPO). (2009). Copyright and related rights. Retrieved April 12, 2009, from http://www.wipo.int/copyright/en/

Suggested Reading

Copyright and fair use. (2008). *ASHE Higher Education Report, 34*, 31-52. Retrieved April 12, 2009, from EBSCO Online Database Academic Search Complete. http://search.ebscohost.com/login.aspx?direct=true&db=a9h&AN=36317447&site=ehost-live

Crawford, J., & Strasser, R. (2008). Management of infringement risk of intellectual property assets. *Intellectual Property & Technology Law Journal, 20*, 7-10. Retrieved April 12, 2009, from EBSCO Online Database Business Source Complete. http://search.ebscohost.com/login.aspx?direct=true&db=bth&AN=35423366&site=ehost-live

Duffin, F., & Watson, B. (2009). Best practices in protecting and enforcing trademarks, copyrights, and other intellectual property rights. *Franchise Law Journal, 28*, 132-180. Retrieved April 12, 2009, from EBSCO Online Database Academic Search Complete. http://search.ebscohost.com/login.aspx?direct=true&db=a9h&AN=36985964&site=ehost-live

Guernsey, L. (2008). New machines reproduce custom books on demand. *Chronicle of Higher Education, 55*, A1-A13. Retrieved April 12, 2009, from EBSCO Online Database Academic Search Complete. http://search.ebscohost.com/login.aspx?direct=true&db=a9h&AN=35633798&site=ehost-live

Mattingly, T., & Samardzija, M. (2009). Minimizing liability for copyright infringement. *Intellectual Property & Technology Law Journal, 21*, 16-20. Retrieved April 12, 2009, from EBSCO Online Database Business Source Complete. http://search.ebscohost.com/login.aspx?direct=true&db=bth&AN=35876120&site=ehost-live

Morgan, M., & Cohn-Sfetcu, S. (2008). Automated software systems for intellectual property compliance. *Intellectual Property & Technology Law Journal, 20*, 14-24. Retrieved April 12, 2009, from EBSCO Online Database Business Source Complete. http://search.ebscohost.com/login.aspx?direct=true&db=bth&AN=35423368&site=ehost-live

Newman, J. M. (2013). Copyright freeconomics. *Vanderbilt Law Review, 66*, 1409-1469. Retrieved November 14, 2013, from EBSCO Online Database Business Source Complete. http://search.ebscohost.com/login.aspx?direct=true&db=bth&AN=91711701&site=ehost-live

Ong, R. (2009). Tackling intellectual property infringement in China. *China Business Review, 36*, 17-21. Retrieved April 12, 2009, from EBSCO Online Database Business Source Complete. http://search.ebscohost.com/login.aspx?direct=true&db=bth&AN=36834857&site=ehost-live

Ouellet, J. (2007). The purchase versus illegal download of music by consumers: The influence of consumer response towards the artist and music. *Canadian Journal of Administrative Sciences, 24*, 107-119. Retrieved April 12, 2009, from EBSCO Online Database Business Source Complete. http://search.ebscohost.com/login.aspx?direct=true&db=bth&AN=26363444&site=ehost-live

Pasquale, R. (2009). The great copyright debate. *Managing Intellectual Property, 1*. Retrieved April 12, 2009, from EBSCO Online Database Academic Search Complete. http://search.ebscohost.com/login.aspx?direct=true&db=a9h&AN=37374320&site=ehost-live

Pike, G. (2008). The financial aid 'stick' against illegal downloading. *Information Today, 25*, 17-20. Retrieved April 12, 2009, from EBSCO Online Database Academic Search Complete. http://search.ebscohost.com/login.aspx?direct=true&db=a9h&AN=34584101&site=ehost-live

Ross, P. (2008, December 29). Copyright laws are working. *U.S. News & World Report, 14*. Retrieved April 12, 2009, from EBSCO Online Database Academic Search Complete. http://search.ebscohost.com/login.aspx?direct=true&db=a9h&AN=35864179&site=ehost-live

Rothstein, J. (2009). Unilateral settlements and retroactive transfers: A problem of copyright co-ownership. *University of Pennsylvania Law Review, 157*, 881-921. Retrieved April 12, 2009, from EBSCO Online Database Academic Search Complete. http://search.ebscohost.com/login.aspx?direct=true&db=a9h&AN=37275911&site=ehost-live

Rott, P. (2008). Download of copyright-protected internet content and the role of (consumer) contract law. *Journal of Consumer Policy, 31*, 441-457. Retrieved April 12, 2009, from EBSCO Online Database Business Source Complete. http://search.ebscohost.com/login.aspx?direct=true&db=bth&AN=36165034&site=ehost-live

Shared and related concerns about intellectual property. (2008). *ASHE Higher Education Report, 34*, 93-113. Retrieved April 12, 2009, from EBSCO Online Database Academic Search Complete. http://search.ebscohost.com/login.aspx?direct=true&db=a9h&AN=36317450&site=ehost-live

The Law of Copyrights. (2008, November). *ASHE Higher Education Report, 34*, 13-30. Retrieved April 12, 2009, from EBSCO Online Database Academic Search Complete. http://search.ebscohost.com/login.aspx?direct=true&db=a9h&AN=36317446&site=ehost-live

The parody defense to copyright infringement: Productive fair use after Betamax. (1984). *Harvard Law Review, 97*, 1395-1414. Retrieved April 14, 2009, from EBSCO Online Database Academic Search Complete. http://search.ebscohost.com/login.aspx?direct=true&db=a9h&AN=7732261&site=ehost-live

Michael Erbschloe

CREATING, MANAGING AND PRESENTING THE ARTS

ABSTRACT

This article will explore how creative arts organizations can effectively manage their businesses, especially in the nonprofit sector. There will be an examination of how marketing, management, labor relations, and funding factors influence the operation of these organizations. In addition, the issue of risk management for the creative arts will be discussed as well as the complexities in arts funding that have placed increasing demands upon arts managers. To help tackle such risks and complexities and ensure a viable future for the arts, many institutions have created graduate arts management programs.

OVERVIEW

Art is a tricky commodity to promote. Although art plays a significant role in educating society on cultural issues, it is not a product that generates large amounts of revenue. "The production of art [became] an international multi-billion dollar industry during the twentieth century" (Kjorkegren, 1993, p. 1). Nonetheless, according to Kjorkegren (1993), most organizations do not make money from the arts, most art initiatives fail, and few yield a profit.

Given the dynamics, many view the art industry as unpredictable. It is difficult to determine which products will be successful because it is not easy to predict the market response. Demographics are other factors that should be considered in marketing campaigns for art. Times are changing and arts managers must make sure that they create programs that appeal to a diverse population. Research has shown that families and senior citizens dominate the population, and new ethnic groups (e.g. Latinos, Asians, and Indians) have emerged (Holtzman, 2000). These variables, along with the fact that Americans are better educated than before, create a need for a different type of event programming. "The market response to art products is also influenced by the act of consumption, since art-producing organizations sell potential meanings rather than finished products" (Kjorkegren, 1993, p. 3). The success of art is determined by how well it is accepted by the target markets. If the product develops into a popular brand, the chances of its success increase as it establishes itself in the minds of potential consumers.

Funding is another concern for arts managers. Over the years, there has been a decline in contributions to the arts. Many organizations have seen a decline in National Endowment for the Arts (NEA) grants as well as a reduction in corporate funding of the arts. Since funding is not coming from the traditional sources, "art organizations will need to increase earned income from audiences and visitors" (Holtzman, 2000, p. 32). New strategies will need to be developed in order to address the changes that are occurring in the arts industry.

Strategies

In order to meet the challenge of managing the unpredictability of the market, Bourdieu (1977) suggests two different business strategies: cultural and commercial. A cultural business strategy is a long-term approach and is driven on the artist's terms. Organizations that prescribe to this type of strategy tend to spend more time and money on developing artists and hoping that their efforts will help the artists become successful. On the other hand, if an organization elects to pursue a commercial strategy, the art product is driven based on the market's terms. This strategy promotes controlling the supply, limiting the amount of the product that is given to the market, and obtaining a rapid return on investment by implementing a strong marketing initiative. Organizations have to decide which approach has the best fit with their mission and vision.

Management

There has been much change in the way organizations conduct their business. "As the non-profit community progresses from founder-dominated to professionally managed institutions, there has been increased emphasis placed on utilizing strategic planning" (Holtzman, 2000, p. 32). Many have concluded that they will need to make changes to their operational practices in order to survive. The first area that an organization should tackle is the management team and structure. Every organization needs a visionary who embraces the need to change at different phases in the life of a company. The leader is the person who has to persuade employees, the board, and other stakeholders of the need to change. It's important that all these groups support the change initiative and work together to improve the organization. One way to ensure success is to develop a viable strategic plan. Holtzman (2000) made some recommendations on how to get off to a good start, and these steps include:

Before a retreat, perform a situational analysis that defines the issues. This step should include developing an understanding of the needs, desires, and innovations of the constituents as well as an understanding of the competition. Many nonprofit organizations tend to overlook analyzing the competition, but it is important to know what the competition is doing and what your organization is good at doing (e.g. niche or unique selling points).

Build your team. Select the best people in the organization to be part of the initial exploration team. These individuals should be open to change management. Once the exploration team has been established, there should be a campaign to include others to participate in the process. Each organization wants to make sure that it avoids group think. The team should not become an "inbred" group, and there has to be members who will not always go along with the popular point of view. Diversity in the skills and opinions of the team members is essential.

Determine the obstacles to change within the organization. It is important to determine where the team expects resistance to come from. There may be people and processes in the current structure that will not support a change initiative. The team must develop strategies to deal with these obstacles.

Determine an action plan that contains deadlines and responsibilities. Although the planning process is important, the team needs to make sure it can show progress. There has to be a beginning and an end. In order to get from one point to the other, the team will need to establish an agreement that is supported by all members. The agreement should list the roles, responsibilities and deadline dates for all the tasks required to implement the plan.

Gain the support of the board and other stakeholders. Everyone has to be on the same page and support the initiative. It is important to get buy-in from all stakeholders. Otherwise, the project may fail before it starts.

Review action plan progress monthly. In order to build momentum, it is important to provide feedback at different intervals of the project. Members will need to know if they should continue as planned or tweak different parts of the plan.

Role of Unions

It has been established that most art products do not produce a profit. One reason is that many nonprofit organizations have a hard time balancing their art and business (Richardson, 2006). This creates a problem for those who are employed in these organizations. Most employees who work in the performing arts industry tend to belong to a union. Unions are responsible for representing these employees and looking out for their best interests. Unions make sure their constituents receive a decent salary on the designated pay dates. As with any organization, payroll is usually the largest item in the budget. If the budget falls short, there may not be sufficient funds to make payroll.

Given the nature of the business, "unions have penetrated more deeply into the management of artistic enterprises than is typically the case for unions in manufacturing and other profit-making sectors, and they are responsible for determining the availability, quality and charter of artistic performances" (Kleingartner & Lloyd, 1972, p. 128). In summary, unions have a lot of power in the art world. They not only have a strong voice in setting wages, they also have some control over the quality of performances since they are responsible for getting the right performers for the available work. Therefore, it is important for struggling artistic organizations to develop a partnership with unions so that they have the available personnel to complete the necessary work for a project. It is also important for the organizations to keep the unions abreast of financial issues.

FUNDING

Studies indicate that up to 70 percent of Americans believe that most charitable organizations misspend and mismanage their funds (Pallotta, 2012). Many people do not believe that nonprofits are held accountable for how their operations are run. The media became part of the equation as it made attempts to expose organizations that were guilty of mismanagement. In order to get past this obstacle, organizations have the opportunity to implement a funding strategy based on two different perspectives.

INTERNAL PERSPECTIVE

An organization can conduct a self-audit and develop a plan that can turn the situation around. The arts managers can select a team of different stakeholders who will assist them in analyzing the situation. One recommendation would be a process that has been utilized. Holtzman (2000) worked on such a project, and the focus was on the number of visitors required to increase revenue. The team projected the different types of scenarios that a visitor would participate in an activity. There were three levels of plans: realistic, mildly optimistic, and highly optimistic. These plans set the foundation for what could be expected. The next step was to look at the competition. By investigating the revenue and range of visitors that other arts institutions realized through auxiliary services such as the gift shop, catering, the café, etc., the team was better able to predict its own figures. Once the results were collected and analyzed, a final document was prepared to share with the board.

External perspective

The external perspective is that nonprofits need objective assistance in revamping their process in order to establish creditability. Based on the nature of their work, grant-makers could be the "knight in shining armor." Robinson (1997) provided several compelling arguments as to why grant-makers should serve as the catalyst in cleaning up the image of nonprofit organizations. Some of the arguments include:

- **Enlightened Self-Interest.** Research has shown that a business can be affected even if it is only marginally affiliated with an organization that is operating poorly. A nonprofit's finances may affect the grant-maker directly. Therefore, it is in the grant-maker's interest to assist in increasing the nonprofits' financial stability.

- **A Powerful Position.** Grant-makers are often a nonprofits' primary customer because they determine whether or not a project will be funded. Therefore, they are in the best position to offer suggestions on how to improve a nonprofit's financial position.
- **A History of Success.** It has been found that grant-makers are successful stabilization proponents. Cutting-edge foundations are encouraging their grant-seekers to improve their financial situation.

In the new economy, management teams at art institutions are challenged to address issues such as competition, marketing campaigns, labor issues, and fundraising and will need to reflect on how they make decisions. They will have to be more creative in the way that they arrive at their final decisions. A study (Barrett, Balloun, & Weinstein, 2005) was conducted and found that arts managers could benefit their organization by:

- Developing their creative climate and learning orientation with the understanding that the former reinforces and leverages the latter.
- Continually scanning their environments for relevant market information, acting upon the gathered information and sharing this information with all levels of the organization.
- Acting proactively to use this knowledge as a starting point to introduce new initiatives to benefit their target markets.
- Using cross-functional, empowered teams to analyze, create, develop, and execute strategic marketing responses into diverse environments.

Implementing this process will assist arts managers in providing better insight, planning, and guidance on how to manage their nonprofit organizations in the new economy.

APPLICATION

Economic Impact Analysis

There is much focus on money in the management of the arts. Therefore, it is important that organizations in this industry understand the impact of their budget on their ability to continue to do business. Economic impact analysis is a way that arts managers can strategically evaluate the financial impact of their programs (Hearney & Hearney, 2003). This approach is an attempt for arts managers to collect data that will assist them in making and justifying their marketing and management decisions. There are three different aspects–direct impact, indirect impact, and induced impact–that managers can utilize in order to measure program effectiveness (Woodward & Teel, 2001).

- **Direct Impact.** This aspect will allow managers to analyze the spending patterns and preferences of the target market.After evaluating the data, managers can determine which programs they should offer based on participation. By offering programs that interest participants, managers may be able to increase participation, satisfaction level, and loyalty. Also, the analysis should be able to assist the managers in determining how much participants are willing to pay for each program.
- **Indirect Impact.** This aspect will allow managers to determine other programs that may be of interest to the target market. Art managers can use the information collected to initiate new marketing campaigns, which may increase community and financial support for their organizations.
- **Induced Impact.** This aspect can be used to increase the stature and validity of the organizations within the community (Hearney & Hearney, 2003). Arts managers will be able to take the data that they have collected and use it to apply for grants, government, and community contributions. It will provide objective information based on reliable and validated data.

By performing an economic impact analysis, arts managers will gain credibility. The information can assist with new marketing campaigns as well as allow the arts managers to run the organizations similar to for-profit organizations. This type of strategy has the capability of assisting managers with understanding and measuring marketing concepts, understanding customer segments, positioning their organizations, determining whether or not they have a loyal customer base, and generating government and community support (Hearney & Hearney, 2003).

ISSUES
Risk Management in the Arts
The market for securing cultural property has soared in the past. "The inflation of values and concentration of risk makes fine arts management a highly complex problem area" (Pfeffer, 1972, p. 117). The nature of fine arts items has created an environment where their high value has made them susceptible to loss or damage. Given the fact that most fine art pieces are authentic and original, many organizations have found it necessary to take actions that may not best serve them in the long term. To protect themselves, many have self-insured to excessive limits instead of allowing private collectors to lend their property to public exhibitions, allocating portions of the budget for insurance premiums, and reducing the public's access to important pieces.

Risk managers have given the arts organizations several ways to deal with this problem. According to Pfeffer (1972), the most popular choices are avoidance, evasion, prevention, protection, transfer, assumption, neutralization, and combination:

- **Avoidance.** A strategy of identifying certain hazards and adhering to a policy of non-exposure to them. If this is selected as the choice, organizations may limit the public's access to items of great value in order to avoid risk.
- **Evasion.** A practical approach of shifting the burden of financial liability by comprising with creditors or filing bankruptcy. Many see this approach as a last resort because they want to avoid the public stigma.
- **Prevention.** If selected, this choice will minimize the chance of loss and its severity before a loss occurs.
- **Protection.** This strategy usually occurs after the onset of a loss. Work completed by such entities as the police and fire authorities falls into this category.
- **Transfer.** This approach occurs when responsibility or liability for potential loss is shifted to another risk-bearer who becomes the insurer. This type of coverage will protect the fine arts from the time it leaves an owner's presence until it is safely returned.
- **Assumption.** This technique is the same as self-insurance. The person who is exposed to the loss absorbs the loss.
- **Neutralization.** This technique is also referred to as hedging, and occurs when offsetting risks may cancel each other out.
- **Combination.** This approach combines risks or pools similar exposures together. By spreading the risk, there is a reduction in the probability of the average loss for each covered interest.

CONCLUSION

Nonprofit organizations often suffer from poor money management, which leads to financial shortfalls that can have an adverse impact on the products that makes them valuable to the community (Richardson, 2006). Arts managers, who are increasingly accountable for their financial and resource allocation decisions, should be able to use economic impact analyses to assist them in predicting, managing, and justifying their managerial decisions (Hearney & Hearney, 2003). By using these three aspects, arts managers will be able to understand and justify their decisions in marketing and management. In addition, the analysis can assist arts managers with creating marketing campaigns to promote new and existing programs, survey customers in order to determine what they are interested in and if they are satisfied with the organization's offerings, and gain support from external entities such as the government and the community. Such an analysis will provide nonprofit organizations with an opportunity to document financial practices with the same level of accountability as maintained by profit organizations (Alexander, 1991).

"From a risk management perspective, an art collection is a target risk with an escalating financial catastrophe exposure" (Pfeffer, 1972, p. 117). Therefore, arts managers must evaluate whether or not they will need to reduce access to the public in order to protect the cultural properties. There are several choices that the organizations may evaluate when selecting an approach to deal with the risk. The key is to select an option that is appropriate for the specific piece of work involved.

Based on the information that has been provided in this article, there is an awareness that cultural funding has become quite complex. As a result, the demands on the arts manager continue to grow. In order to prepare themselves for the challenges that lie ahead, many higher education institutions have developed graduate arts management programs. Although the field of arts administration has been a combination of many professions, master's degree programs have been in place for more than 30 years to provide advanced formal training for arts managers (Bienvenu, 2004).

Individuals are able to earn a master's degree in arts administration or arts management. The programs are designed to provide a foundation in marketing, fund raising, business, management, accounting, law, and other topics of concern to arts managers. Many institutions encourage arts managers to come into the program with a personal project so that they can apply the theoretical concepts to an issue that they are faced with (Reiss, 2001). Many have graduated from these types of programs and provide the management pool for arts organizations (Bienvenu, 2004).

BIBLIOGRAPHY

Alexander, G. (1991, March). Are Non-Profits asleep at the wheel? *Fund Raising Management, 21,* 62-64.

Bienvenu, B. (2004). Opinions from the field: Graduate assessments of the value of master's degrees in arts administration. Ph.D. dissertation, The University of Oklahoma, United States—Oklahoma.

Bjorkegren, D. (1993). Arts management. *Journal of Socio-Economics, 22,* 379-395. Retrieved on May 23, 2007, from EBSCO Online Database Business Source Complete. http://search.ebscohost.com/login.aspx?direct=true&db=bth&AN=9408090225&site=ehost-live

Bourdieu, P. (1977). Cultural reproduction and social reproduction. In J. Karabel, & H. A. Halsey (Eds.), *Power and ideology in education* (pp. 487-511). New York: Oxford University Press.

Barrett, H., Balloun, J., & Weinstein, A. (2005). The impact of creativity on performance in nonprofits. *International Journal of Nonprofit and Voluntary Sector Marketing, 10,* 213-223. Retrieved May 23, 2007, from EBSCO Online Database Business Source Complete. http://search.ebscohost.com/login.aspx?direct=true&db=bth&AN=19497109&site=ehost-live

Heaney, J., & Heaney, M. (2003). Using economic impact analysis for arts management: An empirical application to a music institute in the USA. *International Journal of Nonprofit & Voluntary Sector Marketing, 8,* 251-267. Retrieved on May 23, 2007, from EBSCO Online Database Business Source Complete. http://search.ebscohost.com/login.aspx?direct=true&db=bth&AN=10434081&site=ehost-live

Holtzman, E. (2000). Managing change in the arts sector. *Fund Raising Management, 30,* 32-34. Retrieved May 24, 2007, from EBSCO Online Database Business Source Complete. http://search.ebscohost.com/login.aspx?direct=true&db=bth&AN=3211278&site=ehost-live

Kent, N. (1991). *Naked hollywood.* London: BBC Books.

Kleingartner, A., & Lloyd, K. (1972). Labor-management relations in the performing arts: The case of Los Angeles. *California Management Review, 15,* 128-132. Retrieved on May 23, 2007, from EBSCO Online Database Business Source Complete. http://search.ebscohost.com/login.aspx?direct=true&db=bth&AN=5048526&site=ehost-live

Padanyi, P. (2001). Testing the boundaries of the marketing concept: Is market orientation a determinant of organizational performance in the non-profit sector? Ph.D. dissertation, York University (Canada), Canada.

Pallotta, D. (2012). Charity case: How the nonprofit community can stand up for itself and really change the world. San Francisco: Jossey-Bass.

Pfeffer, I. (1972). Fine Arts: A problem in risk management. *California Management Review, 15,* 117-127. Retrieved on May 23, 2007, from EBSCO Online Database Business Source Complete. http://search.ebscohost.com/login.aspx?direct=true&db=bth&AN=5048431&site=ehost-live

Resiss, A. (2001). Graduate arts management programs grooming new generations of arts fund raisers. *Fund Raising Management, 32,* 27-29. Retrieved on May 23, 2007, from EBSCO Online Database Business Source Complete. http://search.ebscohost.com/login.aspx?direct=true&db=bth&AN=5021590&site=ehost-live

Richardson, N. (2006). The business of art. *Black Enterprise, 36,* 112-122. Retrieved May 23, 2007, from EBSCO Online Database Business Source Complete. http://search.ebscohost.com/login.aspx?direct=true&db=bth&AN=19498086&site=ehost-live

Robinson, B. (1997). Financial stability: The impossible dream? *Nonprofit World, 15,* 40-45. Retrieved May 23, 2007, from EBSCO Online Database Business Source Complete. http://search.ebscohost.com/login.aspx?direct=true&db=bth&AN=13226830&site=ehost-live

Woodward, D., & Teel, S. (2001). The economic impact of the University of South Carolina system (Cover story). *Business and Economic Review, 47,* 3-10. Retrieved May 23, 2007, from EBSCO Online Database Business Source Complete. http://search.ebscohost.com/login.aspx?direct=true&db=bth&AN=3928114&site=ehost-live

SUGGESTED READING

Francis, A. (1998). The culture business. Management strategies for the Arts-related business. *Organization Studies (Walter de Gruyter GmbH & Co. KG.), 19,* 345-346. Retrieved on May 23, 2007, from EBSCO Online Database Business Source Complete. http://search.ebscohost.com/login.aspx?direct=true&db=bth&AN=708178&site=ehost-live

Hume, M., Sullivan Mort, G., Liesch, P., & Winzar, H. (2006). Understanding service experience in non-profit performing arts: Implications for operations and service management. *Journal of Operations Management, 24,* 304-324. Retrieved May 30, 2007, from EBSCO Online Database Business Source Complete. http://search.ebscohost.com/login.aspx?direct=true&db=bth&AN=20822946&site=ehost-live

Experts discuss fine arts risk management. (1997). *Best's Review/Property-Casualty Insurance Edition, 97,* 84. Retrieved May 30, 2007, from EBSCO Online Database Business Source Complete. http://search.ebscohost.com/login.aspx?direct=true&db=bth&AN=9702194664&site=ehost-live Yun, T. (2012).

The efficacy of audience building among nonprofit cultural organizations: The impact of marketing strategies and organizational attributes. *Megatrend Review, 9,* 173–199. Retrieved November 19, 2013 from EBSCO online database, Business Source Complete. http://search.ebscohost.com/login.aspx?direct=true&db=bth&AN=77462370&site=ehost-live

Marie Gould

CUSTOMER INFORMATION SYSTEMS

ABSTRACT

This article focuses on customer information systems, especially as they relate to the marketing function. We are constantly in search of finding ways to satisfy our customers, and we attempt to collect this information so that we can analyze trends. Evaluating a customer's orientation is believed to provide valuable information about customer preferences and habits. There is a discussion of how customer orientation and information systems assist organizations with collecting data on customer behavior. In addition, there is an introduction of customer relationship management (CRM) systems and how the Internet has created a need to be able to collect customer information.

OVERVIEW

There are current trends in the marketing field that suggest that our society is a consumer-oriented economy (Watkins & Vandemark, 1971). We are constantly in search of ways to satisfy our customers, and we attempt to collect this information so that we can analyze trends. "A long standing marketing principle is that understanding and satisfying customers leads to superior business results" (Zhu & Nakata, 2007, p. 187). Evaluating a customer's orientation is believed to provide valuable information about customer preferences and habits. Organizations can collect examples that illustrate that attentiveness to customers, or customer orientation, reaps large rewards (Zhu & Nakata, 2007).

Information systems have been viewed as a mechanism to assist organizations with completing customer intelligence tasks and response activities (e.g. collecting detailed data on purchase habits, distributing this data across functions to analyze critical market trends and developing actionable marketing plans (Day, 1994; Glazer, 1991). "Yet, when information systems for marketing firms are examined, there is little evidence that retailers regularly or systematically attempt to obtain an evaluation of how customers regard their products, service, and performance, or the performance of their competitors in providing an acceptable marketing mix" (Watkins & Vandemark, 1971, p. 50). Therefore, many organizations have resorted to looking at IT capability and information services quality as a way to understand the relations between customer orientation and efficiency (Bharadwai, 2000).

IT Capability, the technological component of information systems, refers to the ability of many computers and similar technologies in a business to conserve, disect, and convey information (Bakos & Treacy, 1985). Storage, processing, and communicating information are viewed as key activities of an IT capability (Molloy & Schwenk, 1995). Given the differences in components and configuration, there is a variation in IT capability as it relates to capacity, quality, and speed in performing these information functions (Zhu & Nakata, 2007).

Information Service Quality, the human component of information systems, is the extent to which information services are provided to system users by computer technicians. The services have desired properties, which include timeliness, appropriateness, and reliability (Pitt, Watson & Kavan, 1995). "The rise of microcomputing, the advent of the Internet, and an explosion of IT products have only increased the demand for and diversity of information services. Services range from the rather mundane (e.g. manning technical help desks) to the highly evolved (e.g. integrating legacy systems)" (Zhu & Nakata, 2007, p. 190). Many of these services fall under customer orientation by providing marketing managers assistance and training in operating customer relationship management (CRM) systems.

Relationship Marketing

Relationship marketing has grown over the past ten years (Sheth & Parvatyar, 2000) based on the belief that the efforts will yield substantial profits. However, there is no data to support this belief, and research is mixed. There needs to be more studies conducted in order to validate these claims. Two of the main issues that will be need to be reviewed focus on the actual payoff when an organization uses different relationship marketing programs to create various forms of relational bonds and norms to create different levels of return (Berry, 1995) and the types and levels of returns an organization receives from a relationship marketing program are based on factors such as participant influence (Reinartz and Kumar, 2000). "Researchers in service and consumer markets have linked relationship marketing activities to intermediate outcomes (i.e. sales growth, higher customer share, lower price sensitivity) that should enhance a firm's profit" (Palmatier, Gopalakrishna, & Houston, 2006). However, the overall findings in both business to business (B2B) and consumer markets is that relationship marketing attempts have a direct effect on the customer's financial worth to the company by extending the length, depth, and extent of the purchasing relationship and the generation of helpful hearsay.

Several criterions are utilized to describe relationship marketing efforts and they include:
- Customer bonds formed
- Exchange control mechanisms used
- Benefits offered
- Functions served
- Content area supported

The criterion uses several perspectives in order to recognize the viable categories for arranging activities intended to build and boost relationships. Most of the categories deal with economic, societal, and structural factors and imply that customer-seller relationships are similarly arranged despite which category they belong to. However, the connections may differentiate by level of effectiveness among the categories. Many researchers have used Berry's (1995) model of explaining economic, societal, and structural relationships and the marketing programs associated with them. According to his model:
- **Financial Relationship Marketing Programs** "include discounts, free products or other financial benefits that reward customer loyalty" (Palmatier, et. al., 2006, p. 479). Organizations, however, must be one-of-a-kind in their offerings so that competitors may not easily duplicate their campaign. Otherwise, there will be no benefit.
- **Social Relationship Marketing Programs** "include meals, special treatment, entertainment, and personalized information" (Palmatier, et. al., 2006, p. 479). Research has shown that social bonds are not easy to duplicate. Therefore, there is a strong possibility of strong customer relationships and

customers will therefore ignore enticing offerings from competitors due to loyalty and satisfaction with a product.
- **Structural Relationship Marketing Programs** "increase productivity and/or efficiency for customers through investments that customers would probably not make themselves (e.g. customized order processing system, tailored packaging) (Palmatier, et. al., 2006, p. 479). These programs tend to offer unique benefits and require substantial setup efforts. Therefore, customers may be reluctant to change vendors given the benefits of the relationship.

In order to keep track of all of the above-mentioned initiatives, some companies have implemented customer relationship management (CRM) systems to track their progress on how well they meet the needs of their customer base. There are two primary types of CRM systems: contact centric and account centric. Contact centric systems tend to be used when the primary organization is around independent contacts. On the other hand, account centric systems are used when there are two separate ranks involved in the simple arrangement. There tends to be a business or account level to which many contacts can be connected.
- **Contact Centric:** The database is organized around individual contacts in this type of system. For example, if an organization is working with 500 different people and they are all employed by the same business, the database would have 500 separate contact records, each listing the name of the corporation. Examples of such a database are GoldMine and ACT!. The advantage of this type of system is that it is useful if an organization is dealing with individuals and there is no need to work with the company's combined history. However, one may experience problems if there is a need to track information about a company separate from contact information.
- **Account Centric:** The databases have a level that lies above the contacts, the organization, or account. There is an ability to tie multiple contacts together. Examples of such databases are Maximizer, SalesLogix, and Sage/ACCPAC CRM. The advantage of this type of system is that it can follow business-related research aside from contact-ori-

ented information. This method can be helpful if one wants to:

- View every opportunity available for an account or business
- View the entire history
- Update addresses
- View the corporation and each of its contacts in one, simple viewing screen
- Easily research the business versus its individuals

The Internet & Customers

Many organizations seek to understand the benefits of the Internet as they move their products to the medium. However, they recognize that having an Internet presence does not guarantee a successful venture. There has to be a significant number of people visiting the site and buying the product. "In reality, many websites have very small traffic with over 90% of Internet traffic flowing through less than 10% of the most popular sites (Ennew, Lockett, Holland & Blackman, 2000). To achieve success, organizations must be able to attract customers and establish a solid customer base.

"If websites exist in a market-space that is so vast that their existence is not a sufficient condition for gaining traffic and the development of a viable Internet venture requires customers, the building of a customer base becomes a key component of any company's marketing strategy toward the Internet" (Lockett & Blackman, 2001, p. 49). Additionally, the growth of a strong customer base will benefit different functions in marketing like market studies and tests (Lockett, Blackman & Naude, 1998). Therefore, having an online customer following is essential for an online marketing strategy.

There are two different methods used to build a customer base through the World Wide Web. The models are based on specific websites and involve symbiotic marketing. In the site-centric model, customers are interested in a particular organization's brand that meets their requirements. The central site focuses on attracting and retaining customers so it invests in building strong brand recognition for the organization. The site-centric approach utilizes an umbrella strategy that has a variety of techniques. All the techniques have the same theme – attract customers to the business's own website. Once the techniques

have been implemented, the Internet company is able to document the characteristics, patterns, and habits of its customer base.

APPLICATION

Customer Relationship Management

Besides relationship marketing, other determinants such as the customers, salespeople, and selling firms might influence the exchange performance in B2B customer interactions. Customer commitment to a selling firm is based on the customer's willingness to maintain a connection with the firm and if the partnership is considered valuable. The customer's perception and interaction frequency are key factors in determining how long the relationship will last. "A customer's sales growth can lead to increased selling firm sales" (Palmatier, Gopalakrishna, & Houston, 2006, p. 480). It has been found that a salesperson's skills and motivations are important factors to successful sales and profits. A motivated sales staff has the ability to find and close opportunities for new relationships, which equates to increased profits. If the customer is satisfied with the sales staff's performance, it can lead to a long and prosperous relationship.

Finally, there are opportunities for a sales firm to utilize subtle and obvious attempts to develop and secure customer relationships that will yield a significant profit. Palmatier, Gopalakrishna, and Houston (2006) identified different techniques to measure how effective the direct and indirect efforts were in securing successful relationships.

- **Direct Efforts:** The employment of customer relationship management (CRM) is evaluated, which would require a deliberate approach to developing shareholder values by building connections with crucial customers by using research, facts, and information technology. Access to the customer database will allow organizations to direct their work more efficiently.
- **Indirect Efforts:** Average tenure of the sales force at the organization is reviewed because tenure causes more powerful customer alliances, more infrequent customer deficiencies, and additional customer-specific information that can help to decrease customer turnover and increase profit margins.

Viewpoint
Building a Customer Base on the Internet

There are two different methods involved in creating an online customer base. The models are specific to certain websites and are also symbiotic marketing. The two models can be viewed as opposite approaches. However, some organizations have used techniques from both approaches. The site centric model will be discussed in this section. This model involves many different techniques that are able to gain customers attention and lead them to a main website offering them a certain product. Ebay is an example of a website that uses the site-centric model. If a person is looking for a particular item, he or she may google the item. One hit may be an eBay link if the product is available on its site.

In the site-centric model, customers are interested in a particular organization's brand that meets their requirements. The central site focuses on attracting and retaining customers, so it invests in building strong brand recognition for the organization. For example, eBay has invested time in building recognition for Gotham Online as a site offering upscale namebrand shoes at discount prices. A customer seeking shoes such as Stuart Weitzman or Kenneth Cole could go through eBay to take advantage of Gotham's discounted prices for these brands. Although Gotham Online has a site, the shoes tend to be cheaper on the eBay site because the auctions start at a lower price. If the customer wants a variety of upscale shoes and is not concerned about price, he or she may go to Gotham Online site for more choices. The purpose of the auctions at the eBay site is to get the customer familiar with Gotham Online. One of the attractions is the low-price bid auctions for upscale shoes. In addition, there is a significant discount on shipping and handling charges for multiple purchases. Once the customer becomes comfortable with the organization, Gotham Online provides opportunities for the customer to sign up for a newsletter regarding upcoming sales on eBay as well as the opportunity to see the latest styles at the organization's site.

The site-centric approach utilizes an umbrella strategy that has a variety of techniques. All the techniques have the same theme—attract customers to the company's own website. According to Lockett and Blackman (2001), some of the techniques include:

- **Portal Sites:** This is either the first site a user sees when logging in or accesses by performing a search on a search engine. The screen upon login is usually arranged by the Internet service provider (e.g. AOL, EarthLink) or the Internet software browser (e.g. Netscape or Microsoft Internet Explorer). Examples of search engines include Google and Yahoo.
- **Purchase Links to a Portal Site:** Companies may develop their own portal links and purchase prominent links in crucial portal sites that already exist. For example, Citigroup agreed to pay Netscape 40 million dollars to contribute to the personal finance information for use by the Netscape Personal Finance website.
- **Purchase Advertising:** After the customer purchases the product from the central site, a direct link is provided so that the customer can pay immediately at the organization's site. The larger portal sites tend to be advantageous, as they sell advertisements that have been directed toward certain groups.
- Keywords can be used to select an appropriate banner advertisement.
- Advertisements can be presented on Internet pages with related topics.
- Regional-specific advertising can be provided on regional-specific search engines.
- Detailed information can be collected to assist buyers with determining the success of specific-banner advertisements.
- **Direct E-mail: Registered Users or Subscribers to Email Services:** Customers can agree to receive regular emails or newsletters when the company has new products.
- **Direct Email: Junk Mail or Spam-Mail:** Spammers use the unprotected servers of other companies to distribute emails about their products.

Although this model has been a successful Internet strategy, some companies are seeking alternatives. One of the concerns with the technique is the additional costs that accompany the process of drawing attention to a key website and developing a strong customer base.

CONCLUSION

There are current trends in the marketing field that suggest that our society is a consumer-oriented economy (Watkins & Vandemark, 1971). We are constantly in search of finding ways to satisfy our customers, and we attempt to collect this information so that we can analyze trends. "A long-standing marketing principle is that understanding and satisfying customers leads to superior business results" (Zhu & Nakata, 2007, p. 187). Evaluating a customer's orientation is believed to provide valuable information about customer preferences and habits. Organizations can collect examples that illustrate that attentiveness to customers, or customer orientation, reaps large rewards (Zhu & Nakata, 2007).

Information systems have been viewed as a mechanism to assist organizations with completing customer intelligence tasks and response activities (e.g. collecting detailed data on purchase habits, distributing this data across functions to analyze critical market trends and developing actionable marketing plans (Day, 1994; Glazer, 1991). "Yet, when information systems for marketing firms are examined, there is little evidence that retailers regularly or systematically attempt to obtain an evaluation of how customers regard their products, service, and performance or the performance of their competitors in providing an acceptable marketing mix" (Watkins & Vandemark, 1971, p. 50). Therefore, many organizations have resorted to looking at IT capability and information services quality in order to understand the relationship between customer orientation and performance (Bharadwai, 2000).

In order to keep track of all of the above-mentioned initiatives, some companies have implemented customer relationship management (CRM) systems to track their progress on how well they meet the needs of their customer base. There are two primary types of CRM systems: contact centric and account centric.

- Contact centric systems tend to be used when the primary organization is around independent contacts.
- Aaccount centric systems are used when there are two different layers to the simple construction.

There tends to a business or account level to which different contacts can be associated.

There are two different methods used in developing a customer base online. The models are site-centric and symbiotic marketing. The two models can be viewed as opposite approaches. However, some organizations have used techniques from both approaches.

BIBLIOGRAPHY

Bakos, J., & Treacy, M. (1985). Information technology and corporate strategy: A research perspective. *MIS Quarterly, 10,* 106-119. Retrieved November 21, 2007, from EBSCO Online Database Business Source Complete. http://search.ebscohost.com/login.aspx?direct=true&db=bth&AN=4678882&site=bsi-live

Berry, L. (1995). Relationship marketing of service-growing interest, emerging perspectives. *Journal of Academic Marketing Science, 23,* 236-245.

Bharadwaj, A. (2000). A resource-based perspective on information technology capability and firm performance: An empirical investigation. *MIS Quarterly, 24,* 169-196. Retrieved November 21, 2007, from EBSCO Online Database Business Source Complete. http://search.ebscohost.com/login.aspx?direct=true&db=bth&AN=3205166&site=bsi-live

Day, G. (1994). The capabilities of market-driven organizations. *Journal of Marketing, 58,* 37-52. Retrieved November 21, 2007, from EBSCO Online Database Business Source Complete. http://search.ebscohost.com/login.aspx?direct=true&db=bth&AN=9410316032&site=bsi-live

Ennew, C., Lockett, A., Holland, C., & Blackman, I. (2000). *Predicting customer visits to Internet retail sites: A cross industry empirical investigation.* Nottingham: University of Nottingham Business School.

Glazer, R. (1991). Marketing in an information-intensive environment: Strategic implications of knowledge as an asset. *Journal of Marketing, 36,* 223-238.

Handley, A. (2013). Behavioral theory. *Entrepreneur, 41,* 72. Retrieved November 24, 2013, from EBSCO Online Database Business Source Complete. http://search.ebscohost.com/login.aspx?direct=true&db=bth&AN=88307882&site=ehost-live

Lambrecht, A., & Tucker, C. (2013). When does retargeting work? Information specificity in online advertising. *Journal of Marketing Research (JMR)*, *50*, 561-576. Retrieved November 24, 2013, from EBSCO Online Database Business Source Complete. http://search.ebscohost.com/login.aspx?direct=true&db=bth&AN=90376388&site=ehost-live

LaPointe, P. (2013). The dark corners where research strategies hide: Throwing light at the intersection of the new and the old. *Journal of Advertising Research*, *53*, 9-10. Retrieved November 24, 2013, from EBSCO Online Database Business Source Complete. http://search.ebscohost.com/login.aspx?direct=true&db=bth&AN=86178717&site=ehost-live

Lockett, A., & Blackman, I. (2001). Strategies for building a customer base on the Internet: Symbiotic marketing. *Journal of Strategic Marketing*, *9*, 47-68. Retrieved on May 3, 2007, from EBSCO Online Database Business Source Complete. http://search.ebscohost.com/login.aspx?direct=true&db=bth&AN=4782033&site=bsi-live

Lockett, A., Blackman, I., & Naude, P. (1998). Using the Internet/WWW for the real time development of financial services: The case of Xenon Laboratories. *Journal of Financial Services Marketing*, *3*, 161-172.

Molloy, S., & Schwenk, C. (1995). The effects of information technology on strategic decision making. *Journal of Management Studies*, *32*, 282-311.

Palmatier, R., Gopalakrishna, S., & Houston, M. (2006). Returns on Business-to-Business relationship marketing investments: Strategies for leveraging profits. *Marketing Science*, *25*, 477-493. Retrieved June 6, 2007, from EBSCO Online Database Business Source Complete. http://search.ebscohost.com/login.aspx?direct=true&db=bth&AN=22883062&site=bsi-live

Pitt, L., Watson, R., & Kavan, C. (1995). Service quality: A measure of information system effectiveness. *MIS Quarterly*, *19*, 173-187. Retrieved November 21, 2007, from EBSCO Online Database Business Source Complete. http://search.ebscohost.com/login.aspx?direct=true&db=bth&AN=9507260424&site=bsi-live

Reinartz, W., & Kumar, V. (2000). On the profitability of long-life customers in a noncontractual setting: An empirical investigation and implications for marketing. *Journal of Marketing*, *64*, 17-35.

Sheth, J., & Parvatiyar, A. (2000). *Handbook of relationship marketing*. Thousand Oaks, CA: Sage Publications.

Watkins, E., & Vandemark, V. (1971). Customer information strengthens market information systems. *Journal of Retailing*, *47*, 50-57. Retrieved November 21, 2007, from EBSCO Online Database Business Source Complete. http://search.ebscohost.com/login.aspx?direct=true&db=bth&AN=4673041&site=bsi-live

Zhu, Z., & Nakata, C. (2007). Reexamining the link between customer orientation and business performance: The role of information systems. *Journal of Marketing Theory and Practice*, *15*, 187-203. Retrieved November 21, 2007, from EBSCO Online Database Business Source Complete. http://search.ebscohost.com/login.aspx?direct=true&db=bth&AN=25741099&site=bsi-live

SUGGESTED READING

Calculating costs of integrating information systems. (2004). *Baseline*, 37. Retrieved November 28, 2007, from EBSCO Online Database Business Source Complete. http://search.ebscohost.com/login.aspx?direct=true&db=bth&AN=15143204&site=ehost-live

Pike, G.H. (2005). Privacy and the database industry. *Information Today*, *22*, 17-19. Retrieved November 28, 2007, from EBSCO Online Database Business Source Complete. http://search.ebscohost.com/login.aspx?direct=true&db=bth&AN=17004162&site=ehost-live

Stonham, L. (2006). Interactive online compliance database. *Pipeline & Gas Journal*, *233*, 68-69. Retrieved November 28, 2007, from EBSCO Online Database Business Source Complete. http://search.ebscohost.com/login.aspx?direct=true&db=bth&AN=20658363&site=ehost-live

Marie Gould

CUSTOMER LOYALTY PROGRAMS

ABSTRACT

This article examines the emergence of customer loyalty programs during the 1900s as well as current perspectives on what companies should consider when launching such a program. The processes of analyzing a company's business goals, customer preferences and habits, and the competitive environment prior to designing a customer loyalty program are reviewed. The importance of aligning a customer loyalty program with business goals, corporate philosophy, and corporate culture is examined. The option of exploiting social context or economic conditions to attract and reward customers is also reviewed. The process of evaluating and reframing analytical models used to evaluate less-than-effective customer loyalty programs is explained.

OVERVIEW

Customer loyalty programs are generally viewed as long-term endeavors in which consumers can accumulate some type of points that can later be redeemed for free merchandise, services, or discounts applied to future purchases. The more value that earned merchandise or services has for customers, the more attractive the program and the more likely customers will participate (Liu & Yang, 2009). The corporate goal of a customer loyalty program is to retain customers and derive more revenue from them in the future, ultimately increasing the profit of the firm (Noone & Mount, 2008). Many loyalty programs have shown some success in raising attitudinal loyalty as well as behavioral loyalty (Daams, Gelderman & Schijns, 2008).

Familiar Point Programs

Loyalty programs have been around for a long time. In the 1920s, General Mills first started a program known as Betty Crocker points. Purchasers received points when buying various General Mills products such as cereal and flour. Betty Crocker points could be redeemed for kitchen utensils or other domestic products. In the 1950s, American tobacco companies launched loyalty programs, which involved placing

coupons on the back of cigarette packs that could be redeemed for catalog items (Thomaselli, 2005).

S&H Green Stamps

The S&H Green Stamps program was established by Sperry & Hutchinson Inc. in 1896. Over the next 65 years, the trading stamp became immensely popular and helped draw customers to Sperry & Hutchinson. In 1964, there were more S&H Green Stamps printed than postage stamps printed by the U.S. Post Office. The green stamps could be taken to a redemption center and exchanged for merchandise.

At their peak, S&H Green Stamps were issued by more than 80,000 retail outlets (Edwards & Keane, 1966). In 1957, it is estimated that one of several competing trading stamps was issued with about 12 percent of all retails sales in the United States (Beem, 1957). However, the popularity of S&H Green Stamps also brought some burdens to the retail outlets that used them as a customer loyalty mechanism. Stamps were popular and therefore valuable and needed to be managed and controlled the same way as cash. The stamps also needed to be manually dispensed at the point of sale (Beem, 1958).

In 1968, the U.S. Federal Trade Commission (FTC) ruled that Sperry & Hutchinson, by then the largest company in the trading-stamp industry, was guilty of unfair trade practices. The U.S. Supreme Court upheld the FTC's power to make the ruling in 1972. The FTC contended that Sperry & Hutchinson had improperly controlled the maximum rate at which retail businesses could dispense trading stamps and that the company had combined with others in the trading-stamp industry to regulate the rate of stamp dispensing. In addition, Sperry & Hutchinson had attempted to suppress the operation of trading-stamp exchanges that redeemed stamps in gray-market operations. The FTC ordered Sperry & Hutchinson to cease and desist from these practices (Werner & Griffiths, 1972).

As times changed, S&H Green Stamps became less popular and grocery stores started phasing out trading-stamp programs, turning their attention to price-based promotions. Gasoline stations started phasing out the stamps during the 1973 petroleum crisis. In 1981, the founding family sold Sperry & Hutchinson (Barker, 2004).

Frequent-Flier Programs

American Airlines launched its customer loyalty program in 1981 called AAdvantage, the airline industry's first frequent-flier program. Customers benefitted by gaining points for miles flown; these points could be applied to free air travel tickets in the future. What was new and different about this loyalty program was that information technology was at the heart of the program. The technology allowed the airline to easily track award points and for fliers to redeem their points (Hederstierna & Sallberg, 2009). Frequent-flier programs were established worldwide, with all major airlines implementing some type of rewards program. The frequent-flier programs, like many customer loyalty programs, have been revamped over the last 25 years as economic conditions have changed (Fickenscher, 1999; Field, 2009; Lederman, 2007).

Once the airline programs gained popularity, the concept of points and reward programs spread to most industries and is now common in travel, lodging, and dining (Noone & Mount, 2008; Russell, 2008). Loyalty programs are catching on across the board in consumer products and services firms and even in toy stores ("Loyalty in Toyland," 2008) and at the gas station (Belanger, 2008). Many leading brand companies have their own reward systems with loyalty cards, and Starbucks has been an innovator in developing new approaches on how reward cards can be used (Dollarhide, 2008).

Technology Helps

Information technology such as point-of-sale systems in retail outlets, customer databases with purchasing history and contact information, and company websites that provide sales or service support have all expanded options to implement and maintain customer loyalty programs. Information technology also allows merchants as well as financial-service companies to develop customized offerings to entice a wider variety of customers (Angrisani, 2008; Gallagher, 2008; Gillen, 2008).

These technologies have even helped to revive the once dying trading stamp, as S&H evolved from lick and stick stamps to a point system. S&H is now partnering with more than 100 online retailers to provide an independent loyalty points exchange. Under the agreement, Points.com members can exchange miles or points from airlines, hotels, and other retailers into Greenpoints that can be used obtain items from the S&H rewards catalog including home goods, jewelry, and electronics. The S&H Greenpoints can also be redeemed at participating grocery stores ("Green Stamps Stick," 2004).

Although customer loyalty programs seem to be offered by businesses everywhere, building an effective program requires considerable effort and can be expensive. In addition, not all loyalty programs have been successful or cost-effective. To determine if a company is achieving a good return on investment from a customer loyalty program requires continuous monitoring and analysis. When results are not adequate, it is time to review what types of programs are attractive to customers and revamp a program to meet changing customer expectations and desires.

APPLICATIONS

Building a Customer Loyalty Program

Companies can increase sales volume by getting existing customers to buy more often and buy greater quantities or by attracting new customers (Adams, 2008). Several factors can affect both sales strategies, including the type of product, economic conditions, and the perceived or actual need for a product (Pringle & Field, 2009). A well-designed customer loyalty program can contribute to repeat purchases by existing customers, help attract new customers, and influence the perceived need for and value of product.

However, designing an effective customer loyalty program requires a realistic and accurate definition of what a company wants to gain from the program. Without clear business goals, it is difficult, if not impossible, to design an effective customer loyalty program and develop appropriate business systems to support the program. The business systems need to be capable of aiding in analyses to determine whether the program is effective and if it provides a favorable return on investment (Nunes & Dreze, 2006).

A loyalty program is not a replacement for good service, ongoing positive customer relations, or failure to deliver upon promises or warranties (Wilson, 2006). In many ways, management perspectives need to be seriously retooled. The principle that a business is customer-satisfaction oriented as opposed to goods-production oriented is one that all managers must grasp. In other words, a business is its customers not its products (Levitt, 2004).

It is also important to have a real-world understanding of a company's customers as well as a company's competitors. The design of an effective customer loyalty program will largely depend on how easy a product or service can be replicated by a competitor and how important price and customer service are to the buyer. In addition, company reputation and the status that customers gain from being a buyer or user of services offered can have a significant impact on creating emotional loyalty. An emotional attachment to a company or brand can drive behavioral loyalty, and the higher the level of emotional loyalty, the more likely a customer will be retained and repeat buying will continue (Hallberg, 2004).

Marketers debate how a loyalty program should benefit a customer. Many, however, do not spend enough time on the emotional side of the loyalty equation. Hallmark observed this and, as a marketer of emotion-focused products, has stepped in to fill the emotional gap in many loyalty programs. The Hallmark Loyalty division has more than 50 large corporate customers who purchase printed as well as electronic loyalty program elements. Hallmark e-cards are easy for corporate sales or communications staff to send and provide a large profit margin for Hallmark (Applebaum, 2004).

When a loyalty program's success depends on the frequency of repeat purchases, then customers need to be motivated beyond a single purchase. Programs with such structures need to also have a consistent and frequent message that convinces the customer to view their relationship with the seller as a long-term relationship and reinforces the point that a long series of purchases will reap a worthwhile reward (Lewis, 2004). But relationship building cannot be left solely to the customer. Company staff should also be trained into the perspective that every transaction with a customer can build loyalty.

Getting a Loyalty Program off the Ground
When loyalty programs have a strong technology element, it is also possible to collect data on customers and design individualized marketing efforts. Such a closed-loop loyalty system enables a seller or service provider to access a database of customers in the loyalty program in order to implement targeted marketing programs. Vendor-supported loyalty programs, of course, come with joining fees starting at about $300 and monthly fees of about $600 (Woodward, 2009).

Many large companies also offer co-branded credit cards through various banks. These programs usually provide some sort of point accumulation that can be redeemed for a product or service. United Airlines, for example, offers a credit card that provides one point for every dollar spent using the card, and the points can be redeemed for airline tickets. Amazon also introduced a co-branded credit card that provides points for dollars spent with the card, and the points can be used toward purchases from Amazon.com. The co-branded card comes with considerable expense to implement and promote for a business. If the potential volume is not readily apparent, then the approach may not meet an organization's needs.

If a company decides to build its own loyalty program, or even if it chooses to contract with a loyalty program vendor, it should keep several principles in mind during the process. Above all, a customer loyalty program should be built on the same business values, management beliefs and attitudes, and the basic business benefits that a company provides its customers (Fowler, 2003). It is also beneficial if a loyalty program is simple and straightforward, so customers can understand and relate to the reward benefits as well as be able to reap those rewards without excessive time and effort (Cebrzynski, 2006).

Social Aspects of Loyalty Programs
The social context of loyalty programs is a key factor to success. The business flyers who managed to keep the points they earned from business trips are able to translate these rewards into family vacations or trips to destinations of their choice. The program benefits are both obvious and easy to understand. Other programs that are more complex may be moderately successful but draw a relatively small number of participants.

Corporate Social Responsibility
Since the environmental awareness movement was revitalized, energy efficiency, pollution, and environmental sustainability are increasingly important factors on the consumer radar. The green movement has also been incorporated into loyalty programs. A

number of companies have added green rewards to their loyalty programs. A few of the pioneers in this approach were already marketing environmentally friendly products. However, it did not take long for a wide variety of companies (including airlines and banks) to start rewarding customers with some type of environmental points.

Typically, a company using environmental points will support environmental programs through its corporate social responsibility (CSR) programs (Cummings, 2008). CSR activities have been used to address consumers' social concerns, create a favorable corporate image, and develop a positive relationship with consumers and other stakeholders (Yoon, Gurhan-Canli, & Schwarz, 2006).

Gift Cards
The use of gift cards as premiums or rewards has caught on rather significantly. American Express markets gift cards for all occasions, and corporate bulk buyers can choose from a variety of themes for their gift cards (Hochstein, 2007). Gift cards are often given to customers, employees, or suppliers to help build loyalty.

As gasoline prices surged upward during the early years of the 2000s, several travel and lodging firms started a contextual marketing program involving free or discounted gasoline. Hotel chains with roadside locations that were convenient for the automobile traveler were using gasoline gift cards as premiums. After three separate stays, guests would receive a $50 gasoline gift card from name-brand oil companies.

ISSUES
When Customer Loyalty Programs Wane
Recent decades have certainly seen a huge growth in loyalty programs. The market has become saturated with programs, and more than 80 percent of the households in the United States are now participating or have participated in one or more rewards program ("Points Mania," 2008). Several retailers offer their own program making it easy for consumers to participate in loyalty or rewards programs at virtually every turn, especially if they use a credit card for purchases. There are many potentially overlapping loyalty programs when credit cards that have point programs are used in retail outlets that also have point programs (Fredericks, Hurd & Salter, 2001).

Many customers are beginning to feel that many reward programs take too long to reap any real benefit (Mazur, 2007). There is also pressure on the companies that offer reward-oriented loyalty programs to provide more flexibility in programs and increase the value of the reward provided to customers (Quittner, 2003).

Corporate executives are on the spot to demonstrate that there is, in fact, a real dollar return on investment for customer loyalty programs (Dowling & Uncles, 1997). The basic methods of examining the results of a loyalty program are not always straightforward and many self-studies of the programs result in a rather shallow and self-serving analysis (Cigliano, Georgiadis, Pleasance & Whalley, 2000).

However, when results from a customer loyalty program are less than expected, it is important to refine measures of activity and success and to reexamine analytical models being used to measure program results. Misleading information from internal as well as external sources can lead to faulty planning and execution. In addition, weak measures and measurement gaps will result in inadequate data and ultimately inappropriate analyses (Crosby & Lunde, 2008).

The most typical problem that corporate executives face with customer loyalty programs is costs, which includes annual maintenance costs as well as the impact of discounts that may be provided to customers through the program. The second challenge that executives face is what to do with a loyalty program when they confirm that its costs are out of control and there is not a good return on investment or possibly a loss for the program. Many customers will view the curtailment of a loyalty program as a betrayal, resulting in negative publicity (Cigliano, Georgiadis, Pleasance & Whalley, 2000).

In addition, digging for answers about the effectiveness of a customer loyalty program is an expensive and time-consuming endeavor. Many companies conduct surveys of loyalty program members, while others conduct focus groups to answer basic questions and gain new insights (Wansink, 2003). These methods can provide important information about how customers view the loyalty program and what drives their participation. This type of feedback can be useful in designing promotional material or in deciding how to expand or modify an existing program.

Customer loyalty programs may very well be profitable in the short run. If they are not, then the cost-effectiveness of the program should be examined and gains to the company reevaluated (Wansink, 2003). If one of the key factors to motivating participation is getting customers to view their participation as a long-term relationship, then the analysis of the return on investment of a loyalty program should also be framed in long-term concepts and based on longitudinal analysis (Lewis, 2004).

Regardless of how company executives view their customer loyalty program, the behavioral and emotional responses of the customer are likely to be the most important measures of a program's success. Awards, accolades, and fame for launching a program that industry observers or marketing gurus' feel is creative, novel, or unique have their appeal. They do not, however, make a customer loyalty program successful.

CONCLUSION

Customer loyalty programs provide consumers with a way to reap benefits from their buying behavior while simultaneously allowing retailers and service organizations to build a long-term relationship the customer. On the surface, this seems to be a win-win situation. However, not all customers will repeat their buying behavior frequently enough to gain a reward, and thus the seller may not recover the cost of gaining the new customer if discounts for programs participation were granted.

In addition to start-up costs, companies that offer customer loyalty programs also face annual maintenance costs as well as any fees from vendors who are contracted to support the program. If sales volume is low for a particular year, a company could end up finding that the customer loyalty program may cost more money than the gain in revenue that it helped generate.

Once corporate managers determines that a customer loyalty program is not a profitable endeavor, they then need to figure out what to do about the problem. Once a loyalty program is established, it may be difficult to terminate because of possible negative publicity such action may generate. It is also often difficult to analyze why a loyalty program is not working, especially if there are insufficient funds to conduct surveys or focus groups of participants.

BIBLIOGRAPHY

Adams, J. (2008). The do's and don'ts of loyalty programs. *Supply House Times, 51,* 24-26. Retrieved May 18, 2009, from EBSCO online database, Business Source Complete. http://search.ebscohost.com/login.aspx?direct=true&db=bth&AN=33373378&site=ehost-live

Angrisani, C. (2008). Thousands of Kroger shoppers embrace E-coupons. *SN: Supermarket News, 56,* 27. Retrieved May 13, 2009, from EBSCO online database, Business Source Complete. http://search.ebscohost.com/login.aspx?direct=true&db=bth&AN=31857024&site=ehost-live

Applebaum, M. (2004). Caring enough about loyalty. *Brandweek, 45,* 16-17. Retrieved May 13, 2009, from EBSCO online database, Academic Search Complete. http://search.ebscohost.com/login.aspx?direct=true&db=a9h&AN=14174689&site=ehost-live

Bagchi, R., & Xingbo Li. (2013). Illusionary progress in loyalty programs: magnitudes, reward distances, and step-size ambiguity. *Journal of Consumer Research, June 2013 Supplement,* S184–S197. Retrieved November 21, 2013 from EBSCO online database Business Source Premier. http://search.ebscohost.com/login.aspx?direct=true&db=buh&AN=87933420

Barker, J. (2004). New life. *Incentive, 178,* 34-36. Retrieved May 18, 2009, from EBSCO online database, Business Source Complete. http://search.ebscohost.com/login.aspx?direct=true&db=bth&AN=15119278&site=ehost-live

Beem, E. (1957). Who profits from trading stamps? *Harvard Business -Review, 35,* 123-136. Retrieved May 18, 2009, from EBSCO online database, Business Source Complete. http://search.ebscohost.com/login.aspx?direct=true&db=bth&AN=6774944&site=ehost-live

Beem, E. (1958). The impact of consumer premiums on marketing efficiency. *Journal of Marketing, 23,* 17-24. Retrieved May 18, 2009, from EBSCO online database, Business Source Complete. http://search.ebscohost.com/login.aspx?direct=true&db=bth&AN=6865693&site=ehost-live

Belanger, M. (2008). ExxonMobil, Chevron launch reward credit cards. *Convenience Store News, 44,* 14-14. Retrieved May 12, 2009, from EBSCO online database, Business Source Complete. http://

search.ebscohost.com/login.aspx?direct=true&db=bth&AN=34876489&site=ehost-live

Brierley, H. (2012). Why loyalty programs alienate great customers. *Harvard Business Review, 90*(7/8), 38. Retrieved November 21, 2013 from EBSCO online database Business Source Premier. http://search.ebscohost.com/login.aspx?direct=true&db=buh&AN=77224719

Cebrzynski, G. (2006). Simplicity, staff training spur loyalty program success. *Nation's Restaurant News, 40,* 76-76. Retrieved May 20, 2009, from EBSCO online database, Business Source Complete. http://search.ebscohost.com/login.aspx?direct=true&db=bth&AN=21139331&site=ehost-live

Cigliano, J., Georgiadis, M., Pleasance, D., & Whalley, S. (2000). The price of loyalty. *McKinsey Quarterly,* Retrieved May 13, 2009, from EBSCO online database, Business Source Complete. http://search.ebscohost.com/login.aspx?direct=true&db=bth&AN=3823411&site=ehost-live

Crosby, L., & Lunde, B. (2008). When loyalty strategies fail. *Marketing Management,* 17, 12-13. Retrieved May 12, 2009, from EBSCO online database, Business Source Complete. http://search.ebscohost.com/login.aspx?direct=true&db=bth&AN=35805367&site=ehost-live

Cummings, B. (2008). Now sprouting everywhere: Eco-friendly loyalty efforts. *Brandweek,* 49, 12-12. Retrieved May 12, 2009, from EBSCO online database, Academic Search Complete. http://search.ebscohost.com/login.aspx?direct=true&db=a9h&AN=31814654&site=ehost-live

Daams, P., Gelderman, K., & Schijns, J. (2008). The impact of loyalty programmes in a B-to-B context: Results of an experimental design. *Journal of Targeting, Measurement & Analysis for Marketing, 16,* 274-284. Retrieved May 12, 2009, EBSCO online database, Business Source Complete http://search.ebscohost.com/login.aspx?direct=true&db=bth&AN=35868007&site=ehost-live

Dollarhide, M. (2008). One card, many options. *Incentive, 182,* 87-88. Retrieved May 12, 2009, from EBSCO online database, Business Source Complete. http://search.ebscohost.com/login.aspx?direct=true&db=bth&AN=33526411&site=ehost-live

Dowling, G., & Uncles, M. (1997). Do customer loyalty programs really work? *Sloan Management Review, 38,* 71-82. *Retrieved May 13, 2009, from EBSCO*

online database, Business Source Complete. http://search.ebscohost.com/login.aspx?direct=true&db=bth&AN=9712235899&site=ehost-live

Edwards Jr., C., & Keane, H. (1966). The honor roll in retailing. *Journal of Retailing, 42,* 53. Retrieved May 18, 2009, from EBSCO online database, Business Source Complete. http://search.ebscohost.com/login.aspx?direct=true&db=bth&AN=4674475&site=ehost-live

Evanschitzky, H., et al. (2012). Consequences of customer loyalty to the loyalty program and to the company. *Journal of the Academy of Marketing Science, 40,* 625–638. Retrieved November 21, 2013 from EBSCO online database Business Source Premier. http://search.ebscohost.com/login.aspx?direct=true&db=buh&AN=78065188

Fickenscher, L. (1999). Amex, Diners Club add perks, services to reward programs. *American Banker, 164, 8. Retrieved May 20, 2009, from EBSCO online database, Business Source Complete. http://search.ebscohost.com/login.aspx?direct=true&db=bth&AN=1537179&site=ehost-live*

Field, N. (2009). Flyers grounded. *Money 14446219.* Retrieved May 12, 2009, from EBSCO online database, Business Source Complete. http://search.ebscohost.com/login.aspx?direct=true&db=bth&AN=37262509&site=ehost-live

Green stamps stick around. (2004). *Marketing News, 38, 23. Retrieved May 13, 2009, from EBSCO online database, Business Source Complete. http://search.ebscohost.com/login.aspx?direct=true&db=bth&AN=15414914&site=ehost-live*

Fowler, M. (2003). Fifteen critical success factors for real-time customer loyalty. *Restaurant Hospitality, 87,* 60-64. Retrieved May 13, 2009, from EBSCO online database, Business Source Complete. http://search.ebscohost.com/login.aspx?direct=true&db=bth&AN=11063524&site=ehost-live

Fredericks, J., Hurd, R., & Salter II, J. (2001). Connecting customer loyalty to financial results. *Marketing Management, 10,* 26-32. Retrieved May 13, 2009, from EBSCO online database, Business Source Complete. http://search.ebscohost.com/login.aspx?direct=true&db=bth&AN=4461338&site=ehost-live

Gallagher, J. (2008). Safeway rewards healthy shoppers. *SN: Supermarket News, 56,* 39-41. Retrieved May 12, 2009, from EBSCO online database, Business Source Complete. http://search.ebscohost.

com/login.aspx?direct=true&db=bth&AN=31957013&site=ehost-live

Gillen, J. (2008). Customer retention strategies evolve one-size-fits-all reward programs. *Banking New York, 5.* Retrieved May 13, 2009, from EBSCO online database, Business Source Complete. http://search.ebscohost.com/login.aspx?direct=true&db=bth&AN=32138994&site=ehost-live

Hallberg, G. (2004). Is your loyalty programme really building loyalty? Why increasing emotional attachment, not just repeat buying, is key to maximising programme success. *Journal of Targeting, Measurement & Analysis for Marketing, 12,* 231-241. Retrieved May 13, 2009, from EBSCO online database, Business Source Complete. http://search.ebscohost.com/login.aspx?direct=true&db=bth&AN=12496953&site=ehost-live

Hederstierna, A., & Sallberg, H. (2009). Bronze, silver and gold: Effective membership design in customer rewards programs. *Electronic Journal of Information Systems Evaluation, 12,* 59-65. Retrieved May 12, 2009, from EBSCO online database, Business Source Complete. http://search.ebscohost.com/login.aspx?direct=true&db=bth&AN=37568217&site=ehost-live

Hochstein, M. (2007). Amex gift card targets businesses. *American Banker, 172,* 6-6. Retrieved May 13, 2009, from EBSCO online database, Business Source Complete. http://search.ebscohost.com/login.aspx?direct=true&db=bth&AN=26971795&site=ehost-live

Jacobs, S. (2007). Gas gift cards get summer travelers moving. *Incentive, 181,* 108-108. Retrieved May 13, 2009, from EBSCO online database, Business Source Complete. http://search.ebscohost.com/login.aspx?direct=true&db=bth&AN=27500180&site=ehost-live

Lederman, M. (2007). Do enhancements to loyalty programs affect demand? The impact of international frequent flyer partnerships on domestic airline demand. *Rand Journal of Economics, 38,* 1134-1158. Retrieved May 13, 2009, from EBSCO online database, Business Source Premier. http://search.ebscohost.com/login.aspx?direct=true&db=buh&AN=32089479&site=ehost-live

Levitt, T. (2004). Marketing myopia. *Harvard Business Review, 82*(7/8), 138-149. Retrieved May 13, 2009, from EBSCO online database, Business Source Complete database. http://search.ebscohost.com/login.aspx?direct=true&db=bth&AN=13621076&site=ehost-live

Lewis, M. (2004). The influence of loyalty programs and short-term promotions on customer retention. *Journal of Marketing Research (JMR), 41,* 281-292. Retrieved May 13, 2009, from EBSCO online database, Business Source Complete. http://search.ebscohost.com/login.aspx?direct=true&db=bth&AN=14365030&site=ehost-live

Liu, Y., & Yang, R. (2009). Competing loyalty programs: Impact of market saturation, market share, and category expandability. *Journal of Marketing, 73,* 93-108. Retrieved May 12, 2009, EBSCO online database, Business Source Complete http://search.ebscohost.com/login.aspx?direct=true&db=bth&AN=35644039&site=ehost-live

Loyalty in Toyland. (2008). *Chain Store Age, 84,* 110. Retrieved May 12, 2009, from EBSCO online database, Business Source Complete. http://search.ebscohost.com/login.aspx?direct=true&db=bth&AN=35218672&site=ehost-live

Mazur, M. (2007). Many small business cardholders find rewards wanting. *Community Banker, 16,* 80. Retrieved May 13, 2009, from EBSCO online database, Business Source Complete. http://search.ebscohost.com/login.aspx?direct=true&db=bth&AN=26939562&site=ehost-live

Noone, B., & Mount, D. (2008). The effect of price on return intentions: Do satisfaction and reward programme membership matter? *Journal of Revenue & Pricing Management, 7,* 357-369. Retrieved May 12, 2009, EBSCO online database, Business Source Complete http://search.ebscohost.com/login.aspx?direct=true&db=bth&AN=35483559&site=ehost-live

Nunes, J., & Dreze, X. (2006). Your loyalty program is betraying you. *Harvard Business Review, 84,* 124-131. Retrieved May 13, 2009, from EBSCO online database, Business Source Complete. http://search.ebscohost.com/login.aspx?direct=true&db=bth&AN=19998917&site=ehost-live

Points mania. (2008). *Consumer Reports, 73,* 12-13. Retrieved May 12, 2009, from EBSCO online database, Academic Search Complete. http://search.ebscohost.com/login.aspx?direct=true&db=a9h&AN=32720508&site=ehost-live

Pringle, H., & Field, P. (2009). Why customer loyalty isn't as valuable as you think. *Advertising Age, 80,* 22-22. Retrieved May 12, 2009, from EBSCO online database, Academic Search Complete. http://search.ebscohost.com/login.aspx?direct=true&db=a9h&AN=37183690&site=ehost-live

Quittner, J. (2003). Loyalty programs' use—and expectations—rising. American Banker, 168, 6A. Retrieved May 13, 2009, from EBSCO online database, Business Source Complete. http://search.ebscohost.com/login.aspx?direct=true&db=bth&AN=9689763&site=ehost-live

Russell, S. (2008). Retailers play loyalty card. B&T Magazine,58(2681), 24-28. Retrieved May 12, 2009, from EBSCO online database, Business Source Complete. http://search.ebscohost.com/login.aspx?direct=true&db=bth&AN=35876692&site=ehost-live

Thomaselli, R. (2005). Who really reaps mileage rewards? Advertising Age, 76, 12-12. Retrieved May 18, 2009, from EBSCO online database, Academic Search Complete. http://search.ebscohost.com/login.aspx?direct=true&db=a9h&AN=17413795&site=ehost-live

Wansink, B. (2003). Developing a cost-effective brand loyalty program. Journal of Advertising Research, 43, 301-309. Retrieved May 13, 2009, from EBSCO online database, Business Source Complete. http://search.ebscohost.com/login.aspx?direct=true&db=bth&AN=11126766&site=ehost-live

Werner, R., & Griffiths, L. (1972). Regulation of product characteristics. Journal of Marketing, 36, 64-65. Retrieved May 18, 2009, from EBSCO online database, Business Source Complete. http://search.ebscohost.com/login.aspx?direct=true&db=bth&AN=25298161&site=ehost-live

Wilson, J. (2006). Schulze: Service remains key to success. Hotel & Motel Management, 221, 4-13. Retrieved May 13, 2009, from EBSCO online database, Business Source Complete. http://search.ebscohost.com/login.aspx?direct=true&db=bth&AN=20450373&site=ehost-live

Woodward, K. (2009). Revenue share, merchant coverage vital in loyalty program choice. ISO & Agent, 5, 12-13. Retrieved May 12, 2009, from EBSCO online database, Business Source Complete. http://search.ebscohost.com/login.aspx?direct=true&db=bth&AN=37325807&site=ehost-live

Yoon, Y., Gurhan-Canli, Z., & Schwarz, N. (2006). The effect of corporate social responsibility (CSR) activities on companies with bad reputations. Journal of Consumer Psychology, 16, 377-390. Retrieved May 20, 2009, from EBSCO online database, Academic Search Premier. http://search.ebscohost.com/login.aspx?direct=true&db=aph&AN=23087782&site=ehost-live

Suggested Reading

Beem, E., & Isaacson, L. (1968). Schizophrenia in trading stamp analysis. Journal of Business, 41, 340-344. Retrieved May 18, 2009, from EBSCO online database, Business Source Complete. http://search.ebscohost.com/login.aspx?direct=true&db=bth&AN=4584614&site=ehost-live

Brønn, P. (2008). Why aren't we measuring relationships? Communication World, 25, 32-34. Retrieved May 13, 2009, from EBSCO online database, Business Source Complete. http://search.ebscohost.com/login.aspx?direct=true&db=bth&AN=28139954&site=ehost-live

Cohen, D. (1974). The concept of unfairness as it relates to advertising legislation. Journal of Marketing, 38, 8-13. Retrieved May 18, 2009, from EBSCO online database, Business Source Complete. http://search.ebscohost.com/login.aspx?direct=true&db=bth&AN=4996673&site=ehost-live

D'Aurizio, P. (2008). Southwest Airlines: Lessons in loyalty. Nursing Economic$, 26 389-392. Retrieved May 12, 2009, from EBSCO online database, Academic Search Complete. http://search.ebscohost.com/login.aspx?direct=true&db=a9h&AN=36452770&site=ehost-live

D.P. (2004). Macy's seeks to engage couples with rewards linked to bridal registry. Executive Technology, 6, 6-6. Retrieved May 13, 2009, from EBSCO online database, Business Source Complete. http://search.ebscohost.com/login.aspx?direct=true&db=bth&AN=14197672&site=ehost-live

Fest, G. (2008). Retailers picking up tab to share in rewards. (cover story). Bank Technology News, 21, 1-31. Retrieved May 12, 2009, from EBSCO online database, Business Source Complete. http://search.ebscohost.com/login.aspx?direct=true&db=bth&AN=33355312&site=ehost-live

Flass, R. (2000). S&H ads tout update. Adweek Eastern Edition, 41, 10. Retrieved May 18, 2009, from EBSCO online database, Business Source Complete. http://search.ebscohost.com/login.aspx?direct=true&db=bth&AN=3261358&site=ehost-live

Garry, M. (2008). Revamp your loyalty program. SN: Supermarket News, 56, 40-42. Retrieved May 12, 2009, from EBSCO online database, Business Source Complete. http://search.ebscohost.com/login.aspx?direct=true&db=bth&AN=35880988&site=ehost-live

Gujarathi, M., & McQuade, R. (2003). Sun Airlines, Inc.: Financial reporting of point and loyalty programs. *Issues in Accounting Education, 18*, 359-368. Retrieved May 13, 2009, from EBSCO online database, Business Source Complete. http://search.ebscohost.com/login.aspx?direct=true&db=bth&AN=11975622&site=ehost-live

Hays, J., & Hill, A. (2006). An extended longitudinal study of the effects of a service guarantee. *Production & Operations Management, 15*, 117-131. Retrieved May 13, 2009, from EBSCO online database, Business Source Complete. http://search.ebscohost.com/login.aspx?direct=true&db=bth&AN=22404170&site=ehost-live

Hart, S., Smith, A., Sparks, L., & Tzokas, N. (1999). Are loyalty schemes a manifestation of relationship marketing? *Journal of Marketing Management, 15*, 541-562. Retrieved May 21, 2009, from EBSCO online database, Business Source Complete. http://search.ebscohost.com/login.aspx?direct=true&db=bth&AN=2514538&site=ehost-live

Jakobson, L., & Casison-Tansiri, J. (2004). Loyalty link: Do reward program participants really want discounts? *Incentive, 178*, 9. Retrieved May 13, 2009, from EBSCO online database, Business Source Complete. http://search.ebscohost.com/login.aspx?direct=true&db=bth&AN=14939155&site=ehost-live

Lal, R., & Bell, D. (2003). The impact of frequent shopper programs in grocery retailing. *Quantitative Marketing & Economics, 1*, 179-202. Retrieved May 13, 2009, EBSCO online database, http://search.ebscohost.com/login.aspx?direct=true&db=bth&AN=16399192&site=ehost-live

Rahman, S. (2005). Loyalty in retail: A strategic success or a management failure. *European Retail Digest*, 57-60. Retrieved May 13, 2009, from EBSCO online database, Business Source Complete. http://search.ebscohost.com/login.aspx?direct=true&db=bth&AN=20398460&site=ehost-live

Rauch, M. (2006). Will they trust you tomorrow? *Incentive, 180*, 46-48. Retrieved May 13, 2009, from EBSCO online database, Business Source Complete. http://search.ebscohost.com/login.aspx?direct=true&db=bth&AN=23144120&site=ehost-live

Schijns, J. (2008). Customer magazines: An effective weapon in the direct marketing armory. *Journal of International Business & Economics, 8*, 70-78. Retrieved May 12, 2009, from EBSCO online database, Business Source Complete. http://search.

ebscohost.com/login.aspx?direct=true&db=bth&AN=35637613&site=ehost-live

Wang, Yanwen, et al. (2016). Enduring effects of goal achievement and failure within customer loyalty programs: a large-scale field experiment. *Marketing Science*. Retrieved June 29, 2017. http://pubsonline.informs.org/doi/abs/10.1287/mksc.2015.0966

Weiwei, T. (2007). Impact of corporate image and corporate reputation on customer loyalty: A review. *Management Science & Engineering, 1*, 57-62. Retrieved May 13, 2009, from EBSCO online database, Academic Search Complete. http://search.ebscohost.com/login.aspx?direct=true&db=a9h&AN=32826012&site=ehost-live

Wetsch, L. (2005). Trust, satisfaction and loyalty in customer relationship Management: An application of justice theory. *Journal of Relationship Marketing, 4*(3/4), 29. Retrieved May 13, 2009, EBSCO online database, Business Source Complete http://search.ebscohost.com/login.aspx?direct=true&db=bth&AN=27651519&site=ehost-live

Wolfe, D. (2008). TSYS product takes rewards beyond cards. *American Banker, 173*, 8-8. Retrieved May 13, 2009, from EBSCO online database, Business Source Complete. http://search.ebscohost.com/login.aspx?direct=true&db=bth&AN=31568566&site=ehost-live

Wood, A. (2004). Loyalty scheming. *Utility Week, 22*, 35. Retrieved May 13, 2009, from EBSCO online database, Business Source Complete. http://search.ebscohost.com/login.aspx?direct=true&db=bth&AN=14951285&site=ehost-live

Zablah, A., Bellenger, D., & Johnston, W. (2004). Customer relationship management implementation gaps. *Journal of Personal Selling & Sales Management, 24*, 279-295. Retrieved May 13, 2009, from EBSCO online database, Business Source Complete. http://search.ebscohost.com/login.aspx?direct=true&db=bth&AN=16913026&site=ehost-live

Zhang, J., & Bruegelmans, E. (2012). The impact of an item-based loyalty program on consumer purchase behavior. *Journal of Marketing Research, 49*, 50–65. Retrieved November 21, 2013 from EBSCO online database Business Source Premier. http://search.ebscohost.com/login.aspx?direct=true&db=buh&AN=70337969

Michael Erbschloe

CUSTOMER RELATIONSHIP MANAGEMENT (CRM)

ABSTRACT

Customer Relationship Management (CRM) employs people, technology, tools, processes, and activities to increase customer retention and a firm's profitability. Early CRM use was fraught with problems, as many firms applied CRM inappropriately. In recent years, however, firms have become selective and prudent with their CRM investments, and many are now reporting success with CRM.

OVERVIEW

Over the years, management thinking has shifted from a focus on acquiring new customers to an understanding of the importance of retaining customers and the need to build loyalty among these customers (Fitzgibbon & White, 2005). It has been recognized that a company's relationship with its customers is one of its most important assets, and this is all the more important in a climate of high customer turnover, decreasing brand loyalty, and lower profitability. As a result, many organizations are moving away from product-centric and brand-centric marketing and toward a customer-centric approach.

Customers are increasingly viewed in terms of their lifetime value to a firm, rather than being measured simply on the value of an individual transaction. Since customers usually engage in many different types of transactions, and since they vary a great deal as to their wants and needs, firms find the management of their relationships with customers very challenging. Customer relationship management (CRM) has emerged as a way of dealing with the challenges thus posed.

CRM evolved out of the field of relationship marketing, which is based on the premise that lifetime connections with customers are more rewarding and advantageous than a short-term transaction-based relationship. Relationship marketing, which became popular in the 1990s, views the customer as an asset that can be controlled, and one that needs an adequate amount of investment, similar to the requirements of tangible assets (Ryals & Payne, 2001). As such, customer retention therefore produces a major foundation of relationship marketing.

Also referred to as customer relationship marketing and customer loyalty marketing, CRM employs information technology to enforce and execute relationship marketing approaches. Through CRM, marketing appears to have come full-circle in its evolution: from straight sales to mass marketing to target marketing to relationship marketing, and now to CRM, which is on the way to completely allowing true one-on-one marketing (Landry, Arnold & Arndt, 2005).

"CRM is based on the belief that developing a relationship with customers is the best way to make them loyal, and that loyal customers are more profitable than non-loyal customers" (Dowling, 2002, p. 87). It is also believed that tiny improvements in customer retention rates can yield significant increases in profits. The goal is to bring about increased customer retention. According to Hamid & Akhir (2013), technology-based CRM is often implemented but not integrated in customer experience or exploited to enhance customer loyalty. Where data on customer behavior is not only collected but also used to maintain communication and entice return business in the form of special offers, it can be very effective in capturing customer loyalty.

True CRM is driven by organizational strategy and technology. It is relationship-centered and allows firms to align their business processes with their strategies to build customer loyalty and the firm's profits. It "requires a holistic approach so that the information that is held about customers across the organization is drawn together in one central source or at least cross-accessed so that it can be compiled and collated" ("CRM demystified," 2001, p. 4). CRM relies on automated processes and technologies; using information systems, software, and call centers.

There is no universally accepted definition of CRM, probably because it is still in the formative stages of development (Tiemo, 2013). It is not surprising, therefore, that there is much variety in the way CRM has been, and is being, defined. Some see it as a marketing strategy: to them, CRM is the creation of customer strategies and processes supported by technology in order to build customer loyalty (Rigby, Reichheld & Schefter, 2002). Others see CRM as a technology for managing customer information.

Stone and Woodcock (2001) have defined CRM as "methodologies, technologies and e-commerce capabilities used to manage customer relationships." Hobby (1999) defines CRM as "a management approach that enables organizations to identify, attract and increase retention of profitable customers by managing relationships with them." Rigby et al (2002) also define CRM as a mechanism for aligning a firm's business processes with its strategies to build customer loyalty and the firm's profits.

A philosophy or approach encompassing people, technology, tools, processes and activities, CRM appears to be a combination of all the above definitions. Its primary purpose is to help firms understand their customers better, to build relationships with them, and to ensure customer retention and therefore, profitability. CRM's secondary purposes include:

- The identification of a firm's customers
- The creation of customer value
- The management of complex customer relationships
- The adaptation of a firm's customer offerings and communications strategy to different customers
- The cultivation of customer-firm dialogue

A CRM strategy provides an effective way for a firm to advance its revenues by providing the specific services and products that precisely meet the requirements of customers through the design and implementation of programs that effectively allocate the appropriate resources to each customer. A good CRM strategy will also allow a firm to offer superior customer service; cross-sell products more effectively; and allow sales staff to acquire deals at a quicker pace. Current customers will be retained, and future customers will be discovered. Customers will also be segmented based on their needs and their profitability.

APPLICATIONS

Rigby, Reicheld and Schefter (2002) have discovered that by tracking communication between firms and their customers, CRM can help firms in many ways, including the following:

- Analyzing customer revenue and cost data to identify current and future high-value customers
- Targeting direct marketing efforts

- Capturing relevant product and service behavior data
- Creating new distribution channels
- Developing new pricing models
- Processing transactions faster
- Providing better information to the front line
- Managing logistics and the supply chain more efficiently
- Deploying knowledge management systems
- Tracking customer defection and retention levels
- Tracking customer satisfaction levels
- Tracking customer win-back levels

To successfully achieve the above objectives, CRM implementations require a holistic approach that integrates internal leadership (in particular, strong executive and business-unit leadership), cautious strategic preparation, precise performance measures, organizational culture and arrangement, business procedures, and information technologies with outside customer touch points (Eichorn, 2004).

In the design of CRM systems, the first variable to consider is knowledge: by collecting and analyzing information, a firm must first discover its customers' wants, needs, and values. Next, the firm must consider the need for interactivity and personal contact and the way in which the customer wants to be contacted (Ling and Yen, 2001).

By integrating customer management activities across a firm, CRM systems should store detailed information about anticipated and existent customers, in admiration of their buying patterns, shopping behavior and usage tendencies of the firm's products and services. The intelligence collected on a CRM database should include:

- Products and services purchased
- Time and date of purchase (frequency of purchase)
- Price paid
- Method of purchase
- Distribution and shipping
- Delivery date
- Requests for service
- Sales calls
- Customer complaints
- All other customer or company-initiated contact
- Demographic information
- Customer lifestyles and goals

- Detailed information for segmentation and other data evaluation aims
- Response to marketing provocation (that is, whether or not the customer responds to a direct marketing approach, a sales contact, or any other direct association)
- Website use

The collection and processing of data for CRM purposes can be facilitated by self-service technologies, natural language processing, and speech recognition technologies with little or no interaction from company staff. Through e-learning technologies, users can quickly learn how to use new systems and enhancements to existing systems.

All the data collected on a CRM system should be represented over time and must be constantly updated to ensure its accuracy. As information pours in, firms must shift emphasis to the development of analytical tools to help them manage the customer information.

ISSUES

After CRM's initial popularity during the 1990s and into 2000, sales of CRM systems fell drastically when early adopters began to see the technology as another overhyped IT investment whose promises would never be fulfilled (Rigby & Ledingham, 2004). However, by 2004, many of the same senior corporate executives who thought that CRM systems were not producing the desired benefits amid high costs began to indicate satisfaction with their CRM investments, and system sales began to increase. The reason for this change in attitude toward CRM was a change in usage by firms.

Rather than depend on CRM to transform entire businesses, firms began to direct their investments toward resolving particular issues within their customer relationship cycle, which comprises product development, sales, service, retention and win back, and targeting and marketing (Rigby & Ledingham, 2004). A broad range of firms are now effectively taking a sensible, habituated approach to CRM.

Although there is no apparent proof regarding either the characteristics of effective CRM methods or the reasons why CRM might be a potential failure, there appear to be some common mistakes that have been made with CRM. First, in evaluating and designing CRM systems, some firms put technological capabilities over business needs. For these firms, CRM becomes more about managing databases and integrated software systems than customer relationships.

It is now known that when managers allow themselves to be distracted by the many capabilities of CRM software, they are likely to lose sight of what CRM *should* do, both for their firms and their customers. Although a large portion of CRM is technology, viewing CRM as a technology-only solution is likely to fail. It is the level of utilization of the information technology, not the mere adoption of the technology, that produces intended outcomes and drives business performance.

As stated above, for CRM to be really successful, a firm should understand its customers and what characteristics they place most value in over the course of a lifetime. The company must then decide what the customers need most and which methods are most effective in providing those necessities. A failure to integrate or align the underlying business processes with information systems causes a gap that leads to inadequate communication and coordination among the differing departments, fragmented data systems, and dissimilar process flows (Eichorn, 2004). A lack of communication between the various parties in the customer connection chain can give way to an unfinished picture of the customer. Inadequate communication can also reveal the situation where technology is put in place without the appropriate support or buy-in from users.

Another common mistake is when CRM efforts within a firm are concentrated within only one functional area of the firm—usually the marketing department or the information technology department. Such an approach causes CRM strategies to be pursued in a vacuum and rarely considers that nearly all business processes utilize more than one certain area within the firm. It has been realized that more integration among all functional areas leads to better treatment and attention given to the customer.

CRM implementations are unlikely to succeed if they are treated and implemented as isolated projects. To enable the firm to have a single view of the customer, and track every interaction it has had with the customer, CRM must be integrated throughout the entire business.

Although it is not yet easy to install a CRM System, the technology is becoming increasingly reliable, and implementation methods are becoming modernized.

As the CRM failure rate declines, firms "apply CRM with greater precision, targeting critical gaps in their customer relationship cycles where performance suffers. By setting priorities for their information requirements carefully, making sure they are guided by overall customer strategy, firms can embark on CRM efforts that will have a greater impact with lower investment and less risk" (Rigby & Ledingham, 2004, p. 129).

A comprehensive CRM system can theoretically automate each aspect of a firm's connection with its customers. However, "smart companies are focusing their CRM implementations, carefully choosing which segment of the CRM cycle and which functions within that segment are likely to deliver the greatest return on an initial CRM investment. When firms achieve success in this first effort, they often progress to subsequent projects, automating additional functions in the same segment, steadily moving from segment to segment, or even moving to critical business processes beyond CRM" (Rigby & Ledingham, 2004, p. 121).

CRM also fails when corporate executives do not comprehend what they are executing, never mind the cost or time involved. Rigby, et. al. (2002) have identified four average pitfalls that managers encounter when attempting to implement CRM. The first pitfall occurs when CRM is implemented before a customer strategy is created. To begin with, when creating a customer strategy, a firm must work out which customers it wants to network further with and which it does not want to build relationships with based on customer needs, wants, and current and potential value to the firm.

Customer strategy addresses issues of segmentation and marketing. Customer segmentation enables firms to clarify their responses to the various customer groups. A firm may choose to invest in certain segments to re-enforce or initiate profitable relations; to control costs to make lower-margin segments worthy of the time and effort; or to divest unappealing segments. Care should be taken to distinguish between profitable and loyal customers, as not every loyal customer is profitable, and not every profitable customer is loyal. Some firms expensively chase after originally profitable customers who lack the potential of securing future profits due to their lack of loyalty.

By mistaking CRM technology for a marketing strategy, many executives allow the vendors of CRM software to steer their firm's approach to customer management. Similarly, some executives wrongly adapt their customer strategy to match their new CRM technology.

The second management pitfall—and probably the most dangerous—occurs when CRM technology is installed before the firm is made customer-focused. For a firm to enhance its relationships with its most advantageous customers, it needs to first overhaul the crucial business processes that relate to customers, from customer service all the way to order fulfillment. Merely having a strategy will not suffice: there should be a coordinated program in place to combine administrative and methodical changes with the employment of new technologies.

CRM will succeed only after the firm and its processes—job descriptions, performance measures, compensation systems, training programs, and the like—have been restructured in order to better meet customers' needs.

The third pitfall occurs when executives assume that the more the CRM technology, the better their relationships with their customers. Many managers take for granted that CRM must be technology intensive, but this is not so. Customer relationships can be controlled in a number of ways, and the aims of CRM can be actualized without the aid of hearty investments in technology by urging employees to pay more attention to the wants of a customer. Simply depending on a technology-based answer, or believing that a high-tech resolution is preferable to a low-tech one, is a pricey hazard. Low-tech, mid-tech, and high-tech firms alike are experiencing success with CRM.

The fourth pitfall occurs when a firm stalks its customers instead of wooing them. The nature of any investment to increase customer loyalty, whether it involves creating a loyalty card or providing more cash registers, should always depend on the kind of firm and the sorts of relationships the firm and its customers would desire of each other. Types of connections can differ depending on the industry, firm, and customers. Those managers who often ignore these developments while using CRM experience horrible results. Sometimes, it results in attempting to enhance relationships with the wrong customers or attempting to enhance relationships with the right customers but in the wrong way. A failure to develop strong, lasting relationships with customers who value their goods and services may lead to the misfortune of losing those customers.

According to Rigby et al (2002), a firm can increase its chances of CRM success when it carries out the following activities:

- Identification of its most valuable customers
- Calculation of the share of the wallet of the most valuable customers for the firm's goods and services
- Study of the products or services its customers need today and will need tomorrow
- Survey of the products or services its competitors offer today and will offer tomorrow
- Identification of the products or services it should be offering
- Research into the best way to deliver its products and services to customers, including the alliances it needs to strike, the technologies it needs to invest in, and the service capabilities it needs to develop or acquire
- Identification of the tools employees need to foster customer relationships
- Identification of the human resource systems that need to be instituted to boost employee loyalty
- Understanding why customers defect and how to win them back
- Analysis of what competitors are doing to win the firm's high-value customers
- Monitoring of customer-defection patterns by senior management

To conclude, a productive CRM strategy requires a customizable approach for businesses, and as a rule, CRM strategies are anticipated to differ from one company to another (Peppers & Rogers, 1996). A blind imposition of CRM will only reduce a firm's profitability (Peterson, 1999).

BIBLIOGRAPHY

Chapter one: Customer relationship management demystified. (2001). *CustomerRelationship Management*, 1–13. Retrieved March 16, 2007, from EBSCO Online Database Business Source Complete. http://search.ebscohost.com/login.aspx?direct=true&db=bth&AN=22377803&site=ehost-live

Agrawal, M. (2003). Customer relationship management (CRM) & corporate renaissance. *Journal of Services Research, 3*, 149–171. Retrieved March 16, 2007, from EBSCO Online Database Business Source Complete. http://search.ebscohost.com/login.aspx?direct=true&db=bth&AN=11718905&site=ehost-live

Arnett, D., & Badrinarayanan, V. (2005). Enhancing customer-needs-driven CRM strategies: Core selling teams, knowledge management competence, and relationship marketing competence. *Journal of Personal Selling & Sales Management, 25*, 329-343. Retrieved March 16, 2007, from EBSCO Online Database Business Source Complete. http://search.ebscohost.com/login.aspx?direct=true&db=bth&AN=19375595&site=ehost-live

Barnes, J. (1994). Close to the customer: But is it really a relationship? *Journal of Marketing Management, 10*, 561–570. Retrieved March 16, 2007, from EBSCO Online Database Business Source Complete. http://search.ebscohost.com/login.aspx?direct=true&db=bth&AN=13500478&site=ehost-live

Bolton, R. (1998). A dynamic model of the duration of the customer's relationship with a continuous service provider: The role of satisfaction. *Marketing Science, 17*, 45. Retrieved March 16, 2007, from EBSCO Online Database Business Source Complete. http://search.ebscohost.com/login.aspx?direct=true&db=bth&AN=825962&site=ehost-live

Chen, I., & Popovich, K. (2003). Understanding customer relationship management (CRM): People, process and technology. *Business Process Management Journal, 9*, 672–688. Retrieved March 16, 2007, from EBSCO Online Database Business Source Complete. http://search.ebscohost.com/login.aspx?direct=true&db=bth&AN=11429583&site=ehost-live

Conlon, G. (2003). Required reading. *CRM Magazine, 7*, 15. Retrieved March 16, 2007, from EBSCO Online Database Business Source Complete. http://search.ebscohost.com/login.aspx?direct=true&db=bth&AN=10615465&site=ehost-live

Dowling, G. (2002). Customer relationship management: In B2C markets, often less is more. *California Management Review, 44*, 87–104. Retrieved March 16, 2007, from EBSCO Online Database Business Source Complete. http://search.ebscohost.com/login.aspx?direct=true&db=bth&AN=6881770&site=ehost-live

Eichorn, F. (2004). Internal customer relationship management (IntCRM): A framework for achieving customer relationship management from the inside out. *Problems & Perspectives in Management,* 154–177. Retrieved March 16, 2007, from EBSCO Online Database Business Source Complete. http://search.ebscohost.com/login.aspx?direct=true&db=bth&AN=13832492&site=ehost-live

Fitzgibbon, C., & White, L. (2005). The role of attitudinal loyalty in the development of customer relationship management strategy within service firms. *Journal of Financial Services Marketing, 9,* 214–230. Retrieved March 16, 2007, from EBSCO Online Database Business Source Complete. http://search.ebscohost.com/login.aspx?direct=true&db=bth&AN=16402535&site=ehost-live

Fitzpatrick, M. (2004). Keep customers coming back with customized relationship management. *Communication World, 21,* 12. Retrieved March 16, 2007, from EBSCO Online Database Business Source Complete. http://search.ebscohost.com/login.aspx?direct=true&db=bth&AN=15065919&site=ehost-live

Gutek, B., Groth, M., & Cherry, B. (2002). Achieving service success through relationships and enhanced encounters. *Academy of Management Executive, 16,* 132–144. Retrieved March 16, 2007, from EBSCO Online Database Business Source Complete. http://search.ebscohost.com/login.aspx?direct=true&db=bth&AN=8951340&site=ehost-live

Hamid, N., & Akhir, R. (2013). Beyond technology-based customer relationship management - it is total customer experience management. *Research in Business & Economics Journal,* 81–15. Retrieved October 31, 2013, from EBSCO Online Database Business Source Complete. http://search.ebscohost.com/login.aspx?direct=true&db=bth&AN=90440226&site=ehost-live

Harness, D., & Harness, T. (2004). The new customer relationship management tool—product elimination? *Service Industries Journal, 24,* 67–80. Retrieved March 16, 2007, from EBSCO Online Database Business Source Complete. http://search.ebscohost.com/login.aspx?direct=true&db=bth&AN=14352907&site=ehost-live

Hobby, J. (1999). Looking after the one who matters. *Accountancy Age,* 28–30.

Karantinou, K. (2005). Customer relationship management. *Blackwell Encyclopedic Dictionary of Marketing,* 1–88. Retrieved March 16, 2007, from EBSCO Online Database Business Source

Complete. http://search.ebscohost.com/login.aspx?direct=true&db=bth&AN=14840507&site=ehost-live

Kim, J., Choi, J., Qualls, W., & Park, J. (2004). The impact of CRM on firm- and relationship-level performance in distribution networks. *Communications of AIS, 2004,* 632–652. Retrieved March 16, 2007, from EBSCO Online Database Business Source Complete. http://search.ebscohost.com/login.aspx?direct=true&db=bth&AN=16744505&site=ehost-live

Kumar, V., Sunder, S., & Ramaseshan, B. (2011). Analyzing the diffusion of global customer relationship management: a cross-regional modeling framework. *Journal of International Marketing, 19,* 23–39. Retrieved October 31, 2013, from EBSCO Online Database Business Source Complete. http://search.ebscohost.com/login.aspx?direct=true&db=bth&AN=58009554&site=ehost-live

Landry, T., Arnold, T., & Arndt, A. (2005). A compendium of sales-related literature in customer relationship management: Processes and technologies with managerial implications. *Journal of Personal Selling & Sales Management, 25,* 231–251. Retrieved March 16, 2007, from EBSCO Online Database Business Source Complete. http://search.ebscohost.com/login.aspx?direct=true&db=bth&AN=18617604&site=ehost-live

Ling, R., & Yen, D. (2001). Customer relationship management: An analysis framework and implementation strategies. *Journal of Computer Information Systems, 41,* 82. Retrieved March 16, 2007, from EBSCO Online Database Business Source Complete. http://search.ebscohost.com/login.aspx?direct=true&db=bth&AN=5094389&site=ehost-live

Nelson, M. (2003). R M needs to shift focus back to customers. *Marketing News, 37,* 41–46. Retrieved March 16, 2007, from EBSCO Online Database Business Source Complete. http://search.ebscohost.com/login.aspx?direct=true&db=bth&AN=11202716&site=ehost-live

Peppers, D. & Rogers, M. (1996). *The one-to-one future: Building relationships with one customer at a time.* New York City, NY: Doubleday.

Peterson, G. (1999). Customer relationship management systems: ROI and results measurement. *Strategic Sales Performance,* March.

Plakoyiannaki, E. (2005). How Do Organisational Members Perceive CRM? Evidence from a U.K.

Service Firm. *Journal of Marketing Management, 21*(3/4), 363–392. Retrieved March 16, 2007, from EBSCO Online Database Business Source Complete. http://search.ebscohost.com/login.aspx?direct=true&db=bth&AN=16845177&site=ehost-live

Rad, H. S., Ghorabi, M., Rafiee, M., & Rad, V. S. (2015). Electronic customer relationship management: Opportunities and challenges of digital world. *International Journal Of Management, Accounting & Economics, 2*(6), 609–619. Retrieved December 3, 2015 from EBSCO Online Database Business Source Premier. http://search.ebscohost.com/login.aspx?direct=true&db=buh&AN=110457118&site=bsi-live

Reinartz, W., & Kumar, V. (2002). The mismanagement of customer loyalty. *Harvard Business Review, 80*, 86–94. Retrieved March 16, 2007, from EBSCO Online Database Business Source Complete. http://search.ebscohost.com/login.aspx?direct=true&db=bth&AN=14365033&site=ehost-live

Reinartz, W., Krafft, M., & Hoyer, W. (2004). The customer relationship management process: Its measurement and impact on performance. *Journal of Marketing Research (JMR), 41*, 293–305. Retrieved March 16, 2007, from EBSCO Online Database Business Source Complete. http://search.ebscohost.com/login.aspx?direct=true&db=bth&AN=6899224&site=ehost-live

Rigby, D., & Ledingham, D. (2004). CRM done right. *Harvard Business Review, 82*, 118–129. Retrieved March 16, 2007, from EBSCO Online Database Business Source Complete. http://search.ebscohost.com/login.aspx?direct=true&db=bth&AN=14874833&site=ehost-live

Rigby, D., Reichheld, F., & Schefter, P. (2002). Avoid the four perils of CRM. *Harvard Business Review, 80*, 101–109. Retrieved March 16, 2007, from EBSCO Online Database Business Source Complete. http://search.ebscohost.com/login.aspx?direct=true&db=bth&AN=6026539&site=ehost-live

Ryals, L. (2003). Making customers pay: measuring and managing customer risk and returns. *Journal of Strategic Marketing, 11*, 165. Retrieved March 16, 2007, from EBSCO Online Database Business Source Complete. http://search.ebscohost.com/login.aspx?direct=true&db=bth&AN=11093346&site=ehost-live

Ryals, L., & Payne, A. (2001). Customer relationship management in financial services: towards information-enabled relationship marketing. *Journal of Strategic Marketing, 9*, 3–27. Retrieved March 16, 2007, from EBSCO Online Database Business Source Complete. http://search.ebscohost.com/login.aspx?direct=true&db=bth&AN=4782035&site=ehost-live

Stone, M., & Woodcock, N. (2001), Defining CRM and assessing its quality. In M. Stone & B. Foss, *Successful customer relationship marketing* (pp. 3–21). Bath: Bath Press.

Stone, M., Woodcock, N., & Wilson, M. (1996). Managing the change from marketing planning to customer relationship management. *Long Range Planning, 29*, 675–683. Retrieved March 16, 2007, from EBSCO Online Database Business Source Complete. http://search.ebscohost.com/login.aspx?direct=true&db=bth&AN=12422285&site=ehost-live

Thomas, J., Blattberg, R., & Fox, E. (2004). Recapturing lost customers. *Journal of Marketing Research (JMR), 41*, 31–45. Retrieved March 16, 2007, from EBSCO Online Database Business Source Complete. http://search.ebscohost.com/login.aspx?direct=true&db=bth&AN=11925402&site=ehost-live

Tiemo, A. J. (2013). Conceptualizing customer relationship management using a descriptive approach. *Journal of Emerging Trends in Economics & Management Sciences, 4*, 337–342. Retrieved October 31, 2013, from EBSCO Online Database Business Source Complete. http://search.ebscohost.com/login.aspx?direct=true&db=bth&AN=90267133&site=ehost-live

Verhoef, P. (2003). Understanding the effect of customer relationship management efforts on customer retention and customer share development. *Journal of Marketing, 67*, 30–45. Retrieved March 16, 2007, from EBSCO Online Database Business Source Complete. http://search.ebscohost.com/login.aspx?direct=true&db=bth&AN=11235600&site=ehost-live

Winer, R. (2001). A framework for customer relationship management. *California Management Review, 43*, 89–105. Retrieved March 16, 2007, from EBSCO Online Database Business Source Complete. http://search.ebscohost.com/login.aspx?direct=true&db=bth&AN=5244752&site=ehost-live

SUGGESTED READING

Buttle, F., & Maklan, S. (2015). *Customer relationship management: concepts and technologies* (3rd ed.). New York City, NY: Taylor & Francis.

Peppers, D., & and Rogers, M., (1999). *The one to one manager: Real world lessons in customer relationship management.* New York City, NY: Currency Doubleday.

Reinartz, W., & Kumar, V. (2002). The mismanagement of customer loyalty. *Harvard Business Review, 80,* 86–94. Retrieved March 16, 2007, from EBSCO Online Database Business Source Complete. http://search.ebscohost.com/login.aspx?direct=true&db=bth&AN=14365033&site=ehost-live

Radut, Carmen and Spinciu, Marius. (2016). Customer loyalty using customer relationship management. *Strategii Manageriale.* Retrieved on June 29, 2017. http://www.strategiimanageriale.ro/papers/160138.pdf

Rigby, D., & Ledingham, D. (2004). CRM done right. *Harvard Business Review, 82,* 118–129. Retrieved March 16, 2007, from EBSCO Online Database Business Source Complete. http://search.ebscohost.com/login.aspx?direct=true&db=bth&AN=14874833&site=ehost-live

Rigby, D., Reichheld, F., & Schefter, P. (2002). Avoid the four perils of CRM. *Harvard Business Review, 80,* 101–109. Retrieved March 16, 2007, from EBSCO Online Database Business Source Complete. http://search.ebscohost.com/login.aspx?direct=true&db=bth&AN=6026539&site=ehost-live

Vanessa A. Tetteh, Ph.D.

CUSTOMER SERVICE

ABSTRACT

Customer service refers to the specific protocols a company follows in dealing with a customer or client in an effort to maximize customer expectations and keep the customer satisfied as a way to ensure that customer's return business. Customer service covers interactions with customers before services are engaged, during the actual transaction in which the customer offers remuneration for a good or service, and, perhaps most important, after the purchase to help customers through any issues that might arise in connection with the goods or service. Customer service is key to building a company brand in a competitive marketplace.

OVERVIEW

Company pledges to provide customers with complete satisfaction seek to assure buyers with an upfront guarantee that they will be happy with their purchase. Indeed, the trials and tribulations of customer service representatives and the trials and tribulations of customers with complaints have become a staple of comedy. The participants in the customer service dynamic have long been reduced to convenient stereotypes and caricatures: Service reps are indifferent, inefficient, slow, snarky, or patronizing; customers are frazzled, confused, harried, not terribly bright, or impatient—and the inevitable inability to resolve the issues brings in a solicitous and inevitably useless supervisor.

Indeed, company guarantees and return policies are often carefully worded customer service policies that appear designed to entangle the customer in rhetorical devices that create loopholes for the company to avoid actually responding to the claim. Sometimes, however, customers may expect a greater degree of accommodation that offered by company policies. For example, the customer would like to return an item but does not have a receipt. The customer does not have the appropriate packaging. The customer is not even sure if the product was actually purchased from the merchant. The customer is really not entirely sure how to operate the product or understands exactly what the product does. Unscrupulous customers lie, and customers can be mistaken.

According to the U.S. Small Business Administration, 72 percent of customers leave a business—whether a restaurant or an airline, a department store or a car repair facility, a grocery chain or an electronics store—directly because of their dissatisfaction with customer service. That means that more than reasonable prices, inventory supplies, efficient service, or even location, customers decide on continuing an association with a company based on how that company handles its customers. The bottom line for businesses, whatever the size of the operation, is simple common sense: It is far cheaper to maintain customer loyalty than to attract entirely new customers. Repeat business keeps businesses in operation.

Word-of-mouth, referrals, and the wide range of customer review platforms available on the Internet make customer service critical. Rather than pursue new customers through elaborate marketing campaigns or saturation advertising, businesses recognize that customer service is the most cost-effective strategy for maintaining profits and expanding revenues. Given the mobile nature of the customer base and that opportunities for securing any good or service are redundant, particularly with the availability of the Internet and company websites, businesses have begun to revisit customer services and the best protocols for addressing customer questions and concerns before, during, and after a purchase is completed.

Customers believe they are entitled to service. When a product malfunctions, when service is slipshod or unprofessional, when guarantees are not met, when goods or services have been overcharged—in short whenever the customer feels slighted—that customer transforms from a customer in search of a product to a complainant in search of redress. At the center of customer service, then, is not the company's need to maintain the integrity of a sale but rather the need of customers simply to be heard, to have their questions answered; their frustrations understood; their emotional range accepted as valid, even reasonable; and ultimately their needs addressed.

Since the advent of Internet customer review platforms, businesses have begun to integrate customer service into the protocol of the business itself. Rather than marginalizing customer service, customer satisfaction emerged as a defining quality of a business. Dissatisfied customers are critical, even inevitable in a business, but they are still customers until through inattention or poorly articulated customer service policies that customer becomes an ex-customer. Customer complaint windows and quick-fix customer complaints cards were displaced as businesses developed entire departments geared exclusively to developing and instituting listening techniques and ways to effectively respond to what is always,

almost by definition, a unique customer interaction. Customers with a question or a complaint or a claim brings to that interaction their history, their emotional makeup, their closed set of expectations, and their particular life situations (Amoako et al., 2016).

Human resources advisory companies in the business of designing effective customer service strategies became elements of the consumer marketplace. Businesses engaged these services, attended their seminars, enlisted their personnel, many of them grounded in behavioral psychology, to come onsite, observe customer service practices, and then help their associates understand the nature and value of a complaint dynamic. Customer service reps were schooled in ways to effectively read a customer's facial features, gestures, inflections, and hand motions as a way to understand the depth and nature of the interaction, strategies for efficient and effective listening, and ways to quick-think solutions, ways to make sure the interaction itself does not make it worse.

Customer service is far more challenging in the digital age as customer service procedures can be conducted entirely through written communications—emails or web postings—or via phone calls, in which deciphering mood, emotions, and intention is far more complicated than in face-to-face interactions. The goal, however, is the same. Let the customer interaction stay centered on the original complaint. Businesses have begun to create protocols to ensure that how customer service is handled does not become, in turn, a whole new problem.

The failure of customer service interactions, after all, could lead to far worse consequences than losing business. A company's reputation can be widely and permanently damaged through Internet customer response platforms. Companies can face litigation stemming from poorly articulated or poorly delivered customer service or investigation from oversight agencies such as the Better Business Bureau (BBB). Ultimately, the accumulated incidents create about a company the reputation of not helping customers, which can in the worst-case scenario actually close that business.

Increasingly, accumulating data and customer research conducted by independent business agencies indicate that effective customer service can no longer be an afterthought for a business. Effective customer negotiations begin from the moment a customer initially indicates an interest in a company's goods or services, service representatives respond politely and confidently to whatever questions they might have, all the way to the point at which the customer is happy with the negotiation. Thus, de facto any business—from a hotel to a hospital, from a shoe store to a software developer—is in the business of customer service. It is imperative to create an effective dynamic in which both the customer and the service representative are both empowered to follow a civil and diplomatic protocol and close on a largely positive solution.

APPLICATIONS

Although there are startup firms that specialize in sophisticated workshops that claim to illuminate the "reality" of customer service, offering pat strategies for successful customer service, the reality is that effective customer service really relies on basic common sense ground rules that define any kind of conversation dynamic, whatever the subject. A customer needs to explain clearly his or her concern. The customer service rep needs to listen with unbiased ears and not make false assumptions about customer motives (Morgen, 2016).

The problem, like all problems, has a number of potential solutions. The two parties need to find the common ground upon which they can reach a mutually satisfying arrangement. Both parties should feel free to stay in touch at least long enough to assure them both that the solution has, indeed, worked. For companies that provide effective customer service—and among companies known for providing critical help support are Apple, Amazon, Walmart, Nordstrom, Disney, Southwest Airlines, Comfort Inn, Wendy's, Humana Health Services, Zappos—the process begins and ends with three basic, even obvious skills: patience, quick thinking, and positivity.

The customer service representative needs not only people skills—that is, those skills directly involved with communication such as eye contact, smiling, and voice modulation—but also the ability to approach an essentially negative interaction with a positive attitude and a calm willingness to sort through the particulars of a problem or a question without distracting asides or redundant gestures. Patience allows the customer service dynamic to find its own pace. Indeed, Jouini and colleagues (2016) actually devised a mathematical formula for deriving

the dimensions of patience needed in particular customer service transactions.

In addition, effective customer service requires quick thinking, the talent for spontaneity and ad libbing—that is, an ability to talk carefully (any word might potentially trigger a far more complicated emotional response) but to think fast and arrive at appropriate solutions. Although the successful customer service engagement, whether through emails or website exchanges, direct face-to-face confrontations or conservations over the phone, involves long-term solutions, the actual customer service negotiation is conducted in a pressing environment of immediate action.

Finally, effective customer service requires positivity, the ability to think and talk in language that builds a sense that solutions are possible, doable, and realistic without seeming patronizing or solicitous. If, for example, an airline is facing massive delays because a trunk line is clogged because of poor weather conditions, an unsatisfactory response might be to tell a customer, "We can't do anything about this bad weather. You are not going anywhere before tomorrow morning, and even then it is not a guarantee. We can't do anything about it." The phrasing deploys multiple negative constructions. An effective customer service representative will address the problem without assuming an adversarial posture: "Yes, we have a problem. We understand your inconvenience. We apologize. The airline is doing everything in its power to keep operations on time overnight. Full operations are expected before dawn." The rep does not lie, the rep does not misrepresent, the rep does not patronize. The negotiation remains upbeat, compassionate, and caring, though the news is no different.

Indeed, businesses explore strategies for maintaining positivity in its customer service negotiations, how to use language to create the possibility of timely and effective resolution. Should the customer service negotiation prove to be moving nevertheless into confrontation and exasperation, the positivity strategy indicates that the customer service rep needs to move the issue (and the customer) to a supervisor, allowing the new face (or voice) to begin again the negotiation with higher stakes. In any event, the customer service dynamic remains positive—somewhere in this, there is a strategy for solution.

Thus, customer service moves from concerns over the product and the sale and focuses on the business and how it conducts business. As Agugliaro (2016) advised business owners, "Make your customers' problems your problems and seek to provide a solution."

VIEWPOINTS

If there is a glitch in this new, evolving customer service dynamic, experts argue, that problem most often arises from what is termed the "human factor"—that is, the essentially unpredictable element of the negotiation inevitable because the customer service rep is, well, a human and given to unlicensed responses, snap judgments, unfocused words, impulsive emotions, and poorly considered phrasing. In fact, customer service reps are among the jobs that are impacted the most by turnover—reps grow weary or frustrated with handling complaints all day. In response to this, companies have begun to investigate the potential for so-called chatbots, response networks that use artificial intelligence software to actually conduct the initial negotiation with customers who use the phone (nearly 3 to 1 the preferred communication avenue for customer service) (Dobocan, 2016).

The communication devices are cheaper and more reliable in some ways than human reps. The customer is fed through a series of questions that use push-button technology to indicate answers until after the machine devises the specific nature of the complaint actually engages the customer in what appears to be actual conversation, offering choices and further information as a way to remediate the problem. Although long seen as an impediment to effective customer service, the emergence of a generation comfortable with computer interactions may enable chatbots to exceed human reps at moving toward a solution, because emotions and the misunderstandings and distractions they can cause are neatly and entirely skirted—at least as far as the chatbot is concerned. Businesses, particularly major department store retailers who must contend with convenience of Internet shopping, have created shopping apps in which customers can have questions answered before or after a purchase (Pitsker, 2016).

In the end, the emerging field of customer service has created something called the product experience, which includes ensuring the product or service meets customer expectations, whatever the level of those expectations. Indeed, customer service research indicates that customers value the follow-up inquiry—the company contacting the person days or weeks after the customer service negotiation to check that the customer is pleased with both the solution and how that negotiation was conducted—even more than the solution itself. Letting the customer know his or her complaint served as a specific evaluation of current company protocols and the company's specific and directed response indicates its desire to not only satisfy a single customer but also provide all its customers with better, more effective service.

BIBLIOGRAPHY

Agugliaro, M. (2016). 4 customer service strategies that create bottom—Line results. *HVACR Distribution Business*, 24. Retrieved October 23, 2016, from EBSCO Online Database Business Source Ultimate. http://search.ebscohost.com/login.aspx?direct=true&db=bsu&AN=120014101&site=ehost-live

Amoako, G. K., Dzogbenuku, R. K., & Doe, J. K. (2016). How service experience leads to brand loyalty: Perspective from the telecom sector in Ghana. *IUP Journal of Brand Management*, *13*(2), 33–56. Retrieved October 23, 2016, from EBSCO Online Database Business Source Ultimate. http://search.ebscohost.com/login.aspx?direct=true&db=bsu&AN=117397839&site=ehost-live

Banyte, J., Gadeikiene, A., Rutelione, A., & Kakneviciene, I. (2016). Expression of personalization while developing long-term relationships with service customers. *Engineering Economics*, *27*(4), 462–471. Retrieved October 23, 2016, from EBSCO Online Database Business Source Ultimate. http://search.ebscohost.com/login.aspx?direct=true&db=bsu&AN=119212060&site=ehost-live

Christopher, M. (1986). Reaching the customer: Strategies for marketing and customer service. *Journal of Marketing Management*, *2*(1), 63–71. Retrieved October 23, 2016, from EBSCO Online Database Business Source Ultimate. http://search.ebscohost.com/login.aspx?direct=true&db=bsu&AN=114780067&site=ehost-live

Dobocan, A. (2016). Get on the Train. *Cabinet Maker*, (6007), 27. Retrieved October 23, 2016, from EBSCO Online Database Business Source Ultimate. http://search.ebscohost.com/login.aspx?direct=true&db=bsu&AN=120090903&site=ehost-live

Jouini, O., Koole, G., & Roubos, A. (2013). Performance indicators for call centers with impatient customers. *IIE Transactions*, *45*(3), 341–354.

Retrieved October 23, 2016, from EBSCO Online Database Business Source Ultimate. http://search.ebscohost.com/login.aspx?direct=true&db=bsu&AN=84423220&site=ehost-live

Morgen, S. D. (2016). The skills of kindness: A guide for sellers, coaches, leaders and facilitators. *Personal Excellence Essentials, 21*(5), 22–23. Retrieved October 23, 2016, from EBSCO Online Database Business Source Ultimate. http://search.ebscohost.com/login.aspx?direct=true&db=bsu&AN=115245385&site=ehost-live

Pitsker, K. (2016). There's more to the mall than shopping. *Kiplinger's Personal Finance, 70*(12), 13–14. Retrieved October 23, 2016, from EBSCO Online Database Business Source Ultimate. http://search.ebscohost.com/login.aspx?direct=true&db=bsu&AN=118766837&site=ehost-live

Suggested Reading

Brcic, J., & Latham, G. (2016). The effect of priming affect on customer service satisfaction. *Academy of Management Discoveries, 2*(4), 392–403. Retrieved October 23, 2016, from EBSCO Online Database Business Source Ultimate. http://search.ebscohost.com/login.aspx?direct=true&db=bsu&AN=120332330&site=ehost-live

Huston, D. (2016). Priceline's CEO on creating an in-house multilingual customer service operation. *Harvard Business Review, 94*(4), 37–40. Retrieved October 23, 2016, from EBSCO Online Database Business Source Ultimate. http://search.ebscohost.com/login.aspx?direct=true&db=bsu&AN=113934208&site=ehost-live

Khan, N., & Steinberg, H. (2016). Customer service, cultural differences, & the big 5 in Great Britain and India. *Allied Academies International Conference: Proceedings of the Academy of Marketing Studies, 21*(2), 19–23. Retrieved October 23, 2016, from EBSCO Online Database Business Source Ultimate. http://search.ebscohost.com/login.aspx?direct=true&db=bsu&AN=120015004&site=ehost-live

Mondal, R., & Steinberg, H. (2016). Accounting customer service, cultural differences, & the big 5 in China and the USA. *Allied Academies International Conference: Proceedings of the Academy of Accounting & Financial Studies, 21*(2), 17–21. Retrieved October 23, 2016, from EBSCO Online Database Business Source Ultimate. http://search.ebscohost.com/login.aspx?direct=true&db=bsu&AN=120015233&site=ehost-live

Piccoli, Gabriele, et al. (2016). The impact of IT-enabled customer service systems on service personalizations, customer service perceptions, and hotel performance. *Tourism Management, 59*, 349-362. Retrieved on June 29, 2017.

Joseph Dewey, Ph.D.

D

DIRECT E-MARKETING

ABSTRACT

Advances in Internet technology and use have created a new channel for businesses to market their goods and services. E-marketing is an evolving discipline in which the Internet is used as the medium for a business's marketing efforts, such as selling goods and services or collecting information about the needs and desires of potential customers. E-marketing can include pay-per-click advertising, banner ads, mass emailings, websites, blogging, and social media. Many tools are available to help businesses increase the traffic to their websites and provide information about the users who view them. However, as these tools allow more and more data to be collected about the user, there is an increasing need to develop enforceable guidelines that balance the needs of the business with the privacy needs of the user.

OVERVIEW

What Is Direct Marketing?

In 1989, the movie *Field of Dreams* introduced the saying, "if you build it, he will come." Although a great tag line in conversation, in the marketing discipline this philosophy has little relevance. Merely having a great product is usually not sufficient to ensure its success in the marketplace. The target market must know that the product or service is available, what customer need the product or service fulfills, and how the product or service is superior to or a better investment than the products or services offered by competitors. To do this, a company needs to market, whether through such activities as simple word of mouth or through major multichannel marketing campaigns; or anything in between.

Direct marketing is a customer relationship management strategy in which the provider of the product or service delivers the promotional message directly to potential customers on a one-to-one basis rather than through the use of mass media. Direct marketing is often a part of a business's marketing mix, or the combination of product, price, place, and promotion that is used to get a product into the hands of the consumer. One of the primary tasks of the marketing function with an organization is to optimize the mix to best position the product for success in the marketplace. With the advent of the Internet, the strategic marketing plans of many businesses have been expanded to include the channel of electronic marketing (e-marketing).

E-Marketing

E-marketing is a relatively new and evolving discipline in which the Internet is used as the medium for a company or an organization's marketing efforts to sell goods and services as well as to collect information about the needs and desires of potential customers. E-marketing can include pay-per-click advertising, banner ads, mass emailings, websites, blogging, and social media.

Using Email

Perhaps the most obvious approach to electronic marketing is through email. In theory, the marketing of a product or service through this channel is simple: Just send out email advertisements to every potential consumer that can be identified, usually from a list purchased through a third party, to increase the exposure of the business's goods or services. Unlike sending out hard-copy advertisements, this approach does not incur an expense for each additional person contacted. Emails can be sent announcing upcoming sales or other promotional events, distributing online coupons for recipients (typically for ordering over the Internet, also called e-commerce), or with electronic newsletters that include short articles of interest to readers, updates on the business's projects and programs, and links to the business's website or blog.

However, for many reasons, this approach is often neither usable nor viable. As the use of the Internet has grown (making it a more attractive medium for marketing), so has its misuse. Mass unsolicited emails (i.e., spam) are often used by cybercriminals to spread computer viruses and spyware. Even when emails are harmless and sent with the best of intentions, if unsolicited, they are likely to be viewed as nuisances by the recipient. According to a 2013 report from IT security firm Kaspersky Lab, about 69.6 percent of emails sent that year were spam (Gudkova, 2014). Further, 3.2 percent of emails contained some sort of malicious attachment. Based on the influx of spam into our daily email boxes, there is no evidence to believe that this trend will reverse. To reduce the amount of spam received, most email software and Web-based email, such as Google Mail, include spam filters to block the most obvious cases of spam. This means that even well-meaning marketing emails may fail to get through to their intended recipients if the latter did not request them.

FURTHER INSIGHTS

Direct marketing on the Internet has become increasingly complicated. Typically, it is important to most businesses to have a website or other Internet presence to be competitive. No matter how well designed, however, a passive website is unlikely to bring in much new business. To be effective, a website needs to be well designed, and potential customers need to know about it and visit it. Fortunately, for

those businesses trying to market their goods and services, there are tools available to help them identify who is actually interested in their offerings and to drive them to their websites.

Search-Engine Marketing

One approach to improving an organization's return on investment for marketing activities is to attempt to drive traffic from search engines to the website based on the words input by the user. Search-engine marketing targets potential customers on the Internet who input specified keywords into a search engine that then directs them to the business's website. Search-engine marketing tools include paid ads (typically with hyperlinks) on the results pages of search engines, and search-engine optimization. Banner ads are a type of Internet advertising that can be used in this way. These ads may be placed on search results pages or on the websites of related but noncompeting organizations. Banner ads, as the name suggests, are spread across the top of a website and direct viewers to the business's website through the use of a hyperlink.

Many websites and search-engine results pages also sell space for the inclusion of other hyperlinked ads. Like physical advertising, online advertisements can be purchased in a number of different ways, including as a onetime advertisement for a set period of time (e.g., one week, three months). A novel approach enabled by Internet technology is the pay per click ad. Payment to the host page for this type of ad is not based on the time that the ad is posted on the site, but by the amount of traffic that the ad actually drives to the business's site. The business purchasing the ad only pays the host for the times that a user is redirected to the business's website by clicking on the hyperlink in the ad.

Search-Engine Optimization

Another way to help drive traffic to one's website is to increase the probability that a search engine will include the business's site in its results-page listings for desired keywords and place the site prominently in the results pages. This approach is called search-engine optimization. Search-engine optimization includes such techniques as adjusting the content of the website to distinguish it from similar websites, correctly indexing the website, using the best keywords to describe the website, and ensuring that the content of the website is unique. There are a number of free online tools available to optimize one's results in search engines. These software tools help determine what words and phrases are most likely to be used by potential customers searching for the goods or services offered by a given business so that these can be included in the website design. Online tools are also available for helping to determine whether or not too many keywords are included; in which case a website may be banned from desirable search engines (Solomon, 2010).

Google

One of the best known search engines is Google. In addition to allowing users to perform keyword searches, Google also offers a suite of tools to help website designers and marketers optimize the effectiveness of their websites. One of the best known tools for helping a business understand the traffic on its website and the effectiveness of its online marketing strategy is Google Analytics (http://www.google.com/analytics/). This free service helps marketers better understand what kind of person is visiting the business's website. Google Analytics summarizes key metrics about how the site is used by visitors and the keywords they used to get there. In addition, Google Insights for Search helps marketers determine which keywords can optimize the number of visitors to their website. Google Display Planner is a tool to help marketers determine the best websites to place their ads.

Cookies & Web Bugs

Although search-engine optimization and web analytics tools can help marketers be more active in marketing efforts through their websites, other, more proactive tools exist, including cookies and web bugs. These tools help marketers capture data regarding how the website is used or how a viewer responds to an email advertisement. These data can then be mined to better understand the effectiveness of the site and improve its performance. Cookies are small, unique text files created by a website and sent to the user's hard drive to record a user's activities on the site (Harding, Reed, & Gray, 2001). Web bugs (also referred to as Web beacons, pixel tags, or clear GIFs) are images included on a website that track the activity on the site. While simultaneously retrieving an image for display on the screen, the beacon also transmits information back to the site (e.g., browser used to retrieve the image, IP address of the viewer's computer, when and for how long the image was viewed). Turning off cookies on the viewer's computer can prevent personal information from being transmitted. However, nonpersonal information will still be transmitted back to the website or third-party monitor of the beacon.

According to Harding, Reed, and Gray (2001), when a user returns to a website, the cookie passes information back to the server concerning the user's activities on the site. This allows the business to target ads to the interests of the user, prevent repetitive ads, and get a higher "click-through" rate. Web bugs have a wider goal and track the number of people in various regions that have accessed the website. This allows a business to manage its website to optimize the content for the users it attracts. Web bugs also allow businesses to build personal profiles of individuals and the sites they have visited. Through data mining, the business can better focus advertising to that user. When web bugs are included in emails, they can be used to not only determine when an email was viewed but also provide the business with the IP address of the viewer even if the viewer does not want to give out that information. Web bugs in emails can also provide the business with information on how often an email was forwarded and read. This information can help marketers gauge the effectiveness of their marketing campaign.

ISSUES
Privacy Concerns

Although technology currently exists that allows the collection of data to better focus online marketing efforts and reach larger numbers of potential customers at lesser cost than ever before, many question how appropriate—or even ethical—such approaches are. As advances in technology continue to support the collection of increasing amounts of personal information, users are increasingly becoming concerned about privacy. In the context of marketing and information technology, this refers not only to the safe storage and dissemination of personal information but also to the legitimacy of collecting information without the subjects' approval in the first place. In the United States, there are a number of laws in place that protect privacy. The Privacy Act of 1974 allows individuals to determine what information others may collect about them and prevents the collectors of such information from using it for a purpose other than the one for which it was collected. This act also allows individuals to have access to the data collected about them and gives them the right to correct or amend faulty records. Under this act, if the organization or individual collecting the data willfully or intentionally violates these rights, they can be sued in civil court. In 1986, the Electronic Communications Privacy Act (ECPA) mandated the protection of privacy of emails sent through public networks (Senn, 2004).

Another privacy concern for Internet users is the receipt of unsolicited email (spam) that has been sent en masse to email addresses acquired from mailing lists. Although the sender is hoping to acquire new customers through spamming, recipients typically view spam as an unwanted nuisance. However, not all unsolicited emails are actually spam. Many websites have a check box (typically already checked) that gives the sender permission to send the recipient emails. Unless the recipient notices this box and unchecks it when registering, he or she will automatically receive emails. Sometimes, this is carried a step further and the business assumes that the recipient is interested in receiving marketing emails merely because that person registered with the site or purchased something from the company. In both these cases, it is good practice to allow the recipient the option to refuse further emails (Senn, 2004). Typically, a statement is included near the bottom of the email that says that the business values the recipient's privacy and either requests that the recipient send an email with the word "unsubscribe" in the subject line or includes a hyperlink that allows the recipient to opt out on the business's website.

Another ethical consideration for online marketing is the use of web bugs. Although these tools are intended for legitimate use by marketers and others interested in the visitors to their website, spammers also use web bugs for less legitimate purposes. In an attempt to allay concerns over privacy and other issues arising from the use of web bugs and to balance the needs of businesses with the needs of potential customers, the Network Advertising Initiative (NAI) has developed guidelines for the use of web bugs. According to these guidelines, online advertisers using web bugs should disclose how web bugs are being used on their site and why they are using them (Marcum, 2003). The initiative's website (http://www.networkadvertising.org/) also allows consumers to opt-out of targeted advertising from all its members.

As Internet use continues to grow, an increasing number of businesses will be likely to include e-marketing efforts in their strategic marketing plans. However, as Internet use rises, abuse is likely to rise, too. It is doubtful that voluntary guidelines are likely to solve the ethical problems of e-marketing. However, they are a good start.

CONCLUSION

The Internet has become not only a source of information, but also a new channel for marketing a business's goods and services. As Internet technologies continue to advance, new and better ways to market online are likely to be developed. However, with increased use typically comes increased abuse. In particular, as tools are developed to help businesses market more effectively online, users become more concerned with issues of privacy. Better policies and regulations are needed to keep the needs of the business and the needs of the customer in balance.

BIBLIOGRAPHY
Enterprise-class web analytics made smarter, friendlier and free. (2010). *Google Analytics*. Retrieved 19 August 2010 from Google http://www.google.com/analytics/

Cochran, B. (2014). How to maximize your e-mail marketing efforts. *Global Cosmetic Industry*, 40-41. Retrieved November 11, 2014, from EBSCO Online Database Business Source Complete http://search.ebscohost.com/login.aspx?direct=true&db=bth&AN=99092424

Gudkova, Darya (2014). *Kaspersky security bulletin. Spam evolution 2013.* Retrieved from http://securelist.com/analysis/kaspersky-security-bulletin/58274/kaspersky-security-bulletin-spam-evolution-2013/

Harding, W. T., Reed, A. J., & Gray, R. L. (2001). Cookies and web bugs: What they are and how they work together. *Information Systems Management, 18,* 17-24. Retrieved 19 August 2010 from EBSCO Online Database Business Source Complete http://search.ebscohost.com/login.aspx?direct=true&db=bth&AN=4549415&site=ehost-live

Kaplan, A. M., & Haenlein, M. (2010). Users of the world, unite! The challenges and opportunities of social media. *Business Horizons, 53,* 59-68. Retrieved November 15, 2013, from EBSCO Online Database Business Source Complete http://search.ebscohost.com/login.aspx?direct=true&db=bth&AN=45641953&site=ehost-live

Lee, C. K. (2012). The Rise, Fall, and Return of E-Marketing Curriculum: A Call for Integration. *Business Education Innovation Journal, 4,* 28-36. Retrieved November 11, 2014, from EBSCO Online Database Business Source Complete http://search.ebscohost.com/login.aspx?direct=true&db=bth&AN=78390447

Lucas, H. C. Jr. (2005). *Information technology: Strategic decision making for managers.* New York: John Wiley and Sons.

Marcum, M. (2003). Controlling web bugs—Online advertisers help shape guidelines. *EContent, 26,* 9-10. Retrieved 19 August 2010 from EBSCO Online Database Academic Search Complete http://search.ebscohost.com/login.aspx?direct=true&db=a9h&AN=9022307&site=ehost-live

Senn, J. A. (2004). *Information technology: Principles, practices, opportunities* (3rd ed.). Upper Saddle River, NJ: Pearson/Prentice Hall.

Solomon, S. (2010). Yours for a song. *Marketing Health Services, 30,* 28-29. Retrieved 19 August 2010 from EBSCO Online Database Business Source Complete http://search.ebscohost.com/login.aspx?direct=true&db=bth&AN=52815673&site=ehost-live

Whitney, L. (2009, 26 May). Report: Spam now 90 percent of all e-mail. *CNET News: Security.* Retrieved 19 August 2010 from CNET http://news.cnet.com/8301-1009%5F3-10249172-83.html

SUGGESTED READING

Brashear, T. G., Kashyap, V., Musante, M. D., & Donthu, N. (2009). A profile of the Internet shopper: Evidence from six countries. *Journal of Marketing Theory and Practice, 17,* 267-281. Retrieved 19 August 2010 from EBSCO Online Database Business Source Complete http://search.ebscohost.com/login.aspx?direct=true&db=bth&AN=40520971&site=ehost-live

Benady, D. (2013). The big data breakdown. *Marketing (Feb. 13, 2013), 28-30. Retrieved November 15, 2013, from EBSCO Online Database Business Source Complete http://search.ebscohost.com/login.aspx?direct=true&db=bth&AN=85711325&site=ehost-live*

Chickowski, E. (2010). Assess for less. *Entrepreneur, 38,* 46. Retrieved 19 August 2010 from EBSCO Online Database Business Source Complete http://search.ebscohost.com/login.aspx?direct=true&db=bth&AN=52095889&site=ehost-live

Chittenden, L. & Ruth, R. (2003). An evaluation of e-mail marketing and factors affecting response. *Journal of Targeting, Measurement, and Analysis for Marketing, 11,* 203-217. Retrieved 19 August 2010 from EBSCO Online Database Business Source Complete http://search.ebscohost.com/login.aspx?direct=true&db=bth&AN=9188413&site=ehost-live

Clark, M., & Melancon, J. (2013). The influence of social media investment on relational outcomes: A relationship marketing perspective. *International Journal Of Marketing Studies, 5,* 132-142. Retrieved November 15, 2013, from EBSCO Online Database Business Source Complete http://search.ebscohost.com/login.aspx?direct=true&db=bth&AN=89899293&site=ehost-live

Eid, R., & El-Gohary, H. (2013). The impact of E-marketing use on small business enterprises' marketing success. *Service Industries Journal, 33,* 31-50. Retrieved November 11, 2014, from EBSCO Online Database Business Source Complete http://search.ebscohost.com/login.aspx?direct=true&db=bth&AN=83864183

Jank, W. & Kannan, P. K. (2005). Understanding geographical markets of online firms using spatial models of customer choice. *Marketing Science, 24,* 623-634. Retrieved 19 August 2010 from EBSCO Online Database Business Source Complete http://search.ebscohost.com/login.aspx?direct=true&db=bth&AN=19243277&site=ehost-live

Joly, K. (2010). Embracing web analytics. *University Business, 13,* 29-30. Retrieved 19 August 2010 from EBSCO Online Database Academic Search Complete http://search.ebscohost.com/login.aspx?direct=true&db=a9h&AN=51445395&site=ehost-live

Martin, D., Hailin, W., & Alsaid, A. (2003). Hidden surveillance by web sites: Web bugs in contemporary use. *Communications of the ACM, 46,* 258-263. Retrieved 19 August 2010 from EBSCO Online Database Academic Search Complete http://search.ebscohost.com/login.aspx?direct=true&db=a9h&AN=25017166&site=ehost-live

Smith, A. D. (2005). Exploring service marketing aspects of e-personalization and its impact on online consumer behavior. *Services Marketing Quarterly, 27,* 89-102. Retrieved 19 August 2010 from EBSCO Online Database Business Source Complete http://search.ebscohost.com/login.aspx?direct=true&db=bth&AN=20423735&site=ehost-live

Spanbauer, S. (2001). Free tools nab web bugs. *PC World, 19,* 182-183. Retrieved 19 August 2010 from EBSCO Online Database Business Source Complete http://search.ebscohost.com/login.aspx?direct=true&db=a9h&AN=5314525&site=ehost-live

Ruth A. Wienclaw, Ph.D.

E

E-BUSINESS ENTERPRISE APPLICATIONS

ABSTRACT

With the explosion of information technology and the Internet over the past few decades, an increasing amount of business is being conducted over communications networks. E-business is the process of buying and selling goods or services electronically rather than through conventional means and includes the support activities and transactions necessary to perform these tasks. E-business can reduce the need for service technicians, increase the responsiveness of the business to the needs to the customer, and allow businesses to add new features to their products and services. Business-to-customer (B2C) applications include online retailing and electronic storefronts, electronic markets, portals, and online services. In addition, information systems can facilitate businesses in dealing with other businesses electronically through such applications as supply-chain management, electronic procurement, and electronic exchanges.

OVERVIEW

With the explosion of information technology and the Internet during the late twentieth and early twenty-first centuries, the normal paradigm of business has changed. Once constrained by communication boundaries in the not-too-distant past, business transactions were only conducted in person or via email, fax, or phone. Since then, an increasing amount of business has been conducted electronically over public and private communications networks. The proliferation of information on the Internet makes it possible to research and compare similar products and features as well as obtain the best price available in seconds or minutes rather than in hours or days. In the comfort of one's own home, one can purchase electronics, furniture, books, music, and more. Rather than going to the grocery store, it is even possible to point and click one's way to a full pantry using online grocery delivery services that will bring food to one's doorstep. Clothing, too, can be purchased online with easy return policies and even virtual models that allow one to "try on" the clothes before purchase. Although these technologies are still evolving, they are mature enough that more and more people rely on the Internet to conduct at least some of their business. For business enterprises in the twenty-first century, e-business, or e-commerce is a fundamental method of conducting business.

The use of communications networks for conducting business is still not an all-or-nothing proposition. Companies can have both traditional capabilities as well as e-business capabilities. Several different strategies are taken by organizations that want to do some or all of their business online. The off-line-focused strategy has a primary channel that is off-line with online marketing efforts playing only a supporting role. The off-line focused strategy may publish a website that provides customers with information about store hours and locations, describes the range of products sold, or offers customer service options. For example, grocery stores often allow customers to go online to read the weekly sales flyer, send a comment to the store or corporate manager, or find driving directions to the store, but one cannot buy groceries online. The off-line-focused strategy is often used when a sophisticated distribution system is needed to provide goods, personal consultation services are offered that can only be done in person (e.g., interior-decoration services), or there are contractual restrictions among the channel partners that prohibit more online involvement. Due to the nature of their goods and services, other organizations can primarily use the online channel for their marketing efforts while others only do business online using traditional marketing methods (e.g., television advertisements; infomercials) to point the customer to their website. This strategy can allow both the business and the customer to bypass the "middleman" or take advantage of the lower costs associated with the online channel (e.g., no need for the overhead associated with a physical retail store).

E-Business

E-business is the process of buying and selling goods or services – including information products and information retrieval services – electronically rather than through conventional means. Although typically conducted over the Internet, e-business can be conducted over any public or private communications network. There are two types of e-business. Business-to-business (B2B) e-business is the electronic marketing and selling of goods and services by one business to another. B2C e-business is the electronic marketing and selling of goods and services by a business directly to the individual consumer.

There are many benefits of e-business. First, it enables a business to extend its geographic reach. With e-business, a business can literally have a global market. For example, software is not only sold over the Internet, but also can be downloaded from the Internet, thereby eliminating the costs of delivery and packaging. Even for instances where the product needs to be physically delivered via a transportation carrier, e-business can facilitate a larger market. In addition, e-business increases the speed at which transactions can take place. Customers no longer have to wait in line to be served as they can complete their own transactions over a secure network. Transaction speeds are also increased because the customer does not physically have to travel to a store to pick up a product. Although the transaction speed is irrelevant if the customer still has to wait for delivery, for those items that are not available locally, time is still saved. Third, e-business can increase productivity. Before the advent of e-business, researching the characteristics of products was a labor-intensive task often requiring a search for review articles and trips from store to store to compare the features of similar products. Today, these activities can be done online for many products. This means that the information can be put to use more quickly and the decision made in a timelier manner. E-business also allows businesses to share information. Product specifications and user manuals can be posted online for

customers to download; troubleshooting databases can also be made available to customers, or customer service can be available by email or chat. These features can both reduce the need for service technicians and increase the responsiveness of the business to the needs to the customer. E-business can also enable businesses to add new features to their products and services. These can include personalization or automatic notification of updates, activities, or new products. Perhaps one of the most attractive advantages of e-business, however, is that it can significantly reduce costs for both the business and its customer. E-business allows customers to reach the business quickly and irrespective of geographic distance for purchasing, technical help, or customer service. These features can combine to give the e-business a competitive advantage over other businesses offering similar products and services.

Another advantage that e-businesses have over conventional businesses is the ability to use web analytics platforms to track usage of e-commerce websites, online advertising campaigns, and online promotions. Enterprises can then use this information to more effectively market their products and services to both B2B and B2C customers and prospects. There is some evidence, however, that few enterprises are taking full advantage of web analytics to analyze online activities. A 2012 study of B2B enterprises found that only 6 percent of marketers surveyed characterized their use of web analytics as "very effective" while only 7 percent of marketers surveyed stated that they were fully engaged with web analytics. Of the marketers surveyed, 44 percent were not at all engaged or only somewhat engaged with web analytics (Hosford, 2012).

APPLICATIONS

There are numerous applications that an enterprise can use in order to facilitate e-business, whether it is selling to other businesses or directly to end users. B2C applications include online retailing and electronic storefronts, electronic markets, portals, and online services. In addition, information systems can facilitate electronic interaction between businesses through such applications as supply-chain management, electronic procurement, and electronic exchanges.

Business-to-Customer (B2C) E-Business Applications
Traditionally, shopping meant physically going to a store, searching aisles for products of interest, comparing product features, and purchasing. With the advent of information technology, customers frequently now have the opportunity to do these tasks electronically by shopping online.

One of the most common applications of B2C e-business applications is online retailing and electronic storefronts. In online retailing, customers are able to visit a business's website on the Internet and examine product pictures and information, compare different products, fill an electronic shopping cart, and checkout and pay for their purchases. The e-business equivalent of the storefront is the home page of the company's website, with the various web pages being the electronic equivalent of the aisles of a traditional store. Rather than going to a brick-and-mortar store, customers can visit the company's website and look for the items they need. Most businesses engaging in e-business allow customers to "stroll the aisles" by having links to various categories of products. Walmart, for example, allows customers to go directly to apparel, baby, electronics, entertainment, home, jewelry, pharmacy, photo, sports, and toys. Amazon has dozens of product categories that customers can browse. Peapod, the online grocery store, allows customers various shopping options including browsing the aisles (e.g., going directly to the baking "aisle" and browsing the items there), express shop (which allows the customer to input a grocery list that the application software uses as key words to search the database so that it can present a list of options from which the customer can choose), and browse the current specials. In addition, most businesses also give customers the ability to search for specific items by various characteristics such as key words, title, product name, item number, or model number so that they can go directly to a specific product.

Another B2C e-business application is the electronic market. These are collections of individual shops that can be accessed through a single location on the Internet. Electronic markets are the virtual equivalent of shopping malls and are also referred to as cybermalls or electronic malls. Just as in brick-and-mortar malls, the shops band together to offer convenience to the customer. This service can be attractive to customers who need a product or service but do not know where to find it. For example, Choice Mall offers shoppers products in a wide variety of areas ranging from arts and entertainment, beauty and fashion, and travel to home and family, professional services, and real estate. Within each of these general categories are hyperlinks to more specific categories. For example, under the "Travel Center" are listed agencies, cruise packages, discounts, general tours, and vacation resorts. If one wanted to find a travel agency, for example, one would click on the "Vacation Resorts" hyperlink, which would bring up a list of travel agencies participating in the e-market along with a brief description and a hyperlink to their home page.

In addition to shopping, a number of other services are available online. Through electronic banking, customers can access their accounts via a secure connection and conduct various banking transactions without physically going to the bank. For example, one can check to see if an electronic paycheck has been deposited, check on an account balance and transaction history, transfer money between savings and checking, and many of the other activities that one does in a bank. Electronic bank statements and scans of checks are also available online and can be used in place of paper documents, thereby saving money for both the bank and the customer. In addition to banking services, other personal financial services are available online. An increasing number of businesses such as credit card companies, utilities, and communications companies allow customers to view their statements and pay their bills electronically. Customers can pay their bills online instead of writing checks or can sometimes have the money automatically withdrawn from their bank account so that they do not have to be involved in the bill-paying process at all (except, of course, to make sure that their account balance will cover the bills). Some companies also give their customers the option to receive their bills electronically rather than through the mail. Consumers are also able to invest, buy airline tickets, concert tickets, and book hotel rooms online.

Business-to-Business (B2B) E-Business Applications
In addition to the opportunities afforded businesses in selling directly to consumers, information technology also enables businesses to do many traditional activities related to dealing with other businesses electronically. One of the areas that is being revolutionized by the application of information technology is

supply-chain management. A supply chain is a network of organizations involved in the production, delivery, and sale of a product. An organization's supply chain may include suppliers, manufacturers, storage facilities, transporters, and retailers, and includes the flow of tangible goods and materials, funds, and information between the organizations in the network. Each of the organizations in the chain provides a value-added activity to the product or service. Supply-chain management is the process of managing the flow of these things within and between the organizations in the chain, a process facilitated through information technology. In supply-chain management, all the parties in the network are linked together into a system where the functioning of each of these affects the functioning of the others. For example, if a supplier is late in delivering a component to the organization, it will affect the organization's ability to produce its product on time and may also affect the ability of the other organizations (e.g., transportation companies, storage companies, retailers) to perform their tasks in a timely manner. Enterprise applications are available to help organizations communicate within the supply chain, improve communication, and optimize the timeliness of deliveries.

In addition to supply-chain management, information technology can also enable businesses to procure supplies and services electronically through the use of electronic procurement systems and electronic exchanges. Electronic procurement systems give employees access to the electronic equivalent of catalogs from multiple suppliers – with whom the organization has often negotiated pre-approved prices. By using e-procurement systems, organizations can reduce purchasing costs, provide employee self-service, and increase their leverage with suppliers. E-procurement typically reduces costs as well as saves time by allowing employees to review catalog and other product information online in order to determine which vendor or product to use as well as to prepare and submit purchase orders electronically. Further, enterprise-wide e-procurement often allows organizations to aggregate their purchases from a single vendor, thereby increasing their purchasing volume and allowing them to negotiate better rates for goods and services. The basic paradigm for e-procurement is shown in Figure 1.

E-procurement software can put vendors' catalogs online for employees to use when choosing

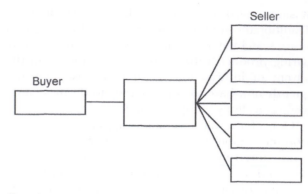

Figure 1

products and services. E-procurement application software can also allow employees to electronically submit purchase orders, automatically route purchase orders for approval when necessary, and eliminate the need for hard-copy documentation. E-procurement software can also be used to generate end-of-month, quarter, or yearly statements that allow the organization to track its spending and enable it to streamline its purchasing and procurement activities.

Another application used by organizations in B2B e-business is electronic exchanges (also known as electronic markets or B2B hubs). These are sites on the Internet where buyers and sellers can come together to exchange information and buy and sell products and services. As shown in Figure 2, electronic interchanges may have one of three structures. Public exchanges (also known as independent exchanges) are electronic markets operated by third parties who operate the electronic market, display information, and provide the tools necessary to conduct e-business. Independent exchanges may be vertical (i.e., serving members of a specific industry) or horizontal (i.e., simultaneously serving businesses in different industries).

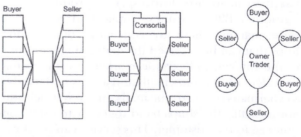

Independent Exchange   Consortia Backed Exchange   Private Exchange

Figure 2

Consortia-backed exchanges are e-markets created by a consortia of traditional firms within an industry thatband together to create a common forum for business-to-business transactions of goods and services. The common goal of consortia-backed exchanges is to drive down costs for all participants. Another electronic exchange structure is the private exchange. Participation in private exchanges is by invitation only. Private exchanges are structured around the needs of a specific sponsoring business and its trading partners. Private exchanges have several advantages over other types of electronic exchanges. First, the owners of these exchanges can regulate access to both buyers and sellers and have the ability to exclude competitors and their suppliers from the exchange. In addition, the owners of a private exchange can offer pricing incentives or alternatives to streamline business processes and benefit participants. Further, as opposed to public exchanges, most private exchanges can be tailored to serve specific products.

BIBLIOGRAPHY

Hosford, C. (2012). B-to-b marketers not taking advantage of Web analytics. B to B, 97(5), S018-1NULL. Retrieved December 4, 2013 from EBSCO Online Database Business Source Premier. http://search.ebscohost.com/login.aspx?direct=true&db=buh&AN=75495718

Hurbean, L., & Fotache, D. (2013). Mobile technology: Binding social and cloud into a new enterprise applications platform. Informatica Economica, 17(2), 73-83. Retrieved December 4, 2013 from EBSCO Online Database Business Source Premier. http://search.ebscohost.com/login.aspx?direct=true&db=buh&AN=88803505

Iqbal, R., Shah, N., James, A., & Cichowicz, T. (2013). Integration, optimization and usability of enterprise applications. Journal of Network & Computer Applications, 36(6), 1480-1488. Retrieved December 4, 2013 from EBSCO Online Database Business Source Premier. http://search.ebscohost.com/login.aspx?direct=true&db=buh&AN=92030307

Lucas, H. C. Jr. (2005). Information technology: Strategic decision making for managers. New York: John Wiley and Sons.

Milchev, G., & Miltchev, R. (2012). Software tool for managing the effectiveness of the enterprise e-business system. Economics & Business, 22125-133. Retrieved December 4, 2013 from EBSCO Online Database Business Source Premier. http://search.ebscohost.com/login.aspx?direct=true&db=buh&AN=82157075

Senn, J. A. (2004). Information technology: Principles, practices, opportunities (3rd ed.). Upper Saddle River, NJ: Pearson/Prentice Hall.

Sila, I. (2013). Factors affecting the adoption of B2B e-commerce technologies. Electronic Commerce Research, 13(2), 199-236. Retrieved December 4, 2013 from EBSCO Online Database Business Source Premier. http://search.ebscohost.com/login.aspx?direct=true&db=buh&AN=87622210

SUGGESTED READING

Anderson, M. C., Banker, R. D., & Ravindran, S. (2006). Value implications of investments in information technology. Management Science, 52(9), 1359-1376. Retrieved August 1, 2007, from EBSCO Online Database Business Source Complete. http://search.ebscohost.com/login.aspx?direct=true&db=bth&AN=22365644&site=ehost-live

Engelstätter, B., & Sarbu, M. (2013). Why adopt social enterprise software? Impacts and benefits. Information Economics & Policy, 25(3), 204-213. Retrieved December 4, 2013 from EBSCO Online Database Business Source Premier. http://search.ebscohost.com/login.aspx?direct=true&db=buh&AN=89730915

Kennedy, A. (2006). Electronic customer relationship management (ECRM): Opportunities and challenges in a digital world. Irish Marketing Review, 18(1/2), 58-68. Retrieved August 1, 2007, from EBSCO Online Database Business Source Complete. http://search.ebscohost.com/login.aspx?direct=true&db=bth&AN=23395030&site=ehost-live

Nguyen, T. N. (2005). Scalable e-business integration. Journal of American Academy of Business, 6(1), 135-142. Retrieved August 1, 2007, from EBSCO Online Database Business Source Complete. http://search.ebscohost.com/login.aspx?direct=true&db=bth&AN=15637421&site=ehost-live

Raymond, L., Bergeron, F., & Blili, S. (2005). The assimilation of e-business in manufacturing SMEs: Determinants and effects on growth and internationalization. Electronic Markets, 15(2), 106-118. Retrieved August 1, 2007, from EBSCO Online

Database Business Source Complete. http://search.ebscohost.com/login.aspx?direct=true&db=bth&AN=17485009&site=ehost-live

Scarle, S., Arnab, S., Dunwell, I., Petridis, P., Protopsaltis, A., & Freitas, S. (2012). E-commerce transactions in a virtual environment: virtual transactions. Electronic Commerce Research, 12(3), 379-407. Retrieved December 4, 2013 from EBSCO Online Database Business Source Premier. http://search.ebscohost.com/login.aspx?direct=true&db=buh&AN=82305043

Smith, L. (2011). Is enterprise mobility at a tipping point?. Enterprise Innovation, 7(4), 15. Retrieved December 4, 2013 from EBSCO Online Database Business Source Premier. http://search.ebscohost.com/login.aspx?direct=true&db=buh&AN=69968913

Thuraisingham, B. (2005). Directions for security and privacy for semantic e-business applications. Communications of the ACM, 48(12), 71-73. Retrieved August 1, 2007, from EBSCO Online Database Business Source Complete. http://search.ebscohost.com/login.aspx?direct=true&db=bth&AN=21048187&site=ehost-live

Ruth A. Wienclaw, Ph.D.

EFFECTIVE MEDIA COVERAGE

ABSTRACT

This article examines the activities and processes that contribute to maximizing positive media coverage. The role of a company's media relations staff is explained along with many of the tasks that the staff performs to obtain positive media coverage. The processes of profiling publications, editors, and writers are reviewed to better understand how to work with them. The various types of publications that can provide press coverage for a company are also reviewed. Ongoing efforts to build relationships with editors and writers are examined along with some of the methods for minimizing damage from negative press coverage.

OVERVIEW

All businesses would like to experience positive media coverage all the time. However, in our world of increased communication, information, and often sensationalist news coverage, this is not possible. Despite this, it is possible to achieve positive media coverage and leverage that coverage to gain more positive coverage, establish goodwill, build a reputation, drive sales, and increase market share. However, this requires time, effort, and a spokesperson who has a positive view toward the media and experience working for positive media coverage (Hong-tao, 2008) (Howard, 1994).

Business managers often seek quick and effective solutions to their problems. However, when it comes to maximizing positive media coverage, success is often far from quick and easy.

MEDIA RELATIONS MANAGEMENT
Staffing

The first challenge of managing media is to hire a media relations staff. In some cases, businesses turn to outside public relations firms or advertising firms for this type of support. In situations where media coverage is fairly constant, it is advisable to have an internal staff person in charge of media relations. This provides for consistency in tone and the ability to adjust and evolve the scope and detail of desired media coverage over time. Members of an internal media relations staff will also be focused solely on their company and will be better able to perform many of the endless small tasks necessary to obtain and maintain positive media coverage (Pellegrino, 2007).

Company Image

The next challenge is getting to know your company and the positive stories you desire to tell about it. A media relations team can help to put the story together, but the details of the article and why it is important are in the minds of the company's employees. Thus, compiling a history of the company as well as material that captures the working spirit and product value of the company is an important step. It may require interviews with dozens or more employees as well as reviewing historical documents (Vanhamme & Grobben, 2009).

Company Contribution

It is also important to know how the company has contributed to the communities in which it is located or contributed to other social causes around the world (Settles, 1996). Volumes of material may need to be reduced down to simple tidbits, but it is essential to provide relevant answers to probable questions. Remember that reporters want to know who, what, when, where, why, and how (Adler, 2007).

Familiarity

Once the history, spirit, product value, and contributions of the company are compiled, edited, and published, it is important that everyone in the company is familiar with these contributions. This is especially true of managers who may have the opportunity to speak on behalf of the company (Morris, 1989).

Newsworthiness

It is also important to develop an understanding about what is newsworthy about the company. This includes what may be appealing on an ongoing basis as well as what might be newsworthy in various circumstances, including boom times, recessions, natural disasters, national elections, and other cyclic events (Schaumleffel & Tialdo, 2006) (Stateman, 1998).

Newsworthiness is often in the eye of the beholder, and, for the most part, it can be situational. Factors that influence newsworthiness will vary considerably from time to time and place to place and may be difficult to determine. There are several ways that a media relations staff can sort through and rank the newsworthiness of various potential stories.

Publication Types

One key to determining newsworthiness is to analyze the actual publications and the type of publications that have previously run stories about your company or similar companies. There are several types of publications that could be interested in your company from a variety of perspectives (Otte, 1992).

Trade Publications

Trade publications cover an industry or a particular type of product or materials used in manufacturing. These publications tend to be read by people in their industry or those who work for companies that use products from an industry or perhaps even sell products to an industry (Peckham, 2007). Trade publications can provide good exposure by increasing awareness about a company or a company's product line. Articles in trade publications can help improve sales and marketing efforts, which in turn increase the return on investment for media and public relations efforts and a company's success at large (McNamara, 2008).

National Newspapers & Magazines

National newspapers and magazines with high circulation numbers as well as distribution in multiple geographical regions also may be interested in news about your company. These publications tend to focus on articles that have a national or global significance. They also tend to be less technical than trade publications because they strive to appeal to a broader audience. The perspective of these publications on almost any topic can also shift over time (Entwistle & Johnson, 2000) (Ott, 1998).

Local & Regional Newspapers & Magazines

Local and regional newspapers and magazines tend to run articles on issues or events that impact their surrounding communities. These publications often have an interest in companies that have facilities located in their circulation areas. Topics or issues that regional and local publications consider newsworthy tend to be those that can impact lifestyles, jobs, businesses, or economics in the community (Martinelli, 2006).

Advocacy Publications

Advocacy publications are those that take a position on a specific issue or segment of the population. Many advocacy publications come and go rather quickly. Examples of the type issues that advocacy publications focus on include the environment, politics, race, business, international relations, immigration, and unionism (Kleinman, 2002). These publications can be a source of positive as well as negative media coverage for a company.

Interest-Specific Publications

There are also a wide variety of publications that target specific demographic segments based on gender, age, race, leisure activities, or hobbies. Many of these publications focus on lifestyle topics ranging from apparel preferences to home decor choices. There is also at least one publication for virtually every type of hobby or leisure activity ranging from plant growing and flower arranging to model railroading and bicycling. Depending on the product or service a company offers, many of these publications can be a source of positive media coverage (Lontos, 2008).

Regardless of the type of publications a company seeks coverage in, the media relations team has a considerable amount of work to do in building and managing those relations. In addition, the media relations team also needs to be prepared to counter any negative media coverage that occurs.

APPLICATIONS

Managing Media Relationships
Awareness of Media Outlets

There are several aspects to the process of managing media relationships. Some publications may have a reputation for being negative and others positive. Some reporters or feature writers may also have a reputation for being negative or positive. Many will tell you that they are looking for the dirt because that is what people like to read. It is important that members of the media relations staff understand the publications that they work with and those that they may work with in the future. Profiling publications, editors, and writers is an important step for maximizing positive media coverage (Lontos, 2008) (Rose, 2001).

Getting to know the publications that cover a company or an industry is a long and sometimes slow process. A review of the last two to three years of the publication's issues is a good start. This review will provide insight into the topics that were covered and how they were covered. It will also provide a good indication as to the slant of the articles published, including if they were negative, positive, or well balanced. A visit to a publication's website can also provide information on its history, mission, and mode of operation (Bradley, 1997).

Awareness of Media Editors

Many publications may be well established and in operation for several years or even several decades. However, few editors remain at a publication for more than ten years. Thus, it is important for the media relations staff to know the styles and preferences of the long-tenured editors and should have an awareness of newer editors. Publications can change

tone relatively quickly if the old guard leaves and there is suddenly a new crop of editors (Carr, 2009).

Awareness of Writers

It is also important to know the writers of each publication. Writers have their own style and have a track record of success. How a writer builds his or her track record varies. Some writers make careers on writing negative stories, and others may build their record on writing well-balanced articles with broad appeal. The importance of building relationships with writers cannot be understated (Youngwirth, 2009).

Preparedness

Once the publications, editors, and writers are known, the process of maximizing positive media coverage will become a bit easier. But it still requires constant hard work. The media relations team needs to stay in tune with editorial and publishing processes. In part, this means being prepared to take advantage of opportunities for possible positive coverage. The media relations staff needs to have a variety of possible positive stories or angles when the media calls, and these stories need to have the right appeal for the publication that is calling (Schultz, 1996).

Being prepared means being able to provide content for an article in progress or to prompt an editor or a writer to be interested in a story. It is important to be able to provide writers with all the information they need to tell the story. In many ways, this means understanding the life of a writer. They are often under deadline, and time is critical. Writers also cannot be expected to readily understand every topic in as much detail as the media relations representative. This means that material provided to writers needs to be readily understandable and that the small details need to have both meaning and context (Jacobs, 2008) (Rembrandt, 2007).

Depending on the publication, writers also like to include quotations from corporate executives, researchers, and scientists. Media relations managers must know which people in their company can be available for an interview and can work with the writer to get positive coverage results. If interviews are set up, it is important that a media relations staff person be present to help coach the interviewee, provide clarification, and perform any follow-up work such as sending along additional information or photographs.

Many trade publications rely heavily on advertising to pay their bills. Generally speaking, publishers deny that there is a relationship between advertising buys and coverage of the advertising buying company. However, there are publications, depending on the industry, that blatantly tie editorial content to advertising buys. The editorial advertising ratio position of a publication is something that should be determined in the profiling process. When possible, companies should take advantage of any positive editorial content offers that come along with advertising buys.

Another way that publications can make money is through the sale of article reprints. In the case of a company or product profile, it is advisable to buy reprints of positive coverage. These reprints are often used in marketing packets, press packets, or as collateral for a trade show table. They are relatively inexpensive and help to build relationships with publishers and editors.

ISSUE

Responding to Negative Press Coverage

Sooner or later negative press coverage will occur. This can happen for a variety of reasons, ranging from a product recall to an injury or a death in the workplace, or even something as far reaching as the economic downturn of 2008, when dozens of companies were being battered in the media. Also bear in mind that negative media coverage can run in trends or cycles (Hannah & Zatzick, 2008).

It is advisable to keep tabs on all media coverage concerning your company. This can be done through traditional clippingservices or by utilizing online services, called media monitoring and media intelligence services, that send you alerts if selected names or topics appear, especially when the company's reputation is at risk (*Treasury & Risk*, 2012).

Sources of Negative Press
Trends / Popular Opinion

Negative press coverage most often occurs for a reason. It is helpful to keep an eye on media trends and public opinion polls. If, for example, a publication that has had a track record of relatively positive coverage of companies or industries suddenly starts turning negative, it may be because of a new editor or even new ownership. Monitoring these changes in style or tone as well as management and ownership can be a sign for media relations staff to start preparing for potential negative coverage. In some situations, once a popular high-circulation publication starts negative coverage of a company or industry, other publications may follow (Eccles & Vollbracht, 2006).

Some publications tend to follow popular opinions to drive their tone and style. Take the case of the war in Iraq. When the war first started, it was popularized by the White House and in turn by the media as a necessary effort to fight terrorism and stop the spread of weapons of mass destruction. As time went by and the war dragged on, the American public became more discouraged with the war. Media coverage about the war became increasingly negative. Some blamed the media for the coverage being negative, while others felt that the tone of the media coverage reflected the feelings of the public (Newport, 2007) (Solomon, 2006).

Misinformation & Errors

In some cases, negative press coverage may occur merely because of misinformation or an error in reporting and fact checking. If this is the case, the media relations staff needs to move quickly to notify the editors and writers that there has been an error and provide documentation of accurate information. In many cases, the publication will print a correction in a later issue. But bear in mind the story will still stand as published and be included in databases and perhaps on websites. The media relations staff needs to be prepared to respond to inquiries about the original story even if a correction was published.

Crises

Sometimes business crises occur and no matter what happens, there may be no stopping the media from being critical and publishing negative stories (Weinberger & Romeo, 1989). Complaining about negative coverage to publishers and editors will yield few if any results and may even create a backlash (Saad, 2008).

If negative media coverage does occur, media relations managers and corporate executives should not be passive. They should be prepared to react to the negative coverage as well as launch a campaign to minimize damage. This requires a coordinated and concerted effort on the part of the company's management team (Miller, 2006). An additional option is to contract for services from a reputation management firm. These firms are relatively new and their effectiveness remains uncertain (Tozzi, 2008).

How a company manages a crisis and responds to overcome, or neutralize, negative media coverage will impact the perception of the public, the media, and stockholders for years to come (Hoggan, 2008). To counter or recover from negative media coverage may take several months or even years. It is also a step-by-step process of overcoming immediate consequences as well as working on long-term reputation repair.

Use of Direct Communication

Direct communication with a company's customer base, through social media, for example, is an effective mechanism to counter negative press coverage and should be done promptly and honestly. To best accomplish direct communication with the customer, media relations staff, public relations staff, and customer service representatives should all play a role in a coordinated, well-tuned effort. If an appropriate customer-focused publication exists, it can be an effective means of communicating and should be used on an ongoing basis (Schijns, 2008). Also, social media, such as Facebook and Twitter, offer public relations staff a way to interact directly with customers (Horn, 2013). Social media is now ubiquitous and cannot be disregarded or ignored.

It is also important to remember that even though the noise about the last episode of negative media coverage will die down after a while, it can crop up again at any time. Editors and writers working on future articles in which the company may be mentioned will have access to all the media from the past. They may read previously published negative media, affecting their point of view about your company. As such, when media relations staff work on future articles with reporters, they need to remember that old negative press may come up and that they need to be prepared to deal with it quickly.

CONCLUSION

Positive media coverage is an asset to a company. It can help drive sales, strengthen marketing campaigns, and help to attract investors. Maximizing positive media coverage requires skill, experience, and diligence. The extent to which a company can achieve positive media coverage dependw on the work of its media relations department.

One of the primary jobs of the media relations staff is to have a working knowledge of the publications, editors, and writers that may cover the company. The staff needs to know which publications may have a reputation for being negative or positive. They also need to know which writers have a reputation for being negative or positive. This knowledge will help them better deal with a media opportunity and work to maximize positive coverage.

Negative press coverage is almost an eventuality and can occur for many different reasons, including that the negative media coverage of corporations is cyclical. Thus, media relations staff need to monitor media coverage concerning the company and watch for changes in ownership or editorial staff of the publications that cover the company. It is also advisable that media relations staff stay current with popular opinion polls because these polls may indicate which way the media will view companies, events, or trends. Media relations staff and corporate executives need to be prepared to react to negative coverage to minimize damage.

BIBLIOGRAPHY

Adler, J. (2007). Positive press. *Professional Builder, 72,* 21-22. Retrieved April 15, 2009, from EBSCO Online Database Business Source Complete. http://search.ebscohost.com/login.aspx?direct=true&db=bth&AN=24104231&site=ehost-live

Bradley, A. (1997). Educators link declining confidence in schools to negative press coverage. *Education Week, 16,* 6. Retrieved April 16, 2009, from EBSCO Online Database Academic Search Complete. http://search.ebscohost.com/login.aspx?direct=true&db=a9h&AN=9705185490&site=ehost-live

Carr, N. (2009). Keys to better coverage. *American School Board Journal, 196,* 41-42. Retrieved April 16, 2009, from EBSCO Online Database Academic Search Complete. http://search.ebscohost.com/login.aspx?direct=true&db=a9h&AN=35628734&site=ehost-live

Eccles, R., & Vollbracht, M. (2006). Media reputation of the insurance industry: An urgent call for strategic communication management. *Geneva Papers on Risk & Insurance—Issues & Practice, 31,* 395-408. Retrieved April 16, 2009, from EBSCO Online

Database Business Source Complete. http://search.ebscohost.com/login.aspx?direct=true&db=bth&AN=23585025&site=ehost-live

Entwistle, V., Watt, I., & Johnson, F. (2000). The case of Norplant as an example of media coverage over the life of a new health technology. *Lancet, 355*(9215), 1633. Retrieved April 16, 2009, from EBSCO Online Database Academic Search Complete. http://search.ebscohost.com/login.aspx?direct=true&db=a9h&AN=3078712&site=ehost-live

Hannah, D., & Zatzick, C. (2008). An examination of leader portrayals in the U.S. business press following the landmark scandals of the early 21st century. *Journal of Business Ethics, 79, 361-377. Retrieved April 18, 2009, from EBSCO Online Database Business Source Complete. http://search.ebscohost.com/login.aspx?direct=true&db=bth&AN=31722501&site=ehost-live*

Hoggan, J. (2008). Positive spin. *Marketing Magazine, 113*, 14-14. Retrieved April 16, 2009, from EBSCO Online Database Business Source Complete. http://search.ebscohost.com/login.aspx?direct=true&db=bth&AN=32765505&site=ehost-live

Hong-tao, T. (2008). Does the reputation matter? Corporate reputation and earnings quality. *Journal of Modern Accounting & Auditing, 4*, 53-59. Retrieved April 16, 2009, from EBSCO Online Database Business Source Complete. http://search.ebscohost.com/login.aspx?direct=true&db=bth&AN=35246648&site=ehost-live

Horn, S. (2013). Social media's online advantage: The evolution of public relations to digital communications. *Public Relations Tactics, 20*, 16. Retrieved November 14, 2013, from EBSCO Online Database Business Source Complete. http://search.ebscohost.com/login.aspx?direct=true&db=bth&AN=84930683&site=ehost-live

Howard, C. (1994). Advertising and public relations. *Vital Speeches of the Day, 60*, 269. Retrieved April 15, 2009, from EBSCO Online Database Academic Search Complete. http://search.ebscohost.com/login.aspx?direct=true&db=a9h&AN=9404061435&site=ehost-live

Jacobs, K. (2008). Improve your placement success: Emphasize quality over quantity. *Public Relations Tactics, 15*, 14-15. Retrieved April 16, 2009, from EBSCO Online Database Business Source Complete. http://search.ebscohost.com/login.aspx?direct=true&db=bth&AN=35778602&site=ehost-live

Kleinman, M. (2002, October 10). Refugee Council fights negative press. *Marketing (00253650)*, 2. Retrieved April 16, 2009, from EBSCO Online Database Business Source Complete. http://search.ebscohost.com/login.aspx?direct=true&db=bth&AN=7683022&site=ehost-live

Lontos, P. (2008). I see your name everywhere!: How to score more positive publicity. *Performance Magazine, 16*, 17-17. Retrieved April 16, 2009, from EBSCO Online Database Business Source Complete. http://search.ebscohost.com/login.aspx?direct=true&db=bth&AN=36371375&site=ehost-live

Martinelli, D. (2006). Strategic public information: Engaging audiences in government agencies' work. *Public Relations Quarterly, 51*, 37-41. Retrieved April 16, 2009, from EBSCO Online Database Business Source Complete. http://search.ebscohost.com/login.aspx?direct=true&db=bth&AN=22431741&site=ehost-live

McNamara, P. (2008). The value of public relations in a softening economy. *Marketing Magazine, 113*, 15-15. Retrieved April 18, 2009, from EBSCO Online Database Business Source Complete. http://search.ebscohost.com/login.aspx?direct=true&db=bth&AN=32765506&site=ehost-live

Media Monitoring Plays Role In Managing Reputation Risk. (2012). *Treasury & Risk, 22*, 10. Retrieved November 14, 2013, from EBSCO Online Database Business Source Complete. http://search.ebscohost.com/login.aspx?direct=true&db=bth&AN=77467191&site=ehost-live

Miller, J. (2006). Damage control. *InsideCounsel, 16*, 42-44. Retrieved April 7, 2009, from EBSCO Online Database Business Source Complete. http://search.ebscohost.com/login.aspx?direct=true&db=bth&AN=23498648&site=ehost-live

Morris, F. (1989). Getting results from a corporate speakers bureau. *Public Relations Quarterly, 34*, 14. Retrieved April 15, 2009, from EBSCO Online Database Business Source Complete. http://search.ebscohost.com/login.aspx?direct=true&db=bth&AN=4466144&site=ehost-live

Newport, F. (2007, January 4). Majority of Americans view media coverage of Iraq as inaccurate: Most likely to say coverage is too negative. *Gallup Poll Briefing*, 1-3. Retrieved April 16, 2009, from EBSCO Online Database Business Source Complete. http://search.ebscohost.com/login.aspx?direct=true&db=bth&AN=24332802&site=ehost-live

Ott, K. (1998). Media study finds more bias in news reports on companies. *Advertising Age's Business Marketing, 83*, 3. Retrieved April 16, 2009, from EBSCO Online Database Business Source Complete. http://search.ebscohost.com/login.aspx?direct=true&db=bth&AN=1150786&site=ehost-live

Otte, R. (1992). Both sides of the media. *Nation's Business, 80*, 71R. Retrieved April 15, 2009, from EBSCO Online Database Academic Search Complete. http://search.ebscohost.com/login.aspx?direct=true&db=a9h&AN=9206222750&site=ehost-live

Peckham, J. (2007). N. American news media seen more positive about diesel. *Diesel Fuel News, 11*, 17-17. Retrieved April 16, 2009, from EBSCO Online Database Business Source Complete. http://search.ebscohost.com/login.aspx?direct=true&db=bth&AN=26747995&site=ehost-live

Pellegrino, J. (2007). Promote yourself. *Wearables Business, 11*, 31-32. Retrieved April 15, 2009, from EBSCO Online Database Business Source Complete. http://search.ebscohost.com/login.aspx?direct=true&db=bth&AN=23640264&site=ehost-live

Rembrandt, M. (2007, October). How to get media coverage without spending a fortune in 5 simple steps. *American Venture*, 34-35. Retrieved April 16, 2009, from EBSCO Online Database Business Source Complete. http://search.ebscohost.com/login.aspx?direct=true&db=bth&AN=30071016&site=ehost-live

Rose, E. (2001). Penetrating the media's psyche. *Communication World, 18*, 10. Retrieved April 16, 2009, from EBSCO Online Database Business Source Complete. http://search.ebscohost.com/login.aspx?direct=true&db=bth&AN=4425293&site=ehost-live

Saad, L. (2008, September 15). Republicans cry foul over media coverage of Palin. *Gallup Poll Briefing*, 2.

Schaumleffel, N., & Tialdo, T. (2006). Hungry for MEDIA attention. *Parks & Recreation, 41*, 54-57. Retrieved April 15, 2009, from EBSCO Online Database Academic Search Complete. http://search.ebscohost.com/login.aspx?direct=true&db=a9h&AN=20459381&site=ehost-live

Schultz, B. (1996). Media mania. *Thrust for Educational Leadership, 26*, 10. Retrieved April 15, 2009, from EBSCO Online Database Academic Search

Complete. http://search.ebscohost.com/login.aspx?direct=true&db=a9h&AN=9612176844&site=ehost-live

Schijns, J. (2008). Customer magazines: An effective weapon in the direct marketing armory. *Journal of International Business & Economics, 8*, 70-78. Retrieved April 16, 2009, from EBSCO Online Database Business Source Complete. http://search.ebscohost.com/login.aspx?direct=true&db=bth&AN=35637613&site=ehost-live

Settles, C. (1996). How to build a press center on the web. *Public Relations Tactics, 3*, 12. Retrieved April 15, 2009, from EBSCO Online Database Business Source Complete. http://search.ebscohost.com/login.aspx?direct=true&db=bth&AN=9706053414&site=ehost-live

Solomon, N. (2006). Blaming the media for bad war news. *Humanist, 66*, 35-36. Retrieved April 16, 2009, from EBSCO Online Database Academic Search Complete. http://search.ebscohost.com/login.aspx?direct=true&db=a9h&AN=20625321&site=ehost-live

Stateman, A. (1998). Positive press for corporate America. *Public Relations Tactics, 5*, 8. Retrieved April 15, 2009, from EBSCO Online Database Business Source Complete. http://search.ebscohost.com/login.aspx?direct=true&db=bth&AN=438890&site=ehost-live

Tozzi, J. (2008, May 1). Do reputation management services work? *Business Week Online*, 11. Retrieved April 16, 2009, from EBSCO Online Database Academic Search Complete. http://search.ebscohost.com/login.aspx?direct=true&db=a9h&AN=31907833&site=ehost-live

Vanhamme, J., & Grobben, B. (2009). "Too good to be true!" The effectiveness of CSR history in countering negative publicity. *Journal of Business Ethics, 85*, 273-283. Retrieved April 20, 2009, from EBSCO Online Database Business Source Complete. http://search.ebscohost.com/login.aspx?direct=true&db=bth&AN=37143239&site=ehost-live

Weinberger, M., & Romeo, J. (1989). The impact of negative product news. *Business Horizons, 32*, 44. Retrieved April 8, 2009, from EBSCO Online Database Business Source Complete. http://search.ebscohost.com/login.aspx?direct=true&db=bth&AN=4527528&site=ehost-live

Youngwirth, J. (2009, March 2). PR for planners: Strategies for gaining credibility and getting results.

Journal of Financial Planning, 22-23. Retrieved April 18, 2009, from EBSCO Online Database Business Source Complete. http://search.ebscohost.com/login.aspx?direct=true&db=bth&AN=37007729&site=chost-livc

SUGGESTED READING

Bagdikian, B. (1992). Journalism of joy. *Mother Jones, 17,* 48. Retrieved April 15, 2009, from EBSCO Online Database Academic Search Complete. http://search.ebscohost.com/login.aspx?direct=true&db=a9h&AN=9206082816&site=ehost-live

Bruck, L. (1995). Bad press–but a fair press? *Nursing Homes: Long Term Care Management, 44,* 10. Retrieved April 16, 2009, from EBSCO Online Database Academic Search Complete. http://search.ebscohost.com/login.aspx?direct=true&db=a9h&AN=9503240508&site=ehost-live

Collins, B. (1997). Bad press tarnishes view of nonprofit8uis for public, Congress. *Corporate Legal Times, 7,* 11. Retrieved April 16, 2009, from EBSCO Online Database Business Source Complete. http://search.ebscohost.com/login.aspx?direct=true&db=bth&AN=9702120489&site=ehost-live

Felix, Reto, et al. (2016). Elements of strategic social media marketing: A holistic framework. *Journal of Business Research, 70,* 118-126. Retrieved on June 29, 2017.

Fisher, J. (2008, October 13). Media darlings. *New American (08856540), 24,* 27-30. Retrieved April 16, 2009, from EBSCO Online Database Academic Search Complete. http://search.ebscohost.com/login.aspx?direct=true&db=a9h&AN=34703061&site=ehost-live

Gergen, D. (1992, January 13). Is the press to blame? *U.S. News & World Report, 112,* 54. Retrieved April 16, 2009, from EBSCO Online Database Academic Search Complete. http://search.ebscohost.com/login.aspx?direct=true&db=a9h&AN=9201130882&site=ehost-live

Joe, J. (2003, March). Why press coverage of a client influences the audit opinion. *Journal of Accounting Research, 41,* 109-133. Retrieved April 16, 2009, from EBSCO Online Database Business Source Complete. http://search.ebscohost.com/login.aspx?direct=true&db=bth&AN=8954789&site=ehost-live

McGee, R. (2008). A media-related plan of attack: Applying the military's practice of embedding reporters to crisis management. *Public Relations Tactics, 15,* 13-26. Retrieved April 18, 2009, from EBSCO Online Database Business Source Complete. http://search.ebscohost.com/login.aspx?direct=true&db=bth&AN=33534445&site=ehost-live

Ryan, L. (2008, November 12). Five lessons for managers from Obama's campaign. *Business Week Online, 10.* Retrieved April 18, 2009, from EBSCO Online Database Academic Search Complete. http://search.ebscohost.com/login.aspx?direct=true&db=a9h&AN=35365829&site=ehost-live

Zachman, W. (1995). Microsoft and the curse of the positive PR. *MC: Marketing Computers, 15,* 16. Retrieved April 16, 2009, from EBSCO Online Database Business Source Complete. http://search.ebscohost.com/login.aspx?direct=true&db=bth&AN=9509084239&site=ehost-live

Zavyalova, A., Pfarrer, M. D., Reger, R. K., & Shapiro, D. L. (2012). Managing the Message: The Effects of Firm Actions and Industry Spillovers on Media Coverage Following Wrongdoing. *Academy of Management Journal, 55,* 1079-1101. Retrieved November 14, 2013, from EBSCO Online Database Business Source Complete. http://search.ebscohost.com/login.aspx?direct=true&db=bth&AN=82571471&site=ehost-live

Zhang, J., & Swanson, D. (2006). Analysis of news media's representation of Corporate Social Responsibility (CSR). *Public Relations Quarterly, 51,* 13-17. Retrieved April 16, 2009, from EBSCO Online Database Business Source Complete. http://search.ebscohost.com/login.aspx?direct=true&db=bth&AN=23907762&site=ehost-live

Zuk, R. (2009). The right kind of writing: Follow simple writing tenets to increase your likelihood of social media success. *Public Relations Tactics, 16,* 7-7. Retrieved April 16, 2009, from EBSCO Online Database Business Source Complete. http://search.ebscohost.com/login.aspx?direct=true&db=bth&AN=36665229&site=ehost-live

Michael Erbschloe

EMPLOYER BRANDING AND MANAGEMENT

ABSTRACT

Employer branding and management refers to the strategies by which a company creates its public image as a desirable place to work. The goal is to recruit top talent and in turn to retain the best employees already hired. However, employer branding is far more than a simple human resources tool to make a company a presence in an increasingly competitive job market. Rather, employer branding and management, when executed correctly, becomes a significant tool for a company to understand its own operations and its own employees, thus making for a more engaged and productive workplace.

OVERVIEW

Traditional Hiring

Before the need for highly specialized talent in fields as diverse as medicine and software development, environmental engineering, and accounting began to far exceed the number of qualified applicants, securing a job was largely the responsibility of the applicant. Applicants had to sell themselves as a good hire. Because internal information was comparatively limited, the applicant might know very little about the company they were applying to or the working conditions to which they would be subject, if hired.

The applicant was at a distinct disadvantage as the company was largely in control of the information provided to make employment there seem attractive. Even if a job interview involved a tour of the facilities and actually meeting employees, the entire interview process could be manipulated to make the best impression. Promises concerning responsibilities and/or company growth potential could be made that really had little foundation.

Indeed, companies largely relied on offering a competitive salary and benefit package as the best—really, only—way to seal the deal. Companies sometimes relied on so-called headhunters—that is, talent acquisition representatives—yet the search still largely relied on a needful applicant field and its own carefully crafted and polished public image to secure needed talent.

The intention was as simple as it was misguided: to hire the best candidate rather than the right candidate. Companies simply filled positions rather than hiring promising workers. The results of the applicant-centered process were predictably uneven. New hires might find that the reality of the selected workplace differed significantly from the impression given during the interview. Talented employees who experienced frustration or were otherwise disappointed in the company or their place in it were motivated to move on, leaving the original company facing the applicant process again.

Attracting Talent

With the advent of the digital era, communication chatter outside a company vastly increased. Through the agencies of mass communication platform outlets, including Facebook and LinkedIn, personal blogs, and review sites that offered individuals the ability to evaluate companies' products, practices, and employment conditions without fear of repercussions, the workforce itself suddenly emerged as a powerful tool for creating the perception of a company. Senior management and human resources departments realized they were no longer in control of the information circulating about their company. They could no longer offer candidates false promises; they could no longer easily create an image of the workplace that did not match the reality; their employees (and their ex-employees) had found a powerful voice to register what conditions were like and what sort of workplace culture defined the company. Was the company a fun place to work? Relaxed and informal? Was it rigid and hierarchical? Did it encourage talent? Did it promote fairly? Were supervisors responsive to employee feedback? Was the technology current? Was there a clear chain of command? Did the company treat its employees with respect? Were there genuine opportunities to engage creatively in the work of the company? Were there legitimate avenues for promotion and significant protocols for job security?

Within a single decade, the pool of qualified applicants fell far below the numbers of openings even as the ability of applicants to choose which employers were the most desirable and best fit for themselves became more refined. Companies realized they needed to engage their own branding—that is, create buzz for their own workplace as a means of attracting the best new talent and retaining their own top management, supervisors, and workers. According to Robertson & Khatibi (2013) 40 percent of applicants considered employee treatment the most important criterion in choosing a place to work, whereas only 29 percent ranked quality of products or services as most important.

Insights such as these significantly impacted the hiring process. Because companies within a field all pitch comparable salary ranges and benefit packages—the tipping point for applicants would have to come from the employer brand. To use the jargon of the fast-emerging field of employer branding, a company might be a talent "magnet" or a talent "repellant."

The emerging theoretical model suggested that in matters of hiring and retaining genuine talent, the best, or most qualified, candidate was not necessarily the right candidate. Promising applicants or recent hires can in fact discover that the workplace environment is simply incompatible with their talents, their skill set, their expertise, their ambitions, or their personality. By managing their employer brand, companies can improve the odds of hiring talent that best fits the company itself, making for a happier, more productive, and more stable workforce and a less stressful workplace. Further, employer branding is not merely about hiring. By defining itself through internal feedback from its employees, companies can retain promising talent (Biswas & Suar, 2016).

The challenge for employers is to discover how a company becomes an employer of choice. Employer branding depends for its success on how well a company can project itself as a vibrant work community in which a person can thrive. The strategy must be able to market a positive, clearly defined, and uncontestable image to the widest possible pool of qualified applicants. Companies can no longer dangle top salaries and wide-ranging benefit packages and expect these to be enough to tap what is termed "top talent"— that is, the most highly qualified and highly desirable applicants.

Conversely, every employee becomes part of the branding process. Virtually any size company, from local grocery stores to multinational corporations, can study their market image as a way to attract the best talent. Employer branding and management is a strategy used by local, state, and federal governments, which employ hundreds of thousands of workers; research facilities; universities; hospitals; financial institutions; law enforcement agencies; and law firms.

APPLICATIONS

The application of employee branding begins with a remarkably simple observation: A company is a community. In addition to the product and/or service it provides to the consumer public, it sustains what is called a workplace culture—that is, maintains a particular signature environment for its employees, a workplace atmosphere created by the interplay between and among its employees and the management team (Verma & Ahmad, 2016). That interplay in turn defines the workplace in which employees, day in and day out, perform their assigned responsibilities. Businesses engaged in identical businesses are not identical.

It is difficult to generalize on exactly how a company can brand itself as an attractive place to work. Ghadeer (2016) terms it a "magic spell that allows organizations to differentiate themselves from others in the market place." Companies routinely identified themselves as having a high-profile and very successful brand marketing strategy. Growth companies such as tech communications conglomerates such as Apple, Google, ESPN, Netflix, and Facebook; business corporations such as Pepsi, Coca Cola, Nike, IBM, and 3M; online retail giants such as Amazon; and transportation services such as Southwest Airlines and Amtrak each follow a brand marketing management strategy that keys to its own identity and its wider business network of competitors.

However, for a company to begin to build its brand as part of a long-term commitment to its employees and more specifically to be competitive for attracting the best and the brightest, branding analysts suggest commitment to a four-stage process. The process is circular—that is, it is never entirely completed but rather once the process has run its course, the company returns to the initial stage as a way to keep the process of branding itself open, flexible, and living.

First, a company must understand its current conditions. This involves not only securing reliable data from its current employees but also gathering data through exit interviews with department employees.

Data collectors also monitor social media sites and investigate conditions at other similar companies, and management looks critically at the company's own operations. With all this information, a company profiles its strengths and weaknesses and reviews its operations and workplace culture from the viewpoint of an applicant. The goal is to discover what might attract a new hire and what might drive that potential hire elsewhere.

Second, research leads to shaping a specific plan, developing a market-based company profile that can be posted online, for example, as an element of a job posting, or as part of a pitch given in an interview. This plan also covers ways of courting current employees who might be thinking of going to a new employer. Hire and retain—those are the prime directives of employer branding and management.

The third stage is critical: the actual execution—that is, the presentation of the brand—live in job interviews, whether in person or through video conferencing. The human resources representative and/or management team responsible for hiring rehearses the critical elements of the company's workplace advantages, hitting critical bullet points, stressing the talking points from the company's developed plan. In addition, the company secures website space to promote its brand marketing, sets up sites on social media platforms—gets the word out. Promotion and communication of a company's brand must be constant (Wilska, 2014).

The fourth stage represents the company's commitment to the ongoing process of managing its brand. Reflection—that is, measuring how successful the current efforts are—is the final process before returning to stage one and beginning again. Constant evaluation is key to success. Companies must discover whether they have shaped a brand image that is both relevant to the contemporary job market and distinctive from the other business entities in the field. At this point, employer branding becomes more than a strategy for hiring better employees; it becomes an essential and ongoing element of a company's sense of its own identity. By creating a forum in which employees and supervisors, junior and senior executives all are respected equally and each help shape a response, brand marketing creates a corporate community, company operations become transparent and the subject of a robust and vibrant critique, the status quo becomes itself a problem, a starting place from which the most promising companies move forward.

VIEWPOINTS

Human resources directors, who are responsible for managing recruitment and retention, view the emerging interest in employer branding as a significant shift in the recruitment paradigm. By using the data generated by its own employees and ex-employees, a company can demonstrate its agility, its ability, indeed its vested interest in listening to problems in operations or personnel, and in changing policies in response to this input. Brand management is useful not merely as a tool for hiring but also as an effective way to ensure a growing company's own corporate integrity, long-term viability, and continuing relevance in its field.

The Internet and social media provide a glut of information, much of it anonymous and unfocused, which can become a distraction, providing unhelpful and conflicting perspectives. Critics doubt that a company managing its own image, deliberately contriving to make its image "sexy," can produce honest self-evaluation. Rather, employee branding and management represents a potentially dangerous sort of propaganda, with a company gathering, censoring, shaping, polishing, and even generating the raw data on the Internet to try to control the conversation about its own reputation.

Workplace psychologists and human resource counselors, however, see a company concerning itself with its own culture as representing a major revision in business management and how it conducts and presents itself to the public in the era of digital communications. By providing a serious evaluation of why a person should want to work there, a business can search not for a good hire but rather for a good fit, taking into consideration how that potential hire, whatever the qualifications and expertise he or she might bring, will ultimately fit into the workplace culture and in turn how the network will nurture that creativity as a way to secure that person's long-term loyalty. It does no good, after all, to hire a qualified candidate who will not fit into the established workplace culture and will be soon gone or, even worse, unhappy and unproductive. A happy and engaged workforce, conversely, networked through social media, becomes the business's best promoters.

Finally, brand marketing and management allows a company the chance to look into the mirror, to define and focus on legitimate and real-time reasons why the company is a challenging and rewarding environment that should attract and keep the best possible talent. Corporations work better when they listen to their employees (Vatsa, 2016). The brand becomes the company's most valuable recruitment tool as well as its identity, its encompassing mission, its pledge to its employees and management teams, and as such represents the ever-evolving, cooperative, and robust nature of its workplace.

BIBLIOGRAPHY

Biswas, M., & Suar, D. (2016). Antecedents and consequences of employer branding. *Journal of Business Ethics, 136*(1), 57–72. Retrieved October 23, 2016, from EBSCO Online Database Business Source Ultimate. http://search.ebscohost.com/login.aspx?direct=true&db=bsu&AN=116146299&site=ehost-live

Ghadeer, M. (2016). Employer branding: What constitutes "an employer of choice?" *Journal of Business & Retail Management Research, 11*(1), 154–166. Retrieved October 23, 2016, from EBSCO Online Database Business Source Ultimate. http://search.ebscohost.com/login.aspx?direct=true&db=bsu&AN=119494341&site=ehost-live

Reis, G. G., & Braga, B. M. (2016). Employer attractiveness from a generational perspective: Implications for employer branding. *Revista De Administração, 51*(1), 103–116. Retrieved October 23, 2016, from EBSCO Online Database Business Source Ultimate. http://search.ebscohost.com/login.aspx?direct=true&db=bsu&AN=119836858&site=ehost-live

Robertson, A., & Khatibi, A. (2013). The influence of employer branding on productivity-related outcomes of an organization. *IUP Journal of Brand Management, 10*(3), 17–32. Retrieved October 23, 2016, from EBSCO Online Database Business Source Ultimate. http://search.ebscohost.com/login.aspx?direct=true&db=bsu&AN=91675188&site=ehost-live

Sengupta, A., Bamel, U., & Singh, P. (2015). Value proposition framework: Implications for employer branding. *Decision, 42*(3), 307–323. Retrieved October 23, 2016, from EBSCO Online Database Business Source Ultimate. http://search.ebscohost.com/login.aspx?direct=true&db=bsu&AN=109091781&site=ehost-live

Vatsa, M. (2016). Leveraging employer branding for organizational success. *Review of Management 6,* (1/2), 9–13. Retrieved October 23, 2016, from EBSCO Online Database Business Source Ultimate. http://search.ebscohost.com/login.aspx?direct=true&db=bsu&AN=116834394&site=ehost-live

Verma, D., & Ahmad, A. (2016). Employer branding: The Solution to create a talented workforce. IUP *Journal of Business Management, 13*(1), 42–56. Retrieved October 23, 2016, from EBSCO Online Database Business Source Ultimate. http://search.ebscohost.com/login.aspx?direct=true&db=bsu&AN=114187526&site=ehost-live

Wilska, E. (2014). Employer branding as an effective tool in acquiring talent. *Journal of Positive Management, 5*(3), 46–54. Retrieved October 23, 2016, from EBSCO Online Database Business Source Ultimate. http://search.ebscohost.com/login.aspx?direct=true&db=bsu&AN=100713372&site=ehost-live

SUGGESTED READING

Blasco- López, M. F., Rodríguez-Tarodo, A., & Fernández-Lores, S. (2014). Employer branding: Estudio multinacional sobre la construcción de la marca del empleador. *Universia Business Review,* (44), 34–53. Retrieved October 23, 2016, from EBSCO Online Database Business Source Ultimate. http://search.ebscohost.com/login.aspx?direct=true&db=bsu&AN=100197992&site=ehost-live

Kaur, P., Sharma, S., Kaur, J., & Sharma, S. K. (2015). Using social media for employer branding and talent management: An experiential study. *IUP Journal of Brand Management, 12*(2), 7–20. Retrieved October 23, 2016, from EBSCO Online Database Business Source Ultimate. http://search.ebscohost.com/login.aspx?direct=true&db=bsu&AN=108447382&site=ehost-live

Kucherov, D., & Zamulin, A. (2016). Employer branding practices for young talents in IT companies (Russian experience). *Human Resource Development International, 19*(2), 178–188. Retrieved October 23, 2016, from EBSCO Online Database Business Source Ultimate. http://search.ebscohost.com/login.aspx?direct=true&db=bsu&AN=113744308&site=ehost-live

Moseley, R. (2014). *Employer Branding Management: Practical Lessons from the world's leading employers.* Hoboken, NJ: Wiley.

Theorer, Christian P., et al. (2016). Employer branding: A brand equity-based literature review and research agenda. *IJMR.* Retrieved June 29, 2017.

Ting, C. (2011). *Employer branding and employee-life-cycle: How to become an attractive employer.* Saarbrucken, Germany: AV Akademikerverlag.

Trudy Mercadal, Ph.D.

ENTREPRENEURIAL MARKETING

ABSTRACT

In many ways, the principles of marketing for the entrepreneur are the same as they are for any business venture. However, because entrepreneurs typically have a limited marketing budget and are trying to sell a new service or product that does not have a track record with the target market, it is particularly important that an entrepreneur's marketing budget be well-spent to help maximize the number of new customers that it generates. For this reason, it is important that the entrepreneur develop a strong marketing plan based on research of the needs and characteristics of the target market and focus the marketing efforts on that specific target market. Marketing efforts do not have to be prohibitively expensive, however. There are a number of low-cost ways to market one's product or service—particularly over the Internet—that allow businesses to reach their target markets without a great outlay of cash.

OVERVIEW

No matter how innovative one's idea is, if potential clients or customers do not know about it, they will not buy the product or service. To survive, one must market. To be successful, one must market well.

If anything, marketing is more important for entrepreneurial firms than for larger organizations with established products or services. This is true for several reasons. First, by definition, entrepreneurial firms are trying to sell something new—an idea, a product, or a service that is as yet unknown to potential customers. Second, even if the entrepreneur or team with the idea is well-known in their current circle of business contacts, it takes effort to turn colleagues into customers. If the entrepreneur or team is not well-known, they will have to convince potential customers not only that they have an idea that the customer needs but also that they will be able to deliver it. In addition, unless the entrepreneur is in the unusual situation of working within an established organization, he or she will typically have little security if the new venture fails. Therefore, unfocused marketing efforts alone are not sufficient: successful marketing is crucial to the viability of the entrepreneurial organization.

Frequently, however, an entrepreneur's enthusiasm is for the technical aspects of the venture—designing the product or providing the service—rather than selling the idea. To make matters worse, marketing is not an isolated activity or even a set of isolated activities but an ongoing process that must continue throughout the life cycle of the organization if it wishes to survive and thrive. So for better or worse, the entrepreneur must recognize the importance of marketing and design a strategy that will maximize the acquisition of customers.

In reality, marketing is everything that the entrepreneur does to promote the business, from picking a name for the company and designing a logo, business card, and brochure to building a website and buying media ads. Marketing also includes such activities as networking—building and maintaining a mutually beneficial relationship with other businesspeople and potential clients or customers. Networking can help one fine-tune ideas by both listening and talking to one's professional peers and potential customers. Networking can also give the entrepreneur new ideas about what the target market would like to see in terms of new products or services. Trade shows and professional conferences are excellent places for networking, where one can make new contacts and exchange business cards. Good networking efforts, however, are not just about selling one's idea; good networking efforts involve listening as well as talking to better understand the target market and how to reach it.

Although most general marketing principles apply equally to the entrepreneurial business and the business world at large, because of their small size, entrepreneurial firms need to be particularly careful about how they spend their limited marketing dollars. Certainly, traditional marketing efforts such as print ads (i.e., advertisements in newspapers, magazines, or trade publications), radio or television ads, or mass mailings of flyers or brochures can be appropriate depending on the product or service being sold and the potential market. However, most entrepreneurs have little budget for marketing and need to be able to get the most bang for their marketing buck. There are a number of low cost and even free ways to do this. For example, electronic newsletters are an excellent way to keep one's company name and products in front of potential customers. One can also gain free publicity through giving away goods or services to local charities. Getting involved in professional organizations, the local chamber of commerce, or other organizations that include members of the target market is a good way to network and gain customers. The entrepreneur can also speak at public events on topics related the company's product or service or write and publish articles (either in journals or on the Web) related to the business. Trade shows and professional conventions are another place where the entrepreneur can spread the word about his or her product. A well-designed business card or brochure and the ability to listen to what potential customers want can go a long way in gaining customers. Combined with strategic traditional or electronic marketing ads, the entrepreneur can target the appropriate audience and become well-positioned within the marketplace.

Although it is important for the entrepreneur to try different ways to market in order to see what works best for the particular product and target audience, it is also important that marketing efforts be focused. It has frequently been observed that one of the biggest marketing mistakes that a small or entrepreneurial business can make is to try to be all things to all people. Many entrepreneurs make the mistake of spreading themselves too thin rather than doing the research to find out what potential customers want or need. For example, to say that one's new widget not only is a better mousetrap but also will scrub floors and feed the cat is not believable. As a result, potential customers will tend to not take the product seriously. Although this is obviously an exaggerated example, many entrepreneurs try to spread themselves too thin with initial marketing efforts, offering consulting services, for example, for anything from performance enhancement to research and development. Although the entrepreneur may have the skills for all these services, without the proven track record of success, potential clients will be hesitant to hire him or her.

Rather than taking a shotgun approach in which one tries to get a little business from a wide variety of markets, it is better to position the company to reach a small market and then to get as many customers from that small market as possible. This allows the company to build the much-needed reputation and proven track record for excellence that will allow it to not only be successful in the short-term but also position itself for expansion and growth in the future. By positioning the company with a smaller, more focused target market, the entrepreneurial organization can distinguish itself from its competitors by stressing unique selling points that appeal to the specific target market. For example, owners of rodent-infested homes are going to be interested in a widget that is a better mousetrap but not care that it can also feed the cat (since if they had cats, they would not need a mousetrap). Similarly, a new boutique could not easily reach a target audience of both high school students and business professionals; the two markets want different types of clothes and will not want to be seen in a shop that is attractive to the other group. Rather, the boutique's marketing efforts would be more effective by focusing on only one of the product lines and making the retail environment as attractive to that market share as possible.

Before starting a marketing effort, the entrepreneur needs to understand the potential market. It is always tempting to just spend one's budget on the most advertising that one can buy, but research has shown that this is not the way to success. Rather, it is important to find out more about the target market so that marketing efforts can be focused to gain as many customers as possible. To accomplish this goal, it is important to do several things. First, before starting a marketing campaign, a market survey should be done. Although this is an often neglected step in many marketing efforts, a market survey enables the entrepreneur to learn more about the needs and wants of the target market as well as the best ways to reach them. Some of this information can be gained through public-access governmental demographic data, and some of it can be collected through surveys conducted in person, over the telephone, or over the Internet.

Once the survey data is analyzed and the nature of the target audience is understood, the entrepreneur can develop a marketing strategy for how best to reach these potential customers. In addition, the marketing strategy should include which media should be used to reach the target audience: the business executives might be reasonably reached through an ad in the *Wall Street Journal*, but the high school students probably would not see an ad there. Once the target market is understood and a marketing strategy is developed, this information can be put together with budgets and other details in the development of a marketing plan that will help the entrepreneur learn from experience and position the company for success and future growth.

APPLICATIONS

As observed earlier, in many ways, marketing strategies for the entrepreneur are little different from those for any business or organization. However, the limited marketing budget of most entrepreneurs makes it imperative that the monies be invested wisely in order to bring the greatest return on investment. One marketing step that is often skipped by entrepreneurs in a misguided attempt to be frugal is the proper positioning of oneself and one's service or product in the marketplace. In addition, the ability to e-market can help entrepreneurs gain data and market products and services much more efficiently than is possible with many traditional media.

Positioning Oneself

As with all things in business, it is important that one perform strategic planning before announcing to the world the availability of a new product or service. Knowing that there is a need and one has a product or service that will fill it is insufficient. Marketing efforts—particularly for entrepreneurs—must be carefully crafted so that the right message is sent and targeted toward a narrow market so that the message has maximum impact.

One important tool for positioning oneself in the marketplace is the marketing plan. This is a strategic planning document that helps the entrepreneur identify the key marketing issues that are critical to long-term success, set goals and objectives for the organization, and develop meaningful measures of success for identifying and attracting potential customers. Marketing plans help the entrepreneur know how best to focus the efforts of the organization to maximize their impact and effectiveness. With a marketing plan in place, one can look back and review how well previous marketing efforts have performed and revise strategies as necessary. Marketing plans also help the entrepreneur to look ahead, and consider the changing nature of the marketplace and trends in the market so that products, services, and marketing efforts can continue to stay abreast of what the market needs or wants. Marketing plans also help the organization's management to focus on the big picture for the organization rather than getting lost in the technical work and day-to-day management of the firm.

There is no one approach to writing a marketing plan, and even the general approaches must be tailored to the individual needs of the company. How one writes a marketing plan depends in part on whether the business is in the start-up phase, is in an aggressive growth phase, or is a mature company. These first two approaches are of particular interest to the entrepreneur as he or she tries to position the company within the marketplace.

Although it is tempting to do a marketing blitz to get out the word about the new product or service, marketing efforts for the start-up company or the business that is still finding its feet should focus on positioning the company within the market and on understanding the dynamics of the marketplace. Laying such strategic groundwork will help the company not only enter into the marketplace but also position itself for growth and continued future success. During the start-up phase of the business, it is typically best to focus on strategic issues and on testing possible marketing approaches. During this phase, entrepreneurs are well-advised to perform pilot studies to test the effectiveness of various marketing strategies (e.g., media ads, websites) to see which works best. Marketing at this point is in many ways carried out by trial and error: entrepreneurs should not spend a great effort on trying to put a mature marketing plan into place when they are just starting their new venture. Rather, marketing at this point in the organization's life cycle will most likely be a series of trial runs to determine where the strengths and weaknesses of the plan are, what approaches to marketing work best, and how best to reach the target market.

Once the entrepreneurial organization develops a marketing plan that is bringing in business, it can spend more time looking at tactics and strategic implementations. As opposed to marketing plans for start-up organizations, the marketing plan for an organization in a growth phase will be more concerned with financial aspects. Marketing plans at this level should include such things as detailed budgets and projected revenues from the various sales thrusts that are mapped on a periodic basis (i.e., monthly or quarterly). These will help the entrepreneur or team keep better track of which strategies are most effective. In addition, marketing plans during the growth phase of an organization are best written to target a particular product line or type of service. For example, if Acme Corporation is trying to sell two products—the widget and the gizmo—there should be a separate marketing plan for each since each product will need to be described differently and even targeted toward a different market. With two separate marketing plans in place, it is easier to tell how each product is doing and whether the approach for either the widget or the gizmo needs to be differently conceptualized. At this phase in the company's life cycle, an initial market share should be established and the strengths and weaknesses of various marketing approaches will have been assessed. Marketing plans during growth phases are typically best when they focus not only on strategy but on implementation, examining the success and failures of marketing from the start-up phase, positioning the organization to gain the market share desired in the future, and implementing plans and strategies in the present that help the organization continue to move toward that goal.

E-Marketing

The rise of the Internet and the ease of designing and maintaining a professional website have allowed the potential to reach far greater numbers of prospective customers than was previously possible. This does not mean, however, that electronic marketing (e-marketing) should be the only strategy used to get the word out about one's product or service. There are still people who do not use the Internet and people who still want to have a hard copy of professional, full-color advertising brochures that they can hold in their hands and ponder at their leisure. Further, e-marketing is not without its weaknesses and pitfalls. However, most businesses today need to consider having some presence on the Internet in order to attract and maintain customers.

The Internet can provide a wealth of information that the entrepreneur can use in marketing efforts. Whether one is offering goods or services, the Internet offers an array of opportunities for gathering information, testing marketing approaches, and advertising. For entrepreneurs offering products for sale, the Internet also offers effective ways to put one's catalog online and even to take orders and receive payment without the expense of a physical storefront or extensive staff.

Among the things that the Internet allows the entrepreneur to do is to research the competition. By searching the web, one can find out what competitors are selling, how and to whom they are advertising, and what the latest buzz words are for attracting potential customers. The Internet is also a source of information about potential customers. One can frequently find government demographic data online or lists of businesses or organizations that might be part of the target market. Internet research will allow one to get ideas for what makes a website attractive or easily navigable so that one can build one's own site.

However, one needs to do more than set up a website and hope that prospective customers or clients will see it when they do a search. It often takes several months for search engines to index and rank a new site highly enough for it to be seen by a significant number of prospective customers. Therefore, if a website is used as a passive marketing tool, it will probably generate little interest. There are, however, things that the entrepreneur can do to encourage potential customers or clients to view the company's website. Writing articles on the entrepreneur's or company's area of expertise is one way to attract new clients. An article on the "Ten Mistakes Most Managers Make" might not only attract readers but also give them a sample of a management consultant's advice. Magazines, e-zines (electronic magazines on the Internet), professional publications, and industry publications are all excellent ways to get one's message to the market. In addition to articles, one can also advertise the new product or service in most of these publications. Another option is to use pay-per-click advertising to reach a highly targeted population with advertising. In pay-per-click (PPC) advertising, the person or company advertising pays a fee for each visitor that clicks on their ad. PPC can include keyword advertising on search engines or other websites. Banner ads (graphical web advertising), flash ads (animated or interactive advertisements), or text ads all can be PPC. Another way to increase traffic to one's website is to use website traffic-builder software that generates metatags (HTML tags that contain descriptive information about the webpage but do not appear in a browser) for the website pages and submits them to numerous search engines and directories. Combined with networking and other traditional marketing approaches, e-marketing can help the entrepreneur reach and win a greater market share.

BIBLIOGRAPHY

Bamping, Y. (2005, Jun). Drive traffic to your site. *Sales and Service Excellence,5*, 9. Retrieved March 26, 2007, from EBSCO Online Database Business Source Complete. http://search.ebscohost.com/login.aspx?direct=true&db=bth&AN=17348799&site=bsi-live

Georgia, B. L. (1999, Oct). Marketing like a pro. *PC Computing, 12*, 230–231. Retrieved March 26, 2007, from EBSCO Online Database Business Source Complete. http://search.ebscohost.com/login.aspx?direct=true&db=bth&AN=2287131&site=bsi-live

Gumpert, D. E. (1992). *How to really create a successful marketing plan.* Boston: Inc. Publishing.

Holtz, H. R. (1982). *The secrets of practical marketing for small business.* Englewood Cliffs, NJ: Prentice-Hall.

Jones, R., & Rowley, J. (2011). Entrepreneurial marketing in small businesses: A conceptual exploration. *International Small Business Journal, 29,* 25–36. Retrieved November 18, 2013, from EBSCO Online Database Business Source Complete. http://search.ebscohost.com/login.aspx?direct=true&db=bth&AN=58645618

Jones, R., Suoranta, M., & Rowley, J. (2013). Entrepreneurial marketing: A comparative study. *Service Industries Journal, 33*(7/8), 705–719. Retrieved November 18, 2013, from EBSCO Online Database Business Source Complete. http://search.ebscohost.com/login.aspx?direct=true&db=bth&AN=87555085

Levinson, J. C. (1993). *Guerrilla marketing: Secrets for making big profits from your small business.* Boston: Houghton Mifflin.

Mort, G., Weerawardena, J., & Liesch, P. (2012). Advancing entrepreneurial marketing: Evidence from born global firms. *European Journal of Marketing, 46*(3/4), 542–561. Retrieved November 18, 2013, from EBSCO Online Database Business Source Complete. http://search.ebscohost.com/login.aspx?direct=true&db=bth&AN=74143794

Thompson, K. D. & Edmond, A. Jr. (1994). Getting the word out. *Black Enterprise, 24,* 28. Retrieved March 26, 2007, from EBSCO Online Database Business Source Complete. http://search.ebscohost.com/login.aspx?direct=true&db=bth&AN=9404257569&site=bsi-live

SUGGESTED READING

Clift, V. (1994). True marketing pros master listening skills. *Marketing News, 28,* 9. Retrieved March 26, 2007, from EBSCO Online Database Business Source Complete. http://search.ebscohost.com/login.aspx?direct=true&db=bth&AN=9410282628&site=bsi-live

Clift, V. (1995). Who's influencing your customer's decisions? *Marketing News, 29,* 33. Retrieved March 26, 2007, from EBSCO Online Database Business Source Complete. http://search.ebscohost.com/login.aspx?direct=true&db=bth&AN=9503074094&site=bsi-live

Lincoln, D. J. & Warberg, W. B. (1987, Apr). The role of microcomputers in small business marketing. *Journal of Small Business Management, 25,* 18–17. Retrieved March 26, 2007, from EBSCO Online Database Business Source Complete. http://search.ebscohost.com/login.aspx?direct=true&db=bth&AN=5274190&site=bsi-live

Lingelbach, D., Patino, A., & Pitta, D. A. (2012). The emergence of marketing in Millennial new ventures. *Journal of Consumer Marketing, 29,* 136–145. Retrieved November 18, 2013, from EBSCO Online Database Business Source Complete. http://search.ebscohost.com/login.aspx?direct=true&db=bth&AN=73374561

McDaniel, S. W. & Parasuraman, A. (1986, Jan). Practical guidelines for small business marketing research. *Journal of Small Business Management, 24,* 1–8. Retrieved March 26, 2007, from EBSCO Online Database Business Source Complete. http://search.ebscohost.com/login.aspx?direct=true&db=bth&AN=5266397&site=bsi-live

Newbert, S. (2012). Marketing amid the uncertainty of the social sector: Do social entrepreneurs follow best marketing practices? *Journal of Public Policy & Marketing, 31,* 75–90. Retrieved November 18, 2013, from EBSCO Online Database Business Source Complete. http://search.ebscohost.com/login.aspx?direct=true&db=bth&AN=74749691

Ruth A. Wienclaw, Ph.D.

EVENT MANAGEMENT

ABSTRACT

This paper will take a comprehensive look at the field of event management, creating a profile of the growth of the event management industry as well as the outlook. It will also review some of the wide range of event types such as meetings, seminars, receptions and conventions. In the process, it will present an illustration of the strategies employed in the development of these types of events.

OVERVIEW

In 1969, four young men decided to invest one of the men's wealth into the creation of a recording studio and musician's retreat in upstate New York. Over time, that idea evolved into presenting a concert whose ticket proceeds would generate money for their institution. The notion was originally for a venue for about 50,000. While the idea seemed reasonable on the surface, the event quickly spiraled out of control. The towns in which the organizers sought to hold the event declined (and even banned) the concert planners the opportunity to host it within their town limits. The organizers had constant issues with vendors and other aspects of the event. Furthermore, the 50,000 expected attendees quickly spiraled into nearly 500,000. The concert festival went on, and at the end, the organizers were faced with 70 lawsuits and over a million dollars in debt. Yet, the Woodstock music festival became etched in American history (Rosenberg, 2009).

A look at Woodstock provides a glimpse into the complex and challenging industry known as event management. The creation, organization and implementation of any major event are an intricate undertaking, requiring the interconnection of a myriad of moving parts. In the modern 21st century business marketplace, however, it is also a vital component to a company's ability to project itself among its clients, employees and the general public.

This paper will take a comprehensive look at the field of event management, creating a profile of the growth of the event management industry as well as the outlook. It will also review some of the wide range of event types such as meetings, seminars, receptions and conventions. In the process, it will present an illustration of the strategies employed in the development of these types of events.

Planning Business Events

The development of such events as meetings, conventions, receptions and similar events requires a great deal of strategic planning. At the very base of the process is a simple question: In what way does the organization wish to convey a message or make an impression? Companies and corporations have certain goals as well as codes of professional behavior that project a certain image. Meeting planners will need to converse with the group to understand the manner in which the company wishes to present the program (as well as the budget used to meet this framework). Doing so assists the planner in proceeding according to a set of general guidelines.

This foundation helps the event planner choose the appropriate venue and build the program. At the next level, the event planner will locate the proper site for the event to take place. The venue may be a hotel, reception room, convention hall, conference room, or private room at a restaurant or a similar location. Understanding the event parameters will also enable the planner to determine the type of facilities that will be necessary for the event to proceed successfully; such as booth space, audio/visual technologies, computer capabilities and transportation resources.

The next phase in the planning of the event is the communications step. The planner will coordinate a public relations outreach about the event, in order to entice attendee participation. Although formal, paper invitations are also sent out to potential participants, e-mail invitations often represent an optimal vehicle for quick information distribution to a wide audience. This important step may also help the planner gauge the number of participants that plan to attend. As a result, the event planning process, including the date of the reception or meeting as well as the venue, may be altered to account for any change in numbers.

Concurrent with the communications are the logistical planning elements. In this arena, the planner will determine the application of relevant technology and lighting, room setup, staffing and labor, food and/or cocktail menus, vendors, check-in tables and booth configuration. The event planner will, at this stage, work consistently as a communications hub for the client and the venue staff to ensure that each detail is given attention and, where necessary, altered to meet the needs of the client. The planner will also work with the client to ensure that contracts are developed and signed so that there are no disruptions in the event's development phases.

Finally, the event itself demands careful management. The planner and the client will work to ensure that there are no last-minute issues with vendors or food, that the equipment is operating properly and all audio-visual presentation materials are prepared for the program, that signs and decorations are appropriately posted, that attendees are seated in the proper seats and that transportation to and from the event for guests is operating smoothly. The execution of the event is often just as complex as the event planning stages. In fact, given the heightened atmosphere and the fact that there is no more time to revise the program, it is arguably the most intense and emotionally draining stage of the event management process.

As demonstrated above, the field of event management requires that those who work within it manifest a number of important personal and professional qualifications. For example, an event manager must be able to handle multiple tasks in often intense

environments. He or she must also demonstrate exceptional diplomatic skills, which are called into service when dealing with higher-level clients during both the development and implementation phases. Event managers must also be able to quickly comprehend the client's corporate philosophy, since the event will be a reflection of that ideology.

In light of the nature of the work performed in the field of event management, it is useful to next analyze the industry itself and how it operates.

FURTHER INSIGHTS
The Event Management Industry

Event management spans across a broad range of industries and therefore, each manifestation is distinct. In many cases, the event management aspect of a company's activities is handled internally, either by an onsite event manager or by personnel who handle other tasks in addition to organizing such meetings. Then again, the event management industry continues to thrive in industrialized nations around the world.

According to the U.S. Bureau of Labor Statistics (BLS), there were 51,000 event planners in the United States in 2006. Thirty-nine percent of those jobs were held by those who worked in corporate and convention planning companies, while 27 worked in civic, religious, or professional organizations. The BLS forecasts a 20 percent increase in the workforce in this industry over a 10-year period, a significant growth in comparison to other industries. The salaries for those employees were above the national average as well—by May 2006, the BLS reported that personnel in this field earned a median salary of about $42,000, while some earned close to $71,000 per year (U.S. Bureau of Labor Statistics, 2009).

Coinciding with the growth of the event management industry is the increased development of event management associations. These organizations are trade associations; networks comprised of member representatives of a given industry. Event management associations provide a number of benefits to their membership, including vendor services, government lobbying and networking opportunities. In many cases, event management associations seek common ground among seemingly disparate event planning companies. In a growing number of these trade associations, event management networks are seeking to establish common codes of industry professional conduct and standards. One study revealed that of 152 professional event management associations, nearly 40 percent had stated codes of ethical behavior and professional conduct. Such codes center around themes like effective business practices, reputation, respect and personal conduct, and communications (Arcodia & Reid, 2008).

Event management professionals undergo a great deal of diverse training. A growing number of them are college-educated, receiving degrees in business, communications, hospitality, or event management. These professionals may also have academic training in industry-specific categories, such as health care, finance, and education. Such training helps them develop knowledge of the industries for which they will be developing event programs.

Academic training is important, but many experts in the field of event management believe that "real-world practical and applied experience" is the true hallmark of an accomplished planner. In one study, students in event management courses were required to plan, market, manage, and evaluate an actual event. The analysis of this program revealed that participatory training in this manner was an effective educational tool for giving students a true taste of the intricacies and pressures of event planning (Moscardo & Norris, 2004).

Event management is a complex industry spanning across a wide range of other industries. To further illustrate the scope of this industry and its presence in the twenty-first century economy, it is useful to better understand the types of events being managed.

Types of Business Events

From small meetings involving fewer than 10 people to conventions whose participants require the resources of nearly an entire metropolitan area, business events are manifest in a wide range of forms. As such, the industry of event management must also show diversity in organizing and executing them.

Meetings

On the smaller end of business events are meetings. These types of gatherings may only involve a few individuals. Meetings require venues, either in-house or off-site locations like hotels or restaurants. In many cases, food and beverage services (such as continental breakfast, lunch, and coffee stations) are also utilized. Depending on the size of the meeting, audio-visual hardware such as microphones, computer monitors, laptop projectors, and screens may be used for presentations. Smaller meetings of this nature may not necessarily require the efforts of a professional meeting or event planner—they are often assembled by administrative professionals who, in addition to coordinating the meeting development, are also charged with ensuring the proper information is disseminated to participants.

Seminars

Some smaller events are educational in nature rather than internal meetings of business executives and personnel. Seminars, for example, are informal meetings designed for participants to share information about an important issue, system, or program. Seminars are similar to formal classes, although in this case, they are brief presentations of topics of importance to a company or its personnel. Managing the development of a seminar entails not just selection of a venue but also the selection of speakers and materials that will effectively communicate the subject matter to participants. Business seminars may be stand-alone in nature, but are often part of a larger conference or meeting program. Seminars are typically used for training purposes; in fact, many companies and associations hold seminars on event management so that corporate personnel may receive training in this field and, as a result, minimize the need for a company to employ an external event planning vendor for its own meetings and gatherings (Kovaleski, 2003).

Receptions

Receptions are less business-oriented and more celebratory events. They vary in size, scope, and substance, depending on the purpose of the event and the corporate profile and philosophy. For example, some receptions are small-scale, formal cocktail hours, with drinks and hors d'oeuvres and low-volume music. This form of reception is typically held off-site in a hotel ballroom, private room at a restaurant, or similar venue. They may honor one or two individuals or simply be designed to facilitate networking (meeting new business contacts and company representatives) among potential business partners. On a larger scale, receptions are more theatrical events, often including live music and/or performers, video presentations, and other forms of entertainment as well as greater quantities of food and drinks. These events may be simple celebrations while others may be designed to give a portion of the proceeds to charity. As is the case for smaller receptions, these types of events are designed according to the tastes of the client and thus vary in terms of size and spectacle.

The largest of business events is the convention. Conventions are large-scale, formal gatherings of one or more groups and corporations with a given industry. They are typically multifaceted, with seminars, guest speakers, marketplaces (spaces filled with booths and kiosks managed by vendors), and other activities. Similar to (and often interchangeable with) trade shows, conventions may last more than one day and have specific programs of events that are designed to ensure that participants (many of whom travel great distances to take part) are given a full complement of activities from which to choose during their stay. Some conventions are called "citywides," as they draw so many participants to a given convention center and municipal area that it directly impacts hotel room occupancy, transportation services, restaurant business, and other commercial sectors. For this reason, conventions are considered invaluable economic contributors for cities and regions that have the resources to support them.

Event management pertaining to each of these types of events entails a specific type of approach. Some events may take a few days to organize and take shape, while conventions may take months. Event planners must work closely with clients to ensure that the meeting, reception, or convention satisfies their needs.

Conclusions

In 1969, a storeowner in Kauneonga Lake, New York, saw a significant uptick in the sales of nails and cold cut meats, as construction workers descended on a nearby farm to build the stage for the Woodstock festival. The shopkeeper, Art Vassmer, later reflected on his dismay at the volume of sales his store saw thanks to these workers: "They told me, 'Mr. Vassmer, you ain't seen nothing yet,' and by golly, they were right" (Tiber, 1994). In truth, no one expected Woodstock to be a venue at which 500,000 people would descend at one of the most iconic sights of the era. Even the festival's organizers did not anticipate the concert to

grow into the event it would eventually become—the debt and lawsuits they saw afterward served as a testament to that naïveté.

The Woodstock example provides evidence of the reasons the event management industry has flourished in the modern economy. In the United States alone, the event management industry generates more than $300 billion each year (Douglas & Gregory, 2009). Events of all shapes and sizes remain as critical for business in the twenty-first century as they were in the twentieth century. Events, after all, provide a venue for the exchange of ideas, networking, and information dissemination. Event management was born of the need to ensure that such programs avoid budget overruns, are executed with minimal technical glitches and, perhaps most importantly, that the goals of the meetings are met without being clouded by mishaps and errors.

This industry remains diverse, due in no small part to the breadth of meeting types and industry environments in which they take place. Planners must be as experienced in the field of events they are organizing as well as the industries that sponsor them. Some are employed by professional event management organizations, while others are in-house event planners.

From the small board meeting to the citywide convention, business-oriented events are continuing to evolve to meet the needs of the ever-diversifying corporate characters of twenty-first-century businesses. This field will, according to forecasts, continue to grow as part of the twenty-first-century business environment due to the continued demand for successful networking and presentation venues.

BIBLIOGRAPHY

Arcodia, C. & Reid, S. (2008). Professional standards: The current state of event management associations. *Journal of Convention and Event Tourism, 9,* 60-80. Retrieved September 16, 2009 from EBSCO Online Database Academic Search Complete. http://search.ebscohost.com/login.aspx?direct=true&db=a9h&AN=33918576&site=ehost-live.

Dakle, S. (2013). Event management: A study of problems and prospects. *Global Conference on Business & Finance Proceedings, 8,* 202-207. Retrieved November 15, 2013, from EBSCO Online Database Business Source Complete. http://search.ebscohost.com/login.aspx?direct=true&db=bth&AN=89496816&site=ehost-live

Douglas, M-R. & Gregory, S. (2009). Not all politics are local: Exploring the role of meetings and events coordinators in the political arena. *Journal of Convention & Event Tourism, 10,* 134-145. Retrieved September 18, 2009 from EBSCO Online Database Academic Search Complete. http://search.ebscohost.com/login.aspx?direct=true&db=a9h&AN=40627973&site=ehost-live.

Kovaleski, D. (2003). New tool for event management. *Association Meetings, 15,* 19. Retrieved September 17, 2009 from EBSCO Online Database Business Source Premier. http://search.ebscohost.com/login.aspx?direct=true&db=buh&AN=12444005&site=ehost-live.

Ledger, A. (2013). The big debate event management degrees: Are they a waste of time?. *Conference & Incentive Travel,* 14. Retrieved November 15, 2013, from EBSCO Online Database Business Source Complete. http://search.ebscohost.com/login.aspx?direct=true&db=bth&AN=91598237&site=ehost-live

Moscardo, G. & Norris, A. (2004). Bridging the academic practitioner gap in conference and events management: Running events with students. *Journal of Convention and Event Tourism, 6,* 47-62. Retrieved September 16, 2009 from EBSCO Online Database Academic Search Complete. http://search.ebscohost.com/login.aspx?direct=true&db=a9h&AN=16571140&sit e=ehost-live.

Thomas, J. (2013). Develop your own best practice set. *Conference & Incentive Travel,* 16. Retrieved November 15, 2013, from EBSCO Online Database Business Source Complete. http://search.ebscohost.com/login.aspx?direct=true&db=bth&AN=91598239&site=ehost-live

Tiber, E. (1994). How Woodstock happened. *The Times Herald-Record.* Retrieved September 17, 2009 from http://www.discoverynet.com/~barnes/wsrprnt1.htm.

U.S. Bureau of Labor Statistics. (2009). Meeting and convention planners. *Occupational Outlook Handbook, 2008-09 Edition.* Retrieved September 14, 2009 from http://www.bls.gov/oco/ocos298.htm.

SUGGESTED READING

Arcodia, C. & Reid, S. (2003). Goals and objectives of event management associations. *Journal of Convention and Exhibition Management, 5,* 57. Retrieved September 18, 2009 from EBSCO Online Database Academic Search Complete. http://search.ebscohost.com/login.aspx?direct=true&db=a9h&AN=11856551&site=ehost-live.

Landey, J. & Silvers, J. (2004). The miracle of training in event management. *The Journal of Convention & Event Tourism, 6,* 21-46. Retrieved September 18, 2009 from EBSCO Online Database Academic Search Complete. http://search.ebscohost.com/login.aspx?direct=true&db=a9h&AN=16571139&site=ehost-live.

Phelan, K., Kavanaugh, R., Mills, J. & SooChong, J. (2009). Current convention course offerings at the top 25 ranked hospitality management undergraduate programs. *Journal of Teaching and Travel in Tourism, 9*(1/2), 37-62.

Scofidio, B. (Ed). (2007). All about events. *Corporate Meetings and Incentives, 26,* 33. Retrieved September 18, 2009 from EBSCO Online Database Business Source Premier. http://search.ebscohost.com/login.aspx?direct=true&db=buh&AN=24419579&site=ehost-live.

Tassiopoulos, D. (2005). *Event management: A professional and developmental approach—2nd edition.* Juta & Co.

Michael P. Auerbach, M.A.

EXTERNAL BUSINESS COMMUNICATIONS

ABSTRACT

External business communications are the activities through which a company transmits information generated within the company to one or more constituencies outside of the company. Information can be transmitted in this way to a wide variety of constituencies, from customers and shareholders to industry regulators and even business competitors. Some communications are made deliberately, but some become external inadvertently, such as confidential information that is leaked to outside sources. Most information, however, is distributed deliberately with the purpose of improving the company's position in some way.

OVERVIEW

Business communication is often categorized based on what parts of the company the communication concerns, and the most important factor in making this determination is the boundary between what goes on inside the company and what occurs outside of company control. "Internal communication" is the term used to describe all the information exchanges that occur within the firm, and includes types of communication such as employee training, interoffice memos and presentations, and office coordination activities—ordering office supplies, requesting help from the information technology department, and so on. Because these types of information transfer occur inside the company, the company can exercise more control over them, setting rules or establishing official procedures, ensuring that these are followed by everyone, and imposing consequences if they are not followed.

External communication is much less under the company's control, because it involves all the ways in which information is communicated by the company to the outside world. Although the company can try to control what information is sent out, it cannot do much to regulate what happens to that information once it is outside the company or how it is interpreted by others. The most that a company can do with regard to external communications is to try to exert influence over information that is released by selecting what information can be released and then phrasing that information in a way that is most beneficial to the company (Rollins & Lewis, 2014).

External business communication is not monolithic—there are many different types and forms that it can take, just as there are numerous audiences at which it may be directed. The different groups that have an interest in learning about a company are known as stakeholders—they have a stake in what happens to the company, either because they own shares of the company, the value of which they would like to see increase, or because they or their friends and relatives work at the company or do business with it (Stoykov, 2007).

Even customers and potential customers are stakeholders. A person who is considering the purchase of an expensive product, for example, would be very interested to hear about whether or not the company that manufactures it is expected to remain in business for the next few years, because this will affect the type of support the purchaser could expect to receive in the event that the product malfunctions.

Corporations are aware of the differing interests of their stakeholders, and when they prepare external communications, they craft them to better fit the needs of the group or groups they are targeted at. Advertising messages emphasize the company's products and the ways they enhance people's lives, financial reports focus on how the company is positioning itself in order to take advantage of expected conditions in the marketplace, and so on (Waldeck, Durante, Helmuth & Marcia, 2012).

Press Kits

One of the most important external groups that a company can communicate with is made up of representatives of the media. These can include journalists working for newspapers, television stations, or Internet news sites. Some journalists may regularly monitor companies as part of their business and finance coverage, while others will inquire only about unusual events such as a product recall or the release of a much-anticipated product. Still others may be hostile to the corporation due to a conflict between their personal beliefs and the corporation's real or perceived activities—these journalists may conduct investigative reports intended to reveal information that the company might prefer to keep obscure.

Whatever the motivation of members of the media, corporations seek to manage their communication with them accordingly in an effort to encourage them to provide favorable or at least neutral coverage of the company. One way this is done is by preparing and distributing press kits, which are sets of pre-packaged background information about the company and its products (Mileti & Đurovi , 2015). The purpose of a press kit is to make it easier for a journalist to prepare a story about the company by gathering together basic facts about the firm. Since companies create the press kits themselves, they invariably include the information that will improve their corporate image. When the average person picks up a newspaper or tunes in to a television segment, he or she is often unaware that a significant part of the report is taken directly from the press kit—that is, the company's own public relations department.

Advertising

Another major component of external business communication is advertising, which involves the company informing customers and potential customers about its products and services to encourage them to purchase those products and services or improve their opinion about the company. Advertising is vital to the success of most businesses because people cannot support the company by buying its products if they do not know that those products exist.

Even when consumers are aware of a product, there may be other products that have been developed by competing firms with which the product must vie for favor—in these situations, advertising is used to explain to consumers why they should choose one product over others. Because the livelihood of a business largely depends on encouraging people to buy what it is selling and because advertisers have time to carefully craft their advertising to influence customers, advertising is the form of external business communication in which companies invest the most time and attention, spending large portions of their budgets to develop marketing plans and advertising campaigns (Patrutiu-Baltes, 2016).

Financial Reports

In addition to the forms of external communication that a company produces more or less voluntarily, there are some types of information that companies may be required to reveal to the outside world. Often this has to do with the financial state of the company, as government regulations require that certain kinds of data be released periodically, so that investors and those who are considering making an investment can base their decisions on current performance figures.

In some cases this does not present a problem, apart from the company's need to expend sufficient resources to collect and organize the information in preparation for its release; this may require hiring accountants and financial analysts to pore over the firm's balance sheets and create quarterly and annual earnings reports, for example. This is usually the case when the company is performing well, and the news that is to be shared with the public is good. When the news is bad, however, this can have a severe impact on the company and its employees, because it may cause investors to decide to pull their money out of the company by selling their shares or avoid purchasing shares in the first place, placing the company

in an even more precarious situation (Gerdewal & Seçim, 2014).

WEBSITES

Regardless of the type of information being externally communicated or its intended audience, a company's website is one of the main tools used to distribute it. In the days before the Internet, company information was primarily distributed in annual reports printed and mailed to investors and in financial statistics gathered and published by business news outlets and later collected in reference sources that compiled such information from many different firms. The Internet has revolutionized external business communications in the same way that it has affected so many other aspects of modern life.

Instead of having to publish hard-copy reports in huge numbers, company information and annual reports can easily be made available online and delivered worldwide in a matter of seconds instead of days or weeks. There is virtually no limit to the types of company information that a corporation may choose to place on its website, from directories of its officers and staff to detailed research data used to help develop and test its products; for example, a drug manufacturer might use its website to link to copies of the scientific research that establishes that its medicines are safe and effective in the hope that doing so will increase consumer confidence in the medication and result in higher sales (Shrivastava, 2012).

Lobbying

Some types of external communication are controversial by their very nature, and prominent among these is the practice of lobbying. Lobbying is the practice of meeting with elected representatives and other government officials in an attempt to influence official policies and legislation to favor the interests of the person or organization doing the lobbying. Many companies, especially large corporations, spend large sums on lobbying each year. Critics of lobbyists argue that corporations' use of lobbyists and campaign donations results in these entities having an unfair amount of influence, since average citizens lack the resources to lobby for protection of their interests.

Lobbyists and the corporations that employ them respond that all they are really doing is communicating their needs to legislators and anyone can do the same. Lobbyists explain to government officials the challenges that a company is facing and the government actions that would be most helpful in allowing the corporation to overcome them. Typically, these actions involve the modification or elimination of regulations that restrict how the company can operate, or the provision of tax incentives for the corporation that will make it less costly to conduct its business (Bruyer, Jacobs & Vandendaele, 2016).

FURTHER INSIGHTS

In part because businesses must manage their communications with so many different external interest groups, it happens that some types of external communication can interfere with each other. The overall goal of external business communication is always to portray the company in a favorable light, but this means different things to different groups. The company might wish to communicate with environmental groups about how safe its products are for the environment and how much research and development has gone into making sure they do not contaminate the natural world, but when investors hear about this message, they may become concerned that too much time and money is being spent on unnecessary, eco-friendly activities. This could have the unintended consequence of causing investors to reconsider their support of the company. Similarly, lobbying often has negative effects on the public's perception of the company, because some people feel that companies unfairly use their political connections and financial resources to convince legislators to protect them from unfriendly laws and regulations. Companies must therefore be extremely cautious in developing their external communication strategy, so they can attempt to compartmentalize each communication to the greatest degree possible, by using media channels specific to each target audience (Gramatnikovski, Stoilkovska & Serafimovic, 2015).

Since the early part of the twenty-first century, social media networks have proliferated and are now many people's primary source for news and information. Most people in the developed world belong to multiple social networks, and membership in at least one or two is common even in less developed regions. This presents a dilemma for companies seeking to manage their external communications, on at least two levels. First, most companies feel the need to have a presence on the larger social media networks,

so that users of those networks can find out about the company, contact the company's support staff, and stay up to date on new developments.

Just as with any other form of external communication, corporate social media accounts must be carefully managed and integrated into the firm's overall communication plan. At the same time, employees of the company all belong to their own social networks, and the "inside information" that they have access to by working at the company can therefore be put at risk by even the most innocent of social media posts. This has led corporations to implement strict policies about what may and may not be shared on social media by employees.

At the same time, some companies have realized that their own employees can use social media to help support the company's activities by posting about the company's products and helping to spread enthusiasm about them. Still, even this type of activity must be well thought out, lest it be perceived as contrived or even manipulative; there have been a number of cases where a company tried to get its employees to spread the word about a product while concealing the fact that the company was pressuring them to do so. If and when consumers find out this has occurred, there is often a backlash against so-called astroturfing. The name is derived from the observation that the company is trying to fake a grassroots community (Beckers & Bsat, 2014).

BIBLIOGRAPHY

Beckers, A. M., & Bsat, M. Z. (2014). An analysis of intercultural business communication. *Journal of Business & Behavioral Sciences, 26*(3), 143.

Bruyer, T., Jacobs, G., & Vandendaele, A. (2016). Good pharma? How business communication research can help bridge the gap between students and practitioners. *Business & Professional Communication Quarterly, 79*(2), 141. Retrieved October 23, 2016, from EBSCO Online Database Business Source Ultimate. http://search.ebscohost.com/login.aspx?direct=true&db=bsu&AN=116081281&site=ehost-live

Gerdewal, M. T., & Seçim, H. (2014). A business communication design for information technology (IT) organizations based on information technology infrastructure library (ITIL). *Business Management Dynamics, 4*(5), 12. Retrieved October 23, 2016, from EBSCO Online Database Business

Source Ultimate. http://search.ebscohost.com/login.aspx?direct=true&db=bsu&AN=110258089&site=ehost-live

Gramatnikovski, S., Stoilkovska, A., & Serafimovic, G. (2015). Business communication in function of improving the organizational culture of the company. *UTMS Journal of Economics, 6*(2), 267.

Miletić, S., & Đurović, Đ. (2015). Improving enterprise interests through the process of business communication. *Ekonomika, 61*(1), 43. Retrieved October 23, 2016, from EBSCO Online Database Business Source Ultimate. http://search.ebscohost.com/login.aspx?direct=true&db=bsu&AN=101773177&site=ehost-live

Patrutiu-Baltes, L. (2016). The impact of digitalization on business communication. *SEA: Practical Application of Science, 4*(2), 319.

Rollins, W., & Lewis, S. (2014). A comparison of processes used by business executives and university business communication teachers to evaluate selected business documents. *Journal of Organizational Culture, Communications And Conflict,* (1), 139. Retrieved October 23, 2016, from EBSCO Online Database Business Source Ultimate. http://search.ebscohost.com/login.aspx?direct=true&db=bsu&AN=100277127&site=ehost-live

Shrivastava, S. (2012). Identifying the major components of business communication and their relevance: A conceptual framework. *IUP Journal of Soft Skills, 6*(4), 51–66. Retrieved October 23, 2016, from EBSCO Online Database Business Source Ultimate. http://search.ebscohost.com/login.aspx?direct=true&db=bsu&AN=85170846&site=ehost-live

Stoykov, L. (2007). Nature and definitions of business communication. *Language in India, 7*(2), 2–37.

Waldeck, J., Durante, C., Helmuth, B., & Marcia, B. (2012). Communication in a changing world: Contemporary perspectives on business communication competence. *Journal of Education for Business, 87*(4), 230–240. Retrieved October 23, 2016, from EBSCO Online Database Business Source Ultimate. http://search.ebscohost.com/login.aspx?direct=true&db=bsu&AN=92042451&site=ehost-live

SUGGESTED READING

Chernobaeva, G. (2013). Importance of integration of marketing communications in the project activity. *Proceedings of the International Conference on Management, Leadership & Governance,* 372–378. Retrieved October 23, 2016, from EBSCO Online Database Business Source Ultimate. http://search.ebscohost.com/login.aspx?direct=true&db=bsu&AN=87746756&site=ehost-live

Conrad, D., & Newberry, R. (2011). 24 business communication skills: Attitudes of human resource managers versus business educators. *American Communication Journal, 13*(1), 4–23.

Kovac, Kristina, et al. (2016). Neuromarketing: The effect of attitudes on the perception of external business communication. *Rediscovering the Essentiality of Marketing,* pp 95-96. Retrieved on June 29, 2017.

International journal of business communication special issue: Social collaboration and communication (open invitation). (2015). *International Journal of Business Communication, 52*(2), 163. Retrieved October 23, 2016, from EBSCO Online Database Business Source Ultimate. http://search.ebscohost.com/login.aspx?direct=true&db=bsu&AN=101689611&site=ehost-live

Sinha, A. B. (2012). Business communication: The mainstay of an efficient business. *IUP Journal Of Soft Skills, 6*(1), 7–15. Retrieved October 23, 2016, from EBSCO Online Database Business Source Ultimate. http://search.ebscohost.com/login.aspx?direct=true&db=bsu&AN=78153525&site=ehost-live

Turpen, R., & Dyer, H. (2015). Working with external auditors. *Internal Auditor, 72*(1), 17–19. Retrieved October 23, 2016, from EBSCO Online Database Business Source Ultimate. http://search.ebscohost.com/login.aspx?direct=true&db=bsu&AN=108974428&site=ehost-live

Scott Zimmer, J.D.

F

FRANCHISING

ABSTRACT

Franchising is a business model with a track record that spans more than 500 years. In its contemporary form, dozens of industries around the world have companies that use the franchise model. The many benefits of franchising—diminished risk, strong franchisor company support, and affordability—make it a popular option for many entrepreneurs, both new and experienced. Critics, however, claim that the franchising model hinders innovation and autonomy and has higher rates of labor standards violations.

OVERVIEW

The term "franchise" originated from the French "franche," which referred to the privilege of being allowed to invest. Although scholars believe the earliest form of franchise originated in ancient China, in its modern form it began in the Middle Ages, as a privilege granted by rulers to merchants and purveyors. A franchise also authorized individuals to build roads, collect taxes, organize market fairs, and other profitable endeavors. The individual granted the franchise, or the franchisee, was awarded monopoly rights for a specific business and period of time, usually in exchange for a payment or fee. In essence, the franchise fee was a "tax" paid for the monopoly over a certain good and its endorsement by the ruler. Such businesses often had to give the monarch a portion of their profits, hence the term "royalty." Variations on these early systems survive in modern franchises (Dant & Grunhagen, 2014). With the rapid expansion of globalization and telecommunication technologies, contemporary franchise systems are increasingly varied and complex.

Franchising in its current inception refers to a legal contract that cements a business agreement between a grantor firm (franchisor) and a grantee (franchisee), in which the franchisee pays the franchisor for the rights to sell the product or service under the franchisor's brand or trademark. The rights are usually limited to a specific geographic territory and time frame. There are many different types of franchise but most identify closely with an originating business or manufacturer. Some of these were founded between the 1880s and 1920s and have continued into the twenty-first century, such as General Motors dealerships and Hertz car rentals.

The boom in fast food franchises began in the mid-1950s, with the launch of Burger King, followed shortly after by McDonald's, which opened in 1955. These served as the model for the homogenization and standardization typical of modern franchises. The model proved so efficient, it soon spread across industries as diverse as convenience stores, gas stations, childcare services, beauty salons, real estate, accounting services, and many other types of business (Dant & Grunhagen, 2014).

The franchise system became popular early on because it offered a business model in which both parties enjoyed higher levels of certainty than were the norm and both stood to benefit. Franchisees knew they could count on known quantities and franchisors could count on a guaranteed income flow. In most franchise agreements, both sides must contribute to the success of the franchise. Franchisees must prove successful at selling and representing the product, and the franchisor must provide a quality product and know-how.

Franchises are very popular business models because they offer the opportunity to own a business representing a known product or service without the effort, expense, and uncertainty of starting a business from scratch. Franchisors provide logistical support, policies, technical information, and guidance, but selling the product or providing the service is up to the franchisee. In short, it may be a very rewarding arrangement for both parties if all goes well (Laughlin, 2015).

By 2015, approximately 3,700 franchises existed in the United States, representing about 20 industries and 70 categories (Laughlin, 2015). Franchises, then, run the gamut, and while some are modestly affordable, others run into the millions. Franchisees usually acquire their franchise by paying an entry fee and then royalties based on their revenue or gross income. Although a franchise agreement can be a win-win situation for the companies involved, they may often share different goals. For example, franchisors profit from the establishments they own as well as from those owned by their franchisees. Franchisees, on the other hand, need only worry about maximizing the profits of the subset of establishments they own. This often implies two different sets of incentives, priorities, risks, expectations, and costs (Ji & Weil, 2015).

The most common types of franchise businesses are in the restaurant industry. Studies show that in the United States, the eating and drinking industries account for more than 20 percent of franchises. A significant portion of this segment is represented by Top 20 restaurants, which account for about 68 percent of annual sales and 48 percent of employment in the restaurant industry (Ji & Weil, 2015). Other important examples of American franchising businesses are automobile dealerships, gasoline stations, and bottled soft drinks (Dant & Grunhagen, 2014).

FURTHER INSIGHTS

Many different types of franchise exist, such as turnkey franchise, retail franchise, distribution franchise, trademark franchise, banking franchise, cooperative franchise, and product manufacturing franchise. Each may present some variations according to geographic, economic, or social criteria. Franchises are usually temporal agreements limited to a specific territory or geographic area.

Because there are many variables involved in a franchise's success, experts counsel that both sides do their respective due diligence in order to ensure that they are a good fit. Many successful franchisees find a niche business or one that is recession-proof. Another important factor is the size of the territory that a franchisee is allocated as well as the demography and competition. In short, it requires a great deal of research and legwork.

Unsuccessful franchisees often acquire a business model that is not a good fit for his or her skills, personality, and level of motivation. Therefore, critical thinking and self-evaluation are important skills. Franchisees with little capital may be attracted to an inexpensive franchise, yet not take into account that he or she must often not only sell product but also network and manage teams of people (Laughlin, 2015).

On the other hand, franchisees may not need to hire marketing, branding, quality control, or IT personnel because the franchisor often provides those services in its package deal. In other words, they offer the expertise that a franchisee may lack.

A good franchisor can appraise a franchisee's performance and offer advice and guidance. Having to calculate these without access to the larger picture can be burdensome, but with modern technology, franchisors can increasingly help their franchisees connect to software and telecommunications that save much time and money (Laughlin, 2015). Despite these advantages, experts warn that modern franchising contracts have changed since the 1990s, when they experienced a surge. Modern franchising contracts are often extremely long and complex documents and require many different fees. Large franchisors may be inflexible and very reliant on codes and specifications that control every aspect of the business performance and relationship. More often than not, they have become non-negotiable deals, and renewals may depend upon changing business procedures, investing in new branding, or other potentially onerous conditions. This occurs as businesses are faced with the need to ensure homogeneity and standards across national and even international territories. Moreover, franchisors may refuse to offer territorial exclusivity or any individualized provisions. Experts believe that the growing popularity of franchises and the trend toward exponential growth among businesses have created a power imbalance in favor of franchisors, a situation that will probably continue unabated (Dant & Grunhagen, 2014).

However, other experts argue that global developments may ameliorate the one-sidedness of franchising agreements. The twenty-first century experienced a growing tendency toward multi-unit franchisees, that is, those who acquire and operate multiple franchises establishments, nationally and internationally. These franchise aggregates gain power within the network hierarchy. This development has been accompanied by the rapid worldwide expansion of franchising. Experts believe that an explosive expansion of U.S. businesses toward foreign markets is underway, a phenomenon that is replicated across countries and enterprises around the world. Advanced countries such as the United States used to franchise close to its borders or in cultures with which they shared some commonalities, such as the same language.

With the emergence of rapidly industrializing economies such as Brazil, Russia, India, and China—sometime called the BRIC countries—U.S. companies have expanded their franchising efforts across very different cultures. Advanced nations increasingly offer master international franchising agreements in countries across the globe. International master franchising is a contract between a franchisor and an international franchisee, which gives the franchisee a wider span of control in a specific country and for a specified period of time. In fact, by the beginning of the twenty-first century, reports showed that close to 90 percent of quick-service franchisors and 70 percent of restaurant franchisors in foreign markets acquired international master franchises. These developments have given foreign franchisees unprecedented power in their relationship with franchisors; the latter, unfamiliar in foreign markets, need to rely on and trust their franchisees abroad (Dant & Grunhagen, 2014).

Multi-unit franchising, then, is an important trend at the national and international level. For example, the average McDonald's franchisee owns about three restaurants. Another franchisee chain, the Flynn restaurant group, owns more than 500 restaurants across the United States (Lafontaine, 2014).

Franchising has long been considered by many experts as an important system of economic development. When a country shows economic growth, it is associated with business opportunities. First, it decreases the entrepreneurial risk that usually accompanies internationalization efforts by large companies because it uses management and operational processes that have been proven successful. Nevertheless, risk is never reduced absolutely, and social phenomena such as cultural and political factors may affect franchising performance. For example, individualistic cultures seem to prefer holding more control over their businesses than that which franchising often allows. Therefore, there are higher rates of franchising in countries with higher levels of cultural collectivism (Baena & Cervino, 2014).

Moreover, businesses prefer to invest in cultures nearby or that they are familiar with; therefore, the United States is the largest franchise operator in Latin America, with Spain running second. Since the late 1900s, many franchises have opened in Latin American countries such as Argentina, Chile, and Mexico. Studies suggest that the successful expansion of franchising across Latin America correlates with its cultures, which are traditionally low in individualism and prone to avoid uncertainty. In consequence, many Latin American entrepreneurs prefer to open businesses that minimize risk and provide the security of known factors, rather than starting a business from scratch or engaging in much innovation (Baena & Cervino, 2014).

According to an Iberoamerican Federation of Franchising Report in 2012, franchising in Latin America is growing exponentially, not only by way of business from advanced nations penetrating its markets, but also from some Latin American nations to others (Baena & Cervino, 2014). In fact, several Latin American franchises have begun to penetrate the North American markets and those of other nations abroad, such as the Guatemalan fried chicken brand Pollo Campero, which now has many franchises across the United States, Latin America, and China.

Beyond Latin America, franchising is proliferating in other emerging economies. Besides cultural elements mentioned above, experts also point to economic and financial factors. For example, the risks involved in new projects by untried entrepreneurs make it very difficult to find access to capital. In other words, few investors want to risk their capital in developing nation entrepreneurship and innovation, finding it too risky. Lack of funds prevents entrepreneurs in developing nations not only from opening new businesses from scratch, but also from networking in the national and international markets. Because they lack experience, they are not attractive to investors. These are common scenarios that make franchising a very attractive option. Franchises are often affordable for many, depending upon industry and brand, and offer growth opportunities for entrepreneurs without ample financial capital and field experience, but enough motivation and discipline to succeed (Lewandoska, 2014).

VIEWPOINTS

Despite the advantages and popularity of franchising, the proliferation of the business model and the relatively low levels of oversight have been cause of some concern among some scholars, activists, and public officials. Critics argue, for example, that franchising is ubiquitous in the food and beverage industry, an area that is already rife with labor violations related to minimum-wage and work-hours regulations. There are many complaints by workers who claim they have been pressured to do unpaid work before clocking in and after clocking out of their work shifts, as well as other abuses common to low-wage industries. In fact, government and academic studies find that franchise businesses are often guilty of noncompliance with labor standards and regulations (Ji & Weil, 2015).

Experts have examined industry practices to determine the reasons for the increase in labor standards violations overall and for franchise businesses' decisions to comply or not with labor standards. Results suggest that the business model or organization is often related to noncompliance precisely because of the prevalence of low-wage industries in franchising, such as restaurants and hotels. Large franchisors benefit from the incoming capital from franchisees; however, they are also concerned with maintaining and enhancing the reputation of their company or brand.

Franchisees also operate their own establishments, for which they usually operate directly through managers and staff. Franchisees, however, tend to own a small number of establishments and have different concerns and costs than the franchisor. For example, Burger King owns approximately 600 establishments, while the average franchisee owns one to three. This makes franchisees, then, less invested in the upkeep of standards and regulations than are franchisors (Ji & Weil, 2015). In addition, franchisees run a relatively low risk of investigation by labor standards inspectors, because they own fewer establishments than the franchisor. Moreover, even for larger establishments, the risk of investigation is low, given funding cuts to government agencies that are charged with inspecting businesses and investigating complaints.

Franchisors and franchisees also face differences in operational costs. Franchisees' profits are the difference between their operating expenses (costs for overhead, labor, supplies, and such) and their revenue (sales minus royalty fees paid to the franchisor). In other words, because the franchisor receives a portion of the franchisee's revenues, a franchisee will always profit less from its products or services than does the franchisor. As experts posit, then, the higher the fees paid by the franchisee, the less the incentive to comply with labor standards, which come at a cost. In short, this may explain why there is higher compliance with labor standards in company-owned establishments than in their franchised establishments (Ji & Weil, 2015).

Finally, both franchisors and franchisees are stakeholders in the reputation of the company brand. In fact, the brand's reputation is likely to have been an investment incentive for the franchisee. On the other hand, the average franchisee owns a small number of franchised establishments, so that its stake is lower than that of the franchisor. In other words, a franchisee has less to lose than a franchisor if the company reputation suffers a detrimental impact and franchisors, then, are more concerned about the brand's reputation. Moreover, the decreased profits and other costs incurred by franchisees diminish the overall importance of brand reputation. This lower concern for brand reputation, according to experts, is also a motivator for higher noncompliance with labor standards among franchise companies (Ji & Weil, 2015).

However, these issues, although serious, are not to say that franchising is not a good business model. Many franchisees exhibit excellence in labor standards compliance, and many instances of noncompliance may be the result of error or misinformation. Franchisors could collaborate with their franchisees to educate them as to Fair Labor Standards Act, compensable hours, and best business practices. Contractual agreements between franchisors and franchisees may include periodic hour, wage, and workplace audits. The many benefits of franchising—risk avoidance, higher purchasing power, assistance with marketing, operations, logistics, and training—are among the many reasons franchising has maintained a track record of success.

BIBLIOGRAPHY

Baena, V., & Cervino, J. (2014). International franchising decision-making: A model for country choice. *Latin American Business Review, 15*(1), 13–43. Retrieved December 27, 2015 from EBSCO

Online Database Business Source Complete. http://search.ebscohost.com/login.aspx?direct=true&db=bth&AN=94873048&site=ehost-live

Dant, R. P., & Grunhagen, M. (2014). International franchising research: Some thoughts on what, where, when, and how. Journal of Marketing Channels, 21(3), 124–132. Retrieved December 27, 2015 from EBSCO Online Database Business Source Complete. http://search.ebscohost.com/login.aspx?direct=true&db=bth&AN=96920460&site=ehost-live

Edger, C., & Emmerson, A. (2015). Franchising: How Both Sides Can Win. Oxfordshire, UK: Libri Publishing.

Ji, M., & Weil, D. (2015). The impact of franchising on labor standards compliance. Industrial & Labor Relations Review, 58(5), 977–1006. Retrieved December 27, 2015 from EBSCO Online Database Business Source Complete. http://search.ebscohost.com/login.aspx?direct=true&db=bth&AN=110155332&site=ehost-live

Lafontaine, F. (2014). Franchising: Directions for future research. International Journal of the Economics of Business, 21(1), 21–25. Retrieved December 27, 2015 from EBSCO Online Database Business Source Complete. http://search.ebscohost.com/login.aspx?direct=true&db=bth&AN=94381259&site=ehost-live

Laughlin, F. (2015). How to Succeed in Franchising. Nulkaba, AU: Lioncrest Publishing.

Lewandoska, Lucyna. (2014). Franchising as a way of creating entrepreneurship and innovation. Comparative Economic Research, 17(3), 163–181. Retrieved December 27, 2015 from EBSCO Online Database Business Source Complete. http://

search.ebscohost.com/login.aspx?direct=true&db=bth&AN=99346623&site=ehost-live

Meiklejohn, A. (2014). Franchising: Cases, materials & problems. Chicago, IL: American Bar Association.

SUGGESTED READING

Gerhardt, S., Hazen, S., Lewis, S., & Hall, R. (2015). Entrepreneur options: "Franchising" vs. "licensing" (McDonald's vs. Starbucks and Chick-Fil-A). ASBBBS Ejournal, 11(1), 80–88. Retrieved December 27, 2015 from EBSCO Online Database Business Source Complete. http://search.ebscohost.com/login.aspx?direct=true&db=bth&AN=108548019&site=ehost-live

Lewandoska, Lucyna. (2014). Franchising as a way of creating entrepreneurship and innovation. Comparative Economic Research, 17(3), 163–181. Retrieved December 27, 2015 from EBSCO Online Database Business Source Complete. http://search.ebscohost.com/login.aspx?direct=true&db=bth&AN=99346623&site=ehost-live

Merrilees, B. (2014). International franchising: Evolution of theory and practice. Journal of Marketing Channels, 2(3), 133–142. Retrieved December 27, 2015 from EBSCO Online Database Business Source Complete. http://search.ebscohost.com/login.aspx?direct=true&db=bth&AN=96920461&site=ehost-live

Suh, Taewon, et al. Brand resonance in franchising relationships: A franichisee-based perspective. *Journal of Buisness Research*, 69, 10, 3943-3950. Retrieved on June 29, 2017.

Trudy Mercadal, Ph.D.

FUTURE OF INTEGRATED MARKETING COMMUNICATIONS

ABSTRACT

Changes in the business environment, along with technological innovation, increasing consumer sophistication, and changes in marketing communications practices have led organizations to seek to improve relationships with their consumers and strive to deliver consistent messages to all stakeholders across a wide range of marketing communications channels in order to effectively reinforce their core proposition. Although Integrated Marketing Communications (IMC) is an emerging field with a seemingly underdeveloped theoretical base, it appears to be an unavoidable trend that will continue into the future.

OVERVIEW

Marketing is the way companies strategically develop, price, promote, and distribute their products to increase customer interest and attain organizational goals. Marketing communications refers to the messages and related media used to communicate with a market. The idea of integrating marketing and communications dates back to early marketing literature, but the term Integrated Marketing Communications (IMC) only became popular in the 1980s. Even so, it was not until 1991 that a task force of academics and professionals began looking into issues such as appropriate terminology and definitions.

IMC can be defined as "the concept and process of strategically managing audience-focused, channel-centered, and results-driven brand communication programs over time" (Kliatchko, 2005, p. 23). By drawing from the fields of psychology, marketing and mass communications, IMC reveals the subtle ways in which consumers respond to marketing communications, thus helping marketers to better manage their marketing communications choices and maximize their effectiveness.

In addition, IMC helps organizations maximize their resources and link their communications activities. IMC integrates elements of the promotional mix as well as the creative elements, organizational factors, and the promotional mix with other marketing mix factors. IMC also integrates information and database systems, communications to internal and external audiences, and corporate communication, and promotes geographical integration.

A major feature of IMC is the shift from traditional, one-way marketing communications and advertising channels like advertising, public relations, sales promotion, specialty items, merchandising, packaging, and licensing; to two-way channels such as personal sales, direct response marketing, events and sponsorships, trade shows and exhibitions, e-commerce, customer loyalty programs, plant tours and other customer service activities (McGrath, 2005b).

Scholars and practitioners have begun to recognize a growing need to integrate marketing communications. Many factors have contributed to this need, including:

- Communications agency mergers and acquisitions
- An increasing sophistication of clients and retailers, causing marketers to develop more elaborate and quicker response systems
- The desire of firms for interaction and synergy with their stakeholders
- The need for firms to save costs, causing companies to pursue new methods to increase productivity and value from marketing and media expenses
- The increasing cost and decreasing effectiveness of traditional marketing and advertising, due to the rapid development and increasing effectiveness of integrative and interactive information technology
- The decreasing cost of database development and usage
- Increasing global competition
- Increasing global and regional coordination

The rise of corporate brands companies use to communicate core values to different stakeholders, as against individual brands that are costly to manage and promote

Organizations that are well integrated will maximize the impact on their consumers and other end users at a minimal cost for all of the organization's communications, whether business-to-business, customer-focused, or internally oriented. Such organizations will enjoy consistent messages with a consistent style and theme. Consistency will be maintained across a wide range of communications channels; costs will be reduced through the prevention of duplication of effort; corporate cohesion will increase; and dialogue and relationships with customers will also improve ("Chapter 5," 2003).

Generally, IMC is not easy to implement, but some firms find it easier to implement than others. For instance, according to Low (2000), small, consumer-focused, service-oriented companies in industries like manufacturing, agriculture, forestry, and mining are more likely to have IMC programs, since they typically target fewer market segments and therefore require fewer messages than large, product-oriented companies. It is also believed that IMC has the potential to thrive in conditions where there is the availability of experienced managers; where the market share for products or services is growing; and where competitive intensity is high.

FURTHER INSIGHTS

Theoretical Foundations—IMC & the Consumer.

According to McGrath (2005b), IMC is based on three theoretical foundations. The first foundation proposes that IMC is based on an ongoing and dynamic two-way dialogue or relationship between consumers and marketers, with marketers seeking ways to strengthen their brand's relationship with the consumer and with consumers using their own resources to develop a relationship with the brand.

In order to have effective relationships with their customers through IMC, marketers first need to know *why* consumers respond to marketing communications. Research in social psychology implies that consumers respond to marketing communications because of a natural desire or need to "complete" their concepts of themselves, otherwise known as their 'self-concepts.' A person feeling 'incomplete' might fill a perceived gap through the buying of material goods, and marketing communications can be used to influence or define which specific brands can best fill the gap. Additionally, marketers may position their products as desired, or even required, extensions of a person's self-concept, as is the case with luxury items such as clothing, luxury automobiles, and exotic vacations.

Marketers also need to know *how* consumers respond to marketing communications. The field of cognitive psychology has given insight into the ways in which human beings process external stimuli, including marketing communications messages. It is known that "individuals base many decisions concerning products on their attitudes toward individual brands, and these attitudes can be influenced by marketing communications" (McGrath, 2005b, p. 4).

Consumers respond to marketing communications stimuli in three stages: cognitive, affective, and conative. The cognitive stage involves conscious intellectual activity, while the affective involves feelings and emotion. The conative stage is where consumers are inclined to take action. Equipped with the knowledge of how their own consumers respond to marketing communications, marketers can employ media planning models to determine the optimum amount of exposure that will help consumers receive the intended message.

It is also known that there are two routes to persuasion: central and peripheral. Marketing communications messages that encourage central processing can "lead to the creation of relatively strong and long-lasting attitudes about the messages" (McGrath, 2005b, p. 5). On the other hand, marketing communications messages that "employ superficial or peripheral techniques (such as the attractiveness of the message presenter, the credibility of the message source, etc.) will not be as long lasting or as resistant to change as those processed centrally" (McGrath, 2005b, p. 5).

Consumers develop opinions about brands through product or service use and through exposure to marketing communications messages: This knowledge helps marketers advertise brands in a way that encourages consumers to link their opinion of a brand with values that are important to them.

The second theoretical foundation of the IMC concept highlights the need to maintain a consistent message throughout all marketing media outlets and especially across all marketing communications messages. It is important that organizations and brands maintain a clear and consistent visual image (including color schemes, logos, symbols, and other design elements), position, verbal and/or text theme (including body copy, typography, tag lines, and other devices) across all marketing communications channels to ensure "one-voice" or "one personality" consistency and "seamless" communications. A corporate manual will help to ensure a consistent corporate brand.

It is believed that messages that are consistent across different channels may create traces in the consumer's memory and that these traces may be revived and intensified upon exposure to subsequent messages from different channels that the same conceptual themes. Thus, a brand using the IMC strategy of integrating different types of communications channels may be more memorable to the consumer and processed more easily than a series of brand messages that offer relatively inconsistent information across different channels. Message consistency simplifies mental message processing by today's consumers, who are inundated with increasing amounts of competing message stimuli.

The third theoretical foundation of IMC suggests that all facets of a brand's relationship with a consumer must be taken into consideration. Both traditional promotion channels and non-traditional means of promotion must be considered, and likewise, the various internal and external communications functions must be strategically integrated. A consistent brand message that is integrated across the entire range of marketing communications will allow for consistent clarity and reinforcement of an organization's (or a brand's) main proposition.

"The theory of an IMC program is that it has one basic communications strategy for each major target audience. This one strategy is then used as the basis for executing each communications function (advertising, PR, sales promotion, etc.) throughout a variety of communications channels" (Duncan, 1993, p. 31).

Firms with high integration of marketing channels will have their channel integration including everything from the design of the product itself to its packaging, its distribution, its pricing, and its marketing communications efforts (McGrath, 2005b). Also, the integration of common messages must span all market segments and geographical regions. The Internet is particularly helpful in this regard, enabling organizations to have an international presence and enabling the integration of communication around individual customers and stakeholders through means such as cookie technology, which reveals information about the behavior of individual consumers through site visits.

Each element of the communications mix must support consumer expectations of a brand that in turn must be integrated and coordinated so it supports the others. Even the timing of each message must be coordinated to ensure maximum synergy.

IMC & the Organization. Since IMC requires the strategic management of audience-focused, channel-centered, and results-driven brand communication programs over time, any organization that desires to develop IMC must first make some key internal changes, phased over time. The nature and speed of adoption of IMC will vary from organization to organization: There is no single formula for the development of IMC (Fill, 2001).

IMC requires a strong blending of internal and external communications in order for it to be identified with the strategy and direction of an organization. As such, IMC must first involve the entire organization in an internal reorientation so that the organization's entire internal audience—employees, managers and members of the board of directors—become customer-focused, speak with 'one voice,' and have their attitudes and behaviors reflecting the brand that they represent. As internal positive relationships are built

and strengthened, internal stakeholders will develop a sense of loyalty and business ownership.

Organizations should also establish a market-oriented organizational structure instead of the traditional brand management setup. This requires that responsibility for communications functions be given to a single position within the organization (typically a senior manager with relevant experience), who would handle strategic direction and planning. Creative and media services should be outsourced to a single agency that should be accountable for maintaining message coherence and coordinating communications programs.

Organizations and their agencies become channel-centered by planning and managing the coordinated use of appropriate and multiple communications channels such as advertising, public relations, direct marketing, sales promotions, and the Internet. In addition, the use of all other sources of information and brand contact points must also be planned and coordinated so that they may reach and connect with target audiences.

To achieve IMC, an organization must prepare a plan with full senior management support. In order to decide which elements of the communications mix should be selected and integrated into a marketing campaign, the organization must carry out a situation analysis, looking at internal factors such as core competencies, strengths and weaknesses, product and service objectives, budgets and strategies adopted, as well as external factors such as competitor analysis, customer needs analysis and channels for delivery, and environmental scanning ("Chapter 5," 2003).

The plan must then be communicated to all other staff in the organization so that each internal stakeholder will understand it and actively support its implementation in his or her day-to-day activities. Once the internal reorientation and plan implementation are underway, the messages to be communicated must be integrated in all the chosen media to all target external audiences, including customers, consumers, prospective customers, government, and other entities outside the organization.

With IMC, it is audience or the target consumer, and not the interest of the marketer or communications agency, that must drive the planning and selection process. Therefore, it is important that organizations maintain media neutrality in planning media channels or the message delivery system, treating all communications channels equally without bias or preference for one medium over the others.

IMC must be results-driven, with its effectiveness tracked through customer valuation of the identified markets, and through return on customer investments. The financial measurement of IMC programs involves observing and tracking their impact along with the behavioral responses and effects on target audiences over time.

Organizations developing IMC must use the knowledge and skills of strategic management (such as planning, directing and controlling) to enable both the IMC process and an entire brand communication program to fit in with the overall corporate vision and business objectives. Many initiatives should be put in place to support the outworking of IMC. For instance, top management must be closely involved; organization structures should be supportive; employees should undergo cross-functional training; and a 'culture of marketing' should be created as part of the organization's corporate philosophy.

Since market conditions are continually changing, IMC planners should, as much as possible, adopt a zero-based planning approach, where all objectives and strategies should be formed at the time as opposed to relying on previous plans ("Chapter 5," 2003). In this regard, budget allocations should be based on the marketing communications objectives that need to be achieved, rather than being constrained by budgets imposed by management.

IMC is not easy to develop—it takes time, and all the more so in the case of diversified organizations with multiple products, multiple market segments, and multiple functional divisions across multiple geographical locations. Organizations will have to contend with many barriers to integration including the following:

- Fear of change and loss of control
- Hierarchical organizational structures
- Traditional command-and-control organizational structures
- Functional competition (with issues of power, coordination, and control)
- Multiple budgeting processes
- Profit goals set internally and not based on customers
- Short-term planning focused only on the acquisition of new customers, not on long-term customer loyalty and retention

- Lack of database development
- Media fragmentation
- Agency resistance to integration and a lack of willingness to work across the media and promotional mix
- Incomplete understanding of the integration process
- Junior and inexperienced employees in charge of developing communications
- Lack of cross-discipline management skills

VIEWPOINTS

While IMC has been lauded by many, it also has many critics, some of whom have gone as far as pronouncing IMC's demise on the grounds that there is too much misunderstanding surrounding this emerging field. According to Kliatchko (2005), the divergent viewpoints and criticisms stem from the following:

- Disagreements on definitional issues and scope of IMC
- Difficulties arising from the view that IMC is both a concept and a process
- Contentions on whether IMC is merely a fad or a management fashion
- Debate over measurement methods used in evaluating IMC programs
- Controversy over turf battles and on who leads the integration process
- Conflicts on agency-client relationships, organizational structures, and compensation issues

Academics and practitioners still disagree on definitional issues concerning IMC, as well as the scope of IMC. Even the term Integrated Marketing Communications has many other names, such as new advertising, orchestration, 360 branding, total branding, whole egg, seamless communication, relationship marketing, one-to-one marketing, integrated marketing and integrated communications (Kliatchko, 2002, p. 7). The literature also lacks empirical evidence to support the theoretical underpinnings of IMC. In addition, when it comes to the practice of IMC, there remains much controversy and debate over its actual adoption, content, and effect. Likewise, the view that IMC is both a concept and a process impedes the formation of definitions and other foundational issues.

While some scholars believe that IMC is a fad without a solid theoretical base, others believe that IMC is not new at all. Specifically, some suggest that IMC reinvents existing marketing theory by using different terminology for existing concepts. To support this view, the proponents of this argument cite the fact that small marketing departments have always had a quasi-integrated approach, since everyone in the department is involved in all the major communications programs. Also cited is the fact that smaller communications agencies have long been practicing coordinated planning for their clients and the fact that textbooks with marketing communications emphases have been in circulation for years (Duncan, 1993).

The supporters of IMC also say that IMC is an unavoidable trend. According to them, changing marketing factors inevitably require such a marketing strategy. Due to technological advancements, modern customers tend to integrate marketing communications, obtaining information and making decisions as and when they want, regardless of whether marketers and agencies integrate *their* communications. Likewise, globalization and global forces favor—and probably require—IMC for the successful marketing of global businesses and global brands. Proponents of IMC also say that it cannot be a fad since it reflects major changes in the ways in which organizations and their agencies approach marketing communications.

The quest is still on for a means to effectively evaluate and measure IMC. Effective evaluation requires 'thinking outside the box'—using new criterion instead of the existing models. Controversy over turf battles and on who leads the integration process has also contributed to the widening disparity of viewpoints on IMC, including conflicts on agency-client relationships, organizational structures, and compensation issues. Such issues are difficult to generalize because, as Kim and Schulz (2004) point out, agency-client relationships are influenced by agency and client interests, as well as by the specific social, cultural, institutional, and organizational factors in each country. Therefore, the client and agency situation varies from country to country.

Criticisms of IMC have been fueled by the fact that many of the few quantitative studies in IMC research are inconclusive, leaving many unanswered questions. Moreover, some main empirical studies on factors related to IMC contradict each other. In response to the critics, however, the supporters of IMC affirm that IMC is still developing as a field and that many of the matters being raised by critics are typical of "an evolutionary field, still undergoing a process of definition and redefinition" (McGrath, 2005b, p. 3).

For IMC to be effective into the future and mature as a field of study and practice, much more research must be undertaken to help formalize and reinforce IMC theory—or to simply help confirm or negate its validity.

BIBLIOGRAPHY

Barger, V. A., & Labrecque, L. I. (2013). An integrated marketing communications perspective on social media metrics. *International Journal of Integrated Marketing Communications, 5*, 64–76. Retrieved November 15, 2013, from EBSCO Online Database Business Source Complete. http://search.ebscohost.com/login.aspx?direct=true&db=bth&AN=87965639&site=ehost-live

Chapter 5: The tools of corporate reputation: Integrated marketing communications (IMC). (2003). *Managing Corporate Reputation, 103*–128. Retrieved May 26, 2007, from EBSCO Online Database Business Source Complete. http://search.ebscohost.com/login.aspx?direct=true&db=bth&AN=22377418&site=ehost-live

Clow, K., & Baack, D. (2005). Integrated marketing communications. *Concise Encyclopedia of Advertising, 97*–98. Retrieved May 26, 2007, from EBSCO Online Database Business Source Complete. http://search.ebscohost.com/login.aspx?direct=true&db=bth&AN=22573943&site=ehost-live

Cornelissen, J. (2003). Change, continuity and progress: The concept of integrated marketing communications and marketing communications practice. *Journal of Strategic Marketing, 11*, 217–234. Retrieved May 26, 2007, from EBSCO Online Database Business Source Complete. http://search.ebscohost.com/login.aspx?direct=true&db=bth&AN=11763013&site=ehost-live

Duncan, T., & Everett, S. (1993). Client perceptions of integrated marketing communications. *Journal of Advertising Research, 33*, 30–39. Retrieved May 26, 2007, from EBSCO Online Database Business Source Complete. http://search.ebscohost.com/login.aspx?direct=true&db=bth&AN=9309136066&site=ehost-live

Fill, C. (2001). Essentially a matter of consistency: Integrated marketing communications. *Marketing*

Review, 1, 409. Retrieved May 26, 2007, from EBSCO Online Database Business Source Complete. http://search.ebscohost.com/login.aspx?direct=true&db=bth&AN=5776082&site=ehost-live

Gonring, M. (1994). Putting integrated marketing communications to work today. *Public Relations Quarterly, 39,* 45–48. Retrieved May 26, 2007, from EBSCO Online Database Business Source Complete. http://search.ebscohost.com/login.aspx?direct=true&db=bth&AN=9412092110&site=ehost-live

Gronstedt, A. (1997). Internet: IMC on steroids. *Marketing News, 31,* 9. Retrieved May 26, 2007, from EBSCO Online Database Business Source Complete. http://search.ebscohost.com/login.aspx?direct=true&db=bth&AN=9706055169&site=ehost-live

Hart, N. (1999). Chapter 1: Integrated marketing communications planning. *Implementing an Integrated Marketing Communications Strategy,* 1–12. Thorogood Publishing Ltd. Retrieved May 26, 2007, from EBSCO Online Database Business Source Complete. http://search.ebscohost.com/login.aspx?direct=true&db=bth&AN=22386401&site=ehost-live

Hartley, B., & Pickton, D. (1999). Integrated marketing communications requires a new way of thinking. *Journal of Marketing Communications, 5,* 97–106. Retrieved May 26, 2007, from EBSCO Online Database Business Source Complete. http://search.ebscohost.com/login.aspx?direct=true&db=bth&AN=3960635&site=ehost-live

Hill, D., Fink, R., & Morgan, A. (1998). Plant tours as a customer contact tool: An integrated marketing communications framework. *Journal of Marketing Management (10711988), 8,* 44–51. Retrieved May 26, 2007, from EBSCO Online Database Business Source Complete. http://search.ebscohost.com/login.aspx?direct=true&db=bth&AN=18078408&site=ehost-live

Keller, K. L. (2016). Unlocking the power of integrated marketing communications: how integrated is your imc program?. *Journal of Advertising, 45*(3), 286–301. doi:10.1080/00913367.2016.1204967. Retrieved December 28, 2016, from EBSCO online database Business Source Ultimate. http://search.ebscohost.com/login.aspx?direct=true&db=bsu&AN=117922895&site=ehost-live&scope=site

Kim, I., Han, D., & Schultz, D. (2004). Understanding the diffusion of integrated marketing communications. *Journal of Advertising Research, 44,* 31–45. Retrieved May 26, 2007, from EBSCO Online Database Business Source Complete. http://search.ebscohost.com/login.aspx?direct=true&db=bth&AN=13045723&site=ehost-live

Kitchen, P., & Li, T. (2005). Perceptions of integrated marketing communications: A Chinese ad and PR agency perspective. *International Journal of Advertising, 24,* 51–78. Retrieved May 26, 2007, from EBSCO Online Database Business Source Complete. http://search.ebscohost.com/login.aspx?direct=true&db=bth&AN=16626096&site=ehost-live

Kliatchko, J. (2002). *Understanding integrated marketing communications.* Pasig City, Philippines: Inkwell Publishing.

Kliatchko, J. (2005). Towards a new definition of integrated marketing communications (IMC). *International Journal of Advertising, 24,* 7–34. Retrieved May 26, 2007, from EBSCO Online Database Business Source Complete. http://search.ebscohost.com/login.aspx?direct=true&db=bth&AN=16626064&site=ehost-live

Low, G. (2000). Correlates of integrated marketing communications. *Journal of Advertising Research, 40,* 27. Retrieved May 26, 2007, from EBSCO Online Database Business Source Complete. http://search.ebscohost.com/login.aspx?direct=true&db=bth&AN=3351535&site=ehost-live

Luo, L. (2011). Product line design for consumer durables: An integrated marketing and engineering approach. *Journal of Marketing Research (JMR), 48,* 128–139. Retrieved November 15, 2013, from EBSCO Online Database Business Source Complete. http://search.ebscohost.com/login.aspx?direct=true&db=bth&AN=57434514&site=ehost-live

McArthur, D., & Griffin, T. (1997). A marketing management view of integrated marketing communications. *Journal of Advertising Research, 37,* 19–26. Retrieved May 26, 2007, from EBSCO Online Database Business Source Complete. http://search.ebscohost.com/login.aspx?direct=true&db=bth&AN=1841&site=ehost-live

McGrath, J. (2005a). A pilot study testing aspects of the integrated marketing communications concept. *Journal of Marketing Communications, 11,*

191–214. Retrieved May 26, 2007, from EBSCO Online Database Business Source Complete. http://search.ebscohost.com/login.aspx?direct=true&db=bth&AN=17926963&site=ehost-live

McGrath, J. (2005b). IMC at a crossroads: A theoretical review and a conceptual framework for testing. *Marketing Management Journal, 15*, 55–66. Retrieved May 26, 2007, from EBSCO Online Database Business Source Complete. http://search.ebscohost.com/login.aspx?direct=true&db=bth&AN=19403280&site=ehost-live

Schlinke, J., & Crain, S. (2013). Social media from an integrated marketing and compliance perspective. *Journal of Financial Service Professionals, 67*, 85–92. Retrieved November 15, 2013, from EBSCO Online Database Business Source Complete. http://search.ebscohost.com/login.aspx?direct=true&db=bth&AN=85802252&site=ehost-live

Spiller, L. D. (2013). Using metrics to drive integrated marketing communication decisions: Hi-Ho Silver. *International Journal of Integrated Marketing Communications, 5*, 24–38. Retrieved November 15, 2013, from EBSCO Online Database Business Source Complete. http://search.ebscohost.com/login.aspx?direct=true&db=bth&AN=87965636&site=ehost-live

Suggested Reading

Batra, R., & Keller, K. L. (2016). Integrating marketing communications: New findings, new lessons, and new ideas. *Journal of Marketing, 80*(6), 122–145. doi:10.1509/jm.15.0419. Retrieved December 28, 2016, from EBSCO online database Business Source Ultimate. http://search.ebscohost.com/login.aspx?direct=true&db=bsu&AN=119129833&site=ehost-live&scope=site

Finne, Ake, et al. (2017). Communication-in-use: customer-integrated marketing communication. *European Journal of Marketing*. Retrieved on June 29, 2017.

Gould, S., Lerman, D., & Grein, A. (1999). Agency perceptions and practices on global IMC. *Journal of Advertising Research, 39*, 7–20. Retrieved May 26, 2007, from EBSCO Online Database Business Source Complete. http://search.ebscohost.com/login.aspx?direct=true&db=bth&AN=1898809&site=ehost-live

Kitchen, P., & Schultz, D. (2003). Integrated corporate and product brand communication. *Advances in Competitiveness Research, 11*, 66–86. Retrieved May 26, 2007, from EBSCO Online Database Business Source Complete. http://search.ebscohost.com/login.aspx?direct=true&db=bth&AN=13380272&site=ehost-live

McGrath, J. (2001). Integrated marketing communications: Some new experimental evidence. *AMA Winter Educators' Conference Proceedings, 12*, 318.

Schultz, D.E. & Schultz, H.F. (1998). Transitioning marketing communication into the twenty-first century. *Journal of Marketing Communications 4*, 9–26.

Vanessa A. Tetteh, Ph.D.

G

GLOBAL MARKETING

ABSTRACT

This article will focus on how organizations can position themselves for successful global marketing. When entering the global market, social, economic, political, technological, and institutional factors are added into the equation as multinational corporations develop global marketing strategies. In order to be successful in global marketing, organizations will have to integrate their marketing initiatives into different countries. Given the changes that are occurring in the way business is conducted today, marketing professionals must be prepared to create campaigns that appeal to a global clientele. Global marketing is successful when there is coordination between the marketing policies for different countries and when the marketing equation for different countries can be adapted to the local market.

OVERVIEW

There is much activity between people, products, and organizations crossing over borders, which has led to the creation and growth of new global market segments. In addition, many forces are transforming markets and changing the way that business is conducted. Factors that influence marketing include the marketing environment, types of customers, and competition in the market. When entering the global market, social, economic, political, technological, and institutional factors are added into the equation as multinational corporations develop global marketing strategies.

In most cases, global marketing generally manifests itself in two different phases (Caslione, 2003). The first phase is usually when an organization experiences rapid growth, high sales, and high profits. During this period, there tends to be an increased level of competition for limited resources. In addition, customers, suppliers, and governments tend to be difficult to work with, and it is hard to develop relationships among these groups. However, "there is a specific infrastructure and unique behavioral mode of collective thinking and actions, which is referred to as the accelerated reactivity phase of globalization" (Caslione, 2003, p. 1).

The second phase occurs when an organization experiences slower economic growth, lower sales and profits, and reduced competition for limited sources. During this period, it is easier to gain access to customers, suppliers, and governments. Collaboration between these three groups is positive as all are attempting to find ways to improve the situation. Unlike the first phase, this period is categorized as a "decelerated proactivity phase of globalization due to a different type of infrastructure and behavioral mode dominating" (Caslione, 2003, p. 2).

Caslione (2003) believes that successful marketing professionals will be able to recognize and master the two different phases mentioned above by:

- Measuring results within each country and region
- Using a combination of marketing communication media
- Using a globally centered mix of communications, marketing, and advertising
- Building the corporate brand globally, country by country
- Appointing an experienced, highly motivated multicultural marketing team

Marketing professionals will be required to understand the marketing concepts and practices needed to penetrate the political, economic, and social environments of potential markets (Kahle, Marshall & Kropp, 2003). In the era of global marketing, many organizations will be challenged to keep abreast of events affecting the marketing environment if they want to survive (Lin & Kao, 2004). In order to be successful in global marketing, organizations will have to integrate their marketing initiatives into different countries.

Preparing Marketing Professionals

Given the changes that are occurring in the way business is conducted today, marketing professionals must be prepared to create campaigns that appeal to a global clientele. Globalization is reshaping business strategy, especially marketing strategy, and marketing professionals will have to transition from a domestic focus to a global focus (Caslione, 2003). It will be imperative for marketing professionals to become well versed in the profiles of different segments that their organization plans to pursue. Unfortunately, many in the field are not prepared to make the transition. In a study conducted by the Massachusetts Institute of Technology (MIT), researchers found that 29 percent of the organizations surveyed did not have enough global marketing leaders in their organizations, 56 percent of the organizations believed that they did not have sufficient numbers of global marketing leaders to take their organization to the next level, and 80 percent were concerned that they lacked the global marketing professionals needed to staff their global marketing initiatives (Caslione, 2003). Therefore, marketers will need to upgrade their skill set in the field in order to be competitive in the market. As the marketing professionals become equipped for the challenge, they will be tasked to deal with the issues that have arisen in the field.

APPLICATION

Global Marketing Strategies

Globalization is not a new trend (IMF, 2002). With the prospect of conducting business on a global scale, global marketing professionals should create global strategies that will allow their organizations to reap benefits instead of getting trapped by pitfalls. In order to be successful in global marketing, organizations will have to integrate their marketing initiatives into different countries. Reddy and Vyas (2004) created a list of advantages and disadvantages of globalization as it pertains to marketing; information that is beneficial as global marketing professionals continuously improve upon their strategies in order to stay competitive.

Advantages

- Globalization leads to more economic growth. Economic growth is important to every country because it makes it feel strong, safe and secure.

Effective marketing approaches will lead to economic growth. Therefore, marketing is essential for economic growth and development (Reddy, 1996), and a major reason for globalization for multinationals, governments, and United Nation agencies.

- Globalization causes rapid technology transfer. Rapid technology transfers from one country to another are a result of increased globalization. Once there is a transfer of an organization's management and logistic expertise, there is potential for improvement in efficiency and reduction of costs for products and services across the world.

- Globalization is becoming effective as a result of more countries becoming democracies. There were many communist countries seeking a democratic state after the fall of the Soviet Union. In a globalized economy, democratization became easier than in a closed communist world where the information flow is restricted.

- The rapid spread of free enterprise system; capitalism has been key in the success of the United States and western countries, and many countries desired to pursue their model in order to own and operate business corporations.

- Unification of culture, living norms, and work ethic; values and work ethic are becoming homogenous as a result of globalization, which has led to improved marketing effectiveness.

- Globalization will flourish as a result of increased communication through the Internet and other media. The Internet has provided many organizations with the ability to transmit media files quickly, which allows them to operate on an international level. Corporations can share who they are, what they market, and how customers may obtain their product.

- Instant news worldwide; satellite and Internet communications, such as CNN and MSNBC, allows everyone to see news 24 hours a day in several languages. International media eliminates barriers to information flow.

- Worldwide improvement of health and living conditions; globalization has brought improved quality of life throughout the world. Many products and services can be shared across the world with a mutual exchange of information.

- People are living longer. Life expectancy rates have increased across the world due to medical breakthroughs and new products that encourage health benefits. Globalization provides this type of information to an international audience.

- Multinational corporations are the greatest beneficiaries of the globalization trend. Corporations have the ability to use the same advertising themes and customize them for different countries by using marketing and distribution strategies to transfer the same message throughout the world.

Disadvantages

- Increasing unemployment in developed countries. Globalization has caused the unemployment rate to rise in developed countries because corporations outsource and manufacture their products outside otheir countries. According to Cateora (2002), there has been an increase in protests against global organizations such as World Trade Organization (WTO) and the International Monetary Fund (IMF) because there is a perception that "globalization creates global worker exploitation, cultural extinction, higher oil prices, and diminished sovereignty of nations" (p. 51).
- Increasing trade deficit in developed countries. Increased imports of manufactured goods and services from other nations has led to trade deficits.
- Terrorism; since people are able to migrate between countries so freely, there has been an increase in terrorism from other countries.
- Loss of competitiveness in developed nations; technology transfer has allowed underdeveloped countries to go from traditional manufacturing to modern manufacturing, which brings underdeveloped countries to the same level as the developed countries that provided them with the technology.
- Poorer nations feel that they are being taken advantage of by advanced nations. Poor countries have limitations in education, health care, and transportation, which keep them in a poor state (Kenny, 2002). Pirages (2000) believes that there are other issues (such as weakening of political authority without substitutions, increase of economic maladies, and destruction of culture) that create problems for poorer countries.
- Increasing economic gap between the rich and poor nations; many poor countries believe that globalization has given the Western world more control over its economies. Wealthy countries tend to use cheap labor to get wealthier and do not help the poorer countries.
- Tradition- and religion-based countries feel that their norms and religious practices are violated. Some citizens believe that corporations will do anything to make a profit, even if it means violating some of their cultural practices and values.
- Comparison with wealthy nations makes poorer nations unhappy. With the increased use of satellites, citizens of the poorer countries have the opportunity to see the quality of living in the countries where corporations reside. When comparing the two ways of living, the citizens of the poorer countries perceive that they are being exploited to make the corporations and quality of life for their countries richer.
- Increasing pollution through manufacturing and transport worldwide. When corporations grow, there is an increase in manufacturing and traffic, which results in an increase in pollution. As a result, the pollution spreads globally.
- Globalization increased the spread of AIDS, the West Nile virus, various kinds of flu, and other diseases.
- As organizations develop their global marketing strategies, they will need to be mindful of the above-mentioned advantages and disadvantages of globalization as they relate to the countries that have been identified as their target markets.

Overseas Expansion

Licensing, franchises, and joint ventures that are undertaken overseas are sometimes refered to as global marketing.

- Licensing. Licensing occurs when a target country grants the right to manufacture and distribute a product under the licenser's trade name in a target country. The licensee pays a fee in exchange for the rights. Small and medium-sized companies tend to grant licenses more often than large companies. Since little investment is required, licensing has the potential to provide a large return on investment. However, it is seen as the least profitable way to enter the market because most companies use licensing to supplement manufacturing and exporting. Licensing tends to be a viable option to enter a the market when the exporter does not have sufficient capital, when foreign government import restrictions forbid other ways to enter the market or when a host country is not comfortable with foreign ownership.

- Franchises. According to Edwards (2006), there are a number of reasons why a franchise may consider going global, and some of these reasons include opportunities to: "build more brand and shareholder value, add revenue sources and growth markets, reduce dependence on the company's home market, leverage existing corporate technology, supply chains, know-how, and intel-

Table 1 (From Witkowski, T. (2005). Fair trade marketing: An alternative system for globalization and development. Journal of Marketing Theory & Practice, 13(4), p. 25)

Fair Trade versus	Ideological Similarities	Ideological Differences
Antiglobalization	• Both philosophies show great concern for disadvantaged producers, gender equity, and environmental protection. • Both disdain the dominant international trading regime. • Both are infused with idealism and utopianism.	• Fair trade achieves economic development via north-south trading relationships. • Fair trade uses branding and other elements of the marketing mix to achieve its ends. • Fair trade cultivates "positive" consumer demand. • Fair trade partners with large corporations.
Marketing Management	• Both philosophies apply managerial principles. • Both emphasize building brands and other elements of the marketing mix. • Both stress creating trust among supply chain members. • Both apply social marketing concepts.	• Fair trade gives priority to producers, not consumers. • Fair trade applies moral criteria to consumer decisions. • Fair trade favors communalism and cooperation over competition. • Fair trade is concerned with market failures.
Ethical Sourcing	• Both philosophies assume responsibility for other key people in the supply chain.	• Fair trade maintains price floors for producer products. • Fair trade emphasizes external auditing of supply chain.
Ethical Consumerism	• Both philosophies care about the environmental impact of production processes. • Both seek information on how, where, and by whom goods are produced. • Both play up humanitarian ideals and morality.	• Fair trade encourages spending and consumption, rather than voluntary simplicity.

lectual property, and award more franchises in the home country by being global."

- Joint Ventures. Joint ventures occur when an organization enters a foreign market via a partnership with one or more companies already established in the host country. In most cases, the local company provides the expertise on the target market while the exporting company manages and markets the product. A joint-venture arrangement allows organizations with limited capital to expand into international markets and provides the marketers with access to its partner's distribution channels. According to QuickMBA.com, "Key issues in a joint venture are ownership, control, length of agreement, pricing, technology transfer, local firm capabilities and resources, and government intentions. Potential problems include conflict over new investments, mistrust over proprietary knowledge, how to split the pie, lack of parent company support, cultural clashes, and when and how to terminate the relationship" if it is necessary to take such action (2007).

VIEWPOINT
Fair Trade Marketing

Fair trade marketing provides consumers with the opportunity to pay higher prices for imported goods so that producers in developing countries can have a decent standard of living (Witkowski, 2005). Supporters of this philosophy believe that prices need to be high enough so that multinational corporations in developing countries can have a living wage, safe working conditions, and human dignity. In addition, there is a belief that trading has become unfair because the cost of developing global commodities has been undervalued when compared to commodities imported from industrialized countries.

When reviewing the concept of fair trade, it is important to analyze various ideological viewpoints. One could compare fair trade to antiglobalization; marketing management, ethical sourcing, and ethical consumerism in order evaluate the different opinions and arguments on the topic. Witkowski (2005) has summarized some of the views by comparing and contrasting the positions.

CONCLUSION

Organizations that conduct business on a global level realize that it tends to be more complex, competitive,

Table 2 International Fair Trade Association (IFAT), Fair Trade Federation & Ten Thousand Villages (From Witkowski, T. (2005). Fair trade marketing: An alternative system for globalization and development. Journal of Marketing Theory & Practice, 13(4), 26.

International Fair Trade Association (IFAT)	Fair Trade Federation	Ten Thousand Villages
• Creating opportunities for economically disadvantaged producers. Fair Trade is a strategy for poverty alleviation and sustainable development. • Transparency and accountability. Fair Trade involves transparent management and commercial relations to deal fairly and respectfully with trading partners. • Capacity building. Fair trade is a means to develop producers' independence. • Payment of a fair price. A fair price in the regional or local context is one that has been agreed through dialogue and participation. • Gender Equity. Fair Trade means that women's work is properly valued and rewarded. • Working conditions. Fair Trade means a safe and healthy working environment for producers. • The environment. Fair Trade actively encourages better environmental practices and the application of responsible methods of production.	• Fair Wages. Producers are paid fairly for their products, which mean that workers are paid at least that country's minimum wage. • Cooperative workplaces. Cooperatives and producer associations provide a healthy alternative to large-scale manufacturing and sweatshop conditions. • Consumer education. Fair Trade Organizations educate consumers about the importance of purchasing fairly traded products which support living wages and healthy working conditions. • Environmental sustainability. Fair Trade Organizations encourage producers to engage in environmentally friendly practices which manage and use local resources sustainability. • Financial and technical support. Small-scale farmers and artisans in the developing world lack access to affordable financing, impeding their profitability. • Respect for cultural identity. Fair Trade Organizations encourage the production and development of products based on producers' cultural traditions adapted for Western markets. • Public accountability. FTF members' finances, management policies, and business practices are open to the public and monitoring by the Fair Trade Federation.	• They honor the value of seeking to bring justice and hope to the poor. • They trade with artisan groups who pay fair wages and demonstrate concern for their members' welfare. • They provide consistent purchases, advances and prompt final payments to artisans. • They increase market share in North America for fairly traded handicrafts. • They market quality products that are crafted by underemployed artisans. • They build sustainable operations using a variety of sales channels, including a network of stores with a common identity. • They choose handicrafts that reflect and reinforce rich cultural traditions, that are environmentally sensitive and which appeal to North American consumers. • They encourage North American customers to learn about fair trade and to appreciate artisans' cultural heritage and life circumstances with joy and respect. • They use resources carefully and value volunteers who work in their North American operations.

and difficult to manage. When entering the global market, social, economic, political, technological, and institutional factors are added into the equation as multinational corporations develop global marketing strategies. The companies that successfully master these challenges tend to be recognized for their best practices and excel in global marketing (Caslione, 2003).

Globalization is reshaping business strategy, especially marketing strategy, and marketing professionals will have to transition from a domestic focus to a global focus (Caslione, 2003). Unfortunately, many in the field are not prepared to make the transition. Therefore, marketers will need to upgrade their skill set in the field in order to be competitive in the market. As the marketing professionals become equipped for the challenge, they will be tasked to deal with the issues that have arisen in the field.

The Fair Trade Movement promotes trading partnerships, and organizations exist that work to make this effort successful. Common themes among these organizations include helping disadvantaged producers; promoting gender equity, transparent relations, and economic and environmental sustainability; reforming conventional international trade relationships; and creating consumer awareness of these issues (Witkowski, 2005, p. 24).

Witkowski (2005) presented the principles and goals of fair trade as defined by three organizations, and the results are listed below.

BIBLIOGRAPHY

Alden, D. L., Kelley, J. B., Riefler, P., Lee, J. A., & Soutar, G. N. (2013). The effect of global company animosity on global brand attitudes in emerging and developed markets: does perceived value matter?. Journal of International Marketing, 21(2), 17-38. Retrieved November 15, 2013, from EBSCO Online Database Business Source Complete. http://search.ebsco-host.com/login.aspx?direct=true&db=bth&AN=87742599&site=ehost-live

Caslione, J. (2003). Globalization demands new marketing skills. Marketing News, 37(14), 7-8. Retrieved May 22, 2007, from EBSCO Online Database Business Source Complete. http://

search.ebscohost.com/login.aspx?direct=true
&db=bth&AN=10089707&site=ehost-live

Cateora, P. & Graham, J. (2002). International marketing, 11th ed. New York: McGraw-Hill.

Edwards, W. (2006). Why go global? Franchising World, 38(12), 38-40. Retrieved May 22, 2007, from EBSCO Online Database Business Source Complete. http://search.ebscohost.com/login.aspx?direct=true&db=bth&AN=23508136&site=ehost-live

Ersun, A., & Karabulut, A. (2013). Innovation management and marketing in global enterprises. International Journal of Business & Management, 8(20), 76-86. Retrieved November 15, 2013, from EBSCO Online Database Business Source Complete. http://search.ebscohost.com/login.aspx?direct=true&db=bth&AN=91583049&site=ehost-live

Gao, T., & Shi, L. (2011). How do multinational suppliers formulate mechanisms of global account coordination? an integrative framework and empirical study. Journal of International Marketing, 19(4), 61-87. Retrieved November 15, 2013, from EBSCO Online Database Business Source Complete. http://search.ebscohost.com/login.aspx?direct=true&db=bth&AN=67729121&site=ehost-live

International Monetary Fund. (2000). Globalization: Threat or opportunity? An IMF issue brief. Retrieved May 22, 2007, from http://globalization.about.com/library/weekly/aa080901.ahtm.

Kahle, L., Marshall, R., & Kropp, F. (2003). The new paradigm marketing model. Journal of Euromarketing, 12(3/4), 99-121. Retrieved May 22, 2007, from EBSCO Online Database Business Source Complete. http://search.ebscohost.com/login.aspx?direct=true&db=bth&AN=11902084&site=ehost-live

Kenny, C. (2003). Development's false divide. Foreign Policy, January/February, 76-77.

Kolk, A. (2014). Linking subsistence activities to global marketing systems: The role of institutions. Journal of Macromarketing, 34(2), 186–98. Retrieved November 17, 2014, from EBSCO Online Database Business Source Complete. http://search.ebscohost.com/login.aspx?direct=true&db=bth&AN=95830912

Lin, C., & Kao, D. (2004). The impacts of country-of-origin on brand equity. Journal of American Academy of Business, Cambridge, 5(1/2), 37-40.

Retrieved May 22, 2007, from EBSCO Online Database Business Source Complete. http://search.ebscohost.com/login.aspx?direct=true&db=bth&AN=13200704&site=ehost-live

Pirages, D. (2000). Globalization: A cautionary note. Retrieved on May 24, 2007, from http://www.aaas.org/spp/yearbook/wooo/ch9.pdf.

Reddy, A., & Campbell, D. (1996). Marketing's role in economic development. Connecticut: Quorum Books.

Reddy, A., & Vyas, N. (2004). The globalization paradox: A marketing perspective. International Journal of Management, 21(2), 166-171. Retrieved May 22, 2007, from EBSCO Online Database Business Source Complete. http://search.ebscohost.com/login.aspx?direct=true&db=bth&AN=13989766&site=ehost-live

Steenkamp, J.-B. (2014). How global brands create firm value: The 4V model. *International Marketing Review, 31*(1), 5–29. Retrieved November 17, 2014, from EBSCO Online Database Business Source Complete. http://search.ebscohost.com/login.aspx?direct=true&db=bth&AN=94622236

Witkowski, T. (2005). Fair trade marketing: An alternative system for globalization and development. Journal of Marketing Theory & Practice, 13(4), 22-33. Retrieved May 22, 2007, from EBSCO Online Database Business Source Complete. http://search.ebscohost.com/login.aspx?direct=true&db=bth&AN=21031867&site=ehost-live

SUGGESTED READING

Field, A. (2007). Breaking down barriers. Journal of Commerce, 8(16), 28-28. Retrieved May 22, 2007, from EBSCO Online Database Business Source Complete. http://search.ebscohost.com/login.aspx?direct=true&db=bth&AN=24872329&site=ehost-live

Hult, G., Cavusgil, S., Kiyak, T., Deligonul, S., & Lagerström, K. (2007). What drives performance in globally focused marketing organizations? A three-country study. Journal of International Marketing, 15(2), 58-85. Retrieved May 22, 2007, from EBSCO Online Database Business Source Complete. http://search.ebscohost.com/login.aspx?direct=true&db=bth&AN=25020790&site=ehost-live

Laser, R. (2007). BP takes global branding role away from marketing. Marketing Week, 30(5), 3-3.

Retrieved May 22, 2007, from EBSCO Online Database Business Source Complete. http://search.ebscohost.com/login.aspx?direct=true&db=bth&AN=24013433&site=ehost-live

Manrai, Ajay K. (2016). New emerging business models, frameworks, and trends in global marketing. *Journal of Marketing*, 29, 4. Retrieved on June 29, 2017.

Yung K. C. & Schellhase, R. (2014). Exploring globalization and marketing performance at the 2012 Global Marketing Conference in Seoul. *Journal of Business Research, 67*(10), 2053–5. Retrieved November 17, 2014, from EBSCO Online Database Business Source Complete. http://search.ebscohost.com/login.aspx?direct=true&db=bth&AN=97173453

Marie Gould

I

Integrated Marketing Communications (IMC)

ABSTRACT

The proliferation of high technology communications media and methods has changed the way that many people communicate in the twenty-first century. To be successful in this environment, marketing communications need to take into account not only these new approaches to communication, but also the way that people best receive and retain information. Prospective customers today are bombarded with information about competing products. Just running more advertisements is likely to only add to the confusion. Integrated Marketing Communications (IMC) is an approach to marketing communications that combines and integrates multiple sources of marketing information to maximize the effectiveness of a marketing campaign. To be effective, an IMC approach needs to be based on research and analysis of the target market, including its needs and motivations and the ways to communicate with the targeted market segment. The results of the analysis can be used to develop a plan of action for integrating multiple sources of communication about the organization and its products and services to optimize the effectiveness of the marketing effort.

OVERVIEW

In the late twentieth century, communication technology was much simpler than it is today. Although most people had land-line telephones, the mobile phone was an almost inconceivable luxury only for the very rich. Correspondence was done by mail and one patiently waited for a reply by return mail. In the evening, those families with television sets sat down and watched their favorite shows with rapt attention. Those days, however, are long over. In many sectors of the culture, those without a cell phone or email capabilities are viewed as technophobes, hopelessly behind the times. The fax machine that revolutionized the speed of communication in the latter part of the twentieth century is considered passé for many applications, as messages and documents fly through cyberspace at incredible speeds.

In many ways, this surge in communications technology has been a boon to the businessworld in general and the marketing function in particular. It is easy to pick up a cell phone or a computer mouse and communicate virtually instantaneously with a colleague or customer halfway around the world. The Internet can be mined for data to keep up with one's competition or to gain more knowledge about current or prospective customers (e.g., through social media). However, the proliferation of new communications technologies is not an unmixed blessing. The radio that was once a prime advertising medium has become, for the most part, nothing more than background noise or has been replaced completely with commercial-free Internet radio stations or music downloads. Even the value of television as an advertising medium has been diminished as people multitask (e.g., on tablets or smart phones) while watching, or record their favorite programs using DVR technology so they do not have to watch the commercials. Many people prefer sound bites to long speeches and do not even process much advertising because they are so inundated with data they cannot comprehend it all. Many people have learned to automatically discard the junk mail that fills mail boxes daily and have software applications that automatically remove the spam from email boxes. As a result, these medias are no longer as effective for advertising goods and services as they once were.

To help solve this problem and get their message across to customers and prospective customers, an increasing number of businesses are utilizing the approach of Integrated Marketing Communications (IMC). This approach to marketing combines and integrates multiple sources of marketing information (e.g., advertising, direct response, sales promotions, publicity) to maximize the effectiveness of a marketing campaign. The concept of IMC emphasizes that the organization coordinates all its marketing efforts to present a consistent face to customers while focusing the marketing campaign in an attempt to give the organization a competitive edge.

A number of factors led to the development of IMC. First, the proliferation of messages that one sees for various products frequently results in a situation of information overload in which the consumer receives more inputs than he or she can reasonably process. As a result, merely putting more advertisements in the marketplace is no longer likely to be successful since the consumer is already receiving too many inputs. Second, the growth of high-technology approaches to information management has led to a decrease in the cost of database marketing. This means that it is easier and relatively inexpensive to acquire a list of single mothers, veterinary technicians, or whatever market segment the organization is interested in targeting so that advertisements can be sent out. Third, as discussed above, communication via mass media is becoming increasingly less effective while concomitantly becoming more expensive. In addition, the changing composition of marketing communications agencies resulting from mergers and acquisitions has allowed them to more easily compile comprehensive teams that can develop integrated marketing campaigns than can be done by separate agencies. As a result, knowledge and theory about how to better craft IMC has increased. In addition, differentiation within and among the media is fragmenting the audience. For example, someone who listens to a classical radio station is unlikely to look favorably on an organization that tries to sell its product or service with a hard-rock soundtrack and vice versa. Similarly, the demographics of people who watch the History Channel differ from those who watch MTV. Although in the past, advertising on the three major networks could get an organization's product or service recognition among a large market demographic, that is no longer true.

To better understand the purpose of IMC, it is helpful to understand the marketing communication process. At its simplest, communication starts when the organization decides to transmit a message to the receiver. The organization decides what it wants to convey to the customers, for example, that their widgets can walk the dog and take out the garbage.

This message is then sent to the receiver through the medium that the organization thinks will best reach the target market (e.g., television commercial, newspaper advertisement). However, this information does not reach the prospective customer directly, but goes through a series of filters that screen the message and may alter its meaning. For example, suppose that Widget Corporation is not the only organization that is trying to reach the customer; both Acme and Gizmo are also sending messages that their products can more effectively walk the dog and take out the garbage, and do these things for a lower price. The customer unconsciously screens the message for other reasons, too. For example, he or she may not have a dog and also misses the fact that widgets take out the garbage. Or, he or she may not like the background music played in the commercial and the layout of the print advertisement and so chooses to ignore them. The potential customer then decodes what the filtered message says and encodes an appropriate response. This leads to either positive or negative feedback to the organization that sent the message (e.g., the customer does or does not buy a widget).

The literature discusses several levels of development for IMC. At the first level, the organization is simply aware of the need for implementing an integrated approach to its marketing efforts. For example, when trying to create a consistent image for excellence in its given field or for developing cutting-edge products, an organization may eventually realize that it would be helpful to consistently present this image across all its marketing efforts. This level of awareness regarding the need for IMC is then followed by efforts to integrate the organization's image to ensure that a consistent message is being sent to potential consumers. This includes integrating the messages and visual themes of the entire marketing communications effort to maximize its impact on potential customers. In addition, at this level, the organization focuses on the benefits of its products and services to the customer rather than merely trying to persuade the customer to purchase.

At the next level of development of an IMC campaign, the organization begins the process of functional integration. At this level, each component of the marketing communications is analyzed and evaluated to determine strengths and weaknesses and the value it adds to the campaign as a whole.

This evaluation takes into consideration the marketing goals of the campaign, including the market share that the organization is trying to achieve. At the next level, the integration of these components is integrated with the personal selling effort, with marketing representatives interacting with prospective customers one-on-one in an attempt to demonstrate the benefits of the product or service vis a vis the customer's unique requirements. At this level, specific knowledge and data about the prospective customer base to which the organization wishes to sell its products or services is integrated into the marketing approach. This activity can include data collection and analysis of such factors as understanding the needs and motivations of the target market, determining which customers are more likely to purchase the organization's products or services, and structuring the marketing effort in a way that positions it to help show potential buyers the benefits of the product or service as well as persuading them to purchase it. At this level, the marketing strategy becomes integrated and all marketing efforts are shaped to better reach the target market and convince prospective customers to buy the product or service.

In addition to understanding the market demographics and its motivations and needs and determining the best way to shape a campaign that will show the market the benefits of the organization's products or services, the organization must also consider its other stakeholders when determining the appropriate mix for an IMC approach. Stakeholders are persons or groups that can affect or be affected by a decision or action. In marketing, stakeholders may include the organization's employees, suppliers, distributors, and stockholders. The IMC campaign must not only communicate effectively with prospective customers, but also with any stakeholders to show them how the new product or service will benefit them (e.g., more job security for the manufacturing department, more profits for the stockholders).

APPLICATIONS

IMC is not a shotgun approach to marketing where any and all media and methods are used in the hope that something will attract the customer's attention. Rather, to be successful, an IMC needs to be based on careful analysis and planning and then coordinated in order to maximize its impact. As discussed above, to be successful, a marketing strategy needs to be based on a rigorous analysis of empirical data, including market needs and trends, competitor capabilities and offerings, and the organization's resources and abilities. From this analysis, the organization can determine the best way to meet its goals and develop a plan of action to implement the plan. Although this is not a minor undertaking, it is an important step. Without collecting and analyzing data to determine the needs and motivations of the target market and determining how best to position the organization's product or service to best attract the targeted potential customers, any results will be merely hit or miss and will not leverage the capabilities of the organization and its offerings into a successful marketing plan.

Considerations for Planning an Integrated Marketing Communications (IMC) Campaign

Several considerations need to be taken into account when planning an IMC effort. First, the organization needs to consider the nature and makeup of the target market. This analysis can include any or all of several groups within the potential marketplace. The most likely group to purchase a new product or service from the organization is its current customers, particularly those who are loyal to the organization's brand. A successful marketing plan must be crafted to take into account these differences and marketing efforts must be targeted to reach each of the groups as determined by the organization.

A successful marketing plan, however, strives not only to keep the organization's current customers, but also to increase its market share. However, there are other types of current customers including those who buy the product or service out of habit but could easily be persuaded to switch to another brand and those who use several brands indiscriminately. This means that individuals who could benefit from the organization's product or service need to be targeted appropriately to turn them from non-customers into customers. These groups include new users who have never purchased a similar product or service, customers who are loyal to other brands, and customers who use other brands out of habit without seriously weighing its costs and benefits. Once the various categories of potential customers have been identified, the organization must next decide which of these is most likely to switch brands and the best way to persuade them to do so. When this is done, the organization can determine the best way to communicate its message to them in a way that encourages a positive response and drives the customer to purchase from the organization.

To do this, one must determine what the objectives for the marketing campaign are. From a consumer perspective, the organization wants the consumer to take some kind of action – either trying the product or service or continuing to use it. In either case, the objective of the organization will more than likely be for the consumer not only to continue using the product or service, but also to recommend it to other potential customers. This can be done at several different levels. At the level of category need, the members of the target market need to be aware that they need what the organization is offering. This level of marketing effort is necessary when the new product or service is innovative and has not been offered before or when the product or service is being offered to prospective customers who have not used this type of product before. However, if the prospective customers are only made aware of a need, they will not necessarily purchase the product or service from the organization. Therefore, it is also to make prospective customers aware of the brand. At this level of communication, the organization's marketing communications are aimed at getting prospective customers to recognize the organization and recall the product or service that they offer. In addition, marketing communication should be targeted toward helping prospective customers develop a positive attitude toward the product or service because of its benefits or its capability to satisfy the needs that have been illuminated by other parts of the marketing strategy. The organization should also help the prospective customers form the intention to buy their brand of product or service and then help them to do so. This can be done through numerous methods including free samples, discounts, and coupons.

Approaches to Planning an Integrated Marketing Communications (IMC) Campaign

Planning for an IMC campaign also includes consideration of how the campaign will be designed. Although some agencies or organizations attempt an ad hoc approach to integrate the various elements of their campaigns, these are much less likely to be successful than an integrated approach based on strategic planning as discussed above. The "one

look" approach helps customers more easily identify the brand. This may be done through such techniques as using the same graphics, colors, and logo in all marketing communications. For example, the Apple logo appears on all their marketing materials, and Campbell's Soup is easily recognized by its red, white, and gold labels. Although this approach helps with brand recognition, on its own it is typically not sufficient.

Another approach to design is the theme-line approach. In this approach, the same slogan is used in all the marketing communications. For example, the phrase "Xerox, the document company" has been used across the company's marketing materials, including in its logo and commercials. The purpose of this consistent approach is to connect the name "Xerox" in people's minds with the concept of "document company." That way, when business customers determine that they need a document company, the name Xerox should spring to their mind. Research has been done on this approach to marketing and it has been found that when key visuals or slogans are also placed on product displays and packaging, customers better remember the message of the advertising. In addition, research has found that another way to reinforce the message of the advertising is to present it through both visual media (e.g., television) and auditory media (e.g., radio). Psychologically, some people are visual learners and some are auditory learners. This dual approach helps reach both kinds and provides reinforcement for the message. Similarly, research has found that running print and radio advertisements before television commercials acts to peak the consumer's interest in the product. Like the "one look" approach, the theme-line approach is helpful, but these activities are not sufficient alone for a successful marketing campaign.

A third approach to IMC planning is the supply-side approach. In this approach, the organization signs with an agency that has an agreement with representatives of several different media to provide discounted rates in a "package deal" (e.g., newspaper ads, local radio station commercials, and a local television station commercial). However, although this moves the organization closer to an integrated approach to marketing communications, the package deal may not include all the media that are appropriate to its campaign or may include media that will not help in its marketing effort.

Finally, there are consumer-based approaches that help the organization identify the market and segment of the market that it wants to reach, identify messages and communication vehicles that are most appropriate to each segment, allocate resources, and evaluate the effectiveness of the effort as a whole. The most popular of these models was developed by Schultz, Tannenbaum, and Lauterborn. This model also stresses the development of a database of customer information including demographics, buying history, and other factors that might influence their buying decisions. The data are further segmented into the type of prospective customer: those who are loyal to the organization's products or services, those who are loyal to another brand, and those who are willing to switch brands. Other considerations include when or where the advertisement should occur. For example, a television ad for an expensive piece of business equipment would probably not result in a high return on investment if aired during the day when the people who make the decision to buy that kind of equipment are in the office and not watching television. This model also stresses the need to develop a communications strategy. This includes determining what points the organization would like the prospective customer to remember and how to most effectively craft the message to do this. Similarly, the marketing plan needs to consider the marketing objectives: to maintain or increase sales to loyal customers, convince customers loyal to other brands to switch to the organization's product or service, or to help turn swing users into loyal users. The customer-based model also considers what marketing tools should be used in the creation of an optimal mix and what tactics should be used to get the organization's point across.

BIBLIOGRAPHY

Keller, E., & Fay, B. (2012). Word-of-mouth advocacy: A new key to advertising effectiveness. Journal of Advertising Research, 52 (4), 459-464. Retrieved November 20, 2013 from EBSCO Online Database Business Source Complete. http://search.ebscohost.com/login.aspx?direct=true&db=bth&AN=84295240&site=ehost-live

Mihart, C. (2012). Impact of integrated marketing communication on consumer behaviour: Effects on consumer decision – making process. International Journal of Marketing Studies, 4 (2), 121-129. Retrieved November 20, 2013 from EBSCO Online Database Business Source Complete. http://search.ebscohost.com/login.aspx?direct=true&db=bth&AN=75333802&site=ehost-live

Percy, L. (1997). Strategies for implementing integrated marketing communications. Lincoln, IL: NTC Business Books.

Super Bowl ads are pricey, very risky, executives say. The Boston Globe. Retrieved May 5, 2007, from The Boston Globe Online Database http://www.boston.com/business/globe/articles/2007/01/25/super%5fbowl%5fads%5fare%5fpricey%5fvery%5frisky%5fexecutives%5fsay?mode=PF.

Schlinke, J., & Crain, S. (2013). Social media from an integrated marketing and compliance perspective. Journal of Financial Service Professionals, 67 (2), 85-92. Retrieved November 20, 2013 from EBSCO Online Database Business Source Complete. http://search.ebscohost.com/login.aspx?direct=true&db=bth&AN=85802252&site=ehost-live

Schultz, D. E., Tannenbaum, S. I., & Lauterborn, R. F. (1993). Integrated marketing communications. Lincoln, IL: NTC Business Books.

Sirgy, M. J. (1998). Integrated marketing communications: A systems approach. Upper Saddle River, NJ: Prentice Hall.

SUGGESTED READING

Keller, Kevin Lane. (2016). Unlocking the power of integrated marketing communications: How integrated is your IMC program? Journal of Advertising, 45, 3. Retrieved on June 29, 2017.

Laurie, S., & Mortimer, K. (2011). 'IMC is dead. Long live IMC': Academics' versus practitioners' views. Journal of Marketing Management, 27 (13/14), 1464-1478. Retrieved November 20, 2013 from EBSCO Online Database Business Source Complete. http://search.ebscohost.com/login.aspx?direct=true&db=bth&AN=67698755&site=ehost-live

Paley, N. (2005). Promotional strategies: Plan a total communications mix. In Paley, N. Manager's Guide to Competitive Marketing Strategies (3rd ed.), 333-362. Retrieved May 5, 2007, from EBSCO Online Database Business Source Complete. http://search.ebscohost.com/login.aspx?direct=true&db=bth&AN=22355290&site=ehost-live

Rossiter, J. R., & Percy, L. (2013). How the roles of advertising merely appear to have changed. International Journal of Advertising, 32 (3), 391-398. Retrieved November 20, 2013 from EBSCO Online Database Business Source Complete. http://search.ebscohost.com/login.aspx?direct=true&db=bth&AN=89594088&site=ehost-live

Semenik, R. J. (2002). Promotion and integrated marketing communications. Cincinnati, OH: South-Western/Thomson Learning.

Smith, T. M, Gopalakrishna, S., & Chatterjee, R. A. (2006). Three-stage model of integrated marketing communications at the marketing-sales interface. Journal of Marketing Research, 43 (4), 564-579. Retrieved May 5, 2007, from EBSCO Online Database Business Source Complete. http://search.ebscohost.com/login.aspx?direct=true&db=bth&AN=22754671&site=ehost-live

Ruth A. Wienclaw, Ph.D.

INTERNATIONAL ADVERTISING

ABSTRACT

This article will focus on how organizations can create an effective international advertising program for their business. Many corporations have seen the need to venture into the international market. As a result, they have challenged their marketing departments to develop advertising campaigns that will highlight their products and services in targeted countries. Although the field is growing, organizations face several challenges as they determine the types of strategies their businesses will utilize in order to make their presence known in the international market. Although there is no one way to create an effective international advertising program, one practitioner has provided three easy steps that can serve as a guideline when developing an effective international advertising strategy.

OVERVIEW

Many corporations have seen the benefits of expanding their brand presence into the international market. As a result, they have challenged their marketing departments to develop advertising campaigns that will highlight their products and services in targeted countries. Given the popularity, academicians and practitioners have contributed to the literature in terms of what the most effective practices are in international advertising. George Zinkhan (1994) discussed some of the important issues in international advertising in the 1994 special issue of *Journal of Advertising*. Corporations have increased their international advertising budgets. Global advertising expenditures exceeded $322 billion in 2000 (Burberry, 2000) and continued to grow pass the $400 billion mark (O'Guinn, Allen, & Semenik, 2003). In 2013, global advertising expenditures surpassed $500 billion.

Although the field is growing, organizations face several challenges as they determine the types of strategies their businesses will utilize in order to make their presence known in the international market. Marla Royne Stafford (2005) emphasized four of the major challenges that corporations need to address. Corporations should work on their positions regarding message issues, standardization versus adaptation, media issues, and advertising regulations.

- **Message Issues.** Corporations must develop a message that accurately reflects the culture of interest. It has been found that specific aspects and psychological factors may differ significantly across cultures (Cateora & Graham, 2002) even though the outcomes may be the same. In most cases, there is a possibility that these variables may have a significant impact on the advertising message. Researchers (Nevett, 1992; Koudelova & Whitelock, 2001) have conducted content analysis to explore this phenomenon. These researchers may use "a coding system to distinguish the differences in appeals, executions, tactics, or cues across two or more countries" (Stafford, 2005, p. 66).

- **Adaptation versus Standardization.** Many in the field continue to debate whether standardization or adaptation is the best method for international advertising. As a result of the different perspectives, three schools of thought have emerged: standardization, adaptation, and contingency.

Supporters of the standardization model believe that international advertising should highlight the similar desires of buyers regardless of the country of origin. The adaptation model seeks to ensure that cultural issues are addressed in advertisements. The contingency model falls in the middle of the two previously mentioned approaches. This perspective encourages corporations to make a decision based on the specific circumstance. The suggested approach could change depending on the factors involved.

- **Media Issues.** "Media options are critical to services, and existing media infrastructures may hamper service providers' efforts to communicate effectively with their potential customers" (Stafford, 2005, p. 66). For example, some countries monitor what can be seen on television (Kotabe & Helsen, 2001), which may hinder an organization's advertising message. The use and growth of the Internet has provided corporations with new opportunities to get their message across the global network. The Internet can be used to minimize some of the challenges previously identified. The Internet offers corporations the ability to advertise goods and services in foreign markets. Organizations must select the appropriate media strategies that will effectively convey their message. The media message is critical because it is a key factor in the success of the advertising campaign, especially in the international marketplace.
- **Advertising Regulations.** International advertisers must be aware of the various advertising regulations in each of their target markets.

APPLICATION

International Advertising Programs

Although there is no one way to create an effective international advertising program, Peter Holt (2004) has provided three easy steps that can serve as a guideline when developing an effective international advertising strategy. He created this design to assist organizations with thinking about how they would like to generate leads in a global market. Holt (2004) believed that an international advertising strategy was the first step in this process. Having a plan will allow the organization to develop a proactive approach in its international expansion. His plan was based on three steps:

STEP 1
Prioritize the World
There are nearly 200 countries in the world, but that does not mean that an organization should advertise in all of them. Rather, a corporation needs to target which markets make the most sense for its products, and the advertising campaign should be geared toward those countries and cultures that are selected. When conducting an analysis of whether or not to enter a specific market, the organization should identify the challenges facing the country, determine if it will be hard or easy to conduct business in the country, create a grid of the factors that have led to an organization's success with specific products and/or services in the target country, consult the U.S. Department of Commerce to research the target countries, and contact the International Franchise Association (IFA) since it has significant information on international development.

STEP 2
Establish a Profile for Leads
Many U.S. franchisors have found that utilizing a master franchising method has provided a level of success when attempting to expand into another country. If this option is pursued, the first step will be to determine who the master licensee will be. When selecting this individual, the organization should ask itself certain questions when reviewing the qualifications. Some of these questions include "What kind of business experience will the organization require?" "Is it important that the master licensee has business experience?" "What kind of human resources will be required?" and "What type of financial requirement is needed?" If the organization is specific with the types of question it asks, it will be able to utilize its time more effectively when determining which resources to use when generating leads. According to Holt, "with the exception of business acumen and financial requirements, the most important element to consider is a shared vision of what you are trying to create and a shared sense of values that drive the relationship" (Holt, 2004, p. 58).

STEP 3
Establish a Budget for a Lead Generation Program
An organization can use a variety of tactics when generating international leads. Each type of tactic has its own costs and benefits. It is the organization's

responsibility to determine which programs will yield the greatest profit. Some of the tactical programs include:

- **Franchise Trade Missions** – Many have viewed this option as one of the most successful lead generation activities, especially when it is arranged by the U.S. Department of Commerce or the International Franchise Association (IFA). In most cases, the staff at U.S. embassies or consulates arrange meetings between multinational corporations and prequalified businesses. There will be opportunities to have a firsthand view of the target country as well as meet with other international franchise executives. New contacts inside the target country may provide valuable information for international expansion. Unfortunately, there are a few downsides to the tactic. There are only approximately three trade missions per year, and they may not be within the areas that the corporations would like to venture.

- **Gold Key Programs** – Another similar tactic is to work with the U.S. Foreign Commercial Service (FCS) in the target country. In most cases, the U.S. embassies and consulates sponsor a one- or two-day Gold Key Program during which they invite prequalified businesses to come in and meet with corporate executives. The meetings are coordinated based on the criteria that the corporations have established. This tactic is very cost-effective and can be an alternative to the franchise trade missions.

- **Franchise Trade Shows** – This option is becoming very popular in the global marketplace. The approach has been found to be helpful, especially if the corporation is looking for a specific business. However, only a small number of master licensees attend these types of events.

- **Industry-Specific Trade Shows** – Some countries have sponsored trade shows geared toward a specific industry. They would invite those corporations that were interested in the target industry and provide information to corporations so that they could expand into the country. By using this approach, there are opportunities to generate leads that could turn into multiple contacts.

- **Direct Advertising** – This option is one of the most expensive methods. Some corporations have found it difficult to convey their message effectively in print format, especially in a target country

that is unfamiliar with the corporation's product or service. In addition, there is a need to keep printing the message in order to generate a sufficient number of responses. This practice adds to the cost of the initial kickoff campaign message.

- **Public Relations** – Corporations can get favorable press by writing articles for publications and taking out advertisements. This approach can be a good source of lead generation, especially when used in conjunction with efforts such as trade missions and the Gold Key Program.

Each corporation will be challenged with evaluating each tactic and determining which options would be appropriate for its international advertising strategy. There is no magic formula or right combination. The final decision should be based on the tactics that support the target goals of the organization.

VIEWPOINT
The Great Debate

One of the debates that continues to be a source of contention is the value of standardization in the advertising field, especially as it relates to the international market. In 1923, David Brown, a manager at Goodyear, became the first advocate of standardization by supporting the practice of standardizing advertisement across countries (Melewar & Vemmervik, 2004).

Advertising Approaches

There are two extreme schools of thought when developing advertising strategies. As mentioned in the overview, the different approaches are standardization, adaptation, and contingency. T. C. Melewar and Claes Vemmervik (2004) believed that one could categorize each of these approaches on a continuum when developing advertising strategies. One end of the spectrum evaluates the degree to which an advertisement campaign is considered to be standardized. The other end focuses on the geographical coverage of the campaign. When analyzing the relationship between the schools of thought and the two dimensions, the following hypotheses can be made:

- **Standardization** – There is an assumption that markets (i.e. arts, tastes, religious beliefs, culture) are converging as a result of faster communication and technology, and consumers are becoming more similar over time. Supporters challenge the belief that markets are heterogeneous and do not believe interventions proposed by the adaptation school are necessary. Although people in various cultures may be different, their basic physiological and psychological needs are the same. This belief is in alignment with Abraham Maslow's hierarchy of needs theory. Maslow's theory suggests that all people must satisfy the same five basic needs: physiological needs, safety, love, self-esteem, and self-actualization. According to the theory, people seek to satisfy their needs in a step progression. Therefore, a set of universal guidelines governs all people regardless of cultural differences. Gordon Link (1988) supported this viewpoint and inferred that advertisers should focus on developing a global brand image, which is referred to as global advertising.

- **Adaptation (Individualization)** – There is an assumption that advertising must adapt to cultural differences in order to achieve a successful international advertising campaign. Adaptation is necessary because there is a need to create a differential advantage via effective communication and sensitivity toward the local cultures (Hite & Fraser, 1990). Many supporters of this school of thought highlight the differences between countries (i.e. culture, consumer values, and political systems) and the need to consider barriers to standardization (i.e. taste, economic conditions, media options).

- **Contingency (Compromise)** – Although there is recognition of local cultural differences, there is equal recognition that standardization may be needed in order to create an effective international advertising strategy. Supporters of this school of thought view advertising to be on a global continuum. The degree of support for the other two schools of thought is based on each individual campaign. "On the left side are companies with highly centralized, multi-domestic operations and products. On the right side are the totally integrated and globally advertised brands and companies. In the middle are companies that increasingly standardize brands or projects, but still adapt to local differences" (Melewar & Vemmervik, 2004, p. 871). There is a strong belief that

Table 1: Advantages & Disadvantages

	Standardization	Adaptation
Benefits	• Cost reduction from economies of scale and scope. • Consistent brand image across the world. • Consistent positioning arguments through the world. • Sharing of experience. • Effective use of advertising budget. • Consistency of communication. • Less duplication of effort • Pre-selling of the company's products.	• Adaptation is usually linked to a decentralized advertising function, which allows for responsiveness to culture, infrastructure and competition. • Adaptation of creative presentations and decentralized implementations of campaigns usually offer greater benefits than less culturally led functions (Hite & Fraser, 1990). • Accurate positioning arguments • Price discrimination
Challenges	• Ignoring the target group's needs as a result of attempting to keep costs down. • Probability for communication breakdown increases if the focus is on homogenous segments. • Costs are not really reduced, especially when there is a lack of economies of scale for media costs.	• Increased costs • Inconsistent brand image

there are internal and external factors that influence the approach that an organization will utilize when developing its international advertising campaign.

When an organization is evaluating which approach to use, its decision-making process is based on how the organization views the world. If the team prefers standardization, the members focus on issues such as reducing advertising costs and presenting a

Table 2

Researcher	Basis of Model
Harvey (1993)	There were six factors that influenced the level of standardization in a campaign. The variables were product variable (the degree of universality of the product); competitive variables (the structure of the competitive environment); organizational experience and control variables (the level of organizational experience in the corporation); infrastructure variables (the degree of similarity of the media infrastructure); government variables (the restrictions on mass-communication); and cultural and societal variables (the cultural differences between the home and export markets). Product, competitive and organizational variables have the most influence on how an organization determines which model to use.
Grein & Gould (1996)	A model was created for the Globally Integrated Marketing Communications based on factors such as horizontal (across countries) and vertical (across disciplines). Horizontal factors include target market, market position and organizational factors, whereas, vertical factors include overall promotion mix, advertising creation and public relations.
Shoham (1999)	Model asserts that there are only three environmental factors which effect whether or not a company will select standardization or adaptation. The factors are local government, level of competition and physical environment.

consistent brand image across the world. However, if the team prefers adaptation, the members will highlight how to achieve differential advantage through local adaptation.

After reviewing the pros and cons of both approaches, many who support the contingency model will start to develop a formula to evaluate the benefits and costs of each method based on the dynamics of campaign. A number of researchers have created contingency models to assist advertisers with making the right decision.

CONCLUSION

Many corporations have seen the need to venture into the international market. Corporations have increased their international advertising budgets significantly in recent decades. Global advertising expenditures exceeded $322 billion in 2000 (Burberry, 2000) and surpassed the $500 billion mark in 2013.

Although the field is growing, organizations face several challenges as they determine the types of strategies their businesses will utilize in order to make their presence known in the international market. Corporations should work on their positions regarding message issues, standardization versus adaptation, media issues, and advertising regulations. Holt (2004) has provided three easy steps that can serve as a guideline when developing an effective international advertising strategy. Having a plan will allow the organization to have a proactive approach in its international expansion. Holt's plan (2004) was based on prioritizing the world, establishing a profile for leads, and establishing a budget for lead generation programs.

Corporations will be challenged with evaluating each tactic and determining which options would be appropriate for their international advertising strategy. There is no magic formula or right combination. The final decision should be based on the tactics that support the target goals of the organization.

BIBLIOGRAPHY

Burberry, R. (2000). U.S. fuels growth in global advertising. Australian Financial Review, 33.

Cateora, P., & Graham, J. (2002). International marketing (11th ed.). New York: McGraw-Hill.

Ford, J. B., Mueller, B., & Taylor, C. R. (2011). The tension between strategy and execution: challenges for international advertising research. Journal of Advertising Research, 51, 27-44. Retrieved November 19, 2013 from EBSCO online database Business Source Premier. http://search.ebscohost.com/login.aspx?direct=true&db=buh&AN=59487708

Garret, J., Iyer, R. (2013). International advertising research: a literature review, 1990-2010. International Journal of Management, 30(1), 143-159.

Retrieved November 19, 2013 from EBSCO online database Business Source Premier. http://search.ebscohost.com/login.aspx?direct=true&db=buh&AN=85634494

Grein, A., & Gould, S. (1996). Globally integrated marketing communications. Journal of Marketing Communications, 2, 141-158.

Harvey, M. (1993). Point of view: A model to determine standardization of the advertising process in international markets. Journal of Advertising Research, 33(4), 57-64. Retrieved July 8, 2007, from EBSCO Online Database Business Source Complete. http://search.ebscohost.com/login.aspx?direct=true&db=bth&AN=9401195885&site=ehost-live

Hilliard, H., Matulich, E., Haytko, D., & Rustogi, H. (2012). An International Look at Attitude towards Advertising, Brand Considerations, and Market Expertise: United States, China, and India. *Journal of International Business Research*, 1129-41. Retrieved December 1, 2014, from EBSCO Online Database Business Source Complete. http://search.ebscohost.com/login.aspx?direct=true&db=bth&AN=82601388

Hite, R., & Fraser, C. (1988). International advertising strategies of multinational corporations. Journal of Advertising Research, 28(4), 9-17. Retrieved July 8, 2007, from EBSCO Online Database Business Source Complete. http://search.ebscohost.com/login.aspx?direct=true&db=bth&AN=8832147&site=ehost-live

Hite, R., & Fraser, C. (1990). Configuration and coordination of global advertising. Journal of Business Research, 21(4), 335-344. Retrieved July 8, 2007, from EBSCO Online Database Business Source Complete. http://search.ebsco-host.com/login.aspx?direct=true&db=bth&AN=18811820&site=ehost-live

Holt, P. (2004). Marketing for growth: How to create a great international advertising program. Franchising World, 36(1), 58-59. Retrieved July 5, 2007, from EBSCO Online Database Business Source Complete. http://search.ebsco-host.com/login.aspx?direct=true&db=bth&AN=12011483&site=ehost-live

Kotabe, M., & Helsen, K. (2001). Global marketing management (2nd ed.). New York: John Wiley.

Koudelova, R., & Whitelock, J. (2001). A cross-cultural analysis of television advertising in the United Kingdom and the Czech Republic. International Marketing Review, 18(3), 286-300. Retrieved July 5, 2007, from EBSCO Online Database Business Source Complete. http://search.ebscohost.com/login.aspx?direct=true&db=bth&AN=6449779&site=ehost-live

Link, G. (1988). Global advertising: An update. Journal of Consumer Marketing, 5(2), 69-75. Retrieved July 8, 2007, from EBSCO Online Database Business Source Complete. http://search.ebscohost.com/login.aspx?direct=true&db=bth&AN=5335549&site=ehost-live

Melewar, T., & Vemmervik, C. (2004). International advertising strategy: A review, reassessment and recommendation. Management Decision, 42(7), 863-881. Retrieved July 5, 2007, from EBSCO Online Database Business Source Complete. http://search.ebscohost.com/login.aspx?direct=true&db=bth&AN=14741055&site=ehost-live

Nevett, T. (1992). Differences between American and British television advertising: Explanations and implications. Journal of Advertising, 21(4), 61-73. Retrieved July 8, 2007, from EBSCO Online Database Business Source Complete. http://search.ebscohost.com/login.aspx?direct=true&db=bth&AN=9308265330&site=ehost-live

O'Guinn, T., Allen, C., & Semenik, R. (2003). Advertising and integrated brand promotion, (3rd ed.). Mason, OH: southWestern.

Okazaki, S., Mueller, B., & Diehl, S. (2013). A multi-country examination of hard-sell and soft-sell advertising: comparing global consumer positioning in holistic- and analytic-thinking cultures. Journal of Advertising Research, 53(3), 1-23. Retrieved November 19, 2013 from EBSCO online database Business Source Premier.

Shoham, A. (1999). Bounded rationality, planning, standardization of international strategy, and export performance: A structural model examination. Journal of International Marketing, 7(2), 24-50. Retrieved July 8, 2007, from EBSCO Online Database Business Source Complete. http://search.ebscohost.com/login.aspx?direct=true&db=bth&AN=2501258&site=ehost-live

Stafford, M. R. (2005). International services advertising (ISA). Journal of Advertising, 34(1), 65-86. Retrieved July 5, 2007, from EBSCO Online Database Business Source Complete. http://search.ebscohost.com/login.aspx?direct=true&db=bth&AN=14741055&site=ehost-live

Taylor, C. R. (2014). Corporate Social Responsibility and Advertising. *International Journal of Advertising, 33*(1), 11-15. Retrieved December 1, 2014, from EBSCO Online Database Business Source Complete. http://search.ebscohost.com/login.aspx?direct=true&db=bth&AN=94699146&site=ehost-live

SUGGESTED READING

Daechun An. (2013). Cultural influence on perceptions of advertising creativity: a cross-cultural comparison of U.S. and Korean advertising students. International Journal of Marketing Studies, 5(5), 75-87. Retrieved November 19, 2013 from EBSCO online database Business Source Premier. http://search.ebscohost.com/login.aspx?direct=true&db=buh&AN=91906576

Hoeken, H., van den Brandt, C., Crijns, R., Dominguez, N., Hendriks, B., Planken, B., et al. (2003). International advertising in Western Europe: Should differences in uncertainty avoidance be considered when advertising in Belgium, France, The Netherlands and Spain? Journal of Business Communication, 40(3), 195-218. Retrieved July 5, 2007, from EBSCO Online Database Business Source Complete. http://search.ebscohost.com/login.aspx?direct=true&db=bth&AN=10564790&site=ehost-live

Kumar, V., Sharma, A., Shah, R., & Rajan, B. (2013). Establishing Profitable Customer Loyalty for Multinational Companies in the Emerging Economies: A Conceptual Framework. *Journal Of International Marketing, 21*(1), 57-80. Retrieved December 1, 2014, from EBSCO Online Database Business Source Complete. http://search.ebscohost.com/login.aspx?direct=true&db=bth&AN=85872955

Taylor, C. (2005). Moving international advertising research forward. Journal of Advertising, 34(1), 7-16. Retrieved July 5, 2007, from EBSCO Online Database Business Source Complete. http://search.ebscohost.com/login.aspx?direct=true&db=bth&AN=16683236&site=ehost-live

Zou, S. (2005). Contributions to international advertising research. Journal of Advertising, 34(1), 99-110. Retrieved July 5, 2007, from EBSCO Online Database Business Source Complete. http://search.ebscohost.com/login.aspx?direct=true&db=bth&AN=16683320&site=ehost-live

Marie Gould

INTERNATIONAL MARKETING

ABSTRACT

This article focuses on how organizations use international marketing to gain entry into foreign markets. In order to have a successful international marketing strategy, organizations adapt, manage, and oversee marketing campaigns in foreign locales. Most organizations that choose to venture into the international market tend to have two similar characteristics. Many organizations have contemplated going into the global marketplace in order to remain competitive and increase their growth. However, this move may not be for all companies. Each organization will need to conduct a SWOT analysis to determine if it should enter this arena. As more businesses seek global opportunities, marketing research that is timely and accurate is a requisite. Marketing researchers must be able to identify creative ways to use the new technologies in order to engage in activities that will assist their organization's marketing strategies.

OVERVIEW

International marketing involves attempts by businesses to sell their products and services to consumers in another country. Although the concept of marketing is the same, an organization's marketing plan can be different based on the geographic location of the target market. Issues such as price, advertising, and distribution tend to be different across geographic locations, and the marketing team will have to address them based on the demands of the various markets. In order to have a successful international marketing strategy, organizations will need to adapt, manage, and oversee a marketing campaign in a foreign territory. Most organizations that choose to venture into the international market tend to have two similar characteristics. They tend to go abroad to market products and services that they believe have a high potential to earn money in the specified foreign markets, and they have committed themselves to making an international presence.

Many organizations have contemplated going into the global marketplace in order to remain competitive and increase their growth. However, this move may not be for all companies. Each organization will need to conduct a SWOT analysis to determine if it should enter this arena. There are many factors to consider before embarking on such an endeavor. Lisle (n.d.) has provided a guideline to assist organizations with determining whether or not international marketing is an option. Each organization should research and respond to the following points for analysis:

- **Determine if the organization has advantages as compared to other possible entrants or existing organizations.** An organization may be able to overcome barriers to entry due to its uniqueness in the market. When an organization has an advantage over other possible entrants or existing competitors, it is the best time for market entry.
- **Identify an unmet market need or underserved market niche.** Organizations will need to research and identify market niches that have not been discovered or are underserved. There may be a possibility that the organization can meet the need before competitors discover that it existed.
- **Find the "Goldilocks" sized market.** Organizations should take the size of the market opportunity into consideration. Sometimes, the best market is one that is not too large or too small. It's safer to go with a market that is average size.
- **Growing markets are advantageous so that an organization's success does not have to come at the expense of other organizations.** A market's growth rate is an important factor to consider; growing markets are easier to enter than those which are overcrowded. If there are too many players in the game, organizations will be forced to steal from each other in order to survive.
- **Conduct a competitive analysis of each market under consideration.** The level of competition in the industry is an important factor. A perfect market would be one that has a customer base

that is dependent on the industry's competitors, a large number of similar suppliers to the organization and its competitors so that the customers' bargaining power is low, an innovative industry with barriers to entry that lower the threat of substitute products and new competitors, and enough competitors and price elasticity so that competition would not be too high.

- **Identify markets that are in a state of "disequilibrium."** When a market is in disequilibrium, it means that it is experiencing some type of change or transformation. Stagnant industries tend not to welcome new entrants; whereas an industry seeking new solutions would provide opportunities for entry.
- **Seek out dissatisfied customers with low switching costs.** Customer satisfaction is a hot issue in many industries. Although many organizations spend substantial amounts of money soliciting customers, they lack the personnel to maintain quality customer service. Therefore, opportunities rise for new entrants who can market their ability to service customers after the sale has been made.
- **Understand that the customers' purchase decision is essential.** Organizations will need to research the potential markets to determine what would be successful. Unfortunately, many organizations have attempted to take a product's marketing campaign and product development to foreign countries only to fail. Different markets have different preferences. For example, a French manufacturer cannot utilize the process for its French facility to produce the same product in Germany. The German customer base may have a different set of needs and standards. Therefore, it would be best to determine what those needs are versus assuming the same process can be successfully duplicated in another country.
- **Choose the more profitable of two markets.** If an organization has followed all of the above-mentioned steps and found two viable markets, it should enter the market that is the most profitable.
- **Observe macro-level trends.** Organizations should consider "big picture" issues as reason to justify entering a market. For example, are there any themes involving baby-boomers, education and healthcare reform, or global warming? If so, gaining entry may be easier for an organization.

- **Be aware of regulatory obligations.** Identify limitations on trade (i.e. tariffs). Some countries may offer better regulatory conditions than others.
- **Identify the most attractive segment or segments.** Once an organization has identified the ideal market, it will need to be specific about which segments (i.e. in terms of product type, geography, and customer type) are the most attractive.

The decision to go into international marketing must be made only after careful thought has been given to its viability, and organizations should weigh the advantages against the disadvantages. Although doing business internationally can yield great profits, there are some issues that need to be considered. First, cultural and language barriers may be a problem. "Language barriers may present an obstacle when trying to communicate the benefits and advantages of a company's products and services overseas" (Khan, 2005).

Economic and political risks are two additional concerns that need to be considered prior to entering into a foreign market. Organizations will have to research and determine the stability of the host country's government to make sure there are no security threats, and if the foreign exchange is stable and whether there is a risk of not being paid for products and services.

"Developing the required organizational processes and allocating appropriate resources to an international effort often requires creating a separate export department within an organization that is responsible for all aspects of dealing with foreign markets" (Khan, 2005). Organizations will have to decide if it is best to establish the international business function internally or externally. It is important for organizations to assess their current workforce to determine if they will need to rely on expatriates to establish a presence in the host company or whether it is more feasible to hire employees from the host country to minimize cultural and language barriers.

If the organization elects to start internally, it may assign a team to set the budget, ship products, and develop the international marketing plan. However, this can become expensive, so the organization may evaluate two other options. One option is to hire employees from the host countries. Many organizations elect this option to minimize cultural and language barriers and secure labor that is cheaper than its current workforce. If the organization elects to hire employees from the host country, it is important that it assimilates these new hires into its corporate culture so that they will have an understanding of what the organization values and how it operates.

Another option is to use an export management company (EMC). EMCs are beneficial to a company entering the international market because they are organizations focused on this type of business. Such an organization can be a company's international marketing and sales initiative. A good EMC is a reputable organization with established international relationships and has access to key decision makers and buyers; can provide localization services; and has years of experience negotiating with foreign governments and banks.

APPLICATION

"The growing integration of international markets as well as the growth of competition on a worldwide scale implies adoption of a global perspective in planning marketing strategy" (Agnihotri & Santhanam, n.d.). International market efforts take many forms. There are various strategies an organization may take once it has decided to enter the global market. Ways to enter a foreign market include:

- **Exporting.** "Exporting is the marketing and direct sale of domestically-produced goods in another country, and is a traditional and established method of reaching foreign markets" ("Foreign market entry modes," 2007). New companies tend to enter international markets through exporting. One reason may be because this type of entry does not require the organization to produce the goods in the targeted country, which means that the organization would not have to invest in foreign production facilities. Marketing expenses are one of the biggest costs of exporting. There are two ways an organization can make sales in exporting:directly or indirectly. Direct sales can be made via mail order or through offices set up abroad. Indirect sales are made via intermediaries who locate the specific markets for the organization's products. The four players in the exporting business are the exporter, importer, transport provider, and government. Many organizations are able to successfully establish themselves abroad and do not have to expand beyond exporting.

- **Licensing.** Licensing occurs when a target country grants the right to manufacture and distribute a product under the licenser's trade name in a target country. In exchange for manufacturing rights, the licensee pays a fee. Small and medium-sized companies tend to grant licenses more often than large companies. Since little investment is required, licensing has the potential to provide a large return on investment. However, it is seen as the least profitable way to enter the market because most companies use licensing to supplement manufacturing and exporting. Licensing tends to be a viable option to enter a market when the exporter does not have sufficient capital, when foreign government import restrictions forbid other ways to enter the market, or when a host country is not comfortable with foreign ownership.

- **Joint Venture.** Joint ventures occur when an organization enters a foreign market via a partnership with one or more companies already established in the host country. In most cases, the local company provides the expertise on the target market while the exporting company manages and markets the product. A joint venture arrangement allows organizations with limited capital to expand into international markets and provides the marketers with access to its partner's distribution channels. According to QuickMBA.com (2007), these types of partnerships are an asset when (1) the partners' strategic goals converge while their competitive goals diverge; (2) the partners' size, market power, and resources are small compared to the industry leaders; (3) the partners are able to learn from one another while limiting access to their own proprietary skills. Key issues in a joint venture are ownership, control, length of agreement, pricing, technology transfer, local firm capabilities and resources, and government intentions. Potential problems include conflict over new investments, mistrust over proprietary knowledge, determining how to split the pie, a lack of parent company support, cultural clashes, and deciding when and how to terminate the relationship if necessary.

- **Direct Investment.** Direct investment occurs when there is direct ownership of infrastructure in a desired country. This requires high amounts of resources and is a large commitment. This type of market entry may be made via the acquisition of an existing entity or the establishment of a new enterprise. It requires the transfer of resources such as capital, technology, and personnel. Direct ownership can provide a high level of control in the operations as well as the opportunity to better know the potential customers and competitive environment.

ISSUES

As more businesses seek global opportunities, the role of timely and accurate marketing research becomes critical. Organizations will need this type of information to make decisions that affect the business on a daily basis. Information must be evaluated in both developed and developing countries. "Established markets in industrialized countries are becoming more geographically integrated as direct vertical links and information flows are established between customers, retailers and suppliers" (Douglas, 1999). As this continues to occur, international marketing research becomes essential to gather information across many borders "in order to identify regional or global market segments and evaluate opportunities for creating and integrating strategies across national boundaries" (Douglas, 1999). Also, the timely collection and interpretation of data from various sources is crucial in anticipating changes in the market and creating an effective response strategy. Market researchers must have the "ability to interpret and integrate complex data from diverse sources and environments" so that they can provide efficient recommendations for their organization's marketing strategy (Douglas, 1999).

In order to assist this effort, Douglas (1999) has identified four areas where progress must be made:

- **Aligning research efforts and capabilities with market growth potential.** As Douglas recounts (1999): "Although marketing research expenditures are concentrated in the industrialized countries of North America, Europe and Japan, the countries with the highest growth potential are the emerging market economies in Asia, Latin America, Eastern Europe and countries of the former Soviet Union." To be successful in the twenty-first century, market researchers must evaluate markets in these regions and develop the capability to conduct research in these markets. They will need to understand and be sensitive to the differences in these marketing environments as well deal with the lack of a sophisticated market research system. Given the low level of literacy in some of these countries, market researchers will need to develop questions that the respondents are able to understand. In addition, it will be important for market researchers to develop instruments that do not have cultural biases as well as make sure that they do not have any biases when interpreting the data, especially if they are from another culture.

- **Conducting and coordinating research spanning diverse environments.** Researchers must develop research questions as well as "adapt research instruments and administration procedures to different environments" (Douglas, 1999). Having the skills to interpret the results at a global level will be crucial. To avoid bias, research instruments, data collection, and sampling procedures may need to be reformulated to adapt to the environment so that meaningful results can be obtained (Craig & Douglas, 2000). One way to ensure that this goal is accomplished is to have a research team consisting of individuals from different cultural backgrounds and sites.
- **Developing and using new tools.** International market researchers will need to develop new approaches to interpret the results of changing markets. Although most researchers have a preference for quantitative research, a mixed methodology approach may be the best approach given the benefits of qualitative research with international market research. Based on the techniques of the method, researchers may be able to better understand and interpret the collected data in diverse cultural contexts. Additional benefits of qualitative research are that it is unstructured and does not impose the researcher's conceptual model on the respondent. "Qualitative techniques are helpful in probing attitudes and behaviors, providing a deep understanding of situational and contextual factors, and providing input into interpreting observed differences between countries and cultures" (Cooper, 1996).
- **Incorporation of technological advances into research design and methodology.** International marketing researchers must "incorporate the latest technological developments in data collection and dissemination into the research design" (Cooper, 1999). This step will allow the researchers to sig-

nificantly reduce the time required to collect data across global territory and enhance the methods of attaining international marketing data. As advances in computer technology (e.g. scanners, computer-assisted telephone interviewing, and computer-assisted personal interviewing) continue to evolve, they will present new ways to attain data that is conducive for international research issues.

Also, the Internet will have an impact on how international marketing research is conducted. It will provide access to secondary data and a new way to collect primary data. Researchers can surf the Internet for information versus going to a brick-and-mortar library and can collect data by using an electronic survey to send to the respondents. Questionnaires can be sent to potential participants, who can return the information via email or complete the survey via a link.

CONCLUSION

Organizations may elect to enter into the international marketing business to remain competitive. Although such an act can extend the life cycle of a particular product or service, there are other issues that a company should investigate before entering this arena. Companies need to investigate issues such as cultural and language barriers, political atmosphere, and business negotiation styles to determine if international marketing is a good fit for the organization. Khan (2005) has identified two steps that an organization can take to prepare for foreign entry. The first step is to develop an international marketing plan, and the second step is to determine how it will enter the new market.

An organization's nature provides the foundation for the type of international marketing plan it can develop. Organizational structure, management process, personnel, and culture are four factors that affect an organization's ability to create and implement a successful global strategy (Yip, Loewe & Yashino, 1988). To become globally competitive, organizations will need to focus on developing a marketing plan with global appeal, helping employees understand its global vision, selecting the right partners for joint ventures in foreign markets, and learning from mistakes that other organizations have made.

Marketing researchers must be able to identify creative ways to use the new technologies to engage in activities that will assist their organization's marketing strategies. In addition, they must develop methods to conduct market research in developed and developing countries simultaneously. There has been an increase in the number of multinational marketers who design and sell global brands, and they need international market research to assist them in making decisions in a diverse business market (Douglas, 1999).

BIBLIOGRAPHY

Abbreviations & acronyms. (2000, January). Acronyms from US OMB. Retrieved May 3, 2007, from http://crcwater.org/allacronyms.html

Agnihotri, P., & Santhanam, H. (n.d.). *International marketing strategies for global competitiveness*. Retrieved May 3, 2007, from http://blake.montclair.edu/~cibconf/conference/DATA/Theme5/India1.pdf

CAPI. (2007). *ISP Glossary*. Retrieved May 3, 2007, from http://isp.webopedia.com/TERM/C/CAPI.html

Craig, C., & Douglas, S. (2000). *International marketing research* (2nd ed.). Chichester, UK: John Wiley & Sons.

Cooper, P. (1996). *Internationalization of qualitative research*. ESOMAR Congress, Monte Carlo.

Douglas, S. (1999). Conducting international marketing research in the 21st century. Retrieved May 3, 2007, from http://pages.stern.nyu.edu/~sdouglas/rpbus/imr.html

Evers, N., Andersson, S., & Hannibal, M. (2012). Stakeholders and Marketing Capabilities in International New Ventures: Evidence from Ireland, Sweden, and Denmark. Journal Of International Marketing, 20, 46-71. Retrieved November 19, 2013 from EBSCO online database Business Source Complete with Full Text:http://search.ebscohost.com/login.aspx?direct=true&db=bth&AN=83698982&site=ehost-live

Foreign market entry modes. (2007). *Strategy*. Retrieved May 3, 2007, from http://www.quickmba.com/strategy/global/marketentry/

Khan, A. (2005). Deciding to go international. Retrieved May 3, 2007, from http://www.hispanicsmb.com/LinkClick.aspx?fileticket=tmS%2B7IKQYco%3D&tabid=62&mid=497

Lisle, C. (n.d.). Going global: Assess market opportunities. Retrieved May 3, 2007, from http://industrialmarketer.m.xtenit.com/files/1/industrialmarketer/412/pa/Going%20Global–%20Assess%20Market%20Opportunities.pdf

QuickMBA.com (n.d.). *Foreign market entry modes*. Retrieved May 3, 2007, from http://www.quickmba.com/strategy/global/marketentry/

Seggie, S. (2012). Transaction Cost Economics in International Marketing: A Review and Suggestions for the Future. Journal Of International Marketing, 20, 49-71. doi:10.1509/jim.11.0119 Retrieved November 19, 2013 from EBSCO online database Business Source Complete with Full Text:http://search.ebscohost.com/login.aspx?direct=true&db=bth&AN=76488174&site=ehost-live

Tan, Q., & Sousa, C. P. (2013). International Marketing Standardization. Management International Review (MIR), 53, 711-739. doi:10.1007/s11575-013-0172-5 Retrieved November 19, 2013 from EBSCO online database Business Source Complete with Full Text:http://search.ebscohost.com/login.aspx?direct=true&db=bth&AN=90471170&site=ehost-live

Yip, G., Loewe, P., & Yashino, M. (1988). How to take your company to the global market. *Columbia Journal of World Business, 23*, 37-48. Retrieved May 3, 2007, from EBSCO Online Database Business Source Complete. http://search.ebscohost.com/login.aspx?direct=true&db=bth&AN=5550336&site=bsi-live

SUGGESTED READING

Dong, M., Li, C., & Tse, D. (2013). Do Business and Political Ties Differ in Cultivating Marketing Channels for Foreign and Local Firms in China?. Journal Of International Marketing, 21, 39-56. doi:10.1509/jim.12.0088 Retrieved November 19, 2013 from EBSCO online database Business Source Complete with Full Text:http://search.ebscohost.com/login.aspx?direct=true&db=bth&AN=85872957&site=ehost-live

Douglas, S., & Craig, C. (2006). On improving the conceptual foundations of international marketing research. *Journal of International Marketing, 14*, 1-22. Retrieved May 3, 2007, from EBSCO Online Database Business Source Premier. http://search.ebscohost.com/login.aspx?direct=true&db=bth&AN=19918696&site=ehost-live

Eteokleous, Pantelitsa P., et al. (2016). Corporate social responsibility in international marketing: review, assessment, and future research. *International Marketing Review.* Retrieved on June 29, 2017.

Katsikeas, C., Samiee, S., & Theodosiu, M. (2006). Strategy fit and performance consequences of international marketing standardization. *Strategic Management, 27,* 867-890. Retrieved May 3, 2007, from EBSCO Online Database Business Source Premier. http://search.ebscohost.com/login.aspx?direct=true&db=bth&AN=21786389&site=ehost-live

Young, R., & Javalgi, R. (n.d.). International marketing research: A global project management perspective. *Business Horizons, 50,* 113-122. Retrieved

May 3, 2007, from EBSCO Online Database Business Source Premier. http://search.ebscohost.com/login.aspx?direct=true&db=bth&AN=23868537&site=ehost-live

Zhou, L., Wu, A., & Barnes, B. R. (2012). The Effects of Early Internationalization on Performance Outcomes in Young International Ventures: The Mediating Role of Marketing Capabilities. Journal Of International Marketing, 20, 25-45. Retrieved November 19, 2013 from EBSCO online database Business Source Complete with Full Text:http://search.ebscohost.com/login.aspx?direct=true&db=bth&AN=83698981&site=ehost-live

Marie Gould

INTERNET MARKETING STRATEGIES

ABSTRACT

This article will focus on Internet marketing and the strategies used to make the efforts successful. The Internet poses both opportunities and threats to the field of marketing. When developing a strategic marketing plan, organizations will need to determine if and when Internet marketing will be utilized. The success of the Internet as a medium for marketing depends upon how well the system outperforms alternative systems. This article will also explore how an organization can establish a customer base with the site-centric and symbiotic marketing approaches.

OVERVIEW

The use of the Internet continues to grow, in the United States and around the world. People spend a lot of time on the Internet because there is a wealth of information to be found. In addition, many consumers feel comfortable purchasing online and value the Internet's capacity for providing information about different products and services. As a result, Internet marketing has blossomed and become a key part of many companies' advertising efforts. The Internet has reduced costs associated with starting and running a small business (Boaze, 2004), which allows these companies to have an Internet presence because the medium is affordable. Companies have

also found the Internet to be an effective communication tool for customers, potential consumers, and other businesses, and the advent of social media further enabled companies to connect and interact directly with consumers.

As a result, marketing has experienced significant changes in how it operates. The Internet poses both opportunities and threats to the field of traditional marketing (Lemoine, 1999). When creating a marketing plan, organizations must determine if the tool is useful for marketing their products, which products can benefit from Internet marketing, when it is best to use traditional marketing, Internet marketing, or a combination of both, and what pitfalls need to be avoided so organizations do not experience failure when using Internet marketing. Internet marketing research has provided years' worth of valuable findings (Hou & Rego, 2002). The Internet has forever changed the way that organizations, governments, and individuals conduct business. Therefore, companies have responded by changing the way that they market their products.

Opportunities for Internet Marketing

The Internet opened many new avenues for companies to market new products and provided opportunities to restructure how they were marketing their established products. Benefits of the Internet include its ability to market globally, provide a free market

without regulations and barriers to entry, and determine which products sell well in an online format. Companies can decide which products are best to sell online. In addition, they can determine whether they want to sell on their own site or sell products through online retailers such as Amazon. The Internet provides opportunities and challenges for the four Ps of marketing (price, promotion, product, and place) by being an unpredictable distribution channel, a powerful marketing communication and promotional tool, an effective marketing research tool, and an efficient tool for segmenting and targeting consumers and customers (Lemoine, 1999).

The Internet can be considered an Integrated Marketing Communication (IMC) tool. It has the capability to combine the efforts of direct marketing, advertising, and public relations.

- **Direct Marketing:** Companies can communicate and promote products and services to a target market using email, customized pages, and promotional systems. For example, a company can offer a free product if members of a target market go to a particular survey link to answer questions. The feedback can be used to customize a promotional opportunity to that particular market. However, if the company uses email as a mechanism, the company must ensure that its promotional emails are not considered spam—unwanted marketing messages—by their recipients.

- **Advertising:** Companies can target global markets and make sure their ads are seen by consumers who will buy their products. Organizations are able to track the effectiveness of their advertising campaigns by tracking how many people see their ad and how many people visit the site based on a particular ad. In addition, the cost of online advertising is typically cheaper than traditional advertising methods such as print or television advertising. In some cases, a company may pay for an advertisement only when a user clicks on it; this system is known as pay-per-click (PPC) advertising. The Internet also allows advertisers to take advantage of data mining, if budgeting allows. Companies can use different tactics, such as cookies, to track the sites people visit, the music they listen to, the things they shop for, and more online. This information, once analyzed by algorithms, can then be used to offer ads targeted more specifically to these users.
- **Public Relations:** Companies may also use the Internet to provide corporate information about the organization and its products. Potential customers will be able to find information such as the names and background of the senior management team, investor information, history, and product information. Through the use of social media, companies can respond to complaints or other customer concerns quickly and effectively, thus managing their online reputation and establishing rapport with consumers.

The success of the Internet as a medium for marketing depends upon how well the system outperforms any alternative systems. The features of the Internet must be better than any of these alternative systems, and consumers must be able to benefit. Studies have indicated that the Internet is, in fact, one of the best venues for marketing products and services. These studies include one that distinguishes online and traditional retail formats with regard to the costs and benefits for consumers (Alba, Lynch, Weitz, Janiszewski, Lutz, Sayer & Wood, 1997) and another that illustrates how the Internet shares some of the same characteristics as other mediums but also offers new and unique features (Peterson, Balasubramanian, and Bronnenberg, 1997). Some of the unique features of the Internet are:
- Ability to store larger amounts of information at lower costs

- Ability to provide information that is interactive and can be customized
- Provision of power and inexpensive ways to search, organize, and distribute information
- Provision to perceive (e.g. 3D image and video preview)
- Capability to serve as a transaction and distribution tool for certain products
- Establishment of a presence at a low cost

Consumers tend to focus on formats that provide them with the most benefits. The Internet provides consumers with many benefits, such as accessibility to goods that are not in the local market, lower prices, the availability of different alternatives within the same product category, and the ability to shop at any time.

Internet Marketing Strategies
Developing a successful Internet marketing strategy is necessary if an organization wants to make an impression online. A successful strategy should include a great product, a website designed to sell, and an outstanding marketing strategy (Lowery, n.d.). All three of these areas are important and must be developed. If one area fails, chances of success may be reduced. Lowery suggests a three-step process for ensuring the success of an Internet marketing strategy.
- **Step 1: Develop Product**—A company should create a unique product that gives potential customers what they want. The product should fill a void in order to overcome the threat of competition. The company must also develop a target market. Researching the market is key. The company will need to find out what people want in order to develop a unique, quality product presentation.
- **Step 2: Develop Website**—The website should be designed to sell the product(s). The purpose of the website is to convince the consumer to buy the product. Therefore, words become important. Although graphics are impressive, words mean more. Consumers seek information and want to find out about the product and whether they should buy it. The objective of this step is to create a website that provides information to potential customers that would lead them to purchase the product.
- **Step 3: Develop a Marketing Strategy**—The marketing strategy is the final step in the process and

should include short- and long-term planning. The purpose of short-term strategies is to temporarily boost traffic to the site. Some examples of short-term strategies are purchasing advertising and optimizing the site for search engines. The purpose of long-term strategies is to bring a steady flow of targeted traffic over a period of time. Examples of long-term strategies include opt-in email lists, free gifts, and content.

Borgeon (1999) provided additional tips to take to make a site successful. These suggestions include:

- Feature new products regularly because it encourages repeat business
- Invite feedback and follow-up to those who contact the site by email
- Select products that speak to the target markets
- Build an easy navigation system on the web pages
- Present the website with a professional look
- Do not rely on "one-shot" outside expertise to build the site

APPLICATION

Having an Internet presence does not guarantee a successful venture. There has to be a significant number of people visiting the site and buying the product. In order to achieve success, the organizations must be able to attract customers and establish a solid customer base.

"If websites exist in a market-space that is so vast that their existence is not a sufficient condition for gaining traffic and the development of a viable Internet venture requires customers, the building of a customer base becomes a key component of any company's marketing strategy toward the Internet" (Lockett & Blackman, 2001, p. 49). "In addition, the development of a customer base will benefit other functions in the marketing process such as market research and testing" (Lockett, Blackman & Naude, 1998). Therefore, having an Internet customer base is essential for an Internet marketing strategy.

Developing an online customer base can be accomplished using two approaches: site-centric and symbiotic marketing. The two models can be viewed as opposite approaches; however, some organizations have used techniques from both approaches. The site-centric model relies upon the use of a central site that offers a specific product and solicits traffic. The

auction site eBay is an example of a website that uses the site-centric model. If a person is looking for a particular item, he or she may search for the item using a search engine such as Google. One search result may be an link to eBay if the product is available on that site.

In the site-centric model, customers are interested in a particular organization's brand that meets their requirements. The central site focuses on attracting and retaining customers, so it invests in building strong brand recognition for the organization. The site-centric approach utilizes an umbrella strategy that has a variety of techniques. All the techniques have the same theme—attract customers to the company's own website. According to Lockett and Blackman (2001), some of the techniques include:

- Portal sites—A portal site is either the first site a user sees when logging in or a search engine used to identify other sites. The default portal site may be operated by the Internet service provider (such as Yahoo!) or the provider of the browser (such as Google, provider of Chrome). Examples of search engines include Google and Bing. Companies may develop their own portal links and purchase prominent links in existing key portal sites.
- Purchase advertising—After the customer purchases the product from the central site, a direct link is provided so that the customer can pay immediately at the organization's site. The large portal sites have advantages in selling targeted advertisements. Some of these advantages are that (1) advertisements can be presented on Internet pages with related topics; (2) regional-specific advertising can be provided on regional-specific search engines; and (3) detailed information can be collected to assist buyers indetermining the success of specific banner advertisements.
- Direct email: Registered users or subscribers to e-mail services—Customers can agree to receive regular emails or newsletters when the company has new products.

ISSUES

Organizations may consider different strategic options as they attempt to build a customer base on the Internet. As the traditional site-centric approach continues to be plagued with increased costs and decreased effectiveness, alternatives are being sought. An alternative strategy is the symbiotic marketing approach, which is based on the concept of mutuality (Lockett & Blackman, 2001).

Symbiotic marketing assumes that it is not impossible to protect content such as intellectual property and concentrates on what needs to be done in order to build and defend a customer base. The model works under the assumption that by making the service available to a multitude of sites, the probability of new customers finding the service is increased. "This strategy seems to be appropriate for business-to-business markets since the most important site for a service to be referenced is their own company's Intranet site or access page Internet coverage of the service" (Lockett & Blackman, 2001).

The symbiotic marketing model has a centralized site, but other sites are asked to incorporate the service on their own sites. "The service is taken to the site the customer wants to use rather than the customer having to go to the service provider's central site" (Lockett & Blackman, 2001). An example of this is Amazon. Amazon encourages other sites to become associates and provides Amazon services on their sites, and the companies have a number of different ways to link to Amazon's site.

The symbiotic marketing model is the best strategy to use when building a customer base if "the service is based on changing data;" "the service is viewed as adding value to the host site and not seen as a competitive threat;" "the service is simple for other sites to implement;" and "the feedback from clients can be immediately used to enhance the service" (Lockett & Blackman, 2001). In addition to the above-mentioned scenarios, the nature of the targeted service market may be a factor in an organization deciding whether or not to use the symbiotic marketing model. Lockett and Blackman (2001) highlighted three examples of situations where this model may be the best strategy:

- "Where markets are fragmented and there are no big established dominant players in the industry"
- "Where market segments have had traditionally long product development cycles"
- "Where the customer base is in a business-to-business (B2B) rather than a consumer context"

One of the disadvantages of this model is that building links requires time, more time than some companies are willing to commit. In addition, the model may be difficult to implement in a large

organization with a well-developed marketing strategy. The symbiotic strategy is cheap, is slow to generate results, and has the potential to impact the brand value of an organization. An organization evaluating this method would have to evaluate the features mentioned above to determine if it is the best choice.

CONCLUSION

The Internet will continue to play a significant role in the field of marketing. Social media is another area in which companies can take advantage of marketing opportunities—Facebook ads directly targeting users is an example of the expansion of Internet marketing. Many will need to further their studies on the benefits and drawbacks of Internet marketing. Theorists may gain new ideas about the Internet and evaluate whether existing marketing theories can continue to be applied to the study of the Internet. Practitioners may continue to conduct market research to determine what consumers want, and policymakers must address topics such as security, consumer protection, and taxes (Hou & Rego, 2002).

As the field of Internet marketing explodes, there still will be a need for traditional advertising. Internet marketing does not threaten the existence of traditional marketing techniques but instead compliments them. Although Internet marketing provides valuable assets such as an increased awareness of brand names, traditional marketing efforts still can address some of the disadvantages of online shopping. For example, traditional marketing efforts can promote brick-and-mortar shopping experiences based on the opportunity for social interaction and allow consumers to actually see and physically touch a product before purchasing.

Two popular Internet marketing strategies are site-centric and symbiotic marketing. Although the site-centric model has the central site as its foundation and base, the techniques can be expensive and unaffordable for small businesses. The symbiotic marketing strategy is more cost-effective and provides organizations with an avenue to develop "a presence on the key portal sites in the business-to-business market" (Lockett & Blackman, 2001). However, it has its downside, especially for large organizations. There tends to be a need for a longer lead time, and it may require more persistence than the site-centric model.

BIBLIOGRAPHY

Alba, J., Lynch, J., Weitz, B., Janiszewski, C., Lutz, R., Sawyer, A., & Wood, S. (1997). Interactive home shopping: Consumer, retailer, and manufacturer incentives to participate in electronic marketplaces. *Journal of Marketing, 61*, 38–53. Retrieved May 3, 2007, from EBSCO Online Database Business Source Complete. http://search.ebscohost.com/login.aspx?direct=true&db=bth&AN=9707205120&site=bsi-live

Boaze, S. (2004, November 22). Two kinds of advertising for a marketing strategy. *EzineArticles.* Retrieved May 3, 2007, from http://ezinearticles.com/?Two-kinds-of-Advertising-for-a-Marketing-Strategy&id=5536.

Borgeon, M. (1999). Linking the Internet to your marketing strategy. *International Trade Forum, 17.* Retrieved May 3, 2007, from EBSCO Online Database Business Source Complete. http://search.ebscohost.com/login.aspx?direct=true&db=bth&AN=1953204&site=ehost-live

Dahlström, P., & Edelman, D. (2013). The coming era of 'on-demand' marketing. *Mckinsey Quarterly,* 24–39. Retrieved November 21, 2013, from EBSCO Online Database Business Source Complete. http://search.ebscohost.com/login.aspx?direct=true&db=bth&AN=87315649

Dinner, I. M., Van Heerde, H. J., & Neslin, S. A. (2014). Driving Online and Offline Sales: The Cross-Channel Effects of Traditional, Online Display, and Paid Search Advertising. *Journal of Marketing Research (JMR), 51*, 527–45. Retrieved November 11, 2014, from EBSCO Online Database Business Source Complete. http://search.ebscohost.com/login.aspx?direct=true&db=bth&AN=98472595&site=ehost-live

Ennew, C., Lockett, A., Holland, C., & Blackman, I. (2000). *Predicting customer visits to Internet retail sites: A cross industry empirical investigation.* Nottingham: University of Nottingham Business School.

Flosi, S., Fulgoni, G., & Vollman, A. (2013). If an advertisement runs online and no one sees it, is it still an ad? Empirical generalizations in digital advertising. *Journal of Advertising Research, 53*, 192–199. Retrieved November 21, 2013, from EBSCO Online Database Business Source Complete. http://search.ebscohost.com/login.aspx?direct=true&db=bth&AN=88284679

Hou, J., & Rego, C. (2002). Internet marketing: An overview. Retrieved May 3, 2007, from http://72.14.205.104/search?q=cache:Yp3Bnoyz%5fT8J:www.ebusinessforum.gr/engine/index.php%3Fop%3Dmodload%26modname%3DDownloads%26action%3Ddownloadsviewfile%26ctn%3D742%26language%3Del+internet%2Bmarketing%2Boverview%2Bhou&hl=en&ct=clnk&cd=1&gl=us

Lemoine, V. (1999). The role of the Internet in marketing. Retrieved May 3, 2007, from http://cci.mccombs.utexas.edu/research/white/int%5fmark.htm

Lipsman, A., Mud, G., Rich, M., & Bruich, S. (2012). The power of "like": How brands reach (and influence) fans through social-media marketing. *Journal of Advertising Research, 52*, 40–52. Retrieved November 21, 2013, from EBSCO Online Database Business Source Complete. http://search.ebscohost.com/login.aspx?direct=true&db=bth&AN=73177656

Lockett, A., & Blackman, I. (2001). Strategies for building a customer base on the Internet: symbiotic marketing. *Journal of Strategic Marketing, 9*, 47–68. Retrieved May 3, 2007, from EBSCO Online Database Business Source Complete. http://search.ebscohost.com/login.aspx?direct=true&db=bth&AN=4782033&site=bsi-live

Lockett, A., Blackman, I., & Naude, P. (1998). Using the Internet/WWW for the real time development of financial services: The case of Xenon Laboratories. *Journal of Financial Services Marketing, 3*, 161–172.

Logan, K. (2016). Have perceptions of internet advertising value changed over time? *American Academy of Advertising Conference Proceedings*, 18–26. Retrieved December 21, 2016 from EBSCO Online Database Business Source Ultimate. http://search.ebscohost.com/login.aspx?direct=true&db=bsu&AN=118578198&site=ehost-live&scope=site

Lowery, S. (n.d.) Internet marketing strategies—Part one: Three step formula. Retrieved on May 3, 2007, from http://www.web-source.net/3steps.htm

Peterson, R., Balasubramanian, S., & Bronnenberg, B. (1997). Exploring the implication of the Internet for consumer marketing. *Journal of the Academy of Marketing Science, 25*, 60–75. Retrieved

May 3, 2007, from EBSCO Online Database Business Source Complete. http://search.ebscohost.com/login.aspx?direct=true&db=bth&AN=9710093159&site=bsi-live

Vien, C. L. (2015). The future of marketing: Thriving in a digital world. *Journal of Accountancy, 219*(6), 1–4. Retrieved December 2, 2015, from EBSCO Online Database Business Source Complete. http://search.ebscohost.com/login.aspx?direct=true&db=bth&AN=109211098&site=ehost-live&scope=site

Yadav, M. S., & Pavlou, P. A. (2014). Marketing in Computer-Mediated Environments: Research Synthesis and New Directions. *Journal Of Marketing, 78*, 20–40. Retrieved November 11, 2014, from EBSCO Online Database Business Source Complete. http://search.ebscohost.com/login.aspx?direct=true&db=bth&AN=93641514&site=ehost-live

SUGGESTED READING

Agarwal, A., Hosanagar, K., & Smith, M. (2011). Location, location, location: An analysis of profitability of position in online advertising markets. *Journal of Marketing Research (JMR), 48*, 1057–1073. Retrieved November 21, 2013, from EBSCO Online Database Business Source Complete. http://search.ebscohost.com/login.aspx?direct=true&db=bth&AN=67729140

Dodson, I. (2016). *The art of digital marketing: The definitive guide to creating strategic, targeted and measurable online campaigns.* Hoboken, NJ: John Wiley & Sons.

Eid, R., Elbeltagi, I., & Zairi, M. (2006). Making business-to-business international Internet marketing effective: A study of critical factors using a case-study approach. *Journal of International Marketing, 14*, 87–109. Retrieved May 3, 2007, from EBSCO Online Database Business Source Complete. http://search.ebscohost.com/login.aspx?direct=true&db=bth&AN=23047726&site=ehost-live

Nesamoney, D. (2015) *Personalized digital advertising: How data and technology are transforming how we market.* Old Tappan, NJ: Pearson Education.

Pitta, D., Franzak, F., & Fowler, D. (2006). A strategic approach to building online customer loyalty: Integrating customer profitability tiers. *Journal of Consumer Marketing, 23*, 421–429. Retrieved May 3, 2007, from EBSCO Online Database Business Source Complete. http://search.ebscohost.com/login.aspx?direct=true&db=bth&AN=20712635&site=ehost-live

Pashkevich, M., Dorai-Raj, S., Kellar, M., & Zigmond, D. (2012). Empowering online advertisements by empowering viewers with the right to choose: The relative effectiveness of skippable video advertisements on YouTube. *Journal of Advertising Research, 52*, 451–457. Retrieved November 21, 2013, from EBSCO Online Database Business Source Complete. http://search.ebscohost.com/login.aspx?direct=true&db=bth&AN=84295239

Smith, S. (2013). Conceptualising and evaluating experiences with brands on Facebook. *International Journal of Market Research, 55*, 357–74. Retrieved November 11, 2014, from EBSCO Online Database Business Source Complete. http://search.ebscohost.com/login.aspx?direct=true&db=bth&AN=87975676&site=ehost-live

Survey: Business authors cite Internet marketing as top strategy. (2006). *Book Publishing Report, 31*, 4. Retrieved May 3, 2007, from EBSCO Online Database Business Source Complete. http://search.ebscohost.com/login.aspx?direct=true&db=bth&AN=20712635&site=ehost-live

Yucelt, U. (2007). Online consumers around the globe. *Journal of International Marketing & Marketing Research, 32*, 17–24. Retrieved May 3, 2007, from EBSCO Online Database Business Source Complete. http://search.ebscohost.com/login.aspx?direct=true&db=bth&AN=23638743&site=ehost-live

Marie Gould

L

LAUNCHING NEW VENTURES THROUGH TECHNOLOGY

ABSTRACT

The business environment of the early twenty-first century affords entrepreneurs the opportunity to launch new ventures through technology. The need to use up-to-date technological innovations in business is increasingly becoming a necessity, as firms strive to obtain good business partners and achieve competitive advantage. New firms must avoid adopting technology for technology's sake: sound business practices must prevail, and any technology that is adopted must be the right fit.

OVERVIEW

The field of entrepreneurship comprises three main elements: organizational creation, organizational renewal, and innovation—within or outside an existing organization (Sharma and Chrisman, 1999). The formation of new business ventures amounts to organizational creation with innovation, as an individual or organization pioneers, innovates, and takes risks for growth and development.

According to Sharma and Chrisman (1999), "entrepreneurs are individuals or groups of individuals, acting independently or as part of a corporate system, who create new organizations, or instigate renewal or innovation within an existing organization" (p. 18). Entrepreneurs carry out new business permutations out of a quest for growth through innovation.

A business venture is an entrepreneurial activity in which capital is exposed to the risk of loss weighed against the possible reward of profit. New ventures may be formed within preexisting organizations, or they may be formed independently, 'from scratch.' The formation of new business ventures by preexisting organizations is known as corporate venturing. Specifically, corporate venturing refers to the corporate entrepreneurial efforts that lead to the creation of totally new business organizations within preexisting corporate organizations (Sharma and Chrisman, 1999). This is different from strategic renewal, where corporate entrepreneurial efforts result in significant changes to an organization's preexisting business or corporate level strategy or structure, but not the formation of new business organizations.

New businesses formed from scratch are termed startups. Startup activity is related to the macroeconomic growth rate, cost of capital, and unemployment rate of a country as well as industry-specific characteristics, especially the technological conditions underlying the industry.

While starting a company is much easier than before, succeeding is as difficult as ever. "Only about a third of all startups ever turn a profit; another third operate at break-even level, and the rest end in failure. Top among the reasons young companies fail are problems such as incorrect market focus and misguided executive leadership" (Copeland and Malik, 2006, par. 3).

In developed economies like tthe United States, new firms play two essential roles. First, they are engines of innovation, more so than large firms, which only innovate within limits. Secondly, new firms in such economies help to smooth out the oscillations in the business cycle, fueling rebounds during slump periods.

High-impact entrepreneurs are those who start new firms, often with new ideas, not necessarily ideas for new products, but sometimes with ideas for new business strategies, and innovative production and marketing ideas. Apart from ideas, new firms also need money, skilled people, and other resources: in developed economies, these are often obtained from large, mature firms.

High-impact entrepreneurship thrives most in countries that pay proper attention to the entrepreneurial system, which comprises four sectors: high-impact entrepreneurs, large mature firms, the government, and the universities (Copeland and Malik,

2006). Large mature firms assist new ventures by becoming their customers, outsourcing to them, buying them, and training and providing human capital to start or join them. The government formulates and implements policies to actively encourage entrepreneurship. It, therefore, creates an enabling environment for entrepreneurship, provides funding, sponsors research, and buys products from new firms. The universities invest in education: they help broaden access to higher education and carry out research and idea-generation for new businesses.

Technology is the systematic knowledge and use, usually of industrial processes but applicable to any recurrent activity. It refers to developed applications for business and industry and the use of applied science for the development of technical applications. There are two types of developments in technology: those that reduce manual labor and those that enhance existing services (de Bunen, 2003).

There are several branches of technology: applied science (including computer technology, electronics, and nanotechnology); athletics and recreation; information and communication; industry; military science; domestic/residential; engineering; health and safety; and transport.

The use of technology in business has grown dramatically due to increases in the speed of communication and business processes, decreases in the cost of technology, decreases in the importance of businesses activities that take place in fixed geographical locations, globalization, and increases in global competition, major investments in infrastructure, and a leading-edge mentality in firms.

The use of technology in business has even given rise to a new management science called Business Technology Management (BTM). BTM unifies business and technology decision-making at every level in an organization. BTM provides a set of guiding principles, known as BTM Capabilities. The capabilities are combined to form BTM solutions, which organize and improve a company's practices.

As a global society, we have evolved from the industrial age to the information age; information has replaced physical products and inventories as the real driving force of business success. According to Amine and Botterton (2002), "clearly, there has been a profound transition in methods of doing business, especially in the way market players (both individuals and companies) communicate" (p. 1). Copeland

writes, "New technologies are creating new business opportunities on the Internet, on mobile phones, in consumer products, and in information services" (2006, Par. 2).

As with the other branches of technology, the use of information technology (IT) in new businesses has many advantages. Internet and web-related technologies offer real savings in time, money, effort, and valuable gains in efficiency and scope for many organizations, through the following capabilities (Amine and Botterton, 2002): global information dissemination, interactive communication, mass customization, collaboration, transactional support.

Companies "exploit one or more of these capabilities to reach a wider customer base, offer a broader range of value-added service offerings, and develop closer affiliations with customers" (Looney and Chatterjee, 2002, p. 76). Firms now have a relatively economical medium for marketing their products and services to a wider customer base and over long distances. They also offer a broader range of value-added service offerings. Through Customer Relationship Management, firms can also adapt their customer offerings and communications strategy to different customers, cultivate two-way customer-firm dialogue, and drastically improve the firm's image through demonstrated responsiveness (Looney and Chatterjee, 2002).

Geographic Information Systems (GIS) are computer systems designed to collect, store, retrieve, manipulate, and display spatial data. These systems can be used by new firms to geographically reference useful information such as census data, mailing addresses, telephone numbers, demographic traits, population distributions, location of shopping malls and residential housing, and much more.

New markets can be identified on the basis of demographics such as age, income, gender, housing preference, and census block. Advertising expenditure can be allocated to population areas containing appropriate demographic characteristics for the target market, and outdoor advertising can be purchased based on the routes residents are likely to take from work to home. Maps can be prepared to assure efficient routing for delivery of goods and services. Salespeople can access information on customer locations as well as availability of alternative sources (McBane, 2003). GIS can be combined with Global Positioning Satellite (GPS) technology, providing roadside assistance, driving directions, and mobile yellow pages.

According to Diana (2005), the technological capabilities offered by computers, software and the Internet have become indispensable in the performing of most business processes, and the reach of this technology is becoming almost unlimited as handheld computing devices and wireless networking technologies improve. . . Increasingly, cars are being designed with computer networking capabilities so that company vehicles can be virtual rolling offices (p. 22).

Advances in technology like email, video conferences, and online conferencing save time by reducing the number of face-to-face meetings needed to make decisions, conclude transactions, and manage projects.

Along with the Internet, "the concept of the intranet and extranet have developed which have added to the single communication standard. The intranet means that a company uses the Internet technology for communication within the company. The extranet further extends the intranet by allowing outside companies to gain access to selected internal company data" (Kanter, 1999, p. 13).

New firms can also use technology for their internal operations. For instance, Internet and web-related technologies can be used to recruit employees and give employees direct access to their own HR and payroll information, thereby allowing them to perform by electronic means transactions that used to be performed by administrative staff on paper forms. Touch-tone telephones can also be used for employee self-service, through Interactive Voice Response (IVR) systems (Nielson, 2002).

APPLICATIONS

E-business (technologies or uses) refers to the use of information and communications technologies to perform any type of business-related operation. E-business refers to "the ability of a firm to electronically connect, in multiple ways, many organizations, both internal and external, for many different purposes. It allows a firm to execute electronic transactions with any individual entity along the value chain, which includes suppliers, logistics providers, wholesalers, distributors, service providers, and end customers. E-business also allows an organization

to establish real-time connections simultaneously among numerous entities for specific purposes, such as optimizing the flow of physical items like raw materials, components and finished products, through the supply chain" (Fahey, Srivatava, Sharon & Smith, 2001, p. 892).

Fahey, et al. write that "one of the key characteristics of the e-business world is that companies will inevitably move more and more into a customer-centric approach in order to increase competitiveness" (2001, p. 892). All the processes in an organization can be affected by e-business, while subcategories with labels such as e-commerce and e-marketing are confined to certain key business processes (Meckel et al., 2004).

E-commerce refers to technologies and uses related to the performance of market transactions (getting in touch, negotiating, agreeing on deals, and making payments). "The rapid growth of the Internet, networking systems such as electronic data interchange systems, and the penetration of ISDN based applications are stimulating an ever-increasing number of businesses to participate in e-commerce worldwide" (Papazoglou, 2001, p. 71).

E-marketing is a component of e-commerce. It uses the Internet to advertise and sell goods and services. It can sometimes include information management, public relations, and customer service.

Brousseau and Chaves (2005) write that firms

make multiple uses of Internet for business, but selling online is the least frequent one. . . . This is because selling online is more complex, not only because it requires more complex technologies (essentially to manage security and payments), but also because it requires a re-engineering of the company's operations. . . . There may also exist 'natural' barriers to selling online, in particular when the provision of a good or a service requires 'face-to-face' interactions because it is complex, because there are uncertainties about quality, and so on (p. 7-8).

E-business technologies are also used to "support coordination between business partners, for instance, exchanging operational data, forecasts, and sharing technical information" (Brousseau and Chaves, 2005, p. 3).

Fahey, et al. report that "business offers the platform for new forms of marketplace strategy models, and it also requires firms to refocus and reconfigure almost every type of tangible and intangible asset. . .

Many new start-up e-business-based entities such as Travelocity, E*TRADE, and amazon.com create integrated networks of relationships with channels, end customers, suppliers, providers, and even rivals that would not be possible in the absence of the ever-increasing electronic interconnectivity. These relationships afford the e-business-driven organization the ability to access and influence the assets of external entities" (2001, p. 893).

In effect, "e-business is dramatically reshaping every traditional business process: from developing new products and managing customer relationships to acquiring human resources and procuring raw materials and components. By enabling major new tasks to be added to individual processes, e-business broadens their scope, content, and value-generating capability... by integrating traditionally largely separate processes, e-business creates what might well be described as new business processes" (Fahey et al., 2001, p. 893).

E-business is first and foremost developed to improve coordination with partners, then to expand markets, and then to increase competitiveness (Brousseau and Chaves, 2005). Indeed, the use of e-business can provide an important source of competitive advantage in the current business environment; it is rapidly becoming a competitive necessity in order to do business with larger firms.

For firms that want to launch their business through technology, technological reasons are often secondary to commercial considerations. The powerful external pressure to start with e-business technologies comes both from potential customers and competitors (Meckel et al., 2004). The pressure is greatest for small and medium-sized enterprises (SMEs), which are "frequently not in a position to dictate terms and are dependent on larger companies where they are suppliers of products (goods or services) or buyers of products" (p. 262). Such SMEs thus face two major problems:

- Disproportionate implementation costs because they have to adapt to the IT solution of the large company. The solution would most likely have to be implemented from scratch and would be tailored to the needs of the large company rather than the SME.
- Technological 'lock-in' with specific trading partners when the IT solution of the large company involves unique and exclusive standards, rather than open standards (Meckel et al., 2004, p. 261-2).

New ventures launching through technology would have to have a technology-capable workforce. They may save funds by buying and using commercial, off-the-shelf applications, including desktop applications like word processors, accounting systems, human resources systems, and other sophisticated business applications. Such commercial, off-the-shelf applications have quelled the need for in-house programming staff (Phillips, 2001). On the other hand, if the new venture has any custom-made systems or programs, it may have to provide specialized training for its employees.

Many new ventures—especially startups—may not have enough money to successfully launch their businesses, and therefore they may need to raise money. According to Copeland and Malik, "The right time to raise the first round of money varies from startup to startup. Some companies—mostly software or Web-based ventures—need relatively little funding to get off the ground." Firms looking to build a physical product will look for funding much earlier on. That's where "angel investors come in: unlike venture capitalists, who usually wait until a company has a working product, they specialize in early-stage startups" (Copeland and Malik, 2006).

In general, many of the new technologies have "radically reduced the costs associated with launching a new venture." In the late 1990s, a typical venture capital–funded startup needed roughly $10 million to put together the infrastructure and staff required to carry the company from its first business plan to its first product launch. In 2006, that cost was reduced to just $4 million—and in many cases much less, meaning that the "barriers to entry have never been lower" (Copeland and Malik, 2006).

ISSUES

There is a continuing debate about whether technology is actually the driving force in the development of new business processes or merely the facilitator or enabler (Kanter, 1999). The answer notwithstanding, it would be wrong for new firms to bank their success wholly on technology; new firms also need appropriate leadership, strategies, structures, systems, processes, organizational environments, human resources, and other resources.

A new venture launched through technology is not likely to succeed if the plan for an innovation looks only at the project as originally conceived, and not at underlying capabilities that may be created. Neither will the venture succeed if no explicit plan has been made to articulate and test assumptions and update the project according to what is learned ("The value captor's process," 2007). Web companies that learn quickly from their mistakes are more likely to succeed. The strategy is to launch quickly, listen to customers by examining user data, and see what works and what does not. Defects are embraced as a means toward improvement.

Project funding for a new venture should be linked to requirements that certain post-launch milestones must be successfully achieved. In addition, the firm should ensure good management of its cash flow. In the marketing arena, it has been said that it is better for a new venture to start with an existing market rather than a revolutionary product ("Startups that work," 2005). The market size should be well-estimated, and the firm should protect its competitive position, creating an unforgettable brand for its product or service. The initial founding team should include a marketing or salesperson.

Rewards allocated to the new venture's project team members should not only be tied to the successful launch of the firm: the project team should not be made to suffer negative consequences if the venture dies prematurely. Similarly, pressure should not be placed on the business leaders to quickly achieve large revenues or market share.

Technology in business does not operate on its own; it is driven by people. The human resource systems and strategies for a new venture must be built early, preferably in conjunction with an educational institution. The firm must have a talented management team in place, with a board of directors to offer strategic guidance. Management team members should have experience handling uncertain or ambiguous situations.

It is uncommon for firms to be able to acquire or afford all the technological and human resources that they need. Increasingly, they form interdependent and flexible relationships with other firms—including suppliers and competing firms—to be able to focus on what they do best. A new venture should consider outsourcing and choose all its partners wisely.

A new venture should also seek to constantly develop its product or service range, and in doing so, it should not shy away from making acquisitions. In fact, acquisitions can turn out to be the cheapest way to expand the business. Entrepreneurs should not think that their company's products and assets have to be brand new in order to be their own.

The firm must establish a strategic business model. The new venture should not be evaluated on a calendar schedule, as established businesses are—instead, it should be evaluated according to the achievement of specific milestones. Additionally, if the new venture is a project of a preexisting company, it should not be managed in isolation from other parts of the company.

Lastly, progress in achieving the planned goals should not be seen as the only way to measure project benefits. Intangible assets, new opportunities uncovered, or platforms on which future ideas could build should be identified and monitored ("The value captor's process," 2007).

Once launched, new ventures should be careful not to rely on pure technology to solve its problems. They must be sure to review their business processes and interaction with trading partners as carefully as they evaluate new technology (Burnell, 2001).

With new ventures that wish to—or are compelled to—launch through technology, the main thing is to use the right technology in the right place to deliver the biggest benefit. New technologies should not be used unless they have a business or a performance benefit and have proven security and robustness.

BIBLIOGRAPHY

Acs, Z., & Preston, L. (1997). Small and medium-sized enterprises, technology, and globalization: introduction to a special... *Small Business Economics, 9*, 1. Retrieved April 26, 2007, from EBSCO Online Database Business Source Complete. http://search.ebscohost.com/login.aspx?direct=true&db=bth&AN=9711300204&site=ehost-live

Amine, L., & Botteron, P. (2002). Guest editors' introduction: global e-business: a progress report. *Thunderbird International Business Review, 44*, 1–3. Retrieved April 26, 2007, from EBSCO Online Database Business Source Complete. http://search.ebscohost.com/login.aspx?direct=true&db=bth&AN=13638319&site=ehost-live

Audretsch, D., & Acs, Z. (1994). New-firm startups, technology, and macroeconomic fluctuations. *Small Business Economics, 6*, 439–449. Retrieved April 28, 2007, from EBSCO Online Database

Business Source Complete. http://search.ebsco-host.com/login.aspx?direct=true&db=bth&AN=16913165&site=ehost-live

Brousseau, E., & Chaves, B. (2005). Contrasted paths of adoption: is e-business really converging toward a common organizational model? *Electronic Markets, 15*, 181–198.

Burnell, J. (2001). No secrets, no shortcuts. *Frontline Solutions, 2*, 8. Retrieved April 26, 2007, from EBSCO Online Database Business Source Complete. http://search.ebscohost.com/login.aspx?direct=true&db=bth&AN=9078389&site=ehost-live

Carlozzi, C. (1999). Make your meetings count. *Journal of Accountancy, 187*, 53–55. Retrieved April 26, 2007, from EBSCO Online Database Business Source Complete. http://search.ebscohost.com/login.aspx?direct=true&db=bth&AN=1541368&site=ehost-live

Copeland, M., & Malik, O. (2006). How to build a bulletproof startup. *Business 2.0, 7*, 76–92. Retrieved April 28, 2007, from EBSCO Online Database Business Source Complete. http://search.ebscohost.com/login.aspx?direct=true&db=bth&AN=21115804&site=ehost-live

Cotterill, K. (2012). A Comparative Study of Entrepreneurs' Attitudes to Failure in Technology Ventures. International Journal Of Innovation Science, 4, 101-116. Retrieved December 3, 2014, from EBSCO Online Database Academic Source Complete. http://search.ebscohost.com/login.aspx?direct=true&db=a9h&AN=77495924

Cusumano, M. A. (2013). Evaluating a startup venture. *Communications of the ACM, 56*, 26–29. Retrieved November 19, 2013, from EBSCO Online Database Business Source Complete. http://search.ebscohost.com/login.aspx?direct=true&db=bth&AN=90502519

Davis, J. (2000). Traditional vs on-line learning: It's not an either/or proposition. *Employment Relations Today (Wiley), 27*, 47–60. Retrieved April 26, 2007, from EBSCO Online Database Business Source Complete. http://search.ebscohost.com/login.aspx?direct=true&db=bth&AN=3115771&site=ehost-live

De Bunsen, J. (2003). Facilitating meetings. *Business Travel World*, Retrieved April 26, 2007, from EBSCO Online Database Business Source Complete. http://search.ebscohost.com/login.aspx?direct=true&db=bth&AN=11477258&site=ehost-live

Diana, T. (2005). Technology–a pervasive and growing presence in business credit. *Business Credit, 107*, 22–25. Retrieved April 26, 2007, from EBSCO Online Database Business Source Complete. http://search.ebscohost.com/login.aspx?direct=true&db=bth&AN=18525150&site=ehost-live

Fahey, L., Srivastava, R., Sharon, J., & Smith, D. (2001). Linking e-business and operating processes: the role of knowledge management. *IBM Systems Journal, 40*, 889.

Jolly, D. R., & Thrin, F. (2007). New venture technology sourcing: Exploring the effect of absorptive capacity, learning attitude and past performance. *Innovation: Management, Policy & Practice, 9*, 235-248. Retrieved December 3, 2014, from EBSCO Online Database Business Source Complete. http://search.ebscohost.com/login.aspx?direct=true&db=bth&AN=28118660&site=bsi-live

Kanter, J. (1999). Knowledge management, practically speaking. *Information Systems Management, 16*, 7. Retrieved April 26, 2007, from EBSCO Online Database Business Source Complete. http://search.ebscohost.com/login.aspx?direct=true&db=bth&AN=2795219&site=ehost-live

Looney, C., & Chatterjee, D. (2002). Web-enabled transformation of the brokerage industry. *Communications of the ACM, 45*, 75–81. Retrieved April 26, 2007, from EBSCO Online Database Business Source Complete. http://search.ebscohost.com/login.aspx?direct=true&db=bth&AN=11863434&site=ehost-live

McBane, D. (2003). Getting the horse to drink: teaching technology to marketing students. *Marketing Education Review, 13*, 1–6. Retrieved April 26, 2007, from EBSCO Online Database Business Source Complete. http://search.ebscohost.com/login.aspx?direct=true&db=bth&AN=10297980&site=ehost-live

Meckel, M., Walters, D., Greenwood, A., & Baugh, P. (2004). A taxonomy of e-business adoption and strategies in small and medium sized enterprises. *Strategic Change, 13*, 259–269. Retrieved April 27, 2007, from EBSCO Online Database Business Source Complete. http://search.ebscohost.com/login.aspx?direct=true&db=bth&AN=17073632&site=ehost-live

Nielson, N. (2002). How technology affects the design and administration of pensions and benefits.

Journal of Labor Research, 23, 417–431. Retrieved April 26, 2007, from EBSCO Online Database Business Source Complete. http://search.ebscohost.com/login.aspx?direct=true&db=bth&AN=6795090&site=ehost-live

Papazoglou, M. (2001). Agent-oriented technology in support of e-business. *Communications of the ACM, 44,* 71–77. Retrieved April 26, 2007, from EBSCO Online Database Business Source Complete. http://search.ebscohost.com/login.aspx?direct=true&db=bth&AN=12026105&site=ehost-live

Phillips, J. (2001). Embracing the challenge of leadership. *Information Management Journal, 35,* 58. Retrieved April 26, 2007, from EBSCO Online Database Business Source Complete. http://search.ebscohost.com/login.aspx?direct=true&db=bth&AN=5348423&site=ehost-live

Schramm, C. (2004). Building entrepreneurial economies. *Foreign Affairs, 83,* 104–115. Retrieved April 26, 2007, from EBSCO Online Database Business Source Complete. http://search.ebscohost.com/login.aspx?direct=true&db=bth&AN=13478435&site=ehost-live

Sharma, P., & Chrisman, J. (1999). Toward a reconciliation of the definitional issues in the field of corporate entrepreneurship. *Entrepreneurship: Theory & Practice, 23,* 11–27. Retrieved April 27, 2007, from EBSCO Online Database Business Source Complete. http://search.ebscohost.com/login.aspx?direct=true&db=bth&AN=2311216&site=ehost-live

Shiffman, K. (2006). 5 smart strategies of super startups. *Profit, 25,* 63-66. Retrieved April 28, 2007, from EBSCO Online Database Business Source Complete. http://search.ebscohost.com/login.aspx?direct=true&db=bth&AN=22619469&site=ehost-live

Simmons, G., Armstrong, G. A., & Durkin, M. G. (2011). An exploration of small business website optimization: Enablers, influencers and an assessment approach. *International Small Business Journal, 29,* 534–561. Retrieved November 19, 2013, from EBSCO Online Database Business Source Complete. http://search.ebscohost.com/login.aspx?direct=true&db=bth&AN=69671749

Sood, S. (2012). The death of social media in start-up companies and the rise of s-commerce: Convergence of e-commerce, complexity and social media. *Journal of Electronic Commerce in Organizations, 10,* 1–15. Retrieved November 19, 2013, from EBSCO Online Database Business Source Complete. http://search.ebscohost.com/login.aspx?direct=true&db=bth&AN=82357002

Startups that work: Surprising research on what makes or breaks a new company. (2005). *Publishers Weekly,* Retrieved April 28, 2007, from EBSCO Online Database Business Source Complete. http://search.ebscohost.com/login.aspx?direct=true&db=bth&AN=17725026&site=ehost-live

The value captor's process. (2007). *Harvard Business Review,* Retrieved April 26, 2007, from EBSCO Online Database Business Source Complete. http://search.ebscohost.com/login.aspx?direct=true&db=bth&AN=24647412&site=ehost-live

SUGGESTED READING

Acs, Z., & Preston, L. (1997). Small and medium-sized enterprises, technology, and globalization: introduction to a special... *Small Business Economics, 9,* 1. Retrieved April 26, 2007, from EBSCO Online Database Business Source Complete. http://search.ebscohost.com/login.aspx?direct=true&db=bth&AN=9711300204&site=ehost-live

Audretsch, D., & Acs, Z. (1994). New-firm startups, technology, and macroeconomic fluctuations. *Small Business Economics, 6,* 439–449. Retrieved April 28, 2007, from EBSCO Online Database Business Source Complete. http://search.ebscohost.com/login.aspx?direct=true&db=bth&AN=16913165&site=ehost-live

Brousseau, E., & Chaves, B. (2005). Contrasted paths of adoption: Is e-business really converging toward a common organizational model? *Electronic Markets, 15,* 181–198. Retrieved April 27, 2007, from EBSCO Online Database Business Source Complete. http://search.ebscohost.com/login.aspx?direct=true&db=bth&AN=18396415&site=ehost-live

Kandel, B. K., & Hota, J. (2012). Information technology adoption in small family businesses for developing economies. *IUP Journal of Entrepreneurship Development, 9,* 7–37. Retrieved November 19, 2013, from EBSCO Online Database Business Source Complete. http://search.ebscohost.com/login.aspx?direct=true&db=bth&AN=78120176

Mohamad, R., & Ismail, N. (2013). The extent of e-business usage and perceived cumulative benefits: A survey on small and medium-sized enterprises.

Information Management & Business Review, 5, 13–19. Retrieved November 19, 2013, from EBSCO Online Database Business Source Complete. http://search.ebscohost.com/login.aspx?direct=true&db=bth&AN=87965748

Savitz, E., & Lea, W. (2011). Social Business: You're Doing It All Wrong. Forbes.Com, 30. Retrieved December 3, 2014, from EBSCO Online Database Business Source Complete. http://search.ebscohost.com/login.aspx?direct=true&db=bth&AN=66640183&site=bsi-live

Vanessa A. Tetteh, Ph.D.

LAW OF MARKETING AND ANTITRUST

ABSTRACT

Every company must market its products to make a profit; however, the allowable methods of marketing are limited. The United States and other market economies are committed to the principle of competition because it protects consumers, encourages efficiency and innovation in producers, and maximizes overall wealth. Society, in the form of the antitrust law, has announced its strong policy against monopolies, cartels, and other arrangements that threaten competition. The company seeking to market its products is well advised to steer clear of any practices that hamper competition. Excessive market power, tying agreements, and cartel violations can all attract the attention of government regulators seeking to enforce the antitrust law. This article reviews these concepts and the criminal penalties for violation of the antitrust law.

OVERVIEW

All businesses operate by offering some good or service within some market. The basic forces that drive those markets economies are supply, demand, and competition. Market economies are dedicated to the principle that people are in the best position when they can make voluntary exchanges of goods and services at prices controlled by competitive markets. When exchanges are made in competitive markets, society will be better off because markets remain open, and output can expand, thereby maximizing national wealth. Antitrust laws are designed to control private economic power by preventing monopolies, punishing cartels, and otherwise ensuring competitive markets. A market is competitive if goods are priced at the cost of production giving sellers and producers enough profit to maintain their investment in the industry and if all consumers willing to pay that price are able to purchase those goods (Hovenkamp, 1985).

As an economic model, a perfectly competitive market is characterized by the existence of several factors. First, sellers would produce identical products such that consumers are indifferent regarding which supplier they buy from. Second, each supplier is so small as compared to the overall market that fluctuations in its output, or its withdrawal from the market, would not affect the decisions of other sellers. Third, all sellers would have the same access to the material required to produce their goods. Fourth, all participants in the market would have perfect knowledge about prices, output, and other market information. The closer a market comes to meeting all four standards, the more competitively that market will perform (Hovenkamp, 1985).

A monopoly is essentially the opposite of perfect competition. Monopolies seek to maximize profits through substantial or total market power and restrict output in a way that limits supply and causes prices to rise. This practice reduces overall production and likely relieves the producer from competitive market pressures to be innovative and efficient. Monopoly markets are characterized by three factors. First, a single seller occupies the entire market. Second, that dominant seller sells a unique product. Third, there are substantial barriers to entry for other firms, and exiting the market is also difficult. This third factor is likely the most important to monopolistic behavior. Without such barriers, other firms would be likely to enter the market when the monopolist raises prices or lowers quality from the competitive norm (Hovenkamp, 1985).

The Development of the Antitrust Law

The law has developed over the years in order to protect markets from monopolies and anti-competitive behavior. Courts in England, dating back to 1414, sought to protect fair commercial activity by declaring void clauses in agreements between master and apprentice whereby the apprentice was prevented from entering the trade for a certain period of time or in a given location. Courts were, and are, hesitant to deprive a person of the ability to use his or her skills to earn a living and to deprive the public of the advantages of competition. However, the principle of freedom of contract held that people should be able to make agreements, and courts should enforce those freely entered agreements without dictating how a person can or should dispose of the property or effort. The competing principles of market regulation and freedom of contract came to a head in the famous English case of *Mitchell v. Reynolds* in 1711. The case laid down the doctrinal principles to determine the enforceability of a restraint on trade. General restraints on trade were invalid because their only purpose was to limit competition. Society was justified in intervening in an agreement in order to protect a person who agreed to such a general restraint before the person became a burden to the state or deprived the public of the benefits of competition. Particular or specific restraints may be valid if they are limited in duration and scope and otherwise reasonable. The common law view was that the public was protected if the legal right to trade was guaranteed.

The inadequacy of the safeguard provided by the common law became apparent in the railroad industry where high capital expenditures to enter the market made competition sparse, even though all potentially interested parties had a legal right to enter the market. The concern was that a railroad could inflate rates on routes where it enjoyed a monopoly and then unfairly cut rates on competitive routes. In the United States, during the second half of the nineteenth century, rising public concern about the abusive practices of railroads and corporate giants led to antitrust legislation. Congress first responded with the Interstate Commerce Act and the Sherman Antitrust Act, both passed in 1890. The Sherman Act enjoyed overwhelming support and passed in Congress with only one vote cast against the measure. However, continuing corporate abuse along with disappointing judicial interpretation of the acts fueled continued public pressure for additional regulation. The antitrust issue dominated the 1912 presidential election and led to the Clayton Act and the Federal Trade Commission Act of 1914.

The operative provisions of Sherman Antitrust Act of 1890 are few and brief. Section 1 of the Sherman Act declares illegal all contracts, combinations, or conspiracies that unreasonably restrain interstate or foreign trade. The act applies to agreements among competitors that attempt to fix prices, rig bids, and allocate customers. Section 2 of the act declared illegal any monopoly or attempt to monopolize any part of trade. The violation of either section is punishable as a criminal felony. The Sherman Act did not create authority for active regulation of business. On the other hand, the general prohibition on monopolies and restraints of trade was more restrictive than the common law approach that only refused to enforce offensive contracts. The main effect of the Sherman Act was to bring the enforcement of the antitrust law within the executive branch of government. The initial judicial reaction was to give the Sherman Act a very narrow reading followed by a very broad reading that made it unworkable. Eventually, the courts settled on the "rule of reason" and condemned only unreasonable conduct under the act (Hovenkamp, 1985).

Under the "rule of reason" businesses had little guidance as to what was illegal and courts had no specific mandate to enforce. To provide some guidance, in 1914 Congress passed the Clayton Act, which declared four restrictive or monopolistic activities against the law but not criminal offenses: price discrimination (selling the same product at different prices to similar buyers); exclusive dealing contracts (selling on the condition that the buyer would not deal with seller's competition); corporate mergers (acquisition of competing companies), and interlocking directors (common board members among competing companies). Each of these practices was illegal only when its effect was to considerably lessen competition or when it tended to create a monopoly in any line of commerce. The Federal Trade Commission Act of 1914, as amended in 1938, declared unlawful unfair methods of competition and deceptive trade acts (Hovenkamp, 1985).

APPLICATIONS

The application of the antitrust law, for example section 2 of the Sherman Act, requires the finding that a company has monopolistic power. As a general matter, courts describe market power as the ability to raise prices or eliminate competition. When a firm raises prices to sell at higher than competitive price, that firm will lose customers. Market power refers to a firm's ability to raise prices without losing so many sales that the price increase becomes unprofitable. Monopolistic power is a high degree of market power. Therefore, a monopolist can deviate significantly from competitive or marginal cost and pricing and will enjoy increased profits. To determine market power, courts rely on the positive correlation between market share and market power. For example, suppose that a market is composed of ten firms each with 10 percent market share. If the competitive price is $1.00 and Firm X attempts to raise its price to $1.25, Firm X's customers will look to the competition to purchase the item at the competitive price. If each of those competitors can raise output by a little more than 10 percent, Firm X will lose all of its sales. However, if Firm X has an 80 percent market share, Firm X's customers will still look to competitors but those competitors will have to substantially raise their output to take all of Firm X's sales. Firm X's increased prices would encourage other new firms to enter the market and cause current competitors to increase competition. While Firm X's position would eventually erode, it would be able to charge the higher price for quite some time. The firm with a large market share has market power because it may raise prices and, at least for a while, charge higher than competitive prices (Hovenkamp, 1985).

To infer the market power deemed illegal by the antitrust law, a court will typically determine the relevant product market and geographic area and then compute the firm's output in that relevant market. A particular company may have a number of product markets but many of those potential markets are not relevant for antitrust purposes. The relevant market is the smallest for which a firm with 100 percent of the market could profitably reduce output and raise prices. Consider the product market of "Ford cars," of which Ford has 100 percent of the market. If Ford raised the prices of Ford cars, then customers would likely turn to some other manufacturer; "Ford cars" is therefore not a relevant market. If the holder of 100 percent market share of "American passenger cars" raised prices, once again consumers would likely turn to manufactures from another country. However, if the holder of 100 percent of the market for "passenger cars" raised prices, consumers would have to switch to trucks, bicycles, or simply do without cars. In reality, because the demand for cars is sufficiently inelastic, a large percentage of consumers would pay the higher price. The elasticity of demand is the relationship between a change in the price for a product and the corresponding change in demand for that product. While the price increase would motivate related manufacturers to enter the market, causing GM to lose its monopolistic pricing, it would likely take several years. Of the examples listed above, the "passenger car" market is the smallest market that could result in monopoly pricing given 100 percent market share and therefore likely to be the relevant product market (Hovenkamp 1985).

The above analysis is focused upon the ability, or likelihood, that consumers would substitute one product for another. That concept of substitution of alternative products is known as the cross elasticity of demand. For two products that are close substitutes, a raise in the price of one will encourage consumers to buy the other. For example, corn and wheat are often used interchangeably for many purposes and the products would have a high cross elasticity of demand. For antitrust purposes, those two products would be in the same relevant market.

In addition to evaluating the cross elasticity of demand, antitrust law also evaluates the elasticity of supply. The elasticity of supply is the relationship between the changes in price and the amount of the product produced. As a general rule, as prices increase, more companies will produce the products to earn those higher prices. Therefore, if producers of a product have a large amount of excess production capacity, the holder of a large percentage of the market would not be able raise prices. A price increase would prompt other producers to flood the market with those same products at the lower price.

Goal of Antitrust Policy

The overall goal of antitrust policy is to assure the efficiency of market economies by protecting competition, and the law accomplishes this goal by prohibiting a number of activities. Although breaking up a massive company's market power is certainly a popular notion, another practice called a tie-in can catch the attention of the antitrust law. A tie-in or tying arrangement may be illegal under the Sherman Antitrust Act, as an act in restraint of trade, or the Clayton Act, as an act that substantially lessens competition. A tying arrangement is the sale of one product on the condition that the consumer takes another product as well. Generally, the practice of tying is illegal where the seller has sufficient economic power in one market to force the sale of the tied product and where the seller coerces the buyer to take the tied product. Many products are and may be legally tied or bundled; the law of tying agreements is aimed at those forced sales that are anti-competitive or cause injury to the seller's customers. However, that does not mean that the law seeks a solution that makes every consumer better off in every instance. The law seeks to make most consumers better off most of the time.

According to the U.S. Department of Justice (DOJ), cartel violations are the worst antitrust violations. Cartel violations include price fixing, bid rigging, and customer allocation. Price fixing happens when two or more competitors agree on a price to charge as when they agree to raise prices by a certain amount or agree not to sell below a certain price. Bid rigging occurs when two or more companies agree to bid so that a predetermined firm receives the contract. Bid rigging typically occurs in contracts for government work. Customer allocation agreements split customers between companies to reduce or eliminate competition. The allocation may be by geographic area or some other method. These types of cartel agreements are usually secret and the participants defraud consumers by pretending to be competitors even though they have made an agreement not to compete. These agreements harm consumers by forcing them to pay more for products and services and by removing the usual benefits of competition, such as innovation. It has been estimated that cartel arrangements can raise the price of products by 10 percent or more. The Department of Justice considers people who take consumer money by using one of these methods to be thieves (U.S. Dept. of Justice).

Enforcement of Antitrust Law

Antitrust laws are enforced by the Antitrust Division of the United States Department of Justice (DOJ) (both civil and criminal actions), the Federal Trade Commission (FTC) (civil actions only), and by private parties asserting damage claims. DOJ attorneys investigate cases with the help of the Federal Bureau of Investigation (FBI) and other investigative agencies. Most states also have antitrust laws very similar to the federal laws that are applied to antitrust violations that occur entirely within one state. State antitrust laws are generally enforced through the office of the state attorney general. Currently, the penalties for violations of the federal acts are fines up to $1 million and up to 10 years in prison for each offense committed by an individual and fines up to $100 million for each corporate offense. In certain circumstances, the fine can exceed these maximums and go to twice the actual gain or loss.

Cartel violations are the DOJ's top antitrust priority. The DOJ has prosecuted and convicted many cartel violation cases in a number of industries, including soft drink, vitamins, trash hauling, auto parts, road building, and electrical contracting. Industries producing fax paper, display materials, explosives, plumbing supplies and doors, among others, have been investigated for possible violations. In the late 1990s, the DOJ began an investigation into a large-scale vitamin cartel that was affecting more than $5 billion in U.S. commerce. The cartel had agreements on the production for each company, on the amount it should charge, and on the customers it should serve. The victims of the cartel included such corporations as General Mills, Kellogg, Coca Cola, Tyson Foods, and Procter & Gamble. The effects of the cartel conspiracy were eventually felt in the form of higher prices for a decade by all Americans who took vitamins, drank milk, or ate cereal. The DOJ investigations led to the condemnation of Swiss, German, Canadian, Japanese, and U.S. firms and many top executives from those companies went to prison and paid unprecedented fines of $850 million in 1999 alone (U.S. Dept. of Justice).

CONCLUSION

Companies must market their products to make a profit; however, the allowable methods of marketing are limited. The United States and other market economies are committed to the principle of competition because competition protects consumers, encourages efficiency and innovation from producers, and maximizes overall wealth. The U.S. government, in the form of the antitrust law, has announced its strong policy against monopolies, cartels, and other arrangements that threaten competition. The company seeking to market products is well advised to steer clear of any practices that prevent competition. Excessive market power, tying agreements, and cartel violations can all attract the attention of government investigators seeking to enforce the antitrust law.

BIBLIOGRAPHY

Gates, B. (2000). The case for Microsoft. *Time, 155*(20), 57. Retrieved June 14, 2007, from EBSCO Online Database Business Source Complete. http://search.ebscohost.com/login.aspx?direct=true&db=bth&AN=3074549&site=ehost-live

Gellhorn, E. (1986). *Antitrust law and economics in nutshell* (3rd ed.). St. Paul, MN: West Publishing.

Giving the invisible hand a helping hand. (2002). *Economist, 365*(8298), 14-15. Retrieved June 14, 2007, from EBSCO Online Database Business Source Complete. http://search.ebscohost.com/login.aspx?direct=true&db=bth&AN=7799641&site=ehost-live

Hovenkamp, H. (1985). *Economics and federal antitrust law* (Hornbook series student ed.). St. Paul, MN: West Publishing.

Kwoka, J. E., & Moss, D. L. (2012). Behavioral merger remedies: evaluation and implications for antitrust enforcement. *Antitrust Bulletin, 57*(4), 979–1011. Retrieved November 19, 2013 from EBSCO online database Business Source Premier. http://search.ebscohost.com/login.aspx?direct=true&db=buh&AN=85404112

Levy, S., Sandberg, J., Stone, B., & Thomas, R. (1999). Bill takes it on the chin. *Newsweek, 134*(20), 52. Retrieved June 14, 2007, from EBSCO Online Database Business Source Complete. http://search.ebscohost.com/login.aspx?direct=true&db=bth&AN=2457810&site=ehost-live

Markham, J. W. (2012). Sailing a sea of doubt: a critique of the rule of reason in U.S. antitrust law. *Fordham Journal of Corporate and Financial Law, 17*(3), 591–664. Retrieved November 19, 2013 from EBSCO online database Business Source Premier. http://search.ebscohost.com/login.aspx?direct=true&db=buh&AN=77931207

McDonald, M. (2013). Antitrust immunity up in smoke: pre-emption, state action, and the master settlement agreement. *Columbia Law Review, 113*(1), 97–137. Retrieved November 19, 2013 from EBSCO online database Business Source Premier. http://search.ebscohost.com/login.aspx?direct=true&db=buh&AN=84955965

U.S. Department of Justice Antitrust Enforcement and the Consumer Brochure, available at http://www.usdoj.gov/atr/public/div%5fstats/211491.htm

SUGGESTED READING

Dassiou, X. & Glycopantis, D. (2006). The economic theory of price discrimination via transactions bundling: An assessment of the policy implications. *Review of Law & Economics, 2*(2), 323-348. Retrieved July 11, 2007, from EBSCO Online Database Business Source Complete. http://search.ebscohost.com/login.aspx?direct=true&db=bth&AN=22934555&site=ehost-live

Dvorak, J. (2000). Not a monopoly, marketing. *PC Magazine, 19*(2), 69. Retrieved July 11, 2007, from EBSCO Online Database Business Source Complete. http://search.ebscohost.com/login.aspx?direct=true&db=bth&AN=2639439&site=ehost-live

Peritz, R. J. R. (2013). Taking antitrust to patent school" the instance of pay-for-delay settlements. *Antitrust Bulletin, 58*(1), 159–171. Retrieved November 19, 2013 from EBSCO online database Business Source Premier. http://search.ebscohost.com/login.aspx?direct=true&db=buh&AN=88876653

Ulanoff, L. (2007). Google? A monopoly? *PC Magazine, 26*(14), 56-56. Retrieved July 11, 2007, from EBSCO Online Database Business Source Complete. http://search.ebscohost.com/login.aspx?direct=true&db=bth&AN=25425988&site=ehost-live

Seth M. Azria, J.D.

LEGAL ASPECTS OF MARKETING

ABSTRACT

The success of any given business relies heavily on how effectively that business can bring its products or services to market. This marketing objective is both regulated and assisted by the law. The government has an interest in protecting its citizens from unfair dealing on the part of dishonest or overzealous marketers. However, the government also has an interest in promoting innovation and invention for the benefit of society. To achieve these goals, the law seeks to regulate the acceptable methods of marketing and allow inventors to profit from the fruits of their labor. Two ways the federal government accomplishes those goals are with the Federal Trade Commission (FTC) and the intellectual property law. These two bodies of law join together with other areas of law, like contracts and torts, to form the fabric that governs the marketplace.

OVERVIEW

Marketing is an essential function of most all businesses; as the saying goes, nothing happens until something is sold. As with any other profession, knowledge of legal rights and responsibilities that affect a given area is fundamental to success, and the lack of that that understanding can be dangerous. Marketing a product or service typically involves exposure of a message to a large number of people in an attempt to persuade their behavior in a particular manner. That wide and public exposure increases the chances that injury may occur to a member of the target audience. Aside from deliberate wrongful acts, a marketer may inadvertently violate the law with potentially severe consequences. A marketer may embroil its company in an expensive lawsuit, do significant damage to the company's professional reputation, and damage its profits and market position. There is also the possibility that such problems end in a prison sentence. Accordingly, marketers would be wise to keep informed of the legal implications of marketing activities. In the current digital age, it is especially important for marketers to be aware of legal developments because the field of marketing changes quickly in response to consumer needs and new technology. While ignorance of the law may cause many difficulties, knowledge and use of certain laws can provide a significant advantage to the marketer of products in the form of intellectual property rights.

The law that can affect any given attempt to market any given product would be a large undertaking. In truth, comprehensive coverage of any area of law is generally reserved for the writers of multi-volume legal treatises. Those treatises are not read cover to cover but are used as research materials to resolve a particular legal problem as they arise. Moreover, many legal problems include issues from several categories of law. Such is the case with marketing. Marketing a product may raise potential issues in the law of contracts, torts (e.g. defamation, products liability), intellectual property rights, advertising and labeling, broadcasting, licensing and merchandising, promotions and incentives, lobbying and online marketing rules. Understanding that the law often imposes many requirements from several areas that areissued by different governmental organizations is critical. Here we will take a closer look at two areas of the law that are generally applicable to nearly all marketers: federal regulation through the Federal Trade Commission (FTC) and federal intellectual property law.

MARKETING & THE FTC
Deceptive Practices

When designing and implementing a marketing campaign, marketers and advertising agencies must take into account federal law. Through the FTC, a federal agency formed to administer the Federal Trade Commission (FTC) Act, the U.S. government seeks to protect all consumers from deceptive and unfair trade practices. Generally, the FTC requires marketers to tell the truth, not mislead consumers, and substantiate the claims made about their products. As interpreted by the FTC, a practice is deceptive if it is likely to mislead consumers and affect a consumer's decision about the product or service. That is, the consumer would have chosen differently in the absence of the deception. Deceptions that affect consumer decisions are called material; the FTC is concerned with material acts.

In addition to a material representation or act, the FTC imposes marketer liability based on the behavior of a *reasonable* consumer. The word "reasonable" is a critical adjective in the law and imposes an important qualification of the noun it modifies. There is a vast different between "consumers" and "reasonable consumers." "Consumers" means all consumers and would impose liability on marketers for potential deceptions that arise from the understandings or misunderstandings of any consumer. "Reasonable consumers" means that a marketer is only liable for potential deceptions interpreted by a specific subset of consumers. That subset of reasonable is defined by certain specific factors relevant to a chosen marketing practice. Examples of factors that may define the reasonable consumer in a target audience are age, education, profession, and experience. For example, if a company seeks to sell a sophisticated MRI machine to doctors, the marketing practices would be judged by how a typical doctor in that field of practice would interpret the information. An advertisement does not become false or misleading simply because it could be unreasonably misunderstood by a member of the general public; an advertiser is not liable for all possible interpretations by all consumers.

While the reasonable consumer qualification limits the potential liability of consumers, the FTC interpretation of deception broadens the range of impermissible acts. When the FTC considers whether a marketing practice is deceptive, the critical issue is whether a practice or an act is likely to mislead, rather than whether it actually causes deception. The FTC presumes that certain types of claims are material or likely to influence consumer behavior. Express claims and omitted information are presumed material. Express claims are material because the willingness of business to promote its products with those claims reflects a belief that the public is interested in that advertising. Omitted information is material if the advertiser knew or should have known that a reasonable consumer would need the omitted information to evaluate their product or service.

To determine whether a practice is fair, the FTC generally looks to whether the practice injures consumers, whether the practice violates public policy, and whether the practice is unethical or unscrupulous. The most important factor is the issue of injury. The FTC is concerned with substantial injury not outweighed by benefits, caused by benefits of the practice. A substantial injury typically involves monetary harm, as when a seller coerces consumers into buying unwanted goods or services or when consumers are sold defective goods and are unable assert the defect as a defense against payment.

The FTC does not protect consumers against injuries they could have reasonably avoided themselves. Again, notice the use of the word reasonable. In this context, the word means that consumers need not take all possible steps to avoid the injury. It means that a consumer must take the similar precaution that the average consumer would take when presented with the same claim or marketing practice.

FTC Regulations

The FTC's Division of Marketing Practices implements these general prohibitions against unfairness and deception in marketing practices by enforcing specific rules that address a wide variety of initiatives. For example, initiatives seek to shut down Internet and telephone scams; end deceptive and misleading telemarketing and direct-mail marketing; stop fraudulent business opportunity scams; govern labels on merchandise; prohibit deceptive sales pitches; protect consumers from abusive, unwanted, and late night calls; require warning labels on commercial email containing sexually oriented material; requiring franchise sellers to disclose certain information to enable a buyer to make an informed decision; require sellers of 900 number pay-per-call services to clearly disclose the price of their services; prohibit sellers from targeting children; and, require merchants to disclose warranty information prior to purchase, just to mention a few.

Two FTC initiatives address two topics that are consistently on the forefront of business concerns in the twenty-first century and deserve a closer look: online marketing and environmental marketing concerns. The Internet has been an extraordinary and transformative force in marketing that can reach consumers all over the globe and seems destined to have a huge effect on marketing. While the FTC regulates sellers and makes them responsible for claims they make about their products, the responsibly to avoid deception and unfairness extends to third parties, such as advertising agencies and website designers. These third parties are integral to Internet advertising and may also be liable for inappropriate claims made on behalf of their clients. Due to this potential source of liability, advertising agencies and web designers must take measures to ensure that they have received sufficient information from their clients to substantiate advertising claims. It is not enough for an agency or a designer to rely on their client's assurance that such claims are substantiated.

To determine third-party liability, the FTC looks at the extent of an agency's or a designer's involvement in the preparation of the advertisement and whether the agency knew or should have known that the marketing practice contained deceptive or false information. The third party can protect itself by asking the manufacturer to back up its claims about its products. Substantiation is especially important for claims regarding performance, health, or weight loss benefits or earnings guarantees. While disclaimers are usually insufficient to remedy a false or misleading claim, marketers should make sure that disclaimers are clear and conspicuous. Disclaimers should be presented so that consumers notice and understand the information. Product demonstrations, when used, must show product performance under normal use. And refunds, if promised, must be made. Moreover, special care must be taken when advertisers target children. The FTC implemented the Children's Online Privacy Protection Act (COPPA) to restrict websites from collecting personal information from children under 13 years old. COPPA requires parental consent for online marketers to collect information on websites targeted to children or where the marketer actually knows that children are part of the website's general audience.

FTC regulations also cover product and service testimonials, endorsements, warranties, and guarantees; both generally and online. Testimonials and endorsements must reflect the typical consumer experience unless the advertisement clearly and conspicuously states otherwise. Typically, a statement that not all consumers will get the same results is not enough to qualify the claim, and the advertiser must be able to substantiate all claims. The connection between an endorser and the company—paid endorser, or ownership interest etc.—must also be made clear and expert endorsement can be made only by a person who has mastered the subject matter. To enforce the online marketing rules, the FTC periodically joins with other law-enforcement agencies to monitor the Internet for potentially false or deceptive advertising claims. Advertisers in violation of FTC rules face cease and desist orders combined with fines up to $11,000, injunctions, and civil or criminal contempt proceedings if orders are disobeyed.

The FTC & Environmental Marketing

The FTC has the authority to take action against false and misleading marketing claims that involve environmental or "green" marketing claims. The FTC environmental compliance guides apply to all forms of marketing for goods and services including advertisements, labels, package inserts, promotional materials, words, symbols, logos, product brand names, and marketing through digital or electronic media like email or the Internet. The FTC evaluates green claims from the consumer's perspective and ascribes meaning as a consumer would and not necessarily the technical or scientific meaning. As a general matter, all claims made by marketers must be substantiated; that is, a marketer must have a reasonable basis for the claim. In the context of environmental claims, the requirement of substantiation often requires competent and reliable scientific evidence such as tests, analysis, research, and other evidence collected by experts according to generally accepted procedures in the field.

Specific claims, such as claims regarding recycled content, should be specific and not exaggerate or overstate the benefits. For example, a marketer may make a claim that a package contains 50 percent more recycled content than a previous package. But when the content has increased from 2 percent to 3 percent, the claim is likely to convey a false impression of improvement, even though technically correct. General claims about products such as phrases like "eco-friendly" are more difficult to substantiate and more susceptible to liability for being deceptive than specific environmental claims. Thus, such general claims should contain limited language that the marketer can substantiate. In the above example, "eco-friendly" may be qualified by such language as "this cloth bag is reusable and made from 100 percent recycled fibers."

The FTC & Intellectual Property Rights

The FTC is concerned with protecting the public from marketer misconduct. On the other hand, intellectual property rights protect the marketer and can give rise to significant advantages in business. For most small and medium-size businesses, marketing products or services is a major challenge. Successful marketing strategies should establish a clear link between products or services and the producer or provider of those products or services. Ideally, customers should be able to easily distinguish between products or services offered in the marketplace and associate those with desired qualities as intended by the marketer. Intellectual property is an important tool to accomplish that goal. Intellectual property rights generally refer to the category of intangible rights that protect commercially valuable products of human intellect, including patents, trademarks, and copyrights. A trademark is a distinctive design, picture, emblem, logo, or wording (or combination) affixed to goods for sale to identify the manufacturer as the source of the product. Words that give a generic name for a product or merely name the maker, without particular lettering, are not trademarks. Trademarks are valuable to differentiate a product or service in the marketplace; a distinctive mark that provides an assurance to consumers that they are buying authentic goods. Trademarks may be registered with the U.S. Patent Office to prove use and ownership. Use of another's trademark, or one that is confusingly similar, is infringement and the basis for a lawsuit for damages for unfair competition and/or a petition for an injunction against the use of the infringing trademark (www.dictionary.law.com).

A patent is an exclusive right by the federal government to the inventor to make, use, or sell an invention for a specified period, usually 17 years. Inventions may qualify for a patent if the device or process is novel, useful, and non-obvious. Applications for patents involve technical information and patent attorneys, typically with an engineering or other technical background, often assist individuals and companies through the application process. This type of protection encourages innovation by assuring a party can benefit from their efforts. A patent may be thought of as a government granted private monopoly.

A copyright is the exclusive right of the author or creator of a literary or artistic property such as a book, movie or musical composition, to print, copy, sell, license, distribute, transform to another medium, translate, record or perform, or otherwise use—or not use—and to give it to another by will. As soon as a work is created and is in a tangible form, such as writing or taping, the work automatically has federal copyright protection. On any distributed

and/or published work a notice should be affixed stating the word copyright, copy or (c), with the name of the creator and the date of copyright, which is the year of first publication. The notice should be on the title page or the page immediately following and for graphic arts on a clearly visible or accessible place.

A work should also be registered with the U.S. Copyright Office by submitting a registration form and two copies of the work together with a fee. The filing establishes proof of the earliest creation and publication, is required to file a lawsuit for infringement of copyright, and if filed within three months of publication, establishes a right to attorneys' fees in an infringement suit. Copyrights cover literary, musical, and dramatic works, periodicals, maps, works of art (including models), art reproductions, sculptural works, technical drawings, photographs, prints (including labels), movies, and other audiovisual works, computer programs, compilations of works and derivative works, and architectural drawings. Short phrases, titles, extemporaneous speeches or live unrecorded performances, common information, government publications, mere ideas, and seditious, obscene, libelous, and fraudulent work are not entitled to copyright protection. For any work created from 1978 to date, a copyright is good for the author's life plus 50 years, with a few exceptions such as work "for hire," which is owned by the one commissioning the work for a period of 75 years from publication. After that, it falls into the public domain. Many, but not all, countries recognize international copyrights under the "Universal Copyright Convention," to which the United States is a party (www.dictionary.law.com).

CONCLUSION

The success of any given business relies heavily on how effectively that business can bring its products or services to market. That objective is both regulated and assisted by the law. The government has an interest in protecting its citizens from unfair dealing on the part of dishonest or overzealous marketers. However, the government also has an interest in promoting innovation and invention for the benefit of society. To achieve these goals, the law seeks to regulate the acceptable methods of marketing and allow inventors to profit from the fruits of their labor. Two ways the federal government accomplishes those goals are with the Federal Trade Commission (FTC) and the intellectual property law. Those two bodies of law join together with other areas of law, like contracts and torts, to form the fabric that governs the marketplace.

BIBLIOGRAPHY

Avery, R., Cawley, J., Eisenberg, M., & Cantor, J. (2013). Raising red flags: The change in deceptive advertising of weight loss products after the federal trade commission's 2003 Red Flag initiative. *Journal of Public Policy & Marketing, 32*, 129-139. Retrieved November 15, 2013, from EBSCO Online Database Business Source Complete. http://search.ebscohost.com/login.aspx?direct=true&db=bth&AN=87372138&site=ehost-live

Bureau of Consumer Protection. (2000). *Advertising and marketing on the internet.* Washington, DC: U.S. Federal Trade Commission Publication. http://www.ftc.gov/bcp/conline/pubs/buspubs/ruleroad.pdf

Bureau of Consumer Protection. (2000). *Complying with environmental marketing guides.* Washington, DC: U.S. Federal Trade Commission Publication. http://www.ftc.gov/bcp/conline/pubs/buspubs/greenguides.pdf

Federal Trade Commission. (1984). *FTC policy statement on deception.* Washington, DC: U.S. Federal Trade Commission Publication. http://www.ftc.gov/bcp/policystmt/ad-decept.htm

Federal Trade Commission. (1984). *FTC policy statement on unfairness.* Washington, DC: U.S. Federal Trade Commission Publication. http://www.ftc.gov/bcp/policystmt/ad-unfair.htm

Masters, R.M., Leung, L.Y., Syverson, K., & Fabre, R.D. (2013). Intellectual property outlook: Cases and trends to follow. *Intellectual Property & Technology Law Journal, 25*, 3-13. Retrieved November 15, 2013, from EBSCO Online Database Business Source Complete. http://search.ebscohost.com/login.aspx?direct=true&db=bth&AN=87117367&site=ehost-live

Miller, A.R. & Davis, M.H. (1990). *Intellectual property in a nutshell.* St. Paul, MN: West Publishing.

Sater, G.J., & Alexander, B. (2011). Four legal issues stare down social marketing planners. *Response, 19*, 55. Retrieved November 15, 2013, from EBSCO Online Database Business Source Complete. http://search.ebscohost.com/login.aspx?direct=true&db=bth&AN=58149055&site=ehost-live

Wootton, B.H., & Shultz, M. (2012). Federal Trade Commission continues to put a spotlight on pharmaceutical patent agreements. *Intellectual Property & Technology Law Journal, 24*, 15-19. Retrieved November 15, 2013, from EBSCO Online Database Business Source Complete. http://search.ebscohost.com/login.aspx?direct=true&db=bth&AN=83466179&site=ehost-live

SUGGESTED READING

Dames, K. (2007). Trade agreements as the new Copyright Law. *Online, 31*, 16-20. Retrieved May 22, 2007, from EBSCO Online Database Academic Search Premier. http://search.ebscohost.com/login.aspx?direct=true&db=aph&AN=24121559&site=ehost-live

Hesseldahl A. (2007, May 2). 'Brandjacking' on the web. *Business Week Online*, pp. 13-13. Retrieved May 29, 2007, from EBSCO Online Database Business Source Complete. http://search.ebscohost.com/login.aspx?direct=true&db=bth&AN=24952521&site=ehost-live

Hailey, G., & Knowles, J. (2007). Finding the limit to 'Brother's Keeper' regulations. *Response, 15*, 61-61. Retrieved May 29, 2007, from EBSCO Online Database Business Source Complete. http://search.ebscohost.com/login.aspx?direct=true&db=bth&AN=25040242&site=ehost-live

Truth in advertising. (2006). *Economist, 381*(8505), 13-14. Retrieved May 22, 2007, from EBSCO Online Database Business Source Complete. http://search.ebscohost.com/login.aspx?direct=true&db=bth&AN=23263251&site=ehost-live

Seth M. Azria, J.D.

M

MARKETING (STATISTICS) AND APPLIED PROBABILITY MODELS

ABSTRACT

The success of the marketing function within an organization is key to the success of the organization as a whole. Mathematical models can help marketers answer questions about marketplace needs and buyer behavior by providing a mathematical representation of the system or situation being studied. Despite the fact that the real world is an infinitely complex entity, models should still strive to be succinct and parsimonious. Empirical observations in combination with a review of the literature will give the analyst a good starting point from which to decide which variables to include or exclude in the model-building process. A number of approaches are available to help analysts determine which variables will be most predictive in a model. Marketing models can be used in a wide variety of situations. Three of these include the determination of customer lifetime value, optimizing sales-force deployment, and optimizing the mix between expert judgment and statistical technique in building the best model for direct marketing.

OVERVIEW

The success of the marketing function within an organization is key to the success of the organization as a whole. Marketing involves creating, communicating, and delivering value to consumers in ways that benefit the organization and its stakeholders. In addition, modern marketing theory emphasizes customer relationship management, the process of identifying prospective customers, acquiring data concerning these prospective and current customers, building relationships with customers, and influencing their perceptions of the organization and its products or services. Because of the importance and the complexity of these tasks, many marketing departments rely on the use of mathematical models to help them forecast buyer behavior under various sets of variables and "what if" scenarios. Marketing is concerned with both the description of actual, observed behavior and the prediction of future behavior. For example, one might be interested to know why customers prefer a widget over a gizmo. One might also be interested to know whether customers might prefer a gizmo if it were redesigned to improve certain characteristics. Mathematical models can help marketers answer these questions by providing a mathematical representation of the system or situation being studied.

Despite the fact that the real world is an infinitely complex entity, models should still strive to be succinct and parsimonious. The state of modeling science is such that it can only take into account a finite amount of variables. It is part of the modeler's task to determine which variables should and should not be included in the model-building process. In general, this means considering only those things that are relevant to the central research question. For example, if one is interested in predicting if a proposed turquoise widget will appeal to women, the question could be broken down according to infinite demographic variables such as age range, education, area of the country, national origin, and whether or not they were cat lovers. Although these variables may have some effect on prospective customers' decision to purchase the new widget, they are less relevant to the central question concerning women and the color turquoise and should, therefore, probably be eliminated from the model unless they are theorized to be central to the question at hand. A good model needs to have both fit (i.e., accurately models the real-world situation) and robustness (i.e., accurately predicts future behavior). A model that attempts to consider all observations usually predicts poorly or yields predictions that are too ambiguous to be of much practical use. To achieve stronger predictions, one must often compromise and predict fewer situations. The best models make the appropriate compromise between predicting in all circumstances and predicting accurately. Anything else will not have much applicability. Two well-known and established statistical techniques used in mathematical modeling for market analysis are conjoint analysis and the Dirichlet model.

Empirical observations in combination with a review of the literature will give the analyst a good stating point from which to decide which variables to include or exclude in the model-building process. Typically, theorists and researchers will have given serious thought to the relationship between variables, and the literature will express the state-of-the-art thinking about various aspects of the universe of data at which one is looking and will have built upon previous research and models. Similarly, empirical observations of trends and relationships by the marketing personnel or management in the organization can lead to other strong assumptions that are good points of departure for building a model of buyer behavior. However, strong assumptions alone are insufficient: To be useful, a model also needs to be testable. Models are only of use if they have validity and reliability. Validity means that the model accurately predicts what it is intended to predict. Reliability means that the model consistently measures what it is intended to measure. A model cannot be valid unless it is reliable.

There are a number of approaches to selecting variables for marketing models:

- Forward selection approach
- Backward elimination approach
- Stepwise approach
- R-squared approach
- Rule of thumb approach

Forward Selection Approach

The forward selection approach adds variables to the model until no variable that adds significance to the model is not incorporated into it. As each variable is added to the model, a test statistic is first calculated to determine the variable's contribution to the model. If the test statistic is greater than a predetermined value, it is added to the model; if the test statistic is less than the predetermined value, it is not added. This process is completed for each potential variable of interest until the model is populated with all variables that make a significant contribution to the model.

Backward Elimination Approach

Whereas the forward selection approach starts with an empty model and adds variables to it, the backward elimination approach starts with a model fully populated with all potential variables and then subtracts those that do not add significance to the model. As with the forward selection approach, the backward elimination approach ends with a model in which all the included variables have a test statistic that is greater than the predetermined value.

Stepwise Approach

A third approach to selecting variables is the stepwise approach, which is a variation of the forward selection approach. As opposed to the forward selection approach, however, in the stepwise approach, not all the variables already in the model necessarily remain in it. As in the forward selection approach, variables are added one at a time after being tested with the test statistic. However, the stepwise approach also examines the variables already included to delete any that do not have a test statistic value greater than the predetermined number.

R-squared Approach

A fourth approach to variable selection is the R-squared approach. This approach is used to find multiple subsets of variables that best predict the dependent variable using an appropriate test statistic. This approach can be used to find the best one-variable model, the best two-variable model, and so forth.

Rule-of-Thumb Approach

Another approach is the rule-of-thumb approach. This approach selects the variables best associated to the dependent variable as determined by the Pearson correlation coefficient r. The variables are then ranked by their r values and the top k (as predetermined) ranked variables are included in the model. If a regression model with these variables demonstrates that all the variables have test statistic values greater than the predetermined value, then the set is determined to be the best.

Although it is important to choose the right variables for building a model, it is also important to remember that models are not set in stone. Model building is an iterative process and a model that does not meet the tests of validity and reliability can be refined to better model the real world. Indeed, the factors influencing customer behavior change over time and the marketing model needs to be flexible to reflect those changes. Based on empirical observation, expert judgments, and the insights of the literature, one posits a theory and develops a model based on its assumptions. The model is then tested against the real world and modified to better reflect the real-world experience. This process is repeated as necessary until the model reaches the desired level of accuracy.

Similarly, it is also important to remember that the needs of the marketplace are not static. For example, in the mid-1950s, grocery stores stressed having all the ingredients available that the homemaker needed to make meals from scratch. At that time, frozen dinners were almost unheard of. Today, however, many people are more concerned with convenience and fewer people cook from scratch. As a result, grocery stores today offer a wide array of frozen foods that can be popped into a microwave or prepared meals that can be easily cooked or reheated and served with a salad from the salad bar. The marketing model that was appropriate for the mid-twentieth century grocery store is no longer appropriate in the twenty-first century.

APPLICATIONS

Marketing models can be used in a wide variety of situations. Three of these are the determination of customer lifetime value, optimizing sales-force deployment, and optimizing the mix between expert judgment and statistical technique to build the best model for direct marketing.

One of the reasons that many marketing departments turn to modeling is because of the complexities of customer relationship management. Marketing departments strive not only to win the customer for a one-time purchase, but also to gain customer loyalty to the business or brand and thereby win continuing sales over the long term. In customer relationship management, the business identifies prospective customers, acquires data concerning prospective and current customers, builds relationships with customers, and attempts to influence their perceptions of the organization and its products or services. However, it would be impossible to perform this function for all possible customers; so, many marketing departments tend to cultivate deeper relationships with those customers who will spend more money with a business or brand over the course of their lifetimes. This concept is called customer lifetime value. This information theoretically allows a business to know how much each customer is worth in terms of dollars of income which, in turn, allows businesses to better know how to spend their marketing budget. For example, if the 20-35-year-old demographic will potentially spend ten times as much money on widgets during their lifetime than the 60-75-year-old demographic, most businesses would place more marketing effort on the younger demographic. However, calculating customer lifetime value tends to be complex (e.g., the customer's need or desire for the product may change, the competition may bring out a product that better fits the customer's needs), and reliable data to build a usable model and net cash flow from the customer are difficult to gather. Haenlein and Libai (2013) highlight the benefit of targeting customers with high lifetime value, also known as "revenue leaders." The authors argue that targeting revenue leaders can create high value by accelerating adoption among these customers and because of the greater-than-average value that revenue leaders generate by influencing other customers with similarly high lifetime value.

Although knowing how much the "average" customer will spend on a company's products over the course of his or her lifetime is of interest in general, it is particularly where markets are mature and there is significant competition. This situation is a good example of how mathematical marketing models can be of use. Berger and Nasr (1998) present a series of five general marketing models of customer lifetime value. The simplest of these models assumed one sale per customer a year with both the cost of marketing efforts to retain customers and their actual retention rate remaining constant over time. The second generic model removed the assumption of once-yearly sales and allowed examination of time periods both longer and shorter than one year. The third and fourth models examined the effects of gross contribution margin and promotion costs that vary over time. The final model was based on the assumption of a shrinking customer base in which customers are lost over time and treated as new customers when they return. All these models can be used by marketers for a variety of purposes including making decisions concerning the allocation of marketing dollars for advertising campaigns and forecasting the effect of a marketing strategy particularly *vis a vis* acquisition and retention of customers and the associated costs and tradeoffs.

Another area in which mathematical models can be useful for marketing is sales force management. This is the process of efficiently and effectively making sales through the planning, coordination, and supervision of others. The sales manager must make the best use possible of both the human and financial resources available to sell the organization's goods and services to potential customers. Sales managers must determine how best to use the resources available to optimize the effectiveness and efficiency of the sales force as a whole. This requires understanding numerous variables and their interactions including the qualifications, abilities, and experience of the sales force as well as the target market and its demographics, needs, and motivations. Data on sales-force capabilities and prospective customer needs can be used in the development of a model that allows the sales manager to leverage the strengths of the individual sales personnel and enables each to reach his or her optimal sales potential.

The activities of sales management include recruiting and selecting sales personnel, enabling the sales force to sell (e.g., training, print materials, or samples), supervising and coordinating sales efforts (e.g., assigning territories or routes), and other motivating and human resource activities. Deploying a sales force requires simultaneously solving four inter-related problems:

- Determining the size of the sales force needed (i.e., how many salespersons are needed within a territory)
- Determining the optimal location for sales personnel (i.e., how many salespersons are needed within a given sales coverage unit)
- Aligning sales territories (i.e., how best to group sales coverage units into larger geographic clusters)
- Allocating sales resources (i.e., how best to allocate sales personnel time within the coverage units)
- Drexl & Haase (1999) used a nonlinear mixed-integer programming model to solve all four problems simultaneously. They used approximation methods that could solve large-scale, real-world

instances. These methods also provided lower bounds for the optimal objective function value and were benchmarked against upper bounds. The model has been successfully used to manage the sales force of a beverage company in Germany.

Although mathematical models are important tools for developing marketing models, the understanding of applied probability and stochastic processes is insufficient for developing a robust model. For example, one of the problems with these approaches to selecting variables is that they do not identify structure in the data. When building models, the insights of an experienced marketer who understands the parameters affecting buyer behavior can be invaluable. Such expert judgment is essential for the development of a model that realistically models the marketplace and includes all significant variables. The incorporation of human judgment and statistical models can lead to better models.

Morwitz & Schittlein (1998), for example, found that the combination of management judgment and statistical models can lead to increased effectiveness of marketing models. In fact, a model based on this combination of inputs was able to increase profits by more than 10 percent. Management decisions are based on a rich history of experience and insight that is often not quantifiable. Attempting to replace managerial insights with a mathematical model ignores a very rich source of information. On the other hand, mathematical modeling can better account for a wider range of data and deal with large amounts of data better than can human beings in most situations. Therefore, it is important to include both mathematics and judgments in the model building process.

However, mathematical modeling is not appropriate for every marketing situation. Not only are mathematical models expensive to develop; in some instances, there are insufficient data to apply to quantitative techniques. Even when sufficient data are available, humans still must decide which variables to include in the analysis and must also interpret the results of the forecast. Therefore, no matter how rigorously a model is developed, judgment is still key to determining which data are relevant to the model. Expert judgments can be helpful in understanding the situation and giving the manager insight into the parameters in which the data and subsequent analysis should be interpreted (e.g., "given the current economy and our market plan, we expect widget sales to rise by 2 percent over the next quarter"). As a result, quantitative and qualitative analyses are both indispensable for model building.

Bibliography

Berger, P. D. & Nasr, N. I. (1998). Customer lifetime value: Marketing models and applications. *Journal of Interactive Marketing, 12*, 17-30. Retrieved June 12, 2007, from EBSCO Online Database Business Source Complete. http://search.ebscohost.com/login.aspx?direct=true&db=bth&AN=348356&site=ehost-live

Drexl, A. & Haase, K. (1999). Fast approximation methods for sales force deployment. *Management Science, 45*, 1307-1323. Retrieved July 19, 2007, from EBSCO Online Database Business Source Complete. http://search.ebscohost.com/login.aspx?direct=true&db=bth&AN=2510404&site=ehost-live

Guyon, H., & Petoit, J. (2011). Market share predictions. *International Journal of Market Research, 53*, 831-857. Retrieved November 5, 2013, from EBSCO Online Database Business Source Complete. http://search.ebscohost.com/login.aspx?direct=true&db=bth&AN=67274334&site=ehost-live

Haenlein, M., & Libai, B. (2013). Targeting revenue leaders for a new product. *Journal of Marketing, 77*, 65-80. Retrieved November 5, 2013, from EBSCO Online Database Business Source Complete. http://search.ebscohost.com/login.aspx?direct=true&db=bth&AN=67274334&site=ehost-live

Ho, T. H., Lim, N., & Camerer, C. F. (2006). Modeling the psychology of consumer and firm behavior with behavioral economics. *Journal of Marketing Research, 43*, 307-331. Retrieved June 12, 2007, from EBSCO Online Database Business Source Complete. http://search.ebscohost.com/login.aspx?direct=true&db=bth&AN=21945242&site=ehost-live

Keon, J. W. (1991). Point of view: Understanding the power of expert systems in marketing - when and how to build them. *Journal of Advertising Research, 31*, 64-71. Retrieved June 12, 2007, from EBSCO Online Database Business Source Complete. http://search.ebscohost.com/login.aspx?direct=true&db=bth&AN=9202171002&site=ehost-live

McCabe, J., Stern, P., & Dacko, S.G. (2012). The power of before and after. *Journal of Advertising Research, 52*, 214-224. Retrieved November 5, 2013, from EBSCO Online Database Business Source Complete. http://search.ebscohost.com/login.aspx?direct=true&db=bth&AN=77276980&site=ehost-live

Morwitz, V. G. & Schmittlein, D. C. (1998). Testing new direct marketing offerings: The interplay of management judgement and statistical models. *Management Science, 44*, 610-628. Retrieved July 19, 2007, from EBSCO Online Database Business Source Complete. http://search.ebscohost.com/login.aspx?direct=true&db=bth&AN=812933&site=ehost-live

Ratner, B. (2001). Finding the best variables for direct marketing models. *Journal of Targeting, Measurement & Analysis for Marketing, 9*, 270-296. Retrieved July 19, 2007, from EBSCO Online Database Business Source Complete. http://search.ebscohost.com/login.aspx?direct=true&db=bth&AN=6614028&site=ehost-live

Shugan, S. M. (2002). Marketing science, models, monopoly models, and why we need them. *Marketing Science, 21*, 223-228. Retrieved June 12, 2007, from EBSCO Online Database Business Source Complete. http://search.ebscohost.com/login.aspx?direct=true&db=bth&AN=17463152&site=ehost-live

Wyner, G. A. (2006). Why model? *Marketing Research, 18*, 6-7. Retrieved June 12, 2007, from EBSCO Online Database Business Source Complete. http://search.ebscohost.com/login.aspx?direct=true&db=bth&AN=20577118&site=ehost-live

Suggested Reading

CB Bhattacharya. (2016). Responsible marketing: doing well by doing good. *GfK Marketing Intelligence Review*. Retrieved on June 29, 2017. https://www.degruyter.com/view/j/gfkmir.2016.8.issue-1/gfkmir-2016-0002/gfkmir-2016-0002.xml

Hanssens, D. M. Leeflang, P. S. H. & Wittink, D. R. (2005). Market response models and marketing practice. *Applied Stochastic Models in Business & Industry, 21*(4/5), 423-434. Retrieved July 19, 2007, from EBSCO Online Database Business Source Complete. http://search.ebscohost.com/login.aspx?direct=true&db=bth&AN=18071428&site=ehost-live

Hardey, M. (2012). New visions: capturing digital data and market research. *International Journal of Market Research, 54,* 159-161. Retrieved November 5, 2013, from EBSCO Online Database Business Source Complete. http://search.ebscohost.com/login.aspx?direct=true&db=bth&AN=74637375&site=ehost-live

Ho, T. H., Lim, N., & Camerer, C. F. (2006). How "psychological" should economic and marketing models be? *Journal of Marketing Research, 43,* 341-344. Retrieved July 19, 2007, from EBSCO Online Database Business Source Complete. http://search.ebscohost.com/login.aspx?direct=true&db=bth&AN=21945228&site=ehost-live

Lodish, L. M. (2001). Building marketing models that make money. *Interfaces, 31,* S45-S55. Retrieved July 19, 2007, from EBSCO Online Database Business Source Complete. http://search.ebscohost.com/login.aspx?direct=true&db=bth&AN=5674823&site=ehost-live

Tian, K. T. & McKenzie, K. (2001). The long-term predictive validity of the consumers' need for uniqueness scale. *Journal of Consumer Psychology, 10,* 171-193. Retrieved July 19, 2007, from EBSCO Online Database Business Source Complete. http://search.ebscohost.com/login.aspx?direct=true&db=bth&AN=4437050&site=ehost-live

Ruth A. Wienclaw, Ph.D

MARKETING DECISION MAKING

ABSTRACT

Today's marketing managers are expected to make complex decisions amid an excess of information and a lack of skills, experience, time, and patience. Each marketing decision varies in terms of the problem that has to be solved, the environment in which the problem is solved, and the decision maker who has to solve the problem. To help marketing decision makers make the best possible decisions, marketing science has developed various decision aids, termed Marketing Management Support Systems (MMSSs).

OVERVIEW

Marketing is the process of planning and executing the conception, pricing, promotion, and distribution of ideas, goods, and services to create exchange and satisfy individual and organizational objectives. The academic field of marketing formally began shortly after the turn of twentieth century and is now some 100 years old. Due to the sheer volume of products and brands, the ever increasing amount of market segments, the intensity of competition, and the overall acceleration of change, marketing decision situations are often complex as decisions need to be made under increasing time pressure.

Decision making, also referred to as problem solving, is the process of recognizing a problem or an opportunity and finding a solution to it. Many decisions are relatively simple and routine, but managers are also faced with decisions that can drastically affect the future outcomes of the business. The term marketing decision making refers to the way marketing managers go about making decisions, as well as the decision aids that support marketing managers in the preparation, execution, and evaluation of marketing activities.

It is important that good business decisions are made as wrong decisions can easily lead to the failure of an entire organization. However, decision makers may not have all the requisite information, skills, experience, time, and even patience to make the best decisions all the time. Even if marketing decision makers do have right type of information, it is likely that they will have too much information, since they are confronted with a constant stream of information about the market and the position of products—with formal data and informal cues about customers, distributors, competitors, and so forth (Wierenga & van Bruggen, 1997).

Faced with these challenges and more, marketers have moved from a reliance on intuition in decision making, to the use of tools made possible by developments in statistics, model building, knowledge engineering, and information technology. Marketing decision aids, also called Marketing Management Support Systems (MMSSs), were first developed by marketing scientists in the early 1960s. Initial efforts centered on using computers to build complex models that searched for the optimal solution to a problem. The first concept introduced was a simple but robust marketing model that usually required judgmental input from the manager. This was called a decision-calculus model. The next concepts were marketing information systems, marketing decision support systems, marketing expert systems, and marketing case-based reasoning systems, among others.

FURTHER INSIGHTS

Each marketing decision situation or problem is characterized by three basic factors. These are (1) the problem that has to be solved; (2) the environment in which the problem is solved; and (3) the decision maker who has to solve the problem (Wierenga, van Bruggen & Staelin, 1999).

The Problem that Has to Be Solved

The most important problem characteristics are structuredness and programmability; depth of knowledge; and availability of data. The first problem characteristic, structuredness, and programmability involves the extent to which relevant elements of a problem and the relationships among those elements are known. It is the extent to which a decision can be made by using relatively routine procedures instead of more general problem-solving techniques (Perkins & Rao, 1991).

Programmed decisions are routine and structured with a well-defined starting point, a clear goal, and standardized rules for reaching the goal. They are repetitive enough to allow for the establishment of definite procedures to process them, and the decision maker usually knows from the beginning what the solution and outcome will be.

Non-programmed decisions, on the other hand, are ill-structured and have few guidelines. They involve novel problems that cannot be processed by a pre-specified method and require the decision maker to rely on general problem-solving abilities. Neither the appropriate solution nor the potential outcome is known. When making unprogrammed decisions, managers must exercise judgment, which depends on their experience, insight, and intuition.

Examples of relatively programmable and structured marketing problems are sales management and sales-force decisions, and media planning for advertising. Less-structured problems include designing marketing communication, developing a marketing strategy, and introducing new products.

The second problem characteristic, depth of knowledge, refers to generalized knowledge gleaned from scientific research regarding a problem or an issue. The third problem characteristic, data, helps decision makers to form an impression of the mechanisms in a market.

The Environment in which the Problem Is Solved

Decision environment characteristics, and in particular, time constraints, market dynamics and organizational culture, affect marketing decision making. When time is short, the quickest way to solve a problem is to consult one's memory and search for similar cases experienced before (Wierenga & van Bruggen, 1997). When the market dynamics feature turbulent market conditions, marketers will find it difficult to understand and interpret what is happening. Stable markets, on the other hand, are more structured and thus easier to understand and interpret.

The organizational culture of a company or department will influence the prevailing attitudes and the approach to doing things, including the approach to decision making. This will influence the way in which marketing managers go about problem solving in their domain.

The Marketing Decision Maker

The third factor that characterizes the marketing decision situation is the decision maker: his or her cognitive style, experience, education, and skills. Decision makers select, evaluate, and combine information that is available either internally or externally. Cognitive style refers to the process through which a marketing decision maker perceives and processes information. It is the organization of information in memory and the repertoire of rules for using that information. A low-analytical decision maker is more likely to use a decision aid than a high-analytical decision maker.

A decision maker with a high degree of professional experience (like a marketing decision maker) will have dealt with a large number of practical marketing problems and their solutions. Studies comparing experts and novices suggest that experts have more highly developed cognitive structures, which allow for effective problem structuring and successful problem solution.

The effects of experience are more pronounced in less programmed, unstructured decisions than in the more programmed decisions. Experts are likely to understand the uncertainties and consequences of their decisions better than their inexperienced counterparts. Novices, on the other hand, are more likely to use decision aids (Perkins & Rao, 1991). Experts and knowledgeable decision makers are likely to search for more information than normal, selecting information that is relevant and important. They are also better able to acquire information in a less-structured environment and are more flexible in the manner in which they search for information. They will also agree more than novices regarding what information is important.

On the downside, experts are more likely to focus on rare events, but often at the expense of undervaluing base-rate information. When tasks are extremely unstructured, though, even experts cannot apply known solution strategies. Instead, they must employ heuristics (a method of problem solving that uses trial and error as well as rules of thumb to take shortcuts to a solution), and their judgments are subject to all the biases associated with human judgment processes.

The more relevant the education and skills of a decision maker, the more capable he or she will be in handling decisions. The combination of cognitive style, experience, education, and skills of a decision maker results in his or her choice of Marketing Problem-Solving Modes (MPSMs). Different marketing decision makers may use different MPSMs, and the same decision maker may use different modes at different times.

There are four different MPSMs: optimizing, reasoning, analogizing, and creating. When optimizing, the decision maker has clear insight into the way processes work. This is represented by a mathematical model, which describes the relationships between the relevant variables in a quantitative way. When reasoning, decision makers also translate external events into internal models, which they manipulate.

Analogizing refers to a decision maker's natural inclination to bring to bear the experience gained from solving similar problems. Unlike analogizing, during the creating mode, a marketing decision maker searches for concepts, solutions, or ideas that are novel in order to respond to a situation that has not occurred before (Wierenga & van Bruggen, 1997). The decision maker combines known but previously unrelated facts and ideas in such a way that new ones emerge.

Creating can refer to all aspects of marketing management, including the generation of ideas for new products or services, innovative advertising or sales-promotion campaigns, new forms of distribution, and ingenious pricing. Creativity is often the means for firm survival and growth (Wierenga & van Bruggen, 1997).

When confronted with a single unique decision and no extensive past history, marketing decision makers often rely on the judgments of several individuals. Since it is unlikely that several individuals would agree on the same decision, the marketing manager must process their assessments according to his or her own judgment and the degree of belief assigned to each assessment.

In general, group decision making allows for the generation of more input and more possible solutions to a situation. There is shared responsibility for the decision and its outcome, so that no single person has total responsibility. The disadvantages are that it often takes a long time to reach a group consensus, and group members may have to compromise in order to reach a consensus.

An interesting group decision-making model is the Delphi estimation process, where anonymous judgments are collected through questionnaires. The median responses are summarized as the group consensus, and this summary is fed back along with a second questionnaire for reassessment. This process retains the advantage of several judges while removing the biasing effects that might occur during face-to-face interaction (Best, 1974).

Marketing Management Support Systems (MMSS)
An MMSS can support a decision maker in different ways: It can help the decision maker carry out calculations (for instance, to find an "optimal" value); it can support the analysis and diagnosis of a specific situation; or it can make suggestions for users that stimulate the generation of new solutions. For some, the greatest benefit of MMSSs is that they can help frame the important issues and uncertainties associated with the problem at hand and in the process help the decision maker come to an acceptable decision.

Decision-making aids come in various forms. Some, for instance, are data-driven, while others are knowledge-driven. However, all MMSSs consist of a combination of four components that determine their capability and functionality. These components are as follows:

- Some form of information technology: Hardware such as computers, workstations, optical scanning technology, and telecommunication systems; and software such as database management programs, spreadsheets, and graphical/communication software.

- Analytical capabilities: Statistical packages for analyzing marketing data, parameter-estimation procedures, marketing models, and optimization and simulation procedures, for example.
- Marketing data: Quantitative information about variables such as sales, market shares, prices, one's own and one's competitors' marketing-mix expenditures, distribution figures, and so on.
- Marketing knowledge: Qualitative knowledge about such things as the structure of markets (submarkets and market segments), the suitability of specific sales-promotion campaigns, typical reactions to advertisements, heuristics for the acceptance of clients, and so on (Wierenga & van Bruggen, 1997).

Several types of MMSSs can be distinguished, each type having a different combination of the four components. The oldest type of MMSS is the marketing model, which dates back to the early 1960s, and which aims at finding the best solution to a problem. In this approach, a mathematical representation of the relevant marketing phenomena is first developed. Optimal values for the marketing-mix variables are derived through techniques such as differential calculus and operations research techniques, such as linear and integer programming and simulation. Econometric techniques are also required to handle marketing data, and when there is no data available, a manager's judgment can be used to calibrate the parameters of the model. Examples of marketing models are MEDIAC for media planning and SH.A.R.P. for shelf-space allocation in supermarkets.

Marketing Information Systems (MKISs)

Marketing Information Systems (MKISs) emerged in the second half of the 1960s, when the concept of management information systems was applied to the field of marketing. The main function of an MKIS is to provide information about what is going on in the market and examine the causes of observed phenomena. MKISs answer the questions, "What is happening in the market?" and "Why did it happen?"

MKISs are passive systems: They provide information, but it is up to the marketing decision maker to attach conclusions to this information and decide whether to act on those conclusions. MKISs typically provide data about marketing indicators on a regular basis. Thus, a marketing research or information systems department may send out marketing figures on a monthly basis to relevant employees in the company, sometimes sending different figures to different persons, depending on their responsibilities.

A successful MKIS must incorporate executives' information needs and decision processes, and the user must understand the system structure. Unfortunately, the advantages of many new MKISs are lost because new system developments are not integrated with the information system that already exists in a company.

Marketing Decision Support Systems (MDSSs)

Marketing Decision Support Systems (MDSSs) emerged in the 1970s. Compared with classical operations research, which was the main source of inspiration for marketing models, a decision support system takes a more practical and flexible approach to problem solving. Its purpose is to support rather than replace managerial judgment, and to improve the effectiveness of decision making rather than its efficiency. Companies use MDSSs to gather information from the environment and turn it into a basis for action. Through the data, models, analytical tools, and computing power of an MDSS, marketing managers can model marketing phenomena (major marketing variables such as sales, advertising, promotion, and price) according to their own ideas.

An MDSS can be seen as an extension of an MKIS. Like an MKIS, it is a combination of information technology, marketing data, and analytical capabilities, but with much more emphasis on analytical capabilities. Whereas an MKIS is particularly geared toward answering "what" and "why" questions, an MDSS is especially equipped to answer "what if" questions. Examples of MDSSs are the ADBUDG system, which predicts market shares for given advertising budgets; and ASSESSOR, which predicts the market share of a new product, given its attributes and the introduction campaign.

Marketing Expert Systems (MESs)

Marketing Expert Systems (MESs) are MMSSs that emphasize the marketing knowledge component. The expert system concept emerged in the field of artificial intelligence in the late 1970s. Its basic philosophy is to capture the knowledge from an expert in a particular field and make that knowledge available in a computer program that helps solve problems in the field. The goal of an expert system is to replicate the performance levels of a human expert in a computer model.

In an expert system, knowledge is usually represented in the form of "if-then" rules. For example, "if" you want to stimulate trial, then sampling is an appropriate type of sales promotion" (Wierenga & van Bruggen, 1997). An expert system basically searches for the "best" solution to a given problem. Examples of MESs are Dealmaker, which contains knowledge collected from grocery and drug retailers and can predict the impact of a given special offer; and ADCAD, which is an advisory system for advertising copy and execution.

Marketing Knowledge-Based Systems (MKBSs)

Marketing Knowledge-Based Systems (MKBSs) refer to a broader class of systems than do MESs. In MKBSs, the knowledge originates from any source, not just from human experts, but also from textbooks, cases, and the like. Also, MKBSs do not stand for just one particular approach to dealing with knowledge in marketing; they cover a range of knowledge representation methods, procedures for reasoning, learning, and problem solving that can be brought to bear to support marketing decision making. An example of an MKBS is the Brand Manager's Assistant, which supports brand managers with monitoring, analyzing, and designing tasks related to their brands.

Marketing Case-Based Reasoning Systems (MCBRs)

Marketing Case-Based Reasoning Systems (MCBRs) make cases available in a case library and provide tools for retrieving and accessing them. Historical cases are stored with all the relevant data kept intact, in "raw form." This is different from storage in "compiled form," such as rules that an expert has deduced from previous experiences. Case-based reasoning systems use indexes for representing cases, search-and-retrieval algorithms to find the right cases, and procedures for matching, adapting, and transforming cases. An example of MCBRs is ADDUCE, which infers how consumers will react to a new advertisement by searching relevant past advertising events.

Marketing Neural Nets (MNNs)

Marketing Neural Nets (MNNs) are used to model the way people recognize patterns from signals. An MNN should be able to recognize promising new product opportunities (if properly trained on the relationship between new product characteristics and success on past cases) or distinguish between successful and less successful sales-promotion campaigns. A distinctive feature of neural nets is their ability to learn. Neural nets are more suitable for prediction than for explanation. The technology has been used to predict television audiences, for market segmentation, and for database marketing.

Marketing Creativity-Enhancement Programs (MCEPs)

Marketing Creativity-Enhancement Programs (MCEPs) are computer programs that stimulate and endorse the creativity of a marketing decision maker. An example of a marketing system that has a "creativity module" is the CAAS system for advertising design, which performs a creative search of pictorial motifs for emotional advertising.

Other MMSS Systems

There are other types of MMSS, such as the Profit-Oriented Decision (PROD) system, which is used in evaluating marketing decisions in terms of their contribution to the welfare of the business firm. Another MMSS is the Analytic Hierarchy Process (AHP), which leads to the likely identification of all key components affecting decision making, by building a customized hierarchy to represent each problem. AHP can be used to resolve many complex problems that confront marketing management, including:

- How to reconcile a range of conflicting objectives under scarce resources
- Managing a vast amount of data
- Dealing with subjective and objective data to make a decision
- Managing to resolve conflict amongst multidisciplinary teams (referred to as multi-person problems) (Davies, 1993)

CONCLUSION

According to Wierenga, van Bruggen & Staelin (1999), there is substantial proof that MMSSs can increase firm profit and other measures of performance, depending on the specific characteristics of the situation in which the system is used and specific success measures one is looking at. Since managers can gather partial information, interpret information inaccurately, ignore differences in goals, and lack patience, marketing decision aids can, in many cases, outperform managers in repetitive tasks. Just as there are production and process activities better and more efficiently done by machine than by labor, there are decisions in marketing that may be made better and more efficiently when they are automated (Wierenga & van Bruggen, 1997).

In general, the effectiveness of an MMSS depends on three factors: (1) the extent of top management support; (2) the cognitive style and experience of the MMSS user; and (3) the fit of the MMSS with the decision environment. A successful MMSS should match with the thinking and reasoning processes of the manager.

Although it may appear that there is a proliferation of decision aids in existence today, there is a need for more tools to assist marketing decision makers in carrying out their tasks. It is likely that there will be more automation for decisions regarding existing products and less automation for decisions pertaining to new and innovative products. Markets that are stable are likely to see more automation of decision making than markets that are turbulent (Wierenga & van Bruggen, 1997). While activities such as copy creation will not be automated, models can help guide the appeal to be used and how many creative executions to produce.

As companies shift from a make-and-sell model to a sense-and-respond model of marketing, marketing decision making may shift from the short-run, the tactical, and the maintenance of the established, to the long-run, the strategic, and the launch of the innovative. A word of caution, however: Despite the advantages and attractiveness of marketing decision aids, firms would do well to focus first on the needs of their business, not merely on the enabling technology per se. Expensive software is not the key to marketing success.

BIBLIOGRAPHY

Best, R. (1974). An experiment in delphi estimation in marketing decision making. *Journal of Marketing Research (JMR), 11*, 448-452.

Bucklin, R., Lehmann, D., & Little, J. (1998). From decision support to decision automation: A 2020 vision. *Marketing Letters, 9*, 235-246.

Chen, Y., Hess, J., Wilcox, R., & Zhang, Z. (1999). Accounting profits versus marketing profits: A relevant matric for category management. *Marketing Science, 18*, 208. Retrieved May 23, 2007, from EBSCO Online Database Business Source Complete. http://search.ebscohost.com/login.aspx?direct=true&db=bth&AN=27227531&site=ehost-live

Constantinides, E. (2006). The marketing mix revisited: Towards the 21st century marketing. *Journal of Marketing Management, 22*(3/4), 407-438.

Cressman Jr., G. (1997). Snatching defeat from the jaws of victory. *Marketing Management, 6*, 8-19. Retrieved May 23, 2007, from EBSCO Online Database Business Source Complete. http://search.ebscohost.com/login.aspx?direct=true&db=bth&AN=9712062969&site=ehost-live

Davies, M. (1993). Using the AHP in marketing decision-making. *Journal of Marketing Management, 10*, 57-73. Retrieved May 23, 2007, from EBSCO Online Database Business Source Complete. http://search.ebscohost.com/login.aspx?direct=true&db=bth&AN=10740302&site=ehost-live

Decision making. (n.d.). *Encyclopedia of Business and Finance*. Retrieved May 25, 2007, from Answers.com Web site: http://www.answers.com/topic/decision-making

Greene, M. (1968). Market risk—an analytical framework. *Journal of Marketing, 32*. Retrieved May 23, 2007, from EBSCO Online Database Business Source Complete. http://search.ebscohost.com/login.aspx?direct=true&db=bth&AN=4996795&site=ehost-live

Gronroos, C. (1997). From marketing mix to relationship marketing—towards a paradigm shift in marketing. *Management Decision, 35*(3/4), 322-339. Retrieved May 24, 2007, from EBSCO Online Database Business Source Complete. http://search.ebscohost.com/login.aspx?direct=true&db=bth&AN=9708312642&site=ehost-live

Heuristics. (n.d.). *Dictionary of Marketing Terms*. Retrieved June 25, 2007, from Answers.com Web site: http://www.answers.com/topic/heuristics

Hulbert, J., Farley, J., & Howard, J. (1972). Information processing and decision making in marketing organizations. *Journal of Marketing Research (JMR), 9*, 75-77. Retrieved May 23, 2007, from EBSCO Online Database Business Source Complete. http://search.ebscohost.com/login.aspx?direct=true&db=bth&AN=5001313&site=ehost-live

Little, J. (1979). Decision support systems for marketing managers. *Journal of Marketing, 43*. Retrieved May 23, 2007, from EBSCO Online Database Business Source Complete. http://search.

ebscohost.com/login.aspx?direct=true&db=bth&AN=4999978&site=ehost-live

Martin, W., & Barcus, A. (1980). A multiattribute model for evaluating industrial customer's potential. *Interfaces, 10*, 40-44. Retrieved May 23, 2007, from EBSCO Online Database Business Source Complete. http://search.ebscohost.com/login.aspx?direct=true&db=bth&AN=6692793&site=ehost-live

O'Connor, M. (2011). Early requirements for a marketing management support system for exporters from less developed countries: the case study of Ethiopian coffee. *Journal for Global Business Education,* 1131-44. Retrieved November 15, 2013, from EBSCO Online Database Business Source Complete. http://search.ebscohost.com/login.aspx?direct=true&db=bth&AN=61893857&site=ehost-live

Perkins, W., & Rao, R. (1990). The role of experience in information use and decision making by marketing managers. *Journal of Marketing Research (JMR), 27*, 1-10. Retrieved May 23, 2007, from EBSCO Online Database Business Source Complete. http://search.ebscohost.com/login.aspx?direct=true&db=bth&AN=9602205317&site=ehost-live

Rusetski, A., & Lim, L.S. (2011). Not complacent but scared: another look at the causes of strategic inertia among successful firms from a regulatory focus perspective. *Journal of Strategic Marketing, 19*, 501-516. Retrieved November 15, 2013, from EBSCO Online Database Business Source Complete. http://search.ebscohost.com/login.aspx?direct=true&db=bth&AN=66825344&site=ehost-live

Weiss, D. (1964). Simulation for decision making in marketing. *Journal of Marketing, 28*, 45-50. Retrieved May 23, 2007, from EBSCO Online Database Business Source Complete. http://search.ebscohost.com/login.aspx?direct=true&db=bth&AN=6740880&site=ehost-live

Wierenga, B., Van Bruggen, G., & Staelin, R. (1999). The success of marketing management support systems. *Marketing Science, 18*, 196-207. Retrieved May 23, 2007, from EBSCO Online Database Business Source Complete. http://search.ebscohost.com/login.aspx?direct=true&db=bth&AN=2727530&site=ehost-live

Wierenga, B., & Van Bruggen, G. (1997). The integration of marketing problem-solving modes and marketing management support systems. *Journal of Marketing, 61*, 21-37. Retrieved May 23, 2007, from EBSCO Online Database Business Source Complete. http://search.ebscohost.com/login.aspx?direct=true&db=bth&AN=9707205118&site=ehost-live

Wilkie, W., & Moore, E. (2003). Scholarly research in marketing: Exploring the 4 eras of thought development. *Journal of Public Policy & Marketing, 22*, 116-146. Retrieved May 24, 2007, from EBSCO Online Database Business Source Complete. http://search.ebscohost.com/login.aspx?direct=true&db=bth&AN=11237412&site=ehost-live

Winer, L. (1966). A profit-oriented decision system. *Journal of Marketing, 30*. Retrieved May 23, 2007, from EBSCO Online Database Business Source Complete. http://search.ebscohost.com/login.aspx?direct=true&db=bth&AN=4996983&site=ehost-live

SUGGESTED READING

Agostinho, O. (2012). Proposal of adaptability indexes to support management of engineering and marketing systems. *Proceedings of the European Conference on Information Management & Evaluation,* 1-8. Retrieved November 15, 2013, from EBSCO Online Database Business Source Complete. http://search.ebscohost.com/login.aspx?direct=true&db=bth&AN=82397546&site=ehost-live

Simon, H. (1960). *The new science of management decision.* New York: Harper & Row Publishers, Inc.

Simon, H. (1973). The structure of ill-structured problems. *Artificial Intelligence, 4*, 181-201.

Spence, M., & Brucks, M. (1997). The moderating effects of problem characteristics on experts' and novices' judgements. *Journal of Marketing Research (JMR), 34*, 233-247. Retrieved May 23, 2007, from EBSCO Online Database Business Source Complete. http://search.ebscohost.com/login.aspx?direct=true&db=bth&AN=9705016753&site=ehost-live

Wierenga, B., Van Bruggen, G., & Staelin, R. (1999). The success of marketing management support systems. *Marketing Science, 18*, 196-207. Retrieved May 23, 2007, from EBSCO Online Database Business Source Complete. http://search.ebscohost.com/login.aspx?direct=true&db=bth&AN=2727530&site=ehost-live

Vanessa A. Tetteh, Ph.D.

MARKETING ENVIRONMENT

ABSTRACT

A marketing environment is divided into micro environment, macro environment and meso or intermediate environment, which are affected by internal and external factors. An organization must be able to understand and assess its marketing environment. Since the last decade of the twentieth century, marketing environments have been greatly affected by a boom in information technologies and internationalization, as customers worldwide rely increasingly on the Internet for information and their consuming behavior. This has brought to the fore opportunities and complications, such as growing concerns about personal privacy online and Internet theft.

OVERVIEW

The term "marketing environment" refers to one of the factors of the marketing strategy devised by an organization. A marketing environment is formed by many different factors with characteristics such as national policies, demographics, and consumer behavior. These also include subsets like income, expenses, and resources that directly and indirectly affect the firm, the market, and consumers. Given the changes brought by the digital revolution to social, economic, technological, and market practices, the field of marketing environment has gained greater importance for firms because it helps assess future trends. In other words, marketing environment encompasses all the internal and external factors that constitute the environment in which marketing activities occur and that determine actions such as marketing strategies and marketing mix.

"Marketing mix" is a term coined by Neil Borden in 1950. It refers to a strategic analysis of internal factors, in which firms use a series of tools to analyze the four basic variables of their marketing activities: product, price, place or distribution, and promotion. These variables are also commonly known as "the four Ps." Product is the good or service—tangible or intangible—marketed to consumers. Price is the amount of money stipulated for the market exchange of the product. Place is where the product or service will be commercialized and distributed, and

promotion includes all the communication activities involved in persuading consumers to purchase the product—and, ideally, keep returning for more.

It is important to bear in mind that many of the factors that influence the marketing environment are out of an organization's control. A firm, then, must assess how easy or difficult it is to penetrate a market and look at competition, regulations, and other factors it cannot control. Managers must remain vigilant in order to identify market fluctuations that may bring both opportunities and threats, external and internal. While a firm may not be able to control these factors, it can plan and execute strategies to deal with them. Such strategies might include pricing strategies, location strategies, distribution channel selection, marketing plans, point of sale, outreach, and many others. In addition, a marketing manager must ensure that the marketing environment elements are coherent with all other marketing activities.

The technology sector is one of the most important of marketing environments. The rapid innovation or advances in technology can cause profound changes in firms and their production systems. The competitive environment is another important field, since it includes the varied organizations and consumers the market hopes to serve. Marketing environments are limited by various strictures, which include laws and regulations, production and marketing expenses, tariffs, and social, political, and economic factors.

Micro, Macro, and Meso Environments

A market environment also focuses on different aspects of sales. There are three distinct levels—broken into subdivisions—which represent the focus of sales for an organization's marketing mix, depending upon its product and target customer: micro environment, macro environment, and meso environment.

Microenvironments are organizational in reach; that is, they affect solely the organization and may often be influenced or controlled by the firm's managers. Microenvironments are formed by forces that engage with the organization closely and affect its capacity to satisfy its customers. They include, for example, a store or retailer, providers or suppliers, consumer markets or clients, market intermediaries or resellers, direct competitors, and the public at large. They also include the firm's employees, internal distribution, and technology. Managers may have ways of influencing or managing the dynamics of these elements in ways that do not occur with the macro environment.

Macro environments are contextual, that is, they affect the general context or all related organizations. Usually these changes are global factors, which managers are unable to control, such as demographic, economic, political, and cultural changes, technological innovation, new legislation and government policies, market trends, and acts of nature. These present both threats and opportunities for the firm; in fact, something that may appear to be a threat at first glance, may be turned into an opportunity by using the appropriate marketing strategy. Among the most important tools used by organizations to analyze macro marketing environments is the political-economic-social-technological-environmental-legal, or PESTLE, analysis. Marketers, then, use this framework to study and monitor external marketing environments to identify weaknesses, threats, and opportunities.

The meso environment refers to an intermediate or transactional middle structure between the micro and the macro environments. It has no fixed set of factors but includes the organization's culture, policies and procedures, stakeholders and allies, competitors, suppliers, resellers, and customer relations. Some have described it as the interacting factors between the supply-and-demand infrastructure within the micro and macro systems.

Market Types

Marketing environments are also related to different types of markets; that is, who the target market or direct customers are. These customers may be other businesses, government institutions, members of the public, and employees. The types of markets organizations deal with are usually categorized as export markets, business-to-business (B2B), business-to-consumer (B2C), and government-to-consumer (G2C). Some firms sell to one of these markets only while other firms sell to several different types of market.

An export market refers to a seller located in one country while its buyers are in a different country. B2B marketing refers to sales between organizations. These are often wholesale operations and subject to different regulations than those pertaining to products marketed to consumers in the general public. A can manufacturing firm that sells cans to soda bottling plants is an example of a business operating in a B2B market.

B2C markets are usually those in which individuals buy goods and services directly from a business for individual consumption. G2C markets are those in which interactions are made between government agencies or institutions and citizens acting as consumers; an example for the latter is the use that individuals make of income tax forms and filing government forms online.

As markets globalize and become more complex, market profiles become increasingly sophisticated, including government-to-government, business-to-employee, consumer-to-consumer, and peer-to-peer. For any of these different types of markets, marketing strategies may vary greatly, responding to specific industrial and/or government standards and regulations, economic factors such as tariffs, exchange rates, and interest rates, demographic factors such as gender, age and nationality, and market and economic trends.

FURTHER INSIGHTS

The internal marketing environment consists of all factors that ensure the achievement of organizational goals and includes all its financial, material, and human resources. An organization's material resources include its buildings, equipment, and infrastructure. An external environment consists of the micro and macro environments continuously interacting with each other in order to reach its goals. Customers are the most important factor for a marketing environment and the end goal of all its activities (Manea & Cetina, 2014).

Competitors also form an important part of the marketing environment. Its competitors are often visualized as other markets, of which three main basic types exist: monopolistic markets, oligopolistic markets, and perfect competition. In a monopoly or monopolistic market, one sole vendor or producer exists for a specific product. Penetrating a monopoly market is very costly and risky, as it presents many barriers and expenditures in time and resources. In some countries, a monopoly over a particular good—for example, utilities—is held by the government. In an oligarchy or oligopolistic market, an industrial field is dominated by very few firms, which share the available market. These markets are also difficult to penetrate; in some cases, firms cooperate among themselves to place obstacles in the way of new competition, or alternatively, the barriers may be placed by governments in the form of very exacting or costly conditions and regulations. Finally, market share may be too small to seem attractive except for a few firms (Manea & Cetina, 2014).

The third market structure is perfect competition. In a market system of perfect competition, there are many producers, sellers, and buyers. Obstacles are few or none, and at least in theory, prices are set by market forces of supply and demand. For instance, if a firm sets a higher price for its product, customers have the choice to look for a substitute among the available competition. Most real markets, however, are formed by a combination of different market types and the idea of a perfect free market is more ideal than real. Even in contemporary markets with the least restrictions, the free flow of goods is constrained by many barriers, such as regulations, taxes, tariffs, standards, available technology or raw material, and other legal, social, and political strictures.

ISSUES

Globalization has affected all marketing environments, directly or indirectly, particularly since the last decades of the twentieth century. These changes include technological advances and political and economic disruptions, which have led to new opportunities and business processes. Changes in technology have also led to a great transformation in the speed of conducting business; for instance, a customer may buy and pay for a product online for a business located in a different country and the purchased product will be shipped from a third country.

The globalization of products and services, then, is reflected in the emergence of new forms of doing business and transnational movement of goods in the international market. Moreover, according to experts, modern international trade allows competitive advantages in terms of different types of resources, such as capital, labor, raw materials, and technology. This allows for lower production and transaction costs and economies of scale. As more goods and services are produced cheaply, more people worldwide have access to a wide array of goods and technology produced inexpensively.

One of the most important marketing environments in the contemporary world relates to information technology. Information technology has changed fundamentally the ways in which industries and countries engage in commercial relationships. Customers have different expectations than in the late twentieth century regarding the availability and delivery of products and the customer service they expect from businesses. The channels through which these operations flow is information, and firms know that they need high quality and speedy channels of information to remain competitive and gain an edge in the competitive market.

On the other hand, this has brought to the fore issues of privacy and acceptable consumer trade-offs between individuals' natural concern about their personal information and their willingness to trade some information in exchange for better access to information about available goods and services. Most concerns revolve around fears of illicit and unwarranted use of their personal information. Moreover, consumers have different privacy thresholds. Their concerns may be increased or minimized depending upon the firm collecting the information and the uses it will be given. It follows, then, that it is very important for firms that they be able to convey a feeling of trust to its customers. Some firms—such as health services, which are bound by privacy laws—will seem more trustworthy to consumers than others. But most firms find they must work harder at it. Finally, the growing efforts at increasing citizen surveillance and the abundant cases of Internet identity and information theft, have raised the levels of concern among many consumers.

Marketing environment research has found that age is also a factor in the privacy threshold levels of customers. Millennials—those who reached adulthood in the early 2000s—are found to be extremely comfortable with technology and constantly use a wide range of functions in electronic devices, such as cell phones, than any previous generation. They are considered, by experts, both information seekers and information creators par excellence (Keith & Simmers, 2013).

It is very difficult for experts to predict future changes in the global landscape of globalized digital marketing environments. The growing connectedness and the speed of local/global interactions keeps information managers on the lookout for key trends. These advances have made the use of multiple devices commonplace and communication between businesses and customers, and businesses and suppliers, easier and faster. It makes problem solving easier and the movement of large caches of information efficient and fast. Moreover, current technology allows managers to overview transactional information, such as local and worldwide sales, in real time. Marketing managers, then, understand that technology plays a crucial role in the current and future developments of marketing environments. Technology is considered one of the most important elements in future marketing trends (Danciu, 2013).

Finally, international marketing experts highlight the growing importance of emergent economies in Africa, Asia, Latin America, the Middle East, and some European nations. These countries have been producing a growing number of companies increasingly aggressive in penetrating international markets. They present growing competition to established brands in developed nations, with better offerings in quality and price, lower margins, and greater speed. Many experts also expect that by the mid-twenty-first century most of the middle classes, today located in developed nations, will reside in China and India. It has become extremely important, then, that managers be well-versed in global processes, virtual marketing environments, and, it follows, the wide diversity of cultures that compose the future market worldwide (Danciu, 2013).

BIBLIOGRAPHY

AnaMaria, I. C., Alexandru, L. F., & Constantin, S. (2013). Social networks—Challenge and opportunity in the development of personal brand marketing strategies in the virtual environment. *Ovidius University Annals, Series Economic Sciences, 13*(1), 800–805. Retrieved October 23, 2016, from EBSCO Online Database Business Source Ultimate. http://search.ebscohost.com/login.aspx?direct=true&db=bsu&AN=89442031&site=ehost-live

Andreaiana Mihaescu, V. A., Stoica, S., C., & Ivan, T., C. D. (2014). Influence of the marketing environment on the toy market. *SEA: Practical Application of Science, 2*(1), 48–54.

Ashill, N. J., & Jobber, D. (2014). The effects of the external environment on marketing decision-maker uncertainty. *Journal of Marketing Management, 30*(3-4), 268–294. Retrieved October 23, 2016, from EBSCO Online Database Business Source Ultimate. http://search.ebscohost.com/login.aspx?direct=true&db=bsu&AN=94773134&site=ehost-live

Danciu, V. (2013). The future of marketing: An appropriate response to the environment changes. *Theoretical & Applied Economics, 20*(5), 33–52. Retrieved October 23, 2016, from EBSCO Online Database Business Source Ultimate. http://search.ebscohost.com/login.aspx?direct=true&db=bsu&AN=87923952&site=ehost-live

Keith, N. K., & Simmers, C. S. (2013). Adapting the marketing educational environment for multicultural millenials: The Chinese experience. *Academy of Educational Leadership Journal, 17*(3), 83–92. Retrieved October 23, 2016, from EBSCO Online Database Business Source Ultimate. http://search.ebscohost.com/login.aspx?direct=true&db=bsu&AN=87744079&site=ehost-live

Li, H., & Kannan, P. K. (2014). Attributing conversions in a multichannel online marketing environment: An empirical model and a field experiment. *Journal of Marketing Research, 51*(1), 40–56. Retrieved October 23, 2016, from EBSCO Online Database Business Source Ultimate. http://search.ebscohost.com/login.aspx?direct=true&db=bsu&AN=95682359&site=ehost-live

Luigi, D., Gheorghe, O., & Mircea, F. (2015). Understanding the online consumer behavior and the usage of the internet as a business environment—A marketing research. *Revista Economica, 67*(3), 63–79. Retrieved October 23, 2016, from EBSCO Online Database Business Source Ultimate. http://search.ebscohost.com/login.aspx?direct=true&db=bsu&AN=108596084&site=ehost-live

Manea, N. P., & Cetina, I. (2014). The influence of marketing environment on institutions of higher education in Romania. *Contemporary Readings in Law & Social Justice, 6*(1), 387–392.

SUGGESTED READING

Asare, A., Chelariu, C., Brashear, T., & Awudu, I. (2015). Part B: B2B and interorganizational issues in marketing: new perspectives on channels of distribution in dynamic markets: Value appropriation in dynamic environments: An analysis of digital marketing channels. *AMA Summer Educators' Conference Proceedings, 26*, B-4. Retrieved October 23, 2016, from EBSCO Online Database Business Source Ultimate. http://search.ebscohost.com/login.aspx?direct=true&db=bsu&AN=119938000&site=ehost-live

Burns, A. C., Veeck, A., & Bush. R. E. (2016). *Marketing Research, Eighth Edition.* New York, NY: Pearson.

Gillespie, K., & Hennessey, H. D. (2015). *Global Marketing, Fourth Edition.* London, UK: Routledge.

Jackson, R. W., & Wood, C. M. (2013). The marketing environment: A new paradigm. *Academy of Marketing Studies Journal, 17*(1), 35–50. Retrieved October 23, 2016, from EBSCO Online Database Business Source Ultimate. http://search.ebscohost.com/login.aspx?direct=true&db=bsu&AN=87742556&site=ehost-live

Tantawy, R. Y., & George, B. P. (2016). Cultures within national cultures: international marketing within the domestic marketing environment. *Economic Review: Journal of Economics & Business / Ekonomska Revija: Casopis Za Ekonomiju I Biznis, 15*(1), 26–34. Retrieved October 23, 2016, from EBSCO Online Database Business Source Ultimate. http://search.ebscohost.com/login.aspx?direct=true&db=bsu&AN=119368385&site=ehost-live

Trudy Mercadal, Ph.D.

MARKETING ETHICS

ABSTRACT

Companies that maintain marketing ethics sell their products or services in a way that does not harm, insult, or deceive consumers. Ethical marketing aims to persuade consumers in a truthful way and avoids trying to trick them into making a purchase. While many marketing managers would like to create ethical advertising campaigns, they often cannot do this because unethical advertising is effective and increases sales. To further complicate the dilemma, ethics are subjective; while some consumers might consider an ad unethical, others find it acceptable. Unethical marketing practices include targeting children in advertising, making subjective claims, and stereotyping women. Many companies that strive to maintain ethical marketing practices also integrate social and environmental concerns into their operations, a practice referred to as corporate social responsibility (CRS). These companies may invest in local communities and reduce their own carbon footprint.

OVERVIEW

Marketing ethics refers to the application of standards that define acceptable conduct for marketers and organizations engaging in marketing. According to the American Marketing Association Standard of Ethics, marketers must adhere to these norms: (1) doing no harm, which includes maintaining high ethical standards and obeying laws and regulations; (2) fostering trust in the marketing industry by striving for good faith with customers, promoting fairness, and avoiding deceptions in product designs, pricing, communication, and delivery and distribution; (3) embracing ethical values, which include honesty, responsibility, fairness, respect, transparency, and citizenship.

However, implementing these norms and values is difficult when doing the right thing does not make money for a company and might cause it to fail. Consider a company that manufactures and sells diet pills. While the company's marketing managers may understand that diet pills in general do not work, they may approve advertisements with testimonials from customers who exaggerate their effectiveness. To further promote their product, they may also approve the use of "fake news" websites designed to imitate real news websites such as Fox News and CNN. Without such advertising, the diet pills will not sell and the company, which might employ thousands of people, may go out of business. While the company's ads may trick consumers, they are not illegal.

The relationship between doing what is perceived as right and making money is complicated. Marketing managers are pressured to meet performance objectives—and sometimes, what is considered unethical results in high sales. To further complicate the situation, ethics are subjective. A behavior that one person considers wrong is considered acceptable by another. Those in the field of marketing must struggle to make decisions to balance what is perceived as morally acceptable with what is profitable.

The decision should be easier if the marketing practice under consideration is illegal, yet some major U.S. companies have been charged with illegal marketing practices, such as deceptive advertising. Deceptive advertising involves deliberately misleading consumers through false representation or the omission of information. In 2015, the Federal Trade Commission (FTC) filed a lawsuit against Volkswagen (VW) claiming that the car company deliberately deceived customers with its "Clean Diesel" ad campaign. According to the FTC, VW had been cheating emissions tests on its more than one-half million diesel cars in the United states for seven years. Customers who purchased or leased the cars believed they were low-emissions and environmentally friendly. In 2016, VW pleaded guilty and agreed to pay a $14.7 billion settlement to buy back or repair the vehicles and address the environmental harm caused by its cars (Mehrotra, 2016).

In 2007, the New York Attorney General filed charges against the PC manufacturer Dell, Inc. for an illegal marketing practice known as bait and switch. According to the Attorney General, Dell advertised "no interest" and "no payment" financing. Yet even customers with excellent credit were denied these options and instead offered high-interest financing. The company also did not provide customers with the support services in their warranties. Dell agreed to pay $4 million in restitution and penalties and changed its advertising and promotions O'Leary, 2009).

Ethical Dilemmas

Ethical dilemmas arise for marketing practices that may be considered shady but are not illegal and will likely be profitable. Before the passage of the Public Health Cigarette Smoking Act in 1970, some cigarette companies launched advertising campaigns targeting young people to attract new customers to their brand. These advertisements made smoking look fashionable and sophisticated. While at this time the link between smoking and cancer was not yet proven, most advertisers were aware of the possibility of the negative health effects.

Selling products door to door is considered unethical because the practice invades customers' privacy, yet salespeople have successfully sold water filtration systems this way for years. Companies justify selling the water filtration systems door to door because they claim the privacy invasion is minimal and the customer always has the right to refuse the salesperson's pitch and close the door.

The following are considered unethical marketing practices:

- Targeting children in advertising—creating ads for sugary cereal or other products that appeal to children who are too young to make objective decisions

- Making unverified claims—promising to deliver results without scientific evidence, as in "using this exercise machine for only ten minutes a day will get you in the best shape of your life"
- Making subjective claims (puffery)—making claims that cannot be proven, as in "America's favorite jam"
- Stereotyping women—portraying women as sex objects or housewives
- Using surrogate advertising—finding a way to advertise a product that cannot be advertised legally, as in placing a bottle of water in an ad with a fictitious brand name that is the same as a brand of liquor

Unethical marketing is more effective when a company's goal is to maintain a short-term relationship with a customer. If a company wants to inspire brand-loyalty and a long-term relationship with its customers, it should make only true claims about its products and try to persuade its customers in a truthful way. The Body Shop, which sells bath and body products, makeup, and fragrances, uses organic ingredients and does not test products on animals. The company promotes healthy body images in its advertisements and has a reputation for treating its workers fairly. The company advertises its ethical nature as a way to differentiate itself from competitors and to hopefully convince its customers to shop there again and again.

Corporate Philosophies

Marketing managers should establish a corporate policy regarding their company's marketing ethics. Before they can do this, though, they must first determine the principles that will guide the company; in other words, marketing managers and other executives need to decide how they feel about corporate responsibility. The following are three frames of reference described by Goodpaster and Matthews:

The Invisible Hand: According to this philosophy, "the true and only social responsibilities of business organizations are to make profits and obey the laws." Morality, responsibility, and conscience reside in the invisible hand of the free market system or the legal system rather than in the hands of individual organizations or their managers.

The Hand of Government: According to this philosophy, "the corporation would have no moral responsibility beyond political and legal obedience. Morality, responsibility, and conscience reside in the regulatory hand of the government rather than in the hands of individual organizations or their managers.

The Hand of Management: This philosophy "encourages corporations to exercise independent, noneconomic judgment over matters that face them in their short- and long-term plans and operations. It calls for corporations to implement "moral reasoning and intent." This implies that the managers of corporations should determine the ethics the company will abide by when making decisions.

Corporate Social Responsibility (CSR)

Corporate social responsibility (CSR) refers to a company integrating social and environmental concerns into its operations. Consumers in the twenty-first century expect companies to work to support the world around them. CSR contends that a company can "do well by doing good" (Falck, 2017). CSR is closely linked to marketing ethics because companies seeking to be held in high regard with consumers implement both.

Large corporations significantly harm the environment. They damage local ecosystems and even contribute to climate change via pollution. CSR encourages these orporations to use a portion of their profits to help the environment and the communities in which they operate.

Companies engaging in CSR aim to be transparent, meaning they disclose their actions not only to shareholders and investors but also to the public. These companies help the environment by reducing their carbon footprint by recycling and using renewable resources. They help their local communities by initiating employee volunteer programs, maintaining strict standards regarding product safety, and making charitable contributions, not only in the form of donations but in improvements to public structures such as schools and hospitals. CRS also dictates that companies treat their employees fairly and respectfully. This includes employees working for a company in other countries, where the labor laws may be more lax.

FURTHER INSIGHTS

- In the 2010s, marketing executives continued to struggle to create advertisements that are both successful and profitable. The following are some examples of advertising campaigns consumers considered unethical:
- In 2015, GoDaddy pulled its Super Bowl commercial because of consumer backlash. The advertisement showed a lost puppy who managed to find its way home to its owner, who decided to sell the puppy on her GoDaddy website.
- Also in 2015, McDonald's launched its "Carry On" advertising campaign. The advertisements featured McDonald's signs referencing public tragedies such as 9/11 and the Boston Marathon bombings along with birthday parties and other happy events while the music group Fun's song "Carry On" played in the background. The company's intent was likely to portray itself as being part of its community but consumers thought the ads were in poor taste.
- Dove soap's "Choose Beautiful" campaign angered women. The video showed women from different cities being asked to either walk through a door labeled "beautiful" or one labeled "average." Most women chose the "average" door at first but then realized that they can "choose beautiful" for themselves and walked through the first door.
- In 2016, the brain-training app Luminosity launched an ad claiming that using its app for more than 10 minutes, three times a week could prevent Alzheimer's disease and enable students to better perform in school. The FTC fined the company $2 million for making unfounded advertising claims.

BIBLIOGRAPHY

American Marketing Association Statement of Ethics. AMA. Retrieved https://www.ama.org/AboutAMA/Pages/Statement-of-Ethics.aspx.

Entis, Laura (2015). 5 of the most controversial ads in recent history. *Entrepreneur,* May 21. Retrieved from https://www.entrepreneur.com/article/246532.

Falck, Oliver and Stephen Heblich (2017). Corporate social responsibility: doing well by doing good. *Harvard Business Review,* May 15.

Goodpaster, Kenneth E. and John B. Matthews, Jr. (1982). Can a corporation have a conscience? *Harvard Business Review,* Jan-Feb, 132-41.

Mehrotra, Kartrikay and Margaret Cronin (2016). VW Buybacks to Begin Under $14.7 Billion Diesel Chat Accord. *Bloomberg Markets,* October 25. Retrieved from https://www.bloomberg.com/news/articles/2016-10-25/vw-judge-approves-14-7-billion-diesel-cheating-settlement.

Murphy, Patrick E., et al. *Ethics in Marketing: International Cases and Perspectives*. Routledge, 2012.

O'Leary Noreen (2009). Dell pays $4 mil. in settlement over deceptive ads. *Adweek*, Sept. 17. Retrieved from http://www.adweek.com/brand-marketing/dell-pays-4-mil-settlement-over-deceptive-ads-100367/.

Solomon, Dan (2014). Follow the history of smoking in advertising—from aspirational to shameful. *Fast Company*, Aug. 2017. Retrieved from https://www.fastcompany.com/3034457/follow-the-history-of-smoking-in-advertising-from-aspirational-to-shameful.

SUGGESTED READING

Acquier, A., et al (2011). Rediscovering Howard Bowen's legacy: the unachieved agenda and continuing relevance of social responsibilities of the business-man. *Business & Society*, 50, 580-606.

Gates, Guilvert et al. (2017). How Volkswagen's 'defeat devices' worked. *The New York Times*, May 16. Retrieved from https://www.nytimes.com/interactive/2015/business/international/vw-diesel-emissions-scandal-explained.html.

Lacziak, Gene R. and Patrick E. Murphy (2016). The relationship between marketing ethics and corporate social responsibility: serving stakeholders and the common good. *Marquette University E-publications*, Jan. 1. Retrieved from http://epublications.marquette.edu/market_fac/193/.

Suggett, Paul (2016). What is unethical advertising? *The Balance*, Aug. 12. Retrieved from https://www.the-balance.com/what-is-unethical-advertising-38797.

Wallace, Gregory (2013). Johnson & Johnson to pay $2 billion for false marketing. *CNN Money*, Nov. 4. Retrieved from http://money.cnn.com/2013/11/04/news/companies/johnson-and-johnson-settlement/index.html.

Tracey Biscontini

MARKETING MANAGEMENT

ABSTRACT

Marketing management is the function and process of managing an organization's marketing budget, personnel, and activities. In general, the goal of marketing management is to effectively and efficiently use resources to increase customer base, improve customer perceptions of the organization's products and services, and help the organization meet its goals and objectives as related to the marketing function. Marketing management is a far-reaching function that encompasses the management of every aspect of the marketing within an organization. The role and scope of the marketing management function varies widely between organizations according to organizational characteristics (e.g., size, corporate culture) and industry.

Not long ago, marketing efforts seemed much less complicated affairs. Stories about rag-and-bone men traveling to a village with a dancing bear to grab attention and advertise themselves depict a simpler time. For better or for worse, twenty-first-century marketing efforts are increasingly complicated. The use of a dancing bear in marketing efforts today might bring fleeting attention from potential customers but would probably also result in earning the organization a negative reputation as well as the wrath of the ASPCA. Marketing managers today must be concerned with such concepts as branding, Integrated Marketing Communications (IMC), marketing mix, and control systems for their sales forces.

Marketing management can be defined as the function and process of managing an organization's marketing budget, personnel, and activities. In general, the goal of marketing management is to effectively and efficiently use the organization's marketing resources to increase customer base, improve customer perceptions of the organization's products and services, and help the organization meet its goals and objectives as related to the marketing function. The role and scope of the marketing management function varies widely between organizations based on organizational characteristics (e.g., size, corporate culture) and industry. For example, a high-end consulting company is unlikely to hawk its services on late night TV in the same way as is done for onion choppers. Similarly, the role of the marketing manager in a small start-up company with only one product to sell is unlikely to be the same as that of the marketing manager in a large company or one with an established and varied product line.

General Marketing Functions

No matter the size or type of the organization or the stage of its products or services, there are certain general classes of activities that marketing functions and their managers need to take into account in order to better help the organization meet its goals and objectives: analyzing the market and environment to determine how best to focus one's marketing efforts; determining what the optimal target market or market segment is for the particular market and environmental conditions; setting a marketing strategy and developing a marketing plan; determining the proper marketing mix for persuading potential buyers in the target market or segment to purchase the organization's products or services; and controlling the implementation of the strategy and plan. These efforts are cyclic in nature. To be optimally effective, a marketing manager needs to be constantly engaged in all phases of the process and with refining the marketing plan to better reflect the needs and realities of the real world.

APPLICATIONS

Marketing Management

Although marketing has been viewed by some as a purely personality-driven set of activities whose objective is to persuade potential customers to purchase, it is much more than that. Marketing and the management of the marketing function, like other strategic functions within the organization, needs to be created based on a needs assessment and data analysis to determine what the needs of the market are and how best to position one's product or service to meet those needs. The collection and objective analysis of empirical data allow the marketing manager to make reasoned decisions as to the best way to market the products and services of the organization. Based on the collection and analysis of data regarding the needs, wants, buying habits, and other characteristics of the target market, the marketing management team can then develop a marketing strategy that will best enable the organization to meet its marketing objectives.

A number of factors impact the development of a unique strategy for an organization or product line and the development of a concomitant strategic marketing plan.

- First, the assets and skills that the organization possesses or can readily acquire need to be de-

termined. For example, if an organization selling application software wishes to market itself as a vendor offering superior customer support, it could not do so honestly unless it either had sufficient staff with sufficient time on the payroll to offer such support or could afford to hire the extra personnel needed for such support.

- The development of an effective marketing strategy must also take into account the market drivers for the industry. These are various political, economic, sociocultural, and technological forces that can influence the wants and needs of the consumer base. Increasing reliance on cordless and mobile telephones, for example, might make it a poor strategy for a communications equipment company to focus on the development of more attractive housings for corded phones.

- In addition, marketing management must consider the nature of the competition in the marketplace to help determine whether or not a marketing effort is likely to be successful. Part of the strategic marketing effort is to decide how best to differentiate oneself from the competition and demonstrate that one's product or service is superior to those offered by the competition.

- Not only must one consider the nature of the competition in the marketplace, but one must also consider the stage of the market or the industry life cycle when developing a marketing strategy. Some organizations are innovators and do best when introducing a new product to the marketplace to gain the initial share of the market. While other companies rush to take over some of the market share, innovating companies may be hard at work on another innovative product that can again reshape the demands of the marketplace.

- In addition, strategic windows often affect an organization's ability to successfully compete in the marketplace. These are limited time periods during which there is an optimal fit between the needs of the marketplace and the competencies of the organization. For example, typically only one company can gain a strategic advantage for being the first to market an innovative new product. The competition must be content to improve on the initial design. However, it is often the initial company that retains the reputation for being an innovator and leader in the field. Once the strategic window begins to close (e.g., someone else comes out with the product), it is typically best that the organization looks for another opportunity.

The Marketing Mix

As opposed to the dancing bear approach to marketing referenced above, marketing in the twenty-first century is a complicated thing, requiring a combination of product, price, place, and promotion (called the marketing mix) to get a product into the hands of the consumer. One of the primary tasks of marketing is to optimize the mix to best position the product for success in the marketplace. The marketing mix may contain any number of approaches to marketing a product or service, each of which is designed to move prospective customers closer to a sale (see Figure 3). At the beginning of a marketing effort, these activities are targeted toward making the customer aware of the organization and its products or services. Once the prospective customer is made aware of the organization and what it has to offer, marketing efforts next focus on generating interest in the customer for purchasing the organization's goods or services. These activities also help prospective customers understand the nature and value of the organization's products or services and can help promote the conviction that the product or service being offered is something that is appropriate for the customer. Once this has been accomplished, marketing efforts attempt to turn this conviction that the product or service is appropriate or needed into a desire to purchase it. The marketing strategy should appropriately use the various elements of the marketing mix to improve the probability of a sale. Part of the role of the marketing management function is to develop a marketing plan that will incorporate and articulate these elements.

Customer Relationship Management

Marketing management is also concerned with building and maintaining a positive relationship with the organization's customers. Customer relationship management requires that an organization identify potential customers, acquire data regarding the potential and current customers, build relationships with customers, and influence customer perceptions of the organization and its products or services. As part of the process of customer relationship management, the marketing function identifies prospective

customers, acquires data concerning prospective and current customers, builds relationships with customers, and attempts to influence their perceptions of the organization and its products or services. The activity of the marketing function is often based on an estimate of the customer's lifetime value to the organization. This theoretical information allows the marketing manager to know how much each customer is worth in terms of dollars of income which, in turn, allows the marketing manager to better allocate the marketing budget for a higher return on investment. Calculating customer lifetime value, however, tends to be complex (e.g., the customer's need or desire for the product may change, the competition may bring out a product that better fits the customer's needs), and reliable data to build a usable model and net cash flow from the customer are difficult to gather.

Internal Monitoring

In addition to managing the strategy of the marketing function and the relationship of the organization to the customer, part of the role of marketing management is to manage the marketing or sales personnel who put the plan into action. This includes monitoring the activities of the sales staff to make sure that they are effective and successful. Part of the function of marketing management is to set performance objectives for the marketing personnel as well as present ways to help enable the marketing force to meet those objectives. There are two general approaches to managing marketing or sales staffs. Outcome-based systems focus on the final outcomes of the marketing process (e.g., whether

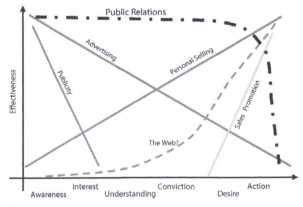

Figure 3: The Marketing Mix

or not a sale was made, total revenues earned by a marketing person in a given period of time). This approach to the management of marketing personnel has the advantage of having standards that tend to be both objective and clear: Either the marketer made the assigned sales quote for a time period or did not. Criteria of success under such management systems tend to be clear and, therefore, require relatively little monitoring or direction by management. Outcome-based control systems are often favored for the management of marketing personnel because of the relative availability of criteria against which performance can be measured such as the number of sales made or the dollar volume earned within a given performance assessment period. Due to the offsite nature of many marketing jobs, such objective measures of performance are sometimes the only way to gather data about how well a marketing person is performing.

Behavior-Based Control Systems vs. Outcome-Based Control Systems

However, outcome-based control systems do not take into account a number of factors. Particularly on big-ticket items, sales often occur over a period of time. In such situations, the marketer may need to establish a relationship with the customer, spend time gathering and analyzing data to assess the customer's needs, defend his or her product against the product of competitors, persuade the customer of the relative value of his or her product, and wait while the customer makes a decision according to the customer's time table. All these activities take time. As a result, there may be performance assessment periods during which a marketer may not have made any sales but is well on his or her way to making a significant sale. Because of such aspects of outcome-based control systems, some people argue that a behavior-based control system is more appropriate for use with marketing personnel. To overcome such potential situations, many marketing managers prefer to use a behavior-based control system. These systems focus more on the behavior of the marketing personnel than on their final sales. As opposed to outcome-based control systems, however, behavior-based control systems require significantly more monitoring of both the activities and the results of the sales force's efforts as well as higher levels of direction and intervention in the activities of marketing personnel.

Behavior-based control systems also tend to be less objective and more complex than outcome-based control systems.

Advantages of Behavior-Based Systems

However, behavior-based control systems overcome a number of the disadvantages associated with outcome-based control systems. First, behavior-based control systems allow marketing managers more control than outcome-based systems. In behavior-based systems, the manager can better ensure that personnel are adhering to the sales plan and policies and procedures of the department. Further, since rewards in behavior-based systems are tied to behavior rather than outcomes, marketing personnel will be more motivated to follow the policies and procedures even if they are not necessarily convinced of their validity. However, fair, objective behavior-based systems are more difficult to develop than outcome-based systems.

CONCLUSION

Marketing management is a far-reaching function that encompasses the management of every aspect of the marketing function within an organization. Although the details of how marketing management is conducted differ from organization to organization and from industry to industry, in general it comprises five elements:

- Analysis of the market and environment
- Setting of the target market
- Setting of a marketing strategy
- Determination of an appropriate marketing mix
- The exercise of control over all these activities and sub-functions.

In addition, it must be remembered that marketing management is an ongoing process. As human, financial, and other organizational resources change, both the strategic marketing plan as well as the way that marketing function is managed will have to change in response. Similarly, as the market or environment changes, marketing management will have to change in order to meet new customer needs or expectation, or changes to the market brought about the competition's activities or the economy in general. Marketing is much more than the application of sales technique to potential customers. It involves strategy, planning, control, and evaluation. It is the function of marketing management to accomplish these tasks.

BIBLIOGRAPHY

AMA definition of marketing. (2007). *MarketingPower, Inc.* Retrieved February 27, 2009, from http://www.marketingpower.com/Community/ARC/Pages/Additional/Definition/default.aspx?sq=an+organizational+function+and+a+set+of +processes+for+creating%2c+communicating+and+delivering+value+to+customers+and+for+managing+customer+relationships+in+ways+that+benefit+the+organization+and+its+stakeholders

Anderson, E. & Oliver, R. L. (1987). Perspectives on behavior-based versus outcome-based salesforce control systems. *Journal of Marketing, 51*(4), 76–88. Retrieved February 17, 2009, from EBSCO Online Database Business Source Complete. http://search.ebscohost.com/login.aspx?direct=true&db=bth&AN=4996249&site=ehost-live

LaPointe, P. (2013). The dark corners where research strategies hide: throwing light at the intersection of the new and the old. *Journal of Advertising Research, 53*(1), 9–10. Retrieved October 31, 2013, from EBSCO Online Database Business Source Complete. http://search.ebscohost.com/login.aspx?direct=true&db=bth&AN=86178717&site=ehost-live

Mintz, O., & Currim, I. S. (2013). What drives managerial use of marketing and financial metrics and does metric use affect performance of marketing-mix activities?. *Journal of Marketing, 77*(2), 17–40. Retrieved October 31, 2013, from EBSCO Online Database Business Source Complete. http://search.ebscohost.com/login.aspx?direct=true&db=bth&AN=85725800&site=ehost-live

Proctor, T. (2000). *Strategic marketing: An introduction.* New York: Routledge.

Ruskin-Brown, I. (2005). *Promoting a service. In I. Ruskin-Brown, Marketing your service business.* London: Thorogood, 199–221. Retrieved July 10, 2007, from EBSCO Online Database Business Source Complete. http://search.ebscohost.com/login.aspx?direct=true&db=bth&AN=22377471&site=ehost-live

Strafford, J. & Grant, C. (1993). *Effective sales management* (2nd ed.). Oxford: Butterworth-Heinemann Ltd.

Tadajewski, M., & Jones, D. (2012). Scientific marketing management and the emergence of the ethical marketing concept. *Journal of Marketing Management,* 28(1/2), 37–61. Retrieved October 31, 2013, from EBSCO Online Database Business Source Complete. http://search.ebscohost.com/login.aspx?direct=true&db=bth&AN=69838525&site=ehost-live

Zekić-Sušac, M., & Has, A. (2015). Data mining as support to knowledge management in marketing. *Business Systems Research, 6*(2), 18–30. Retrieved Dec. 3, 2015, from EBSCO Online Database Business Source Complete. http://search.ebscohost.com/login.aspx?direct=true&db=bth&AN=110526634&site=ehost-live&scope=site

SUGGESTED READING

Ayağ, Z. & Özdemir, R. G. (2007). An analytic network process-based approach to concept evaluation in a new product development environment. *Journal of Engineering Design, 18*(3), 209–226. Retrieved February 16, 2009, from EBSCO Online Database Academic Search Complete. http://search.ebscohost.com/login.aspx?direct=true&db=a9h&AN=24409850&site=ehost-live

Brexendorf, T. O. & Kernstock, J. (2007). Corporate behaviour vs brand behaviour: Towards an integrated view? *Journal of Brand Management, 15*(1), 32–40. Retrieved February 16, 2009, from EBSCO Online Database Business Source Complete. http://search.ebscohost.com/login.aspx?direct=true&db=bth&AN=26435844&site=ehost-live

Iacobucci, D. (2015). *Marketing management.* Stamford, CT: Cengage Learning.

Kotler, Philip, et al. (2016). *Marketing Management.* Pearson Education Ltd., Retrieved June 29, 2017.

Petty, R. D. (2008). Naming names: Trademark strategy and beyond: Part One – Selecting a brand name. *Journal of Brand Management, 15*(3), 190–197. Retrieved February 16, 2009, from EBSCO Online Database Business Source Complete. http://search.ebscohost.com/login.aspx?direct=true&db=bth&AN=27941125&site=ehost-live

Sellers-Rubio, R. & Mas-Ruiz, F. (2007). Different approaches to the evaluation of performance in retailing. *International Review of Retail, Distribution and Consumer Research, 17*(5), 503–522. Retrieved February 16, 2009, from EBSCO Online Database Business Source Complete. http://search.ebscohost.com/login.aspx?direct=true&db=bth&AN=27441981&site=ehost-live

Ruth A. Wienclaw, Ph.D.

MARKETING METHODS

ABSTRACT

Many marketing methods are available to businesses, individuals, and organizations that are looking to sell or promote a product, a service or an idea to a wider audience. While the term "marketing method" can theoretically be applied to just about any action that is taken to promote or sell a product, a set of common marketing methods typically comprises most marketing campaigns. These methods include direct marketing, database marketing, advertising, web marketing, promotions, sponsorship, and public relations. Each of these marketing methods has its own benefits and drawbacks, and no one method is superior to the rest by rule. The general rule of thumb when creating a marketing campaign is to select the method or methods that will allow you to deliver the most effective message to the largest portion of your target audience, while still remaining within your budgetary constraints.

OVERVIEW

The marketing process encompasses designing, developing, and naming a product, a service or an idea; determining how it will be priced, packaged, and distributed; creating a campaign for positioning the product in the marketplace; and touting its features and benefits to a target audience.

Virtually any action that is undertaken by a business or an individual to create demand and desire for a product or service could be considered a "marketing method." You are essentially limited only by your own creative imagination.

However, there are a number of commonly used marketing methods that are important to consider. These methods include database marketing, direct marketing, radio, television, and print advertising, web marketing, promotions, sponsorship, and public relations.

While the largest, loudest, and most dramatic marketing campaigns often draw the most attention, they are not necessarily the most cost-effective. For a smart marketer, it is often possible—and far more financially prudent—to develop a targeted marketing plan that is based on a deep understanding of what your message is, who your target audience is, and what marketing methods your target audience is most likely to respond to.

Research, Analysis, & Market Segmentation

Choosing the right marketing message—and the methods to convey that message—requires a great deal of market analysis and self-examination. It is necessary to determine what is unique about what a company has to offer, what the competition has to offer, and who the target audience is. By gaining a good understanding of these three factors, you will be better equipped to choose the right marketing methods for your campaign.

Determining Differentiating Qualities

The first step in the process is to determine what the differentiating quality or qualities are of the product, service, or idea that a company is hoping to promote. Differentiating qualities are those aspects of the product, service, or idea that are unique, and thus worthy of the customers' specific attention and consideration.

In her book, *Getting More Business* (1999), Sallyann Sheridan suggests that marketers consider a variety of aspects when it comes to determining the differentiating qualities of the products they are trying to promote. Is there something particularly unique about your location, approach to business, service policy, product guarantees, or customer service that is worth highlighting? Perhaps there is something unique about the selection you offer, how much product you have to offer, or the prices at which you offer goods.

Determining this differentiating quality is easy if a company is trying to promote a brand new invention that no one has ever seen before. But what about a men's clothing store along a busy commercial strip, facing competition from several other retail outfitters within a short driving distance? Customers in the area have several options to choose from. Why should they visit a specific company?

Factors that could differentiate one company from another may include selection, better prices, exclusive brands, better customer service, hours of operation, promotions, etc.

Once a company has determined what is special about what it has to offer and what makes it different from the competition, it can start to think about the audience that it is trying to reach.

Determining the Target Audience

A target audience is a group of individuals that a company has identified as being the most important to reach with the message of a particular marketing campaign. A company determines the target audience through the process of market segmentation—division of a market into smaller, more specialized categories based on a variety of factors, including customer buying habits.

A target audience can vary depending on the purpose of the campaign. If the purpose of the campaign is to generate fast sales, the target audience might be existing customers who are likely to make large purchases quickly. If the purpose of the campaign is to broaden the customer base, the campaign could be targeted to individuals who have been identified as a good fit for the company, or former customers that a company is trying to win back.

Customer Characteristics

The more a company knows about its customers, the easier it will be to create a marketing plan that appeals to them. What factors influence their decision-making habits? What do they like about the company? What do they dislike?

There are many ways to gather information about a company's customers and potential customers. A company can host focus groups, visit trade shows, and talk with those in the company who interact with customers on a daily basis. A company can send out customer satisfaction surveys or ask for comments on a web bulletin board.

There are now a variety of data-crunching computer software programs, such as SQL, that can be used to collect and analyze a huge repository of information about customer buying habits. Programs like SQL are able to break down consumer information based on a variety of factors, including geographical location, buying habits, buying frequency, most desired products, and so forth. In the past, advertisers targeted audiences by demographic, for example, running commercials aimed at married women of a certain age during weekday soap operas or ads for breakfast cereals and toys during Saturday morning cartoons. With data collection, campaigns can be crafted almost at the individual level, anticipating the likelihood that a consumer will be interested in a product based on his or her real-time activity. Supermarkets can issue instant coupons in response to purchases. Internet browsers and websites can populate screens with ads based on recent searches. A diaper manufacturer, for example, does not need to waste marketing dollars advertising to all women in the 18 to 34-year-old category but can instead buy ad space on the digital devices of anyone searching for key words indicating pregnancy or the presence of a baby in the consumer's life. Such targeted market is both more efficient (saving dollars) and more effective (increasing sales) (WIND & Nelson-field, 2013). Data collection also helps a company track how well sales are responding to a certain marketing campaign, which is a great help in determining which marketing methods are working and which aren't.

Choosing a Marketing Method

Once a company knows who it is, who its competition is, who the target audience is, and what it wants its message to be, it can start thinking about what marketing methods will work the best for a campaign.

Choosing the best marketing method is not an exact science. There is always an element of chance that comes with any marketing campaign. A company can, however, vastly improve its chances for success by carefully collecting and studying data about the buying habits of its target audience.

It is also important for an organization to maintain a flexible approach. A company shouldn't commit all of its resources and energy to one method until it has had a chance to gauge its success. It may be necessary to alter or abandon a course of action if it is not producing the desired result, and it always helpful to rethink, refresh, and reconfigure an approach from time to time to prevent stagnation.

No matter what methods a company uses, the overall campaign should perform three basic functions: It should implicitly or explicitly set a company apart from the competition; clearly outline the message sent to the target audience; and be crafted in a way that is most likely to generate customer response.

Direct Marketing & Database Marketing

A direct marketing campaign is one that has a specific goal and seeks an immediate response from the customer. Direct marketing can take a variety of forms (including print advertisements, brochures, coupons, and television commercials) but the overall message includes some kind of request: "Ask your cable provider to add the NFL Network to your service package." "Call for free information on this revolutionary exercise machine." "Mail in this subscription card to start receiving National Geographic at home."

The advantage of direct marketing is that it is highly measurable—if a company's campaign desires that the members of its target audience perform a specific task, the effectiveness of the campaign can be gauged by determining how many do what is asked.

One of the drawbacks of a direct marketing campaign is that it is narrow in its focus. A company may lose out on other business opportunities by asking customers to do one specific thing. Direct marketing campaigns can also be expensive to produce, and new regulations on telemarketing and other aspects of direct marketing can make it difficult for marketers to connect with their target audience.

Database marketing is marketing directly to a defined group of individuals whose addresses and/or contact information have been accumulated in database form. The advantage of database marketing is that a company can send its message directly to individuals who have already been identified as interested in the product or service being offered.

These individuals could be existing customers, individuals who have expressed interest in company products in the past, customers who have expressed dissatisfaction with company products and services, or individuals who have been identified through research as likely customers for a product.

Clients who have been identified through a database marketing plan can be contacted using a variety of marketing methods, including email, phone calls, letters, catalogs, brochures, or mailings. A company can also market to them by using promotional items such as coupons, two-for-one deals, or free samples.

Database marketing campaigns can be used to boost business in a variety of ways. A company can try to increase the business of big clients by offering them incentives, exclusives, rewards, or volume-based price breaks. A company can also try to jump-start stagnant accounts by contacting them with information about new products or discounted items, or expanding its

market share in a certain city or state by ramping up its marketing to customers in that geographical area.

The disadvantage to the database marketing is that a company's message is only being sent to the members of an identified group, and thus it is limiting its ability to reach anyone outside that audience base.

Advertising

Advertising is a method of marketing in which a company or an individual pays to deliver a specific message using an outside medium, such as television, radio, newspapers, or magazines.

Advertising is a major component of marketing, and an excellent way to get a message out to target audiences. There have traditionally been three major forms of advertising (television, radio, and print) though web advertising rapidly gained prominence as a marketing method in the twenty-first century and is covered in the web marketing section below.

Television Advertising

Television advertising is perhaps the most prominent and effective way to deliver a marketing message to a mass audience. Because it is so effective, it is also one of the most expensive. A 30-second advertisement during the Colts-Bears Super Bowl in February 2006, for example, cost $2.5 to $2.6 million. Seven years later, in 2013, the same spot cost $4 million. There are, however, many less expensive television venues to advertise in than the Super Bowl; from the big four networks (NBC, CBS, ABC and FOX) to local network affiliates, to basic cable channels (CNN, USA, TNT) all the way down to local access channels.

The nature of television advertising has changed in recent years, as it is becoming increasingly difficult for network executives to assure advertisers that their ads are being seen during commercial breaks. Tivo Machines, Cable DVR boxes, VCRs, and on-demand downloadable programs have fast-forward functions that allow viewers to skip through commercial breaks without watching the ads.

Network executives have tried to solve this problem by finding creative ways to integrate advertisements into the programs themselves. The Fox Television Network, for example, uses "green screen" technology to broadcast computer-generated advertisements onto a blank box behind batters during baseball games. The Fox Network has also been using superimposed graphics to advertise upcoming movies during its television shows, ensuring that the message is reaching viewers who might be fast-forwarding through the ad breaks.

NBC's hit sitcom "The Office" frequently used product placement to highlight the products offered by advertisers Hewlett Packard and Staples. The employees at the fictional company on the show noticeably worked on Hewlett Packard computers, for example, and products from the Staples office supply company were often prominently featured on the show. On one episode, one of the main characters even took a job at a Staples store.

Print Advertising

Print advertising can run the gamut from display ads in newspaper and magazines to billboards, catalogs, leaflets, pamphlets, and brochures. Print advertisements can be a highly effective way to reach a target audience, but they can also be expensive, primarily due to the cost of purchasing advertising space, and/or the cost of designing printing, distributing, and/or mailing brochures, pamphlets, and catalogs.

Radio Advertising

Radio advertising is another effective way to get a marketing message out to a target audience. As Sarah White points out in her book, *The Complete Idiot's Guide to Marketing Basics* (1997), the advantage of radio advertising is that it is easier to target a message to a specific audience. A business that is looking to market a product to young people would likely choose a Top 40 station to advertise on, while someone looking to promote a product to Baby Boomers would be more likely to choose a station that has a classic rock, oldies, or easy-listening format.

Radio has its advantages in that it allows a company to reach a wide audience for less than it costs to advertise on TV, but the medium is also being increasingly challenged for the ears of listeners by other forms of audio entertainment, satellite radio services, streaming and podcasting from station websites, customizable Internet radio sites such as Pandora, and huge, expandable personal music libraries contained on digital music players and smartphones.

Web Marketing

The rapid rise of the World Wide Web over the past 20 years has had a huge impact on the field of marketing, both in terms of the opportunities that it offers, and the challenges it presents.

In terms of opportunity, the Internet has provided marketers with easy, inexpensive access to customers and potential customers from all over the world. Reaching these customers is also incredibly easy and cost-effective. It costs no more to send an email to an address in Perth, Australia, than it does to someone who lives down the street, and costs associated with printing or mailing are avoided.

In terms of challenges, the rise of the Internet has made the marketplace a lot more competitive. Because just about anyone has the ability to start a website or send an email, the marketplace has opened up to businesses of all sizes. Customers are no longer limited by geography when it comes to searching for the products and service they need. It is now much easier to go comparison-shopping. There are many ways for marketers to compete for attention and solicit new customers on the web.

Websites & Search Engine Optimization

Websites can perform a variety of marketing functions. Building and maintaining a professional-looking website can help to improve the public perception of a business. With the careful use of search engine optimization (SEO) terms, a business can ensure that search engines will frequently present its site to users who are searching for the products and services being offered.

The goal of SEO is to guide web users to a business's site by the thoughtful repetition and placement of key marketing phrases. The idea is to figure out what terms are most often searched for when it comes to the product that is offered, and then create text assets that contain these terms. Search engines such as Google, Chrome, Bing, and Yahoo have web crawling software programs that analyze websites based on this target content, and use this analysis to present results to web users who search for specific terms.

SEO is something of an art as well as science. Using too many SEO phrases can work against a business, as many search engines will balk against sites that simply try to overwhelm their search functions with repetition. Not using enough SEO terms, however, could lead to a business being out positioned by a more aggressive competitor.

Search engines are also constantly upgrading and revising their analysis of websites, so it is important to freshen and revise SEO content as the nature of a business—and the nature of its competition—changes.

E-Commerce

Many companies and individuals who have products to sell have set up e-commerce (electronic commerce) enabled websites, where customers can view products and place orders online. By making it possible for customers from all over the world to place orders in an instant, e-commerce-enabled websites have helped companies tap into an incredibly large pool of customers.

E-commerce websites can also help to cut down on other marketing costs. Instead of sending out thick, expensive catalogs that include every product a company has to offer, companies can instead send out smaller, more specialized catalogs that cost less to produce, have a product selection that is carefully chosen to appeal to a certain market segment, and direct readers to the website to find any other products that they need.

Email Marketing

Email marketing campaigns can be used to solicit new business and strengthen existing business relationships. Email marketing messages can take a variety of forms.

Email can be used to create direct response mailings that ask customers to click on a link for more information or sign up for a free trial of a product or service. They can be aggressive selling campaigns that alert customers to new products, seasonal trends, or clearance items. Also, email messages can simply promote a good image for a company by fostering interest in a particular subject. A company that is selling gardening supplies, for example, could send an email with several tips for springtime garden preparation.

Banner Ads

Banner ads can be thought of as the billboards of Internet marketing. Banner ads are paid space that companies purchase on other websites, usually websites that experience a high volume of user traffic. By placing an ad on an outside website, companies hope to draw customers to their own sites, usually by placing an active link on the advertisement itself.

Banner ads can be placed on sites that deal with topics related to the product or service that is being offered or on seemingly unrelated sites that may be appealing to the demographic they are trying to reach.

Promotions

Promotions are rebates, free giveaways, coupons, two-for-one deals, and any other discounts and/or incentives that a company can offer to customers or potential customers to generate sales. The advantage of a promotion is that it is more likely to put a product in the hands of the customer. Promotions are also an excellent way to encourage a sale. Someone who may hesitate to buy a vacuum cleaner for $59.99, for example, might go for the deal if it also includes a free dry mop. Music companies regularly give away posters and other inexpensive items to customers who purchase a new music CD on its first day of release.

Another effective promotional method is to give away free samples of a product at places where members of the target audience are likely to visit. Health clubs regularly have samples of skin cream and shampoos in the bathrooms for members to test out when showering away from home.

The disadvantage of a promotional offer is that it often means that a company is not always operating on its ideal terms for business. Honoring a coupon means taking less than what the original asking price was, while giving away free samples also cuts into the bottom line. As with any marketing method, it is important to monitor the use of promotions and to gauge the effectiveness of each campaign before starting the next.

The spectacular rise and crash of Internet promotional service Groupon provides a cautionary tale for innovative marketing strategists. Groupon, one of the fastest-growing Internet companies in the world, issued an IPO in 2011. Stock quickly tripled in value, and then lost 90 percent of its value when legal troubles and the inherently flawed marketing strategy on which it was built became apparent. Groupon's daring innovation was to offer daily deals, which were 50 percent off the merchant's regular price, via email to subscribers. Merchants signed on in order to attract new business and subscribers were attracted by the deep discounts for quality products and services. The revenue model called for a merchant to offer a good for 50 percent off, then Groupon would claim 40 to 60 percent of the coupon price. The subscriber used the coupon promotional code to purchase a voucher for the good online. Legal issues arose when courts recognized the vouchers as gift certificates, which do not expire, that negatively affected Groupon and the merchant—both of which counted on a large percentage of daily deal vouchers to go unredeemed. Groupon was also challenged to continually replace the majority of merchants, who found the small amount of new business Groupon brought them did not outweigh the hassle and the lost profits that frequently resulted from the deal. Subscribers wearied of the daily emails and began filtering them as spam. Competitors also materialized, grasping the potential of Internet promotional deals but having learned from Groupon's mistakes. Fourteen months after going public, Groupon's founder was ousted, but the company continued to languish in search of improvements to its marketing methods.

Sponsorships

Sponsorships are a way to connect a business, a service, or an idea to a separate entity by entering into some kind of agreement with that entity; usually a financial one. Private companies often become the official sponsors of sporting events, concerts, road races, and charity events.

The advantage of a sponsorship is that it offers companies a chance to link themselves or their products to something that the members of their target audience already admire or are likely to seek out. Sponsorships of this nature create a positive association in the mind of the customer and reflect well on your business.

Sponsorships can also be expensive, however, and there is no guarantee that attaching a company's name to a separate entity will have a beneficial effect on the business.

Public Relations

Public relations is the attempt to influence the public's perception of a product, a service, or an idea by working through public channels such as the media. Common public relations (or PR) tactics include preparing and issuing press releases and press kits, building personal relationships with media members, and organizing special events and celebrations that are designed to generate media coverage.

Public relations professionals can perform a variety of tasks for a company, an individual, or an organization. By building relationships with members of the news media, they can help to generate positive free press for their clients' products, ideas, or services.

PR reps often invite members of the new media to grand opening celebrations or kickoff events, feting them with food and promotional materials as a way to encourage them to report back on events at the company. They also use their press contacts to arrange feature stories about their clients.

PR reps can also be a valuable resource when a company is facing negative publicity. If a chemical plant has an accidental spill, for example, a PR firm can help to control the negative publicity by issuing a carefully crafted and controlled statement to explain what happened and what the plant is planning to do about it. The PR firm can also help by developing a long-term plan to restore the plant's public image, perhaps by contacting the press to talk about new safety features that have been implemented in the wake of the spill or to bring attention to charitable donations the company has made.

The advantage of using public relations is that it is thought to produce a more convincing message than advertising. A news article about new safety features being implemented at the chemical plant in the wake of a spill would probably carry a lot more weight with the community than a paid advertisement. The disadvantage to using public relations is that it is not always easy to control public perception. Media members could choose to ignore your spin on the story or flat out refuse to give you any coverage at all.

CONCLUSION

A variety of marketing methods are available to businesses, individuals, and organizations that are looking to sell or promote a product, a service or an idea to a wider audience. While the term "marketing method" can theoretically be applied to just about any action that is taken to promote or sell a product, there are a set of common marketing methods that typically comprise most marketing campaigns. These methods include direct marketing, database marketing, advertising, web marketing, promotions, sponsorship, and public relations. Each of these marketing methods has its own benefits and drawbacks, and no one method is superior to the rest by rule. The general rule of thumb when creating a marketing campaign is to select the method or methods that will allow you to deliver the most effective message to the largest portion of your target audience, while still remaining within your budgetary constraints.

BIBLIOGRAPHY

Bercovici, J. (2013). The woman(!) behind GoDaddy's tasteless, effective Super Bowl ads. *Forbes.Com,* 49. Retrieved October 31, 2013, from EBSCO Online Database Business Source Complete. http://search.ebscohost.com/login.aspx?direct=true&db=bth&AN=85366340&site=ehost-live

Bly, R. (1998). *Business to business direct marketing: Proven direct response methods to generate more leads and sales.* Lincolnwood, IL: NTC Business Books.

Jacobs, D. L. (2013). Firing CEO Andrew Mason won't end Groupon woes. *Forbes.Com,* 14. Retrieved October 31, 2013, from EBSCO Online Database Business Source Complete. http://search.ebscohost.com/login.aspx?direct=true&db=bth&AN=85869893&site=ehost-live

Kohl, S. (2000). *Getting attention: Leading edge lessons for publicity and marketing.* Boston, MA: Butterworth-Heinemann.

Nash, E. (2000). *Direct marketing: Strategy, planning, and execution.* New York, NY: McGraw-Hill Professional.

Sheridan, S. (1999). *Getting more business: Use proven marketing techniques and get business coming to you.* Oxford : How To Books.

White, S. E. (1997). *The complete idiot's guide to marketing basics.* New York, NY: Alpha Books.

Wind, Y., Sharp, B., & Nelson-field, K. (2013). Empirical generalizations: new laws for digital marketing: How advertising research must change. *Journal of Advertising Research, 53,* 175-180. Retrieved October 31, 2013, from EBSCO Online Database Business Source Complete. http://search.ebscohost.com/login.aspx?direct=true&db=bth&AN=88284642&site=ehost-live ..FT.

SUGGESTED READING

Lerch, R. (2007). Key elements of a successful marketing plan. *Home Business Magazine: The Home-Based Entrepreneur's Magazine, 14,* 50. Retrieved August 13, 2007, from EBSCO Online Database Business Source Complete. http://search.ebscohost.com/login.aspx?direct=true&db=bth&AN=25396747&site=ehost-live

McGoldrick, Peter J. and Liu, Chilling. (2017). Application of mixed methods by consumer marketing practicioners: lessons for the academy? *Creating Marketing Magic and Innovative Future Marketing Trends,* pp 1463-1464. Retrieved on June 29, 2017.

Petrecca, L. (2007, July 16). Marketers flex muscle at gyms. *USA Today, 3b.*

Strauss, S. D. (2007). A whole new radio world. *Home Business Magazine: The Home-Based Entrepreneur's Magazine, 14,* 44. Retrieved August 13, 2007, from EBSCO Online Database Business Source Complete. http://search.ebscohost.com/login.aspx?direct=true&db=bth&AN=25396745&site=ehost-live

Brian Burns

MARKETING PRINCIPLES

ABSTRACT

This article focuses on the principles of marketing and the concept of marketing mix is analyzed. Pricing is one of the four aspects (product management, pricing, promotion, and place) in the marketing mix and directly effects how a product is positioned in the market. Pricing strategies will be discussed. The foundation of business marketing strategy is based on three concepts: segmentation, targeting, and positioning. These three concepts are introduced.

OVERVIEW

Most individuals who study the field of marketing know the foundation of the concept. It is based on a marketing mix, which consists of four basic elements: product, price, promotion, and place. These elements are also known as the 4 Ps of marketing (Golden & Zimmerman, 1980).

- **Products** are what the seller provides for the buyer for a price.

- **Place** refers to how the seller gets the merchandise to the customer.
- **Price** is what the seller charges the buyer for the service or product.
- **Promotion** is the method in which the seller advertises in order to get customers.

The Five Forces

Once the marketers have understood the concept of the marketing mix, it would be advantageous for them to develop a strategic plan for selling their products or services. A popular model for determining competitive advantage is Porter's Five Force Analysis model. This model lists five key areas that marketers and strategic planners should evaluate when analyzing the competitive environment. The five forces are tthreat of entry, the power of buyers, the power of suppliers, the threat of substitutes, and competitive rivalry (Porter, 1985). Each force has a list of questions to be answered as follows.

Threat of Entry

- Are there any benefits associated with bulk purchasing?
- How much will the latest technology cost?
- Do the competitors have a stronghold on most of the distribution channels?
- Are there any cost advantages not associated with the size of the company?
- Will competitors retaliate?
- Will new laws weaken the company's competitive position?
- How important is differentiation?

The Power of Buyers

Are there any large players in the market (e.g. chain restaurants)?

- Will the large players have the support of small suppliers (e.g. companies such as Home Depot receiving flowers from local nurseries)?
- Is the cost of switching between suppliers low (e.g. a conference coordinator switching from Hertz to Avis)?

The Power of Suppliers

- Are the costs high for switching suppliers?
- Is the brand powerful (e.g. Cisco)?
- Is there a possibility of the supplier integrating (e.g. banks offering insurance)?

- Are the customers fragmented so that they have limited bargaining power?

The Threat of Substitutes

- Is there a product-for-product substitution (e.g. cell phones instead of land lines)?
- Is there substitution of need (e.g. lighter textbooks reduces the need for chiropractic care)?
- Is there a generic substitution (e.g. for insurance purposes, getting a generic prescription versus a brand prescription)?
- Can we do without the product (e.g. fast food because it can lead to obesity)?

Competitive Rivalry

- If there is a strong chance of entry, competitive rivalry will be high. There is a danger that involves substitute products as well as suppliers and buyers attempting to take control of the market.

APPLICATION

Pricing

Pricing is one of the four aspects (product management, pricing, promotion, and place) in the marketing mix, and directly effects how a product is positioned in the market. It should take into consideration fixed and variable costs, competition, organizational objectives, proposed positioning strategies, target groups and their willingness to pay the price. When an appropriate price is selected, it should assist the organization in reaching its financial goals; be a realistic price for the target market; and support a product's positioning and be consistent with the other variables in the marketing mix. Many organizations have utilized various factors when determining the pricing strategies for their products and services. However, there are some general guidelines that all share. For example, the marketing representatives may go through a series of steps as follows:

Develop marketing strategy (perform marketing analysis, segmentation, targeting, and positioning). The team will have to determine the mix of each aspect of the marketing mix formula. The first step will be to develop a marketing strategy for the product or service. At this point, a decision is made as to who the target market will be and how the product will be positioned. Another factor will be the response to "is pricing going to be a key point of the positioning"?

For example, if the product is going to be sold on eBay, the company may consider researching how other companies have set up a pricing structure for the same or similar items.

Make marketing mix decisions (define the product, distribution, and promotional campaign). There will be trade offs between the variables in the marketing mix. Pricing will be based on other decisions that have been made in the areas of distribution and promotion. For example, is the expectation to sell a small number of luxury items at high prices so that the product becomes a rare, unique commodity?

Estimate the demand curve (understand how quality demanded varies with price). There tends to be a relationship between price and quantity demanded. Therefore, the marketing team will attempt to estimate the demand curve for the product or service since pricing impacts sales. The first step will be to conduct market research to find out if price will have an effect on the demand for the product. If the product already exists, the marketers may want to survey whether or not the market will accept prices above and below the current price. The results will give the marketing team an idea of the price elasticity of demand for the product.

Calculate cost (include fixed and variable costs associated with the product or service). Once it has been determined that the product will be launched, the marketing team will need to understand all the costs involved. Therefore, they will need to calculate the fixed and variable costs related to the product or service, which is referred to as the total unit cost. The unit cost of the product determines how much is needed in order to break even. Any price set higher than this could set the profit margin.

Understand environmental factors (evaluate potential responses from competitors and understand legal constraints). The marketing team should find out if there are any legal restraints on pricing. For example, offering different prices to different consumers can lead to cases of price discrimination. There may be legislation that dictates how high the price can go. Also, there are laws that prevent predatory pricing, especially in the international trade market.

Set pricing objectives. There are a variety of ways to set the pricing objectives. Some of the most popular objectives include:

- **Profit Maximization.** By taking into consideration revenue and costs, this objective seeks to maximize current profits.
- **Revenue Maximization.** This objective does not take profit margins into consideration when attempting to maximize current revenue.
- **Maximize Quantity.** This objective tries to increase the amount of units or products that are sold and/or the number of customers or the amount of service that is provided as a means to decrease the long-term cost that was estimated by the experience curve.
- **Maximize Profit Margin.** This objective intends to increase the unit profit margin with the understanding that the quantified results will be lower than expected.
- **Differentiation (Quality Leadership).** This objective looks at the difference in price when determining the target market. While some companies may seek to be the low-cost leader, others will highlight quality as the justification for higher prices. For example, a consumer would expect to pay a high price for a Prada handbag.
- **Survival.** This objective is successful when there is a crisis in the marketplace. For example, the market may be experiencing a price war, market decline, or market saturation. Therefore, the company may be forced to temporarily set a lower price that will cover costs and allow the business to continue to operate in order to survive. In this type of situation, survival is more important than profits.
- **Partial Cost Recovery.** An organization may seek only partial cost recovery if it has other sources of income.

Some of the most classical pricing strategies are:
- **Price Skimming.** When the product is introduced, the organization will set a high price in order to attract consumers who are not sensitive to price. However, the prices will eventually fall due to an increase in supply, especially from competitors. This strategy is most appropriate when customers are not sensitive to price, there is no expectation of large cost savings at high volumes, and the organization lacks the proper resources required to pay for the capital expenditures for high-volume manufacturing with lower profit margins.

- **Penetration Pricing.:** When the product is introduced, the price is set at a lower bar as a means to eventually increase the market share. Once market share has been obtained, the prices are increased. This strategy tends to be used by companies attempting to enter a new market or desiring to build a small market share. A penetration strategy may also be used when a company wants to promote complimentary products. The main product is set at a low price in order to get customers to buy the accessories, which are sold at higher prices.
- **Economy Pricing.:** This strategy is considered the "no frills" approach. The cost of marketing and manufacturing are kept low. An example is store brand products or generic drugs.
- **Premium Pricing.** When the product is unique and the company has a competitive advantage, a high price can be set.

Determining pricing utilizes the information gathered in the aforementioned levels involved in selecting a pricing technique, developing a pricing arrangement, and defining discounts available. Once the prices have been set, the marketing team may employ one or more of the following pricing methods in order to achieve their goals.

- **Cost-Plus Pricing.** The price is set at the production cost plus a predetermined profit margin.
- **Target Rreturn Pricing.** The price is set in order to gain a predetermined return on investment.
- **Value-Based Pricing.** A price is set based on the notion that a customer will pay in accordance to the value understood by the customer versus the actual cost of an alternative item or service. Caminal & Vives (1996) research showed that "a higher current market share can be interpreted by future consumers as a signal of higher relative quality and will tend to increase future demand" (p. 222).
- **Psychological Pricing.** A price is set based on factors such as product quality and perceived consumer value. The company perceives that the customer will respond based on emotion versus logic. For cxample, the price may be $1.99 versus $2.00.

The list price is usually the price that is quoted to the target market. However, discounts may be given to distributors and a select group from the target market. Examples of discounts include

- **Quantity Discounts.** Discount offered to customers purchasing large quantities.
- **Cumulative Quantity Discounts.** Discount offered increases as the cumulative purchase increases. This is a good approach for resellers who purchase large purchases over time versus purchase large quantities at one time.
- **Seasonal Discounts.** Discounts offered depending on the time of year the purchase was completed. The purpose is to offset seasonal variations in sales.
- **Cash Discounts.** Discounts offered to customers who pay before the due date.
- **Trade Discounts.** Discounts offered to distributors who successfully perform their responsibilities to the organization.
- **Promotional Discounts.** Discounts offered in order to generate sales. This type of discount is usually set up for a short, specified period. For example, Ford offered $1,000 rebates for the Taurus in an attempt to maintain its lead over the Honda Accord as the number-one selling car in the United States (Naughton, 1997).

VIEWPOINT
Business Marketing Strategy
The foundation of business marketing strategy is based on three concepts: segmentation, targeting, and positioning.

- **Segmentation.** Customers are not the same. They have different needs and place different values on products and services. In order for organizations to respond to the various demands, they may group similar customers together to customize a marketing campaign geared toward each group. This process is an example of market segmentation. Marketers predict that each segment will have similar feelings about specific products. Therefore, there is a high probability that the individuals in the group will be receptive to the marketing campaign.

The purpose of marketing segmentation is to recognize groups of like customers; arrange the groups according to highest priority; understand the potential customers' wants, needs, and behavior patterns;

and respond to the different preferences with the appropriate marketing strategy. If the goal is met, businesses are expected to increase their revenue and marketing effectiveness.

In order to have a successful segmentation, there must be homogeneity with the segment, heterogeneity between segments, segments that can be measured and identified, segments that can be accessed, and segments that supply the vastness necessary to bring in profits. The variables involved in segmentation are geographic variables, demographic variables, psychographic variables, and behavioral variables. When a marketer collects information on the various variables, he or she will combine the information to create a buyer profile. In business-to-business (B2B) marketing, market segmentation can be tricky because market researchers must work with smaller customer populations that are not conducive to large group statistical analysis (e.g. data mining).

- **Targeting.** Once the segments have been identified, the organization must determine which markets it will focus on. This is the next step and it is called targeting. Targeting involves the selection of customers. At this level, the organization must decide which segments need to be targeted, the number of products to make available, and which products will belong to certain segments. Targeting decisions are based on the maturity of the market, the degree of diversity seen in customers' requirements and desires, the stamina of the competitors, and the volume of sales necessary for a respectable profit. Business marketers have to decide which segments are the most profitable, how to assign the sales staff to the various segments, and how to develop distribution channels. Targeting can be selective (e.g. niche marketing) or extensive (e.g. mass marketing).
- **Positioning.** Once segmentation and targeting have been completed, the organization is ready for the final step positioning. A product's position is based on how the customers view the product (i.e. their perception). Therefore, positioning is considered an organization's attempt to instill a picture in the minds of the customers for which the products have been targeted. There are two ways to achieve this goal: re-positioning and de-positioning. Re-positioning occurs when the organization changes the identity of the product based on the identity of other products with which it may

be in competition. De-positioning occurs when the organization attempts to alter the identity of the competitive products based on the identity of its own product.

To fulfill the requirements involved in the positioning process, the organization must:
- Accurately identify and define the market that the product will be targeted toward and compete in.
- Identify the characteristics that help to sufficiently define the product.
- Collect and gather research from trial customers who will offer their opinions, advice, and initial reception of the product based on its relevant characteristics.
- Determine each share.
- Decide where each product will be placed within the overall product category.
- Examine the fit between the position of the organization's product and the ideal vector.

In the positioning phase, organizations are challenged with deciding which elements of their value proposition they will highlight in order to make their product the preferred choice for potential customers. The three elements are uniqueness, differences, and similarity. Uniqueness is when the organization can say it is the only company with the product. Differences are highlighted when the organization compares its product to the competitor's product (e.g. a Sony television has more features than a Toshiba television). Similarity occurs when an organization advertises that its product has the same features, but at a lower price. Organizations may highlight different parts of its value proposition to different target markets. The objective is to position the product or service so that it is the first thing that pops into the minds of potential customers.

CONCLUSION

Pricing is one of the four aspects (product management, pricing, promotion, and place) in the marketing mix, and directly effects how a product is positioned in the market. It should take into consideration the fixed and variable costs, the competing markets and products, the organizational objectives, the suggested positioning techniques, the target audience and the customers' compliance in paying the price. When an appropriate price is selected, it should assist the organization in reaching its financial goals, be a realistic price for the target market, and assist with a product's arrangement while being compatible with the additional variables involved. Many organizations have utilized various factors when determining the pricing strategies for their products and services.

The foundation of business marketing strategy is based on three concepts: segmentation, targeting, and positioning. The purpose of marketing segmentation is to accurately recognize the groups that are akin to the customer-base that will be involved; prioritize which groups a business will focus on; understand the potential customers' wants, needs, and behavior patterns; and respond to the different preferences with the appropriate marketing strategy. If the goal is met, businesses are expected to increase their revenue and marketing effectiveness.

Targeting decisions are based on the maturity of the market, the degree of diversity seen in customers' requirements and desires, the stamina of the competitors, and the volume of sales necessary for a respectable profit. Business marketers have to decide which segments are the most profitable, how to assign the sales staff to the various segments, and how to develop distribution channels. Targeting can be selective (e.g. niche marketing) or extensive (e.g. mass marketing). In the positioning phase, organizations are challenged with deciding which elements of their value proposition they will highlight in order to make their product the preferred choice for potential customers. The three elements are uniqueness, differences, and similarity.

BIBLIOGRAPHY

Bartels, R. W. (1944). Marketing principles. *Journal Of Marketing, 9*, 151-157. Retrieved November 15, 2013, from EBSCO Online Database Business Source Complete. http://search.ebscohost.com/login.aspx?direct=true&db=bth&AN=6739611&site=ehost-live

Caminal, R., & Vives, X. (1996). Why market shares matter: An information-based theory. *RAND Journal of Economics, 27*, 221-239. Retrieved July 3, 2007, from EBSCO Online Database Business Source Premier. http://search.ebscohost.com/login.aspx?direct=true&db=buh&AN=9606192119&site=bsi-live

Challagalla, G., Murtha, B. R., & Jaworski, B. (2014). Marketing doctrine: A principles-based approach to guiding marketing decision making in firms. *Journal of Marketing, 78*(4), 4–20. http://search.ebscohost.com/login.aspx?direct=true&db=bth&AN=97014757&site=ehost-live&scope=site

The Coke side of marketing: The creative principles that took Coke to Cannes. (2013). *Marketing (00253650)*, 58. Retrieved November 15, 2013, from EBSCO Online Database Business Source Complete. http://search.ebscohost.com/login.aspx?direct=true&db=bth&AN=89930665&site=ehost-live

Deshpande, S., & Rundle-Thiele, S. (2011). Segmenting and targeting American university students to promote responsible alcohol use: A case for applying social marketing principles. *Health Marketing Quarterly, 28*, 287-303. Retrieved November 15, 2013, from EBSCO Online Database Business Source Complete. http://search.ebscohost.com/login.aspx?direct=true&db=bth&AN=67040673&site=ehost-live

Golden, L., & Zimmerman, D. (1980). *Effective retailing*. Chicago, IL: Rand McNally College Publishing Company.

Naughton, K., & Light, L. (1997, January 20). Taurus may tumble from the top. *Business Week*, (3510), 4. Retrieved July 3, 2007, from EBSCO Online Database Business Source Premier. http://search.ebscohost.com/login.aspx?direct=true&db=buh&AN=9701145891&site=bsi-live

Porter, M. E. (1980). *Competitive strategy*. The Free Press.

SUGGESTED READING

Driussi, A. (2007, May 11). Pricing: The lost component of the marketing mix? *Professional Marketing Su, 57*, 6-7. Retrieved October 8, 2007, from EBSCO Online Database Business Source Premier. http://search.ebscohost.com/login.aspx?direct=true&db=buh&AN=25227268&site=bsi-live

Graham, J. (2006). Demystifying marketing or what makes it work. *American Salesman, 51*, 14-19. Retrieved October 10, 2007, from EBSCO Online Database Business Source Premier. http://search.ebscohost.com/login.aspx?direct=true&db=buh&AN=22067390&site=bsi-live

Hudson, A. (2006). Marketing principles you can't avoid. *Contractor Magazine, 53*, 46. Retrieved

October 10, 2007, from EBSCO Online Database Business Source Premier. http://search.ebscohost.com/login.aspx?direct=true&db=buh&AN=19628603&site=bsi-live

Kaschyk, H. (2007, May). A new aspect of the marketing mix. *American Drycleaner, 74,* 38-40. Retrieved October 8, 2007, from EBSCO Online Database Business Source Premier. http://search.ebscohost.com/login.aspx?direct=true&db=buh&AN=25031120&site=bsi-live

Kotler, P., & Armstrong, G. (2015). *Principles of Marketing.* Boston, MA: Pearson.

Marie Gould

MARKETING RESEARCH

ABSTRACT

This article concerns marketing research, that is, the methods a business utilizes to gather and analyze information regarding the market for a company's products, its customers and competitors. Essentially, the purpose of marketing research is to sell products at a profit as well as to develop new products by making effective marketing decisions. There are a number of considerations in making those decisions including economic trends, technological advances, and government regulations. The following is a brief study of some of the methods utilized in conducting this research, emerging trends in marketing research, as well as a discussion of privacy and ethical concerns affecting consumers.

OVERVIEW

Factors Affecting Market Structure

Marketing research enables companies to advertise and sell their products as well as to develop new products. In this way, marketing research is similar to advertising research, product research, and business-to-business (B2B) research. This is so because marketing research is essentially aimed at gathering and compiling information about the market structure of a particular business enterprise, its consumers, and its competitors. A number of factors can influence the structure of a market. They include economic trends, technological advances, and government regulations.

Economic Trends

Due to economic trends, a company must rely on forecasts for the economic prospects of a particular line of business as well as general economic indicators to determine how these trends will affect the company's market. For example, energy prices are a significant factor that serve as a leading indicator for the economy at large and also affect a number of other consumer products. As oil prices rise, energy companies have greater profits and these, in turn, can be invested in research and development of new energy sources and the creation of new energy refineries. On the other hand, as energy prices fall, energy companies will not be as profitable and the resulting investment in research, development, and refinery capacity will also decline. It is therefore clear that a company in the refinery business must follow the economic trends in oil prices.

Oil price fluctuations also influence other segments of the economy. Falling energy prices are beneficial to consumers since they will have greater purchasing power (the ability to purchase other goods and services). Moreover, companies will also be able to deliver their products to the market at a lower cost. Obviously, one industry that is greatly affected by the rise and fall of oil prices is the automotive industry due to the way oil prices affect consumers' driving patterns. The fluctuation in oil prices can affect consumer demand for fuel-efficient vehicles like compact cars and hybrid gas-electric vehicles. In order to determine the demand for these products, automakers need to research the economic trends of oil prices as well as consumer demands for new products that are a result of those trends.

Technological Advances

Another factor in marketing research is technological advances. For example, the development and expansion of the Internet has had a tremendous impact on how consumer goods are marketed. In fact,

the Internet has become a new marketplace in and of itself. Companies like Amazon and EBay have applied longstanding techniques of direct marketing to online marketing and in so doing have become quite successful. These companies have also created a new field of business opportunities for many businesses and entrepreneurs. In order to be successful in today's economy, any business enterprise must provide some access to its products, or information about its business, to its customers via the Internet. Further, in order to determine the potential for a product to be successfully sold via the Internet, businesses must also have an understanding of the market structure of the Internet, and the buying patterns of its customers who shop online. This is a new and growing field of marketing research that will invariably lead to new techniques and methods for conducting that research such as cookie tracking, data mining, and tracking social media (Hall, 2012).

Government Regulations

Finally, marketing research must also consider government regulation. Many businesses are subject to extensive regulatory oversight. In particular, companies in the financial services sector must navigate a variety of federal and state laws that impact the company's cost of doing business. As a result, companies seeking to expand into new markets or offer new financial products must have an understanding of the regulatory framework governing these markets and products. This information will enable them to make a riskbased determination as to whether it will be profitable to enter that market or offer a product. In some cases, a banking entity may determine that a regulatory environment is so

onerous that it poses too many risks for such an initiative to be profitable.

As it relates to marketing specifically, one of the most significant regulatory developments in recent years has occurred in the telemarketing sector. In June 2003, the Federal Trade Commission's (FTC's) Telemarketing Sales Rule went into effect. Prior to this, a number of states had already established laws limiting the ability of telemarketers to make unsolicited sales calls to consumers' home phones. The FTC's rule established a federal "do-not-call" registry aimed at protecting consumers from receiving these calls. Basically, people can enter their phone number on the registry, and telemarketers are required to search the registry every 31 days and delete any numbers on their call lists that appear on the registry. Disregarding the registry can result in significant fines; however, the law does not apply to a telemarketer who already has a business relationship with a customer (Simon, 2004).

In addition to the telemarketing sales rule, there are also legislative initiatives aimed at curbing unwanted solicitations on fax lines as well as to limit spam mail that finds its way onto customers personal computers. At the same time, technological advances in this regard already enable customers to purchase software that blocks unwanted email solicitationsl. Federal regulators are also currently legislating marketing via mobile phone and text messages (Gekas, Gilley, & Moskowitz, 2012).

APPLICATIONS

Conducting Marketing Research

By tracking the aforementioned trends and regulations, companies are provided with useful information about the structure of a market. In addition, businesses must also be able to acquire information about customers. In this regard, there are a number of methods for conducting marketing research. These include customer surveys, test marketing, and brand-name testing (Lubin, 2005).

- Customer surveys simply require a business to contact its existing customers to determine their satisfaction with a product, how the product might be enhanced, or the degree to which customers would be interested in new products. In light of the changes brought about by the Internet, many surveys are now conducted online.

- Test marketing is a process whereby a new product is launched in a small-scale market to determine its potential to sell in a larger market. Many of the new soft drinks and vitamin-enhanced bottled waters that are now widely popular were initially brought to the marketplace in this fashion.

- Another type of consumer marketing research is brand-name testing. Essentially, this testing investigates how customers respond to the names of products. Today, companies long to illustrate that their products stand for something. Brands are not only attached to the products being sold, but also to high-profile public personalities who are hired to pitch the products. In fact, it is argued that these personalities are becoming brands in themselves so that the line between entertainers and branding is not so clear (Tischler, 2004).

Loyalty Marketing

There is a common link that ties customer surveys, test marketing, and brand-name testing together. This is an emerging marketing research strategy known as loyalty marketing. In essence, the purpose of loyalty marketing is to retain customers by offering them enhancements to products that they have already consumed as well as to alert existing customers to new products. Moreover, by retaining the loyalties of past customers, it is possible to gain new consumers through satisfied customer referrals and word of mouth. Loyalty marketing is not only a new trend; there are even new means and approaches to the methods of loyalty marketing. One such trend is called customer relationship management (CRM). CRM is a strategy aimed at enhancing the customer's experience with the product and the company. Automakers, video and electronics providers, and sellers of audio components are increasingly involved in this strategy. Loyalty marketing can also assist a company in determining why customers are not being retained.

There are a number of reasons customers are not retained. In some cases, consumers may be able to purchase similar products elsewhere at lower prices. In today's marketplace, thanks in large part to the Internet, customers have greater access to information about products. A host of websites make information about products easily accessible. Because of this trend, customers have more knowledge and are more sophisticated about pricing, product quality, and customer service. Aside from more informed customers, dissatisfaction with a companies' status can also lead to lost customers. It is important to acknowledge the effect that mergers and acquisitions have on a customer's relationship with a company. Because mergers and acquisitions often result in a company changing its name, brand names and product loyalty are adversely affected as loyal customers look to other companies for alternatives (Moloney, 2003).

Business-to-Business (B2B) Research

Once a company has an understanding of the market structure, the forces affecting a market for a particular product and the customers who are purchasing a product, a business enterprise also needs to have an understanding of other businesses that offer similar or like products. The method of gathering and compiling information about other companies is known as business-to-business (B2B) research. Conducting this type of research provides useful information about competitors in the marketplace and also allows a business to establish successful relationships with similar businesses, vendors, and channels of distribution for its products. One of the key developments affecting this aspect of marketing research is enhanced corporate accountability. Such accountability has arisen in the wake of the high-profile accounting scandals and bankruptcies. These incidents have resulted in increased regulatory scrutiny by federal and state government agencies. Further, there has also been an increase in pressure from shareholders who are increasingly concerned about the effectiveness of marketing research (Maddox, 2005). There are a number of other trends affecting how businesses measure each other.

- One of these trends has been termed efficacy. Here, businesses are investigating how effective ad campaigns are in attracting and retaining customers.

- Another trend that businesses are following is developing strategic alliances with similar businesses. These alliances enable a company to draw on the strength of marketing partners and their distribution channels.

- As with customer marketing research, technological advances are also affecting the way in which companies compete for consumers. This can be seen in the growing use of online video ads and instant messaging. As technology has improved the graphics of online content, businesses are able to better create online ads that attract customers. Moreover, companies with e-commerce sites have found that sending an instant message to a customer is more likely to be received than an attempt to call the customer on the phone (Maddox, 2005).

Other Market Research Methods

There are other methods for conducting market research in addition to those referred to above. Some of these include concept testing, sales forecasting and advertising, and promotion research.

- Concept testing is the simple process of determining if certain consumers will accept a concept, and this method is similar to test marketing.
- Sales forecasting enables a company to determine the level of demand for a product as it relates to the cost of delivering it to the consumer.
- Advertising and promotion research allow a business to determine the effectiveness of advertisements. In order to do so, a company needs to determine if consumers recall the ad, comprehend the message, and if the ad influenced the consumer's decision to purchase the product. This type of research is directly related to the emerging trend toward measuring efficacy in B2B research.

Analysis of Data

In addition to the different types of methods used for conducting market research, there are also a number of ways to analyze this data. Regardless of the methods of marketing research a business employs and the qualitative and quantitative factors used in assessing this data, technological advances have enabled businesses to better analyze the data that has been complied on consumer behavior. One method for assessing this information is called database marketing. In short, database marketing is a technological means for conducting market analysis that enables a business to limit its marketing research to consumers who are most likely to purchase its products (Pizzolato, 2004).

Not only have technological advances given businesses enhanced means for compiling and analyzing data about consumers and other businesses, technology offers enhanced means for reaching consumers by providing access to information about the business and its products via the Internet (Mace, 2012). At the same time, the Internet has enabled consumers to become more knowledgeable about products and the companies that provide these products.

VIEWPOINTS

Benefits & Detractors of Technology

Marketing research has undergone dramatic changes in the past 15 years. The most significant change has been the way in which companies gather and use information about markets, customers, and other businesses. Technological advances have enhanced their ability to determine if there is sufficient demand for particular products and devise formulas for determining market trends even before these trends manifest themselves. In order to do so, businesses must be able to develop databases that identify potential opportunities. By having an enhanced method for analyzing data, businesses are now able to know more about the behavioral patterns of potential customers as well as their competitors. This knowledge has the potential to enable a business to influence the choices that consumers make. Further, enhanced means for conducting B2B research enables a company to gather knowledge about other companies' business strategies. This knowledge can be helpful in devising different methods for marketing a product and in determining if there is the possibility for strategic alliances (Pizzolato, 2004).

Consumer Privacy & Ethical Responsibilities

While there may be benefits for both businesses and consumers because of technological advances, some matters require careful consideration. Essentially, consumers are becoming increasingly concerned about their privacy rights since a great deal of personal information can now be compiled, retained, and shared by businesses (Zid, 2004).

Although there has been legislation at the federal and state levels aimed at protecting personal information, especially as it relates to the financial and medical records of consumers, privacy laws cannot prevent security breaches, and there have been a number of incidents where private consumer information has been illegally obtained by computer hackers. In addition to consumers' rising concerns about the protection of personal information being retained by companies, there are also ethical considerations that must be acknowledged (Nunan & Di Domenico, 2013). This is especially relevant because some studies have shown that marketing has been a business sector frequently charged with unethical practices and marketing research presents particular ethical challenges. The essential question here is the extent to which a society can protect consumers from becoming mere research objects used for the sole purpose of creating increased consumption (Michaelides, 2004).

At the same time, consumers in a free society are ultimately responsible for these considerations. They can take steps to ensure their privacy is maintained and that the companies with which they conduct business have measures in place to protect personal information from being shared with third parties or prevent security breaches. Further, consumers should exercise a reasonable degree of discretion when providing information to marketing research firms. By virtue of the do-not-call registries that have been created by government regulations, consumers can protect themselves from unsolicited calls from telemarketers and therefore have no need to provide any information over the phone about their purchasing behavior. Further, while consumers are increasingly purchasing goods through e-commerce sites of companies with whom they conduct business, there are steps a consumer can take to protect his or her privacy. In this regard, it is a prudent idea to limit the amount of personal information provided in online surveys. In order to protect personal financial information, rather than paying for products with credit cards, there are alternative means for doing so such as paying upon delivery or use of an online payment vehicle like PayPal.

In the final analysis, these privacy and ethical considerations are a question of values and the extent to which people have a sense of balance as it relates to being consumers. Consumers have choices about providing information about their purchasing habits. At the end of the day, marketing research serves a valuable purpose as it allows businesses to develop methods to more efficiently deliver consumer products to the marketplace. Ultimately, consumers have the power to choose which products they will purchase and that choice is a matter of deciding if products are necessities or if they serve some other purpose.

BIBLIOGRAPHY

Gekas, J. A., Gilley, C. A., & Moskowitz, A. Z. (2012). Keeping current: FCC clarifies that a text confirming "opt-out" does not violate the TCPA. *Business Law Today, 21,* 1-2. Retrieved on November 15, 2013, from EBSCO Online Database Business Source Complete. http://search.ebscohost.com/login.aspx?direct=true&db=bth&AN=90337462&site=ehost-live

Hall, K. (2012). Gathering retail intelligence. (Cover story). *Computer Weekly,* 20-22. Retrieved on November 15, 2013, from EBSCO Online Database Business Source Complete. http://search.ebscohost.com/login.aspx?direct=true&db=bth&AN=85656046&site=ehost-live

Larson, M. (2005). Trends point to increasing value from Internet sales and meeting specific needs of customers. *Electronics Weekly,* (2221), 26. Retrieved January 5, 2007, from EBSCO Online Database Business Source Premier. http://search.ebscohost.com/login.aspx?direct=true&db=buh&AN=19405621&site=ehost-live

Lubin, P.C. (2005). Is your research any good? *Bank Marketing, 37,* 39-43. Retrieved January 9, 2007, from EBSCO Online Database Business Search Premier. http://search.ebscohost.com/login.aspx?direct=true&db=buh&AN=17085819&site=ehost-live

Mace, T. (2012). Developments and the impact of smart technology. *International Journal of Market Research, 54,* 567-570. Retrieved on November 15, 2013, from EBSCO Online Database Business Source Complete. http://search.ebscohost.com/login.aspx?direct=true&db=bth&AN=78072527&site=ehost-live

Maddox, K. (2005). Top trends. *B to B, 90,* 1-29. Retrieved January 8, 2007, from EBSCO Online Database Business Source Premier. http://search.ebscohost.com/login.aspx?direct=true&db=buh&AN=15842112&site=ehost-live

Moloney, C. (2003). Top 10 trends in loyalty marketing. *Credit Union Newsletter, 29,* 3-4. Retrieved January 4, 2007, from EBSCO Online Database Business Source Premier. http://search.ebscohost.com/login.aspx?direct=true&db=buh&AN=9987320&site=ehost-live

Nunan, D., & Di Domenico, M. (2013). Market research and the ethics of big data. *International Journal of Market Research, 55,* 2-13. Retrieved on November 15, 2013, from EBSCO Online Database Business Source Complete. http://search.

ebscohost.com/login.aspx?direct=true&db=bth&AN=89072042&site=ehost-live

Pizzolato, R. (2004, January). Is your marketing department stuck in 1989? *Direct Marketing*, 1-4. Retrieved January 4, 2007, from EBSCO Online Database Business Source Premier. http://search.ebscohost.com/login.aspx?direct=true&db=buh&AN=15038273&site=ehost-live

Simon, E.Y. (2004). Do-not-call compliance causes confusion. *Hotel & Motel Management, 219*, 20. Retrieved January 5, 2007, from EBSCO Online Database Business Source Premier. http://search.ebscohost.com/login.aspx?direct=true&db=buh&AN=13832682&site=ehost-live

Tischler, L. (2004). The good brand. *Fast Company*, 47-49. Retrieved January 4, 2007, from EBSCO Online Database Business Source Premier. http://search.ebscohost.com/login.aspx?direct=true&db=buh&AN=13660252&site=ehost-live

Zid, L., Abu-Shalaback. (2004). Too much information? *Marketing Management, 13*, 4. Retrieved January 9, 2007, from EBSCO Online Database Business Source Premier. http://search.ebscohost.com/login.aspx?direct=true&db=buh&AN=12123025&site=ehost-live

SUGGESTED READING

Green, P. Johnson, R. Neal, W. (2003). The journal of market research: Its initiation, growth, and knowledge dissemination. *Journal of Marketing Research, 40*, 1-9 Retrieved January 8, 2007, from EBSCO Online Database Business Source Premier. http://search.ebscohost.com/login.aspx?direct=true&db=buh&AN=9190673&site=ehost-live

Hempel, J. Lehman, P. (2005, December 12). The Myspace generation. *Business Week*, (3963), 86-96. Retrieved January 8, 2007, from EBSCO Business Source Premier. http://search.ebscohost.com/login.aspx?direct=true&db=buh&AN=19025357&site=ehost-live

Michaelides, P. & Gibbs, P. (2006). Technical skills and the ethics of market research. *Business Ethics: A European Review, 15* 44-52. Retrieved January 8, 2007, from EBSCO Online Database Business Source Premier. http://search.ebscohost.com/login.aspx?direct=true&db=buh&AN=20506667&site=ehost-live

Stephen, AT, and Lambertson, C. (2016). A thematic exploration of digital, social media, and mobile marketing reacher's evolution from 2000 to 2015 and an agenda for future research. *Oxford University Research Archive*. Retrieved on June 29, 2017. https://ora.ox.ac.uk/objects/uuid:f6995406-9460-40b8-8743-857c8610139a

Richa S. Tiwary, Ph.D., M.L.S.

MARKETING STRATEGY

ABSTRACT

One of the ways that an organization can improve its return on investment for marketing is to base its marketing activities on a well-considered, empirically based strategy for its unique situation. Among the factors that should be considered in the development of this strategy are the assets and skills possessed by the organization, the drivers of the particular market, the nature of the competition, the stage of the life cycle of the industry or market, and any strategic windows that affect the organization's ability to successfully compete in the marketplace. Marketing strategies tend to focus on providing lower-cost products or services than or differentiating their offerings from those of their competition or by focusing on a market niche. Two examples of industries that have had to change their marketing strategies in response to the changing demands of the marketplace include the automotive industry and the pharmaceutical industry.

OVERVIEW

"Build a better mousetrap," the saying goes, "and the world will beat a path to your door." However, as all too many established businesses with new products, entrepreneurs with better mousetraps, and Internet hopefuls have found through bitter experience, if the world does not know that the new mousetrap is, indeed, better or that it is available, it is unlikely that a path will be beaten to one's door. Further, marketing is much more than getting the word out. Both our snail mail and email boxes tend to overflow with advertisements for products we may or may not want, most of which are unsolicited. To send out a flyer announcing one's better mousetrap is unlikely to bring one the success desired. In addition, different types of products require different marketing strategies. For example, an advertisement for a new walker is much more likely to yield positive results if placed in the AARP's magazine (which has a target audience of people 50 years of age and older) than in *Seventeen Magazine*. Similarly, readers of *Sports Illustrated* are more likely to pay attention to an advertisement for sporting goods than readers of *Ladies Home Journal*. In each of these examples, the cited marketing effort is probably doomed to failure because it is not reaching potential buyers. Further, many businesses find that a single approach to marketing is insufficient for attracting customers. Even if an advertisement is placed in an appropriate magazine, for example, it is unlikely to reach other potential customers who do not read that magazine. Part of successfully marketing a product is to determine the target market that one wishes to reach and then determine the right marketing mix to get the target market to purchase one's goods or services.

To improve the return on investment that an organization receives from its marketing efforts, it needs to develop a marketing strategy. This is a plan of action to help the organization reach its goals and objectives. A good business strategy is based on the rigorous analysis of empirical data, including market needs and trends, competitor capabilities and offerings, and the organization's resources and abilities.

Factors to Consider when Developing a Marketing Strategy

Each organization needs to develop its own marketing plan based on a number of factors. Although there is no such thing as a one-size-fits-all marketing strategy, there are a number of factors that should impact the development of a unique strategy for an organization or a product line and the development of a concomitant strategic marketing plan.

- First, one needs to consider the assets and skills that the organization already possesses or can readily acquire. For example, if an organization has a significant engineering department, it would be feasible for it to work on new projects that require engineering skills. However, if these personnel are already involved in other work and are not free to work on a new engineering project, and the organization cannot afford to hire additional engineers, starting a new hardware line would be inadvisable at best.

- In addition, one needs to consider the market drivers when developing a marketing strategy. These are the various political, economic, sociocultural, and technological forces that may influence the wants and needs of the consumer base. For example, a technological force that has influenced the way that many people do business in recent years is information technology. Advances in this area have led to the need for businesses to be able to handle increasing volumes of information and data and the widespread use of information technology in many industries.

- In addition to market drivers, one must also take into account the nature of the competition in the marketplace to determine whether or not a marketing effort will be successful. Even businesses that start as innovators in their field soon find themselves with competition. For example, when buying a computer, one may choose between a Mac and a PC. Similarly, most soft drinks on the market are manufactured by one of two companies that offer very similar products. There are also a variety of choices available when deciding where to fill up one's car, yet most of the fuels available at the pump are virtually the same. Each of the businesses within these industries has its own market position and strives to keep its market share through marketing efforts. Part of their strategic marketing efforts is to decide how best to differentiate themselves from the competition.

- Another external factor that impacts how a business can best position oneself in the marketplace is the stage of the market or the industry life cycle. Some organizations excel as innovators, for example, being the first on the market with an innovation or new product. Other organizations excel at taking the innovation and adapting it to the needs of the marketplace (e.g., lower price, different features).

- Further, there are often various strategic windows that can affect an organization's ability to successfully compete in the marketplace. These are limited time periods during which there is an optimal fit between the needs of the marketplace and the competencies of the organization. For example, advances in computer technology have been accompanied by advances in data storage methods; although cassette tapes for data backup were innovative in their time, that time has passed. A new type of tape backup for home computers would be unlikely to meet success because the strategic window for that type of device (and type of home computer) has passed.

APPLICATIONS

Competitive Strategy

Once goals and objectives have been set, most businesses develop a competitive strategy to help them meet these goals and increase competitive advantage. The three basic approaches for developing a competitive strategy are to focus on:

- The provision of low-cost products or services;
- Differentiation of products from those of the competition; and
- Focus on the market niche.

Although there are generic approaches to developing marketing strategies, in order to be successful, a business's strategy needs to revolve around the nature of competition in the marketplace, stage of the market or industry life cycle, impact of market drivers, assets and skills that the organization possesses or can readily acquire, opening and closing of strategic windows, as well as other factors regarding the nature of the product or service being marketed. For example, if two companies are competing in the marketplace to sell virtually identical items, they will more than likely need different competitive strategies. One of the companies may have a longer track record for the excellence of its products or customer service while the other company may offer the product at a substantially lower price. Each marketing strategy, therefore, would be crafted to take advantage of relative strong points while downplaying the advantages of the other company's offering or exploiting its weaknesses.

To better illustrate how these factors are taken into account in developing a successful marketing strategy, case studies of two familiar industries are presented. Each of these industries has had to change its marketing strategy as market conditions have changed. The first regards the changing business model for the automotive industry with the increase of vehicle leasing and the resultant influx of pre-owned vehicles. The second case study regards the pharmaceutical industry and how its marketing strategy has changed to meet rising research and development costs and the changing sophistication of consumers.

Marketing Strategy in the Automotive Industry

Much has changed both about automobiles and the marketing strategies used to sell them since Henry Ford produced the first Model T. America once seemed to be the preferred country of origin for automobiles whether they were rugged pickup trucks or high-end luxury vehicles. Today, however, there is increasing competition for the automobile market. Vehicles produced in other countries (or even headquartered in other countries with manufacturing plants in the United States) have become known for better gas mileage, lower price tags, and environmental responsibility. Old methods of advertising vehicles with the "bigger is better philosophy" have, therefore, become passé. Another trend in the automotive industry that came into its own in the 1990s is the leasing of automobiles as a popular alternative to purchasing them, particularly among people who want to have the latest edition of a vehicle or be safeguarded against unforeseen repair costs. Not only does this change the way that many people "purchase" cars, it also means that dealers need to be able to deal with the high return rate of slightly used vehicles that have been previously leased. To deal with such new demands of the marketplace, the automotive industry was forced to adopt a new business model and marketing strategy.

Petiti (2008) describes the way in which the Lexus learned to adjust to the changing paradigm of car ownership. With the upsurge in leased vehicles, there was a concomitant upsurge in the number of used cars that need to be resold by automotive dealers. To deal with the necessity of selling these gently used vehicles, the automotive industry developed certified pre-owned sales programs. Far from offering potential customers the same type of used vehicle that had traditionally been offered, the certified pre-owned vehicle program offered customers real value by reducing the risk and stigma typically associated with the purchase of used car. However, marketing efforts were necessary in order to convince the public at large that the greater value of certified pre-owned vehicles warranted a greater price. In addition, automotive dealers found that buyers looking for certified pre-owned luxury vehicles have different characteristics and need to be marketed to in different ways than customers buying traditional used vehicles.

To determine the best marketing strategy for this new type of used vehicle, several steps were taken. First, the potential of the marketplace for pre-owned vehicles was assessed. When the certified pre-owned vehicle programs were first put into effect, there were no secondary data to determine the needs of the marketplace or to develop a new strategy for sales in this area. Therefore, the auto industry assumed that the buyers of certified pre-owned vehicles had the same characteristics as the buyers of other used vehicles. However, when taking this approach, Lexus found that it did not achieve the number of sales that it expected. To better understand the needs of the marketplace and the characteristics of potential buyers, Lexus commissioned a research study to provide data with which it could build a better marketing strategy. Among the things learned from this study was that pricing was not an important factor in the decision to purchase a pre-owned luxury vehicle until later in the process. In this way, the buyers of pre-owned luxury vehicles were more closely aligned with the buyers of new vehicles than with the buyers of traditional used vehicles. The research results also helped Lexus identify which segments of the marketplace were most likely to purchase certified pre-owned luxury vehicles so that it could appropriately tailor its marketing strategy. It was additionally found that buyers of pre-owned luxury vehicles do not shop in the same way as the buyers of used vehicles; they tend to shop for brands and models rather than looking at the entire panoply of used vehicles. Further, approximately two-thirds of those shopping for certified pre-owned luxury vehicles did at least part of their shopping on the Internet. This helped Lexus better determine where to spend its marketing budget for a greater return on investment.

After the characteristics and shopping patterns of potential customers for certified pre-owned luxury vehicles was determined, Lexus then needed to transform its marketing model so that it better reflected the behavior of actual buyers rather than the assumptions and preconceptions of the industry. As a result of its new marketing strategy, Lexus dealers and salespersons saw a 30-percent increase in the sales of certified pre-owned vehicles.

Marketing Strategy in the Pharmaceutical Industry
In mid-century America, pharmaceutical companies did not advertise to the great mass of laypersons. As new drugs came out, they were marketed directly to physicians through advertisements and the efforts of pharmaceutical sales representatives. Times, however, have changed, and the marketing strategy of the pharmaceutical industry has changed with them. One can now see advertisements for various drugs for Alzheimer's disease, premenstrual dysphoric disorder, and clinical depression during prime time on television. This is due in part to the defining of various symptoms that were once considered a natural part of life or not seen as a specific syndrome or disease, the greater willingness of the public to take medication to solve what our ancestors would have considered to be minor symptoms, and the demands of both the public and the healthcare industry to find chemical solutions to these new problems. Although this would seem to be an advantage for the pharmaceutical industry by creating increased demand for new products, the development costs for bringing a new drug to market is estimated to have increased from approximately $54 million in the 1970s to approximately $800 million at the turn of the millennium (Kvesic, 2008). Given such high research and development costs, it is important, therefore, for pharmaceutical companies to increase their return on investment. As a result, they needed to develop a better marketing strategy to deal with the new realities of pharmaceuticals in the twenty-first century. One way this was done was through a new emphasis on life-cycle management.

Life-Cycle Management
There are a number of ways in which to manage the life cycle of a pharmaceutical. One of the ways in which the industry did this was to develop a strategy to maximize brand loyalty. When a new drug is introduced to the market, it is typically under patent, during which time the company has the sole right to manufacture and sell the drug. However, once the patent expires, companies are free to make a generic

version of the drug, often for a significantly lower price. This tends to eat into the profit margin of the original company. To help retain as much of the market share as possible even after the expiration of a patent, therefore, pharmaceutical companies tend to try to increase brand loyalty so that customers are reluctant to switch to a generic drug even when it is significantly less expensive. Another approach to managing the life cycle of a pharmaceutical after patent expiration is to reformulate the drug or launch a second generation version of the drug. For example, the manufacturers of an innovative medication first introduced in the 1990s could add an analgesic to the formula and market it under a new name.

Another way in which the problem of life-cycle management in the pharmaceutical industry has been approached is through the use of fixed-dose combinations. Pharmaceutical companies can potentially extend the period of drug exclusivity by combining products in new ways for the treatment of diseases that were not previously obvious. Pharmaceutical companies can also release their own generic version of a drug when the patent is expiring, thereby helping to maintain its customer base. Similarly, a pharmaceutical company can lower the price on the brand-name drug once the patent expires in order to be more competitive against other manufacturers of generic formulations. Yet another approach is to develop over-the-counter versions of a drug that was once available by prescription only. Legal options for keeping patent exclusivity are another approach to life-cycle management that has been successfully used by pharmaceutical companies in some situations. Finally, a pharmaceutical company is best advised to cut both marketing and research expenses and sell the product or license its manufacture once the patent expires. By strategically using some or all of these approaches, pharmaceutical companies are better able to remain competitive in today's changed marketplace and maximize their return on investment.

CONCLUSION

A marketing strategy is a plan of action to help the marketing function of an organization reach its goals and objectives. A good strategy is based on the rigorous analysis of empirical data, including market needs and trends, competitor capabilities and offerings, and the organization's resources and abilities.

This means that one's marketing strategy is not static, but must change based on the changing needs and expectations of the marketplace as well as changes in the competition's marketing strategy. In addition, a good marketing strategy is not generic, but must take into account market drivers, the assets and skills of the organization, any strategic windows in the marketplace, the nature of one's competition, and the stage of the market or industry life cycle. By taking these factors into account in the development of a strategic marketing plan, an organization can be better prepared to succeed in the marketplace and gain or maintain a greater market share than its competitors.

BIBLIOGRAPHY

AMA definition of marketing. (2007). *MarketingPower, Inc.* Retrieved February 27, 2009, from http://www.marketing-power.com/Community/ARC/Pages/Additional/Definition//default.aspx?sq=an+organizational+function+and+a+set+of+processes+for+ccreating%2c+communicating+and+delivering+value+to+customers+and+for+manaaging+customer+relationships+in+ways+that+benefit+the+organization+and+iits+stakeholders

Kurt, D., & Hulland, J. (2013). Aggressive marketing strategy following equity offerings and firm value: The role of relative strategic flexibility. *Journal of Marketing, 77* (5), 57-74. Retrieved November 20, 2013 from EBSCO Online Database Business Source Complete. http://search.ebscohost.com/login.aspx?direct=true&db=bth&AN=89746481&site=ehost-live

Kvesic, D. Z. (2008). Product lifecycle management: Marketing strategies for the pharmaceutical industry. *Journal of Medical Marketing, 8* (4), 293-301. Retrieved February 12, 2009, from EBSCO Online Database Business Source Complete. http://search.ebscohost.com/login.aspx?direct=true&db=bth&AN=35054499&site=ehost-live

LaPointe, P. (2013). The dark corners where research strategies hide: Throwing light at the intersection of the new and the old. *Journal of Advertising Research, 53* (1), 9-10. Retrieved November 20, 2013 from EBSCO Online Database Business Source Complete. http://search.ebscohost.com/login.aspx?direct=true&db=bth&AN=86178717&site=ehost-live

LaPointe, P. (2012). Measuring Facebook's impact on marketing. *Journal of Advertising Research, 52*

(3), 286-287. Retrieved November 20, 2013 from EBSCO Online Database Business Source Complete. http://search.ebscohost.com/login.aspx?direct=true&db=bth&AN=79983641&site=ehost-live

Leonidou, L. C., Katsikeas, C. S., Fotiadis, T. A., & Christodoulides, P. (2013). Antecedents and consequences of an eco-friendly export marketing strategy: The moderating role of foreign public concern and competitive intensity. *Journal of International Marketing, 21* (3), 22-46. Retrieved November 20, 2013 from EBSCO Online Database Business Source Complete. http://search.ebscohost.com/login.aspx?direct=true&db=bth&AN=90269468&site=ehost-live

Petersen, J. Andrew, Kushwaha, T., & Kumar, V. (2015). Marketing communication strategies and consumer financial decision making: The role of national culture. *Journal of Marketing, 79*(1), 44–63. Retrieved Dec. 3, 2015, from EBSCO Online Database Business Source Complete. http://search.ebscohost.com/login.aspx?direct=true&db=bth&AN=100279006&site=ehost-live&scope=site

Pettit, R. (2008). Learning from winners: How research drove a new model for the automotive industry. *Journal of Advertising Research, 48* (4), 583-590. Retrieved February 12, 2009, from EBSCO Online Database Business Source Complete. http://search.ebscohost.com/login.aspx?direct=true&db=bth&AN=35651393&site=ehost-live

Proctor, T. (2000). *Strategic marketing: An introduction.* New York: Routledge.

SUGGESTED READING

Bell, S. S., & Carpenter, G. S. (1992). Optimal multiple-objective marketing strategies. *Marketing Letters, 3* (4), 383-393. Retrieved February 12, 2009, from EBSCO Online Database Business Source Complete. http://search.ebscohost.com/login.aspx?direct=true&db=bth&AN=7595206&site=ehost-live

Benflah, Jake. (2016). Journal of cultural marketing strategy: bridging the gap between theory and practice. *Henry Stewart Publications.* Retrieved on June 29, 2017. https://www.researchgate.net/profile/Sonja_Poole/publication/308894478_Are_future_business_professionals_ready_for_multicultural_marketing_An_empirical_investigation/links/57f5afbf08ae8da3ce552fb5.pdf.

Burgelman, R. A. & Siegel, R. E. (2008). Cutting the strategy diamond in high-technology ventures.

California Management Review, 50 (3), 140-167. Retrieved February 12, 2009, from EBSCO Online Database Business Source Complete. http://search.ebscohost.com/login.aspx?direct=true&db=bth&AN=32129034&site=ehost-live

Dahlström, P., & Edelman, D. (2013). The coming era of 'on-demand' marketing. *Mckinsey Quarterly,* (2), 24-39. Retrieved November 20, 2013 from EBSCO Online Database Business Source Complete. http://search.ebscohost.com/login.aspx?direct=true&db=bth&AN=87315649&site=ehost-live

Kotler, P., & Armstrong, G. (2015). *Principles of Marketing.* Boston, MA: Pearson.

Rajamäki, H. (2008). Anticipating and managing the challenges of biotechnology marketing. *Journal of Commercial Biotechnology, 14* (3), 225-231. Retrieved February 12, 2009, from EBSCO Online Database Business Source Complete. http://search.ebscohost.com/login.aspx?direct=true&db=bth&AN=32776742&site=ehost-live

Richards, T. J. & Padilla, L. (2009). Promotion and fast food demand. *American Journal of Agricultural Economics, 91* (1), 168-183. Retrieved February 12, 2009, from EBSCO Online Database Business Source Complete. http://search.ebscohost.com/login.aspx?direct=true&db=bth&AN=36034592&site=ehost-live

Wallström, Ä., Karlsson, T., & Salehi-Sangari, E. (2008). Building a corporate brand: The internal brand building process in Swedish service firms. *Journal of Brand Management, 16* (1/2), 40-50. Retrieved February 12, 2009, from EBSCO Online Database Business Source Complete. http://search.ebscohost.com/login.aspx?direct=true&db=bth&AN=33885559&site=ehost-live

Weinstein, A. (2004). *Strategic target marketing. In Handbook of market segmentation: Strategic targeting for business and technology firms* (3rd ed.), p. 133-154. New York: Routledge.

Wind, Y., Sharp, B., & Nelson-Field, K. (2013). Empirical generalizations: New laws for digital marketing: How advertising research must change. *Journal of Advertising Research, 53* (2), 175-180. Retrieved November 20, 2013 from EBSCO Online Database Business Source Complete. http://search.ebscohost.com/login.aspx?direct=true&db=bth&AN=88284642&site=ehost-live

Ruth A. Wienclaw, Ph.D.

MODELS FOR MARKETING STRATEGY

ABSTRACT

Predicting buyer behavior is often a complicated process that must take into account a number of variables affecting buyer behavior. Models can help marketers make decisions and focus their strategic marketing efforts. Although the advent of the personal computer has made model building for marketing strategy a more attainable goal for many organizations, it is important that marketing managers and other key players within the organization contribute the expertise of their experience to the development of the model. In addition, the organization can use secondary data or collect new data through surveys, interviews, or other data-collection techniques to acquire the data needed for the model. Because the real world is so complex, the model also needs to be complex in most cases. One of the essential aspects of model building is to determine which of the innumerable variables that could be potentially built into the model are important and which are not.

OVERVIEW

Arguably, done correctly, marketing is both an art and a science. The art part of the equation tends to be obvious. Businesses need to develop corporate logos, design schemes, and other branding art to catch the buyer's eye, encourage a purchase, and help ensure brand loyalty. The artwork associated with various media advertisements also needs to be both contemporary to demonstrate to prospective buyers that the organization and its products or services are on the cutting edge yet also distinctively target the tastes and expectations of different market segments. Jingles need to attract attention and be memorable without being obnoxious. However, no matter how stylish, contemporary, or eye-catching one's artwork is or how memorable one's slogan or jingle is, if one's marketing efforts are targeted toward the wrong segment of the market, if an appropriate marketing mix is not determined, or if integrated marketing communications are not designed to maximize the return on investment for one's marketing dollar, the marketing efforts will be less than successful.

Buyer Behavior

On its own, buyer behavior is a complex thing. It is often difficult to try to predict what goods and services a buyer might need or want or to design a marketing campaign that will help sway the buying decision. The situation in which a purchasing decision is made can also impact the probability that a potential buyer will actually purchase one's offering. For example, in a bad economy, less money is available for spending on non-essential goods and services whereas in a good economy, consumers have more discretionary funds and are more able and willing to spend money on discretionary items and luxuries. These two factors are further complicated by the buying situation: Those factors influencing buying behavior that cannot be predicted from knowledge of either the buyer or the situation alone. For example, Dr. Pepper's advertising campaign a number of years ago that encouraged consumers to "Be a Pepper" seemed to meet all the criteria for advertising success including upbeat music, a positive image, and high-advertising awareness. Despite the advertisements, however, Dr. Pepper's share of the soft drink market steadily declined (Smith & Swinyard, 1999).

Variables Affecting Buyer Behavior

Predicting buyer behavior is often a complicated process that must take into account any number of variables affecting buyer behavior. Smith and Swinyard list a number of factors that contribute to the complexity of marketing decisions. As mentioned above, determining the right market segment as a focus for one's marketing efforts is an important part of the marketing process. For example, with the right marketing mix and advertising campaign, one might be able to sell the proverbial ice to Eskimos. However, in practice, it would be much easier to focus on a different market segment that actually needs the ice.

Another consideration that needs to be taken into account in developing a marketing strategy is the multiplicity of products that are available to potential customers. One typically needs to take a different marketing task when entering a market in which similar products or services already exist than in a market in which one's offering is innovative. Similarly, if a product or service is part of a line of products or services already offered by the business, a different marketing effort may be required than if the product or service is new to the organization.

Another consideration when determining how best to structure one's marketing efforts is the possibility of the existence of conflicting objectives. For example, if a cereal manufacturer desired to introduce a new cereal to the marketplace with the objective of carving out a share of the market, it would need to be careful that the market share did not come from the share already held by its existing cereal products.

Another factor affecting the complexity of marketing decisions occurs when different functional areas within the organization have objectives that do not easily support each other. For example, the goal of the marketing department may be to sell as many widgets as possible. However, if the manufacturing department is trying to cut down on warehousing costs and does not have sufficient widgets available for potential customers or does not have in place an effective just-in-time manufacturing system, no matter how many widgets the marketing department sells, the manufacturing department will not be able to fulfill the orders. The effectiveness of one's marketing efforts is also dependent on numerous factors related to the competition. If the competition sells comparable widgets at a lower price and has an established customer base with high brand loyalty, for example, it will be more difficult for another business to gain a share of the market. Similarly, although one can design one's own marketing campaign based on the way the competition is currently marketing their products or services, one cannot necessarily predict how the competition's marketing efforts, goods, or services will change in the future and how this will affect the requirements for their own campaign.

The complexity of determining the appropriate approach for one's marketing efforts must also take into account the fact that the effects of a marketing campaign may last for substantial periods of time even when other market factors change. For example, if one's competition has great brand loyalty for its widget, even if a business introduces a better widget, it may take years to overcome the effects of brand loyalty and win a larger share of the market.

Modeling & Statistics

Obviously, accounting for all the factors influencing the probability of success of a marketing effort can be an overwhelming task. One set of tools that can be used to help marketers make such decisions and focus strategic marketing efforts is statistics in general and regression analysis in particular. Statistics and regression analysis allow for the development of various models and decision support systems that help them better understand the intricacies of the real-world processes and how best to target their marketing efforts. At one time, the use of such tools was laborious and time consuming, and readily available only to large corporations with the funds to pay for such models. However, with the advent of the personal computer and its relatively faster and less expensive computing power, the ability to model market and buyer behavior is available to most businesses.

In general, a model is a representation of a situation, system, or subsystem. Conceptual models are mental images that describe the situation or system. Mathematical or computer models are mathematical representations of the system or situation being studied. Models can be used in marketing to either represent the current market situation or what the market might look like in the future. For example, a marketing model might be developed to represent such factors as the existing distribution system for a product, the value structure of potential customers, or how various types of advertising affect the attitudes or behaviors of the target market segment. These variables can then be manipulated to estimate the effects on buyer behavior if one or more of the variables is changed.

There are a number of resources for model building. It is important that marketing managers and other key players within the organization contribute the expertise of their experience to the development of the model. Such inputs are invaluable for developing a model that accurately represents the real-world situation. Data to aid in building a marketing model can come from a variety of sources. The organization can use existing (i.e., secondary) data that were collected for another purpose by the organization, industry, or other source as inputs into the model. Or the organization could engage in the collection of new data through surveys, interviews, or other data collection techniques to acquire the data needed for the model. Examples of the types of data that can be useful in marketing models include the attitudes, perceptions, and preferences of potential consumers, the product usage of various market segments, or how other factors (e.g., the economy, income, gender, educational status) affect one's buying habits.

Because the real world is so complex, in most cases the model also needs to be complex. However, one of the essential aspects of model building is to determine which of the innumerable variables that could be potentially built into the model are important and which are not. As a result, model building is often an iterative process in which the modeler repeatedly tries to develop a marketing model that adequately and accurately models the real world without including extraneous variables that do not account for a significant proportion of the variation. The difficulty of this task is one of the reasons that mathematical modeling is not used more often by businesses to help shape their marketing strategy. On the other hand, if a model is too mathematically complex, it can become useless from a practical point of view. Decision makers will also have to accept that there is some degree of uncertainty even when using the model. Part of the art of using marketing models is to determine what degree of uncertainty is acceptable so that a model that is complex – but not too complex – can be developed. To do this, a model should be simple to use and understand, adaptable to other situations or products, and complete on the salient factors of the situation. Unfortunately, this often seems a daunting task, particularly for managers who are not knowledgeable in the area of modeling or are not willing to spend the time and effort necessary to build (or have built) a marketing model. Another problem in building a model to inform one's marketing strategy is that sometimes the data necessary to build the model simply are not available. This is often true when attempting to build a model to be used in the marketing of an innovative product or service.

A dramatic example of innovation, in terms of both products and services, is Internet commerce. As a new space for buying, selling, merchandising, advertising, and providing customer service, the Internet has entered into the marketing models of every industry and retailer as either variable or strategy. The low cost of entering the marketplace for entrepreneurs, the cost-efficiency of web-based retailing, as opposed to maintaining real stores with large inventories, the dynamics of social media, and data-informed, consumer targeted, pay-per-click advertising pose formidible challenges to brick-and-mortar establishments that must rely on customer loyalty and experience to counterbalance the convenience and discounted pricing of Internet shopping (Azadi & Rahimzadeh, 2012). Advertising outlets expanded well beyond signage, periodical ads, and 30-second commercials on traditional broadcasting and allowed brands to develop more comprehensive marketing strategies, including digital videos ranging from short animated ads to commercials that employ cinematic effects, plot, character, and recognizable actors. The holy grail of advertising became the viral video, which would spread a brand's message through enthusiastic social media (Hof, 2013; Rothenberg, 2013).

APPLICATIONS

Coupon Distribution

Most of us receive many coupons every week both in the newspaper and other publications as well as through the mail. Both manufacturers and local businesses advertise their products this way in an attempt to attract potential customers' attention and get them to try a product or visit their store and hopefully gain brand loyalty. However, from a customer's point of view, not all coupons are created equal. For example, different people may use the envelope of bundled coupons that many local businesses send out differently than the Saturday coupon sections of the regional newspaper.

Because of buyers' different approaches to clipping and using coupons, the decision as to whether or not to advertise one's product or service with coupons can be difficult. The costs of designing, printing, and distributing coupons need to do more than pay for themselves. Coupons need to bring on a sufficient return on investment in the form of new sales in the short term and new customers in the longer term to justify not only investing in coupons but also in using part of one's limited marketing budget for coupons rather than for other marketing efforts. Further, just deciding to use a coupon promotion is only one of a number of decisions that need to be made. One must also determine the face value of the coupon, how many coupons should be distributed, when the coupons should be distributed, and to whom the coupons should be distributed, among other questions.

Modeling the Effectiveness of Coupon Promotions

Neslin and Shoemaker (1983) describe a model for determining how profitable coupon promotions are. In their understanding, the decision as to whether or not to offer a coupon program for one's product is a complex task that needs to take into account a number of factors. Specifically, there are three groups that affect whether or not a coupon program will be successful: the manufacturer, the retailer, and the consumer. Each of these groups makes decisions about different factors that can negatively or positively impact the effectiveness of a coupon program.

Factors to Consider

In addition, three other factors need to be taken into account when determining whether or not to institute a coupon program.

- The first of these factors is the probability of purchase among potential customers before the promotion. If, for example, the majority of targeted customers will purchase the product at full price, it would more than likely not be to the seller's benefit to offer a discount.
- Second, one must take into account whether the effect of a coupon promotion would be to accelerate sales (i.e., buyers purchase the item earlier than they would have so that there is an increase in normally projected sales during the coupon dates with a subsequent drop in sales after the coupon expires). If a coupon only accelerates sales with a subsequent drop-off in sales, the coupon program may not have been of value.
- Third, it must be considered whether the coupon program will attract potential new buyers for a product over time and if it will be a way to gain a larger market share and increase brand loyalty.

Using the techniques of mathematical modeling, a decision-making tool was built for use by marketing managers in determining whether or not a coupon promotion program would be of value in bringing in and retaining customers. Although the model was developed for a specific situation, it shows the complexity of factors and interactions that need to be taken into account in model building for marketing strategy development.

Internet marketing is especially able to exploit the value of promotional coupons. Consumers looking for a place to eat, for example, can find instant coupons on their smartphones delivered to them as part of their restaurant search. Marketers can launch promotional campaigns with short lead times and target campaigns to particular geographic locations or during defined time periods, such as during the weekday lunch hour. Products that might cause the consumer some embarrassment in a store purchase can be openly promoted with coupons for purchase from a website (Promotional pioneers, 2012).

CONCLUSION

Designing a winning marketing strategy can be a complicated and nuanced task. One must understand not only one's product and service, but also the market or segment of the market to which that product or service will most likely appeal. In addition to understanding the potential buyers, one must also take into account the situation in which one is trying to market as well as the buying situation, that ephemeral complex of factors resulting from the interaction of buyer and situation. Based on this knowledge, one must then determine the right marketing mix, the timing of the mix, and make other decisions about how best to market one's product or service. Particularly when marketing innovations or entering a new market, the multitude of possible factors on which such decisions can be made can be overwhelming. Fortunately, with the advent of inexpensive computing power offered today, marketing managers can develop models of their unique marketing situation to use as decision-making tools and optimize their marketing strategy.

BIBLIOGRAPHY

American Marketing Association. (2009). Marketing. AMA Resource Library: Dictionary. Retrieved February 20, 2009, from http://www.marketingpower.com/%5Flayouts/Dictionary.aspx?dLetter=M

Azadi, S., & Rahimzadeh, E. (2012). Developing marketing strategy for electronic business by using McCarthy's four marketing mix model and Porter's five competitive forces. EMAJ: Emerging Markets Journal, 2(2), 47-58. Retrieved October 31, 2013, from EBSCO Online Database Business Source Complete. http://search.ebscohost.com/login.aspx?direct=true&db=bth&AN=90596367&site=ehost-live

Neslin, S. A. & Shoemaker, R. W. (1983). A model for evaluating the profitability of coupon promotions. Marketing Science, 2(4), 361-388. Retrieved

February 14, 2009, from EBSCO Online Database Business Source Complete. http://search.ebscohost.com/login.aspx?direct=true&db=bth&AN=4474166&site=ehost-live

Promotional pioneers keep the classics to hand. (2012). Marketing Week 36(1), 25. Retrieved October 31, 2013, from EBSCO Online Database Business Source Complete. http://search.ebscohost.com/login.aspx?direct=true&db=bth&AN=84617579&site=ehost-live

Smith, S. M & Swinyard, (1999). Introduction to marketing models. Retrieved February 9, 2009, from http://marketing.byu.edu/htmlpages/courses/693r/modelsbook/

SUGGESTED READING

Aake, D. A. & Weinberg, C. B. (1975). Interactive marketing models. Journal of Marketing, 39(4), 16-23. Retrieved February 14, 2009, from EBSCO Online Database Business Source Complete. http://search.ebscohost.com/login.aspx?direct=true&db=bth&AN=4996125&site=ehost-live

Gensch, D. H. (1968). Computer models in advertising media selection. Journal of Marketing Research, 5(4), 414424. Retrieved February 14, 2009, from EBSCO Online Database Business Source Complete. http://search.ebscohost.com/login.aspx?direct=true&db=bth&AN=5004742&site=ehost-live

Hof, R. D. (2013). How Facebook slew the mobile monster. Technology Review, 116(3), 75. Retrieved October 31, 2013, from EBSCO Online Database Business Source Complete. http://search.ebscohost.com/login.aspx?direct=true&db=bth&AN=87418391&site=ehost-live

Jenkins, Roger J., and Samiee, Saeed. (2016). The application of organizational behavior models to the development of effective industrial marketing strategy. *Proceedings of the 1979 Academy of Marketing Science Annual Conference.* Retrieved on June 29, 2017. https://link.springer.com/chapter/10.1007/978-3-319-16934-7_91

Roberts, J. H., Nelson, C. J., & Morrison, P. D. (2005). A prelaunch diffusion model for evaluating market defense strategies. Marketing Science, 24(1), 150-164. Retrieved February 14, 2009, from EBSCO Online Database Business Source Complete. http://search.ebscohost.com/login.aspx?direct=true&db=bth&AN=16384195&site=ehost-live

Rothenberg, R. (2013). Time to jump in. Adweek, 54(17), 23. Retrieved October 31, 2013, from EBSCO Online Database Business Source Complete. http://search.ebscohost.com/login.aspx?direct=true&db=bth&AN=87485206&site=ehost-live

Sarstedt, M. (2008). Market segmentation with mixture regression models: Understanding measures that guide model selection. Journal of Targeting, Measurement and Analysis for Marketing, 16(3), 228-246. Retrieved February 14, 2009, from EBSCO Online Database Business Source Complete. http://search.ebscohost.com/login.aspx?direct=true&db=bth&AN=33869450&site=ehost-live

Sturts, C. S. & Griffis, F. H. (2005). Pricing engineering services. Journal of Management in Engineering, 21(2), 56-62. Retrieved February 14, 2009, from EBSCO Online Database Business Source Complete. http://search.ebscohost.com/login.aspx?direct=true&db=a9h&AN=16606151&site=ehost-live

Weiss, D. L. (1964). Simulation for decision making in marketing. Journal of Marketing, 28(3), 45-50. Retrieved February 14, 2009, from EBSCO Online Database Business Source Complete. http://search.ebscohost.com/login.aspx?direct=true&db=bth&AN=6740880&site=ehost-live

Ruth A. Wienclaw, Ph.D.

MULTIMEDIA PRODUCT PLACEMENT

ABSTRACT

The dawn of the twenty-first century has brought many new technological advances and with them more opportunities for entrepreneurs to market their products. Rather than developing a simple slogan or commercial jingle, advertisers are using various forms of media to engage consumers on a number of levels, enabling them to learn more information about the product, compare it against competitors, and obtain trial usage or samples. There are a number of vehicles through which product placement takes place, including television, movies, and the Internet.

OVERVIEW

In 1968, Arthur C. Clarke's science fiction epic, *2001, A Space Odyssey*, came to the big screen in unique fashion, thanks to the visionary director, Stanley Kubrick. Like many films, *2001* is filled with product brands that were prevalent at the time. However, Kubrick's vision of the future was ill-fated, at least in terms of those household names he believed would last into the twenty-first century. A video telephone call placed by one of the characters is made on a telecommunications system allegedly operated by Bell Telephone, a company that was completely divested in the early 1980s. Additionally, that same character flies into Earth's orbit on a commercial spacecraft run by Pan American airlines, which entered bankruptcy long before the millennium.

Advertising appears in many forms and in every media. Over the course of history, printed advertisements have been joined by radio and television commercials, billboards, banners, and premiums, among other traditional vehicles. Feature films and television shows have increasingly been used for subtle advertising. However, in the twenty-first century, such media has become limited in terms of reach, especially given the fact that so much new technology meant people in every corner of the globe were connected. The Internet and mobile technologies have greatly increased opportunities for entrepreneurs to market their products.

The New Technology for the Twenty-first Century

No one in the late nintennth century could have predicted the technologies that brought moving pictures and radio, nor could the people of the early twentieth century envision a television in every home. In the modern age, people in every corner of the world are able to communicate via handheld mobile phones. Technology has made the world a smaller and vastly more interconnected place.

As technological advancements (especially those involving communication and information) continue to evolve, product and service providers in the world marketplace must consistently adapt to new developments. For decades, advertisers have used roadside billboards to attract the attention of consumers

as well as radio, film, and television to solicit the business of captive audiences. The manner by which these resources are employed for the purposes of product placement and marketing is simple—the viewer or passerby would be captivated by the message and inspired to purchase the product.

Multimedia

Multimedia marketing employs multiple layers of communication. There are two major characteristics of multimedia. First, multimedia employs a number of different types of imagery and sound, layering text, sound, animation, still photos, video—and multiple displays and combinations thereof. Second, unlike traditional marketing methods, multimedia is often interactive—the user can control the information using a mouse, voice controls, and touch-screen devices. Consumers regularly engage in real-time conversation and events and participate with other parties—in person or remotely (Teow, 1999).

Advertisers are turning to this developing form of information exchange and presentation to call attention to their products. Rather than developing a simple slogan or commercial jingle, advertisers are using multimedia to engage the consumer on a number of levels, enabling him or her to learn more information about the product, compare it against competitors' products, and even obtain trial usage or samples. There are a number of vehicles by which product placement is increasingly taking place using multimedia.

APPLICATIONS

The Latest Games

In 1972, Magnavox released its Odyssey home video game console, the first of its kind. Although the games were limited and crude in terms of their graphics, computer game makers seized upon Magnavox's example, and an immensely profitable industry was born. Today, home video game consoles are commonplace—by the end of 2006, 45.7 million American households had such devices, representing more than 41 percent of all U.S. homes ("Nielsen says," 2007). Video games and the Internet have provided advertisers with enormous and creative opportunities to stretch their product placement endeavors.

A major reason for the continuing growth of video game sales is that the games themselves are vastly improved over their predecessors in terms of complexity and graphic quality. 1970s-era games like "Pong" and "Space Invaders" have evolved into "Grand Theft Auto" and "Resident Evil;" games contain story lines, character development and a level of realism never before seen. As part of this realism, game makers have added consumerism. As the "hero" battles his or her enemy, in the background the player sees a billboard advertisement for a beverage brand. Originally, these products added to the realistic feel of the game but were fictitious. Increasingly, however, advertisers have seen an opportunity in such games. As technologies improve, game makers are not exploring fantastic concepts, but rather are attempting to better mimic real life. As one observer comments, such a strategy creates opportunities for advertisers "in mimicking that life, they have, rightly or wrongly, created a virtual arena that accommodates for the movement of advertisers and marketers into the framework of games" (Woolfrey, 2009, par. 11).

In-Game Advertising

That open door represents an enormous boon for advertisers. Rather than feature fictional products and services, "in-game advertising" has become more commonplace. Apparel, toiletries, and other brand-name goods are readily seen in many of the latest video games. Sometimes, the message can be political; in a game called "Burnout Paradise" (released in early 2008) an automobile drives past a presidential campaign billboard for then-Senator Barack Obama.

According to one 2009 study, in-game advertising will drive spending on such games significantly over a short period of time. In 2009, in-game advertisements generated $100 million—by 2014, the study forecasted, that figure would swell to well over the $1 billion mark. At the core of this development is the fact that video game users continue to grow in numbers.

There are two probable reasons for this exponential growth. First, in an economy that has generated a popular search for inexpensive entertainment, video games (many of which are free, accessed on the Internet) represent a low-cost diversion for consumers. As a result, a larger volume of video game players can be expected as economic issues persist (Knight, 2007). Second, the players themselves seem to embrace the advertisements as part of the realism

of the game—with such connections, they may be inspired to purchase the product and/or suggest the products to friends or via online reviews and chat rooms ("In-game Advertising," 2009).

In-game advertising remains in its earliest stages, but has seen great returns for advertisers in just a short period. As business models are developed that utilize the full potential of video gaming, it is likely that this practice will continue to surge (GameZine. co.uk, 2009). In other arenas, however, the potential has been fully appreciated and its advertising tactics have already begun to replace, in many ways, traditional television advertising.

The Viral Video Market

In the 1990s, systems like TiVo, a digital recording device, presented viewers with the ability to watch their favorite television shows and skip commercials. Such devices made television viewing more convenient for many viewers, but also created headaches for advertisers and networks alike. As a result, networks found themselves at a marketing crossroads—hang on to the traditional form of commercial television advertisements (during scheduled breaks), integrate advertisements into television shows, or seek alternative vehicles for broadcasts.

The latter of these options could be found on the Internet. Since the 1990s, the number of websites dedicated to showing brief video clips (known as "viral videos" due to their email-based spread from user to user) has increased significantly. One of the most viewed websites in this arena has consistently been YouTube, but other web giants like Google, Yahoo, and MSN have also joined the environment. It is on these viral video sites that many of these former television commercials have found a home. A viewer may click on a preferred video and, as it loads, be shown a brief commercial. Unlike television viewers using TiVo or other digital recording systems, however, the website user cannot circumvent the advertisement (Ulanoff, 2007).

Marketing products via viral videos is something of an irony in terms of the use of multimedia to advertise goods and services. Multimedia is, after all, by nature an interactive media that enhances the viewer's entertainment experience. Then again, while viral video sites enable the viewer to pick and choose the clip he or she wants to see, the clip itself is in such situations a part of the video—the viewer cannot control its running. In fact, such videos are not dissimilar from the moniker they enjoy—like a virus, the clip spreads from computer to computer, and with it the marketing message to which it is linked. The marketing effort is therefore peer-based, generating buzz simply by attaching itself to the video clip (*Marketing News' Digital Handbook,* 2009).

In addition to their attaching commercials to existing viral videos, advertisers are increasingly producing their own viral videos, with advertisements embedded therein. For example, Ford Motor Company recently created a marketing campaign wherein owners of the company's Fiesta brand urged viewers who had purchased the vehicles to document their experiences via video. These videos were clearly advertisements, thinly veiled as personal videos. Sites like YouTube, Facebook, Google and others added these entertaining videos, without a single charge to the company behind them.

The Fiesta marketing campaign raises an interesting point about the convergence of multimedia advertising with popular Internet video websites. Traditional product placement campaigns involve the purchase of air time on the media in question. However, multimedia (specifically, web-based) advertising is not as clear-cut. Google, YouTube, and others do not receive any money from such campaigns as the Fiesta effort since they do not require members to pay in kind. In economically challenging times, such conditions greatly benefit the corporations but not necessarily the site that broadcasts their advertisements ("Why free-ride," 2009). In response, many such providers are entering into arrangements with many large corporations to ensure their financial viability.

Cellular Technology

Since its introduction in the late 1980s, cellular technology has undergone an extraordinarily quick evolution. Devices shrank in size while ranges of coverage increased rapidly. As the technology grew in capability and popularity, so too did the consumer's need for its continuing evolution. Soon, cell phones became integrated mobile offices of sorts, combining telephone, Internet, email and schedules. Even videos, music, cameras, global positioning systems (GPSs) and other systems have become increasingly commonplace in the device whose original purpose was simply to make mobile calls possible without the use of a telephone booth.

That evolution has intensified with the introduction new mobile technologies. Traditional cellular technology has been rendered obsolete by digital mobile devices and advanced digital networks. Again, advertisers are evolving with such technological advances, looking to take advantage of the growing number smartphone users to market their own products. Application software (programs that enable the user to access email, obtain traveling directions, search the web, and other activities) has become another arena in which companies are seeking to market their products and services.

Applications Software

Advertisers and marketers are looking to this multimedia area because of the enormous potential it represents. Associated Press and Bloomberg News Service, for example, immediately took advantage of the growing market for applications by introducing downloadable links to their news services. Meanwhile, another media leader, British company Thomson Reuters, found itself lagging far behind its competitors, especially after a series of cost-cutting measures that immediately followed the start of the economic downturn in mid- to late-2008. Although Reuters did see appreciable profits during the first quarter of 2009, it still struggled to generate revenues through its usual endeavors. With an economy that showed little sign of recovery, it was imperative that Reuters diversify. The company pledged to invest $1 billion to build up its multimedia capabilities, including the introduction of Blackberry and iPhone applications (Kaplan, 2009).

While applications represent a relatively new medium in which advertisers and marketers are working, the potential returns are evident. Additionally, many are using this medium to sell their wares at minimal cost, making the value of application-based marketing more enticing. One approach is akin to offering free samples of a new food at the grocery store. The multimedia user is offered a free application, which is a stripped-down version of the larger product. The company looks to use these basic "samples" to entice users to purchase the "paid" version. Software maker Adobe, for example, offers via iPhone applications a basic version of its Photoshop suite (O'Brien, 2009), which helps users modify and store digital images.

Applications remain enormously popular, and vendors clearly see the potential returns. In 2012, Apple's App Store registered 20 billion downloads from approximately 500 million active accounts. While many of these downloaded applications are games or simple aesthetically pleasing programs, they remain important marketing vehicles. For example, one application simply shows a container of the popular mint Tic-Tacs on the screen—as the consumer walks with the iPhone, the sound of the mints rattling inside the container can be heard. Although this application is seemingly trivial, it is part of a larger marketing campaign by the parent company, FMCG, that had considerable success—in one week, that application was downloaded 57,000 times (Milman, 2009). With 70 percent of iPhone users in FMCG's targeted 20-29-year-old demographic, the application campaign was considered a major success.

As companies continue to spar over dominance in the "next generation of cellular technology" arena, pursuit of marketing and advertising vehicles within this multimedia technology will likely continue until such systems become obsolete.

CONCLUSIONS

New multimedia vehicles meant that advertisers could market their products in a far more personalized manner than ever before ("Technology is changing," 2001).

Multimedia has helped advertisers place their products in the public eye in newer and more cost-effective ways. Through product placements found in video and online computer games, viral videos and the latest in cellular technologies, marketers are reaching their targeted consumers on levels that television, print, and radio media have never reached.

Because it helps advertisers directly interact with their preferred demographics, multimedia product placement has also proven to be a cost-effective vehicle. In times of recession and economic uncertainty, such as that which enveloped the global economy in 2008, this benefit has become even more salient for companies looking to weather the storm and is illustrative of the long-connected relationship between technology and efficient product placement.

BIBLIOGRAPHY

Beyoncé signs up with PepsiCo. (2013). Chain Drug Review, 35, 45. Retrieved November 19, 2013 from EBSCO online database Business Source Complete with Full Text. http://search.ebscohost. com/login.aspx?direct=true&db=bth&AN=84964 540&site=ehost-live

Cooper, L. (2013). IT'S BUSINESS NOT AS USUAL IN NEW ERA OF CONTENT. Marketing Week (01419285), 29-32. Retrieved November 19, 2013 from EBSCO online database Business Source Complete with Full Text. http://search.ebscohost. com/login.aspx?direct=true&db=bth&AN=88033 277&site=ehost-live

Diehl, M. (2013). Extra Justin: Just What The Fans Ordered. Billboard, 125, 4-6. Retrieved November 19, 2013 from EBSCO online database Business Source Complete with Full Text. http://search. ebscohost.com/login.aspx?direct=true&db=bth& AN=86534977&site=ehost-live

HAIMING, H. (2014). Brand-Placement Effectiveness and Competitive Interference in Entertainment Media. Journal of Advertising Research, 54, 192–99. Retrieved December 1, 2014, from EBSCO Online Database Business Source Complete. http://search.ebscohost.com/login.aspx?d irect=true&db=bth&AN=96555747

In-game advertising to become billion dollar business. (2009, May 26). Retrieved June 4, 2009 from GameZine.co.uk. http://www.gamezine.co.uk/ news/in-game-advertising-become-billion-dollar-business-$1298511.html.

In-game advertising is a massive market. (2009, May 12). Retrieved June 5, 2009 from http://www.telegraph.co.uk/scienceandtechnology/technology/technologynews/5312188/In-game-advertising-is-a-massive-market.html.

Internet Movie Database. (2009). 2001: A Space Odyssey. Retrieved June 1, 2009 from http://www. imdb.com/title/tt0062622/trivia

Kaplan, D. (2009, May 10). Thomson Reuters launches BlackBerry, iPhone apps; first big step in $1 billion multimedia investment. Retrieved June 5, 2009 from PaidContent.org. http://www. paidcontent.org/entry/419-thomson-reuters-launches-blackberry-iphone-apps-first-big-step-in-1-bil/.

Knight, K. (2009, May 27). ScreenDigest: In-game ads to reach $1 billion by 2014. BizReport: Advertising. Retrieved June 5, 2009 from BizReport.com http:// www.bizreport.com/2009/05/screendigest%5Fin-game%5Fads%5Fto%5Freach%5F1%5Fbillion%5 Fby%5F2014.html.

Marketing news' digital handbook. (2009). *Marketing News 43*, 9-18. Retrieved June 5, 2009 from EBSCO Online Database Business Source Complete. http://search.ebscohost.com/login.aspx?direct=true&db=bth&AN=37697708&site=ehost-live

Milian, M., & White, M. (2012). Sony's Scene-Stealing Product Placements. *Bloomberg Businessweek*, (4288), 19-20. Retrieved December 1, 2014, from EBSCO Online Database Business Source Complete. http://search.ebscohost.com/login.aspx?direct=true&db=bth&AN=77732020&site=ehost-live

Milman, O. (2009). The case for iPhone apps. *B&T Magazine, 59* (2691), 10. Retrieved June 8, 2009 from EBSCO Online Database Business Source Complete. http://search.ebscohost.com/login.aspx?direct=true&db=bth&AN=39781620&site=ehost-live

Nielsen says video game penetration in US TV households grew 18% during the past two years. (2007, March 5). [Press release]. Retrieved June 4, 2009 from Nielsen Media Research. http://www.nielsenmedia.com/nc/portal/site/Public/menuitem.55dc65b4a7d5adff3f65936147a062a0/?vgnextoid=998a30a34c121110VgnVCM100000ac0a260aRCRD.

New marketing approach boosts sales. (2011). Cabinet Maker, (5726), 8. Retrieved November 19, 2013 from EBSCO online database Business Source Complete with Full Text. http://search.ebscohost.com/login.aspx?direct=true&db=bth&AN=59151029&site=ehost-live

O'Brien, K. (2009). Marketing focused on premium products provides the best value. *PR Week, 12,* 9. Retrieved June 8, 2009 from EBSCO Online Database Business Source Complete. http://search.ebscohost.com/login.aspx?direct=true&db=bth&AN=37930970&site=ehost-live.

Reager, S. (2012). Blast Heard Round the Globe. Speech Technology Magazine, 17, 33. Retrieved November 19, 2013 from EBSCO online database Business Source Complete with Full Text. http://search.ebscohost.com/login.aspx?direct=true&db=bth&AN=75358824&site=ehost-live

Technology is changing the advertising business. (2001, Jan. 31). Retrieved June 8, 2009 from Knowledge @ Wharton, University of Pennsylvania. http://knowledge.wharton.upenn.edu/article.cfm?articleid=303

Teow, P. (1999, November 17). Multimedia. *SOA Management*. Retrieved June 2, 2009 from SearchSOA.com. http://searchsoa.techtarget.com/sDefinition/0,sid26%5Fgci212612,00.html

Ulanoff, L. (2007). Commercials reborn. *PC Magazine, 26* (7/8), 56. Retrieved June 5, 2009 from EBSCO Online Database Business Source Complete. http://search.ebscohost.com/login.aspx?direct=true&db=a9h&AN=24341241&site=ehost-live

Why free-ride YouTube is finally winning ad dollars. (2009, April 22). Retrieved June 6, 2009 from Advertising News weblog. http://advertisingnews.wordpress.com/2009/04/22/why-free-ride-youtube-is-finally-winning-ad-dollars/.

Woolfrey, C. (2009, June 2). Advertising in games: An unwanted invasion. *Video & Online Games*. Retrieved June 4, 2009 from Suite101.com. http://videoonlinegames.suite101.com/article.cfm/advertising%5Fin%5Fgames%5Fan%5Funwanted%5Finvasion.

SUGGESTED READING

Grosso, F. (2008, Sept.). Harness power of viral video. *Brand Strategy*, 50-51. Retrieved June 8, 2009 from EBSCO Online Database Business Source Complete. http://search.ebscohost.com/login.aspx?direct=true&db=bth&AN=34738648&site=ehost-live

Hui-Fei, L. (2014). The effect of product placement on persuasion for mobile phone games. *International Journal of Advertising, 33*, 37-60. Retrieved December 1, 2014, from EBSCO Online Database Business Source Complete. http://search.ebscohost.com/login.aspx?direct=true&db=bth&AN=94699155

Kirk, J. (2009). Vendors see iPhone for business. *CIO, 22*, 12. Retrieved June 8, 2009 from EBSCO Online Database Business Source Complete. http://search.ebscohost.com/login.aspx?direct=true&db=bth&AN=38698741&site=ehost-live.

Liesse, J. (2008). Media explore content opps. *Advertising Age, 79*, M5-M25. Retrieved June 8, 2009 from EBSCO Online Database Business Source Complete. http://search.ebscohost.com/login.aspx?direct=true&db=a9h&AN=35868487&site=ehost-live

Ritson, M. (2006, April 20). Interactivity means potential mauling. *Marketing*, 17. Retrieved June

8, 2009 from EBSCO Online Database Business Source Complete. http://search.ebscohost.com/login.aspx?direct=true&db=bth&AN=21207364&site=ehost-live.

Ross, C., Johnson, B. & Hodges, J. (1997). Sky's the limit for Sony's ambitious Station plans. *Advertising Age, 68*, 40. Retrieved June 8, 2009 from EBSCO Online Database Business Source Complete. http://search.ebscohost.com/login.aspx?direct=true&db=a9h&AN=9702140579&site=ehost-live.

Winkler, T. & Buckner, K. (2006). Receptiveness of gamers to embedded brand messages in advergames: Attitudes towards product placement. *Journal of Interactive Advertising, 7,* 37-46. Retrieved June 8, 2009 from EBSCO Online Database Business Source Complete. http://search.ebscohost.com/login.aspx?direct=true&db=bth&AN=23266234&site=ehost-live.

Michael P. Auerbach, M.A.

Multinational Marketing

ABSTRACT

Marketing is a complicated discipline requiring the consideration of multiple variables. Multinational marketing is further complicated by the introduction of other factors, including foreign language and idiom and cultural differences. For most instances, successful multinational marketing needs to take into account the culture of the other country. Factors such as cultural, language, and market differences require different strategies. One of the keys to improving the success of multinational marketing efforts is to do market research before entering a new international market. Global marketing is an approach to marketing in which consumer similarities across national borders are emphasized and local differences are minimized. Whether this is truly a different approach to multinational marketing or merely a variation on a theme, however, is debatable.

OVERVIEW

From a business standpoint, the advances of the late twentieth and early twenty-first centuries truly have made the world smaller. In many instances, businesses are no longer limited by geographical location or sheer physical distance in where and with whom they can do business. An increasing number of goods are produced offshore, transported, and then sold in the home country. For example, the clothes worn by many Americans may have been produced in China, while the DVD players in many living rooms may have been produced in Japan. This trend applies not only to tangible products, however. Even some services can be provided in one country and sold in another. Many hospitals, for example, have X-rays read by personnel who are not only outside the hospital but also outside the country. Picking up the phone for technical support with high-tech products often connects one to an expert not in Austin or Salt Lake City but in Manila or Delhi.

Cultural Considerations

Marketing and selling commodities in other countries can be complicated. Not only are there language barriers to deal with in many cases, but also local laws and regulations that differ from those of the home country. International deals need to take these differences into account. However, when trying to market manufactured goods to another country, it is also extremely important to take into account the country's culture, the people's consciously or unconsciously held basic shared assumptions, beliefs, norms, and values. Part of the goal of marketing is to communicate the value of a product or service to potential customers and understanding the target consumers' culture is key to achieving this goal.

Because of these facts, one approach to international marketing is based on the assumption that these efforts need take into account the other country's culture if they are to be successful. Cultural, language, and market differences require different strategies. In addition, this view of international marketing is based on the belief that the savings realized from using a standard campaign across national borders would be neutralized by differences in infrastructure, legal restrictions, and advertising limitations that vary from country to country.

Examples of businesses that failed to heed these warnings and failed in the international marketplace as a result are legion. Sometimes an advertising slogan that makes sense in one language or culture has a widely different effect in another. For example, a literal translation for Schweppes tonic water into Italian had to quickly be changed to *Schweppes tonica* because the expression *il water* is an Italian idiom for the bathroom. An advertising campaign for a detergent in Quebec met a similar fate when it was learned that the French expression for the really dirty parts of the wash (*les parties de sale*) was idiomatic for "private parts." However, language and local idiom are not the only stumbling blocks in cross-cultural marketing. Many marketing campaigns have failed because they did not understand the values of the foreign country in which they were trying to introduce their products. General Mills, for example, attempted to penetrate the breakfast cereal market in Great Britain using packaging that featured a clean-cut, freckle-faced boy who smilingly said, "Gee, kids, it's great!" The campaign was a dismal failure because the designers failed to realize that British households are not as child-centric as their American counterparts, so the packaging had little appeal. Similarly, the Campbell Soup Company's first attempt to penetrate the market in Italy advertised a soup that "tastes as good as homemade." The campaign failed to recognize the Italian emphasis on home cooking and so failed. Similarly, an advertisement for Listerine that was used in Thailand featured a young couple in a public display of affection. Such displays were objectionable in that culture, and the advertisement needed to be changed.

The Necessity of Market Research

One of the keys to avoiding such pitfalls is to perform market research before entering a new international market. Although a simple concept in theory, good market research can be tricky to design. Cross-cultural aspects can make market research even more complicated. As illustrated by the examples above, international marketing research calls for a suspension of many parochial assumptions. Although some concepts are global in nature, such as the avoidance of illness or the satisfaction of hunger, many are not. It is essential to do exploratory research to learn the other culture's idiosyncrasies before building a marketing strategy and concomitant campaign.

There are several issues to be considered in building an international marketing campaign. First, one must consider how best to define one's product. For example, the concept of "heavy-duty detergent" varies from country to country. In Great Britain, many washing machines boil the water for the laundry, a process that kills any enzymatic agents in the detergent. Therefore, heavy-duty detergents in these countries do not have enzymes. In Germany, however, enzymes are a key ingredient in many heavy-duty detergents. Therefore, the characteristic "heavy duty" must change from country to country. Another concept to be considered is how the market in a foreign country is structured. For example, a survey in the 1960s found that significantly more spaghetti was eaten in Germany and France than in Italy. This finding stemmed from the fact that the survey specifically asked about packaged, branded spaghetti. In Italy, however, spaghetti is usually purchased unpackaged and unbranded. As illustrated by the examples of literal translations of advertisements for tonic water and detergent, translation can have a significant impact on how an advertisement is perceived and received. This applies not only to the words used but also to the concepts used.

APPLICATIONS

The Global Marketing Approach

Although the multinational approach discussed above has much support in the corresponding literature, not every successful approach to marketing across national lines takes this approach. Global marketing is an approach in which consumer similarities across national borders are emphasized and local differences are minimized. For example, the controversial United Colors of Benetton strategy of advertising their clothing line using graphic photos of human suffering was an attempt to rise above local culture and target consumers on global issues that are of concern to most people. In some countries, the advertisements were well-received; in others, however, there was an outcry. For example, in the United States, a photograph of a priest and a nun kissing did not cause a furor as it did in Vatican City. Although this example supports the need to take cultural differences into account when developing a multinational marketing strategy, in the end, the ad campaign was hugely successful. In fact, by the time the author of the controversial campaign left the company, Benetton's sales were significantly greater than when he arrived.

The philosophy of the superiority of the global marketing approach is based on three observations. First, research coming from the disciplines of psychology and anthropology supports the contention that all human beings have certain similarities regardless of their culture. This includes basic needs (i.e., the need for love or self-worth). In addition, most human beings share product-related needs as well (i.e., ergonomic design for tools; need for food and clothing). Second, most businesses strive to deliver the best product they can in terms of performance, quality, and value. This means that many businesses are constantly engaged in the cycle of new product development to stay competitive in the marketplace. However, new product development is an expensive undertaking, and many companies need to be able to market globally to remain competitive. Third, not having a global strategy may put an organization at a competitive disadvantage since just as overseas markets are growing, so are overseas competitors.

Whether or not these arguments are sufficient cause for a global marketing approach is debatable, as is shown by continuing discussion in literature. However, the global approach has been proven successful in some cases, just as a multinational approach is successful in others. Although foundational human needs are irrespective of national borders, this does not mean that culture is not also important. As illustrated by the United Colors of Benetton example, some approaches to advertising are just not appropriate in certain cultures due to any number of reasons. Although psychology and anthropology point out similarities among all people, they point out differences, too. In addition, although there are global strategies that work, there are often concomitant exceptions that make them more a multinational approach than a wholly global approach. More research is needed to find out when and why each approach works best.

Success in Global Marketing

Several factors for the success of global marketing have been reported in corresponding literature. The first is to implement a strategy of establishing a world brand that drives the marketing plan. Although there may be local exceptions, this brand should include a consistent name and product characteristics wherever the product is sold. For example, the red can of Coca-Cola and the golden arches of McDonald's are examples of readily recognized brands that transcend national boundaries. A strong world brand will have a consistent name, a standardized product image, and similar features wherever it is sold. Although many organizations attempt to standardize their ads across national boundaries, others find that a global strategy is best served by a local execution.

A second factor that is important to successful global marketing is the ability to segment markets on the basis of consumer similarities rather than geographic differences. For example, an organization could develop one set of advertising for Western countries and another for countries in the Middle East that take into account the cultural sensibilities of each. This approach looks at cultural differences rather than merely looking at geopolitical borders. For example, it is easy to imagine a marketing approach for a product that would be successful in both the United States and Canada—and Great Britain or other Western countries—even though these countries are different geopolitical entities. This strategy would be based on cultural similarities. Missing from this list are countries in Asia, the Middle East, South America, and sub-Saharan Africa, which have decidedly different cultures. For many products, although separate marketing approaches would not be necessary for each country, it might be productive for separate marketing approaches for each cultural grouping. Some theorists posit that the multinational approach necessitates a different marketing mix for each distinct country. A global approach, on the other hand, suggests that the marketing mix can be the same for larger, cultural groupings.

Another factor that may affect the development of a successful global marketing strategy is whether or not the product being introduced is high tech or "high touch." Literature suggests that developing a world brand is more feasible when the product is either high tech or high touch. High-tech products are technical in nature with an emphasis on their technical aspects. Successful advertising for such products tends to be informative rather than persuasive (e.g., if one is considering the purchase of a new computer, a sales pitch emphasizing the machine's features is more likely to be successful than an approach that tries to sell the product through emotional appeals). High-tech products are typically targeted toward specific transnational segments. For example, it would probably be more productive to target small businesses in several nations with a marketing strategy to buy a new computer application software package than to target all potential consumers within one country. In high-touch products, on the other hand, the marketing emphasis is on the image of the product rather than on its features. High-touch products are non-technical in nature and are best marketed using emotional advertising as opposed to informative advertising.

High-Tech Products vs. High-Touch Products

There are three types of high-tech products: those that are purely technical in nature, those that appeal to special interests, and those that are demonstrable. High-tech products tend to do well with special interest audiences that share a common language—for instance, technical computer jargon. One of the reasons that high-tech products can be marketed globally is because of this common language. A gigabyte is a gigabyte, and there is often little to translate in an ad for a high-tech product. Examples of technical products include computers, video equipment, and photography equipment. Special interest products, the second category of high-tech products, are somewhat less technical, but, once again, have a common language known by their users that transcends national boundaries. These products tend to be oriented toward recreation and leisure activities, including sports and hobby equipment. Finally, products that demonstrate are also considered to be high-tech products. This approach, for example, has been successfully used by Polaroid.

There are also three types of high-touch products: those that solve a common problem, global village products, and universal theme products. These products tend to touch a more visceral—albeit international—response and are more image-oriented rather than technology-oriented. Items such as jewelry, fashion, and fragrance fall into this category. Some high-touch products are also high tech. Luxury automobiles, for example, have components of both. Similarly, Apple's iPod may be high tech, but it is also high touch, coming in a variety of styles and emphasizing storage capacity not in terms of bytes but in terms of the number of songs that it can store. Products that solve a common problem can also be marketed globally. For example, a super-strong glue

has been variously demonstrated by gluing a coin to the street and encouraging people to try to pick it up or gluing a hard hat to an I-beam and demonstrating a construction worker holding on to the hat while his feet dangle off the ground. Another example of a product that solves a common problem is illustrated in any one of a number of beverage commercials that show people drinking a product on a hot summer day. Global village products appeal to a pan-national cosmopolitan market segment. Examples include designer fashions and fragrances. Although these are often high-quality or high-priced items, an increasingly universal desire for bottled water, pizza, and ice cream demonstrates that this philosophy can be applied to lower priced items as well. Finally, products with universal themes can be marketed globally. Some universal themes include materialism (which can be advertised through images related to physical well-being or status), heroism (which can be advertised through images and symbols related to altruism and self-sacrifice), play (which can be marketed through images and symbols related to leisure and creativity), and procreation (which can be marketed through images related to sex, courtship, and romance).

BIBLIOGRAPHY

Barela, M. J. (2003). Executive insights: United colors of Benetton—from sweaters to success: An examination of the triumphs and controversies of a multinational clothing company. *Journal of International Marketing, 11*, 113–128. Retrieved June 14, 2007, from EBSCO Online Database Business Source Complete. http://search.ebscohost.com/login.aspx?direct=true&db=bth&AN=11857470&site=ehost-live

Cavusgil, S. S., & Cavusgil, E. (2012). Reflections on international marketing: Destructive regeneration and multinational firms. *Journal of the Academy of Marketing Science, 40*, 202–217. Retrieved November 22, 2013, from EBSCO Online Database Business Source Complete. http://search.ebscohost.com/login.aspx?direct=true&db=bth&AN=71672986

Domzal, T. & Unger, L. (1987). Emerging positioning strategies in global marketing. *Journal of Consumer Marketing, 4*, 23–40. Retrieved June 14, 2007, from EBSCO Online Database Business Source Complete. http://search.ebscohost.com/login.aspx?direct=true&db=bth&AN=5337363&site=ehost-live

Grewal, R., Kumar, A., Mallapragada, G., & Saini, A. (2013). Marketing channels in foreign markets:

Control mechanisms and the moderating role of multinational corporation headquarters-subsidiary relationship. *Journal of Marketing Research (JMR), 50*, 378–398. Retrieved November 22, 2013, from EBSCO Online Database Business Source Complete. http://search.ebscohost.com/login.aspx?direct=true&db=bth&AN=87734971

Kumar, V., Sharma, A., Shah, R., & Rajan, B. (2013). Establishing profitable customer loyalty for multinational companies in the emerging economies: A conceptual framework. *Journal of International Marketing, 21*, 57–80. Retrieved November 22, 2013, from EBSCO Online Database Business Source Complete. http://search.ebscohost.com/login.aspx?direct=true&db=bth&AN=85872955

Mayer, C. S. (1978). The lessons of multinational marketing research. *Business Horizons, 21*, 7–13. Retrieved June 14, 2007, from EBSCO Online Database Business Source Complete. http://search.ebscohost.com/login.aspx?direct=true&db=bth&AN=4530313&site=ehost-live

Suggested Reading

Ayal, I. & Jehiel, Z. (1978). Competitive market choice strategies in multinational marketing. *Columbia Journal of World Business, 13*, 72–81. Retrieved June 14, 2007, from EBSCO Online Database Business Source Complete. http://search.ebscohost.com/login.aspx?direct=true&db=bth&AN=5546187&site=ehost-live

Ayal, I. & Jehiel, Z. (1979). Market expansion strategies in multinational marketing. *Journal of Marketing, 43*, 84–94. Retrieved June 14, 2007, from EBSCO Online Database Business Source Complete. http://search.ebscohost.com/login.aspx?direct=true&db=bth&AN=4999863&site=ehost-live

Buckley, P., & Casson, M. (2011). Marketing and the multinational: Extending internalisation theory. *Journal of the Academy of Marketing Science, 39*, 492–508. Retrieved November 22, 2013, from EBSCO Online Database Business Source Complete. http://search.ebscohost.com/login.aspx?direct=true&db=bth&AN=63899549

Buckley, P., & Casson, M. (2016). The future of the multination enterprise, 2nd ed. *Springer*. Retrieved June 29, 2017.

Cannon, T. (1980). Managing international and export marketing. *European Journal of Marketing, 14*, 34–49. Retrieved June 14, 2007, from EBSCO Online Database Business Source Complete. http://search.ebscohost.com/login.aspx?direct=true&db=bth&AN=5122045&site=ehost-live

Sheth, J. N. (1978). Strategies of advertising transferability in multinational marketing. *Current Issues & Research in Advertising, 1*, 131–141. Retrieved June 14, 2007, from EBSCO Online Database Business Source Complete. http://search.ebscohost.com/login.aspx?direct=true&db=bth&AN=7572088&site=ehost-live

Wind, Y. & Perlmutter, H. (1977). On the identification of frontier issues in multinational marketing. *Columbia Journal of World Business, 12*, 131–139. Retrieved June 14, 2007, from EBSCO Online Database Business Source Complete. http://search.ebscohost.com/login.aspx?direct=true&db=bth&AN=5542899&site=ehost-live

Wu, J. (2013). Marketing capabilities, institutional development, and the performance of emerging market firms: A multinational study. *International Journal of Research in Marketing, 30*, 36–45. Retrieved November 22, 2013, from EBSCO Online Database Business Source Complete. http://search.ebscohost.com/login.aspx?direct=true&db=bth&AN=85250283

Ruth A. Wienclaw, Ph.D.

NEUROMARKETING

ABSTRACT

Neuromarketing is a relatively new field that focuses primarily on using electroencephalography (EEG) and functional magnetic resonance imaging (fMRI) brain scans to examine how consumers respond to advertisements and products. Some scientists argue that the research on neuromarketing is not yet well developed enough to provide marketers with precision techniques to influence consumers. Ethics will be a crucial issue as the accuracy and impact of neuromarketing techniques increase.

OVERVIEW

Neuromarketing is the application of neuroscience to understanding and influencing the consumption of products and services. Marketing has long relied upon social psychological methods of understanding the motivations, emotions, and behaviors of consumers. For instance, marketing groups and researchers frequently utilize scientifically validated questionnaires, interviews, behavioral observations of reactions during laboratory experiments and contributions to focus groups (McDowell & Dick, 2013). These methods have all proven valuable (especially the use of validated questionnaires), but companies competing for consumers see neuromarketing as a better way to attract sales.

Brain scans, such as fMRI's, enable researchers to examine the extent to which an advertisement activates areas of the brain associated with thinking, vision, and emotional responses (Wilson, Gaines & Hill, 2008). Some studies have even located types of motivations, such as the expectancy of obtaining a reward being located in the mesial prefrontal cortex, whereas the perceived value of the reward is located in the subcortical nucleus accumbens region of the forebrain as well as the prefrontal cortex (Wilson et al, 2008). Such findings are exciting for marketers, who hope to exploit the vast array of expectancy-value theory research predicting human behavior.

APPLICATIONS

Motivation to apply effort in an area of life can be estimated by knowing the level of expectation a subject has that he or she will reach a goal or obtain a reward combined with the value placed on reaching the goal or obtaining the reward (Froiland, Peterson & Davison, 2013; Wigfield & Cambria, 2010). Cross-national research indicates that expectancy multiplied by value predicts engagement and long-term intentions (Nagengast, Marsh, Scalas, Xu, Hau & Trautwein, 2011), which would suggest that measures of mesial prefrontal activation and subcortical nucleus accumbens activation could be multiplied to predict how likely a consumer would be to consume a product depicted during an advertisement. Such a multiplication formula would need to account for the fact that the mesial prefrontal cortex is activated during both types of motivation. This is an important example of how the fields of neuromarketing and psychology will need to collaborate to obtain further insights into consumer behavior.

One of the fascinating things about neuroscience is that it can access consciously unidentified preferences. For instance, McClure, Li, Tomlin, Cypert, Montague, and Montague (2004) found that during blind taste tests (tests in which participants did not know which drinks they were imbibing) people equally preferred Coke and Pepsi, suggesting that the drinks tasted equally good among the studied sample. In accordance, the area of the brain associated with appetite and reward was activated for participants. On the other hand, when participants saw a Coke can and then tasted Coke, their hippocampus was activated, which is important because the hippocampus is associated with emotions that contribute to behaviors. Conversely, the hippocampus was not usually activated by Pepsi. This finding was in harmony with the researchers' finding that people generally preferred Coke when they were aware of the labels on the cups (McClure et al., 2004). Effective marketing may have led to the greater stated preference for Coke by affecting the hippocampus with iconic advertisements, such as a holiday commercial featuring a Polar Bear drinking Coke, and associating Coke with happiness through such slogans as "Have a Coke and a Smile."

Historically, advertisements were placed where potential customers were believed to be most likely to see them. Toys and breakfast cereals were marketed to children during children's television programs, for example. This approach, however, left out numbers of real customers, such as the man who buys his own groceries but doesn't read women's magazines. Neuromarketing may be able to help marketers not only pinpoint targets but also catch them when they are most likely to make a purchasing decision. Women who are ovulating, for example, look longer at sexual elements of ads and are more likely to choose to purchase sexually attractive clothing (Durante, Griskevicius, Hill, Perilloux & Li, 2011; Plassmann, Ramsøy & Milosavljevic, 2012). This tendency is heightened when women perceive that females who may be mate competition are present (Durante et al., 2011).

Data collected from an individual's Internet activity can generate real-time profiles, including gender, age, location, interests, habits, and household makeup. Even anonymous online window shoppers can be profiled using certain quick tests. For example, whether a person responds to certain images can be used to tell whether the reader is likely male or female. A study in Germany found that women looked much longer at shoes, whereas men perused motorcycles much more often (Junghöfer, Kissler, Schupp, Putsche, Elling & Dobel, 2010).

ISSUES

In perusing the neuromarketing literature, ethical issues are a frequent concern. For instance, youth are significantly influenced by advertisements for alcohol. McClure, Stoolmiller, Tanski, Engels, and Sargent (2013) found that exposure to alcohol brands in movies and possessing merchandise representing alcohol brands predicted binge drinking. If neuromarketing leads to even more sophisticated alcohol marketing efforts, underage drinking could be further encouraged. Conversely, the same information could be used to avoid marketing to youth and potentially decrease underaged drinking.

Similar suppositions have been used to argue for protecting youth from advertisements encouraging consumption of high-calorie food with low nutrition density (Harris, Brownell & Bargh, 2009). Some or all television marketing to children is banned in Sweden, Quebec, and the United Kingdom; it is likely that children need training in understanding marketing ploys and developing motivation to resist television marketing (Froiland, 2014; Harris et al., 2009). Parents, teachers, and peer groups may serve as good targets for such interventions, but media-based interventions could also help.

Some consider the greatest risk for ethical violations in neuromarketing to involve the potential for extracting valuable information from consumers without their knowledge or consent, and then using that information to manipulate their thoughts, feelings, and behavior (Murphy, Illes & Reiner, 2008). Unlike sociologists or neuroscientists, who are schooled in the ethics of their professions to do no harm to their subjects, marketers strive to stimulate consumption without regard as to whether a potential customer is likely to benefit or suffer from their decision. Ethicists and privacy advocates argue that companies and Internet providers should have to more clearly disclose to customers exactly what information they are extracting and how such information may be used.

Some envision the legal right to access whatever repository of online information exists, so that they can use it to promote their own health and happiness (Havens, 2014). This right to provide informed consent and access one's own consumer data could itself promote greater ethical behavior on the part of companies who wish to sell their products, whether using more traditional forms of marketing, neuromarketing techniques, or some hybrid of the two.

Another issue to consider in neuromarketing is whether certain behavioral measures that are highly correlated with neurological measures could be more cost-effective and even more accurate than neurological measures. For instance, the Duchenne smile (a genuine smile that engages all the smile-related facial muscles) is a good measure of a positive emotional response to stimuli and has an immediate positive effect on EEG brainwave activation in the prefrontal cortex (Ekman & Davidson, 1993). The tourism industry is considering observing for authentic smiles in response to tourism stimuli (Li, Scott & Walters, 2014). Neuromarketing researchers might benefit from doing the same.

Neuromarketing is an exciting young field with much research and many applications yet to be developed.

BIBLIOGRAPHY

Bruce, A. S., Bruce, J. M., Black, W. R., Lepping, R. J., Henry, J. M., Cherry, J. B. C., … & Savage, C. R. (2014). Branding and a child's brain: An fMRI study of neural responses to logos. Social cognitive and affective neuroscience, 9, 118-122. Retrieved March 22, 2015 from EBSCO Online Database Academic Search Complete. http://search. ebscohost.com/login.aspx?direct=true&db=a9h&AN=93398737&site=ehost-live

Durante, K. M., Griskevicius, V., Hill, S. E., Perilloux, C., & Li, N. P. (2011). Ovulation, female competition, and product choice: Hormonal influences on consumer behavior. Journal of Consumer Research, 37, 921-934. Retrieved March 22, 2015 from EBSCO Online Database Business Source Complete. http://search.ebscohost.com/ login.aspx?direct=true&db=buh&AN=67273980&site=ehost-live

Ekman, P., & Davidson, R. J. (1993). Voluntary smiling changes regional brain activity. Psychological Science, 4, 342-345. Retrieved March 22, 2015 from EBSCO Online Database Business Source Complete. http://search. ebscohost.

com/login.aspx?direct=true&db=bth&AN=8561006&site=ehost-live

Froiland, J. M. (2014). Inspired childhood: Parents raising motivated, happy, and successful students from preschool to college. Seattle, WA: Available from Amazon. http://www.amazon.com/dp/B00LT4OX5O

Froiland, J. M., & Davison, M. L. (2014). Home literacy, television viewing, fidgeting and ADHD in young children. Educational Psychology. Retrieved April 1, 2015 from http://www.tandfonline.com/doi/full/10.1080/01443410.2014.963031

Froiland, J. M., Peterson, A., & Davison, M. L. (2013). The long-term effects of early parent involvement and parent expectation in the USA. School Psychology International, 34, 33-50. Retrieved March 22, 2015 from EBSCO Online Database Education Search Complete. http://search.ebscohost.com/login.aspx?direct=true&db=ehh&AN=85042227&site=ehost-live

Harris, J. L., Brownell, K. D., & Bargh, J. A. (2009). The food marketing defense model: Integrating psychological research to protect youth and inform public policy. Social Issues and Policy Review, 3, 211-271. Retrieved March 22, 2015 from EBSCO Online Database Academic Search Complete. http://search.ebscohost.com/login.aspx?direct=true&db=a9h&AN=93588887&site=ehost-live

Havens, J. C. (2014). Hacking happiness: How your personal data counts and how tracking it can change the world. New York, NY: Penguin.

Junghöfer, M., Kissler, J., Schupp, H. T., Putsche, C., Elling, L., & Dobel, C. (2010). A fast neural signature of motivated attention to consumer goods separates the sexes. Frontiers in Human Neuroscience, 4, 179.

Knutson, B., Taylor, J., Kaufman, M., Peterson, R. & Glover, G. (2005). Distributed neural representation of expected value. Journal of Neuroscience, 25: 4806-4812. Retrieved March 22, 2015 from EBSCO Online Database Academic Search Complete. http://search.ebscohost.com/ login.aspx?direct=true&db=a9h&AN=17346481&site=ehost-live

Li, S., Scott, N., & Walters, G. (2014). Current and potential methods for measuring emotion in tourism experiences: A review. Current Issues in Tourism.

http://www. tandfonline.com/eprint/D6chyI4jT-2vjVAXjIzBh/full#.VKGkEl4AU

McClure, A. C., Stoolmiller, M., Tanski, S. E., Engels, R. C., & Sargent, J. D. (2013). Alcohol marketing receptivity, marketing specific cognitions, and underage binge drinking. Alcoholism: Clinical and Experimental Research, 37(s1), E404-E413. Retrieved March 22, 2015 from EBSCO Online Database Academic Search Complete. http://search.ebscohost.com/login.aspx?direct=true&db=a9h&AN=84783260&site=ehost-live

McClure, S. M., Li, J., Tomlin, D., Cypert, K. S., Montague, L. M., & Montague, P. R. (2004). Neural correlates of behavioral preference for culturally familiar drinks. Neuron, 44, 379-387. Retrieved March 22, 2015 from EBSCO Online Database Academic Search Complete. http://search.ebscohost.com/login.aspx?direct=true&db=aph&AN=14714877&site=ehost-live

McDowell, W. S., & Dick, S. J. (2013). The marketing of neuromarketing: Brand differentiation strategies employed by prominent neuromarketing firms to attract media clients. Journal of Media Business Studies, 10, 25-40. Retrieved December 2, 2014 from EBSCO Online Database Business Source Complete. Retrieved March 22, 2015 from EBSCO Online Database Academic Search Complete. http://search.ebscohost.com.source/login.aspx? direct=true&db=buh&AN=88014379&site=ehost-live

Murphy, E. R., Illes, J., & Reiner, P. B. (2008). Neuroethics of neuromarketing. Journal of Consumer Behaviour, 7(4/5), 293-302. Retrieved December 2, 2014 from EBSCO Online Database Business Source Complete. http://search.ebscohost.com/login.aspx?direct=true&db=buh&AN=34074794&site=ehost-live

Nagengast, B., Marsh, H. W., Scalas, L. F., Xu, M. K., Hau, K. T., & Trautwein, U. (2011). Who took the "x" out of expectancy-value theory? A psychological mystery, a substantive-methodological synergy, and a cross-national generalization. Psychological Science, 22, 1058-1066. Retrieved March 22, 2015 from EBSCO Online Database Academic Search Complete. http://search.ebscohost.com /login.aspx?direct=true&db=a9h&AN=67744938&site=ehost-live

Plassmann, H., Ramsøy, T. Z., & Milosavljevic, M. (2012). Branding the brain: A critical review and outlook. Journal of Consumer Psychology, 22, 18-36. Retrieved March 22, 2015 from EBSCO Online Database Business Source Complete. http://search.ebscohost.com/login.aspx?direct= true&db=bth&AN=73286235&site=ehost-live

Whitney, N. & Froiland, J. M. (in press). Parenting style, gender, beer drinking, and drinking problems of college students. International Journal of Psychology: A Biopsychosocial Approach.

Wigfield, A., & Cambria, J. (2010). Students' achievement values, goal orientations, and interest: Definitions, development, and relations to achievement outcomes. Developmental Review, 30, 1-35. Retrieved March 22, 2015 from EBSCO Online Database Education Research Complete. http://search.ebscohost.com/login.aspx?direct= true&db=ehh&AN=48465230&site=ehost-live

Wilson, R. M., Gaines, J., & Hill, R. P. (2008). Neuromarketing and consumer free will. Journal of Consumer Affairs, 42, 389-410. Retrieved December 2, 2014 from EBSCO Online Database Business Source Complete. http://search.ebscohost.com/login.aspx?direct= true&db=buh&AN=34038024&site=ehost-live

SUGGESTED READING

Adhami, M. (2013). Using neuromarketing to discover how we really feel about apps. International Journal of Mobile Marketing, 8, 95-103. Retrieved December 2, 2014 from EBSCO Online Database Business Source Complete. http://search.ebscohost.com/login.aspx?direct= true&db=buh&AN=89412796&site=ehost-live

Booth, D. A., & Freeman, R. J. (2014). Mind-reading versus neuromarketing: How does a product make an impact on the consumer? Journal of Consumer Marketing, 31, 177-189. Retrieved March 22, 2015 from EBSCO Online Database Business Source Complete. http://search.ebscohost.com/login.aspx?direct=true&db=bth&AN=99127542&site=ehost-live

Eser, Z., Isin, F. B., & Tolon, M. (2011). Perceptions of marketing academics, neurologists, and marketing professionals about neuromarketing. Journal of Marketing Management, 27, 854-868. Retrieved December 2, 2014 from EBSCO Online Database Business Source Complete. http://search.ebscohost.com/login.aspx?direct= true&db=buh&AN=63296717&site=ehost-live

Flores, J., Baruca, A., & Saldivar, R. (2014). Is neuro-marketing ethical? consumers say yes. consumers say no. Journal Of Legal, Ethical & Regulatory Issues, 17, 77-91. Retrieved March 22, 2015 from EBSCO Online Database Business Source Complete. http://search.ebscohost.com/ login.aspx?direct=true&db=bth&AN=100277211&site=ehost-live

Green, S., & Holbert, N. (2012). Gifts of the neuro-magi. Marketing Research, 24, 10-15. Retrieved December 2, 2014 from EBSCO Online Database Business Source Complete. http://search.ebscohost.com/login.aspx?direct= true&db=buh&AN=83066537&site=ehost-live

Lee, E., Kwon, G., Shin, H., Yang, S., Lee, S., & Suh, M. (2014). The spell of green: Can frontal EEG activations identify green consumers? Journal of Business Ethics, 122, 511-521. Retrieved December 2, 2014 from EBSCO Online Database Business Source Complete. http://search.ebscohost.com/login.aspx?direct=true&db=buh&AN=96797271&site=ehost-live

Leighton, J., & Dalvit, S. (2011). The branded mind: What neuroscience really tells us about the puzzle of the brain and the brand. International Journal of Advertising, 30, 723-725. Retrieved December 2, 2014 from EBSCO Online Database Business Source Complete. http://search. ebscohost. com/login.aspx?direct=true&db=buh&AN=670 42724&site=ehost-live

McRae, E., Carrabis, J., Carrabis, S., & Hamel, S. (2013). Want to be loved? Go mobile! International Journal of Mobile Marketing, 8, 55-66. Retrieved December 2, 2014 from EBSCO Online Database Business Source Complete. http:// search.ebscohost.com/login. aspx?direct=true&db=buh&AN=95277947&site=ehost-live

Samuel Babu, S., & Prasanth Vidyasagar, T. (2012). Neuromarketing: Is Campbell in soup? IUP Journal of Marketing Management, 11, 76-100. Retrieved December 2, 2014 from EBSCO Online Database Business Source Complete. http:// search.ebscohost.com/ login.aspx?direct=true&db=buh&AN=78153491&site=ehost-live

Staton, Steven J., et al. (2016). Neuromarketing: ethical implications of its use and potential misue. J Bus Ethics. Retrieved June 29, 2017. https://www.researchgate.net/profile/Steven_Stanton/publication/295179863_Neuromarketing_Ethical_Implications_of_its_Use_and_Potential_Misuse/links/56d8a15108aee73df6cd0019.pdf

Va, K. P. (2015). Reinventing the art of marketing in the light of digitalization and neuroimaging. Amity Global Business Review, 10, 75-80. Retrieved March 22, 2015 from EBSCO Online Database Business Source Complete. http://search.ebscohost.com/login.aspx?direct= true&db=bth&AN=1 01518085&site=ehost-live

John Mark Froiland, Ph.D.

NEW PRODUCT MANAGEMENT

ABSTRACT

The proliferation of new products on the market today means that most organizations need to be involved in new product development to stay competitive. This requires the application of systematic methods to all processes from conceptualization through marketing. Management of new product-development efforts, however, can be more difficult than the management of established product lines. To be successful, a new product needs to be managed as if it were an entrepreneurial enterprise. Part of managing a new product-development effort is the function of risk management and control. Although some factors in new product development are beyond the control of the manager, many are not. A number of tools are available to help the new product-development manager successfully bring a new product to market.

OVERVIEW

Although occasionally new products just evolve, more often than not they are the product of a coordinated effort by a product-development team. Members of this team work together to bring a new product to the market that will help the organization maintain or gain a competitive edge. New product development is the application of systematic methods to all processes necessary to bring a new product to the marketplace from conceptualization through marketing. New products can be improvements on existing products or total innovations to what currently exists in the marketplace.

Particularly in the growth industry of high-technology products, change, innovation, and new product development have become a way of life. As a result, new product development is essential to many industries today. More new products are appearing on the market today than ever before. Today's cutting-edge technology frequently becomes tomorrow's distant memory as the proliferation of products on the market continues. This means that for an organization to stay ahead of its competition, it must be on the leading edge of its field. Otherwise, the organization can experience numerous problems that can affect its bottom line including slow or no growth, a decreasing customer base, fewer orders from existing customers, or increasing pressure from the marketplace to lower one's prices. As a result, regular and efficient development and introduction of new products has become a necessity in many industries.

The management of new product development, however, can be more difficult than the management of established product lines due to unpredictability stemming from several sources. First, the new product-development process by definition is a creative process and, therefore, unpredictable. Although less so for products that are merely slight modifications and upgrades to current products, the development of new products or innovations requires the solution to new problems and the development of creative design solutions. These processes cannot be regulated in the same way that calibrating a machine can help to keep widgets on a production line within specification. As such, solutions to problems cannot necessarily be scheduled. Similarly, the reaction of the marketplace to a new product cannot be predicted with 100-percent accuracy. What looks good on the engineering drawing board may be largely ignored by the buying public. On the other hand, what seems like a small change to the designer may receive an overwhelming response in the marketplace. Similarly, although the new product may achieve a great initial response, the demand may quickly die down (e.g., if a competitor releases a more popular product or if there was only a limited

market and the product is durable). In addition, delays in introducing a new product into the marketplace can also increase the risk of the venture due to the possibility of the competition releasing a similar product before and thereby gaining the competitive edge. There are ways to help both technical and marketing managers with these problems. However, new product development always involves a degree of risk.

To be successful, a new product needs to be managed as if it were an entrepreneurial enterprise - which, indeed, it is. New product development may begin with brainstorming activities or from the idea of a creative observer of a marketplace within the organization. These ideas may come from many sources, including monitoring of market changes and the actions of the competition, merger and acquisition possibilities, research and development, or analysis of market or consumer buying trends. In addition to these inputs, new product-development decisions need to consider an economic analysis to determine the risks of the new venture to the organization.

Risk Reduction
One of the major goals when managing new product development is to reduce risk. Risk is the quantifiable probability that a financial investment's actual return will be lower than expected. Higher risks mean both a greater probability of loss and a possibility of greater return on investment. To be successful, managers of new product development need to manage the risks associated with the new venture. This process includes analyzing the tasks and activities of the project, planning ways to reduce the impact if the predicted normal course of events does not occur, and implementing reporting procedures so that project problems are discovered earlier in the process rather than later. The analysis activity of risk management involves the determination of what factors could cause the project to fail, what the consequences of such failure might be, and how likely failure is to occur. Various formulas are available to help managers make tradeoffs between the risks incurred for various options based on the comparative severity and importance of each risk. For example, if there is a high probability that a given activity in the process is likely to go wrong but will have little impact on the overall completion of the project, it is probably less important than an activity that has a smaller chance of failing but that would prevent successful

completion of the project. Such determinations can be used in the development and implementation of a plan to handle the possibility of failure at any one of these points.

Team Creation & New Product Development

Although some factors in new product development are beyond the control of the manager (e.g., the creative process; actions of the competition), many are not. First, it is important that management develops a team with the appropriate resources and expertise for new product development. Most important to the success of a new product venture is technical personnel with the expertise needed to design, develop, and bring the product to market. Included in the technical team should be personnel who can make technical assessments, design products, and manufacture products. However, although technical expertise and excellence are the *sine quibus non* of new product development, they alone are not sufficient for success in the marketplace. In addition, the technical team needs to be supported by a marketing support team that can determine how best to position the new product within the marketplace. This team should include personnel who can perform adequate marketing research, sales personnel, and advertising and promotional personnel. The marketing team should collect and analyze data concerning the needs and trends of the marketplace so that the technical team can better design the new product and the marketing team can better position it. This includes information about the wants and needs of potential customers, factors on which potential customers make their buying decisions for this type of product, and the potential customers' buying power. In addition, the marketing team needs to be able to research the competition and their activities, including their strengths, weaknesses, and strategies. This will enable the new product-development management team to better craft its own strategy so that it can gain or maintain a competitive advantage.

Project managers are not the only level of management who need to be involved in new product development. In a study of more than 700 new product-development teams, it was found that only 7 percent of them became enormous successes. Those that did all had the hands-on involvement of senior-level management (e.g., CEOs, division heads).

This involvement was not just perfunctory, however. Senior-level management on the most successful projects played a very active role in the development process from the first day of the project. Senior managers on successful new development projects tended to work closely with the product-development team to determine what features or resources are essential for its task and then enable the team to do the best job possible by providing these things. Top-level managers also helped the product-development team cut through red tape and circumvent rules as necessary to pave the way for its success. In addition, top management on successful projects tended to encourage the team in its work and ensure commitment to the project throughout the organization. This involvement, however, needs to be consistent. The study found that surprise visits by top management can distract the project team from its task and take away precious time from its development work. Although the involvement of top management is essential, these individuals also need to recognize their limitations. Senior managers who try to impose cosmetic fixes on technical problems did not help the project in the long run and also had a tendency to alienate the project team.

APPLICATIONS

New product development is, in many ways, where the creativity of art or science meets the cold reality of marketing and profits. Although sometimes ideas seemingly occur as sudden, blinding flashes of insight, in most cases they are the end result of a long, hard trail of trial and error; working over a product design until it is a marketable entity. In the best of all possible worlds, the creative process could take place at one's leisure: The new product-development team for the fast food restaurant chain could take its time developing the perfect, flavorful, fat-free, low-calorie burger; the toothpaste manufacturer could take its time developing the all-encompassing toothpaste that eliminates the need to rinse or floss; the engineering company could tweak a hardware or software design until it does not only what it is intended to do but also all that the engineers can design it to do. However, due to pragmatic constraints, very seldom is the creative process allowed such free rein.

Constraints upon New Product Development

Organizations have to be competitive to remain in business. For the most part, the longer the time taken by the creative team to develop a new product, the higher the probability that the competition will release the product first. Therefore, in many cases, the pressure on the organization is not only to be the best, but also to be the first in order to maintain a competitive edge.

In this environment, it is often true that "perfect is the enemy of good enough." Creativity is put on a schedule and must remain within a budget.

Nowhere is this scenario truer than in the high-tech world of hardware and software engineering. Although in other industries, new product development is often part of an effort to stay ahead of the competition, in the engineering arena, new product development is often performed to a schedule with deadlines imposed by the customer. This situation makes management—the process of efficiently and effectively accomplishing work through the coordination and supervision of others—more important than ever.

To do this, most large development projects for new products require careful project management. This is the process of planning, monitoring, and controlling a unique set of tasks that have a discrete beginning, end, and outcome. The project-management process is performed within the three constraints of time, costs, and scope. The goal of project management is to produce a technically acceptable product that is both ontime and within budget. To do this, project management attempts to reduce the risks associated with the project and maximize the benefits;,including profit and marketability.

Risk Control

In addition to the analysis and planning processes discussed above, good risk management also requires risk control. This management responsibility includes monitoring the project risks so that problems can be caught earlier rather than later in the process and the contingency plan can be put into effect as soon as possible. There are a number of tools that the project manager has at his or her disposal in order to work within these constraints. For example, critical path management (CPM) is a tool that helps project managers analyze the activities that need to be performed to accomplish the project in a timely manner and determine when each needs to be accomplished so that the rest of the project can proceed on schedule. Managers can also be helped in their jobs by resource loading, the process of examining the project to determine which resources are most critical to the success of the project, and proportioning them among the various activities. Another widely used project-management tool is the Program Evaluation Review Technique (PERT), which estimates not only the expected length of time to complete each activity in the project, but also the shortest and longest times that each activity could take. This technique gives project managers a window for each activity and helps them better predict future impact on the project if schedule estimates are not met. PERT also helps project managers determine the exact status of the project and predict where any potential trouble areas lie that might negatively impact either the schedule or budget of the project. The Gantt chart is another popular scheduling tool that lists all the tasks to be accomplished for the project and plots them on the time line with an indication of the projected start and end dates for each activity. Kanban is another popular project-management tool, and there are numerous software programs for project managers, including Microsoft Project.

Maximizing the effectiveness of the risk-monitoring process, particularly on large new development projects, also requires a risk-reporting structure so that those working closely on the at-risk activities can report problems to management in a timely manner and appropriate action can be taken to correct the problem. Large projects for new product development that are being designed on contract to a design specification typically build in periodic formal reviews held between both the contractor and the customer to jointly determine the status of the project and whether or not mid-course corrections are needed. Two major reviews that are often conducted on such projects are the preliminary design review (PDR) and the critical design review (CDR). The PDR (or sometimes a series of smaller PDRs) is conducted to determine whether or not the project team understands the preliminary design well enough to start work on a detail design. The review is attended by representatives of all the significant stakeholders in the project: -he technical team, quality-assurance personnel, customer liaisons, management, customer representatives, and user representatives.

Some of the issues addressed at PDR include what factors are driving the system design (e.g., customer requirements, performance, reliability, hardware or software limitations) and how these are prioritized, what tradeoff analyses between performance and costs have been done to determine the most efficient way to meet the requirements of the design specification and the impact of one section of the design on the rest of the product, a critique of the design alternatives, discussions of how the system will be tested, and discussions of schedule, milestones, problems, and risks. At this time, the contractor may also do a live demonstration or other proof-of-concept to support the proposed design.

Another major design performed on large hardware or software projects is the critical design review (CDR). This review is conducted before the design is released for manufacturing. Progressive or incremental CDRs may occur for subsystems of the project (e.g., software engineering, hardware engineering, training), followed by a system-level CDR to determine the completeness and feasibility of the design as a whole. The purpose of the CDR is to determine whether or not the design of the new product is at a point where it is good enough to begin implementation. Participants in the CDR are from the same functions as those in the PDR. Material covered at a CDR may include a discussion and justification of any major changes that have been made to the design since the PDR, a demonstration or discussion of the results of prototyping efforts, specifics of the testing strategy, and discussions of schedule, milestones, problems, and risks.

BIBLIOGRAPHY

Calantone, R. J., Schmidt, J. B., Song, X. M. (1996). Controllable factors of new product success: A cross-national comparison. *Marketing Science, 15,* 341-358. Retrieved June 13, 2007, from EBSCO Online Database Business Source Complete. http://search.ebscohost.com/login.aspx?direct=true&db=bth&AN=149431&site=ehost-live

Capozzi, M.M., Horn, J., & Kellen, A. (2013). Battle-test your innovation strategy. *Mckinsey Quarterly,* 127-131. Retrieved November 15, 2013, from EBSCO Online Database Business Source Complete. http://search.ebscohost.com/login.aspx?direct=true&db=bth&AN=85278086&site=ehost-live

Jae Young, C., Jungwoo, S., & Jongsu, L. (2013). Strategic Management of New Products: Ex-Ante Simulation and Market Segmentation. *International Journal of Market Research, 55,* 289-314. Retrieved December 2, 2014, from EBSCO Online Database Business Source Complete. http://search.ebscohost.com/login.aspx?direct=true&db=bth&AN=86742714

Florén, H., & Frishammar, J. (2012). From preliminary ideas to corroborated product definitions: managing the front end of new product development. *California Management Review, 54,* 20-43. Retrieved November 15, 2013, from EBSCO Online Database Business Source Complete. http://search.ebscohost.com/login.aspx?direct=true&db=bth&AN=78584351&site=ehost-live

Hajek, Victor G. (1984). *Management of engineering projects* (3rd ed). New York: McGraw-Hill Book Company.

Johne, A. (1986). Substance versus trappings in new product management. *Journal of Marketing Management, 1,* 291-301. Retrieved June 13, 2007, from EBSCO Online Database Business Source Complete. http://search.ebscohost.com/login.aspx?direct=true&db=bth&AN=13586646&site=ehost-live

Lynn, G. & Reilly, R. (2002). How to build a blockbuster. *Harvard Business Review, 80,* 18-19. Retrieved June 13, 2007, from EBSCO Online Database Business Source Complete. http://search.ebscohost.com/login.aspx?direct=true&db=bth&AN=7433774&site=ehost-live

Nancy, G. (2014, July 22). New Products, Management Can Drive Stock's Price Higher. *Investors Business Daily.* p. B03. Retrieved December 2, 2014, from EBSCO Online Database Business Source Complete. http://search.ebscohost.com/login.aspx?direct=true&db=bth&AN=97137939

Pessemier, E. A. & Root, H. P. (1973). The dimensions of new product planning. *Journal of Marketing, 37,* 10-18. Retrieved June 13, 2007, from EBSCO Online Database Business Source Complete. http://search.ebscohost.com/login.aspx?direct=true&db=bth&AN=4996022&site=ehost-live

Qiang, L., Maggitti, P.G., Smith, K.G., Tesluk, P.E., & Katila, R. (2013). Top management attention to innovation: the role of search selection and intensity in new product introductions. *Academy of Management Journal, 56,* 893-916. Retrieved November 15, 2013, from EBSCO Online Database Business

Source Complete. http://search.ebscohost.com/ login.aspx?direct=true&db=bth&AN=88418872&site=ehost-live

SUGGESTED READING

Benezra, K. & Khermouch, G. (1996). Silver bullets & brass rings. *Brandweek, 37*, 55-61. Retrieved June 13, 2007, from EBSCO Online Database Business Source Complete. http://search.ebscohost.com/ login.aspx?direct=true&db=bth&AN=9605140082 &site=ehost-live

Kuczmarski, T. D. & Silver, S. J. (1982). Strategy: The key to successful new product development. *Management Review, 71*, 26-32. Retrieved June 13, 2007, from EBSCO Online Database Business Source Complete. http://search.ebscohost.com/login. aspx?direct=true&db=bth&AN=6032221&site=ehost-live

Maile, C. A. & Bialik, D. M. New product management: In search of better ideas. *Journal of Small Business Management, 22*, 40-48. Retrieved June 13, 2007, from EBSCO Online Database Business Source Complete. http://search.ebscohost.com/ login.aspx?direct=true&db=bth&AN=5272343&site=ehost-live

Mercer, D. (1993). A two-decade test of product life cycle theory. *British Journal of Management, 4*, 269-274. Retrieved June 13, 2007, from EBSCO Online Database Business Source Complete. http://search.ebscohost.com/login.aspx?direct=true&db=bth&AN=4527280&site=ehost-live

Murphy, J. H. (1962). New products need special management. *Journal of Marketing, 26*, 46-49. Retrieved June 13, 2007, from EBSCO Online Database Business Source Complete. http://search. ebscohost.com/login.aspx?direct=true&db=bth& AN=6740341&site=ehost-live

Scheuing, E. Z. & Johnson, E. M. (1989). A proposed model for new service development. *Journal of Services Marketing, 3*, 25-34. Retrieved June 13, 2007, from EBSCO Online Database Business Source Complete. http://search.ebscohost.com/login.aspx ?direct=true&db=bth&AN=5692361&site=ehost-live

Yun, H., & Young Seok, Y. (2013). A Comparative Analysis of the New Product Development Practices Trends: U.S.A. Versus Korean Companies. *Academy Of Entrepreneurship Journal, 19*, 97-113. Retrieved December 2, 2014, from EBSCO Online Database Business Source Complete. http:// search.ebscohost.com/login.aspx?direct=true&d b=bth&AN=96115076

Ruth A. Wienclaw, Ph.D.

P

PERSON MARKETING: USING CELEBRITIES TO ENDORSE PRODUCTS

ABSTRACT

This paper will take a closer look at the practice of celebrity endorsements and their marketing value. The use of celebrities to generate greater attention for a given product or service is multifaceted in both the manner in which these endorsements are obtained and the returns for the business they promise. By delving into greater detail about such policies, as well as highlighting the potential returns (both positive and negative), the reader will glean a more complete understanding of one of the most important aspects of marketing a burgeoning product in the twenty-first-century international economy.

OVERVIEW

Throughout the history of commerce, entrepreneurs have consistently sought endorsements of their products and services by high-profile members of society. For example, if a sixteenth-century clothing designer's wares were seen worn by a king or queen, it would follow that sales of that product increased dramatically. Using celebrities to help market products has long been seen as an important catalyst to increased sales and profitability.

This paper will take a closer look at the practice of celebrity endorsements and its marketing value. By delving into greater detail about such policies, as well as highlighting the potential returns (both positive and negative), the reader will glean a more complete understanding of one of the most important aspects of marketing a burgeoning product in the twenty-first-century international economy.

If It's Good Enough for Them . . .

A celebrity is not just someone who has risen to the top of his or her field. Of course, a celebrity may be an expert on a given subject, and therefore, someone whose opinions on the value of a certain product or service matter to the ordinary consumer. Then again, celebrities are also attention-getters, people who live in the spotlight—on the movie screen, in the ballpark, or on the Internet—and have a following among the general public.

Celebrity endorsements speak to that spotlight. For example, by having NBA superstar LeBron James, professional golfer Tiger Woods, and other high-profile athletes affix their names and likenesses to their apparel, Nike creates a perceived link between the extraordinary accomplishments of these individuals and their products; this connection can lead to considerably higher sales and profit generation (Grede, 2008). The appearance of movie stars or the use of popular songs in television and radio commercials can create similar connections among consumers.

APPLICATIONS

Professional Athletes

In 1934, a Kellogg's cereal brand unveiled its newest box, complete with the photo of New York Yankees star Lou Gehrig. For more than seven decades after that iconic moment, Wheaties boxes connected great athletes with consuming the product, claiming, "What's on the box shows that Wheaties fuels champions. What's in the box proves it" (Wheaties.com).

The use of professional and high-profile amateur athletes (such as Olympians) has become commonplace among business marketing endeavors. With the Wheaties perspective in their minds, countless retailers, beverage producers, restaurants, and candy manufacturers have long sought to affix the faces of high-profile sports athletes to their products and services. Many of these athletes are considered to be in the highest echelon of the sport they represent. NBA superstar LeBron James (who was drafted out of high school rather than college) signed a seven-year, $90-million contract with sports retailer Nike right after he signed a contract with the Cleveland

Cavaliers. As part of that relationship, his name was on no fewer than 10 shoe styles, including six "LeBron James" signature models. Additionally, he signed deals with bubble gum maker Bubblicious, sports card maker Upper Deck, and beverage giant Coca-Cola, among others (Horrow & Swatek, 2009). By 2013, even after a controversial, yet highly successful transfer to the Miami Heat, James' endorsement income alone amounted to $40 million (Van Riper, 2013).

The use of athletes in marketing products is not simply lucrative for the athlete. The fact that professional golfer Tiger Woods, one of the most recognizable faces in sports, is also one of the most marketed names in the world is not a coincidence. Consistently the biggest draw at PGA events, Woods also draws high television ratings—a drop in viewership in 2008 and early 2009 could be directly connected to the fact that he was absent with an injury.

Products that bear Woods' name and/or endorsement also sell in high volume. Before 1996, Nike did not even have a golf line to sell. However, when Woods burst onto the scene shortly thereafter, consumer demand for products with his name created a surge in golf apparel, equipment, and other product sales. By 2007, Woods had helped build for Nike a lucrative franchise, Nike Golf, which sold well over $600 million for the company that year (Baker, 2008).

Sports marketing and endorsements are not limited to the most famous athletes, either. In fact, countless athletes have endorsed products and services. Many of them do so at the local level, appearing in advertisements for automobile dealerships, local restaurants, and other places of regional interest. Baltimore Ravens offensive tackle Jonathan Ogden may not be as internationally recognized as Tiger Woods, but his notoriety in greater Baltimore led to his appearances in a local insurance company's advertisements. Boston Red Sox star closer Jonathan Papelbon also holds a strong fan base in New England and, as such, appeared in a number of television and radio spots by a regional auto dealership (Fitch, 2009).

Credibility, Attractiveness, & Product Match-Up

To understand how businesses look to sports figures to help sell their wares, one may look at three theoretical frameworks: source credibility, source attractiveness, and product match-up (Peterson, 2009). The first of these theories, source credibility, looks at how the athlete in question is viewed in terms of his or her knowledge of the product. Tiger Woods, for example, is exceptionally talented at using golf clubs, and his endorsement of Nike's golf line, therefore, is given great credibility.

The second theory, source attractiveness, suggests that consumers will purchase products and services that are endorsed by athletes who have a positive public persona. Athletes such as New York Yankees captain Derek Jeter, former Chicago Bulls player Michael Jordan, and Indianapolis Colts quarterback Peyton Manning all are known by fans and the general public to be friendly with fans, noncontroversial, and inspirational to those around them. Such reputations give an air of trustworthiness to these figures, and as a result, consumers are more likely to consider purchasing a product they endorse.

Finally, product match-up involves congruence between the endorser and the product. This area has proven more difficult to frame for marketing experts as well as psychologists, in light of the myriad factors that play a role in the relationship between the athlete and the products being marketed. In general contexts, however, product match-up looks at two relationships: the logical connection between the endorser and the product (such as Tiger Woods and the Nike golf club line), and what is known as "match-up hypothesis" (Kahle & Riley, 2004). The latter term alludes to a perceived connection between the endorser and the product that creates an impression with the consumer that the product is all the more beneficial because of the athlete's endorsement.

Of course, professional athletes are but one form of celebrity that is called upon to help sell a product or service. Entertainers, movie stars, musicians, and other celebrities are also considered invaluable endorsers.

The Star Treatment

In the 1930s and 1940s, there was a common activity among Hollywood's A-list of actors. Icons such as Clark Gable, Bette Davis, and John Wayne were all featured in advertisements endorsing tobacco products. In fact, many studios scheduled such publicity with the release of the endorsers' films ("Tobacco Companies," 2008). This practice has persisted in other industries on a more widespread basis in the decades that followed.

The entertainment industry has long been seen as a gold mine for businesses looking to give star power to their products. Such endorsements provide the company and its products with a higher degree of perceived legitimacy among consumers who recognize them—the bigger the star, the more effective the advertisement. In 2011, for example, film actor Emma Watson, of *Harry Potter* franchise fame, signed a contract with renowned cosmetics company Lancôme. As a representative of her generation, her endorsement represented a way for the company to expand its pool of potential consumers (Naughton, 2011). She is by no means alone—very few entertainers eschew product endorsements, leading one celebrity broker to assert, "The list of [celebrities] that won't do [advertisements] has gotten a lot smaller" ("Shill and Grace," 2009).

Celebrity endorsements from movie stars and entertainers are somewhat different in nature than those of professional athletes. Whereas athletes have a proven proficiency with certain products and, as a result, tend to generate return on investment (ROI) based on that familiarity, movie stars, musicians, and other non-athlete celebrities often lend little more than a familiar face. Model and actor Cindy Crawford, for example, became a "brand ambassador" for Swiss watchmaker Omega in 1995 and, 18 years later, was still promoting its products (Crawley, 2013). Such brand ambassadors are contractually obligated to exclusively wear that company's product. Another high-profile actor, Charlize Theron, became enmeshed in a tabloid feeding frenzy when she was wearing a watch made by a competitor of the watchmaker to whom she was obligated (Wicks, 2008).

Although connecting the product with the expertise of the endorser seems more appropriate for athletes than it does for movie stars and the like, the enjoyment experienced by the endorser does show positive returns for the company. Talk show mogul Oprah Winfrey, for example, fostered considerable business for book publishers with her endorsements via her long-running book club and, in some cases, created a surge in book sales (Maryles & Sanborn, 1994).

Product Placement

An important aspect of celebrity endorsements from actors and entertainers is product placement. Whereas some celebrities will appear in commercial advertisements or endorse products on their shows, others simply get paid (or in many cases, are simply given the product free of charge) to be seen with the products close at hand. For example, cosmetics company RevitaLash gave away eyelash conditioner at the 2011 Sundance Film Festival to film stars such as Jennifer Love Hewitt, whose praise helped generate media coverage estimated to be worth $2.4 million in advertising (White, 2011).

Using film or television stars for the purposes of marketing products and services is not dissimilar from the same application for professional athletes. In both cases, a familiar and agreeable visage is attached to a product via advertisement, leading the consumer to connect more readily with the message of the ad. However, whereas Tiger Woods' proficiency with golf clubs translates easily into selling such items, he may not prove to be as easily used when endorsing goods outside of his area of expertise.

The use of movie stars, popular singers, and other entertainers, on the other hand, creates a more general and less specific basis for consumer response. In the use of such celebrities, the advertiser is in essence "conditioning" the consumer—an attractive, well-liked, and even trustworthy figure such as a movie star who is seen in the advertisement may stimulate the consumer into connecting the star with the product. Thus, the consumer will demonstrate a desire to purchase the product (Till, Stanley & Priluck, 2008).

Celebrities of all types are seen as effective vessels by which consumer activity may be stimulated. However, this appeal is neither without condition or risk.

ISSUES

The Conditions & Risks of Celebrity Endorsements

The Roman emperor Marcus Aurelius once commented, "All is ephemeral—fame and the famous as well" (Bartlett, 1919). Indeed, fame and celebrity is fleeting as well as subject to surges, plateaus, and doldrums. Because of the fluctuations to which sports and entertainment celebrities are susceptible, using these figures to endorse a given product or service is at times a risky or short-term endeavor.

One of the first conditions to an effective celebrity endorsement is relevance. Using a famous person to market products and services requires that the individual projects a positive image for consumers in order to entice them to buy the advertised goods.

Much of that ability to affect consumer behavior stems from the celebrity's popularity. After all, the goal of the advertisement is to capture the attention of the consumer via a commercial that stands out in a crowded field of other advertisements (Saurbh, 2009). If the individual is not experiencing success on the field or has not been seen in a recent successful movie, he or she is not likely to prove an appealing endorser.

Negative incidents are arguably the greatest risk to a company's celebrity endorsement endeavors. Among these negative incidents is personal injury. A sports star who enjoys a high degree of popularity may be out of action for months due to injury, and in light of this fact, the relationship between endorser and business may be placed in jeopardy. Similarly, an actor who is diagnosed with a debilitating disease that will keep him or her out of the movies for a prolonged period of time runs the risk of losing celebrity status and therefore losing that connectivity with the audience (and consumers). Tiger Woods' 2008 knee injury sent apparent shockwaves through the golf world, sending tournament viewership into a 47 percent drop and his endorsees into a state of concern. When he returned in early 2009, beverage maker Gatorade (which had a relationship with Woods since 2007) took out a large ad in *Sports Illustrated* that featured a golf fan holding aloft a sign that read "Welcome Back, Tiger" (Vranica, 2009). Nike, however, decided that falling revenues in the Nike Golf division between 2009 and 2010 signaled the time to move on without the athlete who had initially inspired it and embarked on a new golf club line without Woods' endorsement (Bustillo, 2010).

Injuries and illness are indeed detrimental to effective use of a celebrity marketing campaign. However, scandal and negative press also pose a tremendous risk for those seeking to use a high-profile name to sell their products. Celebrity chef Paula Deen, for example, earned about $17 million dollars in 2012 through a business empire that included a televised cooking show, food product lines, restaurant deals, and endorsements. In June 2013, however, revelations of Deen having used racial slurs and off-color language, along with allegations of racial discrimination against some of her former restaurant employees, led to a slew of restaurants and retailers, including J. C. Penney, Sears, Kmart, Target, Walgreens, Wal-Mart, and Home Depot, dropping their deals with her, amounting to a $5 million loss of revenue (Lazarowitz, 2013). Particularly affected by Deen's fall from grace were pork producer Smithfield Foods and Novo Nordisk, the manufacturer of a diabetes medication Deen uses, both of which had been endorsees of hers and quickly terminated their contracts with the besmirched cook (Lazarowitz, 2013).

An old axiom states, "The bigger they are, the harder they fall." Indeed, those using celebrity fame, athletic ability, and beauty are taking a gamble that they will see a return on the campaign's investment. It is understandable, therefore, that most of these celebrity endorsement contracts do not last more than a few years. Even though the agreements are ephemeral, there remains great risk that the celebrity's star will rapidly fall and, with it, the company's investment and even reputation.

CONCLUSIONS

Using celebrities to market products is one of the most time-honored practices in the history of commerce. While a product's quality, attractiveness, or practicality may generate increased profits through word of mouth, a famed athlete, movie star, or popular musician who is seen using the product and/or speaking out on its behalf gives it nearly instant and broad-reaching attention. If a campaign is developed in just the right way, the magnitude of the star will correspond with the size of the profits.

There is of course a psychology to celebrity endorsements. Such endeavors must connect the star to the product in such a way that the consumer immediately appreciates. The advertising company must therefore understand the target demographic group and subsequently craft a star-product connection that speaks to that demographic's character.

As shown in this paper, there are potential risks involved with celebrity endorsements. Injury and sickness may lower the celebrity's star power, as another star may take that individual's place in the spotlight. Celebrity scandals that involve drug and/or steroid use, drunk driving, domestic violence, cruelty to animals, or other criminal or unethical activity can also destroy a well-designed and high-level advertising investment. Additionally, by connecting the product to the celebrity, when such occurrences take place, there is a risk that the company will be dragged down with the falling star. Nevertheless, after centuries of using celebrities to market products, it remains clear that entrepreneurs will continue to see such practices as a critical investment.

BIBLIOGRAPHY

Baker, A. (2008, July 11). Tiger Woods, the $1 billion man. *Telegraph*. Retrieved May 27, 2009 from http://www.telegraph.co.uk/sport/columnists/andrewbaker/2305435/Tiger -Woods-the-1-billion-man.html.

Briggs, Bill. (2007, July 18). NFL megastar Vick's endorsements in danger. MSNBC.com. Retrieved May 30, 2009 from http://www.msnbc.msn.com/id/19834805/.

Bustillo, M. (2010, January 18). Nike launches new golf clubs without Tiger Woods. *Wall Street Journal*. Retrieved November 22, 2013, from: http://online.wsj.com/news/articles/SB100014240527487 04541004575011222565583784

Crawley, J. (2013, October 17). Cindy Crawford turns back the hands of time as she dazzles in red and diamonds at luxury watch event. *DailyMail*. Retrieved November 22, 2013, from: http://www.dailymail.co.uk/tvshowbiz/article-2464553/Cindy-Crawford-dazzles-red-luxury-watch-event.html#ixzz2lP6vZq9C

Douglas, J. Y. (2009). A history into celebrity advertising. Unpublished paper, University of Florida. Retrieved May 25, 2009 from http://www.nwe.ufl.edu/~jdouglas/analysis6.pdf.

Fitch, D. (2009, January 14). The 15 most insane commercials featuring sports stars. Retrieved May 29, 2009 from Betfair.com http://betting.betfair.com/sports/oddly-enough/the-15-most-insane-commercials-featuring-sports-st-140109.html.

Grede, R. (2008, June 3). Marketing lowdown: Celebrity endorsements. *Sales and Marketing Management*. Retrieved May 25, 2009 from Managesmarter.com http://www.managesmarter.com/msg/content%5fdisplay/marketing/ e3i5ca4a2c7bdd 71792f172fe3e20c0a8ce.

Horrow, R., & Swatek, C. (2009, April 24). NBA playoffs are paying off. *Business Week Online*. Retrieved May 26, 2009 from EBSCO Online Database Business Source Complete. http://search.ebscohost.com/login.aspx?direct=true&db=a9h&AN=38604054&site=ehost-live.

Insight: Marketers forum celebrity endorsements—When brandendorsers go off the rails. (2012). *Campaign Asia-Pacific*, 25. Retrieved November 22, 2013 from EBSCO online database Business Source Premier. http://search.ebscohost.com/login.aspx?direct=true&db=buh&AN=74572732

Kahle, L. R., & Riley, C. (2004). *Sports marketing and the psychology of marketing communication*. Mahweh, NJ: Lawrence Erlbaum Associates.

Lazarowitz, E. (2013, June 28). Paula Deen has lost as much as $12.5 million in earnings over N-word controversy: Experts. *New York Daily News*. Retrieved November 22, 2013, from: http://www.nydailynews.com/entertainment/tv-movies/deen-lost-12-5-million-experts-article-1.1385469#ixzz2lP10xRjb

Manning-Schaffel, V. (2006, February 13). Brands get celebrity exposure. Retrieved May 29, 2009 from the Brand Channel. http://www.brandchannel.com/features%5feffect.asp?pf%5fid=301.

Marcus Aurelius. (n.d.). In Bartlett's Familiar Quotations (10th ed.). Retrieved May 28, 2009 from http://www.bartleby.com/100/718.37.html.

Maryles, D., & Sanborn, M. (1994). When Oprah speaks … *Publishers Weekly, 241*, 16.

Naughton, J. (2011). Lancôme adds Watson to lineup. *WWD: Women's Wear Daily, 201*, 6. Retrieved November 22, 2013 from EBSCO online database Business Source Premier. http://search.ebscohost.com/login.aspx?direct=true&db=buh&AN=59398044

Peterson, D. (2009, January 12). Endorsements: How sports stars get inside your head.

Retrieved May 28, 2009 from LiveScience.com. http://www.livescience.com/culture/090112-athlete-endorsements.html.

Rose, L. (2006, March 22). The world's best-paid athletes. *Forbes*. Retrieved May 30, 2009 from Forbes.com http://www.msnbc.msn.com/id/11961246.

Shill and grace. (2009). *Entertainment Weekly*. Retrieved May 28, 2009 from EW.com http://www.ew.com/ew/article/0,1043999,00.html.

Till, B. D., Stanley, S. M., & Priluck, R. (2008). Classical conditioning and celebrity endorsers. *Psychology and Marketing, 25*, 179–196. Retrieved May 28, 2009 from EBSCO Online Database Business Source Complete. http://search.ebscohost.com/login.aspx?direct=true&db=bth&AN=28443744&site=ehost-live.

Tobacco companies paid movie stars millions in celebrity endorsement deals. (2008, Sept. 25). *Medical News Today*. Retrieved May 29, 2009 from website http://www.medicalnewstoday.com/articles/122946.php.

Van Riper, T. (2013, June 21). LeBron should net $7 million in new endorsements. Others can score too (or not). *Forbes.com*. Retrieved November 22, 2013, from: http://www.forbes.com/sites/tomvanriper/2013/06/21/lebron-should-net-7-million-in-new-endorsements-others-can-score-too-or-not

Vranica, S. (2009, February 25). Marketers cheer Woods's return. *Wall Street Journal*. Retrieved May 27, 2009 from http://online.wsj.com/article/SB123552209870564841.html.

White, M. (2011). Super swagonomics. *Bloomberg Businessweek, (4217),* 80–81. Retrieved November 22, 2013 from EBSCO online database Business Source Premier. http://search.ebscohost.com/login.aspx?direct=true&db=buh&AN=58665054

Wicks, A. (2008). Giving timepieces a celebrity face. *WWD: Women's Wear Daily, 195,* 22S. Retrieved May 27, 2009 from EBSCO Online Database Business Source Complete. http://search.ebscohost.com/login.aspx?direct=true&db=bth&AN=31723174&site=ehost-live.

SUGGESTED READING

Are celebrity brand ambassadors worth the money. (2012). *Marketing (00253650),* 22. Retrieved November 22, 2013 from EBSCO online database Business Source Premier. http://search.ebscohost.com/login.aspx?direct=true&db=buh&AN=78285670

Biswas, S., Hussain, M., & O'Donnell, K. (2009). Celebrity endorsements in advertisements and consumer perceptions: A cross-cultural study. *Journal of Global Marketing, 22,* 121–137. Retrieved June 1, 2009 from EBSCO Online Database Business Source Complete. http://search.ebscohost.com/

login.aspx?direct=true&db=bth&AN=37155107&site=ehost-live.

Loei, F.W. (2016). Analyzing the effect of celebrity endorsement and brand credibility on brand loyalty (a study on nike shoes in manado). *Jurnal Berkala Ilmiah Efisiensi,* 16, 3. Retrieved on June 29, 2017.

Louie, T., & Obermiller, C. (2002). Consumer response to a firm's endorser (dis)association decisions. *Journal of Advertising, 31,* 41–52. Retrieved June 1, 2009 from EBSCO Online Database Business Source Complete. http://search.ebscohost.com/login.aspx?direct=true&db=bth&AN=9037004&site=ehost-live

Mowen, J., & Brown, S. (1981). On explaining and predicting the effectiveness of celebrity endorsers. *Advances in Consumer Research, 8,* 437–441. Retrieved June 1, 2009 from EBSCO Online Database Business Source Complete. http://search.ebscohost.com/login.aspx?direct=true&db=bth&AN=6430606&site=ehost-live

Ohanian, R. (1990). Construction and validation of a scale to measure celebrity endorsers' perceived expertise, trustworthiness and attractiveness. *Journal of Advertising, 19,* 39–52. Retrieved June 1, 2009 from EBSCO Online Database Business Source Complete. http://search.ebscohost.com/login.aspx?direct=true&db=bth&AN=9605213110&site=ehost-live.

Tripp, C., Jensen, T., & Carlson, L. (1994). The effects of multiple product endorsements by celebrities on consumers' attitudes and intentions. *Journal of Consumer Research, 20,* 535–547. Retrieved June 1, 2009 from EBSCO Online Database Business Source Complete. http://search.ebscohost.com/login.aspx?direct=true&db=bth&AN=9409162879&site=ehost-live

Michael P. Auerbach, M.A.

PERSONAL SELLING AND SALES MANAGEMENT

ABSTRACT

Although there are many ways of marketing products and services to prospective customers, personal selling – the process of communicating with the customer on a one-to-one basis with the intention of persuading him or her to purchase a product or service – continues to represent a significant share of marketing activities. Although other marketing methods may reach more customers more cheaply, personal selling has numerous advantages. To optimize the effectiveness of the sales force, most organizations employ a system of sales management. This function is responsible for enabling and monitoring the sales force in the performance of its tasks. Although a number of automated tools are available to ease the burden on sales representatives and sales managers alike, these are not a panacea and often do not bring sufficient return to justify their cost.

Business organizations use a number of different methods to try to sell their goods and services to consumers. A telvivion or radio commercial may be supplemented by print advertisements in newspapers, magazines, or other publications.

The organization may develop a sales promotion and send advertisements or coupons through the mail or generate publicity to raise the prospective customer's awareness of the organization and its products or services. Stores where a product is sold may position a display to catch the customer's eye and encourage a purchase. The salesperson in the retail store may help the customer make a selection, often stressing the advantages of one particular product over another. Each of these approaches is effective in given circumstances, and many organizations develop an integrated marketing sales campaign utilizing multiple sales techniques to impress the benefits of the product or service in the minds of potential consumers.

Although there are many ways to attempt to persuade a current or prospective customer to buy the business's products or services, many sales are done through personal selling. These are situations in which a sales representative or team communicates with the customer on a one-to-one basis with the intention of persuading him or her to purchase a product or service. Personal selling tasks include developing a relationship with the customer, collecting and analyzing data formally or informally to determine the customer's needs, determining the best match between the customer's needs and the business's products or services, and effectively communicating this information in an attempt to persuade the customer to make a purchase. Personal selling can occur in many different situations ranging from the sales clerk in the retail store who assists a customer in making a purchase to a team of sales representatives who market a document control system to a major corporation.

Personal selling is more than persuading the potential customer to buy a product or service.

Consistently effective personal selling requires that the salesperson work with the customer to determine what the customer actually needs in terms of technical capabilities, price, delivery time, and other relevant factors. Based on an analysis of these factors, the salesperson can then determine which combination of the organization's products or services will best meet these needs. The sales representative then demonstrates to the customer that his or her proposed solution will cost-effectively meet the customer's needs and works with the customer to answer any questions and develop a mutually satisfactory solution to the customer's problem.

Even though at first glance it may not appear to be cost-effective compared with other marketing techniques, personal selling is used in many marketing situations. For example, whereas a print advertisement in a magazine or newspaper may cost only pennies per person reached, the average cost of a sales call is hundreds of dollars. Personal selling persists, however, because it is effective. Because the process involves one-on-one communication with the potential customer, the sales representative can pay more attention to the needs of the customer and tailor the presentation to better demonstrate that the product or service meets those needs. In addition, in personal sales, not only does the sales representative present information, but the customer is also allowed the opportunity to ask questions, thereby getting a better understanding of what the product or service does and how it meets the customer's needs. Further, this two-way communication also gives the sales representative better feedback on how the sales presentation is being received by the potential customer. Nonverbal cues such as yawning, closed-off body language, or an angry look can help the sales representative take a different tack in an attempt to salvage the sale.

Another advantage of personal sales is that it allows the organization to present a large amount of complex or technical information about its products, services, policies, and experience in the field. The personal sales approach also allows the sales representative to work with the customer to find ways to adapt the standard product or service to better fit the customer's needs, develop an integrative solution to the customer's problem, or answer customers' questions regarding the comparison of the organization's products to those of its competitors. Although to some extent such information can be conveyed through other media, it is more effectively and efficiently done through the one-on-one contact of personal sales.

Personal sales are usually accomplished by sales departments with a sales force that works either as individuals or as teams to reach current and prospective customers and persuade them to purchase the organization's products or services. As with other functions in the organization, the sales function requires effective management to enable the sales force to do its job. Sales management is the process of efficiently and effectively making sales through the planning, coordination, and supervision of others. Effective sales management involves much more than performing administrative tasks to coordinate the activities of the sales force. To be successful, the good sales manager is involved in a wide range of activities, including planning; organizing, recruiting, and selecting sales personnel; enabling and motivating the sales force to sell (e.g., training, print materials or samples); supervising and coordinating sales efforts (e.g., assigning territories or routes); and controlling, and monitoring the sales force. Each of these functions is necessary for the successful operation of a sales function within the organization.

Like any other function within the organization, the sales department is not given unlimited resources to persuade customers to buy the organization's goods or services. Therefore, the sales manager must make the best use of both the human and financial resources available to sell the organization's goods and services to potential customers. To do this well requires planning. Sales managers must determine how to use the resources available in the best way to optimize the effectiveness and efficiency of the sales force as a whole. This requires understanding the qualifications, abilities, and experience of the sales force. For example, it would be imprudent to send an experienced salesperson to basic sales training or to give an inexperienced salesperson a large region to cover. To better understand how best to deploy the sales force, the sales manager also needs to understand the target market including its demographics, needs, and motivations. Data on sales-force capabilities and prospective customer needs can then be put together and analyzed in order to come up with a plan that leverages the strengths of the individual sales personnel and enables each to reach his or her optimal sales potential.

After the sales manager has developed a workable plan to help optimize sales performance, the next step in sales management is to organize the sales force to best match the requirements of customers and potential customers. These planning activities should not only occur when a new sales department is being set up, but should be part of a continuing effort to improve the effectiveness and efficiency of the sales force. To determine how best to do this, the sales manager needs to ask several questions. First, how many customers and prospective customers can each salesperson reasonably be expected to call on within a given time period? There are only so many hours in the day, of course, but different salespeople have different selling styles—and radically different styles can be equally effective in different situations. The sales manager needs to understand these differences to better know how to deploy the sales force. To do this, the sales manager needs to take the characteristics of the customer pool and the styles and abilities of individuals on the sales force into account and match them appropriately. Second, the sales manager needs to determine the average number of sales calls each category of sales will require. For example, a sales call to a long-time satisfied customer to replenish a consumable product or update a piece of equipment will more than likely take less of a sales representative's time than would a cold call to a prospective customer who has not used the organization's goods or services before. A third piece of data needed by the sales manager in developing an optimal sales plan is the average call rate per salesperson. Some salespeople are able to make a sale quickly while others require more time to establish a relationship with the customer or to gather the information needed to close the sale. This information, along with the number of work dates per year, will help the sales manager determine how many sales representatives to employ and how these individuals should be deployed.

In addition to analyzing the sales needs of the organization and the needs and motivations of the target market, the sales manager needs to develop a capable sales force that can sell the organization's products or services. With the help of the human resources department, the sales manager develops a job description that specifies the duties and tasks related to a job. Job descriptions may also specify the knowledge, skills, and abilities necessary to do the job as well as the performance standards that differentiate acceptable from unacceptable performance. Candidates for the sales positions are then recruited, their application forms analyzed to determine how well they meet the requirements for the job, and their references checked. From the pool of applicants, the sales manager then interviews those who appear best able to perform the job. The data from all these sources is analyzed in conjunction with the other applicant data, and the sales force is hired.

Once the sales force is hired, it is the sales manager's responsibility to train these individuals to do the tasks of their new job. Although sometimes the human resources department will acquire general training through a third-party vendor, it is the sales manager's job to train new employees on the specifics of the job and the requirements of the organization that differentiate this sales job from other sales jobs. The sales manager is also responsible for updating members of the sales staff on any changes in organizational policy that affect them and for providing new information about the organization's products or services so that they can better do their jobs. Although the sales manager may not do the training him- or herself, it is the sales manager's job to determine what needs to be taught (e.g., basic vs. advanced sales skills, technical training for specific products), where it should be taught (e.g., in the sales office or other onsite venue; in an outside training center), and who should teach it (e.g., the sales or other manager, the human resources department, a consultant or outside vendor).

In addition, it is the sales manager's responsibility to motivate the sales force. Although the factors that motivate differ from individual to individual, some general motivators exist to help encourage sales representatives to do their best. Financial incentives are one of the most common motivators. A reasonable salary in relation to comparable jobs at other companies and the possibility of predictable raises and bonuses for doing one's job well all tend to be motivators. For this reason, many organizations pay their sales staff on commission – a set fee or percentage of the sale that is given to a sales representative for convincing a customer to make a purchase – in addition to a set salary. One of the reasons that sales commissions are an effective motivator is because they tie rewards directly to performance on the job. Other ways to motivate the sales staff are through connecting job performance with various perquisites such as a company car for making sales calls or trips or paid vacations for being a top seller. In addition, job security and status (such as through a promotion, a job title, or other award or recognition) can motivate the sales staff.

In addition to these functions, the sales manager is also responsible for controlling the sales operation and monitoring the activities of the sales staff to make sure that they are effective and successful. To help ensure that the sales force is effective, it is important for the sales manager to set performance objectives for the sales force and set up ways to help enable the sales force to meet those objectives. This activity includes setting standards for behavior (e.g., number of sales calls required during a given period of time), implementing ways to collect data on how well the standards are being met and making sure that the data are collected, analyzing the data to determine where objectives are not being met and why, and determining a plan of action for correcting these situations.

APPLICATIONS

Although the field of personal sales revolves around the personal communication and relationship between the customer and the sales representative, not all communication with the customer needs to be done face to face. Twenty-first-century technology has transformed the way we complete many tasks both at home and at work, including the function of personal sales. For example, the Internet is an invaluable tool for generating sales leads. A visit to a potential customer's website can eliminate hours of work spent tracking down the correct contact person and gathering other information vital to developing a tailored marketing approach. PowerPoint and other presentation software can help boost an organization's image by creating professional-looking, targeted presentations for the customer. Virtual tours of the organization's facilities can be enabled through web-hosted videos, and simulations can help customers better understand the advantages and disadvantages of the organization's product or service. The use of technology in this way is not a mere prop or toy, however; it allows sales representatives to talk to prospective customers in their own language using their own tools, thereby showing themselves to better understand the customer's needs.

Sales representatives' lives can be made easier with other technologies that are common to the business-world. Instant messaging and email allow the sales representative to respond to customer queries in a timely manner no matter where they are, as well as to carry on parts of conversations that previously had to be done in person. Smart phones can help the sales representative receive email and other communications instantaneously.

However, the application of technology to sales tasks goes well beyond these common tools. Organizations spend billions of dollars in various sales technologies to help in tasks such as customer relationship management and sales force automation in an effort to improve the effectiveness and efficiency of the sales team. Customer relationship management tools help identify prospective customers, acquire data concerning these prospective and current customers, build relationships with customers, and influence their perceptions of the organization and its products or services. Customer relationship management software can also be used to manage interactions and transactions with customers. However, as with any software application program, the outputs are only as good as the inputs. Customer relationship management software is only a tool; the salesperson cannot necessarily be taken out of the loop. As a result, the effect on sales of this technology may be insufficient to justify the investment.

Although a host of information technologies are available to assist the sales representative and the sales manager in their tasks, they are not panaceas. The needs of the sales team must be carefully analyzed and compared with the capabilities of the tool before investing significant financial resources into sales technology. In the end, some tasks will always need to be performed by a human being. However, repetitive tasks, arduous data searches, and database management tasks can frequently be made less labor intensive through the application of sales technology, thereby freeing the sales representative or manager to get on with the business of personal selling.

BIBLIOGRAPHY

Asare, A. K., Yang, J., & Alejandro, T. (2012). The state of research methods in personal selling and sales management literature. Journal of Personal Selling & Sales Management, 32 (4), 473-490. Retrieved November 20, 2013 from EBSCO Online Database Business Source Complete. http://search.ebscohost.com/login.aspx?direct=true&db=bth&AN=84086218&site=ehost-live

Churchill, G. A. Jr., Ford, N. M., & Walker, O. C. Jr. (1993). Sales force management (4th ed.). Homewood, IL: Richard D. Irwin, Inc.

Erevelles, S., & Fukawa, N. (2013). The role of affect in personal selling and sales management. Journal of Personal Selling & Sales Management, 33 (1), 7-24. Retrieved November 20, 2013 from EBSCO Online Database Business Source Complete. http://search.ebscohost.com/login.aspx?direct=true&db=bth&AN=84461725&site=ehost-live

Hunter, G. K & Perreault, W. D. (2007). Making sales technology effective. Journal of Marketing, 71 (1), 16-34. Retrieved May 4, 2007, from EBSCO Online Database Business Source Complete. http://search.ebscohost.com/login.aspx?direct=true&db=bth&AN=23368366&site=ehost-live

Kennedy, L. (2000). "Smart" tools will shape the way we sell. Paperboard Packaging, 85(5), 48. Retrieved May 4, 2007, from EBSCO Online Database Business Source Complete. http://search.ebscohost.com/login.aspx?direct=true&db=bth&AN=3129749&site=ehost-live

Peterson, R. (1978). Personal selling: An introduction. New York: John Wiley & Sons.

Shannahan, R. J., Bush, A. J., Moncrief, W. C., & Shannahan, K. J. (2013). Making sense of the customer's role in the personal selling process: A theory of organizing and sensemaking perspective. Journal of Personal Selling & Sales Management, 33 (3), 261-276. Retrieved November 20, 2013 from EBSCO Online Database Business Source Complete. http://search.ebscohost.com/login.aspx?direct=true&db=bth&AN=88834638&site=ehost-live

Strafford, J. & Grant, C. (1993). Effective sales management (2nd ed.). Oxford: Butterworth-Heinemann Ltd.

SUGGESTED READING

Adamson, B., Dixon, M., & Toman, N. (2013). Dismantling the sales machine. Harvard Business Review, 91 (11), 102-109. Retrieved November 20, 2013 from EBSCO Online Database Business Source Complete. http://search.ebscohost.com/login.aspx?direct=true&db=bth&AN=91571500&site=ehost-live

Hunter, G. K. & Perreault, W. D. Jr. (2006). Sales technology orientation, information effectiveness, and sales performance. Journal of Personal Selling & Sales Management, 26(2), 95-113. Retrieved May 4, 2007, from EBSCO Online Database Business Source Complete. http://search.ebscohost.com/login.aspx?direct=true&db=bth&AN=21065989&site=ehost-live

Jacoby, J. & Craig, C. S. (1984). Personal selling: Theory, research, and practice. Lexington, MA: LexingtonBooks.

Krantz, B. (2003). Ramping up with new sales technologies. Gases & Welding Distributor, 47(4), 52-54. Retrieved May 4, 2007, from EBSCO Online Database Business Source Complete. http://search.ebscohost.com/login.aspx?direct=true&db=bth&AN=10840675&site=ehost-live

Sharma, Arun. (2016). What personal selling and sales management recommendations from developed markets are relevant in emerging markets? Journal of Personal Selling & Sales Management, 36. Retrieved on June 29, 2017.

Shepherd, C., Tashchian, A., & Ridnour, R. E. (2011). An investigation of the job burnout syndrome in personal selling. Journal of Personal Selling & Sales Management, 31(4), 397-410. Retrieved November 20, 2013 from EBSCO Online Database Business Source Complete. http://search.ebscohost.com/login.aspx?direct=true&db=bth&AN=66715138&site=ehost-live

Ruth A. Wienclaw, Ph.D.

PRICE ANALYSIS

ABSTRACT

Price analysis is an overly complex task for apprentice scholars especially given its coverage in economics publications. This essay aims to help undergraduate students and other readers develop skills applicable to price analysis. Supply and demand form a foundation for that analysis. On the supply side of the analysis, this foundation and those skills are valuable for understanding the status of a firm in terms of whether it is operating near the shut-down point, the break-even point, or somewhere in between. Value also accrues by helping students and readers determine whether a firm is earning a normal profit or an economic profit. The degree of competition is a key feature in these analyses, which falls under the notion of a market structure. There is a variety of ways in which to conduct price analysis whether one examines supply or demand.

OVERVIEW

The information presented in this essay provides a frame of reference with which to simplify price analysis and distinguish macroeconomic price levels from microeconomic market prices. Though this essay provides a foundation to examine resource markets, its main purpose is to help undergraduate students and other readers develop skills in analyzing prices found in the goods and services market. Specifically, this essay will improve the reader's ability to answer the following questions: Why do prices change or differ? What are the key determinants driving price variations? Which prices are of greatest interest and to whom? How do producer costs interact with the market prices consumers pay and producers receive? Perhaps the most important question is: What do market prices tell us in precise terms about a firm's operating status, profit level, and competition?

In order to answer this last question, a need exists to define the term price. Pearce (1992) informs us in a concise manner what the terms price and price level mean. An input's or an output's price is the amount of money that is required to obtain an item whether it is an input or an output. With its focus on consumer and firm behavior, microeconomics is an area of inquiry that focuses, in part, on production decisions and price theory. At a much broader perspective, macroeconomic inquiry concerns itself, in part, with the general level of prices or a price index, which indicates the extent to which the prices for items within a larger bundle of goods change over time. The index is an average of item prices weighted according to the proportion of total expenditures on each item of the bundle. Price analysis in this essay will touch upon that broad perspective, but it conveys many more crucial details about the narrower perspective, especially with regard to production decisions and price theory.

Prices generally reflect an agreement between sellers and buyers who exchange goods and services as they interact in the marketplace. In addition, most sellers take the price dictated by market forces and very few sellers are able to set the market price. As many undergraduate students experience graph phobia, readers of this essay are encouraged to postpone cross references between the text printed herein and the graphs found in textbooks by Guell (2007), McConnell & Brue (2008), or other economists. In the pages at hand, without the aid from and/or the distraction that graphs provide, the reader will gain a preliminary understanding about the foundations of demand and supply before moving onward to examine how inputs and their costs, production rules and outputs, producer's and consumer's willingness and ability, and market forces and structures converge to determine an item's price.

APPLICATIONS

Foundations of Price Analysis: Demand & Supply

When viewing a two-dimensional graph showing the demand and supply curves in the market for any given item, viewers would notice that its price appears on the vertical axis and its quantity appears on the horizontal axis. Equilibrium price and quantity occur where quantity demanded equals quantity supplied or where the downward-sloping demand curve intersects the upward sloping supply curve. At this juncture, take note that two forms of movement may occur on the graph: movement along a curve and a shift in the curve. To keep these movements straight, price analysts should simply note that a change in price initiates movement along the curve whereas a change in a determinant initiates a shift in the curve. An equilibrium point is static at one instance, but it is also dynamic in nature by virtue of a curve shift that results in a different intersection of the demand and supply curve. New intersections and new equilibrium prices and quantities often result from any inward or outward curve shift.

Determinants of Supply & Demand

The demand curve will shift in accordance with a change in a determinant and so will the supply curve. Keep in mind that five determinants exist each for the demand curve and for the supply curve and each can prompt a shift in one curve or both curves. Because it is quite easy to feel overwhelmed and lose track of a critical sequence when more than one curve shift occurs, the author of this essay encourages students to contemplate only one change in one determinant of supply or demand at a time. In other words, each change will likely produce a shift in the curve under consideration.

Before listing the sets of determinants, price analysis is easier by committing to memory various aspects of curve shifts. A rightward, outward, or upward shift in the demand curve is an increase in demand whereas an opposite shift is a decrease in demand. By extension, an increase (decrease) in demand means consumers will purchase a larger (smaller) quantity of an item at any given price. A rightward, downward, or outward shift in the supply curve is an increase in supply whereas an opposite shift is a decrease in supply. Likewise, an increase (decrease) in supply means producers will supply a larger (smaller) quantity of an item at any given price. In contrast to curve shifts, any movement along a demand curve or a supply curve is respectively a change in quantity demanded or quantity supplied to which there is a corresponding change in price.

The list of five determinants for demand and those for supply is as follows:

Demand	Supply
Consumer income	Prices of alternative outputs
Population or number of buyers	Number of sellers
Consumer tastes and preferences	Technology
Prices of related goods	Resource prices
Expected prices	Expected prices

Correspondence between prices and quantities is revealed through demand and supply schedules. Construction of these schedules occurs at two levels of aggregation. Compilations of a market-level demand schedule and supply schedule originate with individual-level schedules. All individuals who buy or sell an item constitute the market for that item. Individual demand schedules represent the quantities each consumer is willing and able to purchase at each price. The summation of quantities from those individual demand schedules across each price becomes the market demand schedule. In comparison, market supply schedules represent the sum of quantities that individual producers are willing and able to sell at each price as long as the market price makes it feasible for them to do so, which is one of the subjects discussed in the next section.

Firm Operating Status, Profit Level, & Competitiveness

The price at which producers can sell their goods and services is only one constraint. The relationship between market prices and producer costs, which will resume in the pages that remain, often influences whether item production will occur. Firms incur a variety of costs in their production of goods and services.

Costs to a Firm

Total costs are the sum of fixed and variable costs. Fixed costs are those that exist even without any production. Furthermore, they are constant as they do not vary with the scale of production. Some examples of fixed costs include monthly installments paid for machinery, buildings, and land. Variable costs are those that vary with production. Some examples of variable costs include wages, materials, and supplies. Keep in mind that production worker payroll is usually the firm's largest variable cost.

The allocation of costs across larger scales of production results in a variety of cost curve shapes. Graphs depicting these functions show cost on the vertical axis and quantity on the horizontal axis. Average total cost and average variable cost form important U-shaped curves. Their calculation involves dividing them by the production quantity. The lowest points on those curves are significant. At those points is where the marginal cost curve, which is J-shaped, intersects them. Marginal cost is the change in total costs that arises from producing one additional unit.

Firm Revenue

Firms produce and sell items, and they receive a price for each one sold. Total revenue is the mathematical product of price times the quantity sold at each price. Marginal revenue is the change in total revenue that arises from selling one additional unit. Price is equal to marginal revenue in competitive market structures and is greater than marginal revenue in monopolistic market structures. Though graphs can become quite confusing with each addition of a line or curve, keep in mind that the marginal revenue line is horizontal in perfectly competitive market structures and is downward sloping in monopolistic structures; a discussion of market structures will resume later.

Rules of Production

A key relationship exists where marginal revenue equals marginal cost and where these two curves intersect. The intersection determines the profit-maximizing amount of output. Most, if not all, firms attempt to set production to that amount as they exhibit profit-maximizing behaviors. Now, let's bring prices back into the analysis for a short discussion of the rules of production. These rules must be met for a firm to continue its operation as a viable entity.

To comply with the first of two rules, firms must produce at the profit maximizing output; again, where marginal revenue equals marginal cost. The second rule is firms must receive a price that is equal to or greater than average variable cost. Why? Their sales must cover, at the least, average variable costs and contribute something toward average fixed costs. In other words, they must cover their variable inputs, labor costs for instance, and make payments on their plants and machinery. Moreover, they must operate at or above the shut-down point, which is where the marginal cost curve intersects the average variable cost curve and at the latter's lowest point.

Another key reference point is the break-even point. It occurs where the marginal cost curve intersects the average total cost curve and at the latter's lowest point. The break-even point also marks the location at which those costs are equal and the firm earns a normal profit. The term is misleading as it seems to indicate an absence of profit. However, profits become part of an operating cost if the owner is to be consistent with the notion of opportunity costs, which is the value the decision maker assigns to the best foregone alternative. In essence, the firm owner expects to earn a specific minimum level of profit in order to remain in the current business. Otherwise, the owner may sell the business using the proceeds to open another business or placing them in a savings account and then go to work as someone else's employee. Therefore, to remain in business, a firm owner or an entrepreneur will pursue the rate of profit considered normal for the market in which he or she conducts business operations and needs to sell at a market price that covers average total costs.

Market Price Analysis

Any analysis of market prices needs to begin with a focus on whether prices occur at the break-even point, at the shut-down point, or somewhere in between. Depending on the market structures in which they operate, some firms can influence the market price and others merely accept the market price for their outputs. Market structure reflects the firm's ability to make the price or to take the price. In context of microeconomics, structures at the extreme ends of a continuum refer to the presence or the absence of competition in a market for a specific output or item. The book ends of that continuum are perfect competition and monopoly or imperfect competition.

In addition to whether firms are price makers or price takers, market structure descriptors often include the number of sellers and buyers and the ease at which firms can enter or exit a market, and the level of profit. One example of product produced in a perfectly competitive market structure is agriculture. In this instance, there are numerous buyers and sellers of an agricultural product such as corn. Consequently, corn farmers take the price dictated by the market and almost anyone can obtain enough resources to grow corn. An example of a product produced in a monopolistic market structure is a computer operating system. In this instance, there are numerous buyers of the system but only one seller. Consequently, system developers make the price, as they are the only producer, and virtually no one can obtain the resources needed to develop the operating systems software. Furthermore, monopolists produce lower quantities than perfect competitors and charge higher prices as a result. Moreover, those prices are much higher than the break-even point, which provide monopolists with profit greater than the normal level. An economic profit is earned when prices are higher than average total cost, which usually invites entry into the market. However, entry into the market for software as a producer is virtually impossible mostly due to legal constraints such as licenses and patents.

Variants in Price Analysis

Prices can vary across space and time. Residents in some locations experience a higher cost of living than residents in other locations for a host of factors that may include climate, lifestyle, and popularity. It is likely that the prices for most goods and services are higher in those locations than they are elsewhere. Item prices may also vary across seasons or annual cycles. Fluctuations in prices over time are of at least two forms.

Cobweb Model Analysis

One form is the result of sequential yet interrelated shifts in demand and supply. Without reviewing the five determinants of demand and of supply found elsewhere in this essay, changes in those determinants often prompt changes in demand and/or supply. A specific pattern may be observed by following and tracing out a set of perpetual changes in demand and in supply. Cobweb model analysis, by virtue of its name, as introduced by Waugh in 1964, conveys the pattern in equilibrium points established by a series of shifts in the demand curve and the supply curve. Readers can sketch a cobweb on their own simply by taking an initial price and quantity equilibrium and creating new equilibrium points from a sequence such as this: an increase in demand; an increase in supply; a decrease in demand half the distance toward the first demand curve; a decrease in supply half the distance likewise; and so on. The sketch will provide readers with some idea of the amount of time for the market to approximate a point close to the original equilibrium point.

Price Indexes

Another form of temporal price changes is detectable through a macroeconomic price index. One widely used index is the Consumer Price Index (CPI). It portrays changes in the general price level over time in the overall economy. Comparing a past CPI to the current CPI will allow analysts to estimate the rate of inflation or the percentage change in the CPI. Its mention here is to inform price analysts of its existence and to facilitate their understanding of prices in a market, which is a microeconomic mode of analysis, in contrast to price level for the whole economy, which is a macroeconomic mode.

CONCLUSION

In conclusion, prices are a key variable whether one is examining the macroeconomic context or analyzing the microeconomic context. In general, the behaviors of firms and consumers reflect their analysis of prices. Both consumers and producers have schedules that serve as records of their willingness and ability to exchange quantities of items at various prices. Producer schedules may be constrained further by cost functions and market structures. In summary, this essay is an attempt to untangle many strands of price analysis to facilitate learning at the undergraduate level.

BIBLIOGRAPHY

Aguirre, M., & Rodríguez, J. (2013). Relación de causalidad entre el índice de precios del productor y el índice de precios del consumidor incorporando cambios estructurales: el caso de los países miembros del tlcan. (Spanish). Global Conference on Business & Finance Proceedings, 8(1), 848-854. Retrieved November 15, 2013, from EBSCO Online Database Business Source Complete. http://search.ebscohost.com/login.aspx?direct=true&db=bth&AN=87078482&site=ehost-live

Arnold, Roger A. (2005). Economics (7th ed.) Mason, OH: Thomson South-Western.

Guell, R. C. (2007). Issues in economics today (3rd ed.). Boston, MA: McGraw-Hill Irwin.

McConnell, C. R. & Brue, S. L. (2008). Economics (17th ed.). Boston, MA: McGraw-Hill Irwin.

Obadia, C. (2013). Competitive Export Pricing: The Influence of the Information Context. Journal Of International Marketing, 21(2), 62-78. Retrieved November 15, 2013, from EBSCO Online Database Business Source Complete. http://search.ebscohost.com/login.aspx?direct=true&db=bth&AN=87742601&site=ehost-live

Peltier, J.W., Skidmore, M., & Milne, G.R. (2013). Assessing the impact of gasoline sales-below-cost laws on retail price and market structure: Implications for consumer welfare. Journal of Public Policy & Marketing, 32(2), 239-254. Retrieved November 15, 2013, from EBSCO Online Database Business Source Complete. http://search.ebscohost.com/login.aspx?direct=true&db=bth&AN=91886742&site=ehost-live

SUGGESTED READING

Chen, K., Chen, K., & Li, R. (2005). Suppliers capability and price analysis chart. International Journal of Production Economics, 98(3), 315-327. Retrieved September 18, 2007, from EBSCO Online Database Business Source Premier. http://search.ebscohost.com/login.aspx?direct=true&db=buh&AN=18756488&site=ehost-live

Pearce, D. W. (Ed.). (1992). The MIT dictionary of modern economics. Cambridge, MA: MIT Press.

Simmons-Mosley, T.X., Lubwama, C., & Fung-Shine, P. (2013). In retrospect: An early 2000 affordability analysis of house prices in the San Francisco bay area. Journal of International Finance & Economics, 13(4), 49-56. Retrieved November 15, 2013, from EBSCO Online Database Business Source Complete. http://search.ebscohost.com/login.aspx?direct=true&db=bth&AN=91830968&site=ehost-live

Vallarta supermarkets pursues price optimization. (2007). Chain Store Age, 83(2), 38. Retrieved September 18, 2007, from EBSCO Online Database Business Source Premier. http://search.ebscohost.com/login.aspx?direct=true&db=buh&AN=23965869&site=ehost-live

Waugh, F. (1964). Cobweb models. Journal of Farm Economics, 46(4), 732-750

Zaleski, P., & Esposto, A. (2007). The response to market power: Non-profit hospitals versus for-profit hospitals. Atlantic Economic Journal, 35(3), 315-325. Retrieved September 18, 2007, from EBSCO Online Database Business Source Premier. http://search.ebscohost.com/login.aspx?direct=true&db=buh&AN=26218268&site=ehost-live

Steven R. Hoagland, Ph.D.

PRICE DISCRIMINATION

ABSTRACT

Price discrimination is generally defined as charging different prices for the same product or service and may occur on first-, second- or third-degree levels, which are defined according to knowledge of the market and the goals of the seller. In the minds of the general public, price discrimination often conjures up visions of inherent unfairness, but many economists maintain that price discrimination is necessary to keep the market stable. Price discrimination based on such characteristics as race and gender is generally considered unacceptable.

OVERVIEW

Most prices are based on the cost of providing a product or service, plus a profit for the seller. Firms normally establish prices according to reservation prices that are based on what customers/clients are willing to pay and the minimum they, as sellers, are willing to accept. When the reservation price of the buyer and seller are too far apart, no sale is made. From a business owner's perspective, the ideal pricing would always be based on charging each customer what he or she is willing to pay, resulting in higher prices for those willing to pay more and lower prices for those who are unwilling or unable to pay more. Economists have attempted to clarify the meaning of price discrimination by explaining that it occurs only when a firm sells goods at price ratios that are different from the ratios of marginal costs (Edwards, 2014). The classic example of this is when a publisher sells a hardcover book for $30 and an e-book version of the same book for $10 at a ratio of 3:1. Other examples include movie tickets sold at discounted prices to students and seniors, airplane tickets sold at different prices to business travelers, college tuition that is lower for in-state residents than for those from out of state, and store loyalty programs that offer discounted prices to regular customers who allow companies to track their purchases.

Economists agree that price discrimination occurs at different levels. First-degree price discrimination is limited to buyers who possess complete knowledge of the willingness of customers to accept a particular price. In such situations, customers are prevented from seeking out the lowest price available because of market monopolies. With second-degree price discrimination, sellers control large segments of the market and offer lower prices to those who buy in bulk. Since small firms cannot afford to store large quantities of merchandise, they are required to pay higher prices for the same goods.

Third-degree price discrimination is based on the concept of setting prices according to the high and low demands of particular groups. The classic example of third-degree price discrimination is providing student and senior discounts to segments of the populations with lower demands and incomes. Because the different levels of price discrimination may result in injuries to those paying higher prices, different levels of injuries are accepted by the courts. Primary-line injury occurs when sellers engage in predation, offering goods or services at reduced prices solely for the purpose of shutting out local competitors either through forcing them out of business or preventing new competitors from entering the market. Reduced prices in one area may be financed by charging higher prices in another area where no local competitor is present. Second-line injury is often experienced by disfavored firms who pay higher prices than favored firms for the same product.

Most economists agree that price discrimination is dependent on an accurate market segmentation, the ability to prevent the resale of products sold (arbitrage), and control of a particular market (DePasquale, 2015). Business owners may prevent arbitrage through requiring identification for purchase of the product or service, placing maximums on the number of items purchased at a particular price, or prohibiting the transfer of a particular price or service to another customer. Arbitrage is considered beneficial in some instances since buyers are more likely to purchase items from retailers who have some knowledge of a product and its uses. The issue of arbitrage came before the Supreme Court in 2013 in *Kirtsaeng v. John Wiley and Sons* (131 S Ct. 1351). The case involved the actions of Supap Kirtsaeng, a Thai student who purchased textbooks from Asia and resold them on the American market at lower prices than those demanded by the publisher. Wiley was originally awarded $600,000 for copyright infringement, but the Supreme Court overturned the case on the basis of the first-sale doctrine, holding that a buyer had the right to resell a copy of a book bought anywhere in the world without engaging in copyright infringement.

Firms may use predation to force competitors out of business or keep them from entering the market. McGee (1958) was the first to argue that predation was often the result of rational behavior. Building on McGee's foundation, economists developed reputation, long-purse predation, and signaling models to explain the concept of predation. Some predators use the reputation model to assert their right to dominate the market by appearing so tough that no rival is able to compete. Those who practice long-purse predation use their "deep pockets" to survive a period of reduced profits while undercutting all competition. In the signaling model, an incumbent business depends on market signals such as existing prices and advertising to convince competitors that it is inadvisable to enter a given market. Pires and Jorge (2012) argue that all predation models are based on the incomplete information of those who challenge incumbent business owners.

APPLICATIONS

During the rapid industrialization of the late nine-teenth and early twentieth centuries, Americans be-came disillusioned with monopolies that cut down all competitors large and small. New federal legisla-tion was passed, and antitrust suits flourished. The Interstate Commerce Commission was established in 1887 to protect free trade and enforce fair pricing across state lines. Congress passed the Sherman Antitrust Act in 1890, threatening both individuals and corporations with heavy fines and prison terms for engaging in monopolies. In 1911, both *Standard Oil Company v. U.S.* (221 US 1) and *US v. American Tobacco Company* (221 US 106) were used to break up monopolies that had enabled the giant companies to practice widespread price discrimination. Congress passed the Clayton Antitrust Act in 1914 as a means of preventing monopolists from using price discrimina-tion to keep small local companies out of a particular field. The Clayton Act provided for damages of three times injuries suffered for victims who experienced antitrust price discrimination injuries.

By the 1930s, Congress had become concerned with protecting small business owners from being over-ridden by the large chains that had opened across the country. These chains were able to buy items in bulk for low prices and then resell them at higher prices. Congress amended the Clayton Antitrust Act in 1936 by passing the Robinson-Patman Act, providing a means of protecting victims of primary- and second-line injury (Blair, Piette & Durance, 2015). From the beginning, the Robinson-Patman Act was unpopular with economists who believed that Congress had not left enough leeway for price differences related to costs. In cases brought under Robinson-Patman, the plaintiff bore the burden of proving that an antitrust violation had occurred and was required to prove that liability was likely to hamper competition or threaten monopoly (Blair et al., 2015). For example, in *Brunswick Corporation v. Pueblo Bowl-o-Mat, Inc.* (429 US 477), in 1977, the Court held that Brunswick, one of several local bowling centers, had created a likeli-hood of predatory pricing by acquiring Bowl-o-Mat's failing competitors and thereby preventing healthy competitors from adjusting their prices upward.

Before *Brunswick*, the Court had tended to focus entirely on the issue of liability, requiring plaintiffs to demonstrate that an actual antitrust injury had been suffered. The most notorious case dealt with on these grounds was *Utah Pie Company v. Continental Baking Company* (386 US 685, 1967). The case arose out of the entry of Utah Pie into the frozen pie market in Salt Lake City. Before that time, pies had been bought exclusively from Carnation, Continental Baking, and Pet Milk, but the local company sold their pies at lower prices. Within two years, Utah Pie was claiming 67 percent of the frozen pie market, leading to lower prices and increased competition. As other compa-nies increased output and sold pies in Salt Lake City at prices lower than elsewhere, Utah Pie's share of the market fell to 45 percent, and the company filed suit on the grounds of price discrimination under the Clayton and Robinson-Patman Acts. The Court agreed, holding that sellers were prohibited from selling items at different prices with the intention of interfering with the freedom of the market.

The issue of primary-line injury was again visited by the Court in 1993 in *Brook Group Ltd. v. Brown and Williamson Tobacco Corporation* (509 US 209). The case resulted from disputes over prices for generic ciga-rettes, which were introduced as the demand for ciga-rettes fell in the early 1980s. As a way to recoup losses, the Brook Group began selling generic cigarettes at prices 30 percent lower than name-brand cigarettes. A price war erupted when Brown and Williamson began selling generic cigarettes at even lower prices. The Brook Group filed suit, claiming that volume discounts granted by Brown and Williamson were a form of price discrimination. The Court established a two-prong test to determine predatory pricing that required plaintiffs to prove that prices were "below an appropriate measure of its rival's costs" and that a reasonable prospect of recouping investments by selling products below cost prices existed.

ISSUES

Since significant variations exist in what is considered justifiable price discrimination, the courts have consistently been called upon to settle the legal boundaries between what is acceptable and what is not. Cases decided on the basis of Robinson-Patman have involved both first- and second-degree injury (DePasquale, 2015). In the 1940s, the Morton Salt Company began providing five favored grocery store chains with salt that could be bought in bulk for $1.35 a case. Disfavored companies challenged the practice, and *FTC v. Morton Salt* (334 US 37) was heard by the Supreme Court in 1948. The Court held that the bulk discounts were illegal because the cost of the salt was not based on costs involved in producing the product. Some analysts insisted that the Court had erred in its decision because no injury had been suffered by disfavored companies since the sale of salt made up only a small portion of store profits. *Morton Salt* was revisited in 2006 in *Volvo Trucks North America, Inc. v. Reeder-Simco GMC, Inc.* (546 US 164) when the Court held that injury could be proved only when identical products were being sold by favored and disfavored companies.

The standard for judging secondary-line injury was established in *J. Truett Payne Company v. Chrysler Motors Corporation* (451 US 557) in 1981. Chrysler had been providing bonuses to selected dealers that were based entirely on quotas established by Chrysler. The quota required of J. Truett Payne was higher than those of its rivals, and the company did not receive a bonus because it was unable to meet its quota and was subsequently forced out of business. J. Truett Payne then filed suit under the Clayton and Robinson-Patman Acts. A jury awarded the petitioner $111,247.48 in damages, and that amount was trebled by a federal district court. However, the decision was reversed by the Court of Appeals, which argued that the petitioner had failed to produce sufficient evidence of antitrust injury. The Supreme Court also rejected the claim of "automatic damages."

The number of courts challenging price discrimination under Robinson-Patman began a steady decline in the mid-1970s, and the last time the Department of Justice filed a Robinson-Patman case was in 1972. Since 1990, the Federal Trade Commission (FTC) has filed only one Robinson-Patman case (Blair et al., 2015). However, private suits continue to be filed. Robinson-Patman was the basis for *Texaco, Inc. v. Hasbruck* (496 US 543, 1990), which concerned a Spokane gas retailer who had offered discounts to Gull and Dompier distributors in the early 1970s during the oil crisis. Other retailers who were charged higher prices were forced out of business. Ultimately, Texaco was convicted of discriminating against small competitors.

In October 2014, Woodman's Food Market, a 15-store supermarket chain based in Janesville, Wisconsin, brought suit against Clorox, charging the company with price discrimination for selling bulk packages of products such as Clorox, Glad, Hidden Valley, and Bert's Bees only to large retailers such as Sam's Club and Costco. In February 2015, a federal district court dismissed Clorox's claim that the challenge was based on "outdated" FTC rulings and allowed the case to proceed.

In some cases, the unfairness of price discrimination is so obvious that the public is able to win a resolution without resorting to the courts. Such a case occurred in late 2000 when it became known that Amazon, the Internet giant, was selling DVDs to customers at different prices. When customers alleged price discrimination, Amazon CEO Jeff Bezos apologized, explaining that price differences were simply a response to a random price test that had been conducted to determine if more items would be purchased when they were sold at a lower price. Some 6,896 customers were refunded $3.10 each.

Beginning in 1991, Ian Ayers, an economics and law professor at Yale University, has done significant work on the issue of gender and racial price discrimination. In a landmark study (1991), Ayers found that when purchasing automobiles, white women were charged a 40 percent markup. African-American males were charged twice as much for the same car as a white male, and African-American women were charged three times as much. An updated study in 1995 revealed that African Americans and white females were still being charged higher prices than white males. Some price discrimination based on gender is considered acceptable as in the case of haircuts, deodorants, and face creams.

Some price discrimination has occurred at the global level. In the summer of 2015, the European Commission and French authorities learned that Disneyland Paris was charging different prices to citizens of different countries. The same package was being sold to French residents for $1,486, to British residents for $2,065, and to German residents for $2,702 in direct violation of single-market rules established by the European Union (EU). Disneyland claimed that the price differences were a response to promotional packages designed for particular markets.

BIBLIOGRAPHY

Ayers, I. (1991). Fair driving: Gender and race discrimination in retail car negotiations. Faculty Scholarship Series. Paper 1540. Retrieved November 29, 2015 from http://digitalcommons.law.yale.edu/fss_papers/1540/

Blair, R., Piette, D., & Durrance, C. (2015). Private damage actions under the Robinson-Patman act. Antitrust Bulletin, 60(4), 384–401. Retrieved November 21, 2015 from EBSCO Online Database Business Source Complete. http://search.ebscohost.com/login.aspx?direct=true&db=a9h&AN=110970184&site=ehost-live

Cabral, L. (2000). Principles of pricing: An analytical approach. Cambridge, MA: MIT Press.

DePasquale, C. (2015). The Robinson-Patman act and the consumer effects of price discrimination. Antitrust Bulletin, 60(4), 402–413. Retrieved November 21, 2015 from EBSCO Online Database Business Source Complete. http://search.ebscohost.com/login.aspx?direct=true&db=bth&AN=110970185&site=ehost-live

Edwards, M. A. (2014). Teaching consumer price discrimination: An interdisciplinary case study for business law students. Journal of Legal Studies Education, 31(1), 291–324. Retrieved January 3, 2016 from EBSCO Online Database Education Research Complete. http://search.ebscohost.com/login.aspx?direct=true&db=ehh&AN=97177207&site=ehost-live

Elegido, J. M. (2011). The ethics of price discrimination. Business Ethics Quarterly, 21(4), 633–660. Retrieved November 21, 2015 from EBSCO Online Database Business Source Complete. http://search.ebscohost.com/login.aspx?direct=true&db=bth&AN=66804218&site=ehost-live

McGee, J. (1958). Predatory price cutting: The Standard Oil (NJ) case. Journal of Law and Economics, 1, 137–169.

Pires, C., & Jorge, S. (2012). Limit pricing under third-degree price discrimination. International Journal of Game Theory, 41(3), 671. 698.

Retrieved November 21, 2015 from EBSCO Online Database Business Source Complete. http://search.ebscohost.com/login.aspx?direct=true&db=bth&AN=77656540&site=ehost-live

Vohra, R. V., & Krishnamurthi, L. (2012). Principles of Pricing: An Analytical Approach. New York, NY: Cambridge University Press.

SUGGESTED READING

Chao, Y., & Nahata, B. (2015). The degree of distortions under second-degree price discrimination. Economics Letters, 137, 208–213. Retrieved January 3, 2016 from EBSCO Online Database Business Source Complete. http://search.ebscohost.com/login.aspx?direct=true&db=bth&AN=111486081&site=ehost-live

Kain, J. F. (2004). A pioneer's perspective on the spatial mismatch literature. Urban Studies, 41(1), 7–32.

Marcoux, A. M. (2006). Much ado about price discrimination. Journal of Markets and Morality, 9(1), 57–69.

Motta, M. (2004). Competition policy–Theory and practice. Cambridge, UK: Cambridge University Press.

Okada, T. (2014). Third-degree price discrimination with fairness-concerned consumers. Manchester School (14636786), 82(6), 701–715. Retrieved January 3, 2016 from EBSCO Online Database Business Source Complete. http://search.ebscohost.com/login.aspx?direct=true&db=bth&AN=99008355&site=ehost-live

Waldfogel, J. (2015). First Degree Price Discrimination Goes to School. Journal Of Industrial Economics, 63(4), 569-597. Retrieved January 3, 2016 from EBSCO Online Database Business Source Complete. http://search.ebscohost.com/login.aspx?direct=true&db=bth&AN=112000280&site=ehost-live

White, J. B. (2014). Price Discrimination: A Classroom Exercise. Business Education Innovation Journal, 6(2), 100-103. Retrieved January 3, 2016 from EBSCO Online Database Business Source Complete. http://search.ebscohost.com/login.aspx?direct=true&db=bth&AN=101197677&site=ehost-live

Elizabeth Rholetter Purdy, Ph.D.

PRICING POLICY

ABSTRACT

Determining the appropriate price for a product or service is an intricate problem. Three factors need to be considered: the lowest price that can be charged for the product or service without sustaining a loss; the value of the product or service to the potential customer; and the price charged by the competition for similar products or services. These factors are complicated by whether or not a product is durable or consumable as well as whether or not the target market is able to pay. Optimal pricing is also affected by vertical differentiation (i.e., perceived higher quality goods or services) and horizontal differentiation (i.e., different characteristics within a single product line). Prices are not necessarily set in stone, however. It is often advantageous to offer discounts to attract customers and maintain customer loyalty.

OVERVIEW

An old adage cautions that one should not charge more than the market will bear. This is, of course, sound advice. Although one wants to make as much money as possible from a transaction for a number of reasons, it is not feasible to simply set a high price. First, no matter how specific one's market niche, there is virtually no business that is without competition. If a business prices its product or service too high, it is relatively easy for a competitor to set its prices lower and take over a larger portion of the market share. In addition, most consumers have a good idea of what a product or service is worth and what they are willing to pay. For example, although I might be willing to invest a significant amount when purchasing a solid wood dresser, it is unlikely that I would be willing to pay the same amount for a fiberboard replica of the dresser because I know the various advantages and disadvantages of each and what its relative price ranges are. Similarly, although I might like to have an expensive new piece of electronic equipment for my business, if the price is such that the equipment will not save me at least a comparable amount of time and money, I am unlikely to make the purchase no matter how reasonably the price is set vis a vis the value of the item.

From the business's point of view, pricing is as complicated as the buying decision is for the consumer. Sometimes, for example, it is cost-effective for a business to make little or no profit in the short term in order to bring in a larger customer base and higher profits in the long term. This marketing philosophy isillustrated in the Sunday supplement of most major newspapers every week; this supplement carries coupons for products both old and new. Similarly, most days one can find advertisements and coupons in the mail offering first-time customers discounts for trying a product or service. By not making as much profit on the first sale, the businesses offering the products or services hope to earn customer loyalty and continued higher profits over the long term.

Determining Best Price

To enable a business to best price its goods or services, three factors need to be considered and understood. First, as a general rule, the lowest price one can offer a product at is the cost of that product to the business. (There are occasional exceptions where a business prices an item or a service below cost to harm a competitor or gain new customers. However, this approach tends to be successful only as a short-term strategy.) This low price limit must include other factors such as the costs associated with the personnel, equipment, and administration associated with selling and delivering the product or service. Pricing must take into account the salaries of all the personnel involved with that product line such as production, management, human relations, shipping and receiving, and accounting personnel. In addition, pricing needs to take into consideration overhead costs such as the cost to rent facilities, pay for utilities, taxes, and so forth. The second factor that needs to be taken into consideration when setting a price for a product or service is its value—in other words, what is it worth to the customer? This is one of the reasons that purchasing a drink at the movies is more expensive than purchasing a drink at the grocery store. Since the customer cannot bring his or her own soda or water to the theatre, the value of the drink rises. In the grocery store, however, there are more choices not only within the store but at other stores to which the customer can go. So, value places a cap on how much a business can charge for a product or service. Somewhere in the middle between the cost of the product or service to the business and its value to the customer is typically where the actual price of the item will fall. This actual price is influenced by a third factor: the price charged by the competition. Even if one sets the price lower than the value, if a competitor offers the same or a similar product or service at a lower price, it is more likely that the customer will choose the competitor's product or service.

In addition to the old adage about setting prices that the market will bear, there is another old adage that cautions that one gets what one pays for. Indeed, research has found that many consumers do not do sufficient research to differentiate between similar products but often use price as an indicator of quality. There are, of course, limits to this philosophy. Carried to an extreme, this would mean that the higher the price, the more likely people would be to buy a product or service. Although this may be true in some instances, it is not a universal truth. Some purchasing decisions are made not on getting the "best," but on getting the "good enough." Also, some people are out to get a bargain. If offered the same item at two different prices, most people would opt for the less expensive of the two.

Relationship between Price & Purchase Probability

The literature on consumer buying habits reflects the same complicated relationship between price and purchase probability. Recent research into this phenomenon examined three levels of products: a durable product (specifically, a color television set)' a semi-durable product (specifically, a T-shirt); and a non-durable product (specifically, toothpaste). It was found that the relationship between price and consumer buying decisions was complex. For durable goods, the study found that too low a price negatively affected the customer's impression of the product's quality and the probability that the customer would purchase the item. For this level of product, customers tended to purchase a mid- to high-priced product, on the assumption that the price was an indicator of the quality of the item. In fact, customers surveyed in the study believed that it was risky to buy a low-priced product. Another reason that customers hesitated to buy a low-priced product is because they thought it would negatively affect their image. These results

imply that pricing for durable goods such as television sets should not be set too low in order to give the product a higher image. However, this approach is not without its limits. When setting the price of such goods, it is also important to take into consideration competitors' prices on similar products as well as the purchase power of the target market. Whether or not they think that an item is a good value, if it is out of their price range most people will not purchase it.

Semi-Durable Products

For the semi-durable product, price was again found to be a factor. Once again, those consumers surveyed believed that the lower the price of the T-shirt, the lower the quality of the garment. However, customers purchasing semi-durable goods were more skeptical about the relationship between price and value than were those who were purchasing durable goods. For this type of item, purchasing decisions were more likely to be made based on the perceived value of the item (e.g., strength, texture, colorfastness) than on price alone. This makes pricing items of this nature more difficult than pricing for durable goods such as television sets. Part of the problem with pricing T-shirts is that the customers tend to be young and have limited purchasing power. Therefore, even though they might like to purchase a name-brand product, they often chose a less expensive item instead. From a marketing perspective, therefore, it is helpful to select the appropriate segment of the target market and price the item accordingly.

Non-Durable Products

Finally, it was found that customers tended to pay less attention to price when buying the non-durable product than the other types of products. Other factors such as brand loyalty, reputation, and features were more important in the purchase decision than was the price. Although the customers surveyed did believe that there was a relationship between price and product quality, this belief was not as strong as for the durable and semi-durable goods. For non-durable products such as toothpaste, this means that the product should be priced according to the reputation of the brand. However, as with the other types of products studied, pricing the product too low could negatively impact sales and create the impression of an inferior product in the consumer's mind.

Differential Pricing within Multiple Product Lines

Businesses are not only interested in pricing relative to their competitors' products; sometimes they need to determine differential prices for their own multiple product lines. The number of consumer goods offered has been steadily rising for several decades. For example, in the early 1970s, Colgate only offered two varieties of toothpaste; today it offers 19. Similarly, Häagen Dazs only offered three flavors of ice cream when it first started operations in 1961; by 2004 it offered 36 flavors. Even credit card companies differentiate their offers. The industry offered only a small number of cards in the 1960s. Today, tens of thousands of distinct card offers go out daily.

Vertical Presentation

One of the ways that businesses differentiate between their various product lines is to present them vertically; offering different quality levels at different prices. As in the example of T-shirts above, moderately priced garments with fewer features are more likely to be purchased by young people with limited disposable income than are higher priced garments. However, in some businesses or industries, product lines do not differ by quality but by features. For example, Coca Cola offers regular Coke, classic Coke, Diet Coke, decaffeinated Diet Coke, Coke Zero, Cherry Coke, and so forth. This is an example of horizontal differentiation. Items that only differ along this dimension are priced the same.

Horizontal & Vertical Presentation

Sometimes, however, product lines are differentiated both horizontally and vertically. Yoplait, for example, offers numerous product lines including original, light, whips, and thick and creamy as well as smoothies, Yoplait for Kids, etc. (vertical differentiation). Within each product line is a range of flavors (horizontal differentiation). Research into pricing in such situations shows that consumers tend to be more interested in the characteristics of the product line (i.e., the vertical differentiation) than in the flavors (i.e., the horizontal differentiation) offered. In fact, the addition of flavors to a product line does not always increase the worth of the line in the customer's eyes. The standard practice of pricing all items within a line the same is, therefore, optimal.

APPLICATIONS

Discount Pricing

Sometimes an effective pricing strategy is to permanently lower the price of a product or service with the expectation of making up the loss in increased sales volume. For example, the industry average markup on wine purchased by customers in restaurants is typically 100 to 150 percent above wholesale. Many restaurants find, however, this price was often more than the market would bear. However, one restaurant found that when it lowered its markup on wine to 50 percent, it doubled its sales volume in wine, thus retaining its profitability on wine.

As illustrated by this example, offering discounts can sometimes be a worthwhile venture. However, this tactic should only be implemented as part of a well-thought-out strategy as a way to help the organization reach its goals and objectives. The decision as to whether or not to offer a discount should be made based on rigorous analysis of several factors including market needs and trends, competitor capabilities and offerings, and the organization's resources and abilities. For example, a discount can help the business attain such strategic goals as securing customer loyalty (e.g., giving the customer a discount if he or she signs a long-term contract) or customizing products (e.g., giving the customer a discount if he or she bundles several services tailored to his or her needs). In such cases, the business is forcing the customer to decide which products or services are of value and make tradeoffs in determining which products or services he or she most desires. In addition, this approach to discounting requires the customer to work closely with the sales representative. This situation, in turn, will tend to make the customer see the sales representative as a partner helping to determine which products or services to purchase. This gives the business further opportunities to sell to the customer.

Discounting Policy

However, in order for discounting to be an effective way to increase profits, it is important for the business to have a consistent discounting policy made at a level higher in the organization than direct sales. If such a policy is not in place, a discount may aid in the individual sale but will also probably hurt the next several sales. For example, if an individual salesperson offers a customer a discount, the salesperson may make the sale, but when the customer returns, he or she will expect a discount again. Or, if other people find out about the discount, the next several customers will also expect a discount to the disadvantage of the company either in terms of lost revenue or decreased customer satisfaction. However, discounts are not always necessary to attract and keep customers. A product or service that is easily distinguishable from those offered by the competition may add value for which the customer is willing to pay. Superior salespersons who give excellent customer service are another factor that will keep a customer coming back despite a somewhat higher price.

Discount Amount

In addition to deciding whether or not to offer a discount, the organization must also decide how much the discount should be. It should consider two factors when making this decision. First, it must carefully analyze the gross margin. This is the ratio of gross income divided by net sales expressed as a percentage. Gross margin is a measure of the retailer's markup over wholesale. Gross margins are an expression of earnings adjusted for costs associated with producing the product or service. Most businesses attempt to have a gross margin as large as possible, although discount retailers attempt to keep operations efficient so that they can afford a smaller markup. If the business's gross margin is 10 percent and it discounts a product by 5 percent, its income is cut in half, and it must double its sales to keep the same profit. If, on the other hand, the gross margin is 50 percent and the business offers a 5-percent discount, income is only reduced by a tenth, and sales will only need to increase by 10 percent to make up for the difference. Any increased sales over that amount will mean higher overall profits. The second consideration in whether or not to offer a discount is price band analysis. This is a statistical model that measures what customers should pay within a band of prices as opposed to those prices that fall outside the band. Using these two indicators, a business can set pricing and discounting policies that help increase long-term sales, market share, and customer loyalty rather than merely helping the business meet short-term sales goals or quotas.

Customer Relationship Management

One of the ways that businesses can customize their marketing approaches to the needs of individual customers is through the practice of customer relationship management. This is the process of identifying prospective customers, acquiring data that concerns these prospective and current customers, building relationships with customers, and influencing their perceptions of the organization and its products or services. These systems can help businesses develop marketing policies that will adjust to the changing dynamic between with the customer over time. These approaches also seek to increase customer value, an estimate of how much a customer will spend with a business or brand. Analysis of customer value should include consideration of the depth, breadth, and duration of the customer's relationship with the business or brand as well as the cost to acquire, serve, and retain each customer.

A recent study performed by Lewis investigated the effect of discounting on customer relationship pricing in offering discounts for a major metropolitan newspaper. In practice, many newspapers offer new customers a one-time steep discount for starting a new subscription that is not extended to current customers. A dynamic programming model was created that uses a customer transaction history of more than 1,300 customers to develop a Markov chain that determines a way to maximize long-term customer value. As opposed to current practice, however, it was found that such businesses can increase profitability by offering a series of decreasing discounts as customer tenure with the business grows, rather than using a traditional single steep discount to acquire new customers.

BIBLIOGRAPHY

Cai, X., Feng, Y., Li, Y., & Shi, D. (2013). Optimal pricing policy for a deteriorating product by dynamic tracking control. *International Journal of Production Research, 51*, 2491-2504. Retrieved November 15, 2013, from EBSCO Online Database Business Source Complete. http://search.ebscohost.com/login.aspx?direct=true&db=bth&AN=85879208&site=ehost-live

Class, J.N. (2012). Emerging markets and differential pricing policies: A question of global health?. *Journal of Commercial Biotechnology, 18*, 40-43. Retrieved November 15, 2013, from EBSCO Online Database Business Source Complete. http://search.ebscohost.com/login.aspx?direct=true&db=bth&AN=84433070&site=ehost-live

Hosford, C. (2006). The value of good pricing policies. *B to B, 91*, 16. Retrieved June 5, 2007, from EBSCO Online Database Business Source Complete. http://search.ebscohost.com/login.aspx?direct=true&db=bth&AN=23358742&site=ehost-live

Lewis, M. (2005). Research note: A dynamic programming approach to customer relationship pricing. *Management Science, 51*, 986-994. Retrieved June 5, 2007, from EBSCO Online Database Business Source Complete. http://search.ebscohost.com/login.aspx?direct=true&db=bth&AN=17531714&site=ehost-live

Obadia, C. (2013). Competitive export pricing: the influence of the information context. *Journal of International Marketing, 21*, 62-78. Retrieved November 15, 2013, from EBSCO Online Database Business Source Complete. http://search.ebscohost.com/login.aspx?direct=true&db=bth&AN=87742601&site=ehost-live

Verma, D. P. S.; Gupta, S. (2004). Does higher price signal better quality? *The Journal for Decision Makers, 29*, 67-77. Retrieved June 5, 2007, from EBSCO Online Database Business Source Complete. http://search.ebscohost.com/login.aspx?direct=true&db=bth&AN=14024729&site=ehost-live

Voelckner, F. (2006). An empirical comparison of methods for measuring consumers' willingness to pay. *Marketing Letters, 17*, 137-149. Retrieved June 5, 2007, from EBSCO Online Database Business Source Complete. http://search.ebscohost.com/login.aspx?direct=true&db=bth&AN=20743072&site=ehost-live

Walkup, C. (2005). Restaurateurs enjoy higher sales with lower markups on bottled wine. *Nation's Restaurant News, 39*, 4-82. Retrieved June 5, 2007, from EBSCO Online Database Business Source Complete. http://search.ebscohost.com/login.aspx?direct=true&db=bth&AN=18954638&site=ehost-live

SUGGESTED READING

Cattani, K., Gilland, W., Heese, H. S., & Swaminathan, J. (2006). Boiling frogs: Pricing strategies for a manufacturer adding a direct channel that competes with the traditional channel. *Production & Operations Management, 15*, 40-56. Retrieved June 5, 2007, from EBSCO Online Database Business Source Complete. http://search.ebscohost.com/login.aspx?direct=true&db=bth&AN=22404181&site=ehost-live

Draganska, M. & Jain, D. C. (2006). Consumer preferences and product-line pricing strategies: An empirical analysis. *Marketing Science, 25*, 164-174. Retrieved June 5, 2007, from EBSCO Online Database Business Source Complete. http://search.ebscohost.com/login.aspx?direct=true&db=bth&AN=20944037&site=ehost-live

Kehoe, K. (2004). Make your price fit. *Landscape Management, 43*, 46-52. Retrieved June 5, 2007, from EBSCO Online Database Business Source Complete. http://search.ebscohost.com/login.aspx?direct=true&db=bth&AN=14775606&site=ehost-live

Rusmevichientong, P., Van Roy, B., & Glynn, P. W. (2006). A nonparametric approach to multiproduct pricing. *Operations Research, 54*, 82-98. Retrieved June 5, 2007, from EBSCO Online Database Business Source Complete. http://search.ebscohost.com/login.aspx?direct=true&db=bth&AN=19949376&site=ehost-live

Saleh, S. H. (2005). How do you stop a disastrous service pricing practice? *Services Revenue, 3*, 1-10. Retrieved June 5, 2007, from EBSCO Online Database Business Source Complete. http://search.ebscohost.com/login.aspx?direct=true&db=bth&AN=23631642&site=ehost-live

Swami, S. & Khairnar, P. J. (2006). Optimal normative policies for marketing of products with limited availability. *Annals of Operations Research, 143*, 107-121. Retrieved June 5, 2007, from EBSCO Online Database Business Source Complete. http://search.ebscohost.com/login.aspx?direct=true&db=bth&AN=20743058&site=ehost-live

Ruth A. Wienclaw, Ph.D.

PRICING STRATEGIES

ABSTRACT

This article will focus on how marketing professionals develop pricing strategies for their organizations. There will be a review of the guidelines that these individuals process in order to determine the optimal pricing structure for each product or service. The different types of potential pricing strategies (i.e., entrepreneurial, penetration, premium) will be explored. The concept of international countertrade as it relates to pricing will also be introduced.

OVERVIEW

Pricing is one of the four aspects (product management, pricing, promotion, and place) in the marketing mix, and it directly affects how a product is positioned in the market. Pricing should take into consideration fixed and variable costs, competition, organizational objectives, proposed positioning strategies, target groups, and consumer willingness to pay the price. When an appropriate price is selected, it should assist the organization in reaching its financial goals, be a realistic price for the target market, and be cohesive with other marketing mix components as well as with product positioning. Many organizations have utilized various factors when determining the pricing strategies for their products and services. However, there are some general guidelines that all share. For example, the marketing representatives may go through a series of steps such as:

Create a marketing strategy: This entails conducting a market analysis, a product segmentation, targeting, and positioning. The team will have to determine each aspect of the marketing mix formula. The first step will be to develop a marketing strategy for the product or service. At this point, a decision is made as to who the target market will be and how the product will be positioned. Another factor will be based upon whether pricing is going to be a key point of the positioning.

Determine the proper marketing mix. This involves product definition, distribution, and promotion. There will be trade-offs between the variables in the marketing mix. Pricing will be based on other decisions that have been made in the areas of distribution and promotion. For example, is the expectation to sell a small number of luxury items at high prices so that the product becomes a rare, unique commodity?

Be aware of the demand curve: Determine how price affects the quantity demanded. There tends to be a relationship between price and quantity demanded. Therefore, the marketing team will attempt to estimate the demand curve for the product or service since pricing directly affects sales. The first step will be to conduct market research to find out how a particular price point will affect the demand for the product. If the product already exists, the marketers may want to survey whether the market will accept prices above the current price. The results will give the marketing team an idea of the price elasticity of demand for the product.

Determine cost of product: Calculate a product's associated fixed and variable costs. Once it has been determined that the product will be launched, members of the marketing team will need to understand all the costs involved. Therefore, they will need to calculate the fixed and variable costs associated with the product or service, which is referred to as the total unit cost. The unit cost of the product determines how much is needed to break even. Any price set higher than this will help set the profit margin.

Understand environmental factors: Evaluate potential responses from competitors and understand legal constraints. The marketing team should find out if there are any legal restraints on pricing. For example, offering different prices to different consumers can lead to cases of price discrimination. In some markets, legislation may dictate how high prices can go. Also, there are laws that prevent predatory pricing, especially in the international trade market.

Set pricing objectives: There are a variety of ways to set the pricing objectives. Some of the most popular objectives include:

- **Profit maximization**—By taking into consideration revenue and costs, this objective seeks to maximize current profits.
- **Revenue maximization**—This objective does not take profit margins into consideration when attempting to maximize current revenue.

- **Maximize quantity**—The reduction of long-term costs can be achieved by maximizing product or service sales.
- **Maximize profit margin**—In a situation where quantity of sales will be low, unit profit margins can be increased to foster greater returns.
- **Differentiation (quality leadership)**—This objective looks at the difference in price when determining the target market. While some companies may seek to be the low-cost leader, others will highlight quality as the justification for higher prices. For example, consumers expect to pay a high price for a high-end, name-brand designer handbag.
- **Survival**—This objective is successful when there is a crisis in the marketplace. For example, the market may be experiencing a price war, market decline, or market saturation. Therefore, the company may be forced to temporarily set a lower price that will cover costs and allow the business to continue to operate in order to survive. In this type of situation, survival is more important than profits.
- **Partial cost recovery**—An organization may seek only partial cost recovery if it has other sources of income.

Some of the most classical pricing strategies are:

Price skimming—When the product is introduced, the organization will set a high price in order to attract customers who are not sensitive to price. However, the prices will eventually fall due to an increase in supply, especially from competitors. This strategy is most appropriate when customers are not sensitive to price, there is no expectation of large cost savings at high volumes, and the organization cannot produce high volumes of its product at low-profit margins.

Penetration pricing—When the product is introduced, the price is set low in order to gain market share. Once market share has been obtained, the price is increased. This strategy tends to be used by companies attempting to enter a new market or desiring to build a small market share. A penetration strategy may also be used when a company wants to promote complementary products. The main product is set at a low price in order to get customers to buy the accessories, which are sold at higher prices.

Economy pricing—This strategy is considered the "no frills" approach. The cost of marketing and manufacturing are kept low. An example is store brand products or generic drugs.

Premium pricing—When the product is unique and the company has a competitive advantage, a high price can be set.

Determine pricing: Using the information acquired through the steps above, define a pricing method, pricing structure, and discounts.

Once the prices have been set, the marketing team may employ one or more of the following pricing methods in order to achieve its goals.

- **Cost-plus pricing**—The price arrived at by adding the production costs and a selected profit margin.
- **Target return pricing**—The price is set so as to recognize a certain return on investment.
- **Value-based pricing**—A price is set based on the notion that a customer will pay in accordance to the perceived value to the customer versus the cost of an alternative product. Caminal and Vives (1996) research showed that "a higher current market share can be interpreted by future consumers as a signal of higher relative quality and will tend to increase future demand" (p. 222).
- **Psychological pricing**—A price is set based on factors such as product quality and perceived consumer value. The company perceives that the customer will respond based on emotion versus logic. For example, the price may be $1.99 versus $2.00.

The list price is usually the price that is quoted to the target market. However, discounts may be given to distributors and a select group from the target market. Examples of discounts include:

- **Quantity discounts**—Discounts that are awarded to customers based on the quantity purchased.
- **Cumulative quantity discounts**—The discount offered increases as the cumulative purchase increases. This is a good approach for resellers who make large purchases over time versus those who purchase large quantities at one time.
- **Seasonal discounts**—Discounts offered based on the time of year the purchase is made. The purpose is to offset seasonal variations in sales.
- **Cash discounts**—Discounts offered to customers who pay before the due date.
- **Trade discounts**—Discounts offered to distributors who successfully perform their responsibilities to the organization.

- **Promotional discounts**—Discounts offered to generate sales. This type of discount is usually set up for a short, specified period.

APPLICATION

Entrepreneurial Pricing. Although pricing represents one of the most visible decision factors for marketing teams, it tends to be one of the least creative parts of the marketing strategy (Pitt & Berthon, 1997). Many marketers look at pricing from a functional point, and view it only as a means to cover costs and generate revenue. Others have wrongly assumed that they could not be creative in pricing due to competitor pricing or legal constraints. Basically, many marketing managers have not conducted much research into how they price a product because they "did not really understand how to price, and were insecure about the adequacy of the pricing approach they employed" (Pitt & Berthon, 1977, p. 344).

However, this approach may change as many organizations use modern approaches in developing their pricing formulas. The change is being driven by environmental factors such as international legislation forcing firms to open up markets and consumer preference for quality over brand image. For instance, companies such as Coca-Cola and Pepsi experienced a backlash from consumers as they decided to purchase store brand cola over their respective products (Hulbert & Pitt, 1986).

Some researchers have looked to the field of entrepreneurship as a way to add life and creativity to the pricing process. Miller and Friesen (1983) assert that entrepreneurship is based on three dimensions: innovativeness, assumption of risk, and proactiveness. Innovativeness implies that an organization's vision is designed around a unique product, service, or process. Risk-taking infers that the organization is willing to pursue opportunities even if it loses money and takes calculated risks. Miller (1987) defined proactiveness as an organization's willingness to be assertive and take bold risks (i.e., acting versus reacting to market conditions).

As mentioned in the "Overview," developing a pricing structure for a product or service requires decision making on a number of topics. The marketing department must come to a consensus on issues such as price objectives, price strategy, pricing method, promotions, and discounts. In each category, there

are a number of options in which the appropriate selection can be made. However, there is evidence that organizations still need to review their pricing strategy based on four key dimensions:

Cost-based versus market-based. Cost-based strategy occurs when the marketing team focuses on covering its own costs more than any of the other determinants (i.e., demand conditions, competitive market structures, company marketing strategies). It tends to rely on formulas such as cost-plus, keystone, or target return (Pitt & Berthon, 1997). Market-based strategy values the opinion of the consumer. The pricing structure is based on the perceived value that the customer receives from the product or service.

Risk-averse versus risk-assumptive. Risk-averse strategy is the conservative approach. Prices are kept in line with competitors' prices, only changed when necessary, and the process is kept simple. Risk-assumptive strategy is more uncertain because the managers go into uncharted territories with less concern over potential loss in revenue.

Reactive versus proactive. Reactive strategy refers to when a company copies the pricing patterns of its competitors. In most cases, there will not be an adjustment in price if the market does not warrant a change. On the other hand, the proactive approach assumes that the organization is the leader and initiates changes in the market. It will introduce the new pricing schemes and tends to be more aggressive in pricing as well as quick in making adjustments.

Standardization versus flexibility. With standardization a universal price is set regardless of the situation. However, flexibility implies that the organization may fluctuate prices based on "segment or user elasticities, time and place of purchase, as well as in response to opportunities for product or service unbundling or bundling, and anticipated or actual moves by competitors" (Pitt & Berthon, 1997, p. 346).

These are the major dimensions in which organizations must make decisions when analyzing and evaluating factors that are important to the pricing strategy. When participating in the entrepreneurial pricing strategy, the dominant factors in the pricing formula are market based, risk assumptive, proactive, and flexible. In order to combat threats and capitalize on opportunities, organizations are encouraged to design pricing structures based on the entrepreneurial pricing strategy. Organizations have to be ready to respond and adapt to a global economy that constantly changes. Pitt and Berthon (1997) created a checklist for marketing departments to assess whether or not they are positioned to transition to an entrepreneurial pricing system.

VIEWPOINT

International countertrade. During the Clinton administration, the United States experienced high trade deficits. In order to combat the trend, the administration identified 10 emerging markets and committed to assisting American corporations with winning contracts in these areas. The U.S. government created a national exporting strategy that had components such as lowering obstacles to U.S. exports, developing a responsive trade finance strategy, improving access to trade information, and focusing on key markets and sectors (Paun, Compeau & Grewal, 1997). Unfortunately, these efforts had "no clear and consistent policy stance on international countertrade" (Park, 1990, p. 38). Countertrade occurs when "a seller provides a buyer with products and agrees to take some or all of the payment in a form other than money" (Paun, Compeau & Grewal, 1997, p. 69). As the buyer pool decreases and competition among sellers in the global market increases, sellers will participate in countertrade to gain a competitive advantage over noncountertrade bids (Cavusgil & Ghauri, 1990).

Research has shown that countertrade transactions can be very complex, especially when selecting a pricing strategy (Kublin, 1990). Therefore, it is critical for marketing departments to understand pricing strategy as it relates to countertrade (Yoffie, 1984). Pricing is considered to be the primary factor in determining whether or not a countertrade transaction is processed (Cho, 1987). Although exporters wanted to use price as a competitive tool in countertrade, they did not know how to perform this task effectively (Kublin, 1990).

Nagle and Holden (1995) believed that once an organization determined its marketing objectives, there were three potential pricing strategies it could utilize: to sell at premium price, to sell at a going-rate or neutral price, or to sell at a discount price. Countertrade results are based on the contributions of the buyer and seller on the pricing process. The success of a countertrade transaction occurs when there is an intersection between the seller's and buyer's pricing strategies or expectations. Based on the

model that Paun, Compeau, and Grewal (1997) introduced, "a countertrade transaction is more likely to occur when a buyer is willing to pay a price that matches or exceeds the seller's asking price for the countertrade products and less likely to occur when a seller's asking price exceeds what the buyer is willing to pay" (p. 70). Tto close a deal, the difference between the price the seller is seeking and the price the buyer is offering must be minimized. This can occur if the seller lowers the asking price, the buyer raises the offering price, or a combination of both options takes place.

CONCLUSION

Pricing is one of the four aspects (product management, pricing, promotion, and place) in the marketing mix and directly affects how a product is positioned in the market. It should take into consideration fixed and variable costs, competition, organizational objectives, proposed positioning strategies, target groups, and consumer willingness to pay the price. Many organizations have utilized various factors when determining the pricing strategies for their products and services. However, there are some general guidelines that all share.

Although pricing represents one of the most visible decision factors for marketing teams, it tends to be one of the least creative parts of the marketing strategy (Pitt & Berthon, 1997). Many marketers look at pricing from a functional point, and view it only as a means to cover costs and generate revenue. Others have wrongly assumed that they could not be creative in pricing due to competitor pricing or legal constraints. Miller and Friesen (1983) assert that entrepreneurship is based on three dimensions: innovativeness, assumption of risk, and proactiveness.

The marketing department must come to consensus on issues such as price objectives, price strategy, pricing method, promotions, and discounts. In each category, there are a number of options in which the appropriate selection can be made. However, there is evidence that organizations still need to review their pricing strategy based on four key dimensions. When participating in the entrepreneurial pricing strategy, the dominant factors in the pricing formula are market based, risk assumptive, proactive, and flexible. Pitt and Berthon (1997) have created a checklist for marketing departments to assess whether or not they are positioned to transition to an entrepreneurial pricing system.

BIBLIOGRAPHY

Calandro, E., & Chair, C. (2016). Policy and regulatory challenges posed by emerging pricing strategies. *Information Technologies and International Development, 12*(2), 13-28. Retrieved December 28, 2016 from EBSCO online database Business Source Ultimate. http://search.ebscohost.com/login.aspx?direct=true&db=bsu&AN=116161954&site=ehost-live&scope=site

Caminal, R., & Vives, X. (1996). Why market shares matter: An information-based theory. *RAND Journal of Economics, 27*, 221–239. Retrieved July 3, 2007, from EBSCO Online Database Business Source Complete. http://search.ebscohost.com/login.aspx?direct=true&db=bth&AN=9606192119&site=ehost-live

Cavusgil, S., & Ghauri, P. (1990). *Doing business in developing countries.* London, England: Routledge.

Cho, K. (1987). Using countertrade as a competitive management tool. *Management International Review (MIR), 27*, 50–57. Retrieved July 3, 2007, from EBSCO Online Database Business Source Complete. http://search.ebscohost.com/login.aspx?direct=true&db=bth&AN=12254270&site=ehost-live

Danziger, S., Hadar, L., & Morwitz, V. G. (2014). Retailer pricing strategy and consumer choice under price uncertainty. *Journal of Consumer Research, 41*, 761–774. Retrieved November 5, 2014 from EBSCO online database Business Source Premier. http://search.ebscohost.com/login.aspx?direct=true&db=buh&AN=97917327&site=bsi-live

Ellickson, P., Misra, S., & Nair, H. (2012). Repositioning dynamics and pricing strategy. *Journal of Marketing Research (JMR), 49*, 750–772. Retrieved November 15, 2013, from EBSCO Online Database Business Source Complete. http://search.ebscohost.com/login.aspx?direct=true&db=bth&AN=83513328&site=ehost-live

Hellofs, L., & Jacobson, R. (1999). Market share and customers' perceptions of quality: When can firms grow their way to higher versus lower quality? *Journal of Marketing, 63*, 16–25. Retrieved July 5, 2007, from EBSCO Online Database Business Source Complete. http://search.ebscohost.com/login.aspx?direct=true&db=bth&AN=1490355&site=ehost-live

Hulbert, J., & Pitt, L. (1996). Exit left centre stage? The future of functional marketing. *European Management Journal, 14*, 47–60.

Kimpel, M., & Friedrich, C. (2015). The right pricing strategy for offline retailers when expanding into the online sales channel. *Journal of Business and Retail Management Research, 9*(2), 54–67. http://search.ebscohost.com/login.aspx?direct=true&db=buh&AN=103192072&site=ehost-live&scope=site

Kublin, M. (1990). A guide to export pricing. *Industrial Management, 32*, 29. Retrieved July 3, 2007, from EBSCO Online Database Business Source Complete. http://search.ebscohost.com/login.aspx?direct=true&db=bth&AN=4984193&site=ehost-live

Merry QR coding!. (2012). *Chief Marketer, 3*, 52. Retrieved November 5, 2014 from EBSCO online database Business Source Premier. http://search.ebscohost.com/login.aspx?direct=true&db=buh&AN=79362851&site=ehost-live

Miller, D. (1987). Strategy making and structure: Analysis and implications for performance. *Academy of Management Journal, 30*, 7–32. Retrieved July 3, 2007, from EBSCO Online Database Business Source Complete. http://search.ebscohost.com/login.aspx?direct=true&db=bth&AN=4324172&site=ehost-live

Miller, D., & Friesen, P. (1982). Innovation in conservative and entrepreneurial firms: Two models of strategic momentum. *Strategic Management Journal, 3*, 1–25. Retrieved July 3, 2007, from EBSCO Online Database Business Source Complete. http://search.ebscohost.com/login.aspx?direct=true&db=bth&AN=5214672&site=ehost-live

Miniard, P. W., Mohammed, S., Barone, M. J., & Alvarez, C. O. (2013). Retailers' use of partially comparative pricing: From across-category to within-category effects. *Journal of Marketing, 77*, 33–48. Retrieved November 15, 2013, from EBSCO Online Database Business Source Complete. http://search.ebscohost.com/login.aspx?direct=true&db=bth&AN=88789999&site=ehost-live

Nagle, T., & Holden, R. (1995). *The strategy and tactics of pricing* (2nd ed.). Englewood Cliffs, NJ: Prentice Hall.

Naughton, K., & Light, L. (1997). Taurus may tumble from the top. *Business Week,* (3510), 4. Retrieved July 3, 2007, from EBSCO Online Database Business Source Complete. http://search.ebscohost. com/login.aspx?direct=true&db=bth&AN=97011 45891&site=ehost-live

Park, J. (1990, April). Policy response to countertrade and the U.S. trade deficit: An appraisal. *Business Economics, 25,* 38–44. http://search.ebscohost.com/login.aspx?direct=true&db=bth&AN=9 609130007&site=ehost-live

Paun, D., & Compeau, L. (1997). A model of the influence of marketing objectives on pricing strategies in international countertrade. *Journal of Public Policy & Marketing, 16,* 69–82. Retrieved July 5, 2007, from EBSCO Online Database Business Source Complete. http://search.ebscohost.com/ login.aspx?direct=true&db=bth&AN=9706222226 &site=ehost-live

Pitt, L., & Berthon, P. (1997). Entrepreneurial pricing: The Cinderella of marketing strategy. *Management Decision, 35*(5/6), 344–351. Retrieved July 5, 2007, from EBSCO Online Database Business Source Complete. http://search.ebscohost. com/login.aspx?direct=true&db=bth&AN=97083 12644&site=ehost-live

Rohani, A., & Nazari, M. (2012). Impact of dynamic pricing strategies on consumer behavior. *Journal of Management Research, 4,* 143–159. Retrieved November 15, 2013, from EBSCO Online Database Business Source Complete. http://search.ebscohost.com/login.aspx?direct=true&db=bth&AN=8 0232787&site=ehost-live

Yoffie, D. (1984). Profiting from countertrade. *Harvard Business Review, 62,* 8–16. Retrieved July 3, 2007, from EBSCO Online Database Business Source Complete. http://search.ebscohost.com/ login.aspx?direct=true&db=bth&AN=4110384&si te=ehost-live

SUGGESTED READING

Abhik, R., & Walter, H. (1995). Special issue on pricing strategy and the marketing mix. *Journal of Business Research, 33,* 183–185.

Farrell, C. (2015). Global pricing strategies. *Global Marketing: Practical Insights and International Analysis* (pp. 156–176). London: Sage Publications.

Farrell, C., & Fearon, G. (2005). Renting goodwill in international marketing channels: An analysis of pricing strategies and bargaining power. *Atlantic Economic Journal, 33,* 285–296. Retrieved July 5, 2007, from EBSCO Online Database Business Source Complete. http://search.ebscohost.com/ login.aspx?direct=true&db=bth&AN=24105520&s ite=ehost-live

Jobber, D., & Shipley, D. (1998). Marketing-oriented pricing strategies. *Journal of General Management, 23,* 19–34.

Nagle, T. (1998). Make pricing a key driver of your marketing strategy. *Marketing News, 32,* 4. Retrieved July 5, 2007, from EBSCO Online Database Business Source Complete. http://search.ebscohost.com/login.aspx?direct=true&db=bth&AN=1 254489&site=ehost-live

Nicholas, III, A. (1965). Apply value analysis to your own product: Some guides to pricing and marketing strategy. *Management Review, 54,* 4–16. Retrieved July 5, 2007, from EBSCO Online Database Business Source Complete. http://search.ebscohost.com/login.aspx?direct=true&db=bth&AN=6 061268&site=ehost-live

Nagle, T. T., Zale, J., & Hogan, J. E. (2011). *The strategy and tactics of pricing: A guide to growing more profitably.* 5th ed. New York: Routledge.

Petersen, C. D. (2011). Defense and commercial trade offsets: Impacts on the U.S. industrial base raise economic and national security concerns. *Journal of Economic Issues, 45,* 485–492. Retrieved July 5, 2007, from EBSCO online database Business Source Premier. http://search.ebscohost. com/login.aspx?direct=true&db=buh&AN=6080 8375&site=bsi-live

Sharma, S. (2016). Pricing strategy adopted by small-scale entrepreneurs. *IUP Journal of Entrepreneurship Development, 13*(3), 7-24. Retrieved December 28, 2016 from EBSCO online database Business Source Ultimate. http://search.ebscohost.com/ login.aspx?direct=true&db=bsu&AN=120027247 &site=ehost-live&scope=site

Marie Gould

PRINCIPLES OF ADVERTISING

ABSTRACT

This article will focus on the basic principles of advertising. Advertising is crucial to every business. A successful marketing strategy includes an advertising plan that will grow the business. Advertising is a huge investment for an organization. Organizations spend billions of dollars on advertising to support the creation and production of their products as well as to generate income to pay their employees. The benefits of Internet advertising versus traditional advertising will be explored as well as examples of companies that have launched successful advertising campaigns for their online businesses.

OVERVIEW

Advertising is crucial to every business, and a successful marketing strategy includes an advertising plan that will grow the business. Advertising is a type of promotion for a business, and the ad campaign is placed in some form of media venue. In most cases, the advertising representative may have to pay for the message to be placed. However, according to Boaze (2004), there are two types of advertising: the type you pay for and the type that is free. Both types have their place for every organization. Each company must determine when and how to use each type.

Advertising has been viewed as an effective marketing technique because one ad campaign has the potential to reach many people at once. To be effective, the advertising representative must ensure that the message is reaching the appropriate markets. Otherwise, the organization may not be using its advertising budget in the most efficient manner. The use of new advertising technologies and media outlets can assist in preventing the misuse of the budget by providing options for targeted advertising.

Two other characteristics of advertising are also changing because of new technology. In the past, advertising has been viewed two ways: as a one-way form of marketing, in which consumers cannot immediately request additional information about the ad, and as a method that does not elicit immediate demand for the product advertised. Both of these characteristics are changing, as technology has provided target consumers the opportunity to click on a web page, for example, to receive additional information about a product and be interactive with ads as they are being displayed (http://www.knowthis.com) (Dent, 2012). Consumers can now buy products at the same time they view an ad.

Importance of Advertising

Advertising is a huge investment for businesses, which spend billions of dollars on advertising to support product creation and generate income to pay employees. The size of a company may determine how advertising campaigns are implemented. For example, a large business may split its advertising budget by applying half of the budget toward media advertisements and the other half toward efforts conducted by an internal sales team. A small business may elect to place small ads in specific media or promote its product through sources that offer free advertisements. Regardless of the technique, all companies must develop an advertising plan that will support the business's marketing objectives and minimize the risks of costly advertising mistakes.

Six Types of Advertising

An organization can avoid costly mistakes by developing a strategy that focuses on what the message is and what the desired result should be. To accomplish this goal, advertising representatives should determine what type of advertising is best for their organization. Egelhoff (n.d.) identified these six types of advertising that an organization could use in its planning phase:

- **Company image:** Depending on the type of company, it may be beneficial to create an ad campaign that focuses on promoting the company versus its product line. This is especially helpful for new businesses. Name recognition could be valuable in the long term.
- **Name brands:** Many large organizations have developed advertisement strategies that highlight specific brand names. By highlighting brand names, the company is attempting to create an image in the mind of the consumer. The goal is to help the target market identify with the product. For example, Levi-Strauss is recognized for its

jeans. Procter & Gamble is known for hygiene products, especially toothpaste (for, example, Crest).

- **Advertising a service instead of a product:** This type of advertising may be difficult for some organizations to achieve. Services are not tangible products, so it may be hard for the consumer to grasp the intent of the message. The advertising campaign usually has to explain and demonstrate the benefits of the service. In addition, service advertising tends to appeal to the consumer's emotions. For example, AFLAC created a successful campaign using a duck. Many consumers now associate AFLAC with the image and sound of a duck. Once consumers relate to the slogan and visual, they then associate AFLAC's message with the importance of having secondary insurance benefits.
- **Business-to-business (B2B) advertising:** Organizations attempting to market to another business should use direct mail and advertisements in trade journals. For example, pharmaceutical representatives tend to market directly to physicians. These ad campaigns tend to focus on explaining the benefits of specific drugs to doctors so that they recommend and encourage their patients to use them.
- **Co-op advertising:** This type of advertising involves manufacturers absorbing part of the cost and supplying the artwork for the ads. Although this type of advertising could be good for certain companies, such as small businesses, there could be disadvantages. For example, the organization has to follow the manufacturer's guidelines or run the risk of having to cover all the campaign costs.
- **Public service advertising (PSA):** Many companies will set aside a portion of their advertising budget to run campaigns in conjunction with the service of a nonprofit organization or public service event. For example, a business may secure ad time on a local television network for community programs.

Organizations do not have to use all of the different types of advertising. Each advertising department must first determine what it wants to say (the ad campaign) and who it wants to say it to (the target market). Once these questions have been defined, the advertising team can decide which types of advertising it will use to have a successful campaign. Each

campaign is unique. Therefore, organizations may change types based on the campaign.

Pros & Cons of Advertising

There are advantages and disadvantages in the field of advertising. Two advantages of advertising are that it is considered one of the best ways to send a message about a new or existing product or service, and it can lower the cost of the product by increasing sales. The savings from reduced production costs may be passed on to the consumer.

Two disadvantages of advertising are that it creates a temporary need for products and services, and the ad campaign can negatively influence the consumer. Ad campaigns that are directed toward children are examples of the first disadvantage. Advertisers create campaigns directed toward children and run them on Saturday mornings and during the holiday season in December. The ad campaigns are created to entice children to desire products and have their parents purchase them. However, children's interests can wander with each new commercial, and the desire for an item can be for a season, a day, or a minute. An example of the second disadvantage can be seen in the results of studies investigating TiVo users. "Participants in the studies stated that they skipped commercials with their TiVo recorder because once they've seen an ad, they don't want to see it again. They only want to see the ad once or twice" (Smith, 2005). This finding shows that ad campaigns are not enjoyable or desired by the consumer and can lead to negative feelings toward a product.

APPLICATION

Principles of Advertising

Advertising is not a function that operates independently. It works in conjunction with the marketing operation within an organization. To have an effective plan, the marketing and advertising departments will have to work together to obtain their objectives. DePaola (1977) cited the following principles that these two departments need to recognize when coordinating advertising objectives and budgets with the marketing objectives:

- **Marketing and advertising are partners, not adversaries.** Both areas should work together to accomplish the organization's objectives and goals. Most managers in the areas know both functions and appreciate the contributions that each can make to the bottom line.

- **Market identification is the first planning stage.** It is important that the first step in the planning stage is to identify the target market by size, type, and location. The advertising team needs to determine where the business is going to come from and the amount of business expected from the campaign. The next step is to rank the list of sources by the volume and profit that each market is expected to generate. The markets with the greatest potential should be listed at the top.

- **A rational, consistent ranking of markets by potential should precede any thought of allocating advertising dollars.** One should not automatically assume that there is a well-developed marketing plan before advertising decisions are made. Some advertising decisions are made before marketing plans are implemented. Therefore, advertising professionals may have to rely on the results from the planning stage to make budget decisions. The decision makers can determine how many of the potential markets can be served by the established budget. This type of evaluation process will be viewed as an objective method of allocating funds in lieu of having a marketing plan.

- **Successful advertising programs require sound marketing input.** If the marketing side makes an error in judgment regarding the consumer, it could cause the advertising campaign to fail. Testing may be an important step for marketing professionals to perform before launching an advertising and marketing campaign. Information from the testing phase could yield information about the consumers that could prevent an unsuccessful advertising campaign.

Table 1: Organizational Demographics

Organization	Year of Airing	Award	Business	Country
AOL..de	1999/2000	German Effie 2000	ISP	Germany
Confetti.co.uk	1999	IPA Award	Wedding Site	UK
Drugstore.com	1999	US Effie Award	Online Drugstore	USA
Easy Jet	1999	IPA Award	Budget Airlines	UK
FT.com	1999/2000	IPA Award	Financial News	UK
Hotbot.com	1998/1999	US Effie Award	Search Engine	USA
Letsbuyit.com	1999/2000	Euro Effie Award	Buying Club	Europe
Monster.com	1999	US Effie Award	Job Search Site	USA
MoneyExtra.com	1999/2000	IPA Award	Financial Information	UK
Scoot.com	1999/2000	IPA Award	Information Directory	UK

- **Advertisements should target specific audiences.** A popular strategy for an organization is to spend the advertising budget on one market where the organization is strong and has the potential, distribution, and ability to do business. The next step is to formulate an offensive strategy that includes outspending the competitor. Once the organization has made a successful impact on this market, the advertising department could reduce the funding in the market and move some of the budget to the next potential market.

- **The advertising approach should be sensible and factual.** Advertising professionals should be honest with themselves regarding the potential sales a product or service can generate. Being realistic about the product's or service's ability to entice the consumer is a sensible approach when determining how to allocate budget money.

- **Information is more important than persuasion in advertising copy.** The average consumer is intelligent and informed about different products and services. Therefore, advertising professionals should not underestimate the level of knowledge that potential consumers have about a product or service. Providing the consumers with information about a service or product is more important than focusing on persuading a consumer to try a product or service. Consumers value making the final decision based on facts versus emotion.

- **Beware of lists of "10 rules" to instant marketing and advertising success.** These lists tend to leave out more information than they include. In addition, the information can mislead a consumer about a particular service or product.

- **Results of advertising efforts must be measured.** To determine the return on investment, an organization must effectively measure the activities surrounding each campaign. By analyzing consumer feedback about specific campaigns, an advertising professional can evaluate whether or not the amount of money invested in the project was warranted.

VIEWPOINT
Internet Advertising

Internet advertising has many benefits over traditional advertising (http://www.impliedbydesign. com). Advantages include the following:

- **Internet advertising is huge.** People spend a lot of time on the Internet because there is a wealth of information to be found. Also, the Internet is a social place, leaving companies with a vast resource for placing ads. As a result, a new market for Internet advertising, including social media advertising, has blossomed. Given the access to potential consumers, most large companies and many smaller businesses have created an Internet presence for their business. Some of these ads work, others do not (Seymour, 2013).
- **Internet advertising is targeted.** As companies target specific markets, Internet advertising can provide target methods that make sure its ads are seen by consumers who will buy their products.
- **Internet advertising enables good conversion-tracking.** Many companies have not been able to track the effectiveness of their traditional advertising campaigns. However, they can track Internet advertising based on how many people see the ad and how many people visit the website based on a particular ad.
- **Internet advertising has lower entry-level fees.** Traditional advertising can be very expensive, especially if the company (such as a small business) has a tight budget. However, certain Internet advertisements allow a company to only pay when a visitor clicks on the ad.
- **Internet advertising can be much cheaper.** Given the target methods, it is easier to track the effectiveness of Internet advertising.
- **Internet advertising has greater range.** Traditional advertisement tends to focus on a specific geographic location, whereas an Internet audience is global.

Best Practices

Since advertising can be expensive and most advertising departments have to be accountable for the return on investment, research companies have developed testing approaches to evaluate the effectiveness of various strategies used in an ad campaign. The testing models review how the advertising works and look at data collection methods, response measurements, and analytic approaches. Olson (2001) believes professionals should select a testing approach based on the type of advertisement (television spot, print ad), the type of stimulus to be tested (storyboard, commercial), and the measure of effectiveness sought.

Table 2: Successful Practices of Organizations

Organization	Significant Contributions and Highlights of Advertising Campaign
AOL.de	• The campaign objective was to increase brand awareness, attract new users and establish AOL's position, especially in Germany. • The target market was consumers who were fascinated by the internet, but afraid to use it because they felt they lacked the skills to successfully navigate the system. • The commercial campaign increased brand awareness from 28% to 43%. New customers increased by 66% in the first six months and reached 1.5 million by January, 2001.
Confetti.co.uk	• Had the task of building a brand within six months. • Established a target market as the 1% of the UK population that wanted to get married, with a focus on women in the 20-45 year old age range. • Radio and print advertising was used to refer the target markets to the website. • The campaigns boosted the brand awareness by 46% in the target market, and the number of new wedding profiles on the site increased by 500% during the advertising period.
Drugstore.com	• The objective of the campaign was to establish drugstore.com as the online category leader by building brand awareness and preference. • Campaign targeted 25-54 year olds who were comfortable with online shopping and were open to the drugstore category. • Market research showed that many consumers were unsatisfied with their brick-and-mortar drugstore experience, but did not know there was an alternative. • The company launched a nine week campaign with three TV commercials. The last two commercials highlighted a tag line emphasizing "the trip to the drugstore, without the trip to the drugstore." • The campaign doubled brand awareness and new customer orders increased by 356%.
Easy Jet	• A budget airline operating in a low-margin business. • Main concern is to keep costs down. • Low-cost booking was an alternative to an expensive call center facility. • The organization used three key messages in its advertising: (1) displayed prices for specific destinations, (2) offered web surfers a discount for using online booking, and (3) promoted their brand as the web's favorite airline. As a result of these initiatives, online sales doubled during the first two months of the campaign.
FT.com	• The objectives of the campaign were to explain what FT.com was and create a brand image that distinguished it from its parent – the Financial Times paper. • This campaign was the most complex and expensive of all the companies listed. The launch was a three phase program. The first phase's mission was to create awareness and understanding of the product. The second phase's purpose was to communicate the features of the site, and the third phase highlighted the brand's benefits to the target audience. • The target audience was anyone involved in business and risk takers driven by success and effectiveness in business life. • The nine month campaign led to a 342% increase in users, and advertising revenues tripled in the first six months of the campaign.

(continue)

Table 2: Successful Practices of Organizations (*continue*)

Hotbot.com	• The advertising objectives were to increase traffic as well as brand awareness and brand recognition. • Target market was defined as males in the 20-30 year old age range who were savvy with the internet. • Market research showed that this target market consisted of frustrated consumers who were not satisfied with the quality of services provided by search engines. • Launched two commercials that highlighted how other search engines were a waste of time due to old links and outdated information. • As a result of the campaign, brand awareness doubled, daily web site hits increased by 48% and the number of new visitors increased by 91%.
Letsbuyit.com	• The objectives of the campaign were to build awareness and understanding of the concept and to drive visitor's to the site. • The target market was 18-50 year old upscale adults, not just internet users. • A multimedia campaign was launched and it consisted of advertisement via TV, press, radio, the outdoors, transportation and online. • The results of the campaign indicated that brand awareness and understanding was achieved, and the campaign attracted approximately one million new subscribers.
Monster.com	• The advertising objectives of the campaign were to establish itself as the category leader in the online recruiting market as well as increase total number of resumes and job searches. • The target market was individuals dissatisfied with their jobs that were not actively seeking new employment, but were open to new opportunities. • The company launched an advertising campaign during the Super Bowl, which is highly selective and very expensive. • The results of the campaign were measured on the Monday after the Super Bowl. The number of job searches per 24 hours increased to 2.2 million versus 83,000 for the Monday prior to the Super Bowl. Resumes posted per 24 hours increased by 570% and overall traffic increased by 177%.
MoneyExtra.com	• The first campaign was ineffective and did not yield the desired results. Therefore, the advertising department learned from its mistakes and created a second campaign focused on increasing the number of visitor to the site by explaining what MoneyExtra did. • The campaign was directed toward consumers who felt their finances were out of control and consumers who had negative feelings toward the financial industry. • A four month multimedia campaign was launched and it included radio, posters, online advertising and a promotion at railway stations. • As a result of the campaign, there was an increase of visitors to the site and a 300% increase in advertising revenue.
Scoot.com	• The first campaign was ineffective, and there was a re-launch. The second campaign focused on increasing brand awareness and understanding as well as creating a positive image. • TV, radio, print and direct mailing were used in the campaign. • As a result of the campaign, the brand awareness and understanding almost doubled, and usage increased.

CONCLUSION

Advertising campaigns can be expensive. "With the cost of producing a commercial at $500,000 or more—and media budgets of $50 million—there is a natural desire, on the part of advertisers, to make sure that the advertising they are running is effective" (Olson, 2001). Walker (2005) suggested the following four principles to use when evaluating advertising strategies to ensure that advertising campaigns are in line with the marketing objectives:

- Precision: Advertising should be sent to a specific, concise target market.
- Relevance: Advertising should be sent to a market that is interested in the product.
- Power: Advertising should give more control to the target market.
- Reciprocity: Advertising should acknowledge that consumers want quality products and services in exchange for their time commitment to evaluate the products and services.

Advertising professionals should evaluate consumers' attitudes, motivations, and demographics. Simply looking at the demographics is no longer enough. It would be beneficial to review potential consumers' life stage and behaviors as well as why they buy products and services.

BIBLIOGRAPHY

Appelbaum, U. (2001, November). Best practice: The principles of effective advertising for dotcoms – Insights into 10 of the world's most successful advertising campaigns for dotcoms. Retrieved May 3, 2007, from http://www.brandchannel.com/images/papers/FTTdotcomadvertising.pdf

Boaze, S. (2004, November 22). Two kinds of advertising for a marketing strategy. EzineArticles. Retrieved May 3, 2007, from http://ezinearticles.com/?Two-kinds-of-Advertisingfor-a-Marketing-Strategy&id=5536.

Dent, G. (2012). Brand building. BRW, 34(7), 18-21. Retrieved November 19, 2013, from EBSCO Online Database Academic Search Complete. http://search.ebscohost.com/login.aspx?direct=true&db=a9h&AN=78556941&site=ehost-live

DePaola, F. (1977). Ten principles for coordinating advertising budgets and marketing objectives. Management Review, 66(1), 35. Retrieved May 3, 2007, from EBSCO Online Database Business Source Premier. http://search.ebscohost.com/login.aspx?direct=true&db=bth&AN=6072339&site=ehost-live

Egelhoff, T. (n.d.). Six types of advertising and how to use them. Small Town Marketing.com. Retrieved on May 3, 2007, from http://www.smalltownmarketing.com/sixads.html

Best's Review, 105(10), 58. Retrieved May 3, 2007, from EBSCO Online Database Business Source Premier. http://search.ebscohost.com/login.aspx?direct=true&db=bth&AN=15931825&site=ehost-live

Implied By Design, LLC. The advantages of internet advertising vs. traditional advertising. Retrieved May 3, 2007, from http://www.impliedbydesign.com/articles/the-advantages-of-internet-advertising-vs-traditional-advertising.html

Olson, D. (2001). Principles of measuring advertising effectiveness. Retrieved May 3, 2007, from http://www.marketingpower.com/content1025.php

Principles of marketing, Part 13: Advertising. Retrieved May 3, 2007, from http://www.knowthis.com/tutorials/principles-of-marketing/advertising.htm

Rossiter, J. R. (2012). Advertising management principles are derived mostly from logic and very little from empirical generalizations. Marketing Theory, 12(2), 103-116.

Retrieved November 19, 2013, from EBSCO Online Database Business Source Complete. http://

search.ebscohost.com/login.aspx?direct=true&db=bth&AN=77388937&site=ehost-live

Seymour, C. (2013). Brand advertising on the web. Econtent, 36(6), 12-16. Retrieved November 19, 2013, from EBSCO Online Database Academic Search Complete. http://search.ebscohost.com/login.aspx?direct=true&db=a9h&AN=89881560&site=ehost-live

SUGGESTED READING

Eagle, L. (2005). Principles of advertising & IMC, 2nd ed. Journal of Marketing Communications, 11(4), 309-310.

Retrieved May 3, 2007, from EBSCO Online Database Business Source Premier. http://search.ebscohost.com/login.aspx?direct=true&db=bth&AN=19019729&site=ehost-live

Roche, B. (1978). Advertising, principles, problems, and cases. Journal of Advertising, 7(3), 52. Retrieved May 3, 2007, from EBSCO Online Database Business Source Premier. http://search.ebscohost.com/login.aspx?direct=true&db=bth&AN=18560393&site=ehost-live

Snoddy, R. (2002). Core principles omit to mention that advertising can be a waste. Marketing (00253650), 14. Retrieved May 3, 2007, from EBSCO Online Database Business Source Premier. http://search.ebscohost.com/login.aspx?direct=true&db=bth&AN=6047246&site=ehost-live

Marie Gould

PRINCIPLES OF RETAILING

ABSTRACT

This article focuses on the principles of retailing and how they relate to selling on the Internet. Although Business-to-consumer (B2C) e-commerce (electronic commerce) captures the attention of the industry, business-to-business (B2C) e-commerce is the format that is predicted to reap most of e-business activity. B2B e-commerce has exploded. This article includes an exploration of e-commerce and how build a customer base on the Internet.

OVERVIEW

Most individuals who study the field of marketing know the foundation of the concept. It is based on a marketing mix, which consists of four basic elements: product, price, promotion, and place. These elements are also known as the 4 Ps of marketing. According to Golden & Zimmerman (1980), some retailers have expanded the retailer's marketing mix to include variables such as parking, delivery, store layout, displays, public relations, warehousing, transportation, telephone sales, credit extension, and guarantees.

Retailing is based on a transaction. In most cases, the customer will exchange money for goods and services, and the retailer will provide goods and services for dollars (Golden & Zimmerman, 1980). Therefore, one can refer to retailing as an interdependent system because both sides need each other in order to make a smooth transaction. In addition, customers rely on retailers for goods and services, and retailers rely on customers for profits. Up until the mid-1960s, marketing was considered the same as selling with the emphasis being on the seller versus the customer.

History of Retailing

Retailing has been a highly competitive field of business that has been around for a while. "Retailing is a major part of the United State's total distribution system; it is the last link in the system that markets and distributes products and services to consumers" (Golden & Zimmerman, 1980, p. 5). Butcher and McAnelly (1973) provided a timeline that traces the historical background of this field.

The General Store (Early nineteenth century)

This was the typical type of retail store in rural areas, small towns, and villages. As the population became more urban in character, the demands for stores specializing in only one line or a few lines of merchandise increased. General stores carried a broad range of merchandise, but the goods included satisfied only the basic needs of the small local market.

The Specialty Store (1870s)

The specialty store was the most important type of store in the large towns and cities in the United States, and the stores only carried one or a few lines of closely related goods. Specialty store merchants promoted the cash system of selling and offered goods at lower prices for cash.

The Department Store (After 1900)

The department store emerged in response to changing economic and social conditions. Specialty merchants were attempting to develop methods that would improve their competitive position. In the early 1900s, there were more than 8,000 department store merchants in the United States. However, there were signs of decline by the 1930s.

The Mail-Order House (Latter nineteenth century)

This was a cross between a retail store and a wholesale warehouse that sold only by mail. Stores such as Sears and Montgomery Ward were successful in moving their products via the mail order catalogue.

The Chain Store (Began with the Great Atlantic & Pacific (A&P) Tea Company in 1859)

The chain store was one of the most significant innovations in the development of retail institutions. Although data concerning the early growth of chain stores in the United States is limited, A&P had approximately 17,000 stores operation by 1929.

The Discount House (Early 1930s)

Discount houses are modern retail stores that place emphasis on self-service or operate with a minimum of sales clerks whenever self-service is not applicable. They tend to offer a wide variety of discounts without limited customer services. The philosophy of the stores is to sell nationally advertised or brand-named merchandise at substantial discounts from conventional or list prices.

The Supermarket (First appeared in southern California around 1925)

These were primarily large, open-air, self-service stores with drive-in facilities. The first supermarkets were considered to be a device that independent retailers used to meet the competition of the chain store.

Today, we have ventured into the world of the web by selling and buying merchandise on the Internet from various sources around the world.

APPLICATION

E-Commerce

Although B2C e-commerce captures the attention of the industry, B2B e-commerece is the format that is predicted to reap most e-business activity. B2B e-commerce has exploded. This market became a trillion-dollar market by 2003 and was expected to have a 90 percent compound annual growth rate (Sprague, 2000). According to Sprague (2000), "B2B e-commerce represents another revolution that is reshaping business relationships and is causing dramatic shifts in channel power as information and communication imbalances disappear" (p.1). B2B e-commerce provides purchasers and suppliers with value suggestions that can decrease transaction prices and advance the monetary worth gained through corporate relationships. Value propositions such as these are able to provide opportunities for new players to enter the process of facilitating buyer and supplier adoption of e-commerce capabilities.

Effects of eCommerce on Transaction Costs

One of the most important objectives of B2B e-commerce is to change the cost and benefits of transactions. Kaplan and Garicano (2001) developed a framework that describes how B2B e-commerce can change transaction costs. The model presented five ways that this could be done:

- **Changes in the processes.** B2B e-commerce can enhance effectiveness by limiting the prices associated with current company processes. Improvements may occur in two different ways. The first way is to lessen the cost of an activity that is currently occuring (e.g. catalog orders being taken online versus by telephone or fax). The second way is to use the Internet to recreate the current process (e.g. Autodaq establishes Internet auctions for used cars that voids the shipping costs that are usually required with regular auctions). Each process improvement effort should be measured and evaluated to ensure that there are cost savings. This effort can be assessed by documenting the time and costs involved in both the current process as well as the proposed process. The difference between the two is the savings from the process improvement.

- **Changes in the nature of the marketplace.** Use of the Internet can decrease a buyer's cost of searching for appropriate suppliers; offer enhanced information regarding product details to buyers; and supply more adequate research about buyers and sellers.

- **Changes in indirect effects of transaction cost reductions.** "Better information about future demand through B2B e-commerce may allow a seller to improve its demand forecasts, and use that information to change its production decisions to better match demand. As a result, a buyer may obtain better information about existing and future supplies and use the information to change its in-

ventory decisions" (Kaplan & Garicano, 2001, p. 4). Also, if the World Wide Web is able to promote a decline in the costs of dealing with transactions in the market, then even fewer transactions will be dealt with at the corporate, company level.

- **Changes the degree of information incompleteness.** Since buyers and sellers tend to not have similar or accurate information about a certain transaction, one of the parties might be at a disservice when measuring the desirability of a transaction. The Internet has the capability of changing the informational positions of buyers and sellers.

- **Changes the ability to commit.** B2B e-commerce has the ability to advance and hinder the capability of purchasers and sellers to adhere to specific transactions. The Web can also advance a buyer's chances of commitment by standardizing the process of the transaction and leaving an electronic trail.

Internet retail sales were expected to grow from $45 billion in 2000, or 1.5 percent of total retail sales, to $155 billion in 2003, and to $269 billion in 2005, or 7.8 percent of total retail sales expected for that year (Dykema, 2000). eMarketeer reported that B2C Internet retail sales in the United States were $343.43 billion in 2012.

VIEWPOINT
Building a Customer Base on the Internet

Many organizations seek to understand the benefits of the Internet as they move their products to the medium. However, they recognize that having an Internet presence does not guarantee a successful venture. There has to be a significant number of people visiting the site and buying the product. "In reality, many websites have very small traffic with over 90% of Internet traffic flowing through less than 10% of the most popular sites (Ennew, Lockett, Holland & Blackman, 2000). In order to achieve success, the organizations must be able to attract customers and establish a solid customer base.

"If websites exist in a market-space that is so vast that their existence is not a sufficient condition for gaining traffic and the development of a viable Internet venture requires customers, the building of a customer base becomes a key component of any company's marketing strategy toward the Internet"

(Lockett & Blackman, 2001, p. 49). Additionally, the advancement of a customer base proves to be beneficial for other functions in the marketing movement such as market research and experimentation (Lockett, Blackman & Naude, 1998). Therefore, having an online customer base is essential for an Internet marketing strategy.

Approaches to Building a Customer Base

There are two different ways of approaching a potential customer base online. The models are site-centric and symbiotic marketing and can be viewed as opposite approaches. However, some organizations have used techniques from both approaches. The site centric model will be discussed in this section. This model shows a variety of techniques that help to bring customers to a central site that offers a certain product. Ebay is an example of a website that uses the site-centric model. If a person is looking for a particular item, he or she may Google the item. One hit may be an eBay link if the product is available on its site.

In the site-centric model, customers are interested in a particular organization's brand that meets their requirements. The central site focuses on attracting and retaining customers so it invests in building strong brand recognition for the organization. For example, eBay has invested time in building recognition for Gotham Online as a site offering upscale brand-name shoes at discount prices. A customer seeking shoes such as Stuart Weitzman or Kenneth Cole could go through eBay to take advantage of Gotham's discounted prices for these brands. Although Gotham Online has a site, the shoes tend to be cheaper on the eBay site because the auctions start at a lower price. If the customer wants a variety of upscale shoes and is not concerned about prices, he or she may go to Gotham Online site for more choices. The purpose of the auctions at the eBay site is to get the customer familiar with Gotham Online. One of the attractions is low price bid auctions for upscale shoes. In addition, there is a significant discount on shipping and handling charges for multiple purchases. Once the customer becomes comfortable with the organization, Gotham Online provides opportunities for the customer to sign up for a newsletter regarding upcoming sales on eBay as well as the opportunity to see the latest styles at the organization's site.

The Site-centric Approach

The site-centric approach utilizes an umbrella strategy that has a variety of techniques. All the techniques have the same theme to attract customers to the company's own website. According to Lockett and Blackman (2001), some of the techniques include:

Portal sites. It's either the first website a browser visits when logging in or a search engine that is used as a tool to find other websites. The log-in screen is usually put in place by the online service provider or the provider of the software browser. Examples of search engines include Google and Yahoo.

Purchase links to a portal site. Companies may develop their own portal links and buy popular links in current key portal websites. For example, Citigroup agreed to pay Netscape 40 million dollars to allow access to the personal finance information for the Netscape Personal Finance site.

Purchase advertising. After the customer purchases the product from the central site, a direct link is provided so that the customer can pay immediately at the organization's site. The larger portal websites are beneficial in selling advertisements directed at certain consumers. Some of these advantages include:

- Keywords can be used to select an appropriate banner advertisement
- Advertisements can be presented on Internet pages with related topics
- Regional-specific advertising can be provided on regional-specific search engines
- Detailed information can be collected in order to assist buyers with determining the success of specific-banner advertisements.

Direct email: Registered users or subscribers to email services—Customers can agree to receive regular emails or newsletters when the company has new products (Lockett & Blackman, 2001, p. 53).

Direct email: Junk mail or spam-mail—Spammers use the unprotected servers of other companies to distribute emails about their products. Reputable companies do not distribute spam.

CONCLUSION

Most individuals who study the field of marketing know the foundation of the concept. It is based on a marketing mix, which consists of four basic elements:

product, price, promotion, and place. These elements are also known as the 4 Ps of marketing. According to Golden and Zimmerman (1980), some retailers have expanded the retailer's marketing mix to include variables such as parking, delivery, store layout, displays, public relations, warehousing, transportation, telephone sales, credit extension, and guarantees.

Retailing is based on a transaction. In most cases, the customer will exchange money for goods and services, and the retailer will provide goods and services for dollars (Golden & Zimmerman, 1980). Therefore, one can refer to retailing as an interdependent system because both sides need each other to make a smooth transaction. In addition, customers rely on retailers for goods and services, and retailers rely on customers for profits. Up until the mid-1960s, marketing was considered the same as selling with the emphasis being on the seller versus the customer.

The Internet will continue to play a significant role in the field of marketing. Many will need to further their studies on the benefits and barriers that the Internet has on the various marketing mediums. Theorists may gain new ideas about the Internet and evaluate whether current marketing theories can continue to be applied to the study of the Internet. Practitioners may continue to conduct market research to determine what consumers want, and policymakers must address topics such as security, consumer protection, and taxes (Hou & Rego, 2002).

As the field of Internet marketing explodes, there still will be a need for traditional advertising. Internet marketing does not threaten the existence of traditional marketing techniques. Rather, it compliments the efforts. Although Internet marketing provides valuable assets such as an increased awareness of brand name, traditional marketing efforts still can address some of the disadvantages of online shopping. For example, traditional marketing efforts can promote brick-and-mortar shopping experiences based on the opportunity for social interaction, and allow consumers to actually see and physically touch a product before purchasing.

B2B e-commerce has exploded and surpassed the profitability of B2C e-commerce. The new tools and techniques of the digital era have allowed these organizations to understand, develop, and implement processes in a more effective and efficient manner. As a result, they are able to understand, develop, and implement products with a greater value as well

as create new channels for communication, supply-chain integration, demand forecasting, and transaction management.

BIBLIOGRAPHY

Adams, M. (2013). Online sales tax could pump up retail values. *Real Estate Finance & Investment, 23*. Retrieved November 15, 2013, from EBSCO Online Database Business Source Complete. http://search.ebscohost.com/login.aspx?direct=true&db=bth&AN=87804756&site=ehost-live

Butcher, B., & McAnelly (1973). *Fundamentals of retailing*. New York, NY: The Macmillan Company.

Dykema, E. (2000, September). *Online retail's ripple effect*. Cambridge, MA: Forrester Research, Inc.

Ennew, C., Lockett, A., Holland, C., & Blackman, I. (2000). *Predicting customer visits to Internet retail sites: A cross industry empirical investigation*. Nottingham: University of Nottingham Business School.

Golden, L., & Zimmerman, D. (1980). *Effective retailing*. Chicago, IL: Rand McNally College Publishing Company.

Hou, J., & Rego, C. (2002). Internet marketing: An overview. Retrieved May 3, 2007, from http://www.ebusinessforum.gr/engine/index.php

Kaplan, S., & Garicano, L. (2001). The effects of business-to-business e-commerce on transaction costs. *The Journal of Industrial Economics, 44*, 463-485. Retrieved May 3, 2007, from EBSCO Online Database Business Source Complete. http://search.ebscohost.com/login.aspx?direct=true&db=bth&AN=6472761&site=bsi-live

Liu-Thompkins, Y., & Tam, L. (2013). Not all repeat customers are the same: Designing effective cross-selling promotion on the basis of attitudinal loyalty and habit. *Journal of Marketing, 77*, 21-36. Retrieved November 15, 2013, from EBSCO Online Database Business Source Complete. http://search.ebscohost.com/login.aspx?direct=true&db=bth&AN=89746479&site=ehost-live

Lockett, A., & Blackman, I. (2001). Strategies for building a customer base on the Internet: Symbiotic marketing. *Journal of Strategic Marketing, 9*, 47-68. Retrieved on May 3, 2007, from EBSCO Online Database Business Source Complete. http://search.ebscohost.com/login.aspx?direct=true&db=bth&AN=4782033&site=bsi-live

Lockett, A., Blackman, I., & Naude, P. (1998). Using the Internet/WWW for the real time development of financial services: The case of Xenon Laboratories. *Journal of Financial Services Marketing, 3,* 161-172.

Revell, J. (2013). How to survive a retail meltdown. *Fortune, 168,* 64. Retrieved November 15, 2013, from EBSCO Online Database Business Source Complete. http://search.ebscohost.com/login.aspx?direct=true&db=bth&AN=91934167&site=ehost-live

Sprague, C. (2000). B2B eCommerce comes of age and drives shareholder value. ASCET, 2. Retrieved on May 3, 2007, from http://www.ascet.com/documents.asp?grID=149&d%5fID=246

SUGGESTED READING

How big can it grow? (2004). *Economist, 371*(8371), 67-69. Retrieved October 10, 2007, from EBSCO

Online Database Business Source Complete. http://search.ebscohost.com/login.aspx?direct=true&db=bth&AN=12853739&site=bsi-live

Saxtan, J. (2006). Revisiting the "wheel". *Giftware News, 31,* 6. Retrieved October 10, 2007, from EBSCO Online Database Business Source Complete. http://search.ebscohost.com/login.aspx?direct=true&db=bth&AN=20914044&site=bsi-live

Stanton, A. (2006). A view from the other side: Customer behavior from the retailer's perspective. *Marketing Education Review, 16,* 71-74. Retrieved October 10, 2007, from EBSCO Online Database Business Source Complete. http://search.ebscohost.com/login.aspx?direct=true&db=bth&AN=21498850&site=bsi-live

Marie Gould

PRODUCT PLACEMENT

ABSTRACT

Product placement is a form of advertising that seeks to put products before consumers in the form of television and movie props. In traditional broadcast, advertising a television program is interrupted so that the audience can hear or see a message from advertisers. Because technologies now allow viewers to skip commercial breaks in programming and some broadcasters offer ad-free programming, marketers offer compensation in exchange for their product being incorporated into television programs.

OVERVIEW

Product placement involves the use of real-life products in fictional programs. Product placement is most often used in television or movies, but it has also come up in books and even radio. It can be as simple as shooting a scene showing a conversation between two actors and including a soda can on a table in front of them; while the soda can seems like nothing more than an everyday item present to enhance the realism of the scene, viewers will recognize the soda brand, even if unconsciously, and associate it with their experience of watching the movie. Almost any product can be used in this way, from clothing to automobiles, food and

restaurants, and even locations, which can market themselves as tourist destinations by serving as the setting for programs (Venkatadri, Vardarajan & Das, 2015).

Advantages

Advertisers have several reasons for choosing to use product placement. Generally speaking, product placement will almost never be the only marketing strategy used to promote a product. Instead, product placement tends to be used in conjunction with other forms of advertising, and in many cases advertisers prefer to use it with established, well-known products. This is because product placement works best when viewers recognize a product from previous experience with it, and this is less likely to occur if the product is new or relatively unknown to most people.

One of the reasons for choosing product placement is simplicity. Instead of the manufacturer having to come up with its own commercials, hire actors, schedule filming, and all the other steps involved in producing commercials, the manufacturer simply pays a film or television studio to incorporate the product into its production. At most, there may be contract negotiations between the manufacturer and studio to clarify how much screen time the product will receive and how prominently it must be displayed (Patwardhan & Patwardhan, 2016).

Star power is another reason companies choose product placement. For a company to hire an A-list celebrity to promote its product in a commercial, many obstacles could arise: The desired star might want too much money, not have time to make the commercial, not be interested in doing commercials, or not want to endorse the product. By using product placement, a manufacturer can avoid some of these problems and still be able to have its product associated with the star, albeit less directly (Chan, 2015).

Studios, for their part, are usually more than willing to cooperate with product placement efforts. Not only are the fees paid by advertisers for the service quite welcome, but product placement can also help to make a scene appear more realistic, because it includes everyday brands in the scene instead of using items with deliberately generic packaging, which can sometimes look artificial on the screen (Cheng, Liang, Zhang & Fang, 2014).

Consumer Avoidance Behavior

Digital video recording (DVR) devises are set-top boxes that allow consumers to record movies and programs off the television. DVRs are able to record video and audio digitally, meaning that there is essentially no difference between the original broadcast and the recording. Many people prefer to watch recorded programs on their DVR at their own convenience rather than when the program is broadcast. Of concern to advertisers is the DVR user's ability to skip or fast forward through commercials. This ability to bypass advertisements is highly frustrating for advertisers, because an ad is only useful if viewers see it. Advertisers, therefore, have turned to product placement as a method of making their messaging inescapable. Because the product is on display as part of the narrative in the film or program itself, there is no way to avoid exposure to it (Chan, 2016).

FURTHER INSIGHTS

Product placement can take different forms, a fact that is not surprising given the vast array of options available for programs to feature various items. Basic product placement involves the use of a product in such a way that its brand is clearly distinguishable on screen, but not to the extent that the characters in the program actually refer to the product. When characters do make such references, or the product and its brand are included in the performance as an actual element of the story, this is known as advanced product placement.

Basic product placement is far more common than its advanced form. Basic product placement may be arranged for a fee or may be permitted at no cost, since production studios are always in need of materials they can use to arrange scenes and are therefore grateful for being able to use the products in this way (Shears, 2014). The miraculously clean and impervious Hyundai Tuscon that was prominently featured in the 2014 season of *The Walking Dead* was briefly part of the automakers' product line as a limited edition, which was offered as a prize in a viewership contest. The car's peculiar presence in the post-apocalyptic zombie setting was widely parodied, and marketers subsequently sought ways to make tie-ins less jarring.

Cars are frequent beneficiaries of product placement. More successful than the zombie-fighting Tuscon, in terms of both marketing and filmmaking, Aston Martin is among a host of hopeful sports car makers have long been associated with the James Bond franchise, embodying in a car the primary characteristics of the film's protagonist. Moviegoers look forward to seeing what 007 will be driving. For advertisers, ideal product placement results in a transference of positive feelings viewers have toward an actor or a production onto a featured product. Critics of product placement, however, have taken issue with the subtle way in which this type of advertising can infiltrate entertainment media, exerting its influence upon audience members without them being aware of it and having a particularly strong impact upon children and adolescents, who may not possess the critical-thinking skills needed to discern the difference between an innocent visual element and a covert attempt at persuasion.

In the United States, laws are in place requiring advertisers who pay for having their products featured in programs to disclose to the public the fact that they have done so. Failing to disclose in this way is considered a form of bribery and has been condemned since the 1950s. At that time, radio hosts accepted bribes—"payola"— from record companies in exchange for playing certain records as a way of increasing those records' popularity (Paluck et al., 2015).

Product placement has been the subject of a number of interesting studies. Some of this research has been undertaken by the advertising industry itself or by advertisers and seeks to determine how effective various forms of embedded marketing are so that firms can choose an optimal approach. Other analyses are carried out by consumer protection agencies concerned about the effects of "subliminal" advertising on consumers and on society as a whole.

One measure of effectiveness used in product placement research is known as recall, and it attempts to measure how well viewers of a program can remember what products were featured. Measuring recall assumes that the more a viewer recalls a product, the better this is for the advertiser, but in reality this is not always the case. Sometimes, a high recall score can mean that the viewer thought that the product placement in the performance was too obvious, too repetitive, or too jarring, perhaps because it did not fit well with the rest of the scene dressing or with the story itself. If this is the case, then the viewer may have been left with a negative impression of the product and the company that produces it.

ISSUES

Some types of product placement raise strong ethical concerns, generally because they have the potential to encourage people, consciously or subconsciously, to engage in behaviors that may have a negative impact on their health or well-being. The most obvious examples of such behaviors are cigarette smoking and alcohol consumption by television and film characters. For many years, drinking and smoking were regular features of all manner of programs. Young people, in particular, are believed to be persuaded to imitate the habits of characters who are perceived as admirable in part because of their smoking and drinking. Critics blamed increases in the incidence of illnesses associated with cigarette and alcohol consumption on media portrayals. Eventually, stricter regulations about the use of these substances in entertainment media were put into place (Storm & Stoller, 2015).

Other types of products also have raised objections. Sugary sodas are often included as part of product placement efforts, with their brightly colored cans easily identifiable by viewers. Health advocates object to this because childhood obesity in the United States is already at near-epidemic levels, and featuring high-calorie sodas in programs, especially programs for which the primary audience is people under the age of 18, is perceived to exploitative and dangerous.

It has been argued that many of these depictions are not precisely product placement, since it is often not clear what brand of soda a character is drinking, what type of alcohol, or who manufactured the character's cigarettes. Consumer watchdogs point out that the concern about encouraging these practices is not traceable to a particular company, but to the practice itself (Liu, Chou & Liao, 2015).

Many of the objections to product placement have less to do with particular companies or products, and instead come from people's general aversion to feeling that they are being manipulated. All advertising is based on a degree of manipulation because its purpose is to encourage people to behave in a certain way—to buy a product (Srivastava, 2016). Because people are somewhat accustomed to traditional advertising and can see it coming and know what to expect from it, they do not feel that it represents a threat to their autonomy. With product placement, however, there is often a feeling that the advertising is sneaky or otherwise questionable and makes every effort to hide itself from viewers' conscious awareness. This makes people suspicious of this type of advertising and can even cause backfire when people become aware of the advertising message.

BIBLIOGRAPHY

Chan, F. F. Y. (2015). A critical realist and multi-methodology framework for product placement research. *Journal of Promotion Management, 21*(3), 279–295. Retrieved October 23, 2016, from EBSCO Online Database Business Source Ultimate. http://search.ebscohost.com/login.aspx?direct=true&db=asn&AN=103104771&site=ehost-live

Chan, F. F. Y. (2016). An exploratory content analysis of product placement in top grossing films. *Journal of Promotion Management, 22*(1), 107–121. Retrieved October 23, 2016, from EBSCO Online Database Business Source Ultimate. http://search.ebscohost.com/login.aspx?direct=true&db=asn&AN=112901354&site=ehost-live

Cheng, C., Liang, R., Zhang, J., & Fang, I. (2014). The impact of product placement strategy on the placement communication effect: The case of a full-service restaurant. *Journal of Hospitality Marketing & Management, 23*(4), 424–444. Retrieved

October 23, 2016, from EBSCO Online Database Business Source Ultimate. http://search.ebscohost.com/login.aspx?direct=true&db=asn&AN=95678380&site=ehost-live

Liu, S., Chou, C., & Liao, H. (2015). An exploratory study of product placement in social media. *Internet Research, 25*(2), 300–316. Retrieved October 23, 2016, from EBSCO Online Database Business Source Ultimate. http://search.ebscohost.com/login.aspx?direct=true&db=asn&AN=101655595&site=ehost-live

Paluck, E. L., Lagunes, P., Green, D. P., Vavreck, L., Peer, L., & Gomila, R. (2015). Does product placement change television viewers' social behavior? *Plos ONE, 10*(9), 1–18. Retrieved October 23, 2016, from EBSCO Online Database Business Source Ultimate. http://search.ebscohost.com/login.aspx?direct=true&db=asn&AN=109899350&site=ehost-live

Patwardhan, H., & Patwardhan, P. (2016). When fiction becomes fact: Effect of reverse product placement on consumer attitudes. *Journal of Promotion Management, 22*(3), 349–369. Retrieved October 23, 2016, from EBSCO Online Database Business Source Ultimate. http://search.ebscohost.com/login.aspx?direct=true&db=asn&AN=116265555&site=ehost-live

Shears, P. (2014). Product placement: The UK and the new rules. *Journal of Promotion Management, 20*(1), 59–81. Retrieved October 23, 2016, from EBSCO Online Database Business Source Ultimate. http://search.ebscohost.com/login.aspx?direct=true&db=asn&AN=94358442&site=ehost-live

Srivastava, R. K. (2016). Promoting brands through product placement in successful and unsuccessful films in emerging markets. *Journal of Promotion Management, 22*(3), 281–300. Retrieved October 23, 2016, from EBSCO Online Database Business Source Ultimate. http://search.ebscohost.com/login.aspx?direct=true&db=asn&AN=116265552&site=ehost-live

Storm, B. C., & Stoller, E. (2015). Exposure to product placement in text can influence consumer judgments. *Applied Cognitive Psychology, 29*(1), 20–31. Retrieved October 23, 2016, from EBSCO Online Database Business Source Ultimate. http://search.ebscohost.com/login.aspx?direct=true&db=asn&AN=100631217&site=ehost-live

Venkatadri, U., Vardarajan, V., & Das, B. (2015). Product placement within a fast-picking tunnel of a distribution centre. *International Journal of Advanced Manufacturing Technology, 76*(9–12), 1681–1690. Retrieved October 23, 2016, from EBSCO Online Database Business Source Ultimate. http://search.ebscohost.com/login.aspx?direct=true&db=asn&AN=101005427&site=ehost-live

SUGGESTED READING

Begy, G., & Talwar, V. (2016). The economic worth of product placement in prime-time television shows. *International Journal of Market Research, 58*(2), 253–275. Retrieved October 23, 2016, from EBSCO Online Database Business Source Ultimate. http://search.ebscohost.com/login.aspx?direct=true&db=bsu&AN=113837628&site=ehost-live

Ficarra, A., Essenfeld, A., Blonder, M., Tursi, M., Khan, S., & Policastro, P. (2013). The effects of environment and product placement on fruit and candy consumption amongst college students. *Journal of the Academy of Nutrition & Dietetics, 113*, A73.

Gillespie, B., & Joireman, J. (2016). The Role of Consumer Narrative Enjoyment and Persuasion Awareness in Product Placement Advertising. *American Behavioral Scientist, 60*(12), 1510-1528. Retrieved October 23, 2016, from EBSCO Online Database Business Source Ultimate. http://search.ebscohost.com/login.aspx?direct=true&db=sxi&AN=118451512&site=ehost-live

Hudson, S., & Elliott, C. (2013). Measuring the impact of product placement on children using digital brand integration. *Journal of Food Products Marketing, 19*(3), 176–200. Retrieved October 23, 2016, from EBSCO Online Database Business Source Ultimate. http://search.ebscohost.com/login.aspx?direct=true&db=bsu&AN=88353565&site=ehost-live

Kramoliš, J., & Kope ková, M. (2013). Product placement: A smart marketing tool shifting a company to the next competitive level. *Journal of Competitiveness, 5*(4), 98–114.

Manyiwa, S., & Brennan, R. (2016). Impact of materialism on consumers' ethical evaluation and acceptance of product placement in movies. *Social Business, 6*(1), 65–82. Retrieved October 23, 2016, from EBSCO Online Database Business Source Ultimate. http://search.ebscohost.com/login.as

px?direct=true&db=bsu&AN=116959556&site=e
host-live

Marti-Parreno, Jose, et al. (2017). Product placement
in video games: the effect of brand familiarity and
repetition on consumers' memory. *Journal of Interactive Marketing*, 38, 55-63. Retrieved June 29, 2017.

Risner, J. (2016). How I Learned To Stop Worrying
and Grudgingly Accept Product Placement:
Nicolás López, Chilewood and Criteria for A Neo-
liberal Cinema. *Journal Of Latin American Cultural

Studies (13569325), *25*(4), 597-612. Retrieved October 23, 2016, from EBSCO Online Database
Business Source Ultimate. http://search.ebsco-
host.com/login.aspx?direct=true&db=sxi&AN=11
9026702&site=ehost-live

Ruggieri, S., & Boca, S. (2013). At the roots of
product placement: The mere exposure effect. *Europe's Journal of Psychology*, *9*(2), 246–258.

Scott Zimmer, J.D.

PROFESSIONAL SELLING IN BUSINESS TO BUSINESS (B2B) MARKETING

ABSTRACT

This article will focus on the professional selling practices in business to business (B2B) marketing. Many
organizations have identified that managing relationships is an important technique in B2Bmarkets.
They utilize different B2B relationship marketing
programs in an effort to increase their bottom line.
As a result, key account management (KAM) has become an important aspect of many organizations'
marketing strategies.

OVERVIEW

Many organizations have identified that managing
relationships is an important technique in business-
to-business (B2B) markets. These organizations have
invested much time, money, and effort into making
these relationships work. They utilize different B2B
relationship marketing programs in an effort to increase their bottom line. As a result, key account management (KAM) has become an important aspect
of many organizations' marketing strategies. Kotler
(1994) believes that B2B marketing is different from
customer markets in a variety of ways such as there are
usually fewer and larger buyers in a central geographical territory; a derived and fluctuating demand; participation by many in the buying process; professional
buyers and closer relationships, which eliminates the
need for a middleman and technological links to
complete internal and external transactions.

It is important for organizations to develop positive relationships between business customers and
business suppliers, and there are many advantages to
this type of relationship. An organization's customer
base can provide the best opportunities for growth
and long-term profit opportunities, especially in
light of growing competition and market globalization. Filiatrault and Lapierre (1997) reported that
customer retention has more impact on profits than
economies of scale, and it costs five to six times more
to win a new customer than to keep a current one.

"Relationship marketing is based on the premise
that important accounts need focused and continuous attention" (Kotler, 1994). Relationship marketing occurs when organizations realize that they
have to continuously work at having a positive, mutually beneficial relationship with their customers.
When one thinks of the concept in this context, it
supports the marketing belief that marketing is about
exchanges (Hunt, 1983). Gundlach and Murphy
(1993) identified three types of exchanges that support this concept: transactional, contractual, and relational exchanges. Transactional exchanges focus
on single short-term situations, and each transaction yields a profit. Contractual exchange refers to
intermediate formal agreements, which can include
a single contract or a series of contractual exchanges
that include open-ended contracts. Relational exchanges occur over an extended period of time, are
linked together or are an ongoing process, and produce long-term profits. Webster (1992) has found
that many organizations use relationship marketing
as a marketing strategy when the transaction depends
more on negotiation as opposed to market-based
processes. As a result, the market has experienced a
shift to a focus on relationship marketing as opposed
to transactional marketing.

Relationship marketing has grown over the past 10 years (Sheth & Parvatyar, 2000) based on the belief that the efforts will yield substantial profits. However, no data exists to support this belief and research is mixed. More studies need to be conducted to validate these claims. Two of the main issues that will be need to be reviewed focus on the actual payoff when an organization uses different relationship marketing programs to build different types of relational bonds and norms in order to generate varying levels of return (Berry, 1995) and the types and levels of returns an organization receives from a relationship marketing program based on factors such as participant influence (Reinartz & Kumar, 2000). "Researchers in service and consumer markets have linked relationship marketing activities to intermediate outcomes (i.e. sales growth, higher customer share, lower price sensitivity) that should enhance a firm's profit" (Palmatier, Gopalakrishna, & Houston, 2006). However, the overall findings in both B2B and consumer markets is that relationship marketing efforts have a direct effect on a customer's value to the firm by increasing the length, breadth, and depth of the buying relationship and generating positive word of mouth (Verhoef, 2003).

Several criterions are utilized to describe relationship marketing efforts, including customer bonds formed, exchange control mechanisms used, benefits offered, functions served, and content area supported. The criterion use different perspectives to identify the viable categories for grouping relationship building activities. Most of the categories include financial, social, and structural factors and imply that customer-seller relationships are similar within each category, but may vary by level of effectiveness among the categories. Many researchers have used Berry's (1995) model of explaining financial, social, and structural relationship marketing programs. According to his model:

- Financial relationship marketing programs include discounts, free products, or other financial benefits that reward customer loyalty. However, organizations must be unique in their offerings so that competitors may not easily duplicate their campaign. Otherwise, there will be no benefit.
- Social relationship marketing programs include meals, special treatment, entertainment, and personalized information. Research has shown that social bonds are not easy to duplicate. Therefore, there is a good possibility that customer relationships will be strong, and customers will ignore enticing offerings from competitors due to their loyalty and satisfaction with a product.
- Structural relationship marketing programs increase productivity and/or efficiency for customers through investments that customers would probably not make themselves (e.g. customized order processing system, tailored packaging). These programs tend to offer unique benefits and require substantial setup efforts. Therefore, customers may be reluctant to change vendors given the benefits from the relationship.

In addition to relationship marketing, other factors such as the customer, salesperson, and selling firm may influence the exchange performance in B2B customer interactions. Customer commitment to a selling firm is based on the customer's willingness to maintain a relationship with the firm and consider the partnership valuable. The customer's perception and interaction frequency are key factors in determining how long the relationship will last. "A customer's sales growth can lead to increased selling firm sales" (Palmatier, Gopalakrishna, & Houston, 2006, p. 480). It has been found that a salesperson's ability and motivation are important factors to successful sales and profit outcomes. A motivated sales staff has the ability to find and close opportunities for new relationships, which equates to increased profits. If the customer is satisfied with the sales staff's performance, it can lead to a long and prosperous relationship.

Finally, there are opportunities for a selling firm to utilize indirect and direct efforts to develop and secure customer relationships that will yield a significant profit. Palmatier, Gopalakrishna, and Houston (2006) identified different techniques to measure how effective the direct and indirect efforts were in securing successful relationships.

- **Direct efforts**—The use of customer relationship management (CRM) is assessed, which would require a strategic approach to creating shareholder value by developing relationships with key customers and customer segments through the use of data and information technology. Access to the customer database will allow organizations to target their efforts more effectively.

- **Indirect efforts**—Average tenure of the sales force at the organization is reviewed because tenure results in stronger customer relationships, fewer customer defections, and more customer specific knowledge, which can minimize customer turnover and enhance profits.

APPLICATION

Key Account Management

Many organizations have seen the advantages of having a key account management (KAM) strategy for marketing their products and services. "Key account management (KAM) involves targeting the largest and most important customers and providing them with special treatment in the areas of marketing, administration, and service" (Arnett, Macy & Wilcox, 2005, p. 1). Organizations have found a niche where they can provide a holistic approach to satisfying the needs of their client base. They have positioned themselves so that they can satisfy their customers from the beginning of the process to the end. KAM has become popular as a result of customers placing demands on suppliers (Moon & Armstrong, 1994) and organizations realizing the importance of relationship marketing and its emphasis on customers (Morgan & Hunt, 1994).

One of the most important factors in a successful KAM strategy is the core selling team. The core selling team is a group of individuals who have been assigned to a particular customer and are responsible for developing a sales campaign for that client. Most of the research on selling teams focuses on personal selling and sales management. However, the relationship between core selling teams and key customers can be viewed from many perspectives. Two of those perspectives are:

1. The relationship marketing perspective.

This perspective focuses on the characteristics of the core selling team-buyer relationship. This viewpoint highlights the basis for a successful relationship—when each partner increases his or her commitment to the relationship (Morgan & Hunt, 1994).

2. The competitive advantage perspective.

This perspective focuses on the marketing advantages that manifest as a result of the core selling team-buyer partnership. This viewpoint suggests that organizations are able to offer more value and lower

costs than rivals as a result of successful partnerships (Day, 1995).

- Core selling teams can have a tremendous influence on improving the relationship with key customers. Core selling teams have the ability to effect a buyer's perception of the organization. The influences can be seen directly and indirectly in the partnership (Arnett, Macy & Wilcox, 2005).
- Direct Influences
- Enhance the organization's capability to acquire and process market-related information
- Allow organizations to engage in more extensive problem-solving approaches with the buyer
- Facilitate integrative negotiation processes
- Promote increased coordination between sellers and buyers
- Increase the firm's ability to practice joint adaptation with buyers
- Indirect Influences
- Provide access to the learning and knowledge embedded in the routines of the supplier
- Allow the adaptation of the supplier's processes, systems, structures, and market offerings to fit the needs of the buyer
- Increase the investment in resources by the supplier

VIEWPOINT

Trade Fairs in Key Account Management

Trade fairs are an important aspect in the marketing process. However, many exhibitors tend to focus on transactional exchanges. As a result, they do not take the opportunity to pursue relationships that may lead to key accounts. Many exhibitors have different reasons for pursuing relationships at trade fairs. Some may go in order to achieve immediate sales, whereas others may attend in order to build relationships and improve the company's image. Blythe (2001) defined selling and non-selling activities as selling—lead generation, closing sales, finding new customers, qualifying leads and prospecting, and non-selling—meeting existing customers, interacting with existing distributors, enhancing the company image, and taking orders.

There are marketing professionals who do not believe that the non-selling initiatives yield favorable results at a trade fair. However, these efforts are usually the ones that assist in promoting KAM partnerships. Exhibitors must began to understand that trade fairs

Table 1: KAM Development Stages & Strategies

Development Stage	Objectives	Strategies	Visitors' reasons for attendance at trade fair	Exhibitors' reasons for attendance at trade fair
Pre-KAM	Define and identify strategic account potential. Secure initial contact.	Identify key contacts and decision making unit. Establish product need. Display willingness to address other areas of the problem. Advocate key account status in-house.	See new companies. Make business contacts. Compare products and services.	Meet new customers. Launch new products. Meet new distributors. Promote existing products.
Early KAM	Account penetration. Increase volume of business. Achieve preferred supplier status.	Build social network. Identify process-related problems and signal willingness to work together to provide cost effective solutions. Build trust through performance and open communications.	Obtain technical or product information.	Interact with existing customers. Interact with existing distributors. Enhance the company image. Take sales orders.
Mid KAM	Build partnership. Consolidate preference supplier status. Establish key account in-house.	Focus on product-related solutions. Build interorganizational teams. Establish joint systems. Begin to perform non-core management tasks.	Discuss specific problems/talk with the experts.	Interact with existing customers. Interact with existing distributors.
Partnership KAM	Develop spirit of partnership. Build common culture. Lock in customer by being external resource base.	Integrate processes. Extend joint problem solving. Focus on cost reduction and joint value-creating opportunities. Address key strategic issues of the client. Address facilitation issues.	Discuss specific problems/talk with the experts.	Interact with existing customers and distributors (possibly by sharing exhibition space).
Synergistic KAM	Continuous improvement. Shared rewards, quasi-integration.	Focus on joint value creation. Create semiautonomous project teams. Develop strategic congruence.	No real role. At this stage, the companies are very close together, and may even be sharing their promotional activities, including exhibiting at trade fairs.	No real role.
Uncoupling KAM	Disengagement	Withdrawal	To see new customers, products, developments, and companies.	To meet new customers and distributors, and to take sales orders.

provide opportunities for long-term relationships and partnerships with key accounts. Although there may not be an immediate sale to justify the cost of the

fair, there is potential to start to develop a relationship that may provide revenue that is 10 times the expense of the trade fair.

Millman & Wilson (1994) developed the KAM/PPF model that could assist exhibitors in evaluating how their efforts at a trade fair could open the doors to future business. This model can be applied to large and small organizations as they determine what strategies need to be in place at each stage of the KAM relationship. Key personnel must decide what needs to be communicated to potential customers at each stage. In the beginning, the organization may focus on sending written public relations literature about the company to potential clients. However, in the later stages, the focus may be on direct conversations between key players in the process.

CONCLUSION

Managing relationships is an important aspect in business markets, especially among B2B organizations. B2B marketing is considered to be one the fastest-growing sectors. Many professional service firms have engaged in the process, and have found the benefits to be profitable. Filiatrault and Lapierre (1997) developed a four-phase model of the relationship management process that will assist organizations in the B2B relationship. The four phases are (1) before the project, (2) at the beginning of the project, (3) during the project, and (4) after the project. Each phase is characterized by the following activities:

- **Before the project.** Evaluate quality and precision of the answer to the bid; evaluate past experience and distinctive technical competence and ability to work with people; use referrals; and improve linking capabilities.
- **At the beginning of the project.** Seek customer participation early; clearly define needs; assign project responsibility to only one person for both the client and the consultant; define steering committee formalities and procedures, modification, and follow-up procedures; and approve procedures to train customer.
- **During the project.** Assign sufficient authority to project manager; replace incompetent project manager quickly; manage steering committee tightly; closely control schedule and

costs; give and receive feedback; encourage customer participation; discourage over-participation; ensure quick and efficient recovery of errors; and formalize termination procedure.

- **After the project.** Ensure customer satisfaction and nurture relationship through guarantees, follow-up visits, training of technicians and operators, and maintenance contracts; conduct surveys; and facilitate the transfer of responsibilities of project manager to operations manager within the firm by more thorough start-up procedures and extended presence of specialists and technicians (Filiatrault & Lapierre, 1977, p. 216).

KAM is one of the most important developments to occur in marketing strategy. By creating KAM strategies, organizations can position themselves to have a competitive advantage as well as increase their revenue and profitability. In addition, research has shown that KAM can benefit suppliers by increasing profitability, providing greater effectiveness, developing stronger relationships with key accounts, attaining goals, improving customer responsiveness and customer satisfaction, reducing conflict, and creating better business planning (Arnett, Macy, & Wilcox, 2005).

KAM strategies have changed over the years. In the 1950s, the accounts were managed by national account managers who utilized a transaction based approach. In the 1960s and 1970s, there was a shift to highlighting the need to have long-term relationships. National account teams managed the key accounts in the 1960s, and there was a transition to selling center teams in the 1970s. During the 1980s and 1990s, there was a shift toward having formal partnerships. The management of the key accounts was guided by category management teams in the 1980s. Core selling teams/enterprise teams took over in the 1990s and that is the stage the field is currently pursuing. However, horizontal venture teams are expected to manage key accounts in the future, as organizations develop formal alliances with their suppliers.

Trade fairs can be used to promote the establishment of key account relationships. At trade fairs, key account managers have the opportunity to establish the first contact at the pre-KAM or early KAM stage and build partnerships and develop a common culture at the mid-KAM and partnership KAM stages (Blythe, 2002). Many attend trade fairs as a public relations tool. Some believe that by exhibiting at the trade fairs, organizations are showcasing what the company is capable of doing. As a result, the organization solidifies its position in the market as well as credibility. Attendance at a trade fair may show the market that an organization is doing well and not in trouble. In essence, attendance is a way to improve and maintain the organization's reputation and image.

In the past, many exhibitors may not be sure of the reasons why they are attending a trade fair or how to evaluate if attendance and participation was a successful initiative. Although many have attended to make new contacts and interact with existing customers, some have viewed attendance as an opportunity to manage conflict with established partnerships. Visitors and exhibitors have the opportunity to develop a mutually agreeable arrangement as to how the two will interact with one another. A partnership is formed and the guidelines for the working relationship are confirmed through dialogue.

BIBLIOGRAPHY

Agnihotri, R., Kothandaraman, P., Kashyap, R., & Singh, R. (2012). Bringing "social" into sales: the impact of salespeople's social media use on service behaviors and value creation. *Journal of Personal Selling & Sales Management, 32,* 333-348. Retrieved November 15, 2013, from EBSCO Online Database Business Source Complete. http://search.ebscohost.com/login.aspx?direct=true&db=bth&AN=78110795&site=ehost-live

Arnett, D., Macy, B., & Wilcox, J. (2005). The role of core selling teams in supplier-buyer relationships. *Journal of Personal Selling & Sales Management, 25,* 27-42. Retrieved June 6, 2007, from EBSCO Online Database Business Source Complete. http://search.ebscohost.com/login.aspx?direct=true&db=bth&AN=17200366&site=ehost-live

Berry, L. (1995). Relationship marketing of service-growing interest, emerging perspectives. *Journal of Academic Marketing Science, 23,* 236-245.

Blythe, J. (2002). Using trade fairs in key account management. *Industrial Marketing Management, 31,* 627-635.

Borg, S., & Johnston, W.J. (2013). The IPS-EQ model: Interpersonal skills and emotional intelligence in a sales process. *Journal of Personal Selling & Sales*

Management, 33, 39-52. Retrieved November 15, 2013, from EBSCO Online Database Business Source Complete. http://search.ebscohost.com/login.aspx?direct=true&db=bth&AN=84461728&site=ehost-live

Day, G. (1995). Advantageous alliances. *Journal of the Academy of Marketing Science, 23,* 297-300.

Filiatrault, P., & Lapierre, J. (1997). Managing Business-to-Business marketing relationships in consulting engineering firms. *Industrial Marketing Management, 26,* 213-222. Retrieved June 4, 2007, from EBSCO Online Database Business Source Complete. http://search.ebscohost.com/login.aspx?direct=true&db=bth&AN=12495756&site=ehost-live

Gundlach, G. T., & Murphy, P. E. (1993). Ethical and legal foundations of relational marketing exchanges. *Journal of Marketing, 57,* 35-46. Retrieved June 4, 2007, from EBSCO Online Database Business Source Complete. http://search.ebscohost.com/login.aspx?direct=true&db=bth&AN=9402090911&site=ehost-live

Hunt, S. D. (1983). General theories and the fundamental explanada of marketing. *Journal of Marketing, 47,* 9-17. Retrieved June 4, 2007, from EBSCO Online Database Business Source Complete. http://search.ebscohost.com/login.aspx?direct=true&db=bth&AN=5004947&site=ehost-live

Kotler, P. (1994). *Marketing management: Analysis, planning, implementation and control,* (8th ed.). Englewood Cliffs, NJ: Prentice Hall.

Millman, A., & Wilson, K. (1994). From key account selling to key account management. *Journal of Marketing Practice: Applied Marketing Science, 1,* 9-21.

Moon, M., & Armstrong, G. (1994). Selling teams: A conceptual framework and research agenda. *Journal of Personal Selling & Sales Management, 17,* 31-41.

Morgan, R., & Hunt, S. (1994). The commitment-trust theory of relationship marketing. *Journal of Marketing, 58,* 20-38.

Onyemah, V., Pesquera, M., & Ali, A. (2013). What entrepreneurs get wrong. *Harvard Business Review, 91,* 74-79. Retrieved November 15, 2013, from EBSCO Online Database Business Source Complete. http://search.ebscohost.com/login.aspx?direct=true&db=bth&AN=87039867&site=ehost-live

Palmatier, R., Gopalakrishna, S., & Houston, M. (2006). Returns on Business-to-Business relationship marketing investments: Strategies for leveraging profits. *Marketing Science, 25,* 477-493. Retrieved June 6, 2007, from EBSCO Online Database Business Source Complete. http://search.ebscohost.com/login.aspx?direct=true&db=bth&AN=22883062&site=ehost-live

Reinartz, W., & Kumar, V. (2000). On the profitability of long-life customers in a noncontractual setting: An empirical investigation and implications for marketing. *Journal of Marketing, 64,* 17-35.

Sheth, J., & Parvatiyar, A. (2000). *Handbook of relationship marketing.* Thousand Oaks, CA: Sage Publications.

Webster, F. (1992). The changing role of marketing in the corporation. *Journal of Marketing, 56,* 1-17. Retrieved June 4, 2007, from EBSCO Online Database Business Source Complete. http://search.ebscohost.com/login.aspx?direct=true&db=bth&AN=9302070971&site=ehost-live

SUGGESTED READING

Gulati, R., Bristow, D., & Dou, W. (2004). The impact of personality variables, prior experience, and training on sales agents' internet utilization and performance. *Journal of Business-to-Business Marketing, 11*(1/2), 153-179. Retrieved June 4, 2007, from EBSCO Online Database Business Source Complete. http://search.ebscohost.com/login.aspx?direct=true&db=bth&AN=13021067&site=ehost-live

P.M., P. (2002). B2B brand group shakeup. *Catalog Age, 19,* 12-14. Retrieved June 4, 2007, from EBSCO Online Database Business Source Complete. http://search.ebscohost.com/login.aspx?direct=true&db=bth&AN=7208533&site=ehost-live

Piercy, N., & Lane, N. (2006). The underlying vulnerabilities in key account management strategies. *European Management Journal, 24*(2/3), 151-162. Retrieved June 7, 2007, from EBSCO Online Database Business Source Complete. http://search.ebscohost.com/login.aspx?direct=true&db=bth&AN=21266895&site=ehost-live

Marie Gould

PROMOTIONAL POLICIES

ABSTRACT

A promotional policy is a set of principles and guidelines based on an analysis of an organization's goals, objectives, resources, and plans that is used to help develop marketing decisions, strategies, and plans. In addition to the nature of the product or service being offered and the characteristics of the target market, a promotional policy must also take into account the corporate image that the organization desires to portray to the public as well as any ethical considerations about its product or marketing approach. Promotional policies must by their very nature differ from industry to industry and from organization to organization to reflect the nature of business and the characteristics of a particular organization.

Whether one thinks of it as a challenge, a game, or the ultimate boredom, marketing is a fact of life for every business. Even small business owners who swear that they never market their products or services do so through such methods as word of mouth and social or business networking. On the other extreme are large corporations with separate marketing departments and large marketing budgets that enable the creation of a corporate persona, high brand recognition, in-depth research, and a multi-pronged approach to identifying, capturing, and retaining customers.

Strategic Marketing

Whether large or small, the business marketer is faced with a plethora of ways to market the organization's goods and services. Although one could, in theory, stand on the street corner and hawk one's business products, a more solid marketing strategy is necessary. Strategic marketing is a subfunction of marketing that examines the marketplace to determine the needs of potential customers, the strategy of the competitors in the market, and attempts to develop a strategy that will enable the organization to gain or maintain a competitive advantage in the marketplace. Marketing departments can choose from a number of ways to market their company's products or services including advertising, direct response, sales promotions, and publicity. However, no matter how well an advertisement or a marketing campaign is designed, unless one understands the customer's needs, the market, and the industry as well as the strengths and weaknesses of the competition, these approaches are unlikely to be successful. Strategic marketing is an approach to marketing that helps an organization sharpen its focus and successfully compete in the marketplace.

Strategic marketing is concerned with two primary components: the target market and the best way to communicate the value of one's product or service to that market. To develop a viable marketing strategy, one must take into account several key dimensions. First, as with any other strategy within the organization, a marketing strategy needs to be endorsed by top management. Marketing strategy is also political in nature: Powerful units within the organization may disagree on the best marketing strategy and an agreement or compromise may need to be negotiated. Marketing strategies can also be affected by organizational culture and the assumptions that it engenders. For example, if the organization has always marketed its widgets to business executives, it may fail to see the potential for marketing to lower-level personnel within the organization or even for personal use to adults or teenagers, with an important segment of the marketplace not being considered as a result.

Marketing/Promotional Policies

Before one can develop a marketing strategy, determine the appropriate marketing mix, develop and implement a plan that will bring the business a sufficient return on investment for their marketing dollars, or design an advertisement, one must first determine what the parameters within which one must design one's marketing strategy are. Although one could take one's marketing budget and spread it across as many categories of the marketing mix as possible in an attempt to increase coverage of one's product or service, strategic marketing demands a more considered, systematic approach that takes into account not only the product but also the internal and external factors that affect how the product or service might best be marketed. Typically, successful marketing campaigns start with a marketing or promotional policy. This is a set of principles and guidelines based on an analysis of the organization's goals, objectives, resources, and plans.

Figure 1: Factors Informing Promotional Policy

Typically, policies are set by the organization's governing body (e.g., board of directors) and are used to develop strategy and guide decision making in support of meeting the organization's goals and objectives.

Factors to Consider

As shown in Figure 1, promotional policies need to consider at least four factors affecting the best way to market or promote a product or service:

- The characteristics of the product or service;
- The characteristics of the target market;
- The corporate image that the organization wishes to portray;
- Any ethical considerations in the marketing of the product or service.

The characteristics of the products or services being marketed by the organization have an obvious impact on the way that marketing is done. Not all products and services are best promoted in the same way. For example, a television spot advertising a high-end business consulting service would probably yield more results if placed on an all-news channel rather than an all-cartoon channel. In addition, the nature of the target market also influences the way that goods and services are most appropriately marketed. For example, a few years ago, a business bought air time on two local radio stations: one a classical station and the other a rock station. The narrative of the ads was the same, but the background music was different to reflect the musical tastes of the audiences of the respective stations. Unfortunately, somewhere in the process, the ads were switched so that the classical station received the ad with the rock music and the rock station received the ad with the classical

music. Soon thereafter, the stations started playing an apology from the business that had sponsored the ads: Numerous regular listeners of both stations had called in to complain about the appropriateness of the ads. Although the business had attempted to segment the target market into categories and tailor its advertising to appeal to the tastes of the segments, the execution fell short, ending in a lower return on investment than expected.

The characteristics of the product or service and of the target market or market segment are important aspects of marketing, particularly when designing a marketing campaign that will maximize one's return on investment. In addition, an organization must consider what place it wishes to occupy within its industry. Corporate image is the perception of an organization – generally held by the public. To cultivate its corporate image, a business needs to participate in activities that support that image and avoid activities that might tarnish it. Certainly, consulting firms and investment companies that have made the headlines over the past few years have learned this fact the hard way. However, even such decisions as where the organization advertises and how its ads are designed can reflect back on the organization. This is one reason that from time to time organizations change their corporate logo or branding: to realign public perceptions about them or to change their image to reflect new goals and objectives. In addition to activities directly focused on marketing specific products or services for the organization, businesses also typically engage in public relations activities as part of their marketing strategies. A corporate image may change over time depending on the organization's circumstances, publicity, and other publicly known information. Public relations activities help the organization to create and manage its public image or reputation with outside agencies and groups. This marketing function is responsible for developing positive messages about the organization and reducing the impact of negative events and information on the organization's reputation. In addition to considerations of corporate image, businesses also need to be concerned with ethical considerations in marketing and take these into account in the development of their promotional policy and eventual marketing strategy. For example, given the link between smoking and lung cancer, one can no longer view advertisements for cigarettes on television.

Just as there is no such thing as the "ideal" marketing strategy that is appropriate for all organizations, there is also no such thing as the "ideal" promotional policy for all organizations. Different types of organizations and even different industries will market their products and services in different ways. For example, a fast food chain may want to be associated with the concept of "quick and easy" whereas a high-end restaurant would be more likely to want to be associated with a fine dining experience.

APPLICATIONS

Marketing to Children

One area of promotional policy that has been a topic of much debate, particularly within the food industry, is the issue of whether or not one should market directly to children. Obviously, some products are designed specifically for children, including clothes, toys, and certain food products. The question, however, is the degree to which it is ethically appropriate to market these items directly to the children. For the most part, children do not have a great deal of discretionary cash, so marketing directly to children would appear to be a wasted effort. However, the wants of children can have a great effect on the buying behavior of their parents and other adults. In some cases, this is nothing more than the type of influence that is attempted by other marketing efforts and there is little to say when marketing efforts encourage drinking milk or buying comfortable shoes. However, both children and their parents know that milk and shoes are necessary, so little marketing effort is needed.

The ethical dilemma arises, however, when the item being marketed to children is something that may go against the parents' a priori philosophy of what is good or not good for a child to own, eat, or wear (e.g., revealing clothes or high-sugar snacks). The questionability of marketing to children in ethically ambiguous situations has caused companies such as Coca-Cola and the International Council of Beverages Associations (ICBA) to institute guidelines regarding marketing to children. Based on concerns over the rising obesity epidemic, particularly among children, these organizations have issued a statement saying that they take "special care" when deploying advertising practices to children under the age of 12 as children under that age "may lack the necessary

skills and judgements [sic] to properly understand the purpose behind the persuasive techniques commercial advertising represent" (Coca-Cola, 2008). For this reason, they do not market their products directly to children and only show children drinking their products in the company of adult caregivers.

Not only may children not be able to make reasoned judgments about the appropriateness and value of products, but marketing may also change their beliefs and behavior, particularly regarding the marketed product. Bridges and Briesch (2006) developed a model to test the "nag factor" in marketing children's categories. They define the term "nag factor" as an indirect marketing path that begins with promotional activities aimed at influencing the preferences of children who, in turn, request that their parent(s) purchase the product. The promotional activities that are likely to be successful with children tend to be different from those that are successful with adults. Although adults, for example, tend to develop brand loyalty and repeatedly purchase preferred brands, children tend not to focus on brands but make buying decisions (or at least acquisition decisions) based on the characteristics of the product. This is why many products that are aimed at children reflect the latest popular theme or character. In addition, purchasing decisions among children are made differently based on age. Younger children, for example, tend to look for products featuring the latest character, bonus offers, tie-ins with movies, and so forth. Because younger children do not necessarily understand that the general purpose of promotional activities is to sell products, they can, therefore, infer that unhealthy products are good for them because of the "endorsement" of the character. Young children, however, do not remain loyal to a particular brand once they make a purchasing decision, but change brands when a product with a more current character comes out. Teenagers, on the other hand, tend to be more like adults in their buying behaviors, particularly when it comes to brand loyalty, although they continue to respond to image-focused messages.

Given the fact that most children do not have the necessary funds to purchase items even if they form purchasing decisions, one might wonder at the effectiveness of promotional activities that are targeted toward children. However, Bridges and Briesch's review of the literature on marketing to children found that the nag factor has a definite influence on the purchasing behavior of adults with such items as clothing, shoes, fast food and other food items, snacks, and beverages. For example, one study found that the nag factor accounted for one-third of the trips to a fast food restaurant in 2011, up from only one-tenth in 1977. In 2006, 44 food and beverage companies spent $2.1 billion to market food to youth (Federal Trade Commission, 2012). Total advertising expenditures by fast food restaurants totaled $4.6 billion in 2012 (Yale Rudd Center for Food Policy and Obesity, 2013). In 2012, children under the age of 11 viewed half the number of fast food advertisements as adults; McDonald's was the only fast food chain that directed more advertising to children than adults in 2012 (Yale Rudd Center for Food Policy and Obesity, 2013). Research has shown that children tend to be influenced by marketing in categories that are considered unhealthy due to an increase in calorie intake or a decrease in nutrition.

Based on their research, the authors found that the nag factor is a real phenomenon as evidenced by the fact that households with children tend to have more variety in their purchases for such items as soft drinks and cereal than do households without children. Such variety-seeking behavior tends to increase over time as children become more sensitive to the influence of promotional tie-ins with dynamic characters and other popular themes. These findings have ethical implications for the way that organizations market to children so that marketing efforts support their promotional policies.

CONCLUSION

Before one can develop a marketing strategy, one must first develop a marketing or promotional policy. These principles and guidelines will help the marketing department develop a marketing strategy, marketing plan, and marketing mix that will best support the organization in meeting its goals and objectives. The organization's promotional policy must consider not only the characteristics of the product or service being marketed or the concomitant target market, but also the corporate image that the business desires to convey to the public. Any ethical considerations regarding the marketing of their products must also be taken into account. By first developing a well-thought-out promotional policy, marketers can better design marketing strategies and plans that will

support the organization in its goals and objectives and maximize the return on investment that the organization receives for its marketing dollars.

BIBLIOGRAPHY

American Marketing Association. (2009). Marketing. AMA Resource Library: Dictionary. Retrieved February 20, 2009, from http://www.marketingpower.com/%5flayouts/Dictionary.aspx?dLetter=M

Bridges, E. & Briesch, R. A. (2006). The "nag factor" and children's product categories. International Journal of Advertising, 25(2), 157-187. Retrieved February 24, 2009, from EBSCO Online Database Business Source Complete. http://search.ebscohost.com/login.aspx?direct=true&db=bth&AN=21110472&site=ehost-live

Coca-Cola Company, The. (2008). International Council of Beverages Associations guidelines on marketing to children. Retrieved February 24, 2009, from http://www.thecoca-colacompany.com/citizenship/icba.html

Federal Trade Commission. (2012). A review of food marketing to children and adolescents: A follow-up report. Retrieved November 24, 2014, from http://www.ftc.gov/sites/default/files/documents/reports/review-food-marketing-children-and-adolescents-follow-report/121221foodmarketingreport.pdf

Proctor, T. (2000). Strategic marketing: An introduction. New York: Routledge.

Yale Rudd Center for Food Policy and Obesity. (2013). Fast food F.A.C.T.S. 2013: Food advertising to children and teens score. Retrieved November 24, 2014, from http://www.fastfoodmarketing.org/media/FastFoodFACTS%5Freport.pdf

SUGGESTED READING

Challagall, G., B. R. Murtha, & B. Jaworski. (2014). Marketing doctrine: A principles-based approach to guiding marketing decision making in firms. *Journal of Marketing 78*, 4–20. Retrieved November 24, 2014, from EBSCO Online Database Business Source Complete. http://search.ebscohost.com/login.aspx?dircct=truc&db=bth&AN-97014757

Inman, J. J. & McAlister, L. (1993). A retailer promotion policy model considering promotion signal sensitivity. Marketing Science, 12(4), 339-356. Retrieved February 24, 2009, from EBSCO Online Database Business Source Complete. http://

search.ebscohost.com/login.aspx?direct=true&d b=bth&AN=4471790&site=ehost-live

Paley, N. (2005). Promotional strategies: Plan a total communications mix. In N. Paley, Manager's guide to competitive marketing strategies (3rd ed.) (pp. 333-362). London: Thorogood. Retrieved February 24 2009, from EBSCO Online Database Business Source Complete. http://search.ebscohost.com/login.aspx?direct=true&db=bth&AN=2 2355290&site=ehost-live

Ruskin-Brown, I. (2005). Promoting a service. In I. Ruskin-Brown, Marketing your service business (pp. 199-221). London: Thorogood. Retrieved July 10, 2007, from EBSCO Online Database Business

Source Complete. http://search.ebscohost.com/login.aspx?direct=true&db=bth&AN=22377471&s ite=ehost-live

Scott, J. T. (2005). Business marketing and promotion: A checklist. In J. T. Scott, Concise handbook of management: A practitioner's approach (pp. 213-218). New York: Routledge. Retrieved February 24, 2009, from EBSCO Online Database Business Source Complete. http://search.ebscohost.com/login.aspx?direct=true&db=bth&AN=2 1713233&site=ehost-live

Ruth A. Wienclaw, Ph.D.

Public Relations

ABSTRACT

Public relations is the part of the marketing mix designed to build or maintain a positive organizational image among an organization's stakeholders. Public relations is a slow process that gradually changes the impressions, attitudes, and opinions of the various publics over time. Although public relations sometimes can be used to "spin" negative information into a more favorable light, it cannot build a positive reputation for an organization when it is not deserved. Similarly, public relations cannot smother deserved criticisms or malpractice. There are a number of tools for promulgating the organization's message through public relations. In addition to media relations, public relations activities may include face-to-face techniques, research, the use of the Internet, various in-house publications, and the design and protection of the corporate logo and other branding.

OVERVIEW

According to conventional wisdom, if one should "build a better mousetrap, the world will beat a path to your door." The reality, however, is more complex. Whether or not one's "mousetrap" is truly better will depend on a number of factors, including what kind of mousetrap customers want or need and how good the competition's mousetraps are. Pricing, too, will come into play. The potential customer must decide

how much "better" is worth. If the benefit achieved from using the better mousetrap is not worth the price, most customers will not purchase it. However, even if the mousetrap is truly better, needed by the customer, unparalleled by the competition, and gives value for its price, customers still will not purchase the new mousetrap if they do not know about it. For this reason, businesses carry out various marketing activities ranging from word of mouth to elaborate marketing campaigns. The marketing function creates, communicates, and delivers value to customers and manages customer relationships in ways that benefit the organization and its stakeholders.

When thinking about marketing, many people think first about various techniques that directly advertise the organization's goods and services. These include advertising media such as print, television, and radio, billboards and other advertising signage, Internet advertisements, sales promotions, and direct marketing. In addition, another vital part of the marketing effort comprises public relations. This is the process of creating and managing a public image or reputation with outside agencies and groups. In business, the public relations function is responsible for developing positive messages about the organization and reducing the impact of negative events and information on the organization's reputation. The public relations function focuses efforts on various internal and external stakeholders, including stockholders, employees, the government, public interest groups, and society as a whole. It is the function of public relations to monitor its various constituencies and provide positive information to reinforce its Integrated Marketing Communications (IMC) strategy and advertising direction as well as to react quickly to counteract a shift in the desired position of any of its publics.

The Marketing Mix

As shown in Figure 1[CCL1], each of the various elements in the marketing mix is designed to move prospective customers closer to a sale. At first, these activities are targeted toward making the customer aware of the organization and its products or services. Publicity and advertising in particular are effective in achieving this goal. Once the prospective customer is made aware of the organization and what it has to offer, marketing efforts next focus on generating interest in the customer for purchasing the organization's goods or services. Publicity and advertising, again, tend to be particularly successful in generating interest. However, as shown in Figure 1, personal selling efforts tend to become increasingly successful as the customer acquires more information about the organization and what it has to offer. These activities also help prospective customers understand the nature and value of the organization's products or services and can help promote the conviction that the product or service being offered is something that is appropriate for the customer. Once this has been accomplished, marketing efforts attempt to turn this conviction that the product or service is appropriate or needed into a desire to purchase it. At this point, sales promotions can also be effectively used in making a prospective customer a current customer.

In addition to the more direct elements of the marketing effort – publicity, advertising, personal selling, and sales promotion – there is also the public relations function. As shown in the figure, public relations efforts can be effective throughout the process of turning prospective customers into current customers by helping them better understand the organization (or at least the image that the organization wishes to portray).

The marketing mix is the combination of product, price, place, and promotion that is used to get a product into the hands of the consumer. One of the primary tasks of marketing is to optimize the mix to best position the product for success in the

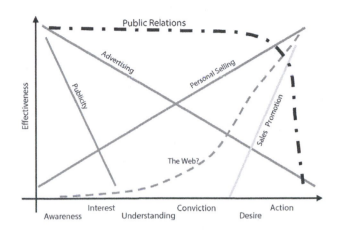

marketplace. The public relations function of the organization can positively contribute throughout the entire marketing program. During new product development, public relations can contribute by monitoring competitor activity and helping to determine the nature of the marketing opportunity. The public relations function can also determine the public relations objectives and strategy. For example, the type of development (whether or not it is an innovation, a reintroduction of a previous product, an extension of the organization's current line, a reappraisal or revitalization of a current product, or a managed decline or withdrawal of a product) will influence whether stakeholders need to be educated about the product, service, or brand, or reassured (e.g., if a product is going off the market); public relations actions need to be taken to support the sales strategy; or if the strategy requires a reassessment. Marketing research can also be used to formulate reports or news stories that can be used in public relations efforts.

In addition to activities directly related to marketing a product or service, public relations has many functions that can help the organization in meeting its goals and objectives. Primarily, public relations is used to build or maintain a positive image among the various stakeholders. For example, public relations can be used to help employees feel good about the organization that they are working for or be used as a selling point to attract and acquire high-quality new employees. Public relations can also be used to raise the awareness of various stakeholders or publics about the organization or its products or services, and educate them in an attempt to build a positive and attractive image. It can also help maintain investor confidence or attract new investors and raise financing. In addition, public relations can help launch new products or services. Public relations efforts can also be used to manage issues that might otherwise negatively affect the organization or its reputation and help defuse potential damaging impact of crisis situations on the organization.

However, public relations is not a magic wand that can immediately gain and maintain customer loyalty. As opposed to other marketing channels, public relations is a slow process that gradually changes the impressions, attitudes, and opinions of the various publics over time. Although public relations sometimes can be used to "spin" negative information into a more favorable light, it cannot build a positive reputation for an organization when it is not deserved. Similarly, public relations cannot smother deserved criticisms or malpractice.

Further, although public relations can help raise the awareness of the organization in the eyes of its various publics or stakeholders, it does not substitute for other elements of the marketing mix (e.g., advertising, publicity, promotion, personal sales) needed to market the organization's products or services. In addition, although good public relations practices can help increase the chances of getting media coverage, it cannot guarantee it. Similarly, although good public relations can increase the likelihood of increased sales, it cannot guarantee them.

APPLICATIONS

Face-to-Face Public Relations
Public relations techniques encompass more than media relations. There are also face-to-face techniques that allow organizations to spread their message and widen their recognition. Venues for face-to-face techniques used in public relations include seminars, meetings, conferences and conventions, and exhibitions. For example, the public relations department of an organization can set up an exhibit of its products, do demonstrations, or pass out literature at one or more conferences or conventions that are held each year. These opportunities allow the organization to choose one or more specific target audiences to whom it wishes to market and focus its message to best communicate with that market. Face-to-face approaches are the most direct of the public relations tools and may be one of the most powerful methods to reach stakeholders. These techniques also

allow the organization to focus the public relations effort so that it can be presented in more detail. If the organization is in charge of the event (e.g., a seminar put on by an investment business that teaches people about retirement planning), it has control over what information is presented and how this is done. If the event is being put on by a larger organization (e.g., exhibiting at a convention), the organization may enjoy a larger audience than if putting on the event independently and have the added benefit of being associated with the reputation of the larger organizer. Face-to-face events, however, are not without their drawbacks. The cost of such events is typically higher than for other public relations techniques. In addition, if working through a third party, one must also work within the parameters set by that party.

Public Relations Research
Another tool of public relations is research. Publishing research on a topic in which the organization has an interest or a proposed solution can not only generate greater interest in the topic but also in the organization's solution. In some cases, the link between the research and the organization's interests may be obvious or overused. However, there are situations where the publication of research findings may be particularly successful. In particular, the publication of research findings is likely to help the organization when it is truly newsworthy or has an interesting angle, is parallel to a strong educational campaign, or includes good case histories. Research can do more than generate media coverage, however. It can also provide a point of departure for discussions with stakeholders or serve as a basis for a conference or other face-to-face method. In addition, research can be used to reinforce the message of an advertising or a direct marketing campaign. However, if an organization decides to use research as a public relations tool, it must be very careful that the research is impeccable; otherwise, it will harm the organization's reputation rather than enhance it.

Mediums for Public Relations Outreach
With advances in electronic communications technology, one of the first choices for many public relations communications is the organization's website. Increasingly, stakeholders turn to this medium for information and updates about the organization and to compare the offerings of one organization to

another. The organization's public relations function should regularly review the organization's website and make recommendations on how to keep it up to date and use it proactively to manage the organization's reputation. The organization's website can be used as a virtual press office and can include press releases, summaries of research, and information about products or services, as well as advertising and contact information. A website can also be used to collect data and report the results of analysis, publicize events, or announce outstanding employee achievement. Electronic communications need not be limited to the Internet, however. Intranets also offer an important medium for public relations efforts with employees. In addition, email newsletters can be sent to employees or other stakeholders.

Electronic communications methods have both advantages and disadvantages. Websites can potentially deliver the organization's message to virtually any place in the modern world not only quickly, but cost-effectively. In addition, electronic communications methods allow two-way communication between the organization and its stakeholders. The information on websites can be quickly and easily updated, a feature essential for getting out information in a timely manner. This feature also means that public relations can issue rebuttals or deal with adverse comments in a timely fashion. However, to be useful from a public relations standpoint, a website needs to be monitored and frequently updated. This requires web-savvy personnel who understand how to update the website. In addition, it must be remembered that public relations information tends require a more subtle presentation than does overt advertising. A light hand is required when developing public relations materials for one's website. Otherwise, the material may have the opposite effect than was intended.

The Internet is not the only modern technology that is useful for public relations activities. Other technologies such as video and audio recordings can be used to promulgate the organization's message to stakeholders. Multimedia efforts can be used for sending out the organization's message in the form of such things as company reports, internal communications, education, recruitment, documentaries, business development, demonstrations, welcome materials for visitors, and issues management. To determine which medium is most appropriate, several considerations need to be taken into account. First, the organization needs to determine what message it is trying to communicate with the stakeholders. Some messages are more appropriate to certain media than are others. For example, if the organization is trying to communicate that it is on the cutting edge of technology, dispersing this message via audio cassette tape may be considered oxymoronic. Another question to be answered is to whom the message is being delivered. Stakeholders who are facile with modern media will appreciate being communicated with in that manner and will interpret the organization's use of such media as a demonstration that their needs are understood. In addition, it must be determined what the purpose of the message is. Just because a medium is available does not mean that it is appropriate to use it. Similarly, just because the message does not utilize all the storage space on the medium does not mean that the message should be longer. In many cases, shorter is better.

Another way that the organization can get out its message to stakeholders is through in-house publications, such as company bulletins, newsletters, newspapers, or magazines. Potential targets of these publications might include internal employees (e.g., workers, management, sales personnel), distributors (e.g., retailers, wholesalers), current or prospective customers, supporters (e.g., donors, guests, passengers), and opinion leaders (e.g., business leaders, academics, politicians).

Similarly, the organization's message can be promulgated through various printed materials – in particular, educational literature, corporate reports, and research or other special reports. For example, a manufacturer of a new drug might provide several different types of information to stakeholders. They might develop a simple leaflet for patients that discusses the disease, the actions of the drugs, and answers patients' frequently asked questions. A more detailed document could be developed for health-care professionals that summarizes scientific research on the drug and explains the actions of the drug on the human body. Package inserts might also be prepared for the patient. All this material might also be posted on the organization's website.

Public Relations & Branding
Last but not least, the public relations department should be involved in the design and safeguarding

of the corporate logo and other branding. These things are closely related to the corporate identity and public relations needs to make certain that they are appropriate to the image that the organization is trying to portray. Careful research needs to be done before changing these things to determine how they will be perceived by the public. Similarly, public relations needs to be watchful that the corporate logo or branding is not infringed by others. For example, several major snack manufacturers filed suit against a person who modified their branding to package drug-laced candy and soda. Organizations need to be vigilant so that their logo and branding only bring up positive associations in the minds of their stakeholders.

BIBLIOGRAPHY

Black, C. (2001). PR Practitioner's desktop guide. London, England: Thorogood.

Clow, K. E., & Baack, D. (2005). Public relations. In K. E. Clow & D. Baack (Eds.), Concise encyclopedia of advertising (p. 133). Binghamton, NY: Haworth. Retrieved July 10, 2007, from EBSCO Online Database Business Source Complete. http://search.ebscohost.com/login.aspx?direct=true&db=bth&AN=22573994&site=ehost-live

Dach, L. (2013). Don't spin a better story. Be a better company. Harvard Business Review, 91(10), 42. Retrieved November 19, 2013 from EBSCO online database Business Source Premier. http://search.ebscohost.com/login.aspx?direct=true&db=buh&AN=90325417

Horn, S. (2013). Social media's online advantage: The evolution of public relations to digital communications. Public Relations Tactics, 20(1), 16. Retrieved November 19, 2013 from EBSCO online database Business Source Premier. http://search.ebscohost.com/login.aspx?direct=true&db=buh&AN=84930683

The PR professional of 2015: Analyzing the future of public relations. (2012). Public Relations Tactics, 19(3), 14-15. Retrieved November 19, 2013 from EBSCO online database Business Source Premier. http://search.ebscohost.com/login.aspx?direct=true&db=buh&AN=73308187

Ruskin-Brown, I. (2005). Promoting a service. In I. Ruskin-Brown (Ed.), Marketing your service business (pp. 199-221). London, England: Thorogood. Retrieved July 10, 2007, from EBSCO

Online Database Business Source Complete. http://search.ebscohost.com/login.aspx?direct=true&db=bth&AN=22377471&site=ehost-live

SUGGESTED READING

Carayol, V., & Frame, A. (2012). Communication and PR from a cross-cultural standpoint: Practical and methodological issues. Brussels, Belgium: Peter Lang. Retrieved November 19, 2013 from EBSCO online database eBook Academic Collection (EBSCOhost). http://search.ebscohost.com/login.aspx?direct=true&db=e000xna&AN=486414&site=ehost-live

Dunn, J. (2001a). Crisis public relations: How to handle emergencies. In J. Dunn (Ed.), Public relations techniques that work pocketbook (pp. 121-137). London, England: Thorogood. Retrieved July 10, 2007, from EBSCO Online Database Business Source Complete. http://search.ebscohost.com/login.aspx?direct=true&db=bth&AN=22377706&site=ehost-live

Dunn, J. (2001b). The nature of public relations. In J. Dunn (Ed.), Public relations techniques that work pocketbook (pp. 3-12). London, England: Thorogood. Retrieved July 10, 2007, from EBSCO Online Database Business Source Complete. http://search.ebscohost.com/login.aspx?direct=true&db=bth&AN=22377695&site=ehost-live

Gottschalk, P. (2011). Corporate social responsibility, governance and corporate reputation. Hackensack, NJ: World Scientific. Retrieved November 19, 2013 from EBSCO online database eBook Academic Collection (EBSCOhost). http://search.ebscohost.com/login.aspx?direct=true&db=e000xna&AN=389603&site=ehost-live

Ikonen, Pasi. (2016) Transparency for sponsored content: analyzing codes of ethics in pulic relations, advertising and journalism. International Journal of Strategic Communication, 11, 2. Retrieved on June 29, 2017.

Knights, K. (2001). Getting out what you put in. In K. Knights (Ed.), Strategic planning in public relations (pp. 16-23). London, England: Thorogood. Retrieved July 10, 2007, from EBSCO Online Database Business Source Complete. http://search.ebscohost.com/login.aspx?direct=true&db=bth&AN=22383614&site=ehost-live

What is strategic planning and why do we need it? (2001). In K. Knights (Ed.), Strategic planning in public relations (pp. 1-6). London, England: Thorogood. Retrieved July 10, 2007, from EBSCO Online Database Business Source Complete. http://search.ebscohost.com/login.aspx?direct=true&db=bth&AN=22383612&site=ehost-live

Moloney, K. (2000). The PR industry from top to bottom. In K. Moloney (Ed.), Rethinking public relations (pp. 17-30). New York, NY: Routledge.

Retrieved July 10, 2007, from EBSCO Online Database Business Source Complete. http://search.ebscohost.com/login.aspx?direct=true&db=bth&AN=17441814&site=ehost-live [CCL1]image is poor quality – remake image from print-out/PDF

Ruth A. Wienclaw, Ph.D.

PUBLIC RELATIONS AND SOCIAL MEDIA

ABSTRACT

The spheres of public relations and social media are in many ways perfectly suited for one another because both are concerned with the flow of information from a small group of people to a potentially much larger audience. Since the dawn of the social media age in the early 2000s, businesses have sought to use social media to manage their public image, partly because social media can reach large numbers of people in a short time, and partly because many social media activities can be conducted with little or no monetary cost.

OVERVIEW

Social media sites are one of many tools used by public relations professionals as part of their mission to communicate information to the public that will portray their clients in the best possible light. Most social media tools are free to use, at least for basic features, meaning that they can benefit public relations staff in two ways. First, the fact that the sites are free encourages large numbers of people to try them. This would not be the case if there were a fee charged to participate in social media. The lack of an admission price encourages the development of a large network of people on a social media platform (Breakenridge, 2012). This works to the advantage of public relations professionals because if they can find a way to join that social media platform, they potentially have access to all the platform's participants; the larger the number of participants, the more people who can be reached by the public relations message. The second benefit of the low cost of social media participation by public relations staff is that even small companies without a sizable budget to devote to public relations can still create a presence for themselves on social media, potentially reaching far more people than they might be able to even by spending substantial amounts of money on advertising and other forms of information dissemination (VanSlyke, Valin & Paluszek, 2014).

However, public relations personnel should exercise caution when using social media as one of the tools within their professional toolkits. While social media can seem to be a fun, exciting, and inexpensive way to connect with others online, it is not without its pitfalls for the unwary. Some of the fundamental features of online communication are that it is difficult to convey subtle nuances of complex issues and impossible to predict who may come across a message that was originally posted for a very different audience (DiStaso & Bortree, 2014). In the few short years that social media sites have existed, there have been countlessscandals, gaffes, faux pas, and assorted backfiring of well-intentioned public relations efforts on social media. This has led many public relations professionals to observe that while using social media is free, that does not mean that it cannot inadvertently become very, very expensive.

Managing social media messages is extremely difficult to do well, a fact that justifies many of the fears and reservations about social media held by those who have been working in the public relations field for a long time. In essence, social media is for public relations staff a double edged sword, because while it is able to reach huge numbers of people with relatively small expenditures of money and effort (the public essentially does most of the work of distribution for free, when users share the public relations message with their social networks), it requires that the public relations staff be willing to relinquish control over the message, and it can backfire in spectacular fashion (Scott, 2010).

This can happen either due to honest error or because of some form of controversy or negativity associated with the subject of the public relations message, which the public relations staff has failed to account for in their campaign plan. An example of the former occurred in 2014 when the clothing manufacturer American Apparel, as part of its promotion of sales and other events around the Fourth of July, posted a photograph of an explosion against a sky blue background. Unfortunately, the image posted was not thoroughly researched by the public relations team to determine its origin, and it turned out to be a photo of the Space Shuttle *Challenger* exploding shortly after being launched in 1986. Members of the public relations team did not mean to offend anyone in this case; they were simply too young to have witnessed and remembered the *Challenger* disaster and did not take the time to verify the nature of the photo they used.

A more distressing incident, and one that is an example of the controversy/negativity type of social media backlash, occurred when the public relations team for famed comedian and actor Bill Cosby launched a social media campaign in which Twitter users were urged to use images of Cosby to create their own memes (Foster & Foster, 2012). The public relations team expected that people would draw on their memories of watching Cosby perform on various programs over the last several decades and use these memories to create images that would celebrate Cosby's incredible career in show business. Instead, the campaign presented an opportunity for critics of Cosby to speak out about numerous, longstanding allegations against him regarding inappropriate and even criminal behavior toward women. What was intended as a social media homage almost instantly transformed into an onslaught of embarrassing and repugnant references to Cosby's alleged conduct—a true public relations disaster and one that was instigated by Cosby's own public relations team.

The incident with Cosby brought home to many public relations professionals the need to be intimately familiar with one's subject matter, both the positive that they want the public to know about and the negative that they would prefer not to discuss. Long ago, when public relations work was under tighter control and moved at a stately pace, it was possible to proclaim the good while covering up the bad (Capozzi & Rucci, 2013). In the modern world, this is rarely an option. Instead, public relations staff are better off knowing everything about their subject so they can spread the good news and prepare to "spin" (a euphemism for reinterpretation) the bad news.

Public relations as a business has fundamentally changed with the advent of social media. In the past, a bad public relations campaign might be ignored by those it targeted, but would be unlikely to cause any harm. In the era of social media, even the most well-intentioned communication can quickly go awry. For each benefit conferred on public relations staff by the wonders of technology, greater risk has been added (Giannini, 2010).

FURTHER INSIGHTS

Despite the huge role that social media use has come to play in the lives of people of all ages, its use as a public relations tool has not been without controversy. In one sense, this can be attributed to factors that have very little to do with social media itself. The workforce is comprised of employees from many different generations, from older workers nearing retirement age, to baby boomers who have been around long enough to ascend to high-level positions, to millennials and generation Z workers just starting their careers (Swann, 2014).

Each of these generations has its own attitudes toward technology such as social media, and its own ideas about what types of communication to the public are in accordance with its notions of professionalism. It is not uncommon for the public relations department of large companies and nonprofits to be led by "the old guard" of a more traditional mindset, with much of the footwork being done by younger staff. There are frequently differences of opinion between the public relations staff, who embrace social media and the technology it runs on, and the administration.

The traditional view of public relations message development is that it is important to take one's time, craft the perfect messaging and distribution plan, and then implement the distribution of information while maintaining tight controls over the whole process, so that the only information released is that which the public relations department wants to have released. Social media, as younger and more technologically literate public relations staff point out, does not work this way. In the world of social media, things move very quickly (Seitel, 2014).

For example, when a newscaster makes a silly mistake on the air—perhaps mispronouncing the name of his own city—within moments, people all around the world have seen the error and used social media to comment on it, thus spreading news of the incident far and wide in a phenomenon known as "going viral." In addition to the factor of speed, social media is also different from the traditional model of public relations because it usually involves a loss of control over the content of the message being conveyed. This happens because users modify the message themselves as they share it with their networks, often adding or removing elements in an attempt at humor or social commentary. For example, a political campaign might wish to send out the public relations message that its candidate cares about what happens to children, so it distributes a photograph of the politician cradling a baby in his arms. In the world of social media, users will take this photo and alter it in ways that they find entertaining. Users might alter the image so that it shows the politician cradling a bag of money, or a life preserver, or even a cheeseburger.

This loss of control can be quite disturbing—even outrageous—to those used to the traditional model of public relations in which the distributor of the message might not have reached as large an audience, but retained more control over the content of the message (Belch & Belch, 2012). The new public relations approach demanded by social media appears to be one that is less about control of the message from start to finish in the communications process, and more about being able to continuously respond to the constantly fluctuating social media landscape in ways that are both graceful and consistent with the branding image of the client, whether an individual or an organization.

BIBLIOGRAPHY

Belch, G. E., & Belch, M. A. (2012). Advertising and promotion: An integrated marketing communications perspective. New York, NY: McGraw-Hill Irwin.

Breakenridge, D. (2012). Social media and public relations: Eight new practices for the pr professional. Upper Saddle River, NJ: FT Press.

Capozzi, L., & Rucci, S. R. (2013). Crisis management in the age of social media. New York, NY: Business Expert Press.

DiStaso, M. W., & Bortree, D. S. (2014). Ethical practice of social media in public relations. New York, NY: Routledge.

Foster, J., & Foster, J. (2012). Writing skills for public relations: Style and technique for mainstream and social media. London, UK: Kogan Page.

Lee, N., Sha, B., Dozier, D., & Sargent, P. (2015). The role of new public relations practitioners as social media experts. Public Relations Review, 41(3), 411–413. Retrieved January 3, 2016, from EBSCO Online Database Business Source Complete. http://search.ebscohost.com/login.aspx?direct=true&db=bth&AN=108299210&site=ehost-live

Giannini, G. T. (2010). Marketing public relations: A marketer's approach to public relations and social media. Upper Saddle River, NJ: Prentice Hall.

Neill, M. S., & Schauster, E. (2015). Gaps in advertising and public relations education: Perspectives of agency leaders. Journal of Advertising Education, 19(2), 5–17. Retrieved January 3, 2016 from EBSCO Online Database Business Source Complete. http://search.ebscohost.com/login.aspx?direct=true&db=bth&AN=111206213&site=ehost-live

Scott, D. M. (2010). The new rules of marketing and PR: How to use social media, blogs, news releases, online video, & viral marketing to reach buyers directly. Hoboken, NJ: John Wiley & Sons.

Seitel, F. P. (2014). The practice of public relations. Boston, MA: Pearson.

Swann, P. (2014). Cases in public relations management: The rise of social media and activism. New York, NY: Routledge, Taylor & Francis Group.

Valentini, C. (2015). Is using social media "good" for the public relations profession? A critical reflection. Public Relations Review, 41(2), 170–177. Retrieved January 3, 2016 from EBSCO Online Database Business Source Complete. http://search.ebscohost.com/login.aspx?direct=true&db=bth&AN=108299204&site=ehost-live

VanSlyke, T. J., Valin, J., & Paluszek, J. (2014). Public relations case studies from around the world. New York, NY: Peter Lang.

SUGGESTED READING

Allagui, Ilhem and Harris Breslow. (2016). Social media for public relations: Lessons from four effective cases. *Public Relations Review*, 42, 1, 20-30. Retrieved June 29, 2017.

Kennedy, A. K., & Sommerfeldt, E. J. (2015). A postmodern turn for social media research: Theory and research directions for public relations scholarship. Atlantic Journal of Communication, 23(1), 31–45.

Khang, H., Ki, E., & Ye, L. (2012). Social media research in advertising, communication, marketing, and public relations, 1997–2010. Journalism & Mass Communication Quarterly, 89(2), 279–298.

Men, L. R., & Tsai, W. S. (2015). Infusing social media with humanity: Corporate character, public engagement, and relational outcomes. Public Relations Review, 41(3), 395–403. Retrieved January 3, 2016, from EBSCO Online Database Business Source Complete. http://search.ebscohost.com/login.aspx?direct=true&db=bth&AN=108299223&site=ehost-live

Vardeman-Winter, J., & Place, K. (2015). Public relations culture, social media, and regulation. Journal of Communication Management, 19(4), 335–353. Retrieved January 3, 2016 from EBSCO Online Database Business Source Complete. http://search.ebscohost.com/login.aspx?direct=true&db=bth&AN=110516941&site=ehost-live

Waddington, S. (2015). Chartered public relations: Lessons from expert practitioners. London, UK: Kogan Page.

Scott Zimmer, J.D.

R

RETAIL MERCHANDISING

ABSTRACT

Retail merchandising comprises the activities, policies and procedures that are intended to help a business sell goods and products directly to consumers. Merchandising activities are important for a retail business whether that business has a brick-and-mortar store or an online one. Far from being an unnecessary expense, appropriate merchandising of retail items can help shape the image of the store and influence its customers' decision to purchase not only a given item, but also related items. To be effective, however, merchandising activities need to be based on marketing data of the customers' wants and needs.

OVERVIEW

A Real-Life Illustration

A few years ago, a long-standing and popular supermarket chain in my area was bought out by another firm. Although the chain had been doing poorly for some time, local residents had mixed feelings about the takeover. On the one hand, if an influx of new money and new ideas was not found quickly, the chain would soon cease to exist. On the other hand, many customers wondered at the wisdom of selling the chain to a firm that was located in an area that was used to much higher grocery prices and very different ways of doing things. After the takeover, one of the first changes to be observed was the renovation of some of the key stores across the area. One such store was not very old, having been built only a few years before as part of a new shopping plaza at the center of a planned community. However, after the takeover, the store soon became a confusing mess as not only stock but the physical shelving were rearranged all for the "convenience" of the shopper. Every morning, the store published a new store directory so that customers could more easily find where the items on the shopping lists happened to be that day. To say the least, it was a time of great confusion, but the local customers had a great deal of loyalty to the original chain and continued to shop there in the hope that as soon as the renovation was complete, all would be better.

Eventually, the renovation was completed, and the store once again took on a bright, shiny new look that welcomed customers. The area near the front door had been rearranged to include most of the items that many people need on quick trips to the grocery store. One entered the store to be greeted by a coffee bar where one could pick up a drink or a snack to make the grocery shopping experience more pleasant. Near the coffee bar was located the bakery, where the aroma of fresh baked goods enticed one to that corner. Along the wall was a very large deli counter that included not only meats and cheeses sliced to one's specifications, but also an assortment of salads, desserts, and even entrees that could be taken home and popped in the microwave for dinner. In the adjoining space was a newly designed produce area with wide aisles, attractive displays, and both salad and olive bars. Then came aisle after aisle of stock, a seemingly virtual paradise for the shopper.

At first, of course, even though the stock was no longer moved every day and signs labeling what was found on each aisle were hung over it, it was still somewhat difficult to locate many items as shoppers learned the new system. Unfortunately, this confusion persisted even several years later for a number of reasons.

- First, the store is no longer laid out as it had been in the past, but is patterned after another American chain owned by the same parent company. This makes some items difficult to find because other local stores—even of different chains—carry them in another place. As a result, on almost every shopping trip, one can find a conversation between shoppers asking each other where one might find X since it was not where it would be logically (at least to the shoppers) located. Store personnel seem to not only be restocking but reshelving the aisles every week in an effort to better display merchandise. The customers, however, do not find this helpful and the chain's revenues continue to drop.

- Second, the signs designating what types of items are kept on each aisle contain different information on each side, which means that if one missed an item as one went through the store, a quick glance at the aisle signs has a 50 percent chance of giving the information needed to locate the item.
- Third, stock keeps moving according to the dictates of the remote corporate headquarters. For example, one might find a national brand of frozen "sliders" next to the frozen hamburgers one week and next to the frozen snack foods another week.

As part of its strategy to recoup some of its losses, the chain next decided to focus on carrying more store brand items and reducing the number of national brand items. As a result, customers with brand loyalty to various items were required to make the decision as to whether or not to continue to shop at the chain or go to another chain that carries the brands for which they are looking. Some customers solve this problem by shopping at other stores for certain items. However, this can often lead to a situation in which an entire grocery list is purchased at a different chain for the sake of convenience. Whether or not the shopper switches to the other store on a more permanent basis, the sales for the chain will decrease to some extent.

Another change that was instituted by the chain after the take over was the concept of "everyday low prices" rather than sales prices. As a result, the weekly flyer for the chain has become much smaller and advertises the regular price (with the implication that it is lower than the competition's or the chain's regular price). This means that those people who sit down with their weekly sales flyer to plan the week's meals based on sales have much fewer options. The concept of low prices is furthered by shelf talkers in the stores, but the higher prices that are used for comparison often come from stores halfway across the county rather than local stores. As a result of these and other

problems with merchandising, several years later, the chain is again in trouble, and newer stores with approaches more in tune with the needs of contemporary shoppers are moving into the area.

The Value & Elements of Merchandising

This case provides a cautionary tale regarding the implications of a number of business concepts. One of the most obvious of these is the effectiveness of the merchandising efforts of a store. In general, retail merchandising can be defined as the activities, policies, and procedures of an organization that are intended to help a business sell goods and products directly to consumers. According to the American Marketing Association (AMA), merchandising encompasses the "planning involved in marketing the right merchandise or service at the right place, at the right time, in the right quantities, and at the right price." Merchandising includes the placement of products (including the layout of the store, where the products are displayed and how the visual display is designed), promotions (including trial offers, bundling, and coupons), and pricing to appeal to the target market. Closely related are the concepts of inventory management (including ordering sufficient stock in time to meet customer demand and how problems of overstock—i.e., having too much of an item on hand so that it needs to be reduced to sell—and understock—having too little of an item on hand so that customers cannot buy their desired items—are handled), warehousing (where the stock will be physically located), and the decision of what categories of products to carry and what range to carry within each category.

As this case study illustrates, there is more to retail merchandising that just arranging goods and products in a retail store in a manner that is pleasing to the eye. In particular, the case study illustrates the importance of both having the appropriate data and having the correct decision makers determining what products are offered in the store, employing appropriate category and product range management, properly allocating space to products, and designing the merchandise displays in ways that are not only eye-catching but appropriate and memorable.

Buying Decisions

Frequently, decisions regarding what to carry in a retail store that is part of a chain are made at a level higher than the individual store. This approach has the advantage of allowing the chain to negotiate better prices with manufacturers, giving marketers consistent data for better forecasting and allowing for better quality control across all stores (Varley, 2000). However, as illustrated above, centralized buying is not without its disadvantages as well. In this case, the decision on what brands and items are to be carried is made by corporate decision makers living in another area of the country where different products and brands are popular. The local manager—who at least in theory has greater understanding of what customers at that particular store or in that particular area of the country want—is allowed little to no input into what is carried in the store.

Category Management

Buying decisions are typically not made based on individual items. For example, a grocery store is unlikely to decide to buy strawberries, lettuce, potatoes, and cabbage in isolation of other factors. Rather, the category of produce would more than likely be broken into the subcategories of vegetables and fruits, which might further be broken down into seasonal, prepackaged, or any one of a number of other categories. Category management is a marketing strategy in which a full line of products is managed together as a strategic business unit. One way to do this is through efficient consumer response, which starts with consumer demand and then organizes the supply chain to meet that demand. In the case above, however, regional differences between consumer purchasing habits was not taken into account,

ending in a situation in which some regions were no longer offering the items and goods desired by the local customers.

Product Display

Once it has been determined what items to carry, one must next determine how best to display the products to encourage customers to purchase them. This aspect of merchandising includes questions of space allocation, store design, and visual merchandising. Like items are typically found together. For example, in a grocery store, one could reasonably expect to find all bread-related products in the same aisle. If pizza crusts are located in the deli section instead (as was done in one of the stores of the chain in the case above), the item becomes difficult to find and the customer becomes frustrated. Similarly, no matter how well a display for potato chips is designed and implemented, for example, if it is in the middle of the juice aisle of the store, it is unlikely to earn the return on investment expected by the store. Even when the chip display is prominently positioned at the entrance to the store the weekend before the big game, if customers are not looking for chips (or even desirous of chips) at that point, it is only wasting retail space and money for merchandising that could be better spent elsewhere. Similarly, it needs to be determined how much shelf space to allot to each item. Devoting an entire aisle to bread and baked goods might make sense in a large supermarket, for example, but would make less sense in a convenience store. In addition, consideration needs to be given to the way that items are displayed within the store. Displays should be designed to attract the customer's attention and elicit a purchase response.

JIT Systems

Another way to increase profitability across the supply chain is to institute just-in-time systems at appropriate places in the chain. Just-in-time (JIT) manufacturing, for example, strives to eliminate waste and continually improve productivity. The primary characteristics of JIT manufacturing include having the required inventory only when it is needed for manufacturing and reducing lead times and set up times. Similarly, JIT inventory management systems attempt to produce, deliver, or receive products just in time to provide the next business in the supply chain with the stock that they need at the time that they need it. (For example, a toy manufacturer would not produce a toy until it could be shipped directly to the retail stores per their request so that the manufacturer did not incur the cost of warehousing the toys.) The major objective of JIT inventories is to reduce the need to physically warehouse stock anywhere within the supply chain.

It can be easy to dismiss a retailer's efforts at merchandising as unnecessary expenses that increase the cost of items without adding value. However, as can be seen in the example above, if a customer cannot locate an item he or she wants or needs or becomes frustrated in the task because of poor merchandising policies, the retailer will lose money. Although merchandising efforts require funds on the front end of the process, when well done, merchandising can help maximize the return on investment of a retail business.

APPLICATIONS

Online Sales

In the twenty-first century, an increasing amount of shopping is no longer being done in brick-and-mortar stores. Customers are turning to the Internet and e-businesses for goods and services. Traditionally, shopping meant physically going to a store, searching aisles for products of interest, comparing product features, and purchasing. With the advent of information technology, customers frequently now have the opportunity to do these tasks electronically by shopping online. One can easily purchase groceries, clothing, electronics, books, and more over the Internet from the comfort of one's own home. Such business-to-consumer (B2C) approaches reduce the costs associated with large sales staffs; rent, utilities, and other overhead costs; and physical inventories for the business. However, because the customer cannot physically see the actual item being purchased (e.g., feel how ripe a tomato is at an online grocery store or try on the shoes at the online shoe store), a number of problems need to be solved. One of these is the determination of how best to merchandise one's products. Many of the approaches to merchandising in the real world have parallels in the virtual world as well: Physical coupons become electronic coupon codes, physical displays become a series of pictures of an item from different angles, shelf talkers may become pop-ups or advertising sidebars. However,

the very nature of virtual sales in a B2C environment versus physical sales in a brick-and-mortar store raises some unique merchandising problems.

A great deal of research and effort has gone into developing techniques and tools that help online retail businesses maximize their return on investment. However, not as much attention has been paid to the merchandising aspect of such online businesses. Although it may be tempting to see merchandising for online stores as the virtual equivalent of merchandising for brick-and-mortar stores, the challenges faced by e-businesses do differ somewhat from those of brick-and-mortar businesses. Lee, Podlaseck, Schonberg, Hoch, and Gomory (2000) examined the merchandising requirements of e-businesses and how these can best be met. As with other types of merchandising, merchandising online requires that the website be effective in order to maximize one's return on investment. Online merchandising, like traditional merchandising, comprises all the activities necessary for a retailer to make products available to consumers at the right price and in a timely manner in order to meet the business's objectives. Similarly, just like retailers with brick-and-mortar stores, online merchants must select the appropriate categories and assortment of merchandise to offer and determine how best to display and promote these.

Merchandising Cues

For an online store to be effective, Lee, Podlaseck, Schonberg, Hoch, and Gomory recommend that online retailers optimize their use of merchandising cues. These are a category of techniques used to present or group products in an online store with the objective of motivating a customer to buy. Commonly used merchandising cues include cross-sells in which a hyperlink refers the visitor to another web page that markets an item complementing the item that the visitor was viewing (e.g., hot dog buns to go along with one's hot dogs). Another type of merchandising cue is the up-sell. This is a hyperlink that refers visitors to a web page the sells a similar, but higher priced, item (e.g., a national brand orange juice rather than the store brand orange juice). Recommendation hyperlinks are another type of merchandising cue that highlight product pages that the shopper (based on past or current behavior) or the population at large might find of interest. Promotion hyperlinks may refer visitors to a product page or high-traffic area (e.g., the home page for the business) to present other information intended to help the visitor make a decision to purchase from the online store. In addition to merchandising cues, online stores also may use shopping metaphors that help visitors find products of interest. For example, a visitor might be able to browse an online "catalog" or use other forms of searching in order to find the product in which he or she is interested. Web design features can also be used in merchandising for online stores.

Smartphones as Directories and Portals

In 2013, more than half of Americans owned a smartphone. Both online and brick-and-mortar retailers saw the necessity of making their establishments smartphone and tablet friendly. Because users defaulted to asking their phones where to find local amenities and services, it became imperative to have a business's online store or storefront appear among the rankings for a relevant search. Social media, websites, business profiles, and online ads were enhanced to capture mobile traffic and direct users to businesses with maps, coupon offers, and instant phone dialing or a direct link to a website. (Savitz, 2013)

CONCLUSION

Retail merchandising comprises the activities, policies, and procedures of an organization that are intended to help a business sell goods and products directly to consumers. Whether merchandising is done for a brick-and-mortar store or for an online one, it is important that merchandising be based on marketing data of the customers' wants and needs. Far from being an unnecessary expense, appropriate merchandising of items in a retail store can help shape the image of the store and influence the customers' decision to purchase not only a given item, but related items as well.

BIBLIOGRAPHY

American Marketing Association. (2009). Marketing. *AMA Resource Library: Dictionary.* Retrieved February 20, 2009, from http://www.marketingpower.com/%5flayouts/Dictionary.aspx?dLetter=M

Briesch, R.A., Dillon, W.R., & Fox, E.J. (2013). Category positioning and store choice: The role of destination categories. *Marketing Science, 32*, 488-509. Retrieved October 31, 2013, from EBSCO Online Database Business Source Complete. http://search.ebscohost.com/login.aspx?direct=true&db=bth&AN=88011113&site=ehost-live

Cant, M. C., & Hefer, Y. (2014). Visual merchandising displays effect—or not—on consumers: The predicament faced by apparel retailers. *Journal of Business & Retail Management Research, 8*, 95–104. Retrieved November 24, 2014, from EBSCO Online Database Business Source Complete. http://search.ebscohost.com/login.aspx?direct=true&db=bth&AN=96566853

Krishnakumar, M. (2014). The role of visual merchandising in apparel purchase decision. *IUP Journal of Management Research, 13*, 37–54. Retrieved November 24, 2014, from EBSCO Online Database Business Source Complete. http://search.ebscohost.com/login.aspx?direct=true&db=bth&AN=95087601

Lee, J., Podlaseck, M., Schonberg, E., Hoch, R., & Gomory, S. (2000). Understanding merchandising effectiveness of online stores. *Electronic Markets, 10*, 20-28. Retrieved February 20, 2009, from EBSCO Online Database Business Source Complete. http://search.ebscohost.com/login.aspx?direct=true&db=bth&AN=3960437&site=ehost-live

Pape, P. (2012). Proper merchandising encourages sales. *Convenience Store Decisions, 23*, 50-54. Retrieved October 31, 2013, from EBSCO Online Database Business Source Complete. http://search.ebscohost.com/login.aspx?direct=true&db=bth&AN=79327201&site=ehost-live

Savitz, E. (2013). Mobile marketing: Reaching the untethered consumer. *Forbes.Com, 17*. Retrieved October 31, 2013, from EBSCO Online Database Business Source Complete. http://search.ebscohost.com/login.aspx?direct=true&db=bth&AN=86066625&site=ehost-live

Varley, R. (2000). *Retail product management: Buying and merchandising.* Oxford: Taylor & Francis.

SUGGESTED READING

Bellizzi, J. A., Krueckeberg, H. F., Hamilton, J. R., & Martin, W. S. (1981). Consumer perceptions of national, private, and generic brands. *Journal of Retailing, 57*, 56-70. Retrieved February 20, 2009, from EBSCO Online Database Business Source Complete. http://search.ebscohost.com/login.aspx?direct=true&db=bth&AN=4667302&site=ehost-live

Bemmaor, A. C., Franses, P. H., & Kippers, J. (1999). Estimating the impact of displays and other merchandising support on retail brand sales: Partial pooling with examples. *Marketing Letters, 10,* 87-100. Retrieved February 20, 2009, from EBSCO Online Database Business Source Complete. http://search.ebscohost.com/login.aspx?direct=true&db=bth&AN=7583634&site=ehost-live

Biswas, D., Labrecque, L. I., Lehmann, D. R., & Markos, E. (2014). Making choices while smelling, tasting, and listening: The role of sensory (dis) similarity when sequentially sampling products. *Journal of Marketing, 78,* 112–126. Retrieved November 24, 2014, from EBSCO Online Database Business Source Complete. http://search.ebscohost.com/login.aspx?direct=true&db=bth&AN=93641519

Hart, C. (1999). The retail accordion and assortment strategies: An exploratory study. *The International Review of Retail, Distribution and Consumer Research, 9,* 111-126. Retrieved February 20, 2009, from EBSCO Online Database Business Source Complete. http://search.ebscohost.com/login.aspx?direct=true&db=bth&AN=4176514&site=ehost-live

Hart, C. & Rafiq, M. (2006). The dimensions of assortment: A proposed hierarchy of assortment decision making. *International Review of Retail, Distribution and Consumer Research, 16,* 333-351. Retrieved February 20, 2009, from EBSCO Online Database Business Source Complete. http://search.ebscohost.com/login.aspx?direct=true&db=bth&AN=22018351&site=ehost-live

Janiszewski, C. (1998). The influence of display characteristics on visual exploratory search behavior. *Journal of Consumer Research, 25,* 290-301. Retrieved February 20, 2009, from EBSCO Online Database Business Source Complete. http://search.ebscohost.com/login.aspx?direct=true&db=bth&AN=1433409&site=ehost-live

King, C. W., Tigert, D. J., & Ring, L. J. (1979). Pragmatic applications of consumer research in retailing. *Advances in Consumer Research, 6,* 20-26. Retrieved February 20, 2009, from EBSCO Online Database Business Source Complete. http://search.ebscohost.com/login.aspx?direct=true&db=bth&AN=6602460&site=ehost-live

McCann, J., Tadlaoui, A., & Gallagher, J. (1990). Knowledge systems in merchandising: Advertising design. *Journal of Retailing, 66,* 257-277. Retrieved February 20, 2009, from EBSCO Online Database Business Source Complete. http://search.ebscohost.com/login.aspx?direct=true&db=bth&AN=4667772&site=ehost-live

Olsen, S. O. (2007). Repurchase loyalty: The role of involvement and satisfaction. *Psychology and Marketing, 24,* 315-341. Retrieved February 20, 2009, from EBSCO Online Database Business Source Complete. http://search.ebscohost.com/login.aspx?direct=true&db=bth&AN=24398334&site=ehost-live

Rosenberg, L. J. & Hirschman, E. C. (1980). Retailing without stores: Will telecommunication and related technologies transform shopping? *Harvard Business Review, 58,* 103-112. Retrieved February 20, 2009, from EBSCO Online Database Business Source Complete. http://search.ebscohost.com/login.aspx?direct=true&db=bth&AN=3867822&site=ehost-live

Smith, S. A., Agrawal, N., & McIntyre, S. H. (1998). A discrete optimization model for seasonal merchandise planning. *Journal of Retailing, 74,* 193-221. Retrieved February 20, 2009, from EBSCO Online Database Business Source Complete. http://search.ebscohost.com/login.aspx?direct=true&db=bth&AN=939279&site=ehost-live

Ruth A. Wienclaw, Ph.D.

S

SALES FORCE MANAGEMENT

ABSTRACT

Sales force management is the process of efficiently and effectively making sales through the planning, coordination, and supervision of others. Effective sales management involves a wide range of activities, including planning; organizing, recruiting, and selecting sales personnel; enabling and motivating the sales force to sell (e.g., training, print materials or samples); supervising and coordinating sales efforts (e.g., assigning territories or routes); and controlling and monitoring the sales force. Two types of control systems are typically used in sales force management: outcome-based and behavior-based. Both approaches have advantages and disadvantages due to the inherent nature of the sales job. Ethics is becoming an increasing concern in many sales departments. However, the treatment of ethical violations is not always consistent across high- and low-performing sales personnel.

OVERVIEW

To the skilled salesperson, sales jobs can offer the potential to earn more than salaried jobs. On the other hand, sales jobs do not offer the security of a salaried job and, therefore, do not appeal to everyone. From a management point of view, the nature of sales jobs can make managing a sales force a different task in some ways than managing other groups of professionals in the workplace. In addition, the fact that much of a salesperson's work may be performed outside the office where he or she cannot be directly observed, makes the task of managing a sales force even more difficult.

Sales Force Management

In general, management can be defined as the process of efficiently and effectively accomplishing work through the coordination and supervision of others. Sales management is the process of efficiently and effectively making sales through the planning, coordination, and supervision of others. Effective sales management involves much more than performing administrative tasks to coordinate the activities of the sales force. To be effective, the management of a sales force must encompass a wide range of activities, including planning; organizing, recruiting, and selecting sales personnel; enabling and motivating the sales force to sell (e.g., training, print materials, or samples); supervising and coordinating sales efforts (e.g., assigning territories or routes); and controlling and monitoring the sales force.

Planning

In order for a sales force to be effective, the objectives and activities of the sales function must be planned in such a way to make the best use possible of both the sales force and the marketing budget necessary to sell the organization's goods and services to potential customers. Activities involved in management planning for a sales force include understanding the qualifications, abilities, and experience of the sales force and how best to use the personnel and other resources of the sales function in the organization. The sales manager also needs to understand the demographics of the target market as well as its needs and motivations in order to better prepare the sales force for success. By better understanding the capabilities of the sales force and the needs of the prospective customers, the sales manager can better develop a plan that will leverage the strengths of the sales force and enable each individual member to reach his or her optimal sales potential. The launch of new product or significantly upgraded product may require a reassessment of strategy, including further training, adjustments to compensation, and potentially a change in sales force personnel. In addition to developing a sales plan to best meet the customers' needs, the sales manager also needs to organize the sales force to best match the requirements of customers and potential customers on an ongoing basis to improve the effectiveness and efficiency of the sales force.

Training & Development

Management of an effective sales force is predicated on the training and development of sales personnel. To do this, one must first articulate what it is that the sales force needs to accomplish. This task involves developing a job description that specifies the duties and tasks related to a job. Job descriptions may also specify the knowledge, skills, and abilities necessary to do the job as well as the performance standards that differentiate acceptable from unacceptable performance. A well-developed job description will not only give the sales manager criteria against which to judge the performance of the individuals in the sales force, but will also give him or her a guide to selecting the best candidates for the sales force. To optimize the effectiveness of the sales force, the manager—typically in conjunction with the human resources function of the organization—is responsible for the training and development of sales personnel. Even if the sales force comprises experienced sales personnel who have worked in other organizations or with other products, sales training needs to include specifics about the way that sales are conducted in the current sales department as well as training on the details of the products or services being sold, so the sales force can accurately and adequately answer the questions of potential customers. Similarly, the sales force needs to receive updated training on any changes in organizational policy that affect them and on new information about the organization's products or services so they can better do their jobs.

Performance Motivation

Just knowing how to do the sales job and knowing the product or service being sold are not enough to create an effective sales force, however. The sales force must also be motivated to perform. For this reason, many sales departments pay their sales personnel at least in part based on commission (a set fee or percentage of every sale made). Such financial incentives are one of the most common motivators for sales jobs. Sales commissions tend to be an effective motivator of superior sales performance because they tie rewards directly to performance on the job. However, financial incentives are not the only way to

motivate sales personnel to perform. Other ways to motivate the sales staff are through connecting job performance with various prerequisites such as a company car for making sales calls or trips or paid vacations for being a top seller. Other motivators include job security and status (such as through a promotion, a job title, or other award or recognition).

Monitoring

Another important activity in sales force management is controlling the sales function and monitoring the activities of the sales staff to make sure they are effective and successful. To do this, management must set performance objectives for the sales force as well as ways to help enable the sales force to meet those objectives. Some ways to do this include setting standards for behavior (e.g., number of sales calls required during a given period of time); implementing ways to collect data on how well the standards are being met and making sure that the data are collected; analyzing the data to determine where objectives are not being met and why; and determining a plan of action for correcting these situations.

Sales Force Behavior Moderation

Determining the best way to control the behavior of members of a sales force is a topic that has been debated in literature for years. Two general approaches to sales force control systems—or the procedures by which an organization observes, guides, appraises, and rewards its employees—have been posited.

Outcome-Based Sales Force Control

The approach of outcome-based sales force control systems focuses on the final outcomes of the sales process (e.g., whether or not a sale was made, total revenues earned by a salesperson in a given period of time). Whether or not a salesperson has met outcome-based standards tends to be both objective and clear: He or she either made the assigned sales quota for a time period or did not. In this way, outcome-based control systems for sales personnel are very similar to management objectives. Criteria of success are set ahead of time, and the employee knows the specifics of what constitutes acceptable behavior. As a result, outcome-based control systems for sales personnel tend to require relatively little monitoring or direction by management. Further, because they are results-oriented, outcome-based control systems allow sales personnel latitude in how they carry out their job and enable them to modify their behavior to fit their personality or the expectations or needs of the customer in order to achieve the desired results rather than following a strict pre-approved procedure for dealing with a customer.

Outcome-based control systems have been the traditional system of choice for most sales force managers. Such systems are often favored because of the relative availability of criteria against which performance can be measured such as number of sales made or dollar volume earned within a given performance assessment period. Since sales personnel tend to spend a majority of their time out of the office (and often on the road), such objective measures of performance are sometimes the only way to gather data about how well a salesperson is performing. Further, there is not only one way to make an ethical sale. Different potential customers need to be treated in different ways and salespersons are typically well-advised to leverage their own personality traits, skills, and experience in making a sale rather than blindly following a specified procedure. However, outcome-based control systems are not without their disadvantages as well. Because sales jobs tend to be performed in isolation, it is easy for sales personnel to actually harm the organization while still making a sale. For example, to make a quick or easy sale, a salesperson might skimp on customer service and follow-up in order to make another sale. In most situations, this will result in a customer who is likely to think twice before purchasing from that salesperson—or even that organization—again. Similarly, in order for their sales figures to look good, salespersons might focus on selling more items with a smaller price tag or on

items or services that have been proven easier to sell. Although this might help the salesperson's performance record, it does not help the organization build its business.

Behavior-Based Control System

Although outcome-based control systems may seem at first to be an objective way to assess the performance of a salesperson, they do not take into account a number of factors. Particularly on big-ticket items, sales often occur over a period of time. The salesperson may need to establish a relationship with the customer, assess the customer's needs, defend his or her product against the product of competitors, persuade the customer of the relative value of his or her product, and wait while the customer makes a decision according to the customer's time table, not the salesperson's. Such activities take time. So, in theory, there may be performance assessment periods during which a salesperson may not have made any sales but is well on his or her way to making a significant sale. On paper, however, this would look no different from the outcomes of a salesperson who had not interacted with a customer at all under an outcome-based control system.

Because of such aspects of outcome-based control systems, some people argue that a behavior-based control system is more appropriate for use with sales forces. These systems focus more on the behavior of the salesperson rather than his or her final sales. However, behavior-based control systems require significantly more monitoring of both the activities and the results of the sales force's efforts. Management employing a behavior-based control system for their sales personnel will also need to give the sales personnel higher levels of direction and intervene more frequently in the sales force's activities than do managers using an outcome-based system. Further, behavior-based control systems tend to be not only more subjective than outcome-based control systems, but more complex as well. Behavior-based regulatory procedures are more reliant than outcome-based control systems on the knowledge, skills, and abilities that the salesperson brings to the job (e.g., aptitudes, personality traits, general or specific product knowledge), the activities of the sales force (e.g., number of calls made), and the sales strategies employed in trying to make a sale (Anderson & Oliver, 1987). These are the types of criteria that are used in behavior-based control systems.

Behavior-based control systems overcome a number of the disadvantages associated with outcome-based control systems. First, behavior-based control systems allow the sales manager more control than do outcome-based systems. In behavior-based systems, the manager can better ensure that the sales force is adhering to the sales plan and the policies and procedures of the department. Since rewards in behavior-based systems are tied to behavior rather than outcomes, sales personnel will be more motivated to follow the policies and procedures even if they are not necessarily convinced of their validity. However, behavior-based control systems also tend to be complex and subjective. When this is the case, the control system is not fair and can easily result in dissatisfied workers.

APPLICATIONS

Unethical Sales Practices

Most people have had experience with an unethical salesperson. Particularly if one is on commission or working under an outcome-based control system, it is too easy to stretch the truth or otherwise prevaricate in an attempt to make a sale by leading the buyer to believe something about a product or service that is not true. As a result, many of us have experienced purchasing such things as a used book online that is not in "like new" condition, but is broken and underlined, or a new kitchen appliance whose warranty was not what was stated by the salesperson. As individual customers who have been conned by unethical sales behavior, we may think that we are not alone in our experience and that the business that employs the unethical individual does not care about his or her behavior as long as the sale is made. The unethical behavior of sales personnel can quickly reflect back on the business that employs them, potentially doing serious damage to both the reputation and revenues of the organization as a result. Therefore, it is important that the sales management be aware of the possibility of such behavior and discourage it from happening if the organization is to build brand loyalty and repeated sales.

However, not every sales manager deals with unethical behavior in the same way. In fact, under outcome-based control systems, it can be difficult to determine whether or not a salesperson was acting in an unethical manner if the "bottom line" is the number of sales made or the amount of revenue earned for the business. Increasingly, organizations are concerned with the development of marketing and sales departments that encourage ethical behavior and discourage unethical behavior (Hunt & Vasquez-Parraga, 1993). However, research has found that how a sales manager actually disciplines a member of the sales force for unethical behavior depends on a number of factors rather than only on the inherent rightness or wrongness of the action. For example, DeConinck (1992) found that managers are more likely to verbally warn top performers for behavior that is deemed unethical while giving more formal, written warnings to or even recommending the firing of poor performers. However, the more severe consequences for poor performers caught in an unethical act may not actually reflect the severity of the unethical action, but may be an excuse for getting rid of a poor performer.

CONCLUSION

Although the management of a sales force has much in common with management activities within other functional departments, the very nature of the sales function does make it different. On the one hand, sales jobs lend themselves easily to the collection of hard performance data that can be used to motivate and control the sales force. However, since most sales personnel perform most of their work outside the office, it is difficult for management to adequately and accurately evaluate their performance in other ways. To best motivate sales personnel to perform in accordance with the standards of the organization and the department, rewards need to be tied to performance not only for objective criteria such as volume of sales, but for other desired behaviors as well.

BIBLIOGRAPHY

Anderson, E. & Oliver, R. L. (1987). Perspectives on behavior-based versus outcome-based salesforce control systems. *Journal of Marketing, 51*, 76-88. Retrieved February 17, 2009, from EBSCO Online Database Business Source Complete. http://search.ebscohost.com/login.aspx?direct=true&db=bth&AN=4996249&site=ehost-live

The art of selling. (2011). *Economist, 401*(8756), 84. Retrieved October 31, 2013, from EBSCO Online

Database Business Source Complete. http://search.ebscohost.com/login.aspx?direct=true&db=a9h&AN=66816353&site=ehost-live

Churchill, G. A. Jr., Ford, N. M., & Walker, O. C. Jr. (1993). *Sales force management* (4th ed.). Homewood, IL: Richard D. Irwin, Inc.

DeConinck, J. B. (1992). How sales managers control unethical sales force behavior. *Journal of Business Ethics, 11*, 789-798. Retrieved February 17, 2009, from EBSCO Online Database Business Source Complete. http://search.ebscohost.com/login.aspx?direct=true&db=bth&AN=5404109&site=ehost-live

Hunt, S. D. & Vasquez-Parraga, A. Z. (1993). Organizational consequences, marketing ethics, and salesforce supervision. *Journal of Marketing Research, 30*, 78-90. Retrieved February 17, 2009, from EBSCO Online Database Business Source Complete. http://search.ebscohost.com/login.aspx?direct=true&db=bth&AN=9511203701&site=ehost-live

Myette, M., & Lambert, B. (2010). Making the shift. *T+D, 64*, 32-35. Retrieved October 31, 2013, from EBSCO Online Database Business Source Complete. http://search.ebscohost.com/login.aspx?direct=true&db=a9h&AN=51189730&site=ehost-live

Rukuižiene, R. (2011). Strategic sales management mix for a launched new product. *Proceedings of the International Scientific Conference: Rural Development, 5*, 229-234. Retrieved October 31, 2013, from EBSCO Online Database Business Source Complete. http://search.ebscohost.com/login.aspx?direct=true&db=a9h&AN=70147277&site=ehost-live

Smith, B., Larsen, T., & Rosenbloom, B. (2009). Understanding cultural frames in the multicultural sales organization: Prospects and problems for the sales manager. *Journal of Transnational Management, 14*, 277-291. Retrieved October 31, 2013, from EBSCO Online Database Business Source Complete. http://search.ebscohost.com/login.aspx?direct=true&db=a9h&AN=46838021&site=ehost-live

Strafford, J. & Grant, C. (1993). *Effective sales management* (2nd ed.). Oxford: Butterworth-Heinemann Ltd.

SUGGESTED READING

Bellizzi, J. A. & Hasty, R. W. (2003). Supervising unethical sales force behavior: How strong is the tendency to treat top sales performers leniently? *Journal of Business Ethics, 43*, 337-351. Retrieved February 17, 2009, from EBSCO Online Database Business Source Complete. http://search.ebscohost.com/login.aspx?direct=true&db=bth&AN=4999418&site=ehost-live

Cravens, D. W., Ingram, T. N., LaForge, R. W., & Young, C. E. (1993). Behavior-based and outcome-based salesforce control systems. Journal of Marketing, 57, 47-59. Retrieved February 17, 2009, from EBSCO Online Database Business Source Complete. http://search.ebscohost.com/login.aspx?direct=true&db=bth&AN=9402090912&site=ehost-live

Henthorne, T. L., Robin, D. P., & Reidenback, R. E. (1992). Identifying the gaps in ethical percepts between managers and salespersons: A multidimensional approach. *Journal of Business Ethics, 11*, 849-856. Retrieved February 17, 2009, from EBSCO Online Database Business Source Complete. http://search.ebscohost.com/login.aspx?direct=true&db=bth&AN=5404114&site=ehost-live

Johnston, Mark W. and Marshall, Greg W. (2016). Sales force management: leadership, innovation, technology. *Routlege.* Retrieved June 29, 2017.

Krafft, M. (1999). An empirical investigation of the antecedents of sales force control systems. *Journal of Marketing, 63*, 120-134. Retrieved February 17, 2009, from EBSCO Online Database Business Source Complete. http://search.ebscohost.com/login.aspx?direct=true&db=bth&AN=2026307&site=ehost-live

Panagopoulos, N. G. & Avlonitis, G. J. (2008). Sales force control systems: A review of measurement practices and proposed scale refinements. *Journal of Personal Selling and Sales Management, 28*, 365-385. Retrieved February 17, 2009, from EBSCO Online Database Business Source Complete. http://search.ebscohost.com/login.aspx?direct=true&db=bth&AN=34882790&site=ehost-live

Ruth A. Wienclaw, Ph.D.

SENSORY MARKETING

ABSTRACT

Sensory marketing is a strategy that seeks to influence purchasing behavior and position a brand or product by engaging customers' senses. The senses mediate an individual's interactions with his or her environment and serve as an interpretative filter—in conscious and unconscious ways—for the information received. In other words, product differentiation originates from the interaction of the consumer with the product through sensorial interplay. Since the late twentieth century, sensory marketing has gained much ground. Growing research illuminates the ways in which senses prompt different responses in people in both positive and negative ways.

OVERVIEW

Sensory marketing refers to the use of marketing strategies—such as branding, positioning, and packaging—to tap into feelings and memories through the engagement of one or several of the senses: sight (visual), sound (auditory), taste (gustative), touch (tactile), and smell (olfactory). All living beings use their five sense or faculties to perceive and interpret stimulation originating internally and externally; that is, from both the psyche and the world around them. Marketing managers, then, create and implement strategies aimed at using these senses to sell goods and services and to ensure that these make a lasting imprint in consumers' minds.

The practice of enticing a potential buyer to purchase a good through the senses is as old as commerce itself. Fabric vendors invited customers to enjoy the tactile smoothness of a silk, and food vendors enticed through taste and smell. In its current incarnation, as a thoughtful and research-based field, however, sensory marketing was born when department store retailers began to use background music and pleasant aromas to influence shoppers' moods and behavior. The idea was to lure shoppers to spend more time and more money at the store. Background music as a retail concept was developed by Muzak in the 1930s, a company that hired bands to record their music and sell it as a service to stores, restaurants, and other firms.

Realizing that heightening the senses led to more sales, retailers began to fine tune the music experience and make it coherent with their visual and scented merchandising, in order to promote particular products, experiences, and lifestyles. Sensory marketing, however, relied on trial and error and was not immune to perils. A music mix that alienates a store's customer base or a faulty sound system can drive shoppers away.

Nevertheless, recent studies continue to support the idea that, in general, marketing expanded to the senses and a sensory environment is a winning proposition. Scientific research suggests that a scented product creates better memory recall in users than unscented equivalents. Scented environments—imbuing an area with a aroma—is used not only by retail shops to promote more sales, but also in the hospitality business and real estate field. Other businesses rely strongly on taste and smell; tasting a product increases the likelihood of purchase, so vendors offer product samples, tasting events, and even cooking classes on their premises.

In the last decades of the twentieth century, marketers and academics began to take more seriously the field of sensory marketing and all the ways in which the senses can intensify perceptions of products and brands. Much of this work relies on the concept of "embodied cognition," the notion that bodily sensations have a strong influence on people's unconscious decision-making processes. These influences are subtle and, to be successful, must be compatible. For instance, some aromas suggest warmth and thus would work better infused in products created to counter cold.

The power of sensory cues or stimuli is in their subtlety because consumers do not perceive them as marketing ploys. Therefore, they do not raise the usual barriers or skepticism to advertising. In fact, sensory marketing has become an established practice in some industrial fields, such as cosmetics, food, hospitality, paper manufacturing, toy manufacturers, and the automobile industry.

Packaging materials may be selected as indicators of a product's quality. People perceive a fashion good differently, for example, if it is shipped in crinkly paper rather than in plastic bubble wrap. Auditory marketing guides the creation of many different products, from luxury car engines to pens, as it has been discovered that the sound of a pen's scratch or an igniting car engine can identify certain brands. The idea, then, is not only to enhance the experience of using the product, but also to fix it in the user's memory.

According to many marketing experts, sensory marketing is a way of placing the customer first and supporting interaction with the customer. Traditional marketing strategies developed one-way communication channels in which a good or service provider pitches to consumers, rather than engaging in a dialogue. Eventually marketers began to understand the importance of listening to the customer by way of feedback and focus groups. With sensory marketing, they are responding to consumers' tastes in the most personal ways possible. On the other hand, some experts raise ethical concerns; they argue that through sensory marketing, some firms are manipulating consumers by cueing their subconscious without their knowledge.

FURTHER INSIGHTS

Marketing experts state that human beings are inherently inclined to enjoy sensory rewards. Among the most intense of these sensations are those that evoke memories and please the olfactory and gustatory senses. Marketing managers, then, must know when consumers are more receptive to such cues and, because individuals perceive and react differently to sensorial stimuli, must also understand how to develop multi-sensory strategies that engage more senses than one. Sensory marketing raises the cost of strategy development and implementation so that firms must be careful and select those likeliest to succeed.

- Sight – Close to 100 percent of the population places great importance on visual factors when buying a product. These include elements such as shape, size, and color. In fact, color can significantly increase brand recognition and shelf visibility. It is usually the first sense that comes into play in a shopping experience, followed by touch.
- Touch – Skin has millions of sense receptors and is the most important sense after sight, in terms of marketing, particularly for the packaging industry. Individuals want to experience how a product feels, the quality of its texture, from the weight of a cell phone in their hand to how a fabric slides against the skin. Packaging, which relies greatly on sight and touch, is also very important element not only for sales, but also for the development of a brand personality.
- Sound – Most individuals are very sensitive to sounds by nature and tend to ascribe meaning to them. Because it does not require a person's full attention, sound can subtly evoke specific memories and feelings. In the contemporary market, almost no retail sales experience and no broadcast advertising exist without music. The career of sound designer was created to professionalize this innovative growing field. Contemporary branding experts increasingly create specific sounds as part of their brand personality.
- Taste – Taste is closely tied to the sense of smell and the two often work together to create a holistic or all-involving experience. Not surprisingly, it is very important in the food industry. However, the perception of "tastiness" is also used in other industries, such as for promoting soaps and scented candles.
- Smell – Some scientific studies suggest that more than 70 percent of feelings and emotions originate in smell. Smell is closely linked to memory and mood. Moreover, it can increase or decrease tension and concentration. While other senses are relatively filtered through the brain, smell is considered the most primeval or instinctive of senses. Marketers use it effectively to evoke memories of childhood –such as through the aroma of baked goods—or perceptions of luxury, as in the aromas of leather, wood, and sandalwood.

A well-designed marketing strategy aims at differentiation; that is, to stand out from competing brands in order to generate memorable experiences, gain competitive advantage, and increase sales. Sensory marketing complements other aspects of a marketing strategy, including brand personality and the process of consumer rationalization (the analysis of a product's benefits versus its defects). Therefore, it is of extreme importance that sensory strategies be coherent with the brand's image and the firm's overall values. According to recent theoretical frameworks, sensory marketing differentiation strategies can be classified as follows:

- Sensory-hedonistic differentiation: This strategy is focused on identifying applicable consumer sensations and designing product or service attributes that appeal to those sensations. The goal is to prompt an emotional and lasting connection between the consumer and the product.

- Sensory-functional differentiation: The purpose of this strategy is to enhance the perception of functionality, such as highlighting a product's innovations or new features, added value, or additional benefits. The idea is that sensory attributes—which in this case are often secondary—serve to lend support to the product's functional benefits.

- Sensory-symbolic differentiation. This strategy mainly seeks to position a product or brand. Positioning is promoting a product or service in a specific market segment or niche and in a specific way. Sensory attributes to be cued are selected to lend support to the positioning process. (Stancioiu, Ditoiu, Teodorescu and Onisor, 2016).

ISSUES

Ideally, a brand means something to the consumer and this meaning is supported by a combination of senses. This is what shapes a brand's personality in the audience's mind and generates customer loyalty or attachment to the brand. The meaning-making that customers experience in relation to a brand, however, is often based in much research and work produced by a marketing team. Some brands emphasize a feeling of sincerity and openness, others of excitement, and yet others of timelessness. Nevertheless, it is often difficult to know beforehand how customers will perceive a brand.

Studies have repeatedly shown that customers will often reject a brand when they feel deceived. Using factors such as packaging to raise consumer expectations is a high-risk strategy. Brands that rely on an image of openness and sincerity risk much if customers perceive the brands as engaging in deceptive practices or failing to satisfy expectations. However, brands that appeal to consumer excitement, for example, have greater latitude in regards to consumers' expectations.

Every firm must give thoughtful consideration to its brand's position in the market and not fall for the common trope that all sensory marketing strategies must provoke surprise (Sundar, 2016). Moreover,

customers' reactions to sensory marketing are often hard to predict and hardly uniform.

Catering absolutely to customer's senses may have counterproductive results, according to some critics. A 2011 study with European organic food consumers is a case in point. The organic food market is in flux, as it moves from goods previously considered niche or exclusive, to more mass market or mainstream. In other words, organic foods are making inroads among large retailers. Whereas marketers initially believed that buyers were motivated by altruistic ideas—protecting the environment, animal welfare, not using chemical products—studies showed that, in fact, organic food consumers demonstrate hedonistic or pleasure-based motives for purchasing organic food. Among the reasons provided, for instance, were taste and wellness.

Organic food consumers' preferences prompted many organic food producers to incorporate sensory factors, such as appearance, smell, feel, and taste into their production practices and marketing strategies. Because organic food is associated with freshness and naturalness, this raised concerns that by satisfying broad-based customer expectations, the value criteria of organic food was shifting toward appearance. Moreover, new consumers were willing to pay the higher prices that come with organic food only if the product also offered a unique experience, such as superior taste and appearance.

Inevitably, this type of situation exerts pressure on organic food producers to standardize some of the characteristics of organic food, such as naturalness of shape, that previously defined it. Critics argued that such a development would run counter to the original philosophy and intent of organic food production and certification.

Studies of such trends illuminate the extent to which sensory marketing affects different people differently. For example, older consumers tend to place greater emphasis on sensory response when buying fresh produce than do younger buyers. This may be because older consumers believe that organic food, being more naturally produced, will replicate the food they used to consume as children. Younger generations, however, raised in different circumstances, seldom make such associations. In other words, the sensorial cues ascribed to organic food both connect with buyer expectations and prompt pleasant memories among older buyers that do not work in the same way with younger ones (Asioli, Canavari, Castellini, de Magistris, Gottardi, Lombardi, & Spadoni, 2011).

Clearly, all senses play very important roles in the daily experience of individuals, and by default, on their consuming behavior. It influences how people perceive and consume specific brands and products, as well as the relationships they may develop with many of these. It is also very effective in differentiating a product from its competitors.

Even though it has been gaining importance in the marketing field, sensory marketing is subject to many limitations besides the difficulties in knowing how individuals will react to their sensory cues or stimuli. One of these is the media outlet by which it promotes its product. A product cannot, for instance, produce taste, touch, and aroma cues by way of film or television. Some firms have resorted to imbuing their print ads with aromatic strips, such as in perfume advertisements so that aroma accompanies the visual impact.

Another potential problem is excess reliance on sensory marketing to the detriment of other important marketing and product aspects. For example, taste, aroma, or sound may have no relationship with a product's actual purpose and performance. It is important, then, to keep always in mind the firm's values, the product's purpose and performance, and the brand's personality when designing a sensory marketing campaign to ensure that coherence and relevance are not lost in the process.

BIBLIOGRAPHY

Asioli, D., Canavari, M., Castellini, A., de Magistris, T., Gottardi, F., Lombardi, P., & Spadoni, R. (2011). The role of sensory attributes in marketing organic food: Findings from a qualitative study of Italian consumers. *Journal of Food Distribution Research*, *42*(1), 16–21. Retrieved October 23, 2016, from EBSCO Online Database Business Source Ultimate. http://search.ebscohost.com/login.aspx?direct=true&db=bsu&AN=95568818&site=ehost-live

Berg, P. O., & Sevón, G. (2014). Food-branding placces—A sensory perspective. *Place Branding & Public Diplomacy*, *10*(4), 289–304. Retrieved October 23, 2016, from EBSCO Online Database Business Source Ultimate. http://search.ebscohost.com/login.aspx?direct=true&db=bsu&AN=99249027&site=ehost-live

Miller, R. K., & Washington, K. (2012). Sensory marketing. In *Consumer Behavior*. n.p.: Richard K. Miller & Associates. Retrieved November 15, 2016 from EBSCO Business Source Ultimate http://search.ebscohost.com/login.aspx?direct=true&db=bsu&AN=66334747&site=ehost-live

Psychology the science of sensory marketing. (2015). *Harvard Business Review*, *93*(3), 28–30. Retrieved October 23, 2016, from EBSCO Online Database Business Source Ultimate. http://search.ebscohost.com/login.aspx?direct=true&db=bsu&AN=101105356&site=ehost-live

Rajain, P. (2016). Sensory marketing aspects: Priming, expectations, crossmodal correspondences & more. *Vikalpa: The Journal for Decision Makers*, *41*(3), 264–266. Retrieved October 23, 2016, from EBSCO Online Database Business Source Ultimate. http://search.ebscohost.com/login.aspx?direct=true&db=bsu&AN=118260703&site=ehost-live

Stach, J. (2015). A conceptual framework for the assessment of brand congruent sensory modalities. *Journal of Brand Management*, *22*(8), 673–694. Retrieved October 23, 2016, from EBSCO Online Database Business Source Ultimate. http://search.ebscohost.com/login.aspx?direct=true&db=bsu&AN=111176023&site=ehost-live

Stncioiu, A., Dioiu, M., Teodorescu, N., Onior, L., & Pârgaru, I. (2014). Sensory marketing strategies. Case study: Oltenia. *Theoretical & Applied Economics*, *21*(7), 43–54. Retrieved October 23, 2016, from EBSCO Online Database Business Source Ultimate. http://search.ebscohost.com/login.aspx?direct=true&db=bsu&AN=108792492&site=ehost-live

Sundar, A., & Noseworthy, T. J. (2016). When sensory marketing works and when it backfires. *Harvard Business Review Digital Articles*, 2–5. Retrieved October 23, 2016, from EBSCO Online Database Business Source Ultimate. http://search.ebscohost.com/login.aspx?direct=true&db=bsu&AN=118686189&site=ehost-live

SUGGESTED READING

Cho, E., Fiore, A. M., & Russell, D. W. (2015). Validation of a fashion brand image scale capturing cognitive, sensory, and affective associations: Testing its role in an extended brand equity model. *Psychology & Marketing*, *32*(1), 28–48. Retrieved

October 23, 2016, from EBSCO Online Database Business Source Ultimate. http://search.ebscohost.com/login.aspx?direct=true&db=bsu&AN=99923075&site=ehost-live

Hulten, B. (2015). *Sensory marketing: Theoretical and empirical grounds.* London, UK: Routledge.

Katsaridou, I. (2012). Sensory marketing: Research on the sensuality of products. *International Journal of Market Research, 54*(1), 147–149. Retrieved October 23, 2016, from EBSCO Online Database Business Source Ultimate. http://search.ebscohost.com/login.aspx?direct=true&db=bsu&AN=70466821&site=ehost-live

Krishna, A. et al. (2016). The power of sensory marketing in advertising. *Current Opinion in Psychology,* 10, 142-147. Retrieved June 29, 2017.

Krishna, A., & Schwarz, N. (2014). Sensory marketing, embodiment, and grounded cognition: A review and introduction. *Journal of Consumer Psychology, 24*(2), 159–168. Retrieved October 23, 2016, from EBSCO Online Database Business Source Ultimate. http://search.ebscohost.com/login.aspx?direct=true&db=bsu&AN=95017212&site=ehost-live

Odell, P. (2016). New study looks at effects of sensory marketing tactics. *Promotional Marketing,* 1. Retrieved October 23, 2016, from EBSCO Online Database Business Source Ultimate. http://search.ebscohost.com/login.aspx?direct=true&db=bsu&AN=115644399&site=ehost-live

Trudy Mercadal, Ph.D.

SOCIAL MEDIA AND BUSINESSES

ABSTRACT

Social media refers to a set of Internet connected tools that allow users to create and participate in online communities, joining other users to share information about themselves and their activities. The creators of social media platforms earn revenue by analyzing the data users share about themselves and sharing it with advertising partners for a fee. Social media has rapidly grown to have a large effect on the economy, and all but the smallest businesses now have a social media strategy in place to derive value from this online marketplace.

OVERVIEW

Social media represents a departure from traditional methods of information dissemination. In the past, media outlets such as television stations and newspaper publishers would collect information and distribute it to their audiences, either for a fee (in the case of newspaper subscriptions) or through the support of advertising revenue (in the case of television commercials). This model has been called the one-to-many approach because it involves a single outlet transmitting the same informational message to a large number of recipients (Close, 2012).

Over time a number of disadvantages were observed with this system. One of these is that one-to-many broadcasting only accommodates a single viewpoint—that of the broadcaster. It is also time consuming for the broadcaster to collect and synthesize information into a form that is ready for broadcasting, so there were often delays between the occurrence of an event and the distribution of information about that event to the public. Social media has addressed each of these concerns by turning the old model on its head. Instead of a one-to-many broadcast, social media makes it possible for participants to experience many-to-many communication, as each user can communicate news and information to his or her entire network. Each member of a user's network can then respond in kind, creating multi-threaded conversations among users who are each able to receive and transmit their own perspectives (Houser, 2013).

The business world has been quick to follow the emergence of social media and find a place for itself in the online world, particularly with regard to advertising. Data shows that each year people spend billions of hours on social media, and for advertisers this represents a treasure trove of time in which they can try to get their messages about their products in front of social media users' eyes. Given the nature of social media, with its emphasis on sharing all kinds of information, advertisers are able to use social media to urge consumers to help advertise products.

Social media not only provides businesses with an additional platform to capture people's attention, but also allows businesses to leverage user-identity construction in order to make their advertising dollars go farther. This works because social media platforms encourage users to construct online identities that parallel their true personalities. Typically, this is done by allowing users to choose "avatars," visual representations of themselves (for example, a drawing of a tooth representing a dentist), and by allowing users to describe themselves by listing personal information such as their date of birth, marital status, the name of their employer, and so on (King, 2012).

Crucially, users often have the additional option to describe themselves in terms of their preferences, including their favorite music, movies and books, favorite color, favorite types of food, preferred brands of clothing, and so on. These data are of great value to businesses engaged with social media. For example, if a business selling sunglasses could convince a popular social media celebrity to wear its brand of glasses and mention the brand on social media, then all the social media users who belong to the celebrity's online network would learn about the glasses and identify them with the celebrity. The business would have essentially achieved an advertising shortcut. Instead of paying a television station to run a commercial about the glasses, which would be seen by millions of people with no interest in sunglasses or the celebrity, the business used the celebrity's social media network to simultaneously create and get in touch with a market for its product (O'Connor, 2012).

Social media is more than simply an advertising platform for businesses, however. It can also be a way for businesses to collect information about current and potential customers. The essence of social media is the sharing of information, so with the application of some creativity, businesses can steer this activity in the direction they specify. This strategy can be seen on the website of almost any business, where there are bound to appear links to Facebook and Twitter, encouraging customers to "follow us online." The purpose for this is for the business to build an online community of users of its products, while getting the word out about the business to the connections of those users.

Each time a person follows a business site on Facebook by "liking" its page, that person's Facebook friends are informed that the person likes and is now following the business. This encourages the person's friends to find out more about the business and perhaps even to follow/like it themselves. What is more, each follower the business gathers online brings along his or her user profile, chock full of information that the business can access and make use of to learn more about its customers. This can help the business tailor its products and services to more closely meet customer needs. So, if a company selling binoculars learned through its social media activities that more than 80 percent of its online followers enjoyed bird watching, it could use this information to develop new products with bird watchers in mind (Springer & Carson, 2012).

APPLICATIONS

Advertising

Pay-per-click advertising involves a business placing an image or a link on a social media site, hoping to entice users of the site to click on it. When a user clicks on the advertisement link or picture, the user is then taken to the website of the business to learn more about the products and services available (Scott, 2013). The phrase "pay per click" refers to the advertising pricing model. The business pays a base rate to have the advertisement appear on the social media site for a specified period (48 hours, for example), and then would pay an additional amount for each referral it received from the site—that is, each time a user clicked on the advertisement. This model is used because each click that an advertisement produces has a chance of resulting in a sale for the business, so over the long term, the more clicks one receives, the more sales one makes.

The pay-per-click model is widely used despite the fact that it has some drawbacks. One limitation is that some users of social media are sophisticated enough to use software that is able to hide most advertisements while displaying the rest of the social media site's information. This frustrates the purpose of the business in paying to place the ad in the first place (Close, 2012). Another concern for advertisers is the phenomenon known as "click farms." Click farms are operations that assemble a large number of people and computers, either in a single location or geographically distributed, and employ the people to sit at the computers clicking on ads, sometimes for hours at a time. The purpose of doing this is to increase the advertising fees that a competing business will be charged and potentially drain the competitor's advertising budget. The click farmer will then be able to bid for advertising space at a lower rate. Alternatively, click farmers may run monetized websites on which other sites advertise. Clicking on these links drives revenue to the click farmer. This is a problem for businesses to be aware of because clicks generated from click farming have no chance of resulting in a sale (O'Connor, 2012).

Professional Networking

Other forms of social media allow businesses to accomplish goals that are not directly related to increasing sales. Some social media sites specialize in professional networking. Instead of allowing users to create profiles and make connections for purely personal reasons as can be done with Facebook, sites such as LinkedIn are geared toward helping professionals manage their network of contacts, communicate with them efficiently and effectively, and expand their network by making new connections. Businesses can use tools such as this to find potential opportunities for partnership and collaboration in new markets, just as they use other types of social media to expand their customer base. In addition, it is also possible to use one's profile on professional networking sites as a modern version of a resume, so that instead of keeping a list of one's accomplishments on file in a word processing document accessible only upon request, one may add work experiences to one's social media profile, and even receive feedback from other social media users about one's strengths (Houser, 2013).

Using a professional networking social media profile in this way allows people to create dynamic resumes that are not only more current but also more accessible and less subject to the selective presentation of information characteristic of traditional résumés. Many companies now turn first to social media sites when they are evaluating job applicants. This is done for a number of reasons. The most obvious purpose is to make sure that a candidate's online presence does not raise any red flags—signs that the person has poor judgment or engages in behavior that could potentially be embarrassing for an employer in the future. Less obvious but just as important, companies can assess a candidate's skills by observing how the candidate interacts with others online and what

others say about the candidate. It even happens that some employers use professional networking social media to recruit employees who are not even looking for work. Companies that specialize in this type of activity are known as headhunters, because they are paid to use social media to locate a specified number of candidates for an employer/client to evaluate (Sponder, 2012).

VIEWPOINTS

With new technologies, excitement often outpaces the amount of information that is actually known about them, and people develop unrealistic expectations about what the technologies can accomplish (Lawton & Marom, 2013). This has certainly been the case with social media and its business applications. Because social media does indeed have much to offer businesses in terms of leveraging their investment in it into a large return, there has been something of a social media "gold rush" as numerous individuals promoting themselves as social media gurus have sought to convince businesses large and small that if they do not act quickly (by hiring the guru as a consultant) then they will be left behind by their competitors in the rush to conquer the social media landscape.

Concentrating too heavily on a particular social media platform is also a danger. It is relatively easy for developers to create social media platforms, but it is much more difficult to design a platform that is appealing to users and fills a need felt by a large community. Social media users have a finite amount of time and attention they are willing to devote to new online services, learning to navigate those services, and developing social networks on those services (Piskorski, 2014). As a result, very few of the many social media sites that have been launched have persisted for more than a year. However, despite this lack of longevity, there has been a tendency in the business literature to latch onto each new technology as if it is a guarantee of business success.

Social media veterans advise businesses that a more useful approach is to concentrate on developing an overall social media strategy rather than on developing strategies for each new tool or network that comes along. For the time being, it appears that the initial rush of enthusiasm over social media has passed and that the phenomenon has begun to mature into an accepted feature of everyday life. What has not yet become clear is whether there will continue to be a proliferation of new social media sites appearing online or if the currently popular sites will remain on top for the foreseeable future. To some extent this depends on users and how quickly social media giants, such as Facebook, are able to adapt to their customers' evolving needs and expectations.

Businesses with substantial investments in the current social media players would prefer that the pace of change slow down, while new and emerging companies have less to lose and are therefore open to the continued emergence of new social media platforms. It seems likely that the services that do emerge in the years to come will have a better chance of surviving than some of their predecessors because more is known today about what is required for a successful social media community to be built.

BIBLIOGRAPHY

Close, A. (2012). *Online consumer behavior: Theory and research in social media, advertising, and e-tail.* New York, NY: Routledge.

Houser, K. A. (2013). *Legal guide to social media: Rights and risks for businesses and entrepreneurs.* New York, NY: Allworth Press.

King, D. L. (2012). F*ace2Face: Using Facebook, Twitter, and other social media tools to create great customer connections.* Medford, NJ: CyberAge Books.

Lawton, K., & Marom, D. (2013). *The crowdfunding revolution: How to raise venture capital using social media.* New York, NY: McGraw-Hill.

O'Connor, R. (2012). *Friends, followers, and the future: How social media are changing politics, threatening big brands, and killing traditional media.* San Francisco, CA: City Lights Books.

Piskorski, M. J. (2014). *A social strategy: How we profit from social media.* Princeton, NJ: Princeton University Press.

Rubin, A., & Ta, L. (2016). How to protect your company's social media currency. *Computer & Internet Lawyer, 33*(8), 19–21. Retrieved December 16, 2016 from EBSCO Online Database Business Source Ultimate. http://search.ebscohost.com/login.aspx?direct–true&db=bsu&AN=116807307&site=ehost-live&scope=site

Scott, D. M. (2013). T*he new rules of marketing & PR: How to use social media, online video, mobile applications, blogs, news releases, and viral marketing to reach buyers directly.* Hoboken, NJ: John Wiley & Sons.

Sponder, M. (2012). *Social media analytics: Effective tools for building, intrepreting, and using metrics.* New York, NY: McGraw-Hill.

Springer, P., & Carson, M. (2012). *Pioneers of digital: Success stories from leaders in advertising, marketing, search, and social media.* London, UK: Kogan Page.

SUGGESTED READING

Annabi, H., & McGann, S. T. (2013). Social media as the missing link: Connecting communities of practice to business strategy. *Journal of Organizational Computing And Electronic Commerce, 23,* 56–83. Retrieved March 22, 2015 from EBSCO Online Database Business Source Complete. http://search.ebscohost.com/login.aspx?direct=true&db=bth&AN=85879575&site=ehost-live

Fuchs, Christian. (2017). Social Media: A Critical Introduction. *SAGE.* Retrieved June 29, 2017.

Humphreys, L., & Wilken, R. (2015). Social media, small businesses, and the control of information. *Information, Communication & Society, 18,* 295–309. Retrieved March 22, 2015 from EBSCO Online Database Business Source Complete. http://search.ebscohost.com/login.aspx?direct=true&db=bth&AN=100099787&site=ehost-live

Li, X. (2012). Weaving social media into a business proposal project. *Business Communication Quarterly, 75,* 68–75. Retrieved March 22, 2015 from EBSCO Online Database Business Source Complete. http://search.ebscohost.com/login.aspx?direct=true&db=bth&AN=75234629&site=ehost-live

Schaupp, L. C., & Bélanger, F. (2014). The value of social media for small businesses. *Journal of Information Systems, 28,* 187–207. Retrieved March 22, 2015 from EBSCO Online Database Business Source Complete. http://search.ebscohost.com/login.aspx?direct=true&db=bth&AN=96548974&site=ehost-live

Shih, C. (2016). *The social business imperative: Adapting your business model to the always-connected customer.* Boston, MA: Prentice Hall.

Weiss, M. (2011). The use of social media sites data by business organizations in their relationship with employees. *Journal of Internet Law, 15,* 16–27. Retrieved March 22, 2015 from EBSCO Online Database Business Source Complete. http://search.ebscohost.com/login.aspx?direct=true&db=bth&AN=63613284&site=ehost-live

Scott Zimmer, M.L.S., M.S., J.D.

STRATEGIC MARKETING

ABSTRACT

In order for an organization's marketing effort to be successful, it needs to be based on a strategic marketing plan to help ensure that the goals and objectives of the effort are appropriate to the needs of the marketplace. Strategic marketing (a subfunction of marketing) examines the marketplace to determine the needs of potential customers, the strategy and market position of competitors, and attempts to develop a strategy that will enable the organization to gain or maintain a competitive advantage in the marketplace. A number of factors should impact the development of a strategic marketing plan. These include internal factors such as the assets and skills of the organization and the organizational culture as well as external factors such as various market drivers, market or industry lifestyle, strategic windows, and the nature of the competition. An optimal strategic marketing plan will also follow a contingency approach that allows flexibility in meeting the unique set of factors that govern the marketplace and the organization's viability within.

OVERVIEW

No matter how good an organization's products or services, unless their value can be communicated to potential customers, the organization will fail in its mission. This communication is the responsibility of the marketing function within the organization. According to the American Marketing Association (AMA), marketing is "an organizational function and a set of processes for creating, communicating and delivering value to customers and for managing customer relationships in ways that benefit the organization and its stakeholders." The marketing function comprises two interrelated subfunctions. Strategic marketing examines the marketplace to determine the needs of potential customers and the nature of the competitors in the market and then attempts to develop a strategy that will enable the organization to gain or maintain a competitive advantage in the marketplace. Operational marketing is built on the foundation set by the strategic marketing function and implements various plans and strategies, including

a development of the appropriate marketing mix, to attract customers and foster customer loyalty.

Methods for Product & Service Marketing

There a number of ways to market one's products or services, including advertising, direct response, sales promotions, and publicity. However, unless one understands the needs of the customer, the market, and the industry as well as the strengths and weaknesses of the competition, these approaches are unlikely to be successful. Strategic marketing helps an organization sharpen its focus and successfully compete in the marketplace. Strategic marketing is concerned with two components: the target market and the best way to communicate the value of one's product or service to that market.

The development of a viable marketing strategy depends on several key dimensions. First, as with any global strategy within the organization, a successful marketing strategy needs to be endorsed by top management within the organization. Marketing strategy is political in nature; powerful units within the organization may disagree on the best marketing strategy, and an accord may need to be negotiated. Marketing strategies may also be affected by organizational culture and the assumptions that this culture engenders. For example, if the organization has always marketed its widgets to business executives, it may fail to see the potential for marketing to lower-level personnel within the organization or even for personal use to adults or teenagers.

Factors That Impact Strategic Marketing Plan Development

There are a number of factors should impact the development of a strategic marketing plan for the organization. The first of these consists of the assets and skills that the organization already possesses or can readily acquire. For example, if an organization has a significant programming department on the payroll, it would be feasible for it to make and market application software. However, if these personnel are too involved in other projects to work on a new software project and the organization cannot afford to hire additional programmers, starting a new software line would be inadvisable at best.

The second factor that must be considered when developing a marketing strategy is the market drivers.

A hybrid marketing strategy process that is primarily visionary command with supporting incrementalism and rational planning is appropriate.	A hybrid marketing strategy process that contains significant amounts of all three components is appropriate.
A hybrid marketing strategy process will suffice.	A hybrid marketing strategy process that is primariy rational planning with supporting command is appropriate.

Relative Market Turbulance (vertical axis)

Relative Market Complexity (horizontal axis)

These are various political, economic, sociocultural, and technological forces that can influence the wants and needs of the consumer base. For example, the need to be able to handle increasing volumes of information and data has led to widespread use of information technology in many industries. Similarly, the need for a college education for an increasing number of jobs has led to a proliferation of for-profit institutions of higher education.

Market drivers, however, are not the only external force that shapes one's market strategy. The nature of the competition in the marketplace is also very important in determining whether or not a marketing effort will be successful. Virtually no business is without competition. When buying a computer, one must choose between Mac and PC. Most soft drinks on the market are manufactured by one of two companies that offer very similar products. There is a variety of choices available when deciding where to fill up one's car, yet most of the fuels available at the pump are virtually the same. Each of these businesses has its own market position and strives to retain its market share through marketing efforts. Part of the strategic marketing effort is to decide how best to differentiate oneself from the competition.

Another external factor that impacts how one can best position oneself in the market is the stage of the market or the industry life cycle. Some organizations excel, for example, at being the first on the market with an innovation or new product. Others excel at taking the innovation and adapting it to the needs of the marketplace (e.g., lower price, different features). In addition, various strategic windows affect an organization's ability to successfully compete in the marketplace. A strategic window is a limited time period during which there is an optimal fit between the needs of the

marketplace and the competencies of the organization. For example, as computer storage technology continues to evolve, the methods by which people store data and information change. Punch cards and magnetic tape gave way to 5.25-inch and 3.5-inch floppy disks. By the 2010s, most people were storing data and information on flash drives or in cloud storage, and computers were no longer made with floppy disk drives. The concept of using punch cards is as foreign and antiquated in most people's minds as using an abacus. Once the strategic window begins to close, it is typically best that the organization look for another opportunity.

Development of Competitive Strategy

To help meet their goals and objectives, many businesses develop a competitive strategy that will increase their competitive advantage. There are three generic approaches for competitive strategies: the provision of low-cost products or services, differentiation of products from those of the competition, and focus on the market niche.

Low-Cost Strategy

The goal of the low-cost strategy is to gain a larger market share. This is done by offering acceptable quality products or services at prices lower than those of the competition. The expectation in this strategy is that the organization will earn an acceptable return on investment by increasing sales volume. The basic methods used in low-cost leadership strategies include reduction of overhead, reduction of buying or production costs, and focused marketing strategies. For example, a restaurant may reduce the price of wine with the intention of making up the shortfall in profits by selling more than it did at the higher price. Similarly, a big box store may use a combination of effective management and information technology practices to reduce operation costs to deliver the lowest possible prices on its merchandise.

Product Differentiation

A second generic approach to competitive strategy is product differentiation. In this approach, the business attempts to differentiate itself from its competitors by producing a product or offering a service that is perceived by customers to have unique features or characteristics that set it apart from similar offerings. This strategy attempts to build customer loyalty by offering something of value that is offered by no one else in the marketplace. In this strategy, keeping the price of the product or service down becomes less important because customers are frequently willing to pay more to get their favorite brand. Value can be a subjective quality, and brand loyalty is not necessarily sufficient to make this strategy successful; there is a point beyond which most customers are no longer willing to pay a premium price. However, if carefully managed, a differentiation strategy can be highly successful. For example, Merrill Lynch was able to differentiate itself from its competitors by offering integrated financial services to attract the most desirable investors. This strategy yielded not only a well-recognized and highly valued brand that differentiated Merrill Lynch from its competitors but also substantial customer loyalty and a competitive advantage in the marketplace.

Niche Marketing
Another generic approach to competitive strategy is niche marketing. In this approach, the organization seeks to gain a proportion of the total sales of a given type of product or service within the marketplace. This strategy requires concentration on one or more specific market segments based on characteristics such as buyer group, portion of a product line or market, or geographical area. For example, rather than marketing itself as a generalist, a management consulting firm might specialize in working with the telecommunications industry or only with businesses on the west side of metropolitan Chicago. A niche-market strategy is indicated in situations where the business believes that it can better serve a segment of the market than it can the entire market. In the example of the management consulting firm, the founding partners may have come out of the telecommunications industry and therefore may be more familiar with the nuances of that industry than they are with other industries. This approach puts the organization in a unique position, through a type of differentiation, to be better able to market to that focused segment than to the whole.

Consideration of Competitors in the Marketplace
To be successful, analysis of the marketplace needs to consider not only the needs of the customer base and the value that can be offered by the organization's product or service but also the state of the industry as a whole and the position of the organization's competition within that industry. As opposed to a market that can be defined as a group of customers with similar buying needs, an industry is a group of organizations (i.e., competitors) that offer similar products or services to the market. Different organizations offering similar products or services will not necessarily have the same window of opportunity. Therefore, it is important to understand how competing firms view the market in order to develop a strategic marketing plan that will yield a significant competitive advantage.

Factors That Influence Industries & the Competition within Them

Several factors influence industries and competition within industries. Government regulation can significantly influence the profitability of an industry. Within the parameters set by this factor, however, are additional factors that influence how competition works within an industry. If a number of organizations all offer similar products or services, for example, competition within the industry will typically be more intense. This is illustrated by the famous marketing slogans of two car-rental agencies. "We're number one!" exclaimed Hertz. "We try harder!" rejoined Avis. Customers, too, can influence the nature of competition within an industry. If the industry becomes larger, it will become more attractive to new entrants offering the same product or service, and competition will tend to concomitantly increase. Similarly, new organizations that enter the industry may bring with them new products that change the nature of the industry. Of particular importance in this regard are new products that improve the relationship between price and performance (e.g., by offering the same quality for a lower price or more quality for the same price) and those produced by industries that earn high profits.

In some industries, a single customer dominates the industry; for example, the federal government is the primary procurer of military ships. This gives the customer more negotiating room for developing higher specifications, tighter deadlines, and lower costs. In addition, buyers can also exert pressure on an industry by searching for lower prices, higher quality, or additional features for a product or service. Organizations willing to meet these requirements will achieve a competitive advantage. However, suppliers can also have bargaining power that affects the competitiveness of an organization or industry. If there is only one or a limited number of suppliers for a component or material needed by the organization, it is the supplier and not the organization that will drive the price of that commodity.

APPLICATIONS

Brian Smith performed a five-year research study with more than 30 organizations and 100 individuals to determine the state of strategic marketing of pharmaceuticals, medical devices and equipment, and related products to physicians, clinicians, and other medical professionals or organizations. Among the questions he asked were why marketing strategy in this arena was of variable quality and how this condition could be improved. The end goal of the study was to develop a model of strategic marketing efforts to improve the marketing efforts within the medical marketplace.

Smith's research found that the optimal marketing strategy was dependent on the appropriate blend of three factors: rational planning processes, visionary command processes, and incremental processes. Using such a hybrid model to develop a marketing strategy tends to be more successful than developing a strategy based on any one of these factors alone. As discussed above, marketing strategy also needs to take into account both internal factors that are intrinsic to the organization (e.g., culture, assets) and external factors (e.g., competition, market stage). In fact, Smith recommends taking a contingency approach in which the best marketing strategy is contingent on the state of these factors. For example, when introducing a new product or innovation to the market, one typically has to convince the customer of the need for and value of the product. However, once the market has assimilated that need, then a different marketing strategy is needed to communicate to the market that the organization's product is superior to (i.e., gives better value than) the similar product of the competition.

The implication of the contingency approach to strategic marketing is that there is no one best way to develop a marketing strategy or to market one's product or service. Rather, organizations need to be flexible in order to be able to successfully market their products or services within an environment that may include strong competition or unfavorable market conditions.

Smith found that the development of an optimal marketing strategy is best approached in five stages. First, the organization needs to assess the conditions of the market, in particular its complexity and turbulence. As shown in Figure 1, this analysis can help the organization determine what hybrid strategy is most likely to succeed in its particular situation. In addition, the marketing strategy needs to be congruent with the external market (macrocongruent) and with the organizational culture (microcongruent). By understanding and incorporating these factors into the marketing strategy, the organization can develop a hybrid strategy that will better help it communicate value to potential customers. The organization should next use various diagnostic tests to determine how well the strategy meets the goals of the organization within the marketplace. Based on the results of the tests, the strategy can be refined to better meet the goals of the organization before it is implemented.

Figure 1: Hybrid Marketing Strategy

A number of characteristics of Smith's approach distinguish it from the more rigid approaches offered by many theorists. First, the model does not prescribe a single method for determining optimal marketing strategy; rather, it helps the organization make strategic marketing decisions based on the characteristics and needs of the situation in which it finds itself. Second, the model takes into account the existing culture of the organization and does not require a systemic change in order to be successful. This means that the development of a successful strategy is more likely to be both practical and possible and less likely to have unexpected consequences that could result from an attempt to implement a wholesale change to the organizational culture. Third, the contingency model advocates testing the strategy before wholesale implementation, supporting the development of a more refined model that will adequately take into account the needs of both the organization and the marketplace and is more likely to be successful in enabling the organization to reach its goals. These characteristics make the model more flexible, better able to meet the demands and needs of the marketplace, and more likely to be useful in helping organizations develop an optimal marketing strategy.

Bibliography

Amoako, G. K., & Dartey-Baah, K. (2012). An analysis of the impact of strategic marketing on profitability of rural banks: A case study of Dangme Bank. International Journal of Marketing Studies, 4(2), 150-156. Retrieved November 25, 2013, from EBSCO Online Database Business Source Complete. http://search.ebscohost.com/login.aspx?direct=true&db=bth&AN=75333804&site=ehost-live

Dickinson, J. (2012). Symbiotic marketing: A network perspective. Journal of Management & Marketing Research, 11, 1-27. Retrieved November 25, 2013, from EBSCO Online Database Business Source Complete. http://search.ebscohost.com/login.aspx?direct=true&db=bth&AN=83536053&site=ehost-live

Iyamabo, J., & Otubanjo, O. (2013). A three-component definition of strategic marketing. International Journal of Marketing Studies, 5(1), 16-33. Retrieved November 25, 2013, from EBSCO Online Database Business Source Complete. http://search.ebscohost.com/login.aspx?direct=true&db=bth&AN=85797513&site=ehost-live

Mathur, M. (2013). Drivers of channel equity: Linking strategic marketing decisions to market performance. *Marketing Review, 13*(4), 393–414. Retrieved November 24, 2014, from EBSCO Online Database Business Source Complete. http://search.ebscohost.com/login.aspx?direct=true&db=bth&AN=95749559

Papasolomou, I., Thrassou, A., Vrontis, D., & Sabova, M. (2014). Marketing public relations: A consumer-focused strategic perspective. *Journal of Customer Behaviour, 13*(1), 5–24. Retrieved November 24, 2014, from EBSCO Online Database Business Source Complete. http://search.ebscohost.com/login.aspx?direct=true&db=bth&AN=99409506

Proctor, T. (2000). Strategic Marketing: An Introduction. New York: Routledge.

Senn, J. A. (2004). Information technology: Principles, practices, opportunities (3rd ed.). Upper Saddle River, NJ: Pearson/Prentice Hall.

Smith, B. (2003). Success and failure in marketing strategy making: Results of an empirical study across medical markets. International Journal of Medical Marketing, 3(4), 287-315. Retrieved June 25, 2007, from EBSCO Online Database Business Source Complete. http://search.ebscohost.com/login.aspx?direct=true&db=bth&AN=10793964&site=ehost-live

Smith, B. (2004). Making marketing happen: How great medical companies make strategic marketing planning work for them. International Journal of Medical Marketing, 4(2), 129-142. Retrieved June 25, 2007, from EBSCO Online Database Business Source Complete. http://search.ebscohost.com/login.aspx?direct=true&db=bth&AN=12483910&site=ehost-live

Suggested Reading

Anderson, D. W. (2012). Strategic marketing planning for the small to medium-sized business: Writing a marketing plan. New York: Business Expert Press. Retrieved November 25, 2013, from EBSCO Online Database eBook Collection. http://search.ebscohost.com/login.aspx?direct=true&db=nlebk&AN=493186&site=ehost-live

Kim, Narwoon et al. (2016). Strategic marketing capability: mobilizing technological resources for new product advantage. *Journal of Business Research*, 69, 12, 5644-5652. Retrieved June 29, 2017.

Rao, P. M. (2005). Sustaining competitive advantage in a high – technology environment: A strategic marketing perspective. Advances in Competitiveness Research, 13(1), 33-47. Retrieved June 25, 2007, from EBSCO Online Database Business Source Complete. http://search.ebscohost.com/login.aspx?direct=true&db=bth&AN=19196897&site=ehost-live

Sausen, K., Tomczak, T., & Herrmann, A. (2005). Development of a taxonomy of strategic market segmentation: A framework for bridging the implementation gap between normative segmentation and business practice. Journal of Strategic Marketing, 13(3), 151-173. Retrieved June 25, 2007, from EBSCO Online Database Business Source Complete. http://search.ebscohost.com/login.aspx?direct=true&db=bth&AN=17941673&site=ehost-live

Vriens, M. (2003). Strategic research design. Marketing Research, 15(4), 21-25. Retrieved June 25, 2007, from EBSCO Online Database Business Source Complete. http://search.ebscohost.com/login.aspx?direct=true&db=bth&AN=12249147&site=ehost-live

Weinstein, A. (2006). A strategic framework for defining and segmenting markets. Journal of

Strategic Marketing, 14(2), 115-127. Retrieved June 25, 2007, from EBSCO Online Database Business Source Complete. http://search.ebscohost.com/login.aspx?direct=true&db=bth&AN=20937022&site=ehost-live

Wiles, M. A., Morgan, N. A., & Rego, L. L. (2012). The effect of brand acquisition and disposal on stock returns. *Journal of Marketing, 76*(1), 38–58. Retrieved November 24, 2014, from EBSCO Online Database Business Source Complete. http://search.ebscohost.com/login.aspx?direct=true&db=bth&AN=69539399

Ruth A. Wienclaw, Ph.D.

T

TRADE SHOW PARTICIPATION

ABSTRACT

A trade show is an exhibition at which businesses within a specific industry demonstrate their products and distribute information about their goods and services. Trade shows offer a unique opportunity for businesses to market their products and services to a large, targeted audience that tends to be seriously interested in purchasing the types of products and services that the organization offers. However, exhibiting at a trade show is not an inexpensive proposition. To maximize the success of the trade show experience as well as the return on investment from trade show participation, one must choose the right show, design an eye-catching exhibit, participate in targeted pre-show marketing efforts, actively work the show, and follow-up on all legitimate sales leads. By using such a concerted approach, participation at trade shows can be an effective addition to many marketing strategies.

OVERVIEW

As globalization widens, the markets for goods and services in many industries and fast-paced advances in technology make it essential to stay on the leading edge of the industry. It is increasingly important for organizations to get information about their products into the hands of potential consumers as quickly as possible. One of the ways that an increasing number of organizations attempt to market to customers is through Integrated Marketing Communications (IMC), an approach to marketing that combines and integrates multiple sources of marketing information (e.g., advertising, direct response, sales promotions, public relations) to maximize the effectiveness of a marketing campaign. This approach to marketing allows an organization to change its strategic marketing plan to better reach different target markets or market niches.

One popular element of the marketing mix for many organizations is the trade show. This marketing venue is an exhibition at which businesses within a specific industry exhibit and demonstrate their products and distribute information about their goods and services. Typically, trade shows are not open to the public but are restricted to representatives within the given industry. Trade shows help organizations and individuals within an industry keep current with the state-of-the-art products and services within the industry as well as offer a single venue for businesses to market to a wide range of customers within their market niche. International trade shows can attract millions of participants. For example, 2007 Cairo International Book Fair—the largest book fair in the world—had 2,000,000 attendees (Voice of America, 2007) and the 2006 Bologna Motor show had 1,123,649 attendees (Motor Show, 2007). Although these trade shows have more attendees than most, many trade shows frequently attract thousands of visitors.

Despite the fact that trade shows offer businesses wide exposure to a specific market niche, trade shows should be only one part of a good marketing strategy. Marketing strategies typically include other media such as advertising, direct response, sales promotions, and publicity to maximize the effectiveness of the marketing campaign. Through an IMC campaign, the organization can coordinate its marketing efforts to present a consistent face to customers while focusing the marketing campaign in an attempt to give the organization a competitive edge.

However, the trade show remains an enduring marketing technique with good reason. It has been consistently found that an average of 85 percent of the typical trade show audience comprises final decision makers or others who influence the products or services that are purchased by the organization. Similarly, 50 percent of qualified sales leads are closed at trade shows (Keobke, 2004). There are a number of reasons for these impressive statistics. First, trade shows offer an opportunity not only to make face-to-face contact with potential customers, but also to do so with a self-selected group of individuals who have indicated by their presence at the show that they are interested in the general types of offerings that the business is trying to sell. Although some attendees at trade shows are merely gathering information, many of them are ready to purchase. In addition, trade shows offer marketing personnel the opportunity to not only make a contact, but also to establish rapport and present their products and services in one encounter.

APPLICATIONS

Ensuring Success at Trade Shows

Although trade shows offer a unique opportunity to businesses to market their products and services to a large, targeted audience, exhibiting at a trade show is not an inexpensive proposition. In addition to the cost of leasing space on the exhibit floor, the business must also develop and print brochures and other literature, design and build an exhibit, transport the exhibit to the venue, hire people who can physically assemble and disassemble the exhibit, transport exhibit staff members to the venue and pay for their expenses, as well as other costs. In addition, success at a trade show requires careful planning starting a year before the event. Further, trade show participation is not a passive marketing tool. It requires an onsite, trained, and knowledgeable staff who can demonstrate products, answer detailed technical questions, and present a polished image to represent the company throughout the show. Despite these costs, however, trade show participation continues to be a popular marketing tool in many industries because of its relatively high potential return on investment.

Choosing a Trade Show

Successful participation in a trade show requires much more than merely setting up a booth and expecting potential customers to walk in. Before even considering what information one will present, it is important to choose the right show. Obviously, one needs to choose a show whose attendees will likely be potential customers. To do this, it is helpful to familiarize oneself with the upcoming trade show opportunities within target industries, and then choose

those that are directly related to the organization's marketing strategy. However, even within an industry, there is often a wide range of shows available. For example, although many book fairs are available, a publisher of medical books would be unlikely to be successful at a book fair focusing on children's publications or even at a trade show focusing on medical equipment. On the other hand, the same publisher might be very successful at a medical trade show targeted toward physicians or at a medical conference even though the show was not specifically focused on medical books. To choose the "right" trade show to attend, several factors to be taken into account:

- First, one must investigate the reputation of the trade shows under consideration. The potential exhibitor must ask whether or not the trade show is in keeping with the organization's image, budget, and overall marketing plan. A manufacturer of high-end goods is unlikely to get much business from exhibiting at a low-end trade show just as a manufacturer of low-end goods is unlikely to get much business from a high-end trade show.
- Another question to ask oneself about a potential trade show is whether or not that particular show has a consistent attendance record and whether or not that record makes attendance worth the investment.
- It is also helpful at this point to find out who has exhibited at that particular show in the past and who the other likely exhibitors are for the upcoming show.

Setting Objectives & Budgets

It is also essential to establish measurable objectives for participation in the show and a budget. Before investing in trade show participation, it is helpful not only to determine the costs of various booth sizes, but also the location of the booths. For example, booths closer to the entrance of the show floor are more likely to attract attendees than booths in a corner off the beaten path. No matter how well designed an exhibitor's display is, if it is located on the show floor in an area where it is unlikely to attract attendees, it is also unlikely to bring in sufficient revenue to justify the cost of participation. Some of the top criteria that many exhibitors use in determining which trade show to attend include audience quality (e.g., proportion of decision makers attending the trade show, proportion of attendees in one's target market), audience quantity (e.g., expected number of attendees, extensive promotion by the show's organizers), exhibit parameters (e.g., booth location on the exhibit floor, ability to specify or negotiate size, location, or other parameters of the exhibit), and logistical aspects (e.g., easy registration or pre-registration and, security, ease of moving in and out of the exhibit space).

Exhibit Size

Another decision that needs to be made early on is what size exhibit one should display. It has been found, for example, that larger booths in trade shows receive a greater response from attendees. However, in general, one should only set up an exhibit with an average of 50 square feet of exhibit space per person who will man the booth. For a minimal staff of one or two salespeople, it is typically not advisable to book more than 200 square feet of space.

Geographic Location

Another type of location that needs to be taken into account when one is considering exhibiting at a trade show is the geographic location of the show. Although one may potentially reach a larger segment of the market in an international show, for example, if one cannot afford the transportation costs for subsequently providing goods and services internationally, the costs of exhibiting at the show will not provide adequate return on investment. Even within the same country, if the cost of extensive travel is prohibitive, the resultant sales will be unequal to the investment.

Sound Design Principles

A good trade show exhibit requires planning and the application of sound design principles. Trade show exhibits should be physically designed to facilitate the movement of attendees at the booth. It is typically sound practice to set aside part of the exhibit area for in-depth discussions with potential customers who need extensive additional information or are ready to make a purchase. In addition, the booth should be designed so that potential customers are not forced to wait outside the exhibit while the staff deals with other potential customers. An exhibit at a trade show is a marketing tool. As with any marketing tool, the message needs to be carefully crafted to make clear what the business has to offer, what the benefit of the business's products and services are, and how

the business's offerings can satisfy the needs of the potential customers. Similarly, the principles of good graphics design should be taken into account when designing a trade show exhibit. For example, bright colors, the use of photographs and graphic art, and hands-on demonstrations are more likely to attract potential customers to the exhibit than are those with only bare walls and black-and-white spec sheets. In addition, any text on display should be clearly visible and easily readable and graphics or photographs used in the display should be clear, simple, and support the organization's message. At all times, the exhibit should reinforce the organization's reputation and message.

Outreach

Although a compelling exhibit design is essential for maximizing the success of trade show participation, the experienced trade show participant understands that there are other activities that can also increase the return on investment achieved by trade show participation. For example, press releases and media kits advertising newsworthy aspects of the company and its products can be sent to the media. In addition, personal invitation letters can be sent to current prospects and trade show attendees to let them know that the organization is exhibiting at the show. Similarly, a direct-mail campaign can be conducted to prospective customers within a 100-mile radius of the show to encourage them to attend and see the organizations exhibit.

Proper Staff Conduct & Expertise

If done correctly, participation in a trade show is hard work. Exhibitors need to do more than passively sit in their booth and wait for potential customers to ask questions. Potential customers who are seriously considering purchasing the business's goods or services will typically have specific questions that cannot be answered by generic brochures and spec sheets. To help maintain the potential customer's interest, exhibit personnel need to be able to answer these questions. In addition, most trade show attendees come to a trade show looking for more than generic information about products or services: They want to evaluate new products, renew business contacts, discuss alternative solutions to specific problems, and make purchasing decisions. Particularly with the ever-increasing high cost of travel, it is important that such questions be answered not only from the point of view of the exhibitor to show a reasonable return on investment for participating in the trade show, but also for the point of view of the attendee who must report back to his or her management on the degree to which their own agenda was met and questions answered at the trade show. Therefore, one's booth needs to be staffed at all times so that the exhibit floor is open with staff members who are well informed in the business's products and services. In addition, it is important that the appearance and conduct of the staff at the exhibit portrays the same type of positive image of the organization as does the exhibit itself. This means that the staff persons should wear business attire appropriate to their industry, be well-groomed, and pay attention to their posture and body language. Similarly, staff personnel should not eat, drink, smoke, or chew gum within the exhibit area. Staff members should remember at all times that this is a business situation and they are representing their organization.

Working a trade show is not only mentally difficult work, but physically difficult as well. Most exhibit areas have concrete floors under a thin layer of carpeting. Because of this, it is helpful to include extra padding for the floor as part of the design of the exhibit. Similarly, experienced trade show staff members know to wear comfortable shoes. Further, it is important for staffers to restrict their evening activities. Some people at trade shows view them as opportunities to spend long nights with their friends. However, this is a business situation, and it is important to restrict such activities in order to maintain a positive image for the organization as well as to be fresh and ready for the next day's activities at the show. Exhibit staff members are also well advised not to carry on conversations with each other even if no attendees are currently in the booth. Conversations between staff members often discourage attendees from visiting the exhibit or asking questions because they do not want to interrupt. In addition, even when there have not been any attendees for an extended period of time during the exhibit hours, it is important to always have one's exhibit staffed until the show is officially over.

Proper Follow-Up

Just as success at a trade show requires groundwork and preparation, so, too, it requires follow-up

in order to be maximally effective. The marketing strategy for trade shows should include a formal process for following up on qualified leads after the show. All legitimate prospects should be personally contacted within the first few days after the trade show, even if the specific material they requested is not yet available. Activities that should be performed as soon as possible after the end of the trade show include compiling a complete list of contact information for distributors, agents, and prospects; sending personal thank-you letters or emails to prospects; and following up on requests for additional information that could not be provided at the show. As when following up on any good sales lead, requested information should be sent to the prospect as soon as possible. In all these matters, the more timely the response, the more professional and customer-oriented the organization will appear.

CONCLUSION

One of the traditional ways in which organizations attempt to market to potential customers is through participation in trade shows. At these exhibitions, businesses can exhibit and demonstrate their products and distribute information about their goods and services. Despite the fact that there are newer, more high-tech marketing techniques available, trade shows continue to prove to be a successful way to reach a large number of potential clients who are ready to purchase. Because of this track record, trade show attendance continues to be an important part of the marketing mix for many organizations. Exhibiting at trade shows, however, is not a passive marketing technique. One must choose the right show, design an eye-catching exhibit, participate in a targeted pre-show advertising and direct-mail campaign, actively work the show, and follow-up on all legitimate sales leads. With such a concerted approach, participation at trade shows can be an effective addition to many marketing strategies.

BIBLIOGRAPHY

American Marketing Association. (2008). AMA adopts new definition of marketing. *Marketing Academics*. Retrieved January 2, 2008, from http://www.marketingpower.com/content24159.php

Eyre, J. (2013). Considering exhibiting?. *Builders Merchants Journal*, 16. Retrieved November 15, 2013, from EBSCO Online Database Business Source Complete. http://search.ebscohost.com/login.aspx?direct=true&db=bth&AN=91623584&site=ehost-live

Kimmick, N. (2013). Practical tips for maximizing the return on your trade show budget. *HVACR Distribution Business*, 22-23. Retrieved November 15, 2013, from EBSCO Online Database Business Source Complete. http://search.ebscohost.com/login.aspx?direct=true&db=bth&AN=89755845&site=ehost-live

Kiobke, B. (2004, Summer). Show stoppers: The power of trade shows. *Export Wise*, 4-5. Retrieved January 2, 2008, from EBSCO Online Database Business Source Complete. http://search.ebscohost.com/login.aspx?direct=true&db=bth&AN=14080855&site=ehost-live

Laurie, C. A. (1993). Getting the most from your trade show exhibit. *Franchising World*, 25(1), 38-39. Retrieved January 2, 2008, from EBSCO Online Database Business Source Complete. http://search.ebscohost.com/login.aspx?direct=true&db=bth&AN=9308306988&site=ehost-live

Motor Show. (2007, 18 Dec). "The first GL events-owned motor show is a resounding success." Retrieved January 8, 2008, from http://www.motorshow.it/uk/news.asp?codcat=87&tab=Pagine&cod=3511

Vanderleest, H. W. (1994). Planning for international trade show participation: A practitioner's perspective. *SAM Advanced Management Journal*, 59(4), 39-44. Retrieved January 2, 2008, from EBSCO Online Database Business Source Complete. http://search.ebscohost.com/login.aspx?direct=true&db=bth&AN=9502151657&site=ehost-live

Voice of America. (2007, 4 Feb). Cairo International Book Fair attracts two million visitors. Retrieved January 8, 2008, from http://www.voanews.com/english/archive/2007-02/2007-02-04-voa16.cfm?CFID=179641025&CFTOKEN=49602115http://www.voanews.com/english/archive/2007-02/2007-02-04-voa16.cfm?CFID=179641025&CFTOKEN=49602115

SUGGESTED READING

Brandl, P. J. (2002). Measuring trade show ROI. *Appliance Manufacturer*, 50(9), 52. Retrieved January 2, 2008, from EBSCO Online Database Business Source Complete. http://search.ebscohost.com/login.aspx?direct=true&db=bth&AN=7385157&site=ehost-live

Friedman, S. (2002). Thinking of cutting your trade show budget—big mistake! *Canadian Manager*, 27(4), 20-21. Retrieved January 2, 2008, from EBSCO Online Database Business Source Complete. http://search.ebscohost.com/login.aspx?direct=true&db=bth&AN=9089394&site=ehost-live

Kramer, K. L. (1998). Capitalizing on your trade show investments. *Adhesives & Sealants Industry*, 5(4), 6. Retrieved January 2, 2008, from EBSCO Online Database Business Source Complete. http://search.ebscohost.com/login.aspx?direct=true&db=bth&AN=563188&site=ehost-live

Mapes, S. & Padden, K. (2006). Conventional wisdom. *Pharmaceutical Executive*, 26(Supp), 14-22. Retrieved January 2, 2008, from EBSCO Online Database Business Source Complete. http://search.ebscohost.com/login.aspx?direct=true&db=bth&AN=20034442&site=ehost-live

Tanner, J. F. Jr. (1992). Trade shows mean bigger business. *Baylor Business Review*, 10(1), 16-18. Retrieved January 2, 2008, from EBSCO Online Database Business Source Complete. http://search.ebscohost.com/login.aspx?direct=true&db=bth&AN=9607036332&site=ehost-live

Tucker, R. B. (2001). Trade show success. *American Salesman*, 46(9), 3-6. Retrieved January 2, 2008, from EBSCO Online Database Business Source Complete. http://search.ebscohost.com/login.aspx?direct=true&db=bth&AN=9509276707&site=ehost-live

Ruth A. Wienclaw, Ph.D.

V

VALUE-BASED STRATEGIES FOR BUSINESS MARKETING

ABSTRACT

Business marketing refers to the marketing operations of businesses whose mission is to serve other businesses, whether companies, government agencies, institutions, or resellers. Since it is known that customers purchase value (and not products, services, or features) suppliers seeking competitive advantage must ensure that they offer the best value to their targeted customers in selected consumer value segments. The trend, therefore, is for companies to move away from cost-based strategies to customer-oriented value-based strategies to ensure optimal value creation and value delivery.

OVERVIEW

Business marketing is the development of strategic plans and the execution of the idea, price, advertisement, and allocation of ideas, goods, and services by organizations (including commercial business organizations, governments, and institutions) to other organizations that resell them, use them as components in their products or services, or use them to support their operations.

Business marketing, also known as business-to-business marketing, (B2B), therefore refers to the marketing operations of businesses whose mission is to serve other businesses. Such businesses usually have a specific business customer and strategy in mind. Consumer marketing, also known as business-to-consumer (B2C) marketing, on the other hand, is generally characterized by organizations offering their goods and services directly to households via the mass media and retail channels.

The practice of traders doing business with each other dates back to time immemorial, but the subfield of industrial marketing has only been in existence since the mid-nineteenth century, and the discipline of business marketing, in its modern form, is even more recent.

There are four broad categories of business marketing customers:

- Companies that consume products or services (either to use in their operations or for their own consumption);
- National and local government agencies;
- Institutions (including schools, hospitals and nursing homes, churches, and charities); and
- Resellers (wholesalers, brokers, and industrial distributors).

In most countries, the largest of the four categories is government agencies.

Since the mid-1970s, business marketing has gradually overtaken consumer marketing in terms of its popularity as an academic discipline and a career choice, as well as in monetary terms. The volume of transactions in the industrial or business market is significantly larger than that of the consumer market. The purchases made by companies, government agencies, and institutions in industrialized countries account for a significant portion of the economic activity in those countries.

B2B marketers in the United States alone spent 10.1 percent of their firm's budgets in February 2013 just in the promotion of their services and 10.8 percent on marketing their goods, the CMO Survey found (Moorman, 2013). This promotional budget is spent on trade shows and events, the Internet and electronic media, promotion and market support, magazine advertising, publicity and public relations, direct mail, dealer and distributor materials, market research, telemarketing, directories, and other promotional efforts.

Business marketing differs from consumer marketing in several ways:

- First, it often involves shorter and more direct distribution channels than consumer marketing.
- Second, the negotiation process between buyers and sellers is more personal in business marketing

than in consumer marketing, where the target markets are larger demographic groups and the main marketing communications vehicles in use are the mass media and retailers.

- Another difference is the fact that most business marketers spend less on advertising than consumer marketers.

The phenomenal growth and development taking place in the business marketing arena is largely due to the fast-paced changes occurring within the fields of technology, entrepreneurship, and marketing. Technological advancement has served and still serves as a catalyst to the development of new products and services. Progress in entrepreneurship has led to leaner, "meaner" reinvented companies, and the twenty-first-century field of marketing is characterized by adaptability, flexibility, speed, aggressiveness, and innovativeness. Relationships, partnerships, and alliances are considered to be prerequisites of success.

Due to the above-mentioned developments, the Internet has become an indispensable tool in helping business marketers manage their relationships with their customers, improve on their customer service in general, and improve the opportunities they have with their distributors. The Internet has also given rise to new e-commerce middlemen, such as infomediaries and metamediaries.

Infomediaries are information intermediaries: They are information providers, such as Google and Yahoo, that collect personal data from customers and market that data to businesses while maintaining consumer privacy, offering consumers a percentage of the brokered deals. Metamediaries, on the other hand, are intermediaries that gather and coordinate the products and services offered by mediators who specialize in specific areas.

The Internet has also paved the way for an increasing amount of collaborations between businesses, with virtual marketplaces allowing companies and their suppliers to conduct business in real time, while simplifying purchase processes and cutting costs.

FURTHER INSIGHTS
The Importance of Value
It is a well-known fact that customers buy value and not products, services, or features. Discerning customers make purchases from the company that generates the greatest benefit for them, making sure that

they purchase the products and services that are in their best interest.

A value-based strategy differs from a mass-marketing strategy in that it is a targeted strategy directed at selected consumer value segments deemed profitable by the supplier. To be successful in highly competitive markets, companies must try to achieve and maintain competitive advantage, and to do so, they must ensure that they offer the best value to their targeted customers. They must be able to show that their product offers better value for the money, and this must be evidenced by higher ratios of value to cost.

B2B marketers must therefore be able to explain to their business customers what the customers are getting from their product, and hence, justify the price they are charging in return for those benefits. Their customers must be persuaded to recognize, purchase, and value the difference between the company and its competitors and also be made to believe that what the supplier is offering them is beyond their expectation.

Offering better value, even when it comes at a higher price, is a customer-oriented approach that has several benefits:

- A customer-oriented approach based on value gives rise to sustainable competitive advantage, since it is relatively difficult for competitors to duplicate advantage that is derived from the overall value generated for the customer.

- This customer-oriented approach can also reinforce the company's reputation for providing high-quality goods or services, which is altogether a better strategy than trying to generate volume and experience advantage through the reduction of costs or rapid growth of market share. In fact, to some, value itself is the best leading indicator of market share (Market Value Solutions, n.d.).

- Value is created for the supplier as well as the customer, especially when the supplier is able to manage costs and run the business effectively.

Value Defined
In marketing parlance, value can be defined both qualitatively and quantitatively. On a purely qualitative level, value is gain perceived by an individual, based on his or her emotional, mental, and physical condition, along with a range of social, economic, cultural, and environmental factors. In pure quantitative terms, on the other hand, value is a tangible

benefit measured by financial numbers, percentages, or actual money.

By combining the qualitative and quantitative definitions, the value of a product or service can be described as the association between a consumer's expectations for product or service quality and the total amount he or she paid for it. Thus defined, value can be expressed in terms of an equation as follows:

Value = Benefits / Price

or:

Value = Quality Received / Expectations

(Argent, 2007, para. 3)

Value-based pricing is a pricing strategy where products or services are uniquely priced for each customer to reflect the precise value delivered to each customer. Prices must be based on how the customer (and not the supplier) measures value. For instance, a customer might measure value based on the number of users of the product, the number of annual transactions, the size of his or her revenues, the amount of money that would be saved through the purchase, and so on. Information on how a customer measures value can be obtained by a thorough evaluation of the customer's operations or feedback from a survey.

Value is dynamic. It is affected by changes in time, location, people, and the environment. For instance, customer expectations are likely to vary from one geographical location to another and from one market to another, since customer expectations are closely related to cultural expectations.

Knowledge of the customer must always be at the core of B2B marketing strategies. It is therefore essential that B2B marketers get to know their customers very well, have a good firm understanding of individual and organizational behavior, and understand how their customers determine value. Business marketers must also know how they themselves can build customer loyalty for their products and services.

Value Creation & Value Delivery

A major prerequisite to the development of a value-based consumer strategy is the identification of a target audience. One of the means of doing so is for a supplier to analyze the customer lifetime value (CLV) of different customer segments and, from the results, identify which customer value segment(s) to target.

DeBonis, Balinsky, and Allen (2002) suggest that in order to create competitive value, companies must follow a sequence in which they must first discover and quantify needs to determine the need their product or service would fulfill and how or why they are different from other companies in the same market. Next, they must commit to impacting their customer, and then they must go on to create meaningful and understandable customer value. Afterward, they must assess how they did, and subsequently, improve upon their value package. They must constantly seek to generate and maintain competitive advantage while delivering value to customers. To compete profitably in their marketplace, companies must follow the following value creation and delivery process:

- Identification of the value expectations of their target customers;
- Selection of the values with which they choose to compete;
- Analysis of their organization's ability to deliver that value;
- Communication of the value and sale of the value message; and
- Distributing the promised value and enhancing the company's value model.

As stated above, business marketers must assess the value of their products and services to their customers, so that they can market them effectively. There are several ways in which a company can determine value and ensure that it delivers value to its customers. These include the consideration of the "total market offering," the "economic value to the customer (EVC)," and the "customer-value model."

Total Market Offering

The total market offering of a product, simply put, compares the totality of the company's reputation, its employees, product advantages, and technological capabilities to competitors' market offerings and the cost of those offerings. Value, in terms of the total market offering, is perceived as the comparison between a company's market offerings and those of its competitors.

Economic Value to the Customer

Economic value to the customer (EVC) is the value a certain product offers to an individual customer in a specific application. In other words, the EVC is the amount that a customer could be expected to pay for a product, assuming that he or she has full information about the product and competitors' offerings. EVC typically corresponds to the sale price of the product the customer is already using, with subtractions or additions made on account of any value difference between the product in use and the product for which the EVC is being determined.

EVC is particularly helpful in cases where a product delivers its benefits over an extended time period; when sales effort, delivery reliability, or other intangible features add significant value to the overall product value; or when the sale price merely constitutes a fraction of the product's total cost to the consumer.

Before calculating the EVC of a product, a supplier must first know the initial costs as well as later costs of his or her own product or service, as well as the life-cycle costs (the total amount of the product's sale price, initial costs, and necessary later costs) of a similar or 'reference' product.

The EVC of a given product A is calculated by subtracting the start-up costs and post-purchase costs of product A from the life-cycle costs of a reference product B, and then adding the amount of extra value that product A offers in relation to product B.

Products that are marketed to several different customer groups and/or have a number of different usages often have a different EVC for each different customer group and each specific application. The variations in customer EVCs serve as the foundation for dividing the market and as a springboard for seeking ways to increase the company's competitive advantage within different market segments. Once this is done, the product price can be established in order to provide sufficient profit and a strategy can be developed to sustain the company's competitive advantage.

The effective use of EVC requires a capable sales force who can maintain close and regular contact with important customers. The well-trained salespeople must endeavor to, on one hand, educate customers and, on the other hand, observe how customers obtain value from the product and funnel this knowledge back to the company.

Many companies, when switching from a cost-based strategy to a value-based strategy, find the transition difficult. As with any change in an organization, there is likely to be some amount of resistance, especially from managers who struggle to change their focus from product costs to value data. The difference between cost-based and value-based strategies is significant: In the case of cost-based strategies, managers have access to cost data that is available at regular intervals, but in the case of value-based strategies, the value data required is difficult to quantify, highly dependent on the internal procedures of the customers, and often partial.

Even when they do make the transaction from cost-based strategies to value-based strategies, the managers of value-based businesses must strive to keep wide the division between value and cost, since the chance of having a sustainable competitive advantage increases as the margin between the EVC and the manufacturer's costs increases. Costs should be kept low enough to induce customers and yet provide sufficient profits to finance essential investments in areas like research and development, facilities, and training.

In companies that choose to use EVC, the concept must be understood and supported by the entire workforce. Among other benefits, EVC helps make employees customer-oriented, and EVC can also reinforce a company's reputation as a provider of high-quality products.

Customer-Value Model

As an alternative to EVC, some business marketers use the customer-value model to compare a product's worth with that of its competitors. Similar to other tools for assessing value, the customer-value model helps companies understand how value is defined by their markets and the way markets view the value of their products and services in relation to their main competitors. This is illustrated in the diagram below.

The customer-value model has two sections. The first is composed of managerial components, and the second is composed of predictive components. The managerial components are known as "quality drivers": These are the criteria on which customers rate their suppliers' performance or quality. Companies conduct qualitative research to discover how customers rate their performance across several performance criteria, which are obtained directly from the customers.

Following statistical analysis, the performance criteria or quality drivers are rated to determine the importance of each one. The ratings of the quality drivers are collated to form the consumer quality index (CQI). Once a company is able to discover which quality components have the biggest impact on customer views of value, and once it discovers the relative impact of each quality component, the company should be able to better manage its quality.

The first three elements among the predictive components are the factors on which customers base their assessment of a product's worth. These are known as "value drivers." They are CQI, image (brand image and/or corporate image), and price. A thorough analysis of customer ratings of the three value drivers will show which value driver is most important to customers and, hence, which driver is the best predictor of value. The gives and takes among the three main elements will also be revealed.

Business marketers will also be able to determine the extent to which value predicts loyalty. The hope is that customer purchase or acquisition will lead to loyalty and that loyalty will in turn lead to customer retention. Customer loyalty would be demonstrated by the customer's eagerness to recommend the product and future buying intentions.

BIBLIOGRAPHY

Argent, D. "Hierarchy of value: Part I." Paper, Film & Foil Converter. Retrieved 30 July 2010 from http://pffc-online.com/mag/paper%5Fhierarchy%5Fvalue%5Fpart/

DeBonis, J. N., Balinski, E. W., & Allen, P. (2002). Value-based marketing for bottom-line success: 5 steps to creating customer value. New York, NY: McGraw-Hill.

Donath, B. (1994). Important commandment: Know thy customer. Marketing News, 28(11), 16. Retrieved June 7, 2007, from EBSCO Online Database Business Source Complete. http://search.ebscohost.com/login.aspx?direct=true&db=bth&AN=9410311415&site=ehost-live

Forbis, J., & Mehta, N. (1981). Value-based strategy for industrial products. McKinsey Quarterly, (2), 35-52. Retrieved November 23, 2007, from EBSCO Online Database Business Source Premier. http://search.ebscohost.com/login.aspx?direct=true&db=buh&AN=6988984&site=bsi-live

Gallarza, M. G., Gil-Saura, I., & Holbrook, M. B. (2011). The value of value: Further excursions on the meaning and role of customer value. Journal of Consumer Behaviour, 10 (4), 179-191. Retrieved November 22, 2013 from EBSCO online database Business Source Premier. http://search.ebscohost.com/login.aspx?direct=true&db=buh&AN=63250263

Haley, F. (2004). Free to be B2B. Fast Company, (85), 88. Retrieved June 7, 2007, from EBSCO Online Database Business Source Complete. http://search.ebscohost.com/login.aspx?direct=true&db=bth&AN=13660262&site=ehost-live

Hinterhuber, A., & Bertini, M. (2011). Profiting when customers choose value over price. Business Strategy Review, 22(1), 46-49. Retrieved November 22, 2013 from EBSCO online database Business Source Premier. http://search.ebscohost.com/login.aspx?direct=true&db=buh&AN=59629141

Infomediary. (n.d.). Computer Desktop Encyclopedia. Retrieved November 27, 2007, from Answers.com website: http://www.answers.com/topic/infomediary-technology

Lawin, D. (2004). Business-to-business marketing: A defined strategy. Franchising World, 36(10), 24-25. Retrieved June 7, 2007, from EBSCO Online Database Business Source Complete. http://search.ebscohost.com/login.aspx?direct=true&db=bth&AN=15119603&site=ehost-live

Market Value Solutions. (n.d.). Using customer value measurement to improve your unique value proposition. Retrieved November 27, 2007, from http://www.marketvaluesolutions.com/customer-value-measurement.htm

Moorman, C. (2013, August). Highlights and insights. CMO Survey.org. Retrieved November 22, 2013, from: https://faculty.fuqua.duke.edu/cmo-surveyresults/TheCMOSurveyHighlightsandInsightsAug%20-%2013-Final.pdf

Pepe, M. (2012). Customer lifetime value: A vital marketing/financial concept for businesses. Journal of Business & Economics Research, 10(1), 1-10. Retrieved November 22, 2013 from EBSCO online database Business Source Premier. http://search.ebscohost.com/login.aspx?direct=true&db=buh&AN=82362686

Singh, S. S., & Jain, D. C. (2013). Measuring customer lifetime value: Models and analysis. INSEAD Working Papers Collection, (27), 1-48. Retrieved November 22, 2013 from EBSCO online database Business Source Premier. http://search.ebscohost.com/login.aspx?direct=true&db=buh&AN=85940750

Walters, D. (1997). Developing and implementing value-based strategy. Management Decision, 35(9/10), 709. Retrieved June 7, 2007, from EBSCO Online Database Business Source Complete. http://search.ebscohost.com/login.aspx?direct=true&db=bth&AN=179984&site=ehost-live

SUGGESTED READING

Anderson, J., & Narus, J. (1998). Business marketing: Understand what customers value. Harvard Business Review, 76(6), 53-65. Retrieved November 23, 2007, from EBSCO Online Database Business Source Premier. http://search.ebscohost.com/login.aspx?direct=true&db=buh&AN=1246475&site=ehost-live

Forbis, J., & Mehta, N. (1981). Value-based strategies for industrial products. Business Horizons, 24(3), 32. Retrieved November 23, 2007, from EBSCO Online Database Business Source Premier. http://search.ebscohost.com/login.aspx?direct=true&db=buh&AN=4528306&site=bsi-live

Jacobides, M. G., &a MacDuffie, J. (2013). How to drive value your way. Harvard Business Review, 91(7), 92-100. Retrieved November 22, 2013 from EBSCO online database Business Source Premier. http://search.ebscohost.com/login.aspx?direct=true&db=buh&AN=88350667

Raab, D. (2005). Customer value models. DM Review, 15(9), 64-68. Retrieved November 23, 2007, from EBSCO Online Database Business Source Premier. http://search.ebscohost.com/login.aspx?direct=true&db=buh&AN=18216730&site=ehost-live

Skugge, G. (2011). The future of pricing: Outside-in. Journal of Revenue & Pricing Management, 10(4), 392-395. Retrieved November 22, 2013 from EBSCO online database Business Source Premier. http://search.ebscohost.com/login.aspx?direct=true&db=buh&AN=62012638

Vanessa A. Tetteh, Ph.D.

GLOSSARY

Adaptation Model: School of thought that supports the assumption that advertising must adapt to cultural differences in order to promote a successful international advertising campaign.

Advertising: Advertising is the paid promotion of a cause, idea, opinion, product, or service by an identified sponsor attempting to inform or persuade a particular target audience through non-personal communication, i.e. media. Media include television or radio; newspapers, magazines, or other publications; direct mail; billboards; catalogs; or the Internet. Advertising also refers to the profession and the business of designing and writing advertisements, along with any related techniques and practices.

Advertising Agency: A company that designs and produces advertising messages, sometimes handling other forms of promotion for its clients.

Advertising Approach: The advertising approach specifies the frequency goals, media impact, media timing, and the reach of an advertising campaign.

Advertising Budget: The amount of money allocated by an organization to be spent on advertising; necessary to weigh the pros and cons of different budget allocations.

Advertising Campaign: A coordinated advertising plan that consists of advertisements, commercials, and related promotional materials that are intended to meet certain objectives during a specified period of time; a series of advertisement messages on the same idea and theme which constitute a consistent, seamless, one-voice integrated marketing communication (IMC).

Advertising Campaign Theme: The central message to be communicated through an advertising campaign.

Advertising Equivalency: The equivalent amount of advertising that results from the exposure gained as a corporate sponsor for an event, organization or individual.

Advertising Frequency: Advertising frequency refers to the number of times an advertisement is repeated during a given time period.

Advertising Management: The application of the principles, concepts, and research of management science, marketing, and communications to the design and evaluation of advertising. Advertising management uses research to determine the needs and characteristics of the target market, strategy development to determine advertising goals and objectives and how to reach them, advertising design and development, and evaluation of advertising and campaign effectiveness.

Advertising Objective: An advertising objective is a statement that specifies the basic message to be delivered by a particular advertising campaign, the target audience to whom the message is to be delivered, the intended effect of the advertising campaign, and the criteria to be used to measure the campaign's effectiveness.

Advertising Strategies: A plan to call the public's attention to your business, usually for the purpose of selling products or services, through the use of various forms of media, such as print or broadcast notices.

Advocacy Publications: Magazines, newspapers, newsletters, and websites that take a position on a specific issue or are dedicated to the advancement of a selected segment of the population and focus on issues such as the environment, politics, race, business, international relations, immigration, and unionism.

Analytic Hierarchy Process (AHP): This process leads to the likely identification of all key components affecting decision-making by building a customized hierarchy to represent each problem. AHP can be used to resolve many complex problems that confront marketing management

Antecedent Demographics: Socio-developmental processes that may influence an individual's intellectual and emotional responses to consumer choices.

Application Software: A software program that performs functions not related to the running of the computer itself. Application software includes word processing, electronic spreadsheets, computer graphics, and presentation software.

Architectural Works: "The design of a building as embodied in any tangible medium of expression, including a building, architectural plans, or drawings" (United States Copyright Office, 2007).

Artificial Intelligence (AI): The branch of computer science concerned with development of software that allows computers to perform activities normally considered to require human intelligence. Artificial intelligence applications include developing expert systems that allow computers to make complex, real world decisions; programming computers to understand natural human languages; developing neural networks that reproduce the physical connections occurring in animal brains; and developing computers that react to visual, auditory, and other sensory stimuli (i.e., robotics).

Attitudes: Consumer attitudes comprise a consumer's beliefs, feelings, and behavioral intentions toward an object. The components of attitude are considered together since they are highly interdependent and together represent forces that influence how the consumer will react to the object.

Attitudinal Loyalty: Customer or buyer loyalty that results in repeat buying as well as ongoing endorsements and recommendations of the product or service to others.

Audiovisual Works (also motion pictures): "Works consisting of a series of related images shown by the use of machines or devices such as projectors, viewers, or electronic equipment, together with accompanying sounds" (United States Copyright Office, 2007).

Avatar: An image or other visual representation chosen by a social media user to represent him or her. Because social media interactions are often not face to face, it can be difficult to identify who a user is. Avatars help to identify which user has shared what content.

Banner Ads: Paid advertising space that companies purchase on websites other than their own.

Behavioral Influence Perspective: The Behavioral Influence Perspective assumes that strong environmental forces propel consumers to action without them necessarily first developing strong feelings or beliefs about a product, service, experience or idea.

Behavioral Loyalty: Customer or buyer loyalty that results in repeat buying but does not generate on-going endorsements of and recommendations of the product or service to others.

Behavioral Perspective: A theoretical model which views the actions of customers as determined by the setting or situation in which consumption takes place, rather than by internal mental processes such as attitudes or intentions.

Bias: The tendency for a given experimental design or implementation to unintentionally skew the results of the experiment due to a nonrandom selection of participants.

Blog: A personal journal that is publicly accessible on the World Wide Web. Blogs include personal thoughts of the author in chronological order, just as in a hard copy journal. The term "blog" is short for "web log."

Body Language: The communication of thoughts or feelings through physical expression such as posture, gesture, facial expression, or other movements. Body language may reinforce or contradict the verbal message being given by the person.

Brand: A trademark or distinctive name that is identified with a particular a product, service, or organization that makes it publicly and easily distinguishable from other products, services, or concepts. A brand may include a name, logo, slogan, or design scheme associated with the product, service, or organization.

Brand Ambassador: A celebrity who, under contract, wears and/or uses a branded product exclusively.

Brand Equity: The value a brand adds to the intrinsic value of a product or service. Or the overall financial value associated with a brand's market strength. Brand equity takes into account all of a brand's various assets and liabilities. It is largely determined by the consumer and by the value the consumer places on a particular brand.

Brand Identity: Ideally created by a brand management team, brand identity ultimately refers to the unique set of characteristics and associations that a brand evokes in the mind of the consumer.

Brand Image: The consumer's perception of a product or brand.

Brand Loyalty: The reluctance of a buyer to switch to another brand of product or service because s/he is familiar and comfortable with the brand s/he is currently using or has used in the past.

Brand Manager: A professional mid-level manager responsible and accountable for supervising all aspects relating to the management of one brand.

Brand Name Testing: The method used to discover how consumers relate to the names of products.

Branding: Working to associate a feeling or awareness to a product or service through the application and use of a name and logo; aimed at increasing a product or service's visibility.

Business Cycle: A predictable long term pattern of alternating periods of economic growth and decline.

Business Marketing: The process of supporting and fostering the sales of products or services to other commercial companies or organizations. This is also referred to as business to business marketing (B2B).

Business Model: The paradigm under which an organization operates and does business in order to accomplish its goals. Business models include consideration of what the business offers of value to the marketplace; building and maintaining customer relationships; an infrastructure that allows the organization to produce its offering; and the income, cash flow, and cost structure of the organization.

Business Process: Any of a number of linked activities that transforms an input into the organization into an output that is delivered to the customer. Business processes include management processes, operational processes (e.g., purchasing, manufacturing, marketing), and supporting processes, (accounting, human resources).

Business-to-Business: The way in which businesses interact, develop alliances, and conduct marketing research on each other.

Business-to-Business Electronic Commerce: Involves computerized processes that occur from one trading partner to another, and is carried out through increased volumes that are higher than other standard business-to-consumer (B2C) applications.

Business-to-Business Marketing: The process of selling goods or services between businesses (see also, business marketing).

Business-to-Consumer (B2C) E-Business: E-business in which a business markets and sells directly to consumers.

Business-to-Consumer Electronic Commerce: A type of electronic commerce where goods and services are sold from a corporation to a consumer.

Business-to-Consumer Marketing: The selling of products or services to individual consumers.

Buyer Behavior: The complex processes by which consumers choose, acquire, use, and dispose of goods and services in order to fulfill their needs and desires.

Buying Center: A group of people who collectively make buying decisions in an organization. Buying centers are also known as decision-making units.

Buying Decision Process: Also known as the decision making process, the buying decision process is comprised of up to six stages, namely: problem recognition, information search, evaluation of alternatives, purchase decision, purchase, and post-purchase evaluation.

Buying Situation: Factors influencing buying behavior that cannot be predicted from a knowledge of either the buyer or the situation alone.

Channel: A route used by a business to market and distribute its products or services (e.g., wholesalers, retailers, mail order, Internet).

Channel Management: The development and implementation of policies and procedures to gain and maintain the cooperation of the various organizations in the channel and to coordinate their activities. Channel management helps organizations manage activities and flow of information between members of the channel. Channel management is also referred to as channel relationship management or partner relationship management (PRM).

Channel Stewardship: An approach to channel management in which the channel processes and communication flow are designed to take into account the best interests of the customer and to optimize profits for all partners in the channel.

Click Farming: The practice of using low wage employees to continuously click online ads in order to generate advertising revenue, at the expense of businesses paying for the online ads in the hope that actual customers will click on them.

Cognitive Style: This is the process through which a marketing decision maker perceives and processes information; the organization of information in memory and the repertoire of rules for using that information.

Cold Call Pitching: Using unsolicited calls to potential clients in an effort to create new business.

Commerce Service Providers: Organization that develops the components necessary to e-commerce websites.

Commission: A set fee or percentage of the sale that is given to a sales representative for convincing a customer to make a purchase.

Competitive Advantage: A firm possesses this when it sustains a profit that exceeds the average profit of its industry competitors.

Competitive Advantage: The ability of a business to outperform its competition on a primary performance goal, such as profitability.

Competitive Strategy: A plan of action by which a business attempts to increase its competitive advantage.

Concept Testing: Process of determining if certain customers will accept a certain concept — similar to test marketing.

Consumer: A person or organization that acquires goods or services for direct use rather than for resale or use in a manufacturing process.

Consumer Behavior: Consumer behavior includes the acquisition, consumption, use and disposal of products, services, experiences or ideas, by consumers.

Consumer Buyer Behavior: The selection and purchase of products, services, experiences or ideas by individual consumers or a group of consumers.

Consumer Buying Decision Process: The Consumer Buying Decision Process comprises six stages, namely: problem recognition, information search, evaluation of alternatives, purchase decision, purchase, and post-purchase evaluation.

Consumer Demographics: Categories such as age, ethnicity, gender, income, mobility, education, and social class, are considered to be predictors of consumer behavior, habits, and patterns.

Consumer Ethnocentrism: Reluctance to buy a foreign product

Consumer Marketing: Refers to the way organizations plan and execute the idea, price, advertisement, and allocation of ideas, goods, and services to households, typically via the mass media and retail channels. Consumer marketing is also known as 'business-to-consumer marketing' and 'B2C marketing.

Consumer Price Index: Used as a measure of inflation or change in overall prices for a national economy; a calculation of the average variation over time in the amount paid by urban consumers for a market basket of goods and services.

Consumer Quality Index (CQI): Formed out of the aggregation of customer ratings of a supplier's performance criteria or quality drivers.

Contingency Model: School of thought that recognizes the importance of local cultural differences as well as the benefits of standardizing the advertising effort.

Contractual Exchanges: Intermediate formal agreements, which can include a single contract or a series of contractual exchanges that include open ended contracts.

Control System: The procedures by which an organization observes, guides, appraises, and rewards its employees.

Cookie: A small, unique text file sent by a website to the user's hard drive to record a user's activities on the site.

Copy Testing: Copy testing is the study and testing of advertisements prior to their release, with the aim of ensuring that the advertisements ultimately contain the best quality messaging, captivate the audience's attention, and lead to the desired behavioral change.

Copyright: The exclusive right of the author or creator of a literary or artistic property (such as a book, movie or musical composition) to print, copy, sell, license, distribute, transform to another medium, translate, record or perform or otherwise use (or not use) and to give it to another by will.

Copyright Infringement: The unauthorized or illegal use of works created by others including reproduction, distribution, or sales.

Corporate Brand Personality: The human personality traits associated with a company. Also, a company's values, purpose, and mission. The brand personality should be apparent in the marketing of all company products and services; it should be exuded by all company employees.

Corporate Image: The perception of an organization that is generally held by the public. A corporate image may change over time depending on the organization's circumstances, publicity, and other publicly-known information.

Created: According to the United States Copyright Office, a work is created when it is "fixed in a copy or phonorecord for the first time."

Criterion: A dependent or predicted measure that is used to judge the effectiveness of persons, organizations, treatments, or predictors. The ultimate criterion measures effectiveness after all the data are in. Intermediate criteria estimate this value earlier in the process. Immediate criteria estimate this value based on current values.

Culture: The basic shared assumptions, beliefs, norms, and values held by a group of people. These may be either consciously or unconsciously held.

Customer Lifetime Value: An estimate of how much a customer will spend with a business or brand during the period when s/he purchases from that business or brand. Analysis of customer value should include consideration of the depth, breadth, and duration of the customer's relationship with the business or brand as well as the cost to acquire, serve, and retain each customer.

Customer Loyalty Programs: Incentive programs that reward customers.

Customer Orientation: The firm-level competency of identifying, analyzing, understanding, and answering the needs of the users.

Customer Relationship Management (CRM): The process of identifying prospective customers, acquiring data that concerns these prospective and current customers, building relationships with customers, and influencing their perceptions of the organization and its products or services.

Customer Surveys: Method of obtaining consumer information directly from customers.

Customer Value Proposition: The promise of benefits delivered to a customer in return for the customer's business and payment.

Customer Value: An estimate of how much a customer will spend with a business or brand. Analysis of customer value should include consideration of the depth, breadth, and duration of the customer's relationship with the business or brand as well as the cost to acquire, serve, and retain each customer.

Customer-Value Model: Derived from customer grading of supplier performance across a range of performance criteria. By assessing the relative impacts that quality, image, and price have on customer perceptions of value, these models enable companies to discover the value their customers place on their products and understand how this value translates into customer loyalty.

Data: (sing. datum) In statistics, data are quantifiable observations or measurements that are used as the basis of scientific research.

Data Mining: The process of analyzing large collections of data to establish patterns and determine previously unknown relationships. The results of data mining efforts are used to predict future behavior.

Database: A collection of data items used for multiple purposes which is stored on a computer.

Database Marketing: Marketing directly to a defined group of individuals whose addresses and/or contact information have been accumulated in database form.

Decision Analysis: A collection of procedures, methods, and tools used to identify, represent, and assess the important aspects of a decision being considered in a decision making process.

Decision Support System (DSS): A computer based information system that helps managers make decisions about semi-structured and unstructured problems. Decision support systems can be used by individuals or groups and can be stand-alone or integrated systems or web-based.

Decision-Making Unit (DMU): A group of people who collectively make buying decisions in an organization. Decision-making units are also called buying centers.

Delphi Estimation Process: A group decision-making tool where anonymous judgments are collected through questionnaire. The median responses are summarized as the group consensus, and this summary is fed back along with a second questionnaire for reassessment.

Demand: The amount of a good or service an individual consumer or a group of consumers wants at a given price.

Demand Schedule: The actual quantities that consumers are willing and able to purchase at various prices.

Demographic Data: Statistical information about a given subset of the human population such as persons living in a particular area, shopping at an area mall, or subscribing to a local newspaper. Demographic data might include such information as age, gender, income distribution, or growth trends.

Dependent Variable: The outcome variable or resulting behavior that changes depending on whether the subject receives the control or experimental condition (e.g., a consumer's reaction to a new cereal).

Design Review: Any of a number of reviews of the product design, usually held between the customer and the contractor to determine the completeness and feasibility of the design at a given time in the contract. Two of the most common design reviews are the preliminary design review (PDR) — held after the completion of the preliminary design but before the start of the detail design — and the critical design review — held before the design is released for production.

Differentiating Quality (Qualities): The aspect or aspects of your product, service or idea that are unique, and thus worthy of your customers' specific attention and consideration.

Direct Advertising: The delivery of promotional materials or messages directly to the consumer, using email, mail, telephone, the Internet, etc.

Direct Marketing: A customer relationship management strategy in which the provider of the product or service delivers the promotional message directly to potential customers on a one-to-one basis rather than through the use of mass media.

Distribution: A set of numbers collected from data and their associated frequencies.

Dramatic Works, Pantomimes, and Choreographic Works: Works that are presented on stage in a theater setting including accompanying sounds.

E-Business: E-business (i.e., electronic business) is the process of buying and selling goods or services electronically rather than through conventional means along with the support activities and transactions necessary to do these tasks. E-business is typically conducted over the Internet.

E-Commerce: See E-Business.

Economic Profit: The amount of profit that exists at the profit-maximizing output when prices are above average total costs, exceeding the rate of profit considered normal for a market; attracts potential new entrants into the market.

Economic Trends: The forces affecting the economy at large and the market for a particular product.

Economic Value to the Customer (EVC): The relative value a given product offers to a specific customer in a particular application. In other words, the EVC is the amount that a customer should be willing to pay for a product, assuming that he or she is fully informed about the product and the offerings of competitors.

Electronic Exchanges: Sites on the Internet where buyers and sellers can come together to exchange information and buy and sell products and services.

E-Marketing: E-marketing (electronic marketing) is an evolving discipline in which the Internet is used as the medium for an organization's marketing efforts to sell goods and services as well as to collect information about the needs and desires of potential customers. E-marketing can include pay-per-click advertising, banner ads, mass emailings, web sites, blogging, and social media.

Empirical: Theories or evidence that are derived from or based on observation or experiment.

Entrepreneur: At its most basic, an entrepreneur is a person who starts a new business. However, the word typically carries with it the connotation of taking risks to turn innovative ideas into profit-making ventures.

Entrepreneurial Pricing: Viewed as the "Cinderella" approach because the strategy deviates from the traditional pricing approaches and takes innovativeness, assumption of risk and proactiveness into consideration when setting prices.

Equilibrium Price: The price at which demand and supply curves intersect reflecting an agreement among consumers and producers.

Equilibrium Quantity: The quantity at which demand and supply curves intersect reflecting an agreement among consumers and producers.

Equilibrium: The price and quantity associated with the intersection of the demand and supply curve reflecting alignments among consumers and producers on an item's price and quantity.

Ethics: In philosophy, ethics refers to the study of the content of moral judgments (i.e., the difference between right and wrong) and the nature of these judgments (i.e., whether the judgments are subjective or objective).

Evaluation of Alternatives: As the third stage in the Consumer Buying Decision Process, the evaluation of alternatives sees a consumer analyzing, ranking or weighing a shortlist of products, services, experiences or ideas, to enable him or her to make a purchase decision.

Evoked Set: This is a list of possible alternatives that the consumer arrives at after his or her Information Search, during the Consumer Buying Decision Process.

Expatriates: Individuals who go overseas to accomplish a job related goal.

Expert System: A decision support system that utilizes artificial intelligence technology to evaluate a situation and suggest an appropriate course of action.

Export Management Company: Within international markets, an organization which sells and distributes goods for domestic companies.

External Audience: All stakeholders outside of an organization, including its customers, consumers, prospective customers, government and other entities outside the organization.

Fair Trade Marketing: A philosophy that supports the marketing and sale of products at greater than fair trade prices.

Fixed Costs: Costs for any level of production or output that remain constant.

Forecasting: In business, forecasting is the science of estimating or predicting future trends. Forecasts are used to support managers in making decisions about many aspects of the business including buying, selling, production, and hiring.

Franchises: Branches of a main company or business which are run and owned by individual entrepreneurs in the manner of the Authorization granted to someone to sell or distribute a company's goods or services in a certain area.

Frequency Goals: The frequency goals specify the number of times that the average consumer should be exposed to the message during the campaign period.

Frequent-Flier Programs: Airline customer loyalty programs that reward customers with points for miles flown. When enough points are accumulated the customer can trade those points for free travel, upgrades in class of seating, or other items or services offered by the airline or business partners.

Functional Brand Management: A style of brand management in which functionally specialized professionals supervise one aspect of brand management across all of an organization's brands.

General Store: Formerly the typical type of retail store in rural areas, small towns and villages. As the population became more urban in character, the demands for stores specializing in only one line or a few lines of merchandise increased.

Global Brands: A brand name recognized all over the world.

Global Marketing: 1. International efforts undertaken by corporations, mostly in the form of licensing, franchises and joint ventures, to expand their product and service offerings overseas. 2. A marketing approach in which consumer similarities are emphasized and local differences are minimized

Global Markets: The economic markets of countries and regions open to foreign trade ad investment.

Globalization: A process of economic and cultural integration around the world caused by changes in technology, commerce, and politics. Globalization creates an interconnected, global marketplace operating outside constraints of time zone or national boundary. Although globalization means an expanded marketplace, products are typically adapted to fit the specific needs of each locality or culture to which they are marketed.

Government Regulations: Federal and state laws and rules that govern a business and the products it sells.

Gross Domestic Product (GDP): The market value of all of the goods and services produced in an economy during a specified period of time.

Gross Margin: The ratio of gross income divided by net sales expressed as a percentage. Gross margin is a measure of the retailer's markup over wholesale. Gross margins are an expression of earnings adjusted for costs associated with producing the product or service. Most businesses attempt to have a gross margin as large as possible, although discount retails attempt to keep operations efficient so that they can afford a smaller markup.

Guerilla Marketing: Everything done to promote the business from the moment the idea is conceived to the point at which clients are doing business with the organization/consultant on a regular basis.

Hashtag: A typographical convention used primarily on the social media site Twitter, and denoted by the symbol "#." A hashtag is similar to a keyword and can be created by any user to make it easy to find all posts ("tweets") mentioning that hashtag. For example, a user could use the hashtag #newyearsday on all her posts that are about New Year's Day. Then, anyone wishing to find all posts about New Year's Day, regardless of who posted them, could simply search for the #newyearsday hashtag to find out what other users had been posting on that topic.

Headhunter: A person or company paid to use social media in order to locate and recruit candidates on behalf of an employer seeking to fill vacant positions. Headhunters often use social media to locate candidates who are looking for work and/or have the desired skill set.

Heuristics: A method of problem solving that uses trial and error as well as rules of thumb to take shortcuts to a solution.

Hierarchy of Needs: A theory of motivation developed by Abraham Maslow. According to Maslow, there are five levels of need: physiological, safety, belongingness, esteem, and self-actualization. The theory posits that people's behavior is motivated by where they are in the hierarchy. People can move up and down the hierarchy and can also experience needs from several levels at once.

Home Based Business: Any business where the primary office is located in the owner's home.

Hub: A business-to-business website that brings together buyers and sellers in a particular industry. Web hubs may charge a transaction fee for purchases. Also known as a vertical portal.

Hypothesis: An empirically-testable declaration that certain variables and their corresponding measure are related in a specific way proposed by a theory.

Income Quintile: A quintile is a fifth portion, as of a pie chart. An income quintile is any of the five

portions of a population divided for statistical analysis into five groups ranked by income.

Inflation: A general rise in the overall level of prices in an economy; see Consumer Price Index.

Infomediaries: Information intermediaries or information providers that collect personal data from customers and market that data to businesses, while maintaining consumer privacy, offering consumers a percentage of the brokered deals.

Information Flow: Refers to the way in which data is collected, processed and reported throughout an organization.

Information Overload: The condition in which a person receives more information than s/he can meaningfully process.

Information Search: The second stage in the Consumer Buying Decision Process, where a consumer searches internally and externally for information that will ultimately help him or her to satisfy a need to purchase a product, service, experience or idea.

Information Service Quality: The human component of information systems, and the extent to which information services offered by computer technicians to systems users having solicited service properties.

Information System: A system that facilitates the flow of information and data between people or departments.

Information Technology: The use of computers, communications networks, and knowledge in the creation, storage, and dispersal of data and information. Information technology comprises a wide range of items and abilities for use in the creation, storage, and distribution of information.

In-Game Advertisements: Product placement found embedded in video and/or computer games

Innovation: Products or processes that are new or significant improvements to previous products or processes and that have been introduced in the marketplace or used in production.

Integrated Marketing Communications: An approach to marketing communications that combines and integrates multiple sources of marketing information (e.g., advertising, direct response, sales promotions, public relations) to maximize the effectiveness of a marketing campaign.

Integrated Strategy: A marketing strategy in which physical and virtual channels are used to complement each other and offer customers a wider range of options.

Integration: In the context of social media, integration refers to the consistency of message across multiple social media platforms. It is important for businesses to have an integrated approach to social media so that their presence on one social media site conveys the same information about the business as is conveyed by its presence on other sites.

Intellectual Property Rights: Refers to the category of intangible rights that protect commercially valuable products of human intellect including patents, trademarks and copyrights.

Internal Audience: All stakeholders within an organization, including its employees, managers and members of the Board of Directors.

Internal Brand Management: The job of managing how employees at all levels of an organization relate to the organization's brands.

International Advertising: The spreading of promotional appeals and messages from one country to another.

International Counter Trade: Agreement in which one country imports goods from a country to which it exports goods.

International Franchise Association: Founded in 1960, is a group of franchisors, franchisees, and suppliers that aims to protect, enhance, and promote worldwide franchises.

International Master Franchising: Franchise in which the franchisor hands off a part of his rights and responsibilities to another individual who then is tasked with developing franchise outlets within other, international territories.

Internet Marketing: The advertising and selling of goods and services on the Internet; includes search-engine marketing (both search-engine optimization and pay-per-click advertising), banner advertising, e-mail marketing, affiliate marketing, and interactive advertising.

Internet Retailing: Selling retail goods or services through the Internet.

Inventory Management: Policies and procedures designed to help a business maintain the optimum quantity of each item in its inventory in order to provide uninterrupted production or sales at the minimum cost. Also referred to as inventory control.

Isolation Strategy: A marketing strategy in which physical and virtual channels are used independently to market products. This strategy is often used to target different market segments.

IT Capability: The technological component of information systems. The ability of many computers and similar technologies within a business to keep, dissect, and relay information.

Job Description: A document that lists the duties and tasks related to a job. Job descriptions may also specify the knowledge, skills, and abilities necessary to do the job as well as the performance standards that differentiate acceptable from unacceptable performance.

Joint Ventures: A partnership or conglomerate, formed often to share risk or expertise.

Just-in-Time (JIT) Inventory: An inventory management system in which products are produced, delivered, or received just in time to provide the next business in the supply chain with the stock that they need at the time that they need it. The major objective of just-in-time inventories is to reduce the need to physically warehouse stock anywhere within the supply chain.

Just-in-Time Manufacturing (JIT): A manufacturing philosophy that strives to eliminate waste and continually improve productivity. The primary characteristics of JIT include having the required inventory only when it is needed for manufacturing and reducing lead times and set up times. Also called "lean manufacturing."

Key Account Management: Involves targeting the largest and most important customers and providing them with special treatment in the areas of marketing, administration, and service.

Leads: Refers to consumers that have expressed interest in an offer, product, or service; potential customers.

Literary Works: "Works, other than audiovisual works, expressed in words, numbers, or other verbal or numerical symbols or indicia, regardless of the nature of the material objects, such as books, periodicals, manuscripts, phonorecords, film, tapes, disks, or cards, in which they are embodied" (United States Copyright Office, 2007).

Localization Services: A service that adapts a company's entire image to fit another culture.

Loyalty Cards: A card issued by a retailer that allows the customer to keep tally of the points gained in the loyalty program. Cards can be in paper form and can be punched at the time of purchase or in magnet/plastic form like a credit card, which can be swiped at the time of purchase to update the database of customer records of points accumulated.

Loyalty Marketing: An emerging marketing research strategy for determining if customers are being retained.

Mail Order House: Was a cross between a retail store and a wholesale warehouse that sold only by mail.

Management by Objectives (MBO): An approach to performance appraisal in which the employee and his or her manager jointly set performance objectives for the coming appraisal period and then review the progress made toward accomplishing these at predefined times. The employee's performance is evaluated in terms of how well s/he met the objectives previously determined.

Management: The process of efficiently and effectively accomplishing work through the coordination and supervision of others.

Marginal Revenue: the contribution to total revenue from the sale of one additional item.

Market Niche: A sub-segment of a particular market in which the consumers' needs are not being met and on which an organization focuses its efforts.

Market Research: The accumulation and examination of information regarding consumers, markets, and the performance of marketing campaigns.

Market Segmentation: The division of a market into specific groups which behave in similar ways or have similar needs. This is done with the assumption that similar groups of people will be affected similarly by marketing strategies.

Market Share: The proportion of total sales of a given type of product or service that are earned by a particular business or organization.

Market Structure: The forces that shape the market for a particular consumer product.

Market: A virtual space where consumers and producers interact while exchanging a specific item in accordance with their demand and supply schedules.

Marketing Case-Based Reasoning Systems (MCBRs): These marketing management support systems make cases available in a case library and provide tools for retrieving and accessing them. Historical cases are stored with all the relevant data kept intact, in "raw form."

Marketing Channels: The multitude of organizations taking part in the creation and distribution of a product or service to customers.

Marketing Communications Agency: A firm that creates, plans, and handles the marketing communications of a client organization.

Marketing Communications Channels: Various means through which marketing messages and related media are used to communicate with a market. They include advertising, public relations, sales promotion, merchandising, personal sales, events and sponsorships, and customer loyalty programs.

Marketing Communications: The messages and media used to communicate with a market.

Marketing Decision Support Systems (MDSSs): These marketing management support systems support rather than replace managerial judgment, and they improve the effectiveness of decision making rather than its efficiency. MDSSs are used to gather information from the environment, and through them, marketing managers can model marketing phenomena according to their own ideas.

Marketing Decision-Making: This refers to the way marketing managers go about solving problems. It also refers to the range of decision aids or tools that support marketing managers in the preparation, execution, and evaluation of their marketing activities.

Marketing Expert Systems (MESs): These are marketing management support systems that emphasize the marketing knowledge component. The expert system concept emerged in the field of artificial intelligence in the late 1970s. Its basic philosophy is to capture the knowledge from an expert in a particular field and make that knowledge available in a computer program for solving problems in that field. The goal of an expert system is therefore to replicate the performance levels of a human expert in a computer model.

Marketing Implementation: The process of delivering products and services to consumers; involving such activities as production, supply chain management, logistics, employee training and motivation, advertising and promotions, and sales and after-sales service.

Marketing Information Systems (MKISs): These marketing management support systems provide information about what is going on in the market, to examine the causes of observed phenomena. MKISs are passive systems: They provide information, but it is up to the marketing decision maker to

attach conclusions to this information and to decide whether to act on those conclusions.

Marketing Knowledge-Based Systems (MKBSs): These are marketing management support systems where the knowledge originates from any source, not just from human experts, but also from textbooks, cases, and the like. MKBSs cover a range of knowledge representation methods, procedures for reasoning, learning, and problem solving that can be brought to bear to support marketing decision making.

Marketing Management: The function and process of managing an organization's marketing budget, personnel, and activities. In general, the goal of marketing management is to effectively and efficiently use resources to increase customer base, improve customer perceptions of the organization's products and services, and help the organization meet its goals and objectives as related to the marketing function. The role and scope of the marketing management function varies widely between organizations based on organizational characteristics (e.g., size, corporate culture) and industry.

Marketing Management Support Systems (MMSSs): Also known as marketing decision aids, the term Marketing Management Support Systems refers to a range of tools which facilitate and support marketing decision making.

Marketing Mix: The combination of product, price, place, and promotion that is used to get a product into the hands of the consumer. One of the primary tasks of marketing is to optimize the mix to best position the product for success in the marketplace.

Marketing Neural Nets (MNNs): These marketing management support systems are used to model the way people recognize patterns from signals. Marketing neural nets are more suitable for prediction than for explanation.

Marketing Plan: A plan that specifies the actions that the organization intends to take to obtain customers for its proffered goods or services. The marketing plan is an organization's marketing strategy (including such things as pricing, budget, specification of target markets) and intelligence about competitors.

Marketing Problem-Solving Modes (MPSMs): These are the various decision-making styles that marketing managers choose to use. MPSMs are the product of the combination of an individual decision maker's cognitive style, experience, education and skills. The four MPSMs are optimizing, reasoning, analogizing, and creating.

Marketing Research: The act of gathering, recording and analyzing customer, competitor and market data so as to aid in the selling of products or services.

Marketing Strategy: 1. Methods by which a business promotes and advertises products and services. 2. A written marketing strategy would include a definition of your business, a description of your products or services, a profile of your target users or clients, and a definition of your company's situation in relation to the competition.

Marketing: This is the process of planning and executing the conception, pricing, promotion and distribution of ideas, goods and services to create exchange and satisfy individual and organizational goals.

Markov Chain: A random process comprising discrete events in which the future development of each event is either independent of past events or dependent only on the immediately preceding event. Markov chains are often used in marketing to model subsequent purchases of products (i.e., the probability of the customer making a purchase from a particular business or brand is dependent only on his/her last purchase of that brand or independent of the brand).

Match-Up Hypothesis: A perceived connection between the endorser and the product that creates an impression with the consumer that the product is all the more beneficial because of the athlete's endorsement.

Media Advertisement: The marketing of products, services, organizations, or ideas through various forms of mass media, including newspaper and television ads.

Media Coverage Inflation: Inflation that occurs when media coverage gained as a corporate sponsor for an event, organization or individual is not properly analyzed and measured.

Media Equivalency: The quality of exposure, size of audience, audience demographics, key messages communicated, type of coverage, type of media and prominence and position of media coverage gained as a corporate sponsor for an event, organization or individual.

Media Impact: Media impact refers to the process of considering the effectiveness of various media outlets by analyzing the strengths and weaknesses of each outlet vis-à-vis its cost.

Media Relations: The process of managing corporate interactions with the news and other media outlets.

Media Timing: Media timing refers to the scheduling of the advertisement messages to be communicated during a particular advertising campaign.

Merchandising Cues: A category of techniques that are used to present or group products in an online store with the objective of motivating a customer to buy.

Message Consistency: The degree of uniformity of visual imagery, verbal and/or text themes across different marketing channels.

Metamediaries: Intermediaries that gather and coordinate the products and services offered by intermediaries who specialize in specific areas.

Mixed Methodology: A research approach that utilizes both quantitative and qualitative research models.

Model: A representation of a situation, system, or subsystem. Conceptual models are mental images that describe the situation or system. Mathematical or computer models are mathematical representations of the system or situation being studied.

Monopoly: The firm that is the sole supplier of a good or service within a market, which can determine output level and price and prevent entry of new suppliers.

Motivation: An internal process that gives direction to, energizes, and sustains an organism's behavior. Motivation can be internal (e.g., I am hungry so I eat lunch) or external (e.g., the advertisement for the ice cream cone is attractive so I buy one).

Multimedia: A form of presentation medium that employs multiple layers of communication and imagery.

Multinational Corporations: Refers to a business organization which operates within more than one country.

Need: A condition in which an organism experiences the deprivation of something necessary for physiological or psychological fulfillment.

Networking: Forming the relationships and partnerships necessary to better position an individual or organization in achieving their pursuits. social contacts by making connections through individuals

New Product Development: The application of systematic methods to all processes necessary to bring a new product to the marketplace from conceptualization through marketing. New products can be improvements on existing products or total innovations.

Newsworthiness: The value that publishers, editors, reporters, and the general public place on media content.

Niche Marketing: The sale and promotion of a product or service to a specific subset of a market; concerns product audience and cost.

Normal Distribution: A continuous distribution that is symmetrical about its mean and asymptotic to the horizontal axis. The area under the normal distribution is 1. The normal distribution is actually a family of curves and describes many characteristics observable in the natural world. The normal distribution is also called the Gaussian distribution or the normal curve or errors.

Normal Profit: The amount of profit considered normal for retaining an entrepreneur in the existing line of business; occurs where price equals average total costs at the profit-maximizing output.

Organizational Buyer Behavior: The selection and purchase of products, services, experiences or ideas by organizations.

Organizational Culture: The set of basic shared assumptions, values, and beliefs that affect the way employees act within an organization.

Output: The quantity of items or services produced by a firm or group of firms in a market.

Patent: An exclusive right granted by the federal government to the inventor to make, use or sell an invention for a specified period, usually 17 years.

Pay per Click: A form of advertising in which businesses pay to have links to their products displayed on social media websites. Each time a person clicks on the link, they are taken to the website for the business, potentially generating a sale, and for each click the business pays the advertiser a fee.

Penetration Pricing: The lowering of prices so as to increase sales and market share.

Perceived Behavioral Control: The perception of how easy or difficult it would be to carry out a behavior.

Perception: Perception comes into play when a person uses his sensory receptors and under the influence of external factors, receives information, accepts and adapts it, and forms his or her personal attitude, opinion, and motive, which will influence further activity and behavior.

Perfect Competition: the condition of a market in which several buyers and sellers exist, but none of them can influence price though entry and exit are easy to accomplish.

Performance Assessment: The process of evaluating an employee's work performance and providing feedback on how well s/he is doing (typically against some standard of performance for that job).

Perquisites ("perks"): Something given to the employee in return for work over and above regular pay or compensation. Perks may include such things as health insurance, a company car, or a private office.

Personal Selling: The process of communicating with the customer on a one-to-one basis with the intention of persuading him/her to purchase a product or service. Personal selling may include developing a relationship with the customer, collecting and analyzing data formally or informally to determine the customer's needs, determining the best match between the customer's needs and the business's products or services, and effectively communicating this information in an attempt to persuade the customer to make a purchase.

Persuasion: The process of convincing someone to take a particular course of action or hold a particular point of view by argument, reasoning, or entreaty.

Pictorial, Graphic, and Sculptural Works: "Include two-dimensional and three-dimensional works of fine, graphic, and applied art, photographs, prints and art reproductions, maps, globes, charts, diagrams, models, and technical drawings, including architectural plans" (United States Copyright Office, 2007).

Points: In a customer loyalty program, customers are rewarded for specific behaviors and those rewards are measured with a point system. In frequent-flier programs, customers are generally given one point for every mile flown. In purchasing-oriented programs, customers are generally given one point for every dollar spent.

Policy: In a business setting, a policy is a set of principles and guidelines based on an analysis of the organization's goals, objectives, resources, and plans. Policies are set by the organization's governing body (e.g., board of directors) and are used to develop strategy and guide decision making in support of meeting the organization's goals and objectives.

Population: The entire group of subjects belonging to a certain category (e.g., all women between the ages of 18 and 27; all dry cleaning businesses; all college students).

Portal: A website that acts as a point of access to the World Wide Web. Portal sites typically offer a search engine or catalog of websites as well as other features.

Positioning: The act of creating a positive perception and identity of a product by instilling such images in the minds of the potential consumers and target market.

Post-Purchase Evaluation: Also known as post-acquisition evaluation, this is the sixth and final stage in the Consumer Buying Decision Process. Here, the consumer assesses the extent to which the product, service, experience or idea purchased, meets his or her need. Post-purchase evaluation may result in satisfaction or dissatisfaction.

Predatory Pricing: Selling products at low prices so as to negatively affect competitors: Could be in order to get rid of them, weaken them for mergers, discipline them or prevent new competitors from entering the market.

Premium Pricing: Pricing that is set high so as to present an air of product exclusiveness.

Price: the amount of money that is required to obtain an item.

Price Band Analysis: A statistical model that measures what customers should pay within a band of prices as opposed to those prices that fall outside of the band.

Price Index: A measure of the overall level of prices in the whole economy.

Price Skimming: Pricing strategy that involves setting prices high initially and then incrementally lowering the price to entice a wider market; objective is to "skim" the market for profits, layer by layer.

Price-based Promotions: These promotions the form of advertised discounts on selected items or store coupons that provide discounts on specific items. These promotions can be store- or chain-specific or can be supported in part by manufacturers or distributors of products.

Pricing: An element of the marketing mix along with product management, promotion, and place.

Pricing Strategies: Creating a plan for pricing structure so as to reflect consumer wants, product characteristics, and competition in a way that generates the most profit.

Probability: A branch of mathematics that deals with estimating the likelihood of an event occurring. Probability is expressed as a value between 0 and 1.0, which is the mathematical expression of the number of actual occurrences to the number of possible occurrences of the event. A probability of 0 signifies that there is no chance that the event will occur and 1.0 signifies that the event is certain to occur.

Problem Recognition: The first stage in the Consumer Buying Decision Process, when a consumer becomes aware of a need caused by a difference between the consumer's desired state and his or her actual condition.

Producers: Firms that supply or provide goods or services desired by consumers.

Product Differentiation: Marketing a product in such a way as to allow consumers in the target market to differentiate the product from its competitors.

Product Match-Up: A marketing theory that involves congruence between an endorser and a product.

Product Placement: Form of paid advertising in which products are used publicly by celebrities or inserted into a high-profile setting like a movie scene in order to increase the product's visibility.

Product Value: The combined value of the products, services, and support a company provides to its customers that provides a competitive advantage over other companies.

Profit-Oriented Decision System (PROD): This marketing management support system is used in evaluating marketing decisions in terms of their contribution to the welfare of the business firm.

Program Evaluation and Review Technique (PERT): A form of the critical path method that organizes project task and activity information in a way that allows project managers and other team members to understand which tasks are critical to keeping the project on track and how the other tasks feed into these.

Programmability: This is the extent to which a decision can be made by using relatively routine procedures instead of more general problem-solving techniques.

Project Management: The process of planning, monitoring, and controlling a unique set of tasks that have a discrete beginning, end, and outcome. The project management process is performed within the three constraints of time, costs, and scope, with the goal of producing a technically acceptable product that is both on-time and within budget.

Promotional Mix: An organization's blend of advertising, personal selling, sales promotion and public relations.

Promotions: Free samples, coupons, discounts and other offers that are used to generate sales.

Psychographics: Quantitative research intended to place consumers on psychological, rather than demographic, dimensions.

Public Relations: The process of creating and managing a public image or reputation with outside agencies and groups. In business, the public relations function is responsible for developing positive messages about the organization and reducing the impact of negative events and information on the organization's reputation.

Publicity: Any general communication about a business or its products or services that is disseminated through mass media (e.g., television, radio, newspaper, online social media) and attracts public notice.

Purchase: This is the fourth stage in the Consumer Buying Decision Process; it involves the consumer acquiring the product, service, experience or idea of his or her choice.

Purchase Decision: As the fourth stage in the Consumer Buying Decision Process, the purchase decision is reached when the consumer has evaluated the alternatives and made a choice of product, service, experience or idea to purchase.

Qualitative Research Model: A research approach that is inductive; it may involve defining a problem, developing a model, acquiring input data, developing a solution, testing the solution, analyzing the results, and implementing the results.

Quantitative Research Model: A research approach that forecasts by using judgments, experiences and data.

Quantity Demanded: The amount of goods or services that consumers desire at given prices.

Quantity Supplied: The amount of goods or services that suppliers are willing and able to produce at given prices.

Reach: The reach of an advertising campaign is the percentage of customers within the target market who will be exposed to the advertising campaign during a given time period.

Reference Group: A group of people used by an individual as a standard of reference against which to compare himself or herself.

Regression: A statistical technique used to develop a mathematical model for use in predicting one variable from the knowledge of another variable.

Reinforcement: An act, process, circumstance, or condition that increases the probability of a person repeating a response.

Relational Exchanges: Occurs over an extended period of time, are linked together or an ongoing process, and produce long term profits.

Relationship Marketing: The strategy of establishing a relationship with the client which continues well beyond the first purchase.

Reliability: The degree to which a psychological test or assessment instrument consistently measures what it is intended to measure. An assessment instrument cannot be valid unless it is reliable.

Retail Merchandising: The activities, policies and procedures of an organization that are intended to help a business sell goods and products directly to consumers. According to the American Marketing Association, merchandising encompasses "planning involved in marketing the right merchandise or service at the right place, at the right time, in the right quantities, and at the right price."

Retailing: Every corporate activity that deals directly or indirectly with the selling of products and services to the individual or corporation that will ultimately consume them.

Return on Investment (ROI): A measure of the organization's profitability or how effectively it uses its capital to produce profit. In general terms, return on investment is the income that is produced by a financial investment within a given time period (usually a year). There are a number of formulas that can be used in calculating ROI. One frequently used formula for determining ROI is (profits − costs) × (costs) × 100. The higher the ROI, the more profitable the organization.

Revenue: The proceeds from the sale of an item; the mathematical product of quantity of item sold times the price of item.

Risk: The quantifiable probability that a financial investment's actual return will be lower than expected. Higher risks mean both a greater probability of loss and a possibility of greater return on investment.

Risk Management: The project management process of analyzing the tasks and activities of a project, planning ways to reduce the impact if the predicted normal course of events does not occur, and implementing reporting procedures so that project problems are discovered earlier in the process rather than later.

Sales Forecasting: A marketing research method used to determine the level of demand for a product.

Sales Management: The process of efficiently and effectively making sales through the planning, coordination, and supervision of others. The activities of sales management include recruiting and selecting sales personnel, enabling the sales force to sell (e.g., training, print materials or samples), supervising and coordinating sales efforts (e.g., assigning territories or routes), and other motivating and human resource activities.

Sales Promotion: A set of activities and concomitant materials intended to attract the attention of potential customers and persuade them to purchase the organization's product or service. Sales promotions frequently offer an incentive to the customer to make a purchase such as coupons, discount prices, rebates, free samples, or contests. Sales promotions are often categorized into two classifications: those that target the ultimate user and those that target the wholesaler or reseller of a product.

Sample: A subset of a population. A random sample is a sample that is chosen at random from the larger population with the assumption that such samples tend to reflect the characteristics of the larger population.

Search Engine Marketing (SEM): An approach to online marketing that targets potential Internet-based customers who input specified keywords into a search engine and direct them to the business's website. Search engine marketing tools include paid ads (typically with hyperlinks) on the results pages of search engines, and search engine optimization.

Search Engine Optimization (SEO): Techniques for guiding web users to a company's site by the thoughtful repetition and placement of key marketing phrases. Optimization increases the probability that a website will be listed in the results of an online search and that it will be placed prominently in the search results. It includes such techniques as adjusting the content of the website to distinguish it from similar websites, correctly indexing the website, using the best keywords to describe the website, and ensuring that the content of the website is unique.

Secondary Analysis: A further analysis of existing data typically collected by a different researcher. The intent of secondary analysis is to use existing data in order to develop conclusions or knowledge in addition to or different from those resulting from the original analysis of the data. Secondary analysis may

be qualitative or quantitative in nature and may be used by itself or combined with other research data to reach conclusions.

Self-Actualization: The need to live up to one's full and unique potential. Associated with self-actualization are such concepts as wholeness, perfection, or completion; a divestiture of "things" in preference to simplicity, aliveness, goodness, and beauty; and a search for meaning in life. In Maslow's hierarchy of needs, this is the ultimate level of motivator for behavior.

Shelf Talker: A printed sign containing information about a product or item in a store (e.g., sales price, new item, compare price) that is attached to a shelf in a store. The objective of shelf talkers is to call the buyer's attention to a particular product or item. Shelf talkers are also referred to as shelf screamers.

Site-centric Model: The use of a central site to direct traffic and sales of a certain product.

SMART: An approach to evaluating advertising goals such as media exposure that can result from event sponsorship when goals are specific, measurable, achievable, results oriented, and time bounded.

Social Media: Social media are Internet-based applications that enable the creation and sharing of user-generated content. Social media sites include Facebook, Twitter, Instagram, and YouTube and rely on the generation of online content by users. Businesses and organizations use social media to market to their customers and potential customers. Social media is a particularly powerful marketing too, as marketers can create content with viral value that is quickly shared across any variety of social media platforms, expanding the campaign's reach beyond its initial target audience.

Sound Recordings: "Works that result from the fixation of a series of musical, spoken, or other sounds, but not including the sounds accompanying a motion picture or other audiovisual work, regardless of the nature of the material objects, such as disks, tapes, or other phonorecords, in which they are embodied" (United States Copyright Office, 2007).

Source Attractiveness: A marketing theory that maintains that consumers will purchase products and services that are endorsed by celebrities that have a positive public persona.

Source Credibility: A marketing theory that looks at how a celebrity endorser is viewed in terms of his or her knowledge of the product.

Spam: Unsolicited commercial e-mails that are sent widely and indiscriminately to various individuals.

Spin: To provide an interpretation to potentially negative information in such a way as to sway public opinion and prevent damage to the reputation of the organization. The term is sometimes used pejoratively.

Sponsorship Effectiveness: How effective a specific sponsorship is at meeting the goals of the sponsor and the organizations, event, or individual being sponsored.

Stakeholder: A person or group that has a stake in an interest or business and can affect or be affected by a decision or action. In marketing, stakeholders may include the organization's employees, suppliers, distributors, and stockholders.

Standardization Model: School of thought that supports the assumption that markets are converging as a result of faster communication and consumers are becoming increasingly similar over time.

Statistics: A branch of mathematics that deals with the analysis and interpretation of data. Mathematical statistics provide the theoretical underpinnings for various applied statistical disciplines, including business statistics, in which data are analyzed to find answers to quantifiable questions. Applied statistics uses these techniques to solve real world problems.

Stochastic: Involving chance or probability. Stochastic variables are random or have an element of chance or probability associated with their occurrence.

Strategic Marketing: A subfunction of marketing that examines the marketplace to determine the needs of potential customers and the strategies of competitors in the market and attempts to develop a strategy that will enable the organization to gain or maintain a competitive advantage in the marketplace.

Strategic Planning: The process of determining the long-term goals of an organization and developing a plan to use the company's resources – including materials and personnel – in reaching these goals.

Strategy: In business, a strategy is a plan of action to help the organization reach its goals and objectives. A good business strategy is based on the rigorous analysis of empirical data, including market needs and trends, competitor capabilities and offerings, and the organization's resources and abilities.

Subjective Norm: Perceived social pressure; one's desire to act as others do, or as others think that one should act.

Supply Chain: A network of organizations involved in production, delivery, and sale of a product. The supply chain may include suppliers, manufacturers, storage facilities, transporters, and retailers. Each organization in the network provides a value-added activity to the product or service. The supply chain includes the flow of tangible goods and materials, funds, and information between the organizations in the network.

Supply Chain Management: The process of efficiently connecting the parties in a value chain in order to reduce costs, improve customer service, develop the organization's knowledge base, increase efficiency, and create barriers to competitors. Supply management includes managing the flow of materials, information, and money within and between organizations in a supply chain.

Supply Schedule: The actual quantities that producers are willing and able to purchase at various prices.

Supply: The amount of a good or service an individual producer or a group of producers will provide at a given price.

SWOT Analysis: A method for evaluating the strengths, weaknesses, opportunities, and threats involved in a project, business venture or in any other organizational situation; includes external and internal monitoring.

Symbiotic Marketing: The process of one organization selling its product to another organization that already has market share and established distribution channels so as to facilitate increased sales.

Tag Line: Usually the theme to a campaign. A slogan or phrase that imparts a product attribute or benefit to the consumer.

Target Audience: The people or businesses to whom the organization wishes to sell goods or services. Also called *target market*.

Targeting: The selection of customers a business wishes to service.

Telemarketing: The use of the telephone to market goods or services directly to prospective customers.

Test Marketing: The introduction of a product into a small market to determine its potential to sell in a larger market.

Theory of Planned Behavior: The Theory of Planned Behavior suggests that behavioral intention — the motivation that determines how hard people are willing to try to perform a behavior — is the most influential predictor of behavior: It assumes that a person does what he or she intends to do.

Total Market Offering: The comparison between the totality of the company's reputation, its employees, product advantages, and technological capabilities, and those of competing companies.

Trade Publications: Magazines, newspapers, newsletters, or websites that exclusively focus on a specific industry or a particular type of product or materials used in manufacturing.

Trademark: A distinctive design, picture, emblem, logo or wording (or combination) affixed to goods for sale to identify the manufacturer as the source of the product. Servicemarks are a related mark used by companies that provided services.

Trading Stamps: A form of customer loyalty program in which the points accumulated took form of a postage-like stamp that were collected by customers and placed in a trading stamp book. When the trading stamp books were full, the customer could take them to a redemption center and trade the stamps for merchandise.

Traditional Advertising: Advertising such as signage, phonebook listings, and newspaper advertising.

Transactional Exchanges: Focus on single short-term situations and each transaction yields a profit.

Trend: The persistent, underlying direction in which something is moving in either the short, intermediate, or long term. Identification of a trend allows one to better plan to meet future needs.

Validity: The degree to which a survey or other data collection instrument measures what it purports to measure. A data collection instrument cannot be valid unless it is reliable.

Value Chain: A network of businesses working together to bring a product or service to the market. Value chains typically comprise one or a few primary suppliers supported by many secondary suppliers each of whom add value to the product or service before it is offered to the customer.

Value: The connection between a consumer's expectations for the value of a product or service quality and the total amount paid for it.

Value-Based Pricing: A pricing strategy in which products or services are priced for each customer or market segment to reflect perceived value.

Value-Based Strategy: A targeted strategy directed at selected consumer value segments that a supplier considers profitable. Value-based strategies are also known as "value delivery marketing strategies."

Variable: An object in a research study that can have more than one value. Independent variables are stimuli that are manipulated in order to determine their effect on the dependent variables (response). Extraneous variables are variables that affect the response but that are not related to the question under investigation in the study.

Variable Costs: Costs for production or output that vary according to activity level.

Vessel Hull Designs: A design for a hull, which is "the exterior frame or body of a vessel, exclusive of the deck, superstructure, masts, sails, yards, rigging, hardware, fixtures, and other attachments" (United States Copyright Office, 2007).

Viral Video: Internet-based video clips that are spread from user to user via instant messaging, e-mail or other forms of internet sharing.

Visual Merchandising: The way in which products are displayed. The goal of visual merchandising is to make products more attractive, appealing, and accessible to customers in an attempt to induce them to purchase the product. Visual merchandising is also known as product merchandising, retail display, or merchandising design.

Web Bug: An image included on a website that tracks the activity on the site. While simultaneously retrieving an image for display on the screen, the beacon also transmits information back to the site (e.g., browser used to retrieve the image, IP address of the viewer's computer, when and for how long the image was viewed). Turning off cookies on the viewer's computer can prevent personal information from being transmitted. However, nonpersonal information will still be transmitted back to the website or third-party monitor of the beacon. (Also referred to as a web beacon, pixel tag, or clear GIF).

Work: "A work is fixed in a tangible medium of expression when its embodiment in a copy or phonorecord, by or under the authority of the author, is sufficiently permanent or stable to permit it to be perceived, reproduced, or otherwise communicated for a period of more than transitory duration" (United States Copyright Office, 2007).

INDEX